Readings in Jurisprudence and Legal Philosophy

— Volume I —

Readings in Jurisprudence and Legal Philosophy

— Volume I —

Morris R. Cohen & Felix S. Cohen

BeardBooks

Washington, D.C.

ISBN 1-58798-144-0

Reprinted 2002 by Beard Books, Washington, D.C.

Printed in the United States of America.

PREFACE

The Scheme of the Volume

A distinguished teacher once gave a series of lectures on law and ethics that made so deep an impression that the notes taken by his students are still being widely circulated. In his final lecture, this teacher commented on the prevailing notion of practical men that legal ideals are other-worldly or utopian, and made the ever-pertinent observation on the nature of ethical doctrine:

> It is not in heaven, that thou shouldest say, Who shall go up for us to heaven, and bring it unto us, and make us to hear it, that we may do it? Neither is it beyond the sea, that thou shouldest say, Who shall go over the sea for us, and bring it unto us, and make us to hear it, that we may do it? But the word is very nigh unto thee, in thy mouth, and in thy heart, that thou mayest do it.

It is with the thought that all of the ethical issues of the law are very near to us, in courtrooms, legislative halls, and city streets, that the materials of this book have been put together.

"To see so far as one may, and to feel, the great forces that are behind every detail," said Holmes, "makes all the difference between philosophy and gossip." [1] So conceived, legal philosophy is not an escape from reality to an easy world of irrefutable imaginings, but rather one of the most rigorous of intellectual disciplines. Abstract questions concerning the nature of law have significance only against a background of concrete controversies. In the modern state such controversies revolve chiefly about private property, contract, tort, liability, crime, and punishment. The first part of this volume therefore deals with the materials of controversy in these varied fields, and provides content for the more abstract considerations of the last three parts: Part II, which explores general theories as to the nature of law, and of its judicial and legislative development; Part III, which surveys legal philosophy at its three major levels—logic, ethics, and metaphysics; and Part IV, which deals with the ties that unite jurisprudence to the social sciences.

The Vocation of Our Age for Jurisprudence and Legal Philosophy

Jurisprudence, as the jurist's quest for a systematic vision that will order and illumine the dark realities of the law, and legal philosophy, conceived as the philosopher's effort to understand the legal order and its role in human life, have come close enough together in our land and our generation to

---

[1] "The Class of '61" in O. W. Holmes, Jr., *Speeches* (privately printed, 1913), 95, 96.

warrant a unified approach to these two overlapping fields. Such, at least, is the premise upon which this volume of readings has been prepared.

This effort at cross-fertilization between legal practicalities and philosophic understanding would be out of place or out of time in many lands today where rational criticism of existing institutions is unwelcome. But it is only as existing institutions are stripped of ancient cruelties by bold philosophical analysis that men escape from the barbaric servitudes of the past; and only as men learn to substitute rigorous reflective thought for hit-or-miss trial-and-error can they escape the barbarisms that the future pins to most human hopes. This is what gives pragmatic significance to the contemporary study of legal philosophy.

Book-burning and other coercive measures may have a short-range efficacy in suppressing unorthodox ideas, but in the long run such methods have proved less powerful, both in the natural sciences and in the affairs of human government, than the method of free competition among ideas. The strength of independent judgment that emerges from such free competition is something that democratic society desperately needs today. Only with such strength can it hope to conquer ideologies that fear free thought more than they fear brute force. This volume seeks to exhibit in their working clothes the ideas that compete for the future loyalties of free men.

Something more it also seeks to establish. It is an attempt to justify the view of jurisprudence and legal philosophy as a great cooperative adventure, pursued across many centuries by men of many races and many faiths. The life of this adventure is the exploration of possible perspectives through which the many-faceted problems of the law may be viewed. This enterprise is based upon the metaphysical premise that radically different views of the same fact may be equally correct and that the coordination of various, and even opposite, perspectives enables us to see more than can be seen from any one of them.[2]

If there is truth in an ancient report that the world's first great cooperative works project failed because fellow-workers did not understand each other's speech, is there not a lesson in the failure for those who would build the foundations of international peace today? Is not peace without understanding merely an accident? Can any of us hope to be understood by men of many political and economic faiths unless we ourselves patiently seek to understand the basic ideas out of which faiths other than our own have emerged?

Contemporary philosophy faces its greatest challenge in the problem of intercultural understanding. Can we devise translation formulae that will permit men to speak to each other across all the gulfs of creed and to understand each other through all the curtains of dogma? A philosophy that resolutely meets this challenge may well avoid the fate of many philosophical movements during the past century that, self-sentenced to solitary confinement, have sunk to an endless puttering with mental tools that removes the tools themselves from use in the world's work. There are those who think that the relative poverty of philosophy in the century following Hegel was closely related to its sustained mood of individual introspection. For nearly a century no first-rate philosopher thought or wrote about the law, although every great figure in philosophic history before the nineteenth century, with the possible exception of Descartes, had made the law a central focus of his thinking.

There is still a powerful drive among many contemporary philosophers to keep their philosophies pure and unpolitical by avoiding contact with the

---

[2] M. R. Cohen, "The Conception of Philosophy in Recent Discussion," 7 *Jour. of Philosophy* 401 (1910), reprinted in *Studies in Philosophy and Science* (1949), 33, 44-45.

realities of human controversy and social disorder. As strong, or even stronger, is the opposition of many practical men to critical reflection upon existing legal institutions. Both these views result in a view of jurisprudence as a maze of inert ideas, a museum of intellectual curiosities far removed from logic or practice. What follows is that analytical, historical, metaphysical, and sociological jurisprudences and their various hybrids and offshoots are exhibited before innocent students like a series of butterflies, all neatly labeled, pinned to their proper cards, and thoroughly dead. The history of law, its logical analysis, the scientific study of its social consequences, and the evaluation of those consequences, instead of being viewed as related problems posed by a common subject matter, come to be viewed as mutually exclusive objectives of conflicting "schools." The pejorative suffix "ism" is invoked to disparage interest in science by calling it "scientism," and interest in history or scholarship can be effectively discouraged by the use of such labels as "historicism" or "scholasticism." It is very easy to dismiss all our predecessors on the ground that they did not know about some recent discovery of psychiatry or sociology or never mastered some modern prestige-vocabulary. But what then? "The notion that we can dismiss the views of all previous thinkers surely leaves no basis for the hope that our own work will prove of any value to others." [3]

The teaching of jurisprudence, so conceived, commonly results only in the suppression of curiosity and the turning of clean-cutting minds into intellectual junk shops. The human product of this process, distrustful of all generalizations and abstractions, is likely to be quite incapable of projecting ideas into the future, since the future is itself an abstraction. But the long-range problems of a social order in competition with rival ideas can certainly not be solved by those who fail to understand the force of ideas. And it is ancient wisdom that in the long run nothing is so powerful as an idea when its time has come. In that moment the "proud men of action," as Heine remarked, "are nothing but unconscious instruments of the men of thought."

The disparagement of ideas by those who mistake short-sightedness for practicality is perhaps part of a "loss of nerve" which attacks the complacent when they face the unfamiliar. But there are many signs today that the pattern of complacency towards the familiar and of mistrust towards all unfamiliar accents and ideas is doomed, that the era of classificatory caricatures in jurisprudence is drawing to a close, and that the value of a multi-dimensional perspective upon legal realities and legal ideals is gradually winning acceptance.

Since 1913, when a handful of philosophers, judges, and law teachers met to organize the Conference on Legal and Social Philosophy, electing John Dewey its President and Morris R. Cohen its Secretary, a great part of our most seminal philosophic thought has revolved about legal problems. It is no longer possible, as it was forty years ago, to write or discourse at length on American philosophy without referring to the philosophy of law. Nor is it possible today, as it was then, for any jurist or philosopher anywhere in the world to deal comprehensively with the problems of jurisprudence and legal philosophy without referring to American writers.

More and more, following the great example of Holmes, our foremost judges have come to see that their daily work involves fundamental ethical, logical, and other philosophical issues; and those judges who have consciously contributed to the literature of legal philosophy,—such men, for example, as Cardozo, Frankfurter, Douglas, Edgerton, Arnold, C. E. Clark, Hutcheson,

---

[3] M. R. Cohen, *Reason and Nature* (1931), p. x.

and Frank,—have greatly illumined the character of American life and American thought. The sister sciences that once completely ignored the law now make legal factors central in their perspectives upon human society: witness the work of Ely, Berle, Hamilton, and Hale in economics, Beard, Bentley, T. V. Smith, and T. R. Powell in political science, Lowie, Hoebel, and Hallowell in anthropology, and John Dewey and T. V. Smith in social ethics. Even the great legal technicians have come, bit by bit, to awareness of the ethical systems in which legal ideals are limited sectors of a larger battle-front. Thus, such masters of specialized legal fields as Walter Wheeler Cook, Oliphant, Llewellyn, Michael, Jerome Hall, Fuller, Lorenzen, Kessler, Horack, Landis, McDougal, Garlan, Boudin, Haines, Patterson, Wechsler, and Gellhorn have all contributed to the philosophic enterprise without departing from their chosen fields of legal study. When to these names are added those of lawyers who have more consciously undertaken to treat of the basic philosophic problems of the legal order,—such men, for example, as Roscoe Pound, Max Radin, and Huntington Cairns,—we have only touched the high spots of a remarkable chapter in the intellectual history of the New World.

The Process of Selection

To select out of the writings of these men, and out of a much larger body of writings of other lands and ages, materials that can provide a useful introduction to the problems of legal philosophy is no easy task. A factor of selection unrelated to the merits of the works involved arises from the objective of this volume. Its editors have tried to present a wide selection of different viewpoints in a brief space. To accomplish this end it has been necessary to pass over many important works that are so solidly integrated that brief excerpts cannot possibly do justice to the viewpoints they develop. This has unfortunately been particularly true in the field of general philosophy, where, as in a system of geometry, no single fragment can reveal the whole. Thus contemporary thinkers such as Ralph Barton Perry and C. I. Lewis appear in the following pages only through the words of their students, as do such distinguished predecessors in philosophic paths as Plato and Spinoza. But even with the aid of such mechanical selectors the choice of materials has been a difficult one. Basically, the process of selection as carried out by the compilers of this volume has consisted in throwing a much larger mass of materials at their students and retaining those fragments that struck sparks.

In this way, in the course of three decades, a good many generations of undergraduate and graduate students at the City College of New York, Chicago University, and the Yale, Columbia, St. Johns, and Oklahoma University law schools have exercised a democratic voice in the selection of these readings. While my own part in this process has been small, I am particularly appreciative of the patience with which my students at Yale Law School and City College have struggled through thousands of pages of tentatively mimeographed materials, to the great detriment of their eyesight, in search of those sparks which no one of the following excerpts will provide for every reader but which each excerpt has struck at least once and may strike again.

Introductions and Footnotes

The chief purpose of any anthology, I suppose, is to save its user the time and carfare that would otherwise be consumed in borrowing from friends or libraries the books he doesn't possess. Were that the only function of this volume, the intervention of an editor between the original authors and the reader would be an impertinence. But since this volume is intended not only for browsing but also for use as a course text and as a beginner's introduction to the main currents of legal thought, I have found it necessary to insert introductory notes at the start of each chapter and a considerable number of footnotes throughout the text. These are intended to clarify the relation of one author or excerpt to another by indicating the various perspectives of time and purpose that orient the works from which these selections have been taken.

Brackets have been used to distinguish editorial footnotes from those of the original authors. Footnotes that appear in the original text I have tried to reproduce faithfully, with occasional bracketed inserts to clarify a reference that is obscure because of the fragmentary character of the excerpt. Footnotes that merely refer to other works or cases have generally been omitted, on the theory that such references are useful only in a library and that in a library it is better to use original works than anthologies. In all such cases the footnote number has been left in the text to indicate the omission.

Translations

In the case of works that were not written originally in English, standard translations have been used, and referred to, wherever they are available. But occasionally the standard translations from the Greek, Latin, German, and French have been revised where they seemed to be unfaithfully obscure or misleading. When Kant, for example, says *"der Gesetzgeber ist heilig,"* the reader has a right to know that in Kant's opinion "the legislator is holy." To assuage Anglo-American sensibilities by a polite circumlocution, such as the standard translation of this work offers,—"the Legislator being rationally viewed as just and holy,"—is to hide from the reader's notice the real difference between Kant's perspective and ours.

Companion Texts

Despite all editorial notes, there must inevitably remain large obscurities in the inter-relations of one excerpt with another. It was intended, when this work was first projected, that a comprehensive treatise on legal philosophy would constitute a companion volume. This purpose was only partially accomplished in the three volumes of essays, *Law and the Social Order*, *The Faith of a Liberal*, and *Reason and Law*, which were completed in the lifetime of the one who conceived this anthology. Today it seems to me that the best single comprehensive treatise on jurisprudence,— to which I constantly refer my students,—is Julius Stone's *Province and Function of Law*, published in 1946. Stone writes with an uncanny sympathy for many different viewpoints and thus is eminently equipped to clarify the social and ideological context in which almost any of the excerpts between these covers found its origin and its purpose.

Acknowledgments

To my wife Lucy Kramer, who searched through hundreds of volumes with me to glean the fragments that are here bound together, to my secretary Pearl Ann Levine, who handled a major part of the proof-reading and a dozen other editorial chores, to my former students and associates Howard

M. Schott and Shirley Fingerhood, who helped with the bibliographical and biographical footnotes and with much of the proof-reading, to Professor Samuel Mermin, who shared with me his experiences in using a preliminary version of this volume at the University of Oklahoma Law School, to Edith Lowenstein, who provided me with a faithful and piquant translation of Von Jhering's dream, "*Im juristischen Begriffshimmel,*" to George and Jane Treister, Evelyn Chavoor, Max Kampelman, and Richard Schifter, who helped so often in finding books and verifying citations and quotations, and to the many other friends and associates who have aided along the way, I give my grateful thanks.

Finally, I should like to give special thanks to all those who freely granted permission to quote from published works. Detailed credits appear in the appropriate places throughout the text.

Epilogue

In completing alone what began as a joint enterprise, I am painfully aware of my many ineptitudes for the appointed task. I have neither the mastery of philosophic and scientific systems, the command of languages and intellectual history, the rich experience as a teacher, nor the many other talents that would be needed to complete this work with the comprehensive and penetrating vision that was present when the work was begun. I must therefore look to the criticisms of colleagues and students for aid in correcting errors of commission and omission in this volume, errors which might have been avoided if it had been possible to complete the task five years ago. But I can only say to my chief guide and collaborator that I have done my best, with clumsy hands, to finish what he began. And I find solace, as he did, in the words of an ancient seer: "The day is short and the task is great. It is not incumbent upon thee to complete the whole work, but neither art thou free to neglect it."

FELIX S. COHEN

WASHINGTON, D. C.

TABLE OF CONTENTS

Volume I

TABLE OF CASES

READINGS IN JURISPRUDENCE

AND

LEGAL PHILOSOPHY

PART I
LEGAL INSTITUTIONS

PROPERTY

Contents

Introductory Note

If the usefulness of a legal theory depends upon the extent to which it illumines legal problems, the field of property must serve as a pre-eminent testing ground for theories of law. Whether or not possession is nine-tenths of the law, it certainly presents more than nine-tenths of the legal problems on which our age calls for illumination. The competing theories on the nature of law that form the substance of most text books on jurisprudence take on serious overtones when they are applied to the unsolved problems of property management and property distribution that face our generation. A significant definition of law must explain the difference between legal and illegal control of a cow or a song or an easement. It must clarify, even if it does not solve, the recurrent question: How far shall the state control the new economic wealth created every day by nature and technology, and how far shall such control be vested in private citizens or private associations? A significant theory of property should illumine such practical problems as the ownership of newly found lands, newly gathered news, or newly invented commercial designs. These are the problems that are dealt with in the following selections from Victoria's epoch-starting essay *De Indis et de Jure Belli*, the Supreme Court's opinion in *International News Service v. Associated Press*, and the evidence brought before Congressional committees considering proposed legislation for the creation of property rights in designs.

A theory of property, to be significant, cannot be a wholesale defense of the status quo, nor can it restrict itself to a socialist or individualist Utopia or a jurist's heaven of legal concepts. It must deal not merely with questions of yes-or-no but more importantly with questions of more-or-less. It is in this light that we need to examine the justifications of private property advanced by such pioneer thinkers as Grotius, Locke, Bentham, Kant, and Hegel, and the modern critiques of these theories advanced by Tawney, Lindsay, Berle and Means, Walton Hamilton, and others who have raised questions that our generation has not yet answered. To stimulate the thinking that may answer those questions is the most useful purpose that can be served by any collection of competing and conflicting views on property.

To grasp the practical significance of Locke's labor theory of property may help us to answer the problems raised during the past century by a socialized labor theory of property. To understand Victoria's appeal to the idea of human rights as a basis of international law may help us to face with more intelligence and less dizziness the parallel problems of our own age.

In relating the thoughts of other generations to contemporary problems, it becomes necessary to remember that different writers have used the word "property" in many ways to mean many different things—some, like Bentham, to mean a verifiable legal fact; others, like Grotius, to mean a human ideal, sought for, but not fully achieved. Formulas for translation are necessary here, as in every other legal field, if we are to understand those who spoke in languages different from our own.

We cannot hope to justify or refute what we do not understand. A good deal of material bearing on the logical structure of property is therefore included in this chapter. Most of the first part of the chapter consists of such material, and most of this material may be viewed as commentary upon the curious conceptions of property advanced by Blackstone and by the American Law Institute. The Blackstonian vision of property as exclusive despotic dominion can perhaps apply to nothing at all in our modern society. The American Law Institute definition of property as equivalent to any right or interest in anything at all (including, no doubt, intangible things like affection and freedom of worship) would bring the whole field of law under the rubric of property. This consequence may be wholly acceptable to the teachers of property law who draft such definitions, but what we are offered is scarcely more useful than the Blackstonian definition as an instrument for the dissection of practical problems.

Perhaps the most serious obstacle to clear thinking on the subject of property is the accumulation of high emotional overtones that cluster about the word itself. In a sense, property is the essence of everything that is proper. To cleanse our terms of question-begging overtones is the first step in a realistic approach to the riddles that modern technology has put to our society. And, as Bentham remarks, we know the traditional penalty for not solving a riddle.

---

1. The Nature and Types of Property

GROTIUS, WAR AND PEACE *

§§ II. Among those things, which belong to no one, there are two that may become the subjects of occupancy; and those are jurisdiction, or sovereignty and property. For jurisdiction and property are distinct from each other in their effects. The objects over which sovereignty may be exercised are of a two-fold description, embracing both persons and things. But this is not the case with property, the right of which can extend only to the irrational and inanimate part of the creation. Though it might originally, for the most part, be the same act by which sovereignty and property were acquired, yet they are in their nature distinct. SOVEREIGNTY, says Seneca, belongs to PRINCES and PROPERTY to INDIVIDUALS. The sovereignty therefore, not only over subjects at home, but over those in the prince's foreign dominions passes with the hereditary descent of the crown.

BLACKSTONE, COMMENTARIES
ON THE LAWS OF ENGLAND †

There is nothing which so generally strikes the imagination, and engages the affections of mankind, as the right of property; or that sole and despotic dominion which one man claims and exercises over the external things of the world, in total exclusion of the right of any other individual in the universe.

---

* [Book II, Chap. 3.

Hugo Grotius (Huig van Groot) (1583–1645), the most influential of all writers on international law, was attorney for the Dutch East India Company when he began to write his treatise on *War and Peace* (*De jure belli ac pacis*, first published in 1625). The brief that served as the starting point for this treatise was written to uphold the legality of the capture by a merchant vessel of the Dutch East India Company of a Portuguese war ship in waters claimed by Portugal. Grotius tried to base his argument on principles that might be accepted alike by Catholic and Protestant countries. His formulation of the doctrine of "freedom of the seas" was perhaps his most successful effort in this direction.]

† [15th ed. (1809), Book II ("*Of the Rights of Things*"), Chap. 1 ("Of Property *in general*"), p. 2.]

BENTHAM, THEORY OF LEGISLATION *

Chapter VIII. Of Property

The better to understand the advantages of law, let us endeavour to form a clear idea of *property*. We shall see that there is no such thing as natural property, and that it is entirely the work of law.

Property is nothing but a basis of expectation; the expectation of deriving certain advantages from a thing which we are said to possess, in consequence of the relation in which we stand towards it.

There is no image, no painting, no visible trait, which can express the relation that constitutes property. It is not material, it is metaphysical; it is a mere conception of the mind.

To have a thing in our hands, to keep it, to make it, to sell it, to work it up into something else; to use it—none of these physical circumstances, nor all united, convey the idea of property. A piece of stuff which is actually in the Indies may belong to me, while the dress I wear may not. The aliment which is incorporated into my very body may belong to another, to whom I am bound to account for it.

The idea of property consists in an established expectation; in the persuasion of being able to draw such or such an advantage from the thing possessed, according to the nature of the case. Now this expectation, this persuasion, can only be the work of law. I cannot count upon the enjoyment of that which guarantees it to me. It is law alone which permits me to forget my natural weakness. It is only through the protection of law that I am able to inclose a field, and to give myself up to its cultivation with the sure though distant hope of harvest.†

But it may be asked, What is it that serves as a basis to law, upon which

---

* ["Principles of the Civil Code," Part I ("Objects of the Civil Law"), pp. 111-113. Dumont, ed., Hildreth, trans. (1864). Reprinted with introduction and notes by C. K. Ogden, London: Routledge and Kegan Paul Ltd., 1931.
Bentham's *Theory of Legislation* is an American translation of a French volume compiled by the Swiss Dumont from otherwise unpublished writings of Jeremy Bentham (1748–1832). Dumont was one of many friends through whom the ideas of Bentham on law, legislation, and semantics were made generally available to public consideration. Others who assisted in presenting Bentham's ideas to a larger public were the Mills, the Austins, and Bowring. Apart from those who avowedly presented Bentham's ideas, there were so many who plagiarized from his writings, even in his own day, that Talleyrand said of him: *"Pillé par tout le monde il est toujours riche."* (Despoiled by all the world, he remains forever rich.) Competent appraisals of Bentham's work and influence will be found in the following writings: Stephens, *The English Utilitarians;* Shientag, *Molders of Legal Thought,* Chap. 4; Wallas, "Bentham as Political Inventor," 129 *Contemporary Rev.* 308 (1926); Association of American Law Schools, *Select Essays in Anglo-American Legal History,* Vol. 1, p. 492; Hepburn, *Development of Code Pleading,* pp. 71-74; Sunderland, "The English Struggle for Procedural Reform," 39 *Harv. L. Rev.* 725 (1926).]
† [Note the empirical evidence for this conclusion given by Bentham later.]

to begin operations, when it adopts objects which, under the name of property, it promises to protect? Have not men, in the primitive state, a *natural* expectation of enjoying certain things,—an expectation drawn from sources anterior to law?

Yes. There have been from the beginning, and there always will be, circumstances in which a man may secure himself, by his own means, in the enjoyment of certain things. But the catalogue of these cases is very limited. The savage who has killed a deer may hope to keep it for himself, so long as his cave is undiscovered; so long as he watches to defend it, and is stronger than his rivals; but that is all. How miserable and precarious is such a possession! If we suppose the least agreement among savages to respect the acquisitions of each other, we see the introduction of a principle to which no name can be given but that of law. A feeble and momentary expectation may result from time to time from circumstances purely physical; but a strong and permanent expectation can result only from law. That which, in the natural state, was an almost invisible thread, in the social state becomes a cable.

Property and law are born together, and die together. Before laws were made there was no property; take away laws, and property ceases.

As regards property, security consists in receiving no check, no shock, no derangement to the expectation founded on the laws, of enjoying such and such a portion of good. The legislator owes the greatest respect to this expectation which he has himself produced. When he does not contradict it, he does what is essential to the happiness of society; when he disturbs it, he always produces a proportionate sum of evil.

UNITED STATES v. PERCHEMAN

UNITED STATES SUPREME COURT 1833
7 Pet. 51

[Facts of the case: Plaintiff, Percheman, claimed two thousand acres in Florida under a grant of 1815 from the Spanish Governor, allegedly acting under color of a royal decree authorizing the allotment of land to veterans. In 1819, Spain ceded Florida to the United States. In 1830, plaintiff petitioned the United States Court for the Eastern District of Florida, asking that Court to confirm his claim of title. The United States appeared as a defendant alleging that it had acquired title under the grant from Spain. The Florida Court decided that Percheman's private claim was superior to the Government's claim. The Supreme Court affirmed the decision. The chief ground of the decisions is set forth in the following passage from Chief Justice Marshall's opinion.]

MARSHALL, C. J. . . . The modern usage of nations, which has become law, would be violated; that sense of justice and of right which is acknowledged and felt by the whole civilized world would be outraged, if private property should be generally confiscated, and private rights annulled. The people change their allegiance; their relation to their ancient sovereign is dissolved: but their relations to each other, and their rights of property, remain undisturbed. If this be the modern rule even in cases of conquest, who can doubt its application to the case of an amicable cession of territory? . . . The language of the second article conforms to this general principle. "His catholic majesty cedes to the United States in full property and sovereignty, all the territories which belong to him situated to the eastward of the Mississippi, by the name of East and West Florida." A cession of territory is never understood to be a cession of the property belonging to its inhabitants. . . . Neither party could consider itself as attempting a wrong to individuals, condemned by the practice of the whole civilized world. . . . [Pp. 86-87.]

ELY, PROPERTY AND CONTRACT IN THEIR RELATION TO THE DISTRIBUTION OF WEALTH *

PART I. PROPERTY, PUBLIC AND PRIVATE

Chapter III. Property Defined and Described

.   .   .   .   .

But what has been said about the subserviency of things to persons does not carry us very far. We find this,—that things exist for the sake of persons; we find established a human control over things. But the essence of property is more than this. *The essence of property is in the relations among men arising out of their relations to things.*

We have not got property when we establish human control over things. That can be exercised by communities recognizing no private property; for example, tribes of a primitive economic type and communistic settlements. In various ways associations of men may exercise control over

* [Vol. I, Book I ("The Fundamentals in the Existing Socio-Economic Order, Treated from the Standpoint of Distribution"). New York: The Macmillan Company, 1914.

Richard Theodore Ely (1854–1943) was a powerful and influential critic of the extreme individualism that dominated American economic thought during most of his life. After studying at Columbia and Heidelberg, Ely became the first head of the Department of Political Economy at Johns Hopkins in 1881. In 1892, he was appointed professor at the University of Wisconsin where he remained until his retirement in 1925. Among his students are numbered Woodrow Wilson, Newton D. Baker, and many leading economists. In 1894, Ely was indicted and tried on a charge of having taught Socialism. Much of the progressive legislation that was enacted in Wisconsin, particularly during the La Follette era, is said to have been inspired by Ely's teachings. Among Ely's best known works are: *Socialism and Social Reform* (1894); *Taxation in American States and Cities* (1888); *Outlines of Economics* (5th ed. 1930); *Studies in the Evolution of Industrial Society* (1903); *Elements of Land Economics* (1924); *Hard Times—The Way In and the Way Out* (1931).]

things, but property means the relations which exist between men arising out of their relations to things, and in the case of slavery, their relations to men who are treated as things. So that we have not gone very far when we say that property is the human control over things. [Pp. 96-97.]

* * * * *

By property we mean an exclusive right to control an economic good.
By private property we mean the exclusive right of a private person to control an economic good.
By public property we mean the exclusive right of a political unit (city, state, nation, etc.) to control an economic good. [Pp. 101-102.]

* * * * *

... Speaking accurately, then, property is not a thing but the rights which extend over a thing. A less strict use of the word property makes property include the things over which the right extends. We say of a farm, this is my property, meaning the land and improvements on it and not merely the right, or rather, the land and its improvements together with the right. But, strictly speaking, property is the right, and not the object over which the right extends.[18] [19] [P. 108.]

Chapter V. The Attributes and Characteristics of Property

* * * * *

Furthermore, *Property is exclusive in its nature and not absolute.* A phrase is found in Roman law which, as a definition of property, is mis-

---

[18] Macleod is emphatic in his statement that "property in its true and original sense means solely a right, title, interest, or ownership; and consequently, to call material things like land, houses, money, cattle, etc., property is as great an absurdity as to call them right, title, interest or ownership. Neither Bacon, nor, so far as we are aware, any writer of his period calls material goods property; such a use of the word is quite a modern corruption, and we cannot say when it began." "Landed property, funded property, house property, real property, personal property, literary property, mean rights to land, rights to houses, rights to realty, rights to personality, rights to payments from the nation, rights to the profits from literature and art, and so on." Nevertheless, although he protests against the usage, he himself employs the term property in the large sense. He says, for instance, that there are three distinct orders of "economic or exchangeable quantities," viz., "I. Material things; II. Labour or Services; III. Rights: typified by the terms money, labour and credit." Now he says that property is the general term covering them all, although he said before that it only referred to rights. It is difficult to see how anyone can avoid using the term property in the large sense. We would have to employ a very awkward circumlocution to avoid its usage. Only we must remember that in the narrow sense property is a right.

Macleod, however, shows that he appreciates the importance of property when he says that it "is the key to all economics."

Henry Dunning Macleod, *Elements of Economics*, 1, pp. 141, 143, 144.

[19] The distinction between property as rights, and the object over which the rights are extended is clearly brought out in Eaton v. The Boston, Concord & Montreal Railroad, 51 N.H. 504, pp. 511-2 (1872).

leading. The phrase is, *"Dominium est jus utendi et abutendi re."* Some
have said that it means that the right of property carries with it the right
to use or to abuse a thing, and so it has been actually claimed that property
is the right to use or misuse a thing, and that the right of property carries
with it the right to make a bad use of things. But such an idea comes from
bad translation. *Abutendi* means to use up or consume a thing, not to
abuse it, and that has been conclusively shown by Knies [4] in his discussion
of the subject. While it means the right of using up or consuming, the
Roman law never intended to give anyone the right of misusing a thing.
This right might have existed in spite of the intent of the law, but it was
contrary to the spirit of the law to give the right. It might have existed
because it could not be prevented, but it was never sanctioned. [5] Wagner
also calls attention to the fact that, added to the phrase, *"Jus utendi et
abutendi re,"* is the generally ignored clause, *"quatenus juris ratio patitur,"*
"in so far as the reason of law permits." But Wagner claims that while
abutendi may mean simply to consume, it does carry with it at least a
suggestion or implication of misuse. [6]

The right of property is an exclusive right, but it has never been an
absolute right. In so far as the right of property existed it was an exclusive
right, that is, it excluded others; but it was not a right without limitations
or qualifications. Notice the distinction between *exclusive* and *absolute*.

The truth is, there are two sides to private property, *the individual side
and the social side.* The social side of property finds illustration in the right
of eminent domain and in the right of taxation. If there were no such
thing as the social side of private property, how could the right of taxation
exist? Take whatever theory you please. Suppose you say that the right
of taxation is payment for protection. I say, 'I do not want any protection,'
and if my right in private property is an absolute right, is not that sufficient, provided, furthermore, that I ask no privileges? The fact that I do
not want protection does not give me exemption, and it shows at once
that there is another side to private property than the individual side.

So also with the right of eminent domain. It is utterly incompatible

---

[4] Knies, *Geld,* p. 88: discussed by Wagner in his *Grundlegung,* 3d ed., Vol. II,
pp. 37-38.

[5] For the view that *"jus utendi et abutendi"* does not give the right of misuse, but
only the right of consuming or using up, see also *Moralphilosophie,* by Viktor
Cathrein, 4th ed., Vol. II, p. 310, note 1.

[6] In Valentin Meyer's *Eigentum nach den verschiedenen Weltanschauungen* the
extreme individualism of the treatment of property by the Romans is discussed
critically and suggestively. On the one hand, the private owner abused his rights
outrageously; on the other hand, he was at times called upon to make unwarranted
sacrifices and was inadequately protected against confiscation. There was a dualism
of private rights and state rights which only in modern times has been replaced by
the social theory of property, a unified concept which is large enough to include
both individual and social rights. On property among the ancient Romans, *v.* Meyer,
ibid. pp. 11-13. The whole first chapter, entitled *"Das Altertum"* is well worth reading.

with the absolute right of private property. *Moreover, this social side of private property is not to be regarded as something exceptional.* On the contrary it is an essential part of the institution itself. It is just as much a part of private property, as it exists at the present time, as the individual side is a part of it. The two necessarily go together, so that if one perishes the other must perish. The social side limits the individual side, and as it is always present there is no such thing as absolute private property. An absolute right of property, as the great jurist, the late Professor von Ihering says, would result in the dissolution of society. [Pp. 135-137.]

. . . . .

Another attribute which is sometimes ascribed to property is perpetuity. The statement is made by Professor H. von Scheel as a characteristic of property that it is unlimited in time, that is, not dependent upon a definite time; in other words, it is perpetual, and its duration is not dependent upon any event or upon the legal action of another person without the consent of the possessor. This same idea is apparent in Austin's definition. Austin defines property or *dominium* in a "strict sense" as denoting a right—indefinite in point of user, etc. But he also mentions various other uses of the term, one of these denoting "a right indefinite in point of user, but limited in duration; for example, a life interest in movables." [25] It is on account of this idea that property must be perpetual that Professor von Scheel does not accept the concept "intellectual property" which is used in Germany and England. The term "intellectual property" means property in books, in inventions, patents and copyrights, property in the product of one's intellect. This property is a limited property, copyrights extending only over an extreme period of fifty-six years (twenty-eight years but renewable for twenty-eight years more) in the United States [26] and having a varying but limited duration in other countries. But it is the opinion of the author that to deny to copyrights, patents, etc., the title property is a mistake, for he agrees with Professor Wagner [27] who considers such property as true property. Why does property need to be perpetual? If by property we mean exclusive control, why need that exclusive control continue for ever? If I have property for fifty-six years, and have full and exclusive control for that period, a control subject to no one else, then I have the full rights of property. Of course, if I had only the right to use a thing for fifty-six years, over which somebody else had a higher right, that would be a different matter. That would be a lease,

---

[25] Austin, *Lectures on Jurisprudence* (London, 1863), Vol. II, pp. 477-8.

[26] Formerly twenty-eight years, and renewable for a period of fourteen years. At present twenty-eight years, and renewable for a period of twenty-eight years by the terms of the Act of March 4, 1909 (Statutes at Large, Vol. XXXV, Pt. 1, pp. 1075-1088).

[27] Professor Wagner discusses this in his *Grundlegung;* he considers copyright as property, as "*geistiges Eigentum.*"

a contract right or limited inheritance or some other limited right. But here the thing itself expires in fifty-six years. My right does not pass over to another but becomes a free good. The single copy of a book which I hold in my hand will be property indefinitely until it is all used up and consumed,—a thousand years, if you please; but the intellectual property is not the paper or the cover of the book; it consists in a certain expression, a form given to certain ideas, and that may expire in twenty-eight years or in fifty-six years, or a longer period as the case may be. It is intellectual property, and, it seems to the author, is full property, but it is property limited in point of time. No valid reason appears why we cannot have many kinds of property with varying duration, which after that duration expire and become free goods. At the end of the fifty-six years at the most anyone in the United States may make copies of a book; likewise he may use an invention when the patent expires.

We must here as elsewhere recognize evolution; we are developing an increasing number of limited rights. *Limitation* is one of the more significant and essential things in the development of property rights. Limitations make it possible to review and revise rights later when larger experience and increasing knowledge give more abundant light. Property has undergone changes in the past and is still undergoing changes now. We cannot look far into the future to see what will be the probable development; therefore we cannot attribute eternity to property even in the limited sense in which we use the term. Why then should we refuse the name of property to economic rights which have a definite duration, which are strictly limited in duration? If these rights during the time of their duration partake of all the characteristics of property, if they give exclusive control over things and rights for a certain time, why should they not be called property?

If one pleases one can classify property with respect to duration— property of unlimited duration, property of indefinite duration (newer franchises, during good behaviour, so to speak), and property definitely limited in time, say, twenty years, fifty years, etc.

We now pass on to the *varying intensivity of property*, of which mention has already been made in a general way. Property extends to various kinds of things and various sorts of rights. It extends to movables and immovables especially, and this is one of the most important distinctions. But it must not be supposed that we have the same laws for all kinds of property, for these laws vary with the varying intensivity of property. This is a point which has been made by various modern writers; among them by Professor Emile de Laveleye who brings out this point in the following words: "It is for economic reasons also that rights of property are more or less extensive,[28] according to the different objects to which

---

[28] According to our terminology, this should be "intensive."

they refer; being almost absolute in relation to objects which are movables, but already limited when we come to arable land, and still more restricted for houses and forests and finally for mines and railways closely hedged in by the intervention of public authority." [29] [Pp. 151-154.]

Chapter VII. Property and the Police Power

.   .   .   .   .

As in the United States all property is held subject to regulations, restrictions, and burdens under the police power, it is appropriate to quote from opinions of the United States Supreme Court giving the views of that high tribunal in noteworthy cases. In the celebrated Slaughter House Cases (1872) we find the following said of the police power:

The power is, and must be from its very nature, incapable of any very exact definition or limitation. Upon it depends the security of the social order, the life and health of the citizen, the comfort of an existence in a thickly populated community, the enjoyment of private and social life, and the beneficial use of property. As says another eminent judge, "... Persons and property are subjected to all kinds of restraints and burdens in order to secure the general comfort, health, and prosperity of the State. Of the perfect right of the legislature to do this, no question ever was, or, *upon acknowledged general principles, ever can be made,* so far as natural persons are concerned." (*Thorpe v. Rutland & Burlington R. R. Co.,* 27 Vt. 139, 1854).

This is clearly stated by Chief Justice Lemuel Shaw: "All property is acquired and held under the tacit condition that it shall not be used so as to injure the equal rights of others, or to destroy or greatly impair the public rights and interest of the community; under the maxim of the common law, *Sic utere tuo ut alienum non laedas.*" [17] [Pp. 218-219.]

.   .   .   .   .

Still more noteworthy is the opinion of the court as expressed by Mr. Justice Holmes in *Noble State Bank v. Haskell.*

"The police power extends to all the great public needs. It may be put forth in aid of what is sanctioned by usage, *or held by the prevailing morality or the strong and preponderant opinion to be greatly and immediately necessary to the public welfare.*" [18]

Now there is more in this police power than regulation of property relations and contractual relations. But there is no difficulty except where property and economic relations are concerned. No one objects to general benevolence—to doing good without cost—so when we consider police power, its essence is the interpretation of property, and when we consider

---

[29] See his book, *Luxury* (Sonnenschein Social Science Series), chapter on "Law and Morals in Political Economy," pp. 159-60.

[17] Commonwealth v. Tewksbury, 11 Metcalf (Mass.), 55 (1846), at p. 57.

[18] Noble State Bank v. Haskell, 219 U.S. 110 (1911), p. 111.

the real essence of the police power as found in the leading American decisions we find that it is consistent with this concept. *It is that power of the courts committed to them by American Constitutions whereby they must shape property and contract to existing social conditions by settling the question of how far social regulations may, without compensation, impose burdens on property.* It seeks to preserve the satisfactory development of the individual and social sides of private property and thus to maintain a satisfactory equilibrium between them. And it is noteworthy that compensation may be given when property is destroyed under the police power. Tuberculous cows are killed in Wisconsin, but a limited compensation is granted to the owner in pursuance of sound public policy, for it lessens the temptation to conceal disease and it diffuses the loss.

Regulation depends on the past—on what was done in England when the Constitution was framed, that is, precedent but likewise on present conditions and sentiments as seen in the quotation given from Mr. Justice Holmes. [Pp. 220-221.]

Chapter XI. A Discussion of the Kinds of Property (Concluded)

. . . . .

The distinction between property in mobilia and property in immobilia is one of great importance. The difference in the periods in which property was developed is one which brings out the difference between property in mobilia and property in immobilia, property in immobilia being of far slower development. There are several reasons for this: In primitive periods abundance of immobilia, including land, and migration rendered the exclusive appropriation of immobilia difficult. Yet another reason is that mobilia or movable things represented at first more labour, more toil and effort than the immobilia. The mobilia stood for an incorporation of labour power. The immobilia in primitive society were the product of nature; they represented the nature factor. In the course of development this particular difference though it does not disappear, is diminished. As time goes on, more and more work is intermingled with the nature factor, with what nature gives. Especially is this true with land, and included in immobilia we have chiefly land.[3] There are bridges, ditches, houses, machinery, etc., connected permanently with the land and improvements, which after a while we cannot distinguish from the land. For instance, we cannot go into a country like Holland and always distinguish between what nature has done and what man has done. Yet even in the case of the steam railways of Wisconsin, the land has been

---

[3] *Cf.* Wagner, *op. cit.* pp. 200-210, where the reader may find a classification similar to that which follows in this chapter. While it is different in important particulars, the author wishes to acknowledge his indebtedness to it for helpful suggestions.

valued separately from the tracts, ties, and other improvements which make the railways and spoil the land for other uses. Probably in few cases would the separate valuation be more difficult.

Land represents more and more the results of human effort of one sort or another. We may therefore say that in this particular, as time goes on, the distinction between mobilia and immobilia is less sharply defined than in primitive times. Doubtless it is on this account that the statute law makes less distinction in later than in earlier times between property in mobilia and in immobilia. Nevertheless, the law may go too far and we may go too far in this respect. The difference which does actually exist even in modern times may be overlooked. But recent discussions, like those of Henry George, sharpen the distinction for us; some of them even exaggerate it.* [Pp. 274-275.]

AIGLER, BIGELOW, AND POWELL, CASES AND MATERIALS ON PROPERTY †

Human beings ... have various needs and desires. Many of these relate to external objects with which they are in some way associated. ... The law of property may be looked at as an attempt upon the part of the state, acting through its courts and administrative officers, to give a systematized recognition of and protection of these attitudes and desires on the part of individuals towards things.‡

AMERICAN LAW INSTITUTE, RESTATEMENT OF PROPERTY

§ 1. *Right.*

A right, as the word is used in this Restatement, is a legally enforceable claim of one person against another, that the other shall do a given act or shall not do a given act.

---

* [In the remainder of this chapter Professor Ely suggests some grounds for the distinctions (to a certain extent already recognized in law) between (*a*) common property and property in severalty, (*b*) public and private property, (*c*) individual, partnership, and corporate property, (*d*) property in human beings and non-human property, (*e*) property in things, services, and relations, (*f*) property in consumption and in production goods, (*g*) property in necessaries, in comforts, and in luxuries, (*h*) fixed, circulating, specialized, and free capital, and (*i*) various types of real estate.

In this connection it is interesting to examine the grounds upon which the early common law established its great distinction between real and personal property. Increasingly in our day the question is raised whether these grounds persist, and whether other basic distinctions in treatment are called for in dealing with capital goods and consumers' goods or with other distinctions of economic significance.]

† [(1943) Part 1, Chap. 1, Sec. 1.]

‡ [*Cf.* 42 *Amer. Jur.* 187 (1942): "In its strict legal sense property signifies that dominion or indefinite rights of user control and disposition which one may lawfully exercise over particular things or objects."]

§ 2. *Privilege.*

A privilege, as the word is used in this Restatement, is a legal freedom on the part of one person as against another to do a given act or a legal freedom not to do a given act.

§ 3. *Power.*

A power, as the word is used in this Restatement, is an ability on the part of a person to produce a change in a given legal relation by doing or not doing a given act.

§ 4. *Immunity.*

An immunity, as the word is used in this Restatement, is a freedom on the part of one person against having a given legal relation altered by a given act or omission to act on the part of another person.

§ 5. *"Interest."*

The word "interest" is used in this Restatement both generically to include varying aggregates of rights, privileges, powers and immunities and distributively to mean any one of them.

§ 10. *"Owner."*

The word "owner," as it is used in this Restatement, means the person who has one or more interests.

INTERNATIONAL NEWS SERVICE v. ASSOCIATED PRESS

UNITED STATES SUPREME COURT, 1918
248 U.S. 215

MR. JUSTICE PITNEY delivered the opinion of the court:

The parties are competitors in the gathering and distribution of news and its publication for profit in newspapers throughout the United States. . . . [P. 229.]

·   ·   ·   ·   ·

The only matter that has been argued before us is whether defendant may lawfully be restrained from appropriating news taken from bulletins issued by complainant or any of its members, or from newspapers published by them, for the purpose of selling it to defendant's clients. Complainant asserts that defendant's admitted course of conduct in this regard both violates complainant's property right in the news and constitutes unfair competition in business. . . . [P. 232.]

·   ·   ·   ·   ·

We need spend no time, however, upon the general question of property in news matter at common law, or the application of the Copyright Act, since it seems to us the case must turn upon the question of unfair competition in business. And, in our opinion, this does not depend upon any general right of property analogous to the common-law right of the proprietor of an unpublished work to prevent its publication without his consent; nor is it foreclosed by showing that the benefits of the Copyright Act have been waived.... [Pp. 235-236.]

. . . . . .

... And although we may and do assume that neither party has any remaining property interest as against the public in uncopyrighted news matter after the moment of its first publication, it by no means follows that there is no remaining property interest in it as between themselves. For, to both of them alike, news matter, however little susceptible of ownership or dominion in the absolute sense, is stock in trade, to be gathered at the cost of enterprise, organization, skill, labor, and money, and to be distributed and sold to those who will pay money for it, as for any other merchandise. Regarding the news, therefore, as but the material out of which both parties are seeking to make profits at the same time and in the same field, we hardly can fail to recognize that for this purpose, and as between them, it must be regarded as quasi property, irrespective of the rights of either as against the public. [P. 236.]

. . . . . .

The peculiar features of the case arise from the fact that, while novelty and freshness form so important an element in the success of the business, the very processes of distribution and publication necessarily occupy a good deal of time. Complainant's service, as well as defendant's is a daily service to daily newspapers; most of the foreign news reaches this country at the Atlantic seaboard, principally at the city of New York; and because of this, and of time differentials, due to the earth's rotation, the distribution of news matter throughout the country is principally from east to west; and, since in speed the telegraph and telephone easily outstrip the rotation of the earth, it is a simple matter for defendant to take complainant's news from bulletins or early editions of complainant's members in the eastern cities, and at the mere cost of telegraphic transmission cause it to be published in western papers issued at least as early as those served by complainant. Besides this and irrespective of time differentials, irregularities in telegraphic transmission on different lines, and the normal consumption of time in printing and distributing the newspaper, result in permitting pirated news to be placed in the hands of defendant's readers sometimes simultaneously with the service of competing Associated Press papers; occasionally even earlier.

Defendant insists that when, with the sanction and approval of complainant, and as the result of the use of its news for the very purpose for which it is distributed, a portion of complainant's members communicate it to the general public by posting it upon bulletin boards so that all may read, or by issuing it to newspapers and distributing it indiscriminately, complainant no longer has the right to control the use to be made of it; that when it thus reaches the light of day it becomes the common possession of all to whom it is accessible; and that any purchaser of a newspaper has the right to communicate the intelligence which it contains to anybody and for any purpose, even for the purpose of selling it for profit to newspapers published for profit in competition with complainant's members.

The fault in the reasoning lies in applying as a test the right of the complainant as against the public, instead of considering the rights of complainant and defendant, competitors in business, as between themselves. The right of the purchaser of a single newspaper to spread knowledge of its contents gratuitously, for any legitimate purpose not reasonably interfering with complainant's right to make merchandise of it, may be admitted; but to transmit that news for commercial use, in competition with complainant,—which is what defendant has done and seeks to justify, —is a very different matter. In doing this, defendant, by its very act, admits that it is taking material that has been acquired by complainant as the result of organization and the expenditure of labor, skill, and money and which is salable by complainant for money, and that defendant, in appropriating it and selling it as its own, is endeavoring to reap where it has not sown, and by disposing of it to newspapers that are competitors of complainant's members is appropriating to itself the harvest of those who have sown. Stripped of all disguises, the process amounts to an unauthorized interference with the normal operation of complainant's legitimate business precisely at the point where the profit is to be reaped, in order to divert a material portion of the profit from those who have earned it to those who have not, with special advantage to defendant in the competition because of the fact that it is not burdened with any part of the expense of gathering the news. The transaction speaks for itself, and a court of equity ought not to hesitate long in characterizing it as unfair competition in business. [Pp. 238-240.]

. . . . .

The contention that the news is abandoned to the public for all purposes when published in the first newspaper is untenable. Abandonment is a question of intent, and the entire organization of the Associated Press negatives such a purpose. The cost of the service would be prohibitive if the reward were to be so limited. No single newspaper, no small group of newspapers, could sustain the expenditure. Indeed, it is one of the most obvious results of defendant's theory that, by permitting indiscriminate publication by anybody and everybody for purposes of profit in competition with the news gatherer, it would render publication profitless, or so little profitable as in effect to cut off the service by rendering the cost prohibitive in comparison with the return. The practical needs and requirements of the business are reflected in complainant's by-laws, which have been referred to. Their effect is that publication by each member must be deemed not by any means an abandonment of the news to the world for any and all purposes, but a publication for limited purposes; for the benefit of the readers of the bulletin or the newspaper as such; not for the purpose of making merchandise of it as news, with the result of depriving complainant's other members of their reasonable opportunity to obtain just returns for their expenditures.

It is to be observed that the view we adopt does not result in giving to complainant the right to monopolize either the gathering or the distribution of the news; or, without complying with the Copyright Act, to prevent the reproduction of its news articles; but only postpones participation by complainant's competitor in the processes of distribution and reproduction of news that it has not gathered, and only to the extent necessary to prevent that competitor from reaping the fruits of complainant's efforts and expenditure, to the partial exclusion of complainant, and in violation of the principle that underlies the maxim *"sic utere tuo,"* etc.

It is said that the elements of unfair competition are lacking because there is no attempt by defendant to palm off its goods as those of the complainant, characteristic of the most familiar, if not the most typical, cases of unfair competition. *Howe Scale Co. v. Wyckoff, Seamans & Benedict,* 198 U.S. 118, 140, 49 L.ed. 972, 986, 25 Sup. Ct. Rep. 609. But we cannot concede that the right to equitable relief is confined to that class of cases. In the present case the fraud upon complainant's rights is more direct and obvious. Regarding news matter as the mere material from which these two competing parties are endeavoring to make money, and treating it, therefore, as quasi property for the purposes of their business because they are both selling it as such, defendant's conduct differs from the ordinary case of unfair competition in trade principally in this: that, instead of selling its own goods as those of complainant, it substitutes misappropriation in the place of misrepresentation, and sells complainant's goods as its own. [Pp. 240-242.]

.   .   .   .   .   .

MR. JUSTICE HOLMES:

When an uncopyrighted combination of words is published there is no general right to forbid other people repeating them,—in other words, there is no property in the combination or in the thoughts or facts that the words express. Property, a creation of law, does not arise from value, although exchangeable,—a matter of fact. Many exchangeable values may be destroyed intentionally without compensation. Property depends upon exclusion by law from interference, and a person is not excluded from using any combination of words merely because someone has used it before, even if it took labor and genius to make it. If a given person is to be prohibited from making the use of words that his neighbors are free to make, some other ground must be found. One such ground is vaguely expressed in the phrase "unfair trade." This means that the words are repeated by a competitor in business in such a way as to convey a misrepresentation that materially injures the person who first used them, by appropriating credit of some kind which the first user has earned. The ordinary case is a representation by device, appearance, or other indirection that the defendant's goods come from the plaintiff. But the only reason why it is actionable to make such a representation is that it tends to give the defendant an advantage in his competition with the plaintiff, and that it is thought undesirable that an advantage should be gained in that way. Apart from that, the defendant may use such unpatented devices and uncopyrighted combinations of words as he likes. The ordinary case, I say, is palming off the defendant's product as the plaintiff's; but the same evil may follow from the opposite falsehood,—from saying, whether in words or by implication, that the plaintiff's product is the defendant's; and that, it seems to me, is what has happened here.

Fresh news is got only by enterprise and expense. To produce such news as it is produced by the defendant represents by implication that it has been acquired by the defendant's enterprise and at its expense. When it comes from one of the great news collecting agencies like the Associated Press, the source generally is indicated, plainly importing that credit; and that such a representation is implied may be inferred with some confidence from the unwillingness of the defendant to give the credit and tell the truth. If the plaintiff produces the news at the same time that the defendant does, the defendant's presentation impliedly denies to the plaintiff the credit of collecting the facts and assumes that credit to the defendant. If the plaintiff is later in western cities, it naturally will be supposed to have obtained its information from the defendant. The falsehood is a little more subtle, the injury a little more indirect, than in ordinary cases of unfair trade, but I think that the principle that condemns the one condemns the other. It is a question of how strong an infusion of fraud is necessary to turn a flavor into a poison. The dose seems to be strong enough here to need a remedy from the law. But as, in my view, the only ground of complaint that can be recognized without legislation is the implied misstatement, it can be corrected by stating the truth; and a suitable acknowledgment of the source is all that the plaintiff can require. I think that, within the limits recognized by the decision of the court, the defendant should be enjoined from publishing news obtained from the Associated Press for hours after publication by the plaintiff unless it gives express credit to the Associated Press; the number of hours and the form of acknowledgment to be settled by the district court.

Mr. Justice McKenna concurs in this opinion.

Mr. Justice Brandeis, dissenting: [Pp. 246-248]

.   .   .   .   .

That news is not property in the strict sense is illustrated by the case of *Sports & G. Press Agency v. "Our Dogs" Pub. Co.* [1916] 2 K.B. 880, 85 L.J. K.B. N.S. 1573, 115 L.T.N.S. 378, 32 Times L.R. 651, where the plaintiff, the assignee of the right to photograph the exhibits at a dog show, was refused an injunction against defendant, who had also taken pictures of the show and was publishing them. The court said that, except in so far as the possession of the land occupied by the show enabled the proprietors to exclude people or permit them on condition that they agree not to take photographs (which condition was not imposed in that case), the proprietors had no exclusive right to photograph the show and could therefore grant no such right. And it was further stated that, at any rate, no matter what conditions might be imposed upon those entering the grounds, if the defendant had been on top of a house or in some position where he could photograph the show without interfering with the physical property of the plaintiff, the plaintiff would have no right to stop him. If, when the plaintiff creates the event recorded, he is not entitled to the exclusive first publication of the news (in that case a photograph) of the event, no reason can be shown why he should be accorded such protection as to events which he simply records and transmits to other parts of the world, though with great expenditure of time and money.

Third: If news be treated as possessing the characteristics not of a trade secret, but of literary property, then the earliest issue of a paper of general circulation or the earliest public posting of a bulletin which embodies such news would, under the established rules governing literary property, operate as a publication, and all property in the news would then cease. Resisting this conclusion, plaintiff relied upon the cases which hold that uncopyrighted intellectual and artistic property survives private circulation or a restricted publication; and it contended that in each issue of each paper a restriction is to be implied that the news shall not be used gainfully in competition with the Associated Press or any of its members. There is no basis for such an implication. But it is also well settled that where the publication is in fact a general one, even express words of restriction upon use are inoperative. In other words, a general publication is effective to dedicate literary property to the public, regardless of the actual intent of its owner.[9] In the cases dealing with lectures, dramatic and musical performances, and art exhibitions,[10] upon which plaintiff relied, there was no general publication in print comparable to the issue of daily newspapers or the unrestricted public posting of bulletins. The principles governing those cases differ more or less in application, if not in theory, from the principles governing the issue of printed copies; and in so far as they do differ, they have no application to the case at bar.

Fourth: Plaintiff further contended that defendant's practice constitutes unfair competition because there is "appropriation without cost to itself of values created by" the plaintiff; and it is upon this ground that the decision of this court appears to be based. To appropriate and use for profit, knowledge and ideas produced by other men, without making compensation or even acknowledgment, may be inconsistent with a finer sense of propriety; but, with the exceptions indicated above, the law has heretofore sanctioned the practice. Thus it was held that one may ordinarily make and sell anything in any form, may copy with exactness that which another has produced, or may otherwise use his ideas without his consent and without the payment of compensation, and yet not inflict a legal injury; [11] and that ordinarily one is at perfect liberty to find out, if he can by lawful means, trade secrets of another, however valuable, and then use the knowledge so acquired gainfully, although it cost the original owner much in effort and in money to collect or produce.[12]

Such taking and gainful use of a product of another which, for reasons of public policy, the law has refused to endow with the attributes of property, does not become unlawful because the product happens to have been taken from a rival and is used in competition with him. The unfairness in competition which hitherto has been recognized by the law as a basis for relief lay in the manner or means of conducting the business; and the manner or means held legally unfair involves either fraud or force or the doing of acts otherwise prohibited by law. In the "passing off" cases (the typical and most common case of unfair competition), the wrong consists in fraudulently representing by word or act that defendant's goods are those of plaintiff. See *Hanover Star Mill. Co. v. Metcalf*, 240 U.S. 403, 412-413, 60 L.ed. 713, 717, 718, 36 Sup.Ct.Rep. 357. In the other cases, the diversion of trade was effected through physical or moral coercion, or by inducing breaches of contract or of trust, or by enticing away employees. In some others, called cases of simulated competition, relief was granted because defendant's purpose was unlawful; namely, not competition, but deliberate and wanton destruction of plaintiff's business.[13]

That competition is not unfair in a legal sense, merely because the profits gained are unearned, even if made at the expense of a rival, is shown by many cases besides those referred to above. He who follows the pioneer into a new market, or who engages in the manufacture of an article newly introduced by another, seeks profits due largely to the labor and expense of the first adventurer; but the law sanctions, indeed encourages, the pursuit.[14] He who makes a city known through his product must submit to sharing the resultant trade with others who, perhaps for that reason, locate there later. *Delaware & H. Canal Co. v. Clark*, 13 Wall. 311, 20 L.ed. 581; *Elgin Nat. Watch Co. v. Illinois Watch*

Co., 179 U.S. 665, 673, 45 L.ed. 365; 378, 21 Sup.Ct.Rep. 270. . . . [Pp. 255–259.]

. . . . .

A legislature, urged to enact a law by which one news agency or newspaper may prevent appropriation of the fruits of its labors by another, would consider such facts and possibilities and others which appropriate inquiry might disclose. Legislators might conclude that it was impossible to put an end to the obvious injustice involved in such appropriation of news without opening the door to other evils, greater than that sought to be remedied. Such appears to have been the opinion of our Senate, which reported unfavorably a bill to give news a few hours' protection; [16] and which ratified, on February 15, 1911, the convention adopted at the Fourth International American Conference; [17] and such was evidently the view also of the signatories to the International Copyright Union of November 13, 1908; [18] as both these conventions expressly exclude news from copyright protection.

Or legislators dealing with the subject might conclude that the right to news values should be protected to the extent of permitting recovery of damages for any unauthorized use, but that protection by injunction should be denied, just as courts of equity ordinarily refuse (perhaps in the interest of free speech) to restrain actionable libels,[19] and for other reasons decline to protect by injunction mere political rights; [20] and as Congress has prohibited courts from enjoining the illegal assessment or collection of Federal taxes.[21] If a legislature concluded to recognize property in published news to the extent of permitting recovery at law, it might, with a view to making the remedy more certain and adequate, provide a fixed measure of damages, as in the case of copyright infringement.[22]

Or again, a legislature might conclude that it was unwise to recognize even so limited a property right in published news as that above indicated; but that a news agency should, on some conditions, be given full protection of its business; and to that end a remedy by injunction as well as one for damages should be granted, where news collected by it is gainfully used without permission. If a legislature concluded (as at least one court has held, *New York & C. Grain & Stock Exch. v. Board of Trade*, 127 Ill. 153, 2 L.R.A. 411, 19 N.E. 855) that, under certain circumstances, news-gathering is a business affected with a public interest, it might declare that, in such cases, news should be protected against appropriation only if the gatherer assumed the obligation of supplying it at reasonable rates and without discrimination, to all papers which applied therefor. If legislators reached that conclusion, they would probably go further, and prescribe the conditions under which and the extent to which the protection should be afforded; and they might also provide the administrative machinery necessary for insuring to the public, the press, and the news agencies, full enjoyment of the rights so conferred.

Courts are ill-equipped to make the investigations which should precede a determination of the limitations which should be set upon any property right in news, or of the circumstances under which news gathered by a private agency should be deemed affected with a public interest. Courts would be powerless to prescribe the detailed regulations essential to full enjoyment of the rights conferred, or to introduce the machinery required for enforcement of such regulations. Consideration such as these should lead us to decline to establish a new rule of law in the effort to redress a newly disclosed wrong, although the propriety of some remedy appears to be clear. [Pp. 264-267.]

M. R. COHEN, PROPERTY AND SOVEREIGNTY *

1. Property As Power

Anyone who frees himself from the crudest materialism readily recognizes that as a legal term "property" denotes not material things but certain rights. In the world of nature apart from more or less organized society, there are things but clearly no property rights.

Further reflection shows that a property right is not to be identified with the fact of physical possession. Whatever technical definition of property we may prefer, we must recognize that a property right is a relation not between an owner and a thing, but between the owner and other individuals in reference to things. A right is always against one or more individuals. This becomes unmistakably clear if we take specifically modern forms of property such as franchises, patents, good will, etc., which constitute such a large part of the capitalized assets of our industrial and commercial enterprises.

The classical view of property as a right over things resolves it into component rights such as the *jus utendi, jus disponendi,* etc. But the essence of private property is always the right to exclude others. The law does not guarantee me the physical or social ability of actually using what it calls mine. By public regulations it may indirectly aid me by removing certain general hindrances to the enjoyment of property. But the law of property helps me directly only to exclude others from using the things which it assigns to me. If then somebody else wants to use the food, the house, the land, or the plough that the law calls mine, he has to get my consent. To the extent that these things are necessary to the life of my neighbour, the law thus confers on me a power, limited but real, to make

---

* [Morris R. Cohen's essay on "Property and Sovereignty" was first delivered as an Irvine Lecture at Cornell University in 1926 and was published in 13 *Cornell L.Q.* 8 (1927) and reprinted in *Law and the Social Order,* pp. 45 *et seq.* New York: Harcourt, Brace and Company, Inc., 1933. Page references are to the latter work.]

him do what I want. If Laban has the sole disposal of his daughters and his cattle, Jacob must serve him if he desires to possess them. In a regime where land is the principal source of obtaining a livelihood, he who has the legal right over the land receives homage and service from those who wish to live on it.

The character of property as sovereign power compelling service and obedience may be obscured for us in a commercial economy by the fiction of the so-called labour contract as a free bargain and by the frequency with which service is rendered indirectly through a money payment. But not only is there actually little freedom to bargain on the part of the steel-worker or miner who needs a job, but in some cases the medieval subject had as much power to bargain when he accepted the sovereignty of his lord. Today I do not directly serve my landlord if I wish to live in the city with a roof over my head, but I must work for others to pay him rent with which he obtains the personal services of others. The money needed for purchasing things must for the vast majority be acquired by hard labour and disagreeable service to those to whom the law has accorded dominion over the things necessary for subsistence.

To a philosopher this is of course not at all an argument against private property. It may well be that compulsion in the economic as well as the political realm is necessary for civilized life. But we must not overlook the actual fact that dominion over things is also *imperium* over our fellow human beings.

The extent of the power over the life of others which the legal order confers on those called owners is not fully appreciated by those who think of the law as merely protecting men in their possession. Property law does more. It determines what men shall acquire. Thus, protecting the property rights of a landlord means giving him the right to collect rent, protecting the property of a railroad or a public-service corporation means giving it the right to make certain charges. Hence the ownership of land and machinery, with the rights of drawing rent, interest, etc., determines the future distribution of the goods that will come into being—determines what share of such goods various individuals shall acquire. The average life of goods that are either consumable or used for production of other goods is very short. Hence a law that merely protected men in their possession and did not also regulate the acquisition of new goods would be of little use.

From this point of view it can readily be seen that when a court rules that a gas company is entitled to a return of 6 per cent on its investment, it is not merely protecting property already possessed, it is also determining that a portion of the future social produce shall under certain conditions go to that company. Thus not only medieval landlords but the owners of all revenue-producing property are in fact granted by the law certain powers to tax the future social product. When to this power of taxation there is added the power to command the services of large numbers who are not economically independent, we have the essence of what historically has constituted political sovereignty.

Though the sovereign power possessed by the modern large property owners assumes a somewhat different form from that formerly possessed by the lord of the land, they are not less real and no less extensive. Thus the ancient lord had a limited power to control the modes of expenditure of his subjects by direct sumptuary legislation. The modern captain of industry and of finance has no such direct power himself, though his direct or indirect influence with the legislature may in that respect be considerable. But those who have the power to standardize and advertise certain products do determine what we may buy and use. We cannot well wear clothes except within lines decreed by their manufacturers, and our food is becoming more and more restricted to the kinds that are branded and standardized.

This power of the modern owner of capital to make us feel the necessity of buying more and more of his material goods (that may be more profitable to produce than economical to use) is a phenomenon of the utmost significance to the moral philosopher. The moral philosopher must also note that the modern captain of industry or finance exercises greater influence in setting the fashion of expenditure by his personal example. Between a landed aristocracy and the tenantry, the difference is sharp and fixed, so that imitation of the former's mode of life by the latter is regarded as absurd and even immoral. In a money or commercial economy differences of income and mode of life are more gradual and readily hidden so that there is great pressure to engage in lavish expenditure in order to appear in a higher class than one's income really allows. Such expenditure may even advance one's business credit. This puts pressure not merely on ever greater expenditure but more specifically on expenditure for ostentation rather than for comfort. Though a landed aristocracy may be wasteful in keeping large tracts of land for hunting purposes, the need for discipline to keep in power compels the cultivation of a certain hardihood that the modern wealthy man can ignore. An aristocracy assured of its recognized superiority need not engage in the race of lavish expenditure regardless of enjoyment.

In addition to these indirect ways in which the wealthy few determine the mode of life of the many, there is the somewhat more direct mode that bankers and financiers exercise when they determine the flow of investment, e.g., when they influence building operations by the amount that they will lend on mortgages. This power becomes explicit and obvious when a needy country has to borrow foreign capital to develop its resources.

I have already mentioned that the recognition of private property as a form of sovereignty is not itself an argument against it. Some form of

government we must always have. For the most part men prefer to obey
and let others take the trouble to think out rules, regulations and orders.
That is why we are always setting up authorities; and when we cannot
find any we write to the newspaper as the final arbiter. But although
government is a necessity, not all forms of it are of equal value. At any
rate it is necessary to apply to the law of property all those considerations
of social ethics and enlightened public policy which ought to be brought
to the discussion of any just form of government. [Pp. 45-49.]

.   .   .   .   .

III. Limitations of Property Rights

The traditional theory of rights, and the one that still prevails in this
country, was molded by the struggle in the seventeenth and eighteenth
centuries against restrictions on individual enterprise. These restrictions
in the interest of special privilege were fortified by the divine (and therefore absolute) rights of kings. As is natural in all revolts, absolute claims
on one side were met with absolute denials on the other. Hence the
theory of the natural rights of the individual took not only an absolute
but a negative form; men have *in*alienable rights, the state must never
interfere with private property, etc. The state, however, must interfere
in order that individual rights should become effective and not degenerate
into public nuisances. To permit anyone to do absolutely what he likes
with his property in creating noise, smells, or danger of fire, would be
to make property in general valueless. To be really effective, therefore,
the right of property must be supported by restrictions or positive duties
on the part of owners, enforced by the state as much as the right to
exclude others that is the essence of property. Unfortunately, however,
whether because of the general decline of juristic philosophy after Hegel
or because law has become more interested in defending property against
attacks by socialists, the doctrine of natural rights has remained in the
negative state and has never developed into a doctrine of the positive
contents of rights based upon an adequate notion of the function of
these rights in society.[12]

Lawyers occupied with civil or private law have in any case continued
the absolutistic conception of property; and in doing this, they are faithful to the language of the great eighteenth century codes, the French,
Prussian, and Austrian, and even of the nineteenth century codes like
the Italian and German, which also begin with a definition of property

---

[12] Thus our courts are reluctant to admit that rules against unfair competition may
be in the interest of the general public and not merely for those whose immediate
property interests are directly affected. Levy v. Walker, 10 Ch. D. 436 (1878);
American Washboard Co. v. Saginaw Mfg. Co., 103 Fed. 281, 285 (C.C.A. 6th,
1900); Dickenson v. N.R. Co., 76 W.Va. 148, 151, 85 S.E. 71 (1915).

as absolute or unlimited, though they subsequently introduce qualifying or limiting provisions.[13]

As, however, no individual rights can in fact be exercised in a community, except under public regulation, it has been left mainly to publicists,[14] to writers on politics and constitutional and administrative law to consider the limitations of private property necessary for public safety, peace, health, and morals, as well as for those enterprises like housing, education, the preservation of natural resources, etc., which the community finds it necessary to entrust to the state rather than to private hands. The fact, however, that in the United States the last word on law comes from judges, who, like other lawyers, are for the most part trained in private rather than in public law, is one of the reasons why with us traditional conceptions of property prevail over obvious national interests such as the freedom of labourers to organize, the necessity of preserving certain standards of living, or preventing the future manhood and womanhood of the country from being sacrificed to individual profits, and the like. Our students of property law need, therefore, to be reminded that not only has the whole law since the industrial revolution shown a steady growth in ever new restrictions upon the use of private property, but that the ideal of absolute *laissez faire* has never in fact been completely operative.

(1) Living in a free land economy we have lost the sense of how exceptional in the history of mankind is the absolutely free power of directing what shall be done with our property after our death. In the history of the common law, wills as to land begin only in the reign of Henry VIII. On the Continent it is still restrained by the system of the reserve. In England no formal restriction has been necessary because of the system of entails or strict settlement. Even in the United States, we have kept such rules as that against perpetuities which is certainly a restraint on absolute freedom of testamentary disposition.

Even as to the general power of alienating the land *inter vivos* history shows that some restrictions are always present. The persistence of dower rights in our own individualistic economy is a case in point. Land and family interest have been too closely connected to sacrifice the former completely to pure individualism.

(2) More important than the foregoing limitations upon the transfer of property are limitations of the use of property. Looking at the matter realistically, few will question the wisdom of Holdsworth's remarks,

---

[13] French Civil Code, § 544; Prussian Landrecht I, 8, § 1; Austrian General Civil Code, § 354; German Civil Code, § 903; Italian Civil Code § 436. *Cf.* Markby *Elements of Law*, 6th ed., 1905, § 310; Aubry & Rau, *Cours de droit civil français*, 5th ed., Vol. II (1897), § 190.

[14] The great Ihering is an honorable exception. The distinction between property for use and property for power was developed by the Austrian jurist, A. Menger, and made current by the German economist Adolph Wagner.

that "at no time can the state be wholly indifferent to the use which the owners make of their property".[15] There must be restrictions on the use of property not only in the interests of other property owners but also in the interests of the health, safety, religion, morals, and general welfare of the whole community. No community can view with indifference the exploitation of the needy by commercial greed. As under the conditions of crowded life the reckless or unconscionable use of one's property is becoming more and more dangerous, enlightened jurists find new doctrines to limit the abuse of ancient rights. The French doctrine of *abus de droit*, the prohibition of chicanery in the German Civil Code, and the rather vague use of "malice" in the common law are all efforts in that direction.[16]

(3) Of greatest significance is the fact that in all civilized legal systems there is a great deal of just expropriation or confiscation without any direct compensation. This may sound shocking to those who think that for the state to take away the property of the citizen is not only theft or robbery but even worse, an act of treachery, since the state avowedly exists to protect people in those very rights.

As a believer in natural rights, I believe that the state can, and unfortunately often does, enact unjust laws. But I think it is a sheer fallacy based on verbal illusion to think that the rights of the community against an individual owner are no better than the rights of a neighbour. Indeed, no one has in fact had the courage of his confusion to argue that the state has no right to deprive an individual of property to which he is so attached that he refuses any money for it. Though no neighbour has such a right the public interest often justly demands that a proprietor shall part with his ancestral home to which he may be attached by all the roots of his being.

When taking away a man's property, is the state always bound to pay a direct compensation? I submit that while this is generally advisable in order not to disturb the general feeling of security, no absolute principle of justice requires it. I have already suggested that there is no injustice in taxing an old bachelor to educate the children of others, or taxing one immune to typhoid for the construction of sewers or other sanitary measures. We may go further and say that the whole business of the state depends upon its rightful power to take away the property of some (in the form of taxation) and use it to support others, such as the needy, those invalided in the service of the state in war or peace, and those who are not yet able to produce but in whom the hope of humanity is embodied. Doubtless, taxation and confiscation may be actuated by malice and may impose needless and cruel hardship on some individuals or

---

[15] Holdsworth, *History of English Law*, (1916), Vol. VIII, Chap. IV, p. 100.

[16] Roussel, *L'Abus du droit*, 1913; German Civil Code, § 226; Walton, "Motive as an Element in Torts," 22 *Harvard Law Review* 501 (1909).

classes. But this is not to deny that taxation and confiscation are within the just powers of the state. A number of examples may make this clearer.

(a) Slavery. When slavery is abolished by law, the owners have their property taken away. Is the state ethically bound to pay them the full market value of their slaves? It is doubtless a grievous shock to a community to have a large number of slave owners, whose wealth often makes them leaders of culture, suddenly deprived of their income. It may also be conceded that it is not always desirable for the slave himself to be suddenly taken away from his master and cut adrift on the sea of freedom. But when one reads of the horrible ways in which some of those slaves were violently torn from their homes in Africa and shamelessly deprived of their human rights, one is inclined to agree with Emerson that compensation should first be paid to the slaves. This compensation need not be in the form of a direct bounty to them. It may be more effectively paid in the form of rehabilitation and education for freedom; and such a charge may take precedence over the claims of the former owners. After all, the latter claims are no greater than those of a protected industry when the tariff is removed. If the state should decide that certain import duties, *e.g.*, those on scientific instruments or hospital supplies, are unjustified and proceed to abolish them, many manufacturers may suffer. Are they entitled to compensation by the state?

It is undoubtedly for the general good to obviate as much as possible the effect of economic shock to a large number of people. The routine of life prospers on security. But when that security contains a large element of injustice the shock of an economic operation by law may be necessary and ethically justified.

This will enable us to deal with other types of confiscation.

(b) Financial loss through the abolition of public office. It is only in very recent times that we have come to forget that public office is and always has been regarded as a source of revenue like any other occupation. When, therefore, certain public offices are abolished for the sake of good government, a number of people are deprived of their expected income. In the older law and often in popular judgment of today this does not seem fair. But reflection shows that the state is not obligated to pay anyone when it finds that particular services of his are unnecessary. At best, it should help him to find a new occupation.

Part of the prerogative of the English or Scotch landlord was the right to nominate the priest for the parish on his land. To abolish this right of advowson is undoubtedly a confiscation of a definite property right. But while I cannot agree with my friend Mr. Laski [17] that the courts were wrong to refuse to disobey the law which subordinated the religious scruples of a church to the property rights of an individual, I do not see

---

[17] Laski, *Studies in the Problem of Sovereignty*, 1912, Chapter II.

that there could have been any sound ethical objection to the legislature changing the law without compensating the landlord.

(c) In our own day, we have seen the confiscation of many millions of dollars' worth of property through prohibition. Were the distillers and brewers entitled to compensation for their losses? We have seen that property on a large scale is power, and the loss of it, while an evil to those who are accustomed to exercise it, may not be an evil to the community. In point of fact, the shock to the distillers and brewers was not as serious as to others, *e.g.*, saloon keepers and bartenders who did not lose any legal property since they were only employees, but who found it difficult late in life to enter new employments.

History is full of examples of valuable property privileges abolished without any compensation, *e.g.*, the immunity of nobles from taxation, their rights to hunt over other persons' lands, etc. It would be absurd to claim that such legislation was unjust.

These and other examples of justifiable confiscation without compensation are inconsistent with the absolute theory of private property. An adequate theory of private property, however, should enable us to draw the line between justifiable and unjustifiable cases of confiscation. Such a theory I cannot here undertake to elaborate, though the doctrine of security of possession and avoidance of unnecessary shock seem to me suggestive. I wish, however, to urge that if the large property owner is viewed, as he ought to be, as a wielder of power over the lives of his fellow citizens, the law should not hesitate to develop a doctrine as to his positive duties in the public interest. The owner of a tenement house in a modern city is in fact a public official and has all sorts of positive duties. He must keep the halls lighted, he must see that the roof does not leak, that there are fire-escape facilities, he must remove tenants guilty of certain public immoralities, etc., and he is compensated by the fees of his tenants which the law is beginning to regulate. Similar is the case of a factory owner. He must install all sorts of safety appliances, hygienic conveniences, see that the workmen are provided with a certain amount of light, air, etc.

In general, there is no reason for the law insisting that people should make the most economic use of their property. They have a motive in doing so themselves and the cost of the enforcing machinery may be a mischievous waste. Yet there may be times, such as occurred during the late war, when the state may insist that man shall cultivate the soil intensively and be otherwise engaged in socially productive work.

With considerations such as these in mind, it becomes clear that there is no unjustifiable taking away of property when railroads are prohibited from posting notices that they will discharge their employees if the latter join trade unions, and that there is no property taken away without due or just process of law when an industry is compelled to pay its labourers a minimum of subsistence instead of having it done for them by private or public charity or else systematically starving its workers. [Pp. 57-63.]

F. S. COHEN, TRANSCENDENTAL NONSENSE AND THE FUNCTIONAL APPROACH*

.   .   .   .   .

3. What's in a Trade Name?

The divorce of legal reasoning from questions of social fact and ethical value is not a product of crusty legal fictions inherited from darker ages. Even in the most modern realms of legal development one finds the thought of courts and of legal scholars trapezing around in cycles and epicycles without coming to rest on the floor of verifiable fact. Modern developments in the law of unfair competition offer many examples of such circular reasoning.

There was once a theory that the law of trade marks and trade names was an attempt to protect the consumer against the "passing off" of inferior goods under misleading lables.[15] Increasingly the courts have departed from any such theory and have come to view this branch of law as a protection of property rights in divers economically valuable sale devices.[16] In practice, injunctive relief is being extended today to realms where no actual danger of confusion to the consumer is present, and this extension has been vigorously supported and encouraged by leading writers in the field.[17] Conceivably this extension might be justified by a demonstration that privately controlled sales devices serve as a psychologic base for the power of business monopolies, and that such monopolies are socially valuable in modern civilization. But no such line of argument has ever been put forward by courts or scholars advocating increased legal protection of trade names and similar devices. For if they advanced any such argument, it might seem that they were taking sides upon controversial issues of politics and economics. Courts and scholars, therefore, have taken refuge in a vicious circle to which no obviously extra-legal facts can gain admittance. The current legal argument runs: One who by the ingenuity of his advertising or the quality of his product has induced consumer responsiveness to a particular name, symbol, form

---

* [35 Col. L. Rev. 809, 814-818 (1935).]

[15] See Nims, Unfair Competition and Trade-Marks (3d ed. 1929) Sec. 8, and cases cited.

[16] See American Washboard Co. v. Saginaw Mfg. Co., 103 Fed. 281, 285 (C.C.A. 6th, 1900).

[17] Nims, op. cit. supra note 15, Sec. 9a; Handler and Pickett, Trade-Marks and Trade Names—An Analysis and Synthesis (1930) 30 Columbia Law Rev. 168, 759; Schechter, The Rational Basis of Trade-Mark Protection (1927) 40 Harv. L. Rev. 813.

of packaging, etc., has thereby created a thing of value; a thing of value is property; the creator of property is entitled to protection against third parties who seek to deprive him of his property.[18] This argument may be embellished, in particular cases, with animadversions upon the selfish motives of the infringing defendant, a summary of the plaintiff's evidence (naturally uncontradicted) as to the amount of money he has spent in advertising, and insinuations (seldom factually supported) as to the inferiority of the infringing defendant's product.

The vicious circle inherent in this reasoning is plain. It purports to base legal protection upon economic value, when, as a matter of actual fact, the economic value of a sales device depends upon the extent to which it will be legally protected. If commercial exploitation of the word "Palmolive" is not restricted to a single firm, the word will be of no more economic value to any particular firm than a convenient size, shape, mode of packing, or manner of advertising, common in the trade. Not being of economic value to any particular firm, the word would be regarded by courts as "not property," and no injunction would be issued. In other words, the fact that courts did not protect the word would make the word valueless, and the fact that it was valueless would then be regarded as a reason for not protecting it. Ridiculous as this vicious circle seems, it is logically as conclusive or inconclusive as the opposite vicious circle, which accepts the fact that courts do protect private exploitation of a given word as a reason why private exploitation of that word should be protected.

The circularity of legal reasoning in the whole field of unfair competition is veiled by the "thingification" of *property*. Legal language portrays courts as examining commercial words and finding, somewhere inhering in them, *property rights*. It is virtue of the property right which the plaintiff has acquired in the word that he is entitled to an injunction or an award of damages. According to the recognized authorities on the law of unfair competition, courts are not *creating* property, but are merely *recognizing* a pre-existent *Something*.

The theory that judicial decisions in the field of unfair competition law are merely recognitions of a supernatural Something that is immanent in certain trade names and symbols is, of course, one of the numerous progeny of the theory that judges have nothing to do with making the law, but merely recognize pre-existent truths not made by mortal men.[19]

---

[18] *Cf.* American Agricultural Chemical Co. v. Moore, 17 F. (2d) 196 (M.D. Ala. 1927) in which an interesting implication of the current theory is carried to its logical conclusion. A fertilizer company is granted an injunction against state officials seeking to prevent the use of a misleading trade name. The argument is: The plaintiff expected to do a larger business under this trade name; such expectations are property, and must be protected against governmental interference.

[19] See M. R. Cohen, The Process of Judicial Legislation, in *Law and the Social Order* (1933) 112, also printed in (1914) 48 *Am. L. Rev.* 161.

The effect of this theory, in the law of unfair competition as elsewhere, is to dull lay understanding and criticism of what courts do in fact.

What courts are actually doing, of course, in unfair competition cases, is to create and distribute a new source of economic wealth or power. Language is socially useful apart from law, as air is socially useful, but neither language nor air is a source of economic wealth unless some people are prevented from using these resources in ways that are permitted to other people. That is to say, property is a function of inequality.[20] If courts, for instance, should prevent a man from breathing any air which had been breathed by another (within, say, a reasonable statute of limitations), those individuals who breathed most vigorously and were quickest and wisest in selecting desirable locations in which to breathe (or made the most advantageous contracts with such individuals) would, by virtue of their property right in certain volumes of air, come to exercise and enjoy a peculiar economic advantage, which might, through various modes of economic exchange, be turned into other forms of economic advantage, e.g., the ownership of newspapers or fine clothing. So, if courts prevent a man from exploiting certain forms of language which another has already begun to exploit, the second user will be at the economic disadvantage of having to pay the first user for the privilege of using similar language or else of having to use less appealing language (generally) in presenting his commodities to the public.

Courts, then, in establishing inequality in the commercial exploitation of language are creating economic wealth and property, creating property not, of course, ex nihilo, but out of the materials of social fact, commercial custom, and popular moral faiths or prejudices. It does not follow, except by the fallacy of composition,[21] that in creating new private property courts are benefiting society. Whether they are benefiting society depends upon a series of questions which courts and scholars dealing with this field of law have not seriously considered. Is there, for practical purposes, an unlimited supply of equally attractive words under which any commodity can be sold, so that the second seller of the commodity is at no commercial disadvantage if he is forced to avoid the word or words chosen by the first seller? If this is not the case, i.e. if peculiar emotional contexts give one word more sales appeal than any other word

---

[20] See M. R. Cohen, Property and Sovereignty, in *Law and the Social Order* (1933) 41; R. L. Hale, Coercion and Distribution in a Supposedly Non-Coercive State (1923) 38 *Pol. Sci. Q.* 470; R. L. Hale, Rate Making and the Revision of the Property Concept (1922) 22 *Columbia Law Rev.* 209.

[21] "Composition is the passage from a statement about *each* or *every* member of a collection, taken severally, in one of the premises, to a statement about the collection as a whole in the conclusion." Eaton, *General Logic* (1931) 340. An instance of the commission of this fallacy, in the present context, would be the statement that the court is adding to the wealth of society because it is adding to the wealth of the particular individuals whose control over the sales device it protects.

suitable for the same product, should the peculiar appeal of that word be granted by the state, without payment, to the first occupier? Is this homestead law for the English language necessary in order to induce the first occupier to use the most attractive word in selling his product? If, on the other hand, all words are originally alike in commercial potentiality, but become differentiated by advertising and other forms of commercial exploitation, is this type of business pressure a good thing, and should it be encouraged by offering legal rewards for the private exploitation of popular linguistic habits and prejudices? To what extent is differentiation of commodities by trade names a help to the consumer in buying wisely? To what extent is the exclusive power to exploit an attractive word, and to alter the quality of the things to which the word is attached, a means of deceiving consumers into purchasing inferior goods?

Without a frank facing of these and similar questions,[22] legal reasoning on the subject of trade names is simply economic prejudice masquerading in the cloak of legal logic. The prejudice that identifies the interests of the plaintiff in unfair competition cases with the interests of business[23] and identifies the interests of business with the interests of society, will not be critically examined by courts and legal scholars until it is recognized and formulated. It will not be recognized or formulated so long as the hypostatization of "property rights" conceals the circularity of legal reasoning.

4. How High Is Fair Value?

Perhaps the most notorious example of circular reasoning in contemporary jurisprudence is that involved in judicial determination of the returns to which public utilities are entitled "under the Constitution."[24] What courts purport to do in rate cases is to ascertain the "value" of the utility's property and then to fix a price to the consumer which assures the utility a fair rate of return upon that value. This would be an understandable procedure if the courts meant by "value" either actual cost or replacement cost. For almost forty years, however, since the famous case of *Smyth v. Ames*, the courts have insisted that it may be "unconstitutional" to allow a utility merely a fair return on the actual cost or replacement cost of its property; it must be allowed a fair return on the "actual value" of the property.

What is the actual value of a utility's property? Obviously it is the capitalization at current market rates of the allowed and expected profit.

---

[22] An example of realistic analysis of consequences in this field is Legis., The Vestal Bill for the Copyright Registration of Designs (1931) 31 *Columbia Law Rev.* 477.

[23] See Schechter, *supra* note 17, at 831.

[24] The circularity of judicial reasoning in this field is discussed in R. L. Hale, Value and Vested Rights (1927) 27 *Columbia Law Rev.* 523; D. R. Richberg, Value by Judicial Fiat (1927) 40 *Harv. L. Rev.* 567; J. C. Bonbright, The Problem of Judicial Valuation (1927) 27 *Columbia Law Rev.* 493.

In a six per cent money market, an enterprise which is allowed to take
six million dollars profit per annum will be valued at one hundred million
dollars, one that is allowed three millions per annum, at fifty million
dollars. *The actual value of a utility's property, then, is a function of the
court's decision,* and the court's decision cannot be based in fact upon
the actual value of the property. That value is created by the court;
prior to the court's decision and aside from information or belief as to
what the court will decide, it is not an economic fact. Nor is it avowedly
an ethical fact based upon a determination of the amount which a given
utility ought, in the light of social facts and social policies, to be allowed
to charge its patrons. Judicial reasoning in this field is thus entirely
mythical, and the actual motivation of courts in reaching given decisions
is effectively concealed, from all true believers in the orthodox legal
theology. [Pp. 814-818.]

PHILBRICK, CHANGING CONCEPTIONS OF PROPERTY
IN LAW *

. . . . .

...Plato and Aristotle did clearly assume in their discussions the
political power exercised by property. The former attacked private
property because its abolishment would prevent the objects of his proposed educational scheme,[24] the future guardians of the state, from being
"enemies and tyrants instead of allies of the other citizens" (and, obviously, of each other). Aristotle criticized at length the particular proposals of Phaleas of Chalcedon to equalize individual fortunes in order to
prevent revolution; but, fully concurring in the view that all civic dis-
sensions arose from inequalities of wealth, suggested the elimination of
gifts *inter vivos* and by will and restrictions upon the right of inheritance
as means by which an oligarchy might preserve itself.[25]

Our ideas of today seem very far removed from the ideas of these two
Greek philosophers. Yet we are probably nearer to them, and to the
relation that actually existed between the Greek city-state and private
property, than we are to the property concept of the Roman Law. The
dominium of Roman Law—that is the *dominium* of the quiritary law
(*dominium ex jure Quiritium*) to which that word was almost wholly
confined—was an absolute right in private property.[26]... [P. 699.]

. . . . . .

* [86 *U. of Pa. L. Rev.* 691 (1938).

Francis Samuel Philbrick (b. 1876), professor emeritus at University of Pennsylvania
Law School, is the author of *Property* (1939, vol. 5 of National Law Library), and
co-author of *A General Survey of Continental Legal History* (1912). He has been a
frequent contributor to legal and historical periodicals in the fields of property and
legal history.]

The doctrine of divided ownership, based upon apportioned use, sprang from the actual economic conditions of medieval times. In it the medieval Germanic law gave us the most fundamental single characteristic of the present Anglo-American law of property.... [P. 703.]

· · · · ·

Now, feudalism was a political system; but also an agrarian system "superimposed upon private ownership and collective ownership."[50] As the latter, it was but an aspect, or an application, of the Germanic doctrine of divided ownership. And its predial character was primary; its political, derivative. The latter sprang from the social status of the overlord, and the economic dominance of land; but its institutional development was made possible by the complete substitution of the Germanic concept of control for the original Roman concept of *dominium* in the use of that word. Its meaning came, apparently, to rest upon the idea of control just as does the meaning of our word dominion. And thus *dominium* came to imply a relationship—in the land law, of general owner to limited owner; in public law, of lord to man or sovereign to subject. This union of concepts of public and private law had momentous consequences. Private law deals with the assertion of one individual's rights and powers against others. Public law deals with duties of individuals to the state; some negative, some affirmative. One is characteristically the field of individualism; and the fact that private law in its origins was predominantly property law must certainly have greatly stimulated absolutistic thinking about private rights. Public law, on the contrary, is the field of social duties. Writing of the political aspect of the union of these ideas in feudalism, Dr. McIlwain has pointed out the influence upon English theories of government of feudalism's "mingling ... of the ideas of proprietary right and governmental authority ... and the corresponding fusion of public and private law".[52] Its influence upon private law was perhaps greater. Ancient proprietary rights of familial and other associations in the land (above referred to) acquired under feudalism a partially political character; and consequently, as individual rights in land became

---

[50] Huebner, *op. cit. supra* note 2, [*History of Germanic Private Law*], at 230. Brissaud, *op. cit. supra* note 2 [*History of French Private Law*], § 60. Of course everybody knows this, but its significance is here emphasized. Mr. McIlwain, for example, speaks of "the feudal conception of the proprietary character of all rights" in *The Growth of Political Thought in the West* (1932) 384; and of course an application of this was a basis of feudalism, but it was not an original concept "of" feudalism.

[52] McIlwain, *op. cit. supra* note 50 [*The Growth of Political Thought in the West*], at 177, 182, 355; citing Gierke, *Grundzüge des deutschen Privatrechts* in i F. v. Holtzendorff, *Encyklopädie der Rechtswissenschaft* (6th ed. 1904) 488-90. See also, 3 Holdsworth, *History of English Law* (3d ed. 1923) 255; W. A. Dunning, *History of Political Theories, Ancient and Mediaeval* (1902) 260-61; H. Rehm, *Geschichte der Staatsrechtwissenschaft* in M. V. Seydel, *Handbuch des Oeffentlichen Rechts* (1896) 170-71, 181 n. 5, 200 n. 9.

stronger they, too, did not become merely proprietary, but became the basis of personal status in private and public law.[53] So it was in Germany. And something of the same character will probably sometime be established for England; for it would apparently explain why in our law all sorts of duties and rights are attached by law, without reference to volition, to various personal relationships—those of husband and wife, bailor and bailee, debtor and surety, partners, and others. This idea of relation, probably introduced into our law *through* rather than from feudalism, Dean Pound regards as almost the most fundamental and fertile in its development.[54]

In all medieval principles of divided ownership and feudalism there is implicit a deduction—or perhaps an assumption—whose consequences, had it been logically, and above all had had it been consciously, developed in our law, would have been of immeasurable importance to society. This assumption or deduction is (I quote again from the German scholar above referred to) that ownership should be "merely the right, and the duty, to control and to use a thing in accordance with socially approved [*sittliche*] purposes."[55] The origins of our basic conceptions of property, and very much of its development (almost wholly judicial), are entirely consistent with that principle. We shall see that its increased assertion is one of the most striking aspects of legal development in the period of industrial expansion and social turmoil that followed the Civil War. What was it, then, which diverted the law from a development in harmony with the principle above expressed, and made necessary the reactive assertion of social control which has been so characteristic an aspect of legislation, alike in this country and in other countries, during the last half-century or more? The answer is found in the decay and abolishment of feudalism and in the several doctrines of economic and political individualism that came to power in Europe in the late decades of the eighteenth century, reinforced in this country by conditions of life in an open continent. [Pp. 707-708.]

. . . . .

The disappearance of any long established social system must involve some losses. And so, in the case of feudalism it is regrettable that there could not have been preserved the idea that all property was held subject to the performance of duties—not a few of them public.[61] In medieval juristic literature, however, although most rights were regarded as creatures of the positive law and at the mercy of the state, a higher origin in the law of nature was attributed to both property and the binding force of contracts.[62]

---

[54] R. Pound, *Spirit of the Common Law* (1921) c. 1; Pound, The End of Law as Developed in Juristic Thought (1917) 30 *Harv. L. Rev.* 201, 212-219.

[62] On contract and property as based upon natural law, see Gierke, *Political Theories of the Middle Age* (Maitland's trans. 1900) 80-1, *cf.* 74 *et seq.* . . .

It was the latter conception that was destined to become dominant in the centuries of our colonial life, and leave with us the problem, still a most formidable one in the twentieth century, of establishing in popular consciousness the doctrine that property rights are not unilateral liberties outside the law, but creatures of the law and subject to the state. In a way, of course, the idea did survive as eminent domain; but that is an inert conception, of too narrow content, limited as it is to *takings* for a public purpose, to be socially important. Modern necessities have compelled us to create a more active and powerful instrument, the police power, with which the state has increasingly met the obstinate individualism of private property in the last three-quarters of a century. Today, everybody concedes that property rights are, to some extent, subject to regulation by the state—in this country, of course, primarily by the forty-eight states, subject to their constitutions and to the due process clause of the fourteenth amendment of the Federal Constitution. But the extraordinary strength among us of doctrines of political and economic individualism has tended to restrict regulation within narrow limits and to make it correspondingly ineffective.

These doctrines became practicalities of politics only in the nineteeth century, although their origins go back to much earlier times. While the bitter convictions of feudal tenants were gathering strength to force the destruction of feudal restraints upon individual proprietorship, these other doctrines were preparing a public opinion certain to invigorate and magnify mightily that concept at the instant of its liberation. The first of these was the doctrine of natural law as developed by medieval jurists and carried forward both by non-legal philosophers and in the modern juristic literature, chiefly German, of *Naturrecht*. The second was the doctrine of economic freedom which the physiocrats and the founders of the English classic school of political economy held in common, and which was only one aspect of the liberalism that spread as an intellectual revolution over western Europe in the eighteenth century, setting up as ideals of government the recognition and protection of personal independence in religion, education, publication, and scientific study. The third was the inflammatory doctrine of Benthamite utilitarianism, which was constructed out of a theretofore torpid principle of utility descended from Locke, and two principles which were common English thought in the second half of the eighteenth century—namely, the identity of individual and social interests and the ability of every man to comprehend and pursue them.[63]

---

[63] On the utility principle, see 2 Leslie Stephen, *English Thought in the Eighteenth Century* (2d ed. 1881) 80 *et seq.* That the other ideas were of the time, see A. Toynbee, *Lectures on the Industrial Revolution* (1913) 149, 158-59. So Blackstone wrote that God had so arranged "that we should want no other prompter to . . . pursue the rule of right, but only our own self-love, that universal principle of action . . . He has so inseparably interwoven the laws of eternal justice with the happiness of each

All the physiocrats were fervent champions of individual ownership. They recognized property as a natural right; to some it was the purest of natural rights, exclusive and absolute. For that reason, they strove for the destruction of feudal privileges and of the myriad of mercantilistic restrictions that hampered trade. With Adam Smith the principle of economic freedom did not operate through the doctrine that property is natural and inviolable; doubtless because he was too much of a realist. He saw that labor (subject then to many restrictions regarding residence and employment) was in fact a creature of law—and he, like the physiocrats, classified the right to labor under property. But he did believe in an inherently desirable economic equality of men. "Two conceptions," wrote Arnold Toynbee, "are woven into every argument of the *Wealth of Nations*—the belief in the supreme value of individual liberty, and the conviction that Man's self-love is God's providence, that the individual in pursuing his own interest is promoting the welfare of all."[64] For that reason he accepted the principle of *laissez faire*. Bentham, also, did not rely upon natural rights; he repudiated that along with all other phrases used to evade the necessity of proof. But he did make happiness primarily dependent upon wealth; he adopted *laissez faire* as the best means of securing the greatest total of community happiness; and he, also, assumed the concurrence of individual and social interests.[65] They were therefore equally exalters of private initiative and—Bentham more directly —of private property. [Pp. 710-712.]

· · · · ·

One may fairly say that it was natural law (with the doctrine of liberalism that adopted its name) and the excesses of the French Revolution

---

individual; that the latter cannot be attained but by observing the former." Introduction to 1 *Bl. Comm.** 40. The same ideas were basic with the physiocrats and even their precursors. See C. Gide and C. Rist, *Histoire des Doctrines Économiques* (5th ed. 1926) 52.

[64] Toynbee, *op. cit. supra* note 63, at 148. With respect to the physiocrats, see W. A. Dunning, *Political Theories from Rousseau to Spencer* (1920) 59; Gide and Rist, *op. cit. supra* note 63, c. 1; *Adam Smith, 1776–1926: Lectures to Commemorate "The Wealth of Nations"* (1928) 63-4, 198-202. Their name signified a government by natural law. Gide describes them as almost wholly men of official position or the higher classes, "*épris avant tout de civilisation, de bon ordre,...de propriété surtout.*" *Op. cit. supra*, at 8. As one of them wrote: "*Propriété, sûreté, liberté, voilà donc l'ordre social tout entier.*" On Smith see 3 Smith, *Works* (D. Stewart's ed. 1811) 319; 2 *id.* (T. Rogers' 2d ed. 1880) 118 (bk. 4, c. 5 at 2nd); also *Adam Smith 1776–1926*, *supra* at 65, 161-72; Toynbee, *op. cit. supra* note 63, at 152-155; 2 Stephen, *op. cit. supra* note 63, at 319-23.

[65] On the happiness principle see J. H. Burdon (ed), *Benthamiana; or Select Extracts From The Works of Jeremy Bentham* (1843) 349, 352, 354, 356; 9 Bentham, *Works* (Bowring's ed. 1843) introduction to the Constitutional Code; 4 *id.* at 537 *et seq.*; 1 *id.* Burton's introd.) 17b, 21b, 22a, 24b. Particularly on property as connected with security and happiness, see Bentham, *The Theory of Legislation* (Ogden's

that exalted individual interests in property above those of society. In the Declaration of 1789 property rights were asserted broadly, but as subject to the law. In the constitutions that followed, their guaranty against the law was definite and extreme.[68] In the eighteenth century French doctrines of social reform had a large history. Proposals to curb private property in the public interest were repeatedly presented in the debates of the Revolutionary period, but they left no trace in the Constitution of 1791 or its successors, nor in the Code Civil and the eighteenth century codes of Prussia and Austria.

In this country no philosophical doctrines were needed to invigorate policies of personal liberty, individual enterprise, and absolute individual ownership; all the circumstances of this continent had dedicated us from the beginning to those ends. But of course men vouched the philosophers to justify their instincts. So it was with Locke's libertarian doctrines, political and economic, and his pronunciamento that "government has no other end but the preservation of property.".... [Pp. 712-713.]

.   .   .   .   .

The practical end and performance of the Constitution's framers is clear. There is little disposition today to question the theses of Mr. Beard that the Constitution was primarily originated and carried through by propertied groups that desired security, and that, so far as it is an economic document, it was based upon the concept that property rights should be beyond the reach of popular majorities.[109] Nor can anyone well deny that the last end has, to some extent, been attained through judicial construction of state and federal constitutions. To indicate, however, to what extent that purpose has been made effective, and with reference to what forms of property, and against which forms of governmental

---

ed. 1931) 98, 102-11, 118-19; 1 Bentham, *Works* (Burton's introd.) 33a-34; Burton, *op. cit. supra* at 360. On *laissez-faire* and identity of self-interest and social interest, see 1 Bentham *Works* 313a, 321a-b; Bentham, *Theory of Legislation* 123, 144-45; Burton, *op. cit. supra* at 356-57, 399, or his introduction to Bentham, *Works* 29a.

[68] The Declaration of 1789 read, "Property is the right that each citizen has to the enjoyment of that portion of goods guaranteed him by the state." Mirabeau declared to the Constituent Assembly: "private property is goods acquired by virtue of the laws. The law alone constitutes property." But the constitution of 1793 read: "No one shall be deprived of the least portion of his property without his consent, except when public necessity, legally proven, evidently demands it, and then only on condition of just compensation previously made." This guaranty (in several respects stronger than that in our Federal Constitution) was preserved in all later constitutions. 1 *Le Code Civil, 1804–1904: Livre du Centenaire* (1904) 336-37; L. Faucher, Property in 3 J. J. Lalor (ed.), *Cyc. Pol. Sci.* (1184) 4 *Code Napoleon, Suivie de L'Exposé des Motifs ... des Rapports ... Opinions ... des Discours* (1808) 25 *et seq.*; 1 *Motifs et Discours Prononcés lors de la Publication du Code Civil* (1838) 286 *et. seq.*

[109] C. A. Beard, *Economic Interpretation of the Constitution of the United States* (1923) 324 and c. 6; *The Supreme Court and the Constitution* (1916) 88-95, 102-12. Cf. the more extreme statements of J. Allen Smith, *op. cit. supra* note 95 [*The Spirit of American Government*], at 294, 298.

action, would require consideration of enormous chapters of public law that lie quite beyond a mere discussion of the concept of property. In a word, it may, perhaps, safely be said that great inroads have been made upon the absolutistic conception of ownership as respects the *use* of mere private property; and that much less has been accomplished in curbing industrial property as respects economic power.

That this country, as compared with the countries of western Europe was, during the first century of its existence, distinctly one in which property received extreme protection under the law cannot be questioned. Our urban concentration was slight. Free lands and loose economic conditions generally made independence easy. An interest in reforms of any kind is, under such conditions, impossible; but we are conscious of no social problems. Cheap land had as one of its consequences that of stimulating and universalizing acquisitive instincts and respect for property rights. Simultaneously, however, with the aggrandizement of political and economic individualism by the modes of thought above referred to, and by the continuance of the frontier mode of life, there arose in the last century an economic society whose problems inevitably demanded restrictions upon individual ownership. It became very evident that inviolability of private property would not work.[110] The close integration of modern society, particularly its urban portion, made it impossible to leave unchecked land's individual use. Hence, the great modern development of the law of nuisances, public and private; and the enormous expansion, almost wholly a creation of the period since the Civil War, of the police power, by virtue of which the use of property is regulated, or the property may even be destroyed, for the furtherance of public order, safety, health, morality, and well-being generally.[111]... [Pp. 723–724.]

.   .   .   .   .   .

It is not, however, the *use* of ordinary property, nor the property of ordinary or "natural" persons, that presents today serious problems of adjusting law to new social conditions. Those problems arise in connection with property for *power*, and therefore primarily in connection with industrial property. "The whole American political and social system"—to quote a conservative and an economist, President Hadley—"is based on industrial property right, far more completely than has ever been

---

[110] "The principle of the inviolability of property means the delivery of society into the hands of ignorance, obstinacy, and spite." Jhering, *op. cit. supra* note 16 [*Law as a Means to an End*], at 389. And *cf. id.* at 396–97. "There is no absolute property—property, that is, independent of consideration of the interests of the community; and history has taken care to engrave this truth upon the minds of all peoples." 1 Jhering, *Geist* 7.

[111] E. Freund, *The Police Power* (1904).

the case in any European country.[118] Guarantees for ordinary property were provided in the Constitution; circumstances have made them applicable to industrial property. Their enforcement by the courts have made these, in effect, "arbiters between the legislature and the property owner".[119] The conception of property for power, scarcely recognized in earlier centuries, acquired great importance as the industrial system developed in the last century. In this country attention has been called to it by the transmission of vast fortunes, by will or inheritance, to persons who perform no service in its creation and by the recent stupendous concentration of wealth in corporations. There are few among us who still adhere to the belief that the distribution of power through the distribution of property is in accord with divine law as understood by President Baer of anthracite coal fame;[120] or with inevitable economic laws;[121] or with natural law, unless in the sense of the survival of the fittest,[122] whose fitness, outside of an industrial jungle, is generally denied. Hence the cry for the abolishment of inheritance;[123] and the protests against taxes which to some degree are doing that. Hence the demand for a redistribution of property; and some efforts of the New Deal in that direction. Hence the appeal (to some) of communism, which, among modern theories in social reform, makes the most definite demand that individual interests in property shall be reduced to a mere privilege of use.

Despite the facts that until 1540 no Englishman could dispose of his realty by will (as distinguished from dispositions "craftily made to secret uses" before that date), and then only to a limited degree until much later; that only a very small proportion of our population is sufficiently propertied to make wills; and that any well informed person would be likely to concur in the opinion that our legislative rules for the descent

---

[118] A. T. Hadley, *Under Currents of American Politics* (1915) 33.

[119] *Id.* at 42.

[120] Who was reported to have written in a letter in 1902 that, "The rights and interests of the laboring man will be protected by the Christian men to whom God in His infinite wisdom has given the property interests of the country." Henry George, Jr., *The Menace of Privilege* (1905) 14. See also Gore, *op. cit. supra* note 15 [*Property: Its Duties and Rights, Historically, Philosophically, and Religiously Considered*], at 76, for a similar opinion.

[121] J. B. Clark, in his *The Distribution of Wealth* (1899), attempted to establish a natural law controlling the distribution of social income, which, operating "without friction" through wage bargains "freely made between individual men would give to every agent of production the amount of wealth which that agent creates." See his preface. This would remove the strongest arguments against Locke's labor theory of property, *supra* note 71.

[122] Andrew Carnegie's idea in his *Gospel of Wealth;* George, *op. cit. supra* note 120 [*The Menace of Privilege*], at 14.

[123] H. E. Read, *The Abolition of Inheritance* (1918). *Cf.* McMurray, *Liberty of Testation and Some Modern Limitations Thereon* (1919) 14 *Ill. L. Rev.* 96; various essays in *Rational Basis of Legal Institutions, op. cit. supra* note 69, at 411-64; Jenks, English Civil Law (1916) 30 *Harv. L. Rev.* 97, 119-20; G. C. Broderick, *English Land and Landlords.* (1881) 336-37.

and distribution of intestate property are decidedly more desirable from a social point of view than the personal preferences and vagaries of the average testator—at least one state court has attempted to make the power of testation a natural right beyond the law's control. This includes, of course, the liberty of disinheriting children or other usually preferred objects of a testator's bounty. But the view is very generally accepted that testation is wholly a creature of law; though certainly not a privilege likely to be abolished. Inheritance taxes are rapidly educating the public to the idea that inheritance, also, is dependent upon the will of the state.

The vast increase in the number and wealth of corporations had begun to attract serious attention fifty years ago.[124] The amazing conditions which now exist in the industrial field were strikingly emphasized a few years ago by Mr. Ripley in his book on *Main Street and Wall Street*, and have more recently been revealed in detail by the exhaustive research of Mr. Berle and Mr. Means. The data compiled by them indicate that two hundred non-banking corporations control "nearly half of all the corporate wealth", and "very much more than half" of the industry of the country.[125] One hundred such corporations as the American Telegraph and Telephone Company would control as much wealth as the total present wealth of the country, and would employ as many persons as all who are now gainfully employed.[126] What is more important, this vast corporate wealth is not controlled by the owners of the corporations—their stockholders; but by managerial groups which very generally, and most particularly those of the large corporations, hold but a small or insignificant amount of stock.[127] And so here again "there has resulted the dissolution of the old atom of ownership" (a dis-

---

[124] Thos. G. Shearman estimated in 1889 that 250,000 persons "practically owned" the country, and that 50,000 would "substantially" own it by 1929 if taxing systems remained unaltered. See Shearman, "Henry George's Mistakes" and "The Owners of the United States" (1889) 8 *The Forum* 40, 262, 271-73. He made no attempt, however, to show to what extent they owned it through corporations. Mr. Justice Field of the Supreme Court expressed an opinion in 1890 that four-fifths of the wealth of the country was owned by corporations, 134 U. S. 742 (1890) (app.); an estimate that was certainly much exaggerated. No source, apparently, shows to what extent this enormous concentration of wealth, necessarily property for power, took place after the Civil War. Mr. Justice Brewer remarked of litigation in 1904 that "formerly there were but two parties: the individual and the Government. Now there are three: the individual, the corporation and the Government." George, *op. cit. supra* note 120, at 263.

See also F. J. Stimson, *Popular Law Making* (1910) 201, 202; Dillon, [*Laws and Jurisprudence of England and America*] *op. cit. supra* note 12, at 376.

[125] A. A. Berle and G. C. Means, *The Modern Corporation and Private Property* (1932) 19, 28, 32, 33.

[126] *Id.* at 3.

[127] W. Z. Ripley, *Main Street and Wall Street* (1927); Berle and Means, *op. cit. supra* note 125, at 4, 47 *et seq.* In 1925, for example, a report of the Federal Trade Commission showed that only 1.4% of the stock of the railroads was held in 1922 by their managers; and in 4,367 corporations selected as representative, an average of only 16.5% of their stock was owned by the managerial groups. *Id.* at 50-52.

solution not at all novel, as we have seen) "into its component parts, control and beneficial ownership."[128] The managers are not themselves controlled by self-interest, as stockholders, to protect with jealousy the interests of the stockholders generally. They cannot be controlled by the latter because of various corporate devices that are available to thwart these; and because great numbers of scattered stockholders cannot unite, the more numerous and scattered they are the greater their helplessness. And they are little controlled by statute, despite the immense mass of legislation regarding corporations now in our statute books. In short, no public duties, direct or indirect, rest upon the managers. [Pp. 726-728.]

.   .   .   .   .

Manifestly we need a modernized philosophy of property. No mere philosophy of words or aspirations, however. In that respect the contrast between Mill and Comte—one looking to individualism to save society, the other to society to save the individual[129]—is precisely the same as that which existed between Aristotle and Plato. The first tenet of an adequate philosophy must be that property is the creature and dependent of law,[130] including, of course, our constitutions—surely no radical doctrine! On one hand, private property, though admitting that it can only exist by virtue of public protection, pleads payment of taxes as the whole price of that protection, and beyond that claims immunity from all social obligations. On the other hand, the thought of the world for two generations has been tending toward collective Utopias. The individualism of Adam Smith's *Wealth of Nations* and of Mill's *Liberty* is an adequate defense against them. The basis for a social philosophy that may be made an adequate bulwark against them, however, was laid long

---

[128] *Id.* at 8; also 2, 7, 345 *et seq.* The instrumentalities by which the economic organization of society is effected are generally thought of as ownership, contract (in its broad sense as in *supra* note 100), and inheritance—*e.g.* Eugen Ehrlich, *Soziologie und Jurisprudenz* (1906) 9, and 1 R. T. Ely, *Property and Contract in Their Relations to the Distribution of Wealth* (1914) 70-93; 2 *id.* at 576-85, and *passim.* Berle and Means would add the corporation, as "both a method of property tenure and a means of organizing economic life." Berle and Means, *op. cit. supra* note 125, at 1. "The surrender of control over their wealth [by stockholders] has efficiently broken the old property relationships...." *Id.* at 2. The managers hold a new power, a power to take from the profits and the underlying corporate assets "by means of purely private processes, without any test of public welfare or necessity.... It is entirely possible...that the corporate profit stream in reality no longer is private property...." *Id.* at 247.

[129] "Comte's ideal is social organization; Mill's ideal is individual development... Comte looked to the elevation of the person through the reaction of society; Mill looked to the progress of society through the improvement of the individual, and the improvement of the individual through freedom and self-help." Frederic Harrison, *On Society* (1918) 205, *cf.* 254.

[130] "Property and law are born together, and die together. Before laws were made there was no property; take away laws, and property ceases." Bentham, *Theory of Legislation* 113.

ago by Marx (I refer to him, of course, solely as an institutional historian [131]) and Jhering. Such has been the influence of Darwin upon modern thought that nearly everyone accepts as a commonplace Marx's idea—revolutionary in his day—that every social institution is the product of development (here some would stop, but Marx went on) whose causes are to be found (here again most of us put in some qualification, such as "partly" or "primarily") in changing material or economic conditions. [Pp. 728-729.]

. . . . .

In all private property there is some public interest, or individual rights therein would not be protected. Yet, since the public interest is most evident in particular cases, we have dealt with these separately under the labels of nuisances, malice torts, the police power, "public utilities", property "affected with a public interest".[134] None of these is a "closed class or category". We need a more unified view, general principles, and less of rubrics. [P. 730.]

BERLE AND MEANS, THE MODERN CORPORATION AND PRIVATE PROPERTY*

Chapter I. Property in Transition

. . . . .

. . . Physical control over the instruments of production has been surrendered in ever growing degree to centralized groups who manage

---

[131] That is, as the first who, in a general and systematic manner, showed that the social process can only be discovered (if at all) by studying interacting social forces; who made history institutional, and, as respects every institution, evolutionary. His exaggeration of the economic element, and his espousal of communism as a cure for the social conditions and tendencies which he believed to exist, are not here involved. See Seligman, *op. cit.* note 8, at 27 [*The Economic Interpretation of History*], 142-44 (quotations from Marx and Engels); *id.* at 7, 22-24, 39, 50-52, 162-64.

[134] Robinson, The Public Utility Concept in American Law (1928) 41 *Harv. L. Rev.* 277; McAllister, Lord Hale and Business Affected with a Public Interest (1930) 43 *id.* 759; Hamilton, Affectation with Public Interest (1930) 39 *Yale L. J.* 1089. Brandeis, J. dissenting in New State Ice Co. v. Liebman, 295 U.S. 262 (1932) said: ". . . the conception of a public utility is not static." *Id.* at 284. ". . . the business of supplying to others, for compensation, any article or service whatsoever may become a matter of public concern. Whether it is, or is not, depends upon the conditions in the community affected." *Id.* at 301. ". . . so far as concerns the power to regulate, there is no difference in essence, between a business called private and one called a public utility or said to be 'affected with a public interest'. . . . The source is the police power. The limitation is that set by the due process clause. . . ." *Id.* at 302.

* [Pp. 7-9. Copyright 1932 by The Macmillan Company and used with their permission.

Berle and Means' treatise on *The Modern Corporation and Private Property*, first published in 1932, and reprinted many times, shows the concentration of economic power in the hands of the two hundred largest corporations and analyzes the implications of this concentration for legal and economic theory.

Adolf A. Berle, Jr. (1895-   ) practiced law in Boston, with the late Justice Brandeis,

property in bulk, supposedly, but by no means necessarily, for the benefit of the security holders. Power over industrial property has been cut off from the beneficial ownership of this property—or, in less technical language, from the legal right to enjoy its fruits. Control of physical assets has passed from the individual owner to those who direct the quasi-public institutions, while the owner retains an interest in their product and increase. We see, in fact, the surrender and regrouping of the incidence of ownership, which formerly bracketed full power of manual disposition with complete right to enjoy the use, the fruits, and the proceeds of physical assets. There has resulted the dissolution of the old atom of ownership into its component parts, control and beneficial ownership.

This dissolution of the atom of property destroys the very foundation on which the economic order of the past three centuries has rested. Private enterprise, which has molded economic life since the close of the middle ages, has been rooted in the institution of private property. Under the feudal system, its predecessor, economic organization grew out of mutual obligations and privileges derived by various individuals from their relation to property which no one of them owned. Private enterprise, on the other hand, has assumed an owner of the instruments of production with complete property rights over those instruments. Whereas the organization of feudal economic life rested upon an elaborate system of binding customs, the organization under the system of private enterprise has rested upon the self-interest of the property owner—a self-interest held in check only by competition and the conditions of supply and demand. Such self-interest has long been regarded as the best guarantee of economic efficiency. It has been assumed that, if the individual is protected in the right both to use his own property as he sees fit and to receive the full fruits of its use, his desire for personal gain, for profits, can be relied upon as an effective incentive to his efficient use of any industrial property he may possess.

In the quasi-public corporation, such an assumption no longer holds. As we have seen, it is no longer the individual himself who uses his wealth. Those in control of that wealth, and therefore in a position to secure industrial efficiency and produce profits, are no longer, as owners, entitled to the bulk of such profits. Those who control the destinies

and later in New York. He has taught courses in the law of corporations and corporate finance at the Harvard Business School and at Columbia Law School. He is the author of many works in those fields and has served in a number of important governmental positions, including those of Assistant Secretary of State and Ambassador to Brazil.

Gardiner C. Means (1896–   ) was for a number of years engaged in economic research at Columbia Law School. In 1933, Dr. Means entered government service and has served as an economist in many agencies. He has written many significant works and articles on modern economic developments.]

of the typical modern corporation own so insignificant a fraction of the company's stock that the returns from running the corporation profitably accrue to them in only a very minor degree. The stockholders, on the other hand, to whom the profits of the corporation go, cannot be motivated by those profits to a more efficient use of the property, since they have surrendered all disposition of it to those in control of the enterprise. The explosion of the atom of property destroys the basis of the old assumption that the quest for profits will spur the owner of industrial property to its effective use. It consequently challenges the fundamental economic principle of individual initiative in industrial enterprise. It raises for reexamination the question of the motive force back of industry, and the ends for which the modern corporation can be or will be run.

The corporate system further commands attention because its development is progressive, as its features become more marked and as new areas come one by one under its sway. Economic power, in terms of control over physical assets, is apparently responding to a centripetal force, tending more and more to concentrate in the hands of a few corporate managements. At the same time, beneficial ownership is centrifugal, tending to divide and subdivide, to split into ever smaller units and to pass freely from hand to hand. In other words, ownership continually becomes more dispersed; the power formerly joined to it becomes increasingly concentrated; and the corporate system is thereby more securely established.

This system bids fair to be as all-embracing as was the feudal system in its time. It demands that we examine both its conditions and its trends, for an understanding of the structure upon which will rest the economic order of the future.

---

2. The Origin and Justification of Private Property

THE INSTITUTES OF JUSTINIAN *

§ 11. Things become the property of individuals in various ways; of some we acquire the ownership by natural law, which, as we have ob-

---

* [8th ed. (1888), Book II, Title I ("*De Rerum Divisione*"). Sandars, ed. and trans.
Justinian's Institutes are probably the most influential set of textbooks ever written for law students. In the study of Roman law, they superseded, and were largely based upon, the *Institutes* of Gaius, which had been the standard authority for some four centuries before the publication of Justinian's *Institutes* in 533 A.D. Gaius was apparently of Greek, and Justinian (483-565 A.D.) of Slavic, origin, although both naturally used the official language of the epoch, Latin. The *Institutes* represent one part of the four-fold work of Justinian known as the *Corpus Juris*. The other parts are the Digest, the Code of Statutes, and a collection of "novel" statutes enacted after the compilation of the Code.

The preparation of the *Corpus Juris* represented the work of two imperial com-

served, is termed the law of nations; of others by the civil law. It will be most convenient to begin with the more ancient law; and it is very evident that the law of nature, established by nature at the origin of mankind, is the more ancient, for civil laws could then only begin to exist, when states began to be founded, magistrates to be created, and laws to be written.

§ 12. Wild beasts, birds, fish, that is, all animals, which live either in the sea, the air, or on the earth, so soon as they are taken by any one, immediately become by the law of nations the property of the captor; for natural reason gives to the first occupant that which had no previous owner. And it is immaterial whether a man takes wild beasts or birds upon his own ground, or on that of another. Of course any one who enters the ground of another for the sake of hunting or fowling, may be prohibited by the proprietor, if he perceives his intention of entering. Whatever of this kind you take is regarded as your property, so long as it remains in your keeping, but when it has escaped and recovered its natural liberty, it ceases to be yours, and again becomes the property of him who captures it. It is considered to have recovered its natural liberty, if it has either escaped out of your sight, or if, although not out of sight, it yet could not be pursued without great difficulty. [P. 95.]

. . . . .

§ 17. The things we take from our enemies become immediately ours by the law of nations, so that even freemen thus become our slaves; but if they afterwards escape from us, and return to their own people, they regain their former condition.

§ 18. Precious stones, too, gems, and other things, found upon the sea-shore, become immediately by natural law the property of the finder. [P. 97.]

. . . . .

§ 20. Moreover, the alluvial soil added by a river to your land becomes yours by the law of nations. Alluvion is an imperceptible increase; and

---

missions of lawyers. The work was begun in 528 A.D., one year after Justinian assumed office, at which time he ordered a collection of all the "constitutions," that is, organic laws and ordinances. The first edition of the *Codex Constitutionum* appeared in 529 and the revised edition (the only one now extant) in 534. In 530, another commission was appointed and it produced in 533 the famous *Digesta* (*Pandecta* or *Pandectai*) which consist of 9,123 excerpts from thirty-nine famous writers on Roman law. The work is, unfortunately, loosely and unscientifically organized. In 533, just before the publication of the *Digesta*, the *Institutes* appeared. Further material, added during the succeeding years, formed a final volume known as the "novels" that is *Novellae Constitutiones Post Codicem*. Altogether the commissions spent seven years in the compilation of the entire work.]

that is added by alluvion, which is added so gradually that no one can perceive how much is added at any one moment of time. [P. 99.]

.   .   .   .   .

§ 25. When one man has given a new form to materials belonging to another, it is often asked which, according to natural reason, ought to be considered the proprietor, whether he who gave the form, or he rather who owned the materials. For instance, suppose a person has made wine, or oil, or wheat, from the grapes, olives, or ears of corn belonging to another; or has cast a vessel out of gold, silver, or brass, belonging to another; has made mead with another man's wine and honey; has composed a plaster, or eye-salve, with another man's medicaments; has made a garment with another's wool; or a ship, a chest, or a bench, with another man's timber. After long controversy between the Sabinians and Proculians, a middle opinion has been adopted, based on the following distinction. If the thing made can be reduced to its former rude materials, then the owner of the materials is also considered the owner of the thing made; but, if the thing cannot be so reduced, then he who made it is the owner of it.* For example, a vessel when cast, can easily be reduced to its rude materials of brass, silver, or gold; but wine, oil, or wheat cannot be reconverted into grapes, olives, or ears of corn; nor can mead be resolved into wine and honey. But if a man has made a new thing, partly with his own materials, and partly with the materials of another, as if he has made mead with his own wine and another man's honey, or a plaster or eye-salve, partly with his own, and partly with another man's medicaments or a garment with his own and also with another man's wool, then in such cases, he who made the thing is undoubtedly the proprietor; since he not only gave his labour, but furnished also a part of the materials. [Pp. 101-102.]

VICTORIA, DE INDIS ET DE JURE BELLI RELECTIONES †

I, 24. The upshot of all the preceding is, then, that the aborigines undoubtedly had true dominion in both public and private matters, just

---

* [The owner of the original materials has in this case a *condictio* or personal action for the value of such materials. *Cf.* the case of United States v. Fullard-Leo, 331 U. S. 256 (1947) at p. 281, in which the Supreme Court held recurrent use of an uninhabited island in the Pacific sufficient to establish private ownership, declaring that the rule recognizing title on the basis of "uninterrupted and long continued possession does not require a constant, actual occupancy where the character of the property does not lend itself to such use."]

† [Ernest Nys, ed. Classics of International Law Series; Washington: Carnegie Institution of Washington, 1917.

The writings of *Franciscus de Victoria* (in Spanish, Francisco de Vitoria) (1480–1546) represent the first comprehensive statement of what is now termed international law. Those portions of the treatise which are here quoted were first formulated by

like Christians, and that neither their princes nor private persons could be despoiled of their property on the ground of their not being true owners. [P. 128.]

.   .   .   .   .

II, 2. A second alleged title to the lawful possession of these lands, and one which is vehemently asserted, is traced through the Supreme Pontiff. For it is claimed that the Pope is temporal monarch, too, over all the world and that he could consequently make the Kings of Spain sovereign over the aborigines in question, and that so it has been done.

In this matter there are some jurists, who hold that the Pope has full jurisdiction in temporal matters over the whole earth, and they even add that the power of all secular princes comes to them from the Pope. This is the tenet of Hostiensis on X, 3, 34, 8; also of the Archbishop (pt. 3, tit. 22, ch. 5, Sec. 8); and also of Augustinus Anconitanus. Sylvester holds the same doctrine.... The sole proof that he gives herefor is in the passages "The earth is the Lord's and the fulness thereof," [1] and "All power is given unto me, both in heaven and in earth." [2] and the Pope is the vicar of God and of Christ, and (Philippians, ch. 2) Christ "for our sake became obedient even unto death," etc. Bartolus ... too, seems to be of this opinion in his comment on the Extravagans, *Ad reprimendum*, and St. Thomas seems to favor it at the end of the second book of the *Sententiae*, the closing words of which are by the way of solution of the fourth argument, which is the last of the whole book, namely, that the Pope holds the summit of both kinds of power, both secular and spiritual, and Hervous is of the same opinion in his *De potestate Ecclesiae*. [Pp. 134-135.]

.   .   .   .   .

Now, inasmuch as I have fully discussed the temporal power of the Pope in my *Relectio de Potestate Ecclesiastica*, I will put my answer to the above into a few brief propositions:

3. First: The Pope is not civil or temporal lord of the whole world in the proper sense of the words "lordship" and "civil power." ...

Victoria, who then held the first chair in moral theology at the University of Salamanca, in response to an inquiry from the Emperor, Charles V, concerning the controversy then raging as to the validity of Spanish land titles in the New World. Accounts of the influence of Victoria on international law in general and on international law concerning subject peoples, specifically, will be found in James Brown Scott, *Spanish Origin of International Law*, (1928) and F. S. Cohen, "The Spanish Origin of Indian Rights in the Law of the United States," 31 *Geo. L.J.* 1 (1942).

The first edition of Victoria's *Relectiones Theologicae* appeared at Lyons in 1557 and was followed in 1565 by a second edition published with emendations at Salamanca. The sections of this general treatise dealing with international law are available in the English translation quoted here.]

[1] Psalm 24, v. 1.
[2] St. Matthew, ch. 28 v. 18.

Further, our Lord's injunction to Peter, "Feed my sheep,"[1] clearly shows that power in spiritual and not in temporal matters is meant. It is, moreover, demonstrable that the Pope has not the whole world for his sphere. For our Lord said (St. John, ch. 10) that there should be "one flock and one shepherd" at the end of the age. This is sufficient proof that at the present day all are not sheep of his flock. Again, assuming that Christ had this power, it is manifest that it has not been entrusted to the Pope. This appears from the fact that the Pope is no less vicar of Christ in spiritual than in temporal matters. But the Pope has no spiritual jurisdiction over unbelievers, as even our opponents admit, and, as seems (1 Corinthians, ch. 5) to have been the express teaching of the Apostle: "For what have I to do to judge them also that are without?" ...

4. Second proposition: Even assuming that the Supreme Pontiff had this secular power over the whole world, he could not give it to secular princes. This is obvious, because it would be annexed to the Papacy. Nor can any Pope sever it from the office of Supreme Pontiff or deprive his successor of that power, for the succeeding Supreme Pontiff can not be less than his predecessor; and, if some one Pontiff had made a gift of this power, either the grant would be null or the succeeding Pontiff could cancel it.

5. Third proposition: The Pope has temporal power only so far as it is in subservience to matters spiritual, that is, as far as is necessary for the administration of spiritual affairs. This is also the view of Torquemada (as above, ch. 114), and of all the doctors. And the proof of it lies in the fact that an art to which a higher end pertains is imperative and preceptive as regards the arts to which lower ends pertain (Ethics, bk. 1). But the end of spiritual power is ultimate felicity, while the end of civil power is political felicity....

6. Fourth conclusion: The Pope has no temporal power over the Indian aborigines or over other unbelievers. This is clear from propositions I and III. For he has no temporal power save such as subserves spiritual matters. But he has no spiritual power over them (I Corinth., ch. 5, v. 12). Therefore he has no temporal power either.

7. ... What has been said demonstrates, then, that at the time of the Spaniards' first voyages to America they took with them no right to occupy the lands of the indigenous population.

Accordingly, there is another title which can be set up, namely, by right of discovery; and no other title was originally set up, and it was in virtue of this title alone that Columbus the Genoan first set sail. And this seems to be an adequate title because those regions which are deserted become, by the law of nations and the natural law, the property of the first occupant (Inst., 2, 1, 12). Therefore, as the Spaniards were the first to

---

[1] St. John, ch. 21 v. 17.

discover and occupy the provinces in question, they are in lawful possession thereof, just as if they had discovered some lonely and thitherto
uninhabited region.

Not much, however, need be said about this third title of ours, because,
as proved above, the barbarians were true owners, both from the public
and from the private standpoint. Now the rule of the law of nations is that
what belongs to nobody is granted to the first occupant, as is expressly
laid down in the aforementioned passage of the *Institutes*. And so, as the
object in question was not without an owner, it does not fall under the
title which we are discussing. Although, then, this title, when conjoined
with another, can produce some effect here (as will be said below), yet
in and by itself it gives no support to a seizure of the aborigines any more
than if it had been they who had discovered us. [Pp. 135-139.]

.   .   .   .   .

16. There remains another, a sixth title, which is put forward, namely,
by voluntary choice. For on the arrival of the Spaniards we find them
declaring to the aborigines how the King of Spain has sent them for their
good and admonishing them to receive and accept him as lord and king;
and the aborigines replied that they were content to do so. Now, "there is
nothing so natural as that the intent of an owner to transfer his property
to another should have effect given to it" (*Inst.*, 2, 1, 40). I, however,
assert the proposition that this title, too, is insufficient. This appears, in the
first place, because fear and ignorance, which vitiate every choice, ought
to be absent. But they were markedly operative in the cases of choice and
acceptance under consideration, for the Indians did not know what they
were doing; nay, they may not have understood what the Spaniards were
seeking. Further, we find the Spaniards seeking it in armed array from
an unwarlike and timid crowd. Further, inasmuch as the aborigines, as
said above, had real lords and princes, the populace could not procure new
lords without other reasonable cause, this being to the hurt of their former
lords. Further, on the other hand, these lords themselves could not appoint
a new prince without the assent of the populace. Seeing, then, that in such
cases of choice and acceptance as these there are not present all the
requisite elements of a valid choice, the title under review is utterly
inadequate and unlawful for seizing and retaining the provinces in question.* [P. 148.]

GROTIUS, WAR AND PEACE †

§ 11. God gave to mankind in general, dominion over all the creatures
of the earth, from the first creation of the world; a grant which was

---

* [Compare the argument of Justice Jackson in Northwestern Bands of Shoshone
Indians v. United States, 324 U.S. 335 (1945).]
† [Book II, Chap. 2, pp. 86-89.]

renewed upon the restoration of the world after the deluge. All things, as Justin says, formed a common stock for all mankind, as the inheritors of one general patrimony. From hence it happened, that every man seized to his own use or consumption whatever he met with; a general exercise of a right, which supplied the place of private property. So that to deprive any one of what he had thus seized, became an act of injustice. Which Cicero has explained in his third book, on the bounds of good and evil, by comparing the world to a Theatre, in which the seats are common property, yet every spectator claims that which he occupies, for the time being, as his own. A state of affairs, which could not subsist but in the greatest simplicity of manners, and under the mutual forbearance and good-will of mankind. An example of a community of goods, arising from extreme simplicity of manners, may be seen in some nations of America, who for many ages have subsisted in this manner without inconvenience. The Essenes of old, furnished an example of men actuated by mutual affection and holding all things in common, a practice adopted by the primitive Christians at Jerusalem, and still prevailing among some of the religious orders. Man at his first origin, requiring no clothing, afforded a proof of the simplicity of manners in which he had been formed. Yet perhaps, as Justin says of the Scythians, he might be considered as ignorant of vice rather than acquainted with virtue; Tacitus says, that in the early ages of the world, men lived free from the influence of evil passions, without reproach, and wickedness; and consequently without the restraints of punishment. In primitive times there appeared among mankind, according to Macrobius, a simplicity, ignorant of evil, and inexperienced in craft: a simplicity which in the book of Wisdom seems to be called integrity, and by the Apostle Paul simplicity in opposition to subtilty. Their sole employment was the worship of God, of which the tree of life was the symbol, as it is explained by the ancient Hebrews, whose opinion is confirmed by the Book of Revelation.

Men at that period subsisted upon the spontaneous productions of the ground: a state of simplicity to which they did not long adhere, but applied themselves to the invention of various arts, indicated by the tree of knowledge of good and evil, that is the knowledge of those things which may be either used properly, or abused; which Philo calls a middle kind of wisdom. In this view, Solomon says, God hath created men upright, that is, in simplicity, but they have sought out many inventions, or, in the language of Philo, they have inclined to subtilty. In the sixth oration of Dion Prusaeensis it is said, "the descendants have degenerated from the innocence of primitive times, contriving many subtile inventions no way conducive to the good of life; and using their strength not to promote justice, but to gratify their appetites." Agriculture and pasturage seem to have been the most ancient pursuits, which characterized the first brothers. Some distribution of things would necessarily follow these different states; and we are informed by holy writ, that the rivalry thus created ended in murder. At length men increasing in wickedness by their evil communications with each other, the race of Giants, that is of strong and violent men appeared, whom the Greeks denominate by a title, signifying those who make their own hands and strength the measure of justice.

The world in progress of time being cleared of this race by the deluge, the savage was succeeded by a softer and more sensual way of life, to which the use of wine proved subservient, being followed by all the evil consequences of intoxication. But the greatest breach in the harmony of men was made by ambition, which is considered in some measure, as the offspring of a noble mind. Its first and most eminent effects appeared in the attempt to raise the tower of Babel; the failure of which caused the dispersion of mankind, who took possession of different parts of the earth.

Still after this a community of lands for pasture, though not of flocks, prevailed among men. For the great extent of land was sufficient for the use of all occupants, as yet but few in number, without their incommoding each other. In the words of the Poet, it was deemed unlawful to fix a land mark on the plain, or to apportion it out in stated limits. But as men increased in numbers and their flocks in the same proportion, they could no longer with convenience enjoy the use of lands in common, and it became necessary to divide them into allotments for each family. Now in the hot countries of the East, wells would be objects of great importance, for the refreshment of their herds and flocks; so that in order to avoid strife and inconvenience, all would be anxious to have them as possessions of their own. These accounts we derive from sacred history, and they are found to agree with the opinions maintained upon this subject by Philosophers and Poets, who have described the community of goods, that prevailed in the early state of the world, and the distribution of property which afterwards took place. Hence a notion may be formed of the reason why men departed from the primaeval state of holding all things in common, attaching the ideas of property, first to movable and next to immovable things.

When the inhabitants of the earth began to acquire a taste for more delicate fare than the spontaneous productions of the ground, and to look for more commodious habitations than caves, or the hollow of trees, and to long for more elegant cloathing than the skins of wild beasts, industry became necessary to supply those wants, and each individual began to apply his attention to some particular art. The distance of the places too, into which men were dispersed, prevented them from carrying the fruits of the earth to a common stock, and in the next place, the WANT of just principle and equitable kindness would destroy that equality which ought to subsist both in the labour of producing and consuming the necessaries of life.

At the same time, we learn how things passed from being held in common to a state of property. It was not by the act of the mind alone that this change took place. For men in that case could never know, what others intended to appropriate to their own use, so as to exclude the claim of every other pretender to the same; and many too might desire to possess the same thing. Property therefore must have been established either by express agreement, as by division, or by tacit consent, as by occupancy. For as soon as it was found inconvenient to hold things in common, before any division of land had been established, it is natural to suppose it must have been generally agreed, that whatever any one had occupied should be accounted his own. Cicero, in the third book of his Offices says, it is admitted as an universal maxim, not repugnant to the principles of natural law, that every one should rather wish himself to enjoy the necessaries of life, than leave them for the acquisition of another. Which is supported by Quintilian, who says, if the condition of life be such, that whatever has fallen to the private use of any individual, becomes the property of such holder, it is evidently unjust to take away any thing which is possessed by such a right. And the ancients in styling Ceres a law-giver, and giving the name of Thesmophoria to her sacred rights, meant by this to signify that the division of lands had given birth to a new kind of right.

LOCKE, TWO TREATISES OF GOVERNMENT *

§ 25. Whether we consider natural Reason, which tells us, that Men, being once born, have a right to their Preservation, and consequently to

---

* [*Works of John Locke*, 6th ed. (1759), Vol. 2, Book II, Chap. 5 ("Of Property"), pp. 174 *ff.*

The *Two Treatises of Government* of *John Locke* (1632–1704) represent the first modern philosophic defense of government and property as based upon popular consent. They were written as an answer to Sir Robert Filmer's *Patriarcha*, a defense of the divine right of kings. Politically, Locke's work amounted to a justification of the English Revolution of 1688 by which James II was driven from the throne and replaced by his daughter and son-in-law, Mary and William of Orange. The theoretical justification put forward by Locke, that James II had forfeited his royal office by violating the terms on which the people assented to his rule, served later as the major philosophical justification of the American Revolution, the Declaration of Independence, and the United States Constitution, as well as many of our state constitutions. Apparently the pattern of government based upon the consent of the governed was suggested to Locke by the American Indian patterns of government, to which he frequently refers.

Locke's thinking on economics was not artificially separated from his thinking on politics. With Sir Isaac Newton he was largely responsible for British currency reforms, initiated by the Government in 1695. The element of consent which is basic in his critique of government is also basic in his theory of value. Locke's labor theory of value, later given a socialized turn by Marx, takes as one of its starting points the difference between the value of frontier land and improved land on the American frontier. Among his many other works, Locke was draftsman of *Fundamental Constitutions of Carolina* (1673).

During the six years (1683-1689) preceding the accession to the English throne of William of Orange, Locke lived in exile in Holland, where he worked on his

Meat and Drink, and such other things, as Nature affords for their Subsistence; Or *Revelation*, which gives us an account of those Grants God
made of the World to *Adam*, and to *Noah*, and his Sons: 'Tis very clear,
that God, as King *David* says, *Psal.* CXV. xvi *has given the Earth to the
Children of Men*, given it to Mankind in common. But this being supposed, it seems to some a very great difficulty how any one should ever
come to have a Property in any thing; I will not content myself to answer,
That if it be difficult to make out *Property*, upon a supposition, That God
gave the world to *Adam* and his *Posterity* in common; it is impossible that
any Man, but one universal Monarch, should have any *Property* upon a
supposition, That God gave the World to *Adam*, and his Heirs in Succession, exclusive of all the rest of his Posterity. But I shall endeavor to show,
how Men might come to have a property in several parts of that which
God gave to Mankind in common, and that without any express Compact
of all the Commoners.

§ 26. God, who hath given the World to Men in common, hath also
given them reason to make use of it to the best advantage of life, and
convenience. The Earth, and all that is therein, is given to Men for the
Support and Comfort of their being. And though all the Fruits it naturally
produces, and Beasts it feeds, belong to Mankind in common, as they are
produced by the spontaneous Hand of Nature; and no Body has originally
a private Dominion, exclusive of the rest Mankind, in any of them, as they
are thus in their natural state: yet being given for the use of Men, there
must of necessity be a means to appropriate them some way or other
before they can be of any use, or at all beneficial to any particular Man.
The Fruit, or Venison, which nourishes the wild *Indian* who knows no
Inclosure, and is still a Tenant in common, must be his, and so his *i.e.* a part
of him, that another can no longer have any right to it, before it can do
him any good for the support of his Life.

§ 27. Though the Earth, and all inferior Creatures be common to all
Men, yet every Man has a *Property* in his own Person. This no Body has
any Right to but himself. The *Labour* of his Body, and the Work of his
Hands, we may say, are properly his. Whatsoever then he removes out
of the State that Nature hath provided, and left it in, he hath mixed his
Labour with it, and joyned to it something that is his own, and thereby
makes it his Property.* It being by him removed from the common state
Nature placed it in, it hath by this Labour something annexed to it, that
excludes the common right of other Men. For this *Labour* being the

---

major contributions to political theory and philosophy. The *Epistola de Tolerantia*
(1689), a plea for religious liberty, followed the general lines of Spinoza's essay on
"Freedom of Thought and Speech," in the *Tractatus Theologico-Politicus* published
nineteen years earlier. The *Two Treatises on Government* and the *Essay on the
Human Understanding* were published in 1690, a few months after his return to
England.]

* [*Cf. Justinian's Institutes*, Book II, Title I, § 25, *supra* p. 50.]

unquestionable Property of the Labourer, no Man but he can have a right to what that is once joyned to, at least where there is enough, and as good left in common for others.

§ 28. He that is nourished by the Acorns he picked up Under an Oak, or the Apples he gathered from the Trees in the Wood, has certainly appropriated them to himself. No Body can deny but the nourishment is his. I ask then when did they begin to be his? When he digested? Or when he eat? Or when he boiled? Or when he brought them home? Or when he picked them up? And 'tis plain, if the first gathering made them not his, nothing else could. That Labour put a distinction between them and common. That added something to them more than Nature, the common Mother of all, had done; and so they became his private Right. And will any one say he had no right to those Acorns or Apples he thus appropriated, because he had not the consent of all Mankind to make them his? Was it a Robbery thus to assume to himself what belonged to all in Common? If such a consent as that was necessary, Man had starved, not withstanding the Plenty God had given him. We see in Commons, which remain so by Compact, that 'tis the taking any part of what is common, and removing it out of the state Nature leaves it in, which begins the Property; without which the Common is of no use. And the taking of this or that part, does not depend on the express consent of all the Commoners. . . . [Pp. 174-175.]

.   .   .   .   .

§ 30. Thus this Law of Reason makes the Deer, that *Indian's* who hath killed it; 'tis allowed to be his Goods who hath bestowed his Labour upon it, though before, it was the common right of every one. And amongst those who are counted the Civilized part of Mankind, who have made and multiplied positive Laws to determine Property, this original Law of Nature for the beginning of Property, in what was before common, still takes place; and by vertue thereof, what Fish any one catches in the Ocean, that great and still remaining Common of Mankind; or what Ambergriese any one takes up here, is by the Labour that removes it out of that common state Nature left it in, made his Property who takes that pains about it. . . . [P. 175.]

.   .   .   .   .

§ 36. The measure of Property, Nature has well set, by the Extent of Men's Labour, and the Conveniency of Life: No Man's Labour could subdue, or appropriate all; nor could his Enjoyment consume more than a small part; so that it was impossible for any Man, this way, to intrench upon the right of another, or acquire, to himself, a Property, to the Prejudice of his Neighbour, who would still have Room, for as good, and as large a Possession (after the other had taken out his) as before it was appropriated.... This I dare boldly affirm. That the same Rule of Propriety, *viz.* that every Man should have as much as he could make use of, would hold still in the World, without straitning any Body, since there is Land enough in the World to suffice double the Inhabitants had not the Invention of Money, and the tacit Agreement of Men to put a Value on it, introduced (by Consent) Larger Possessions, and a Right to them; which, how it has done, I shall, by and by, shew more at large.

§ 37. This is certain, That is the beginning, before the desire of having more than Man needed, had altered the intrinsick value of Things, which depends only on their usefulness to the Life of Man; or had agreed, that a little piece of yellow Metal, which would keep without wasting or decay, should be worth a great piece of Flesh, or a whole heap of Corn; though Men had a Right to appropriate, by their Labour, each one to himself, as much of the things of Nature, as he could use: Yet this could not be much, nor to the Prejudice of others, where the same plenty was still left, to those who would use the same Industry.

Before the Appropriation of Land, he who gathered as much of the wild Fruit, killed, caught, or tamed, as many of the Beasts as he could; he that so employed his Pains about any of the spontaneous Products of Nature, as any way to alter them, from the state which Nature put them in, by placing any of his Labour on them, did thereby acquire a Propriety in them: But if they perished, in his Possession, without their due use; if the Fruits rotted, or the Venison putrified, before he could spend it, he offended against the common Law of Nature, and was liable to be punished; he invaded his Neighbour's share, for he had no Right, farther than his Use called for any of them, and they might serve to afford him Conveniencies of Life. [Pp. 176-177.]

·   ·   ·   ·   ·

§ 39. And thus, without supposing any private Dominion, and property in *Adam*, over all the World, exclusive of all other Men, which can no way be proved, nor any one's Property be made out from it; but supposing the World given as it was to the Children of Men in common, we see how Labour could make Men distinct Titles to several parcels of it, for their private uses; wherein there could be no doubt of Right, no room for quarrel.

§ 40. Nor is it so strange as perhaps before consideration it may appear, that the Property of Labour should be able to over-balance the Community of Land. For 'tis Labour indeed that puts the difference of value on every thing; and let any one consider, what the difference is between an Acre of Land planted with Tobacco, or Sugar, sown with Wheat or Barley; and an Acre of the same Land lying in common, without any Husbandry upon it; and he will find, that the improvement of labour makes the far greater part of the value. I think it will be but a very modest

Computation to say, that of the Products of the Earth useful to the Life of Man 9/10 are the effects of labour: nay, if we will rightly estimate things as they come to our use, and cast up the several Expenses about them, what in them is purely owing to Nature, and what to labour, we shall find, that in most of them 99/100, are wholly to be put on the account of labour.

§ 41. There cannot be a clearer Demonstration of any thing, than several Nations of the *Americans* are of this, who are rich in Land, and poor in all the Comforts of Life; whom Nature having furnished as liberally as any other people, with the materials of Plenty, *i.e.* a fruitful Soil, apt to produce in abundance, what might serve for food, rayment, and delight; yet for want of improving it by labour, have not 1/100 part of the conveniences we enjoy. And a King of a large and fruitful Territory there feeds, lodges, and is clad worse than a day Labourer in *England*. [P. 178.]

· · · · ·

§ 45. Thus Labour in the Beginning, gave a Right of Property, where-ever any one was pleased to employ it, upon what was common, which remained, a long while, the far greater part, and is yet more than Mankind makes use of. Men, at first, for the most part, contented themselves with what unassisted Nature offered to their Necessities; and though afterwards, in some parts of the World, where the Increase of People and Stock, with the Use of Money, had made Land scarce, and so of some value, the several Communities settled the Bounds of their distinct Territories, and by Laws within themselves, regulated the Properties of the private Men of their Society, and so, by Compact and Agreement, settled the Property which Labour and Industry began; and the Leagues that have been made between several States and Kingdoms, either expressly or tacitly disowning all Claim and Right to the Land in the others Possession, have, by common Consent given up their Pretences to their natural common Right, which originally they had to those Countries, and so have, by positive agreement settled a Property amongst themselves, in distinct Parts and Parcels of the Earth; yet there are still great Tracts of Ground to be found, which, (the Inhabitants thereof, not having joined with the rest of Mankind, in the consent of the Use of their common Money) lie waste, and are more than the People, who dwell on it, do, or can make use of, and so still lie in common. Tho' this can scarce happen amongst that part of Mankind that have consented to the Use of Money. [Pp. 179-180.]

· · · · ·

§ 49. Thus in the beginning all the World was *America*, and more so than that is now; for no such thing as Money was anywhere known. Find out something that hath the Use and Value of Money amongst his Neighbours, you shall see the same Man will begin presently to enlarge his possessions.

§ 50. But since Gold and Silver, being little useful to the Life of Man in proportion to Food, Rayment, and Carriage, has its value only from the consent of Men, whereof Labour yet makes in great part the measure, it is plain, that Men have agreed to a disproportionate and unequal Possession of the Earth, I mean out of the bounds of Society and Compact; for in Governments the Laws regulate it, they having by consent found out and agreed in a way how a Man may rightfully, and without injury, possess more than he himself can make use of by receiving Gold and Silver, which may continue long in a Man's possession, without decaying for the overplus, and agreeing those Metals should have a value. [P. 181.]

HAMILTON, PROPERTY–ACCORDING TO LOCKE*

In the history of ideas the names of John Locke and George Sutherland stand somewhat apart. The one was the author of a celebrated "chapter on property";[1] the other was the voice of the United States Supreme Court in the declaration of the invalidity of the minimum wage law;[2] and nearly a quarter of a millennium separates the two intellectual events. The passing of the crowded years belies a causal connection between them; a likeness in thought, and even an occasional turn of expression, betokens more than a coincidence. A comparison of the documents indicates that had it not been for the philosopher, the jurist would not have written as he did.... [P. 864.]

.   .   .   .   .

It was easy enough for America to accept Locke; or, at least, to employ his phrases as sanctions for their own borrowed—or native—political thought. If, in his scribbling, the philosopher had one eye upon the reformed English throne, his other was fixed upon the new continent and the possibilities which it offered for a better ordered society. The great open spaces and the bountiful gifts of the Creator appear constantly in the essay on civil government.... [P. 872.]

.   .   .   .   .

In this country Locke became the gospel of liberty and property. It is true that in its early days the staid authorities at Yale—probably because they were already possessed of "light and truth,"—warned their students against the corrupting doctrines of the Oxford philosopher; but the books got about. Men who were later to shape "the course of human events"

---

* [41 *Yale L.J.* 864 (1932).]

[1] A chapter in *An Essay Concerning the True Original Extent and End of Civil Government* (1690), which is the *Second of Two Treatises of Government*.

[2] Adkins v. Children's Hospital, 261 U. S. 525 (1923).

knew "their Locke" and with him viewed the overthrow of the last of the Stuarts "as an act of reasonable men defending their natural rights against the usurping king who had broken his compact."[19] Friction with the mother country grew,—and out of Locke's arguments[20] a case was contrived against acts of Parliament[21] which threatened the purses of Colonial merchants. The political ties with the crown had to be broken,— and Mr. Jefferson found in the Civil Government the raw material for his organ-like prelude to the Declaration of Independence.[22] A number of erstwhile colonies had to be welded into a union,—and from the same storehouse ideas were drawn for incorporation into a Constitution which was to be "the supreme law of the land." In it "the forces of democracy" were "set over against the forces of property" and a "fundamental division of powers" was effected "between voters on the one hand and property-owners on the other."[23] If, in the provisions engrossed on parchment, the influence of Locke is not explicit, it is manifest in "the bill of rights" which was presently appended to the document.[24]

The Civil War brought its new burst of freedom,—and through the

---

[19] Becker, *The Spirit of '76* (1926) 14.

[20] It is not safe to dogmatize about the native and the borrowed elements in the case of the Colonies against the Mother Country. There was, to be sure, quite an importation of intellectual thunder and no small reliance upon Locke. But the occasion was a novel one, the parties to the struggle had their own distinctive positions, and the events of intellectual combat took their own course. When the smoke of battle and the clouds of dialectic were lifted, our Revolution was discovered to have been a rather different one from the show the English had put on in the preceding century.

[21] A curious twist was given to the dialectic of the great philosopher by the course of events. Locke's argument is a justification of revolution against an irresponsible monarchy; the occasion demanded a protest of humble subjects of His Majesty against acts of Parliament. Locke elevates the rights to life, liberty, and estate above "the legislature"; but he does not distinguish the legislature from the executive. At the time of the break with England, nearly a century later, the supremacy of Parliament had come to be incorporated into the British constitution, and in America the new-fangled theory of the separation of powers was beginning to be in the air. The dialectical attack upon parliament did much to inculcate the idea of the invalidity of legislative acts, and hence played its ideological role in the rise of the doctrine of unconstitutionality.

[22] The turn of events which led to the separation from the crown simplified the argumentative problem, and brought Locke once more to the rescue. For a critical account of the use of borrowed intellectual wares see Becker, *The Declaration of Independence* (1922).

[23] Hadley, The Constitutional Position of Property in America, in *The Independent,* for April 16, 1908, reprinted in Hamilton, *Current Economic Problems* (3d ed. 1925) 764.

[24] "Indeed the remarkable thing about the Constitution is the absence of any declaration of individual rights such as is contained in the Declaration of Independence."—Larkin, *op. cit. supra* note 3 [*Property in the Eighteenth Century*], at 161. The author overlooks the fact that the addition of a "bill of rights,"—the first ten amendments,—was the price paid by the supporters of the document to secure its ratification by the states.

Fourteenth Amendment an injunction against arbitrary interference with "life, liberty, and property," was laid upon the states. The modern industrial system came into being—and the most Lockian phrases in the Constitution were employed to guard its integrity. The property which Locke knew,—or perhaps only wrote about,—receded; and business enterprise won for itself certain immunities from its former over-lord the state. . . . Locke assailed the divine right of kings,—and penned words which have been used to enthrone ownership. . . . [Pp. 873-874.]

. . . . .

In the annals of the law property is still a vestigial expression of personality and owes its current constitutional position to its former association with liberty. If that place is not its by intellectual succession, the fault lies with the march of events which has taken from Locke's principles the support of his own reasons and their relevancy to the world of affairs.

Against the background of a developing industrial culture the position of property in constitutional law is somewhat anomalous. In the world of here and now, justification-by-origin has gone the way of all doctrine. The individual is no longer thought of as a miniature god who has a title to his own creation. It is now impossible to place a mark of personal workmanship upon any chattel; a multitude of men have mixed their labor—and many another personal contribution beside—into such earthly possessions as a motor-car, a sky-scraper, a railroad, a going concern, and a handful of intangibles. In an economic order which comprehends all men the technical contribution of the individual to usable wealth cannot be isolated and measured. Nor can "the worth he has produced" be determined except in terms of the market value of his services or property,— and that is begging the question. Instead his relationship to a gigantic industrial order, into whose keeping he gives his services or his productive possessions and from whose store-house he fetches away his living, depends upon a tangled scheme of social arrangements. The coming of industrialism has made of "liberty" and of "property" convenient names for changeable bundles of specific equities. Personal liberty as an abstraction has no worth; unless it is freedom to think and to express opinion, to seek and to do, it is empty of meaning; its substance lies in a right of access to the opportunities afforded by the prevailing society. Likewise the essence of property is the freedom of the owner in relation to his possession. Neither "liberty" nor "property" is antecedent to the state or beyond the domain of public control. Each is but a name for a cluster of prevailing usages,—certain to change and subject to amendment,— which binds the individual to the social order. The property which Locke justified by natural right was an isolated possession of personal origin;

the property which is the concern of constitutional law is an aggregate of rights inseparable from the gigantic collectivism of business. It was not the fault of Locke that he had to write his immortal lines towards the close of the seventeenth century.

Nor is Locke to blame that he did not anticipate the perils which currently lie in wait for our possessions.[45] The nuisance of royal power had been abated before he wrote, and within a century his checks upon irresponsibility had found expression in constitutional government. But his thinking was not proof against paradox; and to the decree of fate that man contrives his formulas and time and chance rewrite them, he was granted no personal immunity. A supreme law is invented to guard the rights of the people against an unrepresentative government. Then the legislature becomes popular, the judiciary proclaims itself interpreter—and the divine right of kings is replaced by the oligarchy of the robe. An amendment is added to the Constitution to make the people secure in their persons and property against arbitrary acts of an untrusted officialdom. Then corporations become persons, established interests are accounted property, social legislation appears as deprivation—and a democratic provision in the supreme law of the land becomes aristocratic. An argument is contrived to justify the revolt of a people against their rulers—and a judicial institution decades away falls heir to the sanctions invented by the philosophers as a justification of revolution.

In government the technique of averting a threat which is gone is much better understood than the art of taking precautions against prevailing dangers. Today the unemployed walk our streets and securities belie their very name. The ups and downs of business confiscate more property in one month than all our state legislatures and administrative commissions in a decade. Against an unplanned and undirected industrialism, and its imminent hazards to life, liberty, and property, we have no constitutional rights. But thanks to John Locke,—or to the thinkers, statesmen, warriors, business men, and jurists who put the punch in his words,—we have adequate safeguards against the resort by any state to the kind of stuff the Stuart kings used to pull. [Pp. 878-880.]

---

[45] The United States Supreme Court has taken "judicial notice" of the depression, "the outstanding contemporary fact, dominating thought and action throughout the country."—Mr. Chief Justice Hughes, speaking for an undivided court, in Atchison, Topeka and Santa Fe Ry. v. United States, 52 Sup. Ct. 146, 149 (1932). A minority of the court has accorded recognition to some of the hazards which currently lie in wait for property. "There must be power in the States and the Nation to remould, through experience, our economic practices and institutions to meet changing social and economic needs. I cannot believe that the framers of the Fourteenth Amendment, or the States which ratified it, intended to deprive us of the power to correct the evils of technological unemployment and excess productive capacity which have attended the progress of the useful arts."—Mr. Justice Brandeis, dissenting, in New State Ice Co. v. Liebman, 52 Sup. Ct. 371, 386 (1932).

BENTHAM, THEORY OF LEGISLATION*

Chapter X. Analysis of the Evils Which Result From Attacks Upon Property

We have already seen that subsistence depends upon the laws which assure to the labourer the produce of his labour. But it is desirable more exactly to analyze the evils which result from violations of property. They may be reduced to four heads.

1st. *Evil of Non-Possession.*—If the acquisition of a portion of wealth is a good, it follows that the non-possession of it is an evil, though only a negative evil. Thus, although men in the condition of primitive poverty may not have specially felt the want of a good which they knew not, yet it is clear that they have lost all the happiness which might have resulted from its possession, and of which we have the enjoyment. The loss of a portion of good, though we knew nothing of it, is still a loss. Are you doing me no harm when, by false representations, you deter my friend from conferring upon me a favour which I did not expect? In what consists the harm? In the negative evil which results from not possessing that which, but for your falsehoods, I should have had.

2nd. *Pain of Losing.*—Everything which I possess, or to which I have a title, I consider in my own mind as destined always to belong to me. I make it the basis of my expectations, and of the hopes of those dependent upon me; and I form my plan of life accordingly. Every part of my property may have, in my estimation, besides its intrinsic value, a value of affection—as an inheritance from my ancestors, as the reward of my own labour, or as the future dependence of my children. Everything about it represents to my eye that part of myself which I have put into it—those cares, that industry, that economy which denied itself present pleasures to make provision for the future. Thus our property becomes a part of our being, and cannot be torn from us without rending us to the quick.

3rd. *Fear of Losing.*—To regret for what we have lost is joined inquietude as to what we possess, and even as to what we may acquire. For the greater part of the objects which compose subsistence and abundance being perishable matters, future acquisitions are a necessary supplement to present possessions. When insecurity reaches a certain point, the fear of losing prevents us from enjoying what we possess already. The care of preserving condemns us to a thousand sad and painful precautions, which yet are always liable to fail of their end. Treasures are hidden or conveyed away. Enjoyment becomes sombre, furtive, and

---

* ["Principles of the Civil Code," Part I ("Objects of the Civil Law"), pp. 115-119. Dumont, ed. Hildreth, trans. (1864). Reprinted with introduction and notes by C. K. Ogden, London: Routledge and Kegan Paul Ltd., 1931.]

solitary. It fears to show itself, lest cupidity should be informed of a chance to plunder.

4th. *Deadening of Industry.*—When I despair of making myself sure of the produce of my labour, I only seek to exist from day to day. I am unwilling to give myself cares which will only be profitable to my enemies. Besides, the will to labour is not enough; means are wanting. While waiting to reap, in the meantime I must live. A single loss may deprive me of the capacity of action, without having quenched the spirit of industry, or without having paralyzed my will. Thus the three first evils affect the passive faculties of the individual, while the fourth extends to his active faculties, and more or less benumbs them.

It appears from this analysis that the two first evils do not go beyond the individual injured; while the two latter spread through society, and occupy an indefinite space. An attack upon the property of an individual excites alarm among other proprietors. This sentiment spreads from neighbour to neighbour, till at last the contagion possesses the entire body of the state.

Power and *will* must unite for the development of industry. Will depends upon encouragement; *power* upon means. These means are what is called, in the language of political economy, *productive capital*. When the question relates only to an individual, his productive capital may be annihilated by a single loss, while his spirit of industry is not extinguished, nor even weakened. When the question is of a nation, the annihilation of its productive capital is impossible; but a long time before that fatal term is approached, the evil may infect the will; and the spirit of industry may fall into a fatal lethargy, in the midst of natural resources offered by a rich and fertile soil. The will, however, is excited by so many stimulants that it resists an abundance of discouragements and losses. A transitory calamity, though great, never destroys the spirit of industry. It is seen to spring up, after devouring wars which have impoverished nations, as a robust oak, mutilated by tempests, repairs its losses in a few years and covers itself with new branches. Nothing is sufficient to deaden industry, except the operation of a domestic and permanent cause, such as a tyrannical government, bad legislation, an intolerant religion which drives men from the country, or a minute superstitions which stupefies them.

A first act of violence produces immediately a certain degree of apprehension; some timid spirits are already discouraged. A second violence, which soon succeeds, spreads a more considerable alarm. The more prudent begin to retrench their enterprises, and little by little to abandon an uncertain career. In proportion as these attacks are repeated, and the system of oppression takes a more habitual character, the dispersion increases. Those who fly are not replaced; those who remain fall into a state of languor. Thus the field of industry, beaten by perpetual storms, at last becomes a desert.

Asia Minor, Greece, Egypt, the coasts of Africa, so rich in agriculture, in commerce, and in population, at the flourishing epoch of the Roman empire, what have they become under the absurd despotism of the Turkish government? Palaces have been changed into cabins, and cities into hamlets. That government, odious to every thinking man, has never known that a state cannot grow rich except by an inviolable respect for property. It has never had but two secrets of statesmanship,—to sponge the people, and to stupefy them. Thus the finest countries of the earth, wasted, barren, and almost abandoned, can hardly be recognized under the hands of barbarous conquerors.

These evils ought not to be attributed to foreign causes. Civil wars, invasions, natural scourges, may dissipate wealth, put the arts to flight, and swallow up cities. But choked harbours are opened again; communications are re-established; manufactures revive; cities rise from their ruins. All ravages are repaired by time, while men continue to be men; but there are no men to be found in those unhappy countries, where the slow but fatal despair of long insecurity has destroyed all the active faculties of the soul.

If we trace the history of this contagion, we shall see its first attacks directed against that part of society which is easy and well off. Opulence is the object of the first depredations. Apparent superfluity vanishes little by little. Absolute need makes itself be obeyed in spite of obstacles. We must live; but when man limits himself to living, the state languishes, and the lamp of industry throws out only a dying flame. Besides, abundance is never so distinct from subsistence, that one can be destroyed without a dangerous blow at the other. While some lose only what is superfluous, others lose a part of what is necessary; for by the infinitely complicated system of economical connections, the opulence of a part of the citizens is the only fund upon which a part more numerous depends for subsistence.

But another picture may be traced, more smiling and not less instructive. It is the picture of the progress of *security*, and of prosperity, its inseparable companion. North America presents to us a most striking contrast. Savage nature may be seen there, side by side with civilized nature. The interior of that immense region offers only a frightful solitude, impenetrable forests or sterile plains, stagnant waters and impure vapours; such is the earth when left to itself. The fierce tribes which rove through those deserts without fixed habitations, always occupied with the pursuit of game, and animated against each other by implacable rivalries, meet only for combat, and often succeed in destroying each other. The beasts of the forest are not so dangerous to man as he is to himself. But on the borders of these frightful solitudes, what different sights are seen! We appear to comprehend in the same view the two empires of good and evil. Forests give place to cultivated fields; morasses are dried up, and the surface, grown firm, is covered with meadows, pastures, domestic animals, habitations healthy and smiling. Rising cities are built upon regular plans; roads are constructed to communicate between them; everything announces that men, seeking the means of intercourse, have ceased to fear and to murder each other. Harbours filled with vessels receive all the productions of the earth, and assist in the exchange of all kinds of riches. A numerous people, living upon their labour in peace and abundance, has succeeded to a few tribes of hunters, always placed between war and famine. What has wrought these prodigies? Who has renewed the surface of the earth? Who has given to man this domain over nature—over nature embellished, fertilized, and perfected? That beneficent genius is *Security*. It is security which has wrought this great metamorphosis. And how rapid are its operations? It is not yet two centuries since William Penn landed upon those savage coasts, with a colony of true conquerors, men of peace, who did not soil their establishments with blood, and who made themselves respected by acts of beneficence and justice.

KANT, PHILOSOPHY OF LAW*

Chapter I. Of the Mode of Having Anything External as One's Own

§ 2. *Juridical Postulate of the Practical Reason*

It is possible to have any external object of my Will as Mine. In other words, a Maxim to this effect—were it to become law—that any object on which the Will can be exerted must remain objectively in itself *without an owner*, as 'res nullius,' is contrary to the Principle of Right.

---

* [(1887), Book II ("The Science of Right"), Part I ("Private Right: The System of Those Laws which Require No External Promulgation"). Hastie, trans. This translation has been generally followed in these excerpts and in the later excerpts from the same work in Chapters 2, 4, and 10.

Kant's *Philosophy of Law* (*Metaphysische Anfangsgründe der Rechtslehre*) (1796) represents an effort to find in everyday legal doctrine some underlying truths, as one might find in a collection of calendars and almanacs some underlying astronomical truths. *Immanuel Kant* (1724–1804) believed that the methods of natural science, and particularly of Newtonian physics, through which he was able to make several important astronomical discoveries (see his *General Natural History and Theory of the Heavens* [1755]), could also be applied to law, ethics, and philosophy. His chief efforts in this direction are the *Critique of Pure Reason* (1st ed. 1781), the *Metaphysics of Morals* (1785), the *Critique of Practical Reason* (1786), and the *Philosophy of Law* (1797). His practical interest in legal philosophy as a means of overcoming accidental differences and misunderstandings among nations is clarified in his *Essay on Perpetual Peace* (1795), quoted in Chapter 11 of this volume.

The general approach exemplified in Kant's analysis of property is further exemplified in his analysis of contracts (in Chapter 2 of this volume) and in his analysis of crime and punishment (in Chapter 4 of this volume). See the chapter on Kant in Cairns, *Legal Philosophy from Plato to Hegel* (1949), and, for a more critical view, M. R. Cohen, *Reason and Law* (1950), pp. 105-127.]

For an object of any act of my Will, is something that it would be *physically* within my power to use. Now, suppose there were things that *by right* should absolutely not be in our power, or, in other words, that it would be wrong or inconsistent with the freedom of all, according to universal Law, to make use of them. On this supposition, Freedom would so far be depriving itself of the use of its voluntary activity, in thus putting *usable* objects out of all possibility of *use*. In practical relations, this would be to annihilate them, by making them *res nullius*, notwithstanding the fact that acts of Will in relation to such things would formally harmonize, in the actual use of them, with the external freedom of all according to universal Laws. Now the pure practical Reason lays down only formal Laws as Principles to regulate the exercise of the Will; and therefore abstracts from the matter of the act of Will, as regards the other qualities of the object, *which is considered only in so far as it is an object of the activity of the Will.* Hence the practical Reason cannot contain, in reference to such an object, an absolute prohibition of its use, because this would involve a contradiction of external freedom with itself.* . . . [Pp. 62-63.]

.   .   .   .   .

§ 14. *The Juridical Act of this Original Acquisition is Occupancy*

The Act of taking possession (*apprehensio*), as being at its beginning the physical appropriation of a corporal thing in space (*possessionis physicae*), can accord with the Law of the external Freedom of all, under no other condition than that of its *Priority* in respect of Time. In this relation it must have the characteristic of a first act in the way of taking possession, as a free exercise of Will. The activity of Will, however, as determining that the thing—in this case a definite separate place on the surface of the Earth—shall be mine, being an act of Appropriation, cannot be otherwise in the case of original Acquisition than individual or unilateral (*voluntas unilateralis s. propria*). Now, OCCUPANCY is the Acquisition of an external object by an individual act of Will. The original Acquisition of such an object as a limited portion of the Soil, can therefore only be accomplished by an act of Occupation.

The possibility of this mode of Acquisition cannot be intuitively apprehended by pure Reason in any way, nor established by its Principles, but is an immediate consequence from the Postulate of the Practical Reason. The Will as practical Reason, however, cannot justify external Acquisition otherwise than only in so far as it is itself included in an absolutely

---

* [This argument appears to be a *non sequitur*, since the premise that human freedom is impossible if there is *no* property does not justify Kant's conclusion that *all* things must be owned. But the missing link is found in the general Kantian doctrine that what cannot be universalized is wrong, so that the existence of *some* ownerless things cannot be permitted.]

authoritative Will, with which it is united by implication; or, in other words, only in so far as it is contained within a union of the Wills of all who come into practical relation with each other. For an individual, unilateral Will—and the same applies to a Dual or other particular Will—cannot impose on all an Obligation which is contingent in itself. This requires an *omnilateral* or universal Will, which is not contingent, but *a priori*, and which is therefore necessarily united and legislative. Only in accordance with such a Principle can there be agreement of the active free-will of each individual with the freedom of all, and consequently Rights in general, or even the possibility of an external Mine and Thine.

§ 15. *It is only within a Civil Constitution that anything can be acquired peremptorily, whereas in the State of Nature Acquisition can only be provisory*

A Civil Constitution is objectively necessary as a Duty, although subjectively its reality is contingent. Hence, there is connected with it a real natural Law of Right, to which all external Acquisition is subjected.

The *empirical Title of Acquisition* has been shown to be constituted by the taking physical possession (*Apprehensio physica*) as founded upon an original community of Right in all to the Soil. And because a possession in the phenomenal sphere of sense, can only be subordinated to that Possession which is in accordance with rational conceptions of right, there must correspond to this physical act of possession a rational mode of taking possession by elimination of all the empirical conditions in Space and Time. This rational form of possession establishes the proposition, that 'whatever I bring under my power in accordance with Laws of external Freedom, and will that it shall be mine, becomes mine.'

The *rational Title of Acquisition* can therefore only lie originally in the Idea of the Will of all united implicitly, or necessarily to be united, which is here tacitly assumed as an indispensable Condition (*Conditio sine qua non*). For by a single Will there cannot be imposed upon others an obligation by which they would not have been otherwise bound.—But the state of Will actually and universally united for Legislation, constitutes the Civil state. Hence, it is only in conformity with the idea of a Civil state or in reference to it and its realization, that anything External can be acquired. Before such a state is realized, and in anticipation of it, Acquisition, which would otherwise be derived, is consequently only *provisory*. The Acquisition, which is *peremptory*, finds place only in the Civil state.

Nevertheless, such provisory Acquisition is real Acquisition. For, according to the Postulate of the juridically Practical Reason, the possibility of Acquisition in whatever state men may happen to be living beside one another, and therefore in the State of Nature as well, is a Principle of Private Right. And in accordance with this Principle, every one is justified or entitled to exercise that compulsion by which it alone becomes possible to pass out of the state of Nature, and to enter into that state of Civil Society which alone can make all Acquisition peremptory.

It is a question: How far does the right of taking possession of the Soil extend? The answer is: So far as the capability of having it under one's power extends, that is, just as far as he who wills to appropriate it can defend it, as if the Soil were to say, 'If you cannot protect me, neither can you command me.' In this way the controversy about what constitutes a *free* or *closed* Sea must be decided. Thus, within the range of a cannon-shot no one has a right to intrude on the coast of a country that already belongs to a certain State, in order to fish or gather amber on the shore, or such like.—Further, the question is put, 'Is Cultivation of the Soil, by building, agriculture, drainage, etc., necessary to its Acquisition?' No. For, as these processes as forms of specification are only Accidents, they do not constitute objects of immediate possession and can only belong to the Subject in so far as the substance of them has been already recognized as his. When it is a question of the first Acquisition of a thing, the cultivation or modification of it by labour forms nothing more than an external sign of the fact that it has been taken into possession, and this can be indicated by many other signs that cost less trouble.— 'Again, may any one be hindered in the *Act* of taking possession, so that neither one nor other of two Competitors shall acquire the Right of Priority, and the Soil in consequence may remain for all time free as belonging to no one?' *Not at all.* Such a hindrance cannot be allowed to take place, because the second of the two, in order to be enabled to do this, would himself have to be upon some neighbouring Soil, where he also, in this manner, could be hindered from being, and such *absolute Hindering* would involve a Contradiction. It would, however, be quite consistent with the Right of Occupation, in the case of a certain intervening piece of the Soil, to let it lie unused as a neutral ground for the separation of two neighbouring States; but under such a condition, that ground would actually belong to them both in common, and would not be without an owner (*res nullius*), just because it would be *used* by both in order to form a separation between them. [Pp. 89-92.]

HEGEL, PHILOSOPHY OF RIGHT*

Property

§ 41. A person must translate his freedom into an external sphere, in order that he may achieve his ideal existence. Since a person is as yet the

---

* [First Part, First Section.

The *Philosophy of Right* of *Hegel* (1770–1831), like the parallel work of Kant, attempts to find underlying realities in the field of law more important than the superficial details that vary from place to place, from court to court and from

first abstract phase of the completely existent, infinite will, the external sphere of freedom is not only distinguishable from him but directly different and separable.

Addition.—The reasonableness of property consists not in its satisfying our needs, but in its superseding and replacing the subjective phase of personality. It is in possession first of all that the person becomes rational. [Pp. 48-49.]

.   .   .   .   .

§ 44. A person has the right to direct his will upon any object, as his real and positive end. The object thus becomes his. As it has no end in itself, it receives its meaning and soul from his will. Mankind has the absolute right of appropriation over all things.

Note.—There is a philosophy which ascribes to the impersonal, to separate things, as they are directly apprehended, an independent and absolutely complete reality. There is also a philosophy which affirms that the mind cannot know what the truth or the thing in itself is. These philosophies are directly contradicted by the attitude of the free will to these things. Although the so-called external things seem to have an independent reality in consciousness as perceiving and imagining, the free will is the idealization or truth of such reality.

Addition.—A man may own anything, because he is a free will, and is therefore self-contained and self-dependent. But the mere object is of an opposite nature. Every man has the right to turn his will upon a thing or make the thing an object of his will, that is to say, to set aside the mere thing and recreate it as his own. As the thing is in its nature external it has no purpose of its own and contains no infinite reference to itself; it is external to itself. An animal also is external to itself, and is, so far, a thing. Only the will is the unlimited and absolute, while all other things in contrast with the will are merely relative. Thus to appropriate is at bottom only to manifest the majesty of my will towards things, by demonstrating that they are not self-complete and have no purpose of

---

country to country. Unlike Kant, however, Hegel is convinced that these realities are not purely formal or logical in character but constitute the very substance of world history, conceived of as an evolutionary process. The Hegelian conception of history, set forth in Hegel's *Philosophy of History*, had a profound influence on the young Karl Marx. A more conservative development of the Hegelian world-view is found in legal philosophers like Kohler (see Chapter 10 of this volume). Hegel's approach to the problem of property, in the excerpts here quoted, parallels his approach to the problem of contracts (see Chapter 2) and his approach to the problem of crime and punishment (see Chapter 4). For a critique of Hegel's philosophy of law and nature see M. R. Cohen's *Studies in Philosophy and Science* (1949), pp. 176 ff. and see the chapter on Hegel in Cairns, *Legal Philosophy from Plato to Hegel* (1949). The latest available translation of Hegel's *Philosophy of Right* is that of Knox (1942). A less accurate but generally more readable translation is that of Dyde (1896).]

their own. This is brought about my my instilling into the object another
end than that which it primarily had. When the living thing becomes my
property I give to it another soul than it had. I give it my will. Free will
is thus the idealism which refuses to hold that things as they are can be
self-complete. Realism on the other hand declares them to be absolute in
their finite form. Even an animal has gone beyond this realistic philosophy
since it devours things and so proves that they are not absolutely independent. [Pp. 51-52.]

·   ·   ·   ·   ·

§ 46. Since property makes objective my personal individual will, it is
rightly described as a private possession. On the other hand, common
property, which may be possessed by a number of separate individuals,
is a mark of a loosely joined company, in which a man may or may not
allow his share to remain at his own choice.

Note.—The elements of nature cannot become private property.—In the
agrarian laws of Rome may be found a conflict between collective and
private ownership of land. Private possession is the more reasonable, and,
even at the expense of other rights, must win the victory.—Property
bound up with family trusts contains an element which is opposed to the
right of personality and private ownership. Yet private possession must be
kept subject to the higher spheres of right, to a corporate body, e.g., or
to the state, as happens when private ownership is entrusted to a so-called
artificial person, as in mortmain. Yet these exceptions are not to be based
on chance, private caprice or personal benefit, but only on the rational
organization of the state. The idea of Plato's "Republic" does a wrong to
the person, in regarding him as unable to hold property. The theory of a
pious, friendly, or even compulsory brotherhood of men, who are to
possess all their goods in common, and to banish the principle of private
ownership, easily presents itself to one who fails to understand the nature
of freedom of spirit, and the nature of right, through mistaking their definite phases. There is a moral or religious side, also. When the friends of
Epicurus proposed to establish a community of goods, he dissuaded them
on the ground that the plan indicated a lack of confidence in one another
and that those who mistrusted one another could not be friends. ("Diog.
Laert." 1. x. n. vi.)

Addition.—In property my will is personal. But the person, it must be
observed, is this particular individual, and, thus, property is the embodiment of this particular will. Since property gives visible existence to my
will, it must be regarded as "this" and hence as "mine." This is the important doctrine of the necessity of private property. If exceptions may
be made by the state, the state alone can be suffered to make them. But
frequently, and especially in our time, it has restored private possession.
Thus, for instance, many states have rightly abolished monasteries, be-

cause persons, living together in these institutions, have ultimately no such right to property, as the person has. [Pp. 52-53.]

. . . . .

§ 50. It is a self-evident and, indeed, almost superfluous remark that an object belongs to him who is accidentally first in possession of it. A second person cannot take into possession what is already the property of another.

Addition.—So far we have been chiefly concerned with the proposition that personality must find an embodiment in property. From what has been said, it follows that he who is first in possession is likewise owner. He is rightful owner, not because he is first, but because he is a free will. He is not first till some one comes after him. [P. 56.]

. . . . .

§ 64. The form of the object and the mark are themselves external circumstances, deprived of meaning and worth if taken apart from use, employment, or some such manifestation of the subjective will. The presence of the will, however, is in time, and its objective reality is continuance of the subjective manifestation. If the manifestation lapses, the object, abandoned by the real essence of the will and of possession, becomes ownerless. Hence I may lose or acquire property through prescription.* [Pp. 68-69.]

HOLMES, THE COMMON LAW †

Lecture VI. Possession

POSSESSION is a conception which is only less important than contract. But the interest attaching to the theory of possession does not stop with

---

* [Compare Hegel's view with the following dictum of Blackstone: "In the beginning of the world, we are informed by Holy Writ, the all-bountiful Creator gave to man 'dominion over all the earth; and over the fish of the sea, and over the fowl of the air, and over every living thing that moveth on the earth.' This is the only true and solid foundation of man's dominion over external things, whatever airy metaphysical notions may have been stated by fanciful writers upon this subject."]

† [1881. Footnotes have been renumbered.

The Common Law by Oliver Wendell Holmes, Jr. (1841–1935) represents the first great American contribution to the history of the common law. It gained for Holmes, then a practising lawyer, a teacher at Harvard Law School, and editor of *The American Law Review*, an international reputation. In 1882 Holmes was appointed to the highest court of Massachusetts, of which he became Chief Justice in 1889. In 1902 Holmes was appointed to the United States Supreme Court, on which he served until 1933. In 1920 his *Collected Legal Papers*, edited by Harold J. Laski, were published. His correspondence with Sir Frederick Pollock, covering a period from 1874 to 1932, was published under the editorship of Mark DeWolfe Howe in 1941. Some of Holmes' most important writing, including many of his judicial opinions, will be found in Max Lerner's *The Mind and Faith of Justice Holmes* (1943). See, for a more critical appraisal of Justice Holmes' thoughts, pp. 20-31 of M. R. Cohen, *Faith of a Liberal* (1946).]

its practical importance in the body of English law. The theory has fallen into the hands of the philosophers, and with them has become a corner-stone of more than one elaborate structure. It will be a service to sound thinking to show that a far more civilized system than the Roman is framed upon a plan which is irreconcilable with the *a priori* doctrines of Kant and Hegel. Those doctrines are worked out in careful correspond-ence with German views of Roman law. And most of the speculative jurists of Germany, from Savigny to Ihering, have been at once professors of Roman law, and profoundly influenced if not controlled by some form of Kantian or post-Kantian philosophy. Thus everything has combined to give a special bent to German speculation, which deprives it of its claim to universal authority.

Why is possession protected by the law, when the possessor is not also an owner? That is the general problem which has much exercised the German mind. Kant, it is well known, was deeply influenced in his opinions upon ethics and law by the speculations of Rousseau. Kant, Rousseau, and the Massachusetts Bill of Rights agree that all men are born *free* and *equal*, and one or the other branch of that declaration has afforded the answer to the question why possession should be protected from that day to this. Kant and Hegel start from freedom. The freedom of the will, Kant said, is the essence of man. It is an end in itself; it is that which needs no further explanation, which is absolutely to be respected, and which it is the very end and object of all government to realize and affirm. Possession is to be protected because a man by taking possession of an object has brought it within the sphere of his will. He has extended his personality into or over that object. As Hegel would have said, pos-session is the objective realization of free will. And by Kant's postulate, the will of any individual thus manifested is entitled to absolute respect from every other individual, and can only be overcome or set aside by the universal will, that is, by the state, acting through its organs, the courts. [Pp. 206-207.]

· · · · ·

It follows from the Kantian doctrine, that a man in possession is to be confirmed and maintained in it until he is put out by an action brought for the purpose. Perhaps another fact besides those which have been mentioned has influenced this reasoning, and that is the accurate division between possessory and petitory actions or defences in Continental pro-cedure.[1] When a defendant in a possessory action is not allowed to set up title in himself, a theorist readily finds a mystical importance in possession. [Pp. 208-209.]

· · · · ·

[1] Bruns, *R. d. Besitzes,* 499.

Those who see in the history of law the formal expression of the development of society will be apt to think that the proximate ground of law must be empirical, even when that ground is the fact that a certain ideal or theory of government is generally entertained. Law, being a practical thing, must found itself on actual forces. It is quite enough, therefore, for the law, that man, by an instinct which he shares with the domestic dog, and of which the seal gives a most striking example, will not allow himself to be dispossessed, either by force or fraud, of what he holds, without trying to get it back again.[2] Philosophy may find a hundred reasons to justify the instinct, but it would be totally immaterial if it should condemn it and bid us surrender without a murmur. As long as the instinct remains, it will be more comfortable for the law to satisfy it in an orderly manner, than to leave people to themselves. If it should do otherwise, it would become a matter for pedagogues, wholly devoid of reality. [P. 213.]

.   .   .   .   .

The best known theories have been framed as theories of the German interpretation of the Roman law, under the influence of some form of Kantian or post-Kantian philosophy. The type of Roman possession, according to German opinion, was that of an owner, or of one on his way to become owner. Following this out, it was said by Savigny, the only writer on the subject with whom English readers are generally acquainted, that the *animus domini*, or intent to deal with the thing as owner, is in general necessary to turn a mere physical detention into juridical possession.[3] We need not stop to inquire whether this modern form or the ψυχὴ δεσπόζοντος (*animus dominantis, animus dominandi*) of Theophilus [4] and the Greek sources is more exact; for either excludes, as the civilians and canonists do, and as the German theories must, most bailees and termors from the list of possessors.[5] [Pp. 218-219.]

.   .   .   .   .

The effect of this exclusion, as interpreted by the Kantian philosophy of law, has been to lead the German lawyers to consider the intent necessary to possession as primarily self-regarding. Their philosophy teaches them that a man's physical power over an object is protected because he has the will to make it his, and it has thus become a part of his very self,

---

[2] Cf. Wake, *Evolution of Morality*, Part I, ch. 4, pp. 296 *et seq.*

[3] Savigny, *R. d. Besitzes*, § 21.

[4] II. 9, § 4; III. 29, § 2. *Animus domini* will be used here as shortly indicating the general nature of the intent required even by those who deny the fitness of the expression, and especially because Savigny's opinion is that which has been adopted by English writers.

[5] Cf. Bruns, *R. d. Besitzes*, 413, and *ib.* 469, 474, 493, 494, 505; Windscheid, *Pand.* § 149, n. 5 (p. 447, 4th ed.); Puchta, *Inst.* § 226.

the external manifestation of his freedom.[6] The will of the possessor being thus conceived as self-regarding, the intent with which he must hold is pretty clear: he must hold for his own benefit. Furthermore, the self-regarding intent must go to the height of an intent to appropriate; for otherwise, it seems to be implied, the object would not truly be brought under the personality of the possessor.

The grounds for rejecting the criteria of the Roman law have been shown above. Let us begin afresh. Legal duties are logically antecedent to legal rights. What may be their relation to moral rights if there are any, and whether moral rights are not in like manner logically the off-spring of moral duties, are questions which do not concern us here. These are for the philosopher, who approaches the law from without as part of a larger series of human manifestations. The business of the jurist is to make known the content of the law; that is, to work upon it from within, or logically, arranging and distributing it, in order, from its *summum genus* to its *infima species,* so far as practicable. Legal duties then come before legal rights. To put it more broadly, and avoid the word duty, which is open to objection, the direct working of the law is to limit free-dom of action or choice on the part of a greater or less number of persons in certain specified ways; while the power of removing or enforcing this limitation which is generally confided to certain other private persons, or, in other words, a right corresponding to the burden, is not a necessary or universal correlative. Again, a large part of the advantages enjoyed by one who has a right are not created by the law. The law does not enable me to use or abuse this book which lies before me. That is a physical power which I have without the aid of the law. What the law does is simply to prevent other men to a greater or less extent from inter-fering with my use or abuse. And this analysis and example apply to the case of possession, as well as to ownership.

Such being the direct working of the law in the case of possession, one would think that the *animus* or intent most nearly parallel to its movement would be the intent of which we are in search. If what the law does is to exclude others from interfering with the object, it would seem that the intent which the law should require is an intent to exclude others. I believe that such an intent is all that the common law deems needful, and that on principle no more should be required. [Pp. 219-220.]

POUND, AN INTRODUCTION TO THE PHILOSOPHY OF LAW*

Property

Economic life of the individual in society, as we know it, involves four claims. One is a claim to the control of certain corporeal things, the

---

[6] *Supra,* p. 207; 2 Puchta, *Inst.* § 226 (5th ed.), pp. 545, 546.

* [Pp. 191-193. New Haven: Yale University Press, 1922. Originally delivered as the Storrs Lectures for 1921 at Yale Law School.]

natural media on which human existence depends. Another is a claim to freedom of industry and contract as an individual asset, apart from free exercise of one's powers as a phase of personality, since in a highly organized society the general existence may depend to a large extent upon individual labor in specialized occupations, and the power to labor freely at one's chosen occupation may be one's chief asset. Third, there is a claim to promised advantages, to promised performances of pecuniary value by others, since in a complex economic organization with minute division of labor and enterprises extending over long periods, credit more and more replaces corporeal wealth as the medium of exchange and agency of commercial activity. Fourth, there is a claim to be secured against interference by outsiders with economically advantageous relations with others, whether contractual, social, business, official or domestic. For not only do various relations which have an economic value involve claims against the other party to the relation, which one may demand that the law secure, but they also involve claims against the world at large that these advantageous relations, which form an important part of the substance of the individual, shall not be interfered with. Legal recognition of these individual claims, legal delimitation and securing of individual interests of substance is at the foundation of our economic organization of society. In civilized society men must be able to assume that they may control, for purposes beneficial to themselves, what they have discovered and appropriated to their own use, what they have created by their own labor and what they have acquired under the existing social and economic order. This is a jural postulate of civilized society as we know it. The law of property in the widest sense, including incorporeal property and the growing doctrines as to protection of economically advantageous relations, gives effect to the social want or demand formulated in this postulate.

NOTE ON THE VESTAL BILL FOR THE COPYRIGHT REGISTRATION OF DESIGNS*

An important extension of the domain of private property is involved in an act passed in July, 1930, by the House of Representatives [1] and subjected during the past session to senatorial analysis and criticism.[2] The Design Copyright Bill, as submitted to the Senate, provides for the copyright registration of industrial "patterns," "shapes," and "forms," "original" in their application to a given material, artistic or ornamental in effect, and devoid of mechanical utility.[3] Those who copy such designs for commercial[4] purposes or deal in such unauthorized copies[5] are sub-

---

* [31 *Col. L. Rev.* 477-494 (1931).]

[1] H. R. 11852, passed July 2, 1930, by a vote of 112 to 26. 72 *Cong. Rec.* 12367 (1930). For a history of attempts to secure similar bills in recent years, see Solberg, The Present Copyright Situation (1931) 40 *Yale L.J.* 184, 187-189.

jected to the sanctions of injunction, suit for accounting, and action for treble damages.[6]

Although the Design Copyright Bill has been bitterly debated at Congressional committee hearings and unofficial trade conferences,[7] and widely discussed in the public press [8] and in various trade papers,[9] this discussion has moved almost entirely on the plane of impassioned rhetoric and the vital issues involved in the legislation are still somewhat obscure. It is, of course, a patent *ignoratio elenchi* to argue that the copying of designs should be prohibited because piracy and theft are unlawful. Piracy involves the use of violence on the high seas[10] and is clearly irrelevant to the utilization of other people's ideas in the field of industrial design. Robbery involves a taking of property[11] and the precise question at issue is whether any one should have property rights in designs.[12] That question cannot be answered by undiscriminating attacks upon "monopoly" or "communism" or emotional appeals to amorphous abstractions such as "the right of every one to the product of his own labor."[13] Nor do we get much nearer to the issue when we count analogies. True, the writer, the artist, the inventor of useful contrivances, and, more recently, the creator of new plants [14] are given limited property rights in their creations. But on the other hand, the business man who works out a new form of business organization,[15] the lawyer who evolves an ingenious argument, the doctor who discovers a new method of treating tubercu-

---

[8] See Design Piracy (1930) 131 *Nation* 668 for a good presentation of the manufacturer's point of view. The opposite viewpoint is well presented in the speeches of Representatives Stafford (Wis.), Lozier (Mo.), and Strong (Kan.), 72 *Cong. Rec.* 12363-12366 (1930).

[10] See 4 *Bl. Comm.* *72.

[11] See Clark and Marshall, *Law of Crimes* (3d ed. 1927) 495.

[12] "Property, a creation of law, does not arise from value, although exchangeable—a matter of fact. Many exchangeable values may be destroyed intentionally without compensation. Property depends upon exclusion by law from interference, and a person is not excluded by law from any combination of words merely because someone has used it before, even if it took labor and genius to make it." Holmes, J., in International News Serv. v. Assoc. Press, 248 U. S. 215, 246, 39 Sup. Ct. 68, 75 (1918). "By way of preliminary it should be said that the questions involved are obscured and fair discussion of them is prejudiced by a misuse of the term 'piracy' to describe the evil intended to be cured. That evil is the imitation or copying of industrial designs. But it is well settled that imitation of industrial designs of manufactured products is not violative of any right, and therefore is not an actionable wrong, unless the design be patented or unless the imitator is guilty of acts intended or likely to mislead the buying public as to the source of origin of the articles, *i.e.*, 'palming off.' " *Memorandum in Opposition to the Bill for the Copyright Registration of Designs* (H. R. 11852) Submitted by the Committee on Copyrights of the Ass'n of the Bar of the City of New York, read into *Hearings Before the Committee on Patents, U. S. Senate* (71st Cong., 3d Sess.) on H. R. 11852, Part 1, 43.

[13] For a critical analysis of this postulate, see M. R. Cohen, Property and Sovereignty (1927) 13 *Corn. L.Q.* 8, 16-17.

[14] Act May 23, 1930, 46 *Stat.* 376, 35 *U.S.C.A.* (Supp. 1930) §§ 31, 32a, 33, 40, 56a.

[15] For a collection of cases in which relief against the copying of business forms and methods has been sought see Note (1930) 14 *Minn. L. Rev.* 537.

losis, the enterprising mathematician,[16] actress, athletic coach, teacher, legislator, or cook are all denied legal monopolies in their original contributions to human progress or decadence. To sift and weigh these conflicting analogies is clearly an indirect way of attacking the immediate problem. That problem can be solved only by an analysis of the economic and social consequences of the bill and an ethical evaluation of those consequences. Preliminary to these problems is the technical question: To what extent does the proposed legislation add to the domain of private property in industrial designs which is already established by the law of unfair competition, of trade-marks, and existent copyright and patent legislation?

To a limited extent, designs, ornamentation, and the appearance of manufactured goods have been protected from copying under the doctrines of unfair competition. The relief granted is not predicated on the desire to grant a monopoly of design to the manufacturer,[17] nor to permit him perpetual "patent rights" in the mechanical structure under the guise of protecting its appearance.[18] The plaintiff, to obtain relief, must prove

---

[16] For an account of an international treaty under consideration by the League of Nations Committee on Intellectual Cooperation, which proposes to create property rights in scientific ideas generally, and to require the payment of royalties by industrial users to the discoverers of scientific laws, see *New York Times*, Feb. 11, 1931, p. 15. Edward S. Rogers, in a letter to the Department of Commerce, is reported to have said: "Under modern conditions new discoveries do not spring complete out of somebody's brain, but are developed step by step by different people and instead of one discoverer there are likely to be many. Who, for example, discovered electricity? Was it Franklin, Ampère, Ohm or the chap that made the Leyden jar? Every one desires scientific men to be adequately rewarded; they must be; but I am not convinced that the recognition of scientific property is the best way to compensate them."

[17] "... by an ingenious extension of the doctrine of unfair competition, the complainant seeks protection for a monopoly of 'Caslon Bold' type or typography.

"The defendant has not sought to avail itself of the complainant's reputation as a founder, but of its taste and skill as a designer. This it may do. It may copy the complainant's type, so long as it does not pretend that the copy is an original product of the complainant." Keystone Type Foundry v. Portland Pub. Co., 186 Fed. 690, 692 (C.C.A. 1st, 1911); see also Crescent Tool Co. v. Kilborn & Bishop Co., 247 Fed. 299, 301 (C.C.A. 2d, 1917).

[18] "If one manufacturer should make an advance in effectiveness of operation, or in simplicity of form, or in utility of color, and if that advance did not entitle him to a monopoly by means of a machine or a process or a product or a design patent; and if by means of unfair trade suits he could shut out other manufacturers who plainly intended to share in the benefits of the unpatented utilities and in the trade that had been built up thereon, but who used on their products conspicuous name-plates containing unmistakably distinct trade names, trade-marks, and names and addresses of makers, and in relation to whose product no instance of deception had occurred—he would be given gratuitously a monopoly more effective than that of the unobtainable patent in the ratio of eternity to 17 years." Pope Automatic Merchandizing Co. v. M'Coum-Howell Co., 191 Fed. 979, 981-2 (C.C.A. 7th 1911), *cert den.*, 223 U.S. 730, 32 Sup.Ct. 527 (1912); see Harvey Hubbell, Inc. v. General Electric Co., 262 Fed. 155, 160 (S.D.N.Y. 1919); Fairbanks v. Jacobus, 14 Blatchf. 337, 339, Fed. Cas. No. 4608 (C.C.S.D.N.Y. 1877). Many of the cases cited here and in the

(1) that the appearance of his goods has become associated in the mind of the purchasing public with its source, *i.e.*, that a "secondary significance" has been established;[19] (2) that the defendant has copied or colorably imitated some "non-functional" feature of the article,[20] and (3) that the purchasing public has been confused and has purchased the defendant's goods believing them to be the plaintiff's.[21] Where the imitated feature is a "functional" one,[22] one essential to the mechanical efficiency[23] or sale value of the product,[24] even with a showing of confusion, the defendant is free to copy it as he chooses.[25] The sweeping language of the Supreme Court in *International News Service v. Associated Press*[26] indicated that injunctive relief might be granted against the copying of any original works under the rules of unfair competition. But the recent case of *Cheney Bros. v. Doris Silk Corp.*[27] has established that unfair competition may not be invoked to give to a designer a monopoly of the use of his pattern.

Under the copyright laws, "models or designs for works of art" may be copyrighted.[28] Since "works of art" has been interpreted by the Register of Copyrights to cover only the fine arts, *viz.*, painting, drawing, and sculpture,[29] it is impossible to obtain copyrights in designs associated with ordinary manufactured goods. In a recent federal case, a copyright obtained in dress designs was held invalid.[30] Even if such designs could be copyrighted, the necessity of placing the statutory notice[31] on each reproduction of the copyrighted design[32] would render ordinary copyright protection inpracticable for those industries using repeat designs.[33]

Trade-mark law, both statutory[34] and common law, also fails to afford protection to designs on manufactured articles.[35] A trade-mark is an arbitrary device affixed to an article and used only to denote the origin.[36] Reasoning from this definition, the courts hold that a trade-mark may not be obtained in a design where the design either results from the structure of the article[37] (in which case it is clearly functional) or enhances its value[38] by virtue of the appearance[39] (in which case it forms an integral part of the article). Apparently the Federal Trade Commission has no power to act in disputes involving the copying of designs.[40]

Much greater protection for designs is afforded by the Design Patent Law under which "any person who has invented any new, original and ornamental design for an article of manufacture . . . may obtain a patent therefor." [41]...

However, the apparently adequate protection afforded by the Design Patent Law is limited by practical obstacles of time and expense. At pres-

following notes have been collected in Handler, *Cases and Materials in Trade Regulation* (1930 Mimeographed).

[30] Kemp and Beatley v. Hirsch, 34 F(2d) 291 (E.D.N.Y. 1929); see Cheney Bros. v. Doris Silk Corporation, *supra* note 27, at 279. In Rosenbach v. Dreyfuss, 2 Fed. 217 (S.D.N.Y. 1880) designs for balloons and hanging baskets were held not copyrightable.

ent, it probably takes from four to six months to secure a design patent, because of the necessity of making a search of prior patents.[48] In style industries this delay in the grant of a patent greatly reduces the utility of the present law.[49] The present fees constitute a burdensome expense,[50] especially when it is considered that few of the designs which are produced and tried on the public catch the public fancy. The proposed bill obviates these practical difficulties. Immediate protection attaches to the design when the product embodying the design is offered to the public for sale.[51] The technical procedure of the patent has been replaced by the simpler requirements of the copyright laws,[52] resulting in savings of time and expense.[53] Moreover, under the new bill, one marking of the copyright notice is sufficient on products having repeated designs, as wall paper or textiles.[54] A reduction in fees has been made,[55] particularly in respect of the two year copyrights, which will attract those trades using designs the sales value of which is of short duration.

Besides removing the practical difficulties facing the designer who seeks protection under the Design Patent Law, the Vestal Bill purports to widen the scope of protection through the inclusion of many designs unpatentable under the present law. The drafters of the bill seek to eliminate the requirement of "patentable novelty" made by the Design Patent Law,[56] substituting instead the criterion of subjective originality.[57] ... [Pp. 477-485.]

.   .   .   .   .

To the extent that actual enforcement of the Design Copyright Bill is possible, what will be its ultimate effect upon designers, manufacturers, retailers, and consumers?

The "official purpose" of the Vestal Bill is to protect designers and to encourage artistic endeavor in industry.[63] The backwardness of the United States in the field of industrial design[64] is to be cured by copying foreign

---

[63] *H. R. Rep.*, *supra* note 48 [*H. R. Rep.* No. 1372 (71st Cong., 2d Sess.], at 1: "The purpose of this bill is to encourage industrial design in the United States by furnishing adequate protection against piracy of original designs for manufactured products. No adequate protection has heretofore been provided for designs of this character, with the result that notwithstanding the high order or excellence of American artists and designers, and the desire of the manufacturers and merchants to supply such demand, America has failed of leadership in industrial designs, and other countries, particularly France, wherein industrial design is adequately encouraged and protected, have taken and hold that leadership." But *cf.* 72 *Cong. Rec.* 12364 (1930): "This bill is designed to take away from the poor working girl the right to wear the same pattern of goods that the wealthy people do. That is the main purpose of the bill." (Representative Stafford.)

[64] "As a nation we now live artistically largely on warmed-over dishes.... We copy, modify and adapt the older styles with few suggestions of a new idea." *Report of Commission Appointed by the Secretary of Commerce to Visit and Report upon the International Exposition of Modern Decorative and Industrial Art in Paris* (1925) 22-23. But *cf.* Richards, *Art in Industry* (1922) 51, to the effect that in textiles, at least, American designers are now competing successfully with the French.

statutes which secure to the designer "the fruits of his labor."[65] It is
submitted that the problem of artistic achievement is too complex to
admit of so easy a solution. European standards of public taste[66] and
systems of art education[67] are probably more important factors in the
relative superiority of European industrial art than any legal prohibitions
against the copying of designs. Assuming, however, that the profit motive
is an efficacious source of artistic inspiration,[68] it remains doubtful whether
the Vestal Bill will prove of much practical assistance to designers. Section 3 of the bill provides that as a prerequisite to protection, "the author
or his legal representative or assignee must (1) actually cause the design
to be applied to or embodied in the manufactured product." It is only
in the rare instance that a "free lance" designer will be able to comply
with that requirement. Unless he controls essential machinery he will
continue to stand, as he does today, at the mercy of the manufacturer,
who may with impunity copy but reject the submitted design.[69] The
designer who is regularly employed by manufacturer or commercial
studio is not economically able to bargain for an appreciable portion of
the increased value with which the Vestal Bill may endow his products.
Another factor worthy of serious consideration in determining whether
the bill will prove beneficial to American art and artists is the extension
of the privilege of registration to foreigners.[70] As it has been estimated

[65] See testimony of Mr. Paul H. Bonner, *House Hearings supra* note 48 [*Hearings
Held Before the Committee on Patents, House of Representatives* (71st Cong., 2d
Sess.) on H. R. 7243], at 28-29, on inability of American manufacturers to hire designers of repute under present law. See *infra*, note 68 on attitude of designers. See
infra, note 94 on foreign statutes.

[66] Richards, *op. cit. supra* note 64, at 474, also 481.

[67] *Ibid.*, at 494 *et seq.*, 251-434.

[68] "We [the designers] feel no practical incentive to produce artistic and creative
work when the fruits of it may be taken from us." Testimony of William Exton,
House Hearings, supra note 48 [*Hearings Held Before the Committee on Patents,
House of Representatives* (71st Cong., 2d Sess.) on H. R. 7243], at 15. But *cf.* testimony of Miss Bendelari, a shoe designer arguing in support of the bill, at 22: "I must
say that an artist cannot help creating. He will go right on without regard to
whether there is a profit or loss, and do it. I will do more and better designs, not
because I believe in monetary returns, but because I believe I want beautiful things."
And see testimony of C. Adolph Glassgold, at 52.

[69] See *House Hearings, supra* note 48 [*Hearings Held Before the Committee on
Patents, House of Representatives* (71st Cong., 2d Sess.) on H. R. 7243], at 18 *et seq.*,
155; *Senate Hearings, supra* note 12, 110; Artists Organize (1928) 61 *Survey* 357. The
designer may prevent another from copyrighting his design, though not from using it,
by marking it "design copyright reserved." § 19.

[70] Section 1 provides "That any person ... who is a citizen or subject of a foreign
state or nation with which the United States shall have established reciprocal copyright relations [who complies with the requirements] may secure copyright...."
The pending Vestal General Copyright Law, H. R. 12549 (71st Cong. 2d Sess.)
provides for the adherence of the United States to the International Copyright Union.
At present, the United States has established copyright relations with many foreign
countries, by a series of proclamations and treaties. See DeWolf, *An Outline of Copyright Law* (1925) 279 *et seq.*
For a history of the international copyright movement see Solberg, Copyright Law

that about 75% of women's fashions originate in Paris,[71] the American designers in that industry, at least, will not be the primary beneficiaries of the bill. It is probable, then, that the hopes of American designers, who have vigorously supported the present bill, will be, to a great extent, disappointed in actual practice.

The most obvious beneficiaries of the Vestal Bill are the manufacturers of style goods, particularly the silk manufacturers, whose campaign against "piracy" was checked by the *Cheney* case.[72]

The complaint of the manufacturers of high grade silks is understandable. They claim that the fruits of their enormous expenditures[73] for procuring suitable designs are at most a few successes a year, which are promptly copied on the first signs of popularity. The result of this is that buyers of the original often cancel their orders, being unable to compete with rivals who have bought from the "pirate" (who sells without the costs of designing or the loss of the failures).[74]

In the recent hearings before the Senate Committee a number of manufacturers in other industries have opposed the bill.[75] They point out that it will require them to copyright every design produced or bought, because of the difficulty of ascertaining in advance which will prove successful. If all are copyrighted, it is likely in many lines that designs of different houses will be identical or only colorably different.[76] While apparently the later copyright will not be barred by the earlier, where the second was arrived at independently,[77] imputations of "piracy" hurled

---

Reform (1926) 35 *Yale L.J.* 48; Solberg, The International Copyright Union (1927) 36 *Yale L.J.* 68; Solberg, The Present Copyright Situation, *supra* note 1.

[71] A leading manufacturer of ladies' dresses, originally a staunch supporter of the bill, withdrew his support on consideration of this fact. See *Senate Hearings, supra* note 12, at 92. See also Richards, *op. cit. supra* note 64 at 35 *et passim;* Nystrom, *Economics of Fashion* (1928) 167-176; Petition of N. Y. Manufacturers to Paris Couturiers, *Women's Wear Daily,* Jan. 9, 1931, pp. 1, 28.

[72] *Supra* note 27 [Cheney Bros. v. Doris Silk Corp., 35 F.(2d) 279 (C.C.A.2d, 1929)]. The silk manufacturers had attempted, prior to that decision, to solve the problem of "piracy" for themselves, by a design registration bureau, and a code of honor. Their efforts were fruitless; the "pirates" refused to join. See *House Hearings, supra* note 48 [*Hearings Held Before the Committee on Patents, House of Representatives* (71st Cong., 2d Sess.) on H. R. 7243], at 62.

[73] Mr. Cheney testified that his firm alone spends more than half a million annually on design, art and fashion production. *Senate Hearings, supra* note 12, at 18.

[74] *Ibid.,* at 25, and see *House Hearings, supra* note 48 [*Hearings Held Before the Committee on Patents, House of Representatives* (71st Cong., 2d Sess.) on H. R. 7243], at 142.

[75] Automobile, tombstone, glass bottle, furniture, men's clothing, and woolen manufacturers were heard in opposition to the bill. Their arguments, in brief, were that design copyright registration was unnecessary, and fraught with danger in their respective industries. See, *e.g., Senate Hearings, supra* note 12, at 117.

[76] For example, conditions in the men's clothing industry lend themselves readily to this litigation-producing situation. "As a general thing, the ten or twelve leading style manufacturers of men's clothing are producing the same styles, because they have all been watching the same trend." *Senate Hearings, supra* note 12, at 103.

back and forth, and litigation with its attendant costs, are extremely probable consequences.

Where the product is seasonal, and has a selling period of only a few weeks, the danger to a manufacturer from a temporary injunction is obvious.[78] The statutory presumptions of originality in the plaintiff's design, of validity in its registration, and, in the discretion of the court, of copying by the defendant where similarity is shown,[79] and the difficulty of upsetting these presumptions without careful investigation, should render it easy to obtain a temporary injunction.[80] The injunction may well be more disastrous to the honest manufacturer than the pen of the "pirate."[81]

The most determined opponents of the Vestal Bill have been the retailers' organizations.[82] Their chief objection is to the granting of registration without prior examination of the validity of the design copyright. The contention is made that responsibility is thus placed on them to determine whether existing copyrights are being infringed by the merchandise offered to them.[83] They further complain that their liability for purchasing goods after notice of a preliminary injunction against their seller cuts heavily into their profits. Original purchases are often made in small quantities, as "try-outs." If the article proves successful, large re-orders are made.[84] The bill, of course, materially affects this practice. In view of the facility with which a temporary injunction can be obtained by the owner of a copyright, even where there is not an iota of novelty in the design, the retailer naturally fears that the costs of litigation or the losses resulting from the enforced boycott will not be compensated when a court finally determines that the defendant has taken his design from a common source, or that the copyright is invalid.[85] The solution offered by the proponents of the measure, namely, that the retailer secure himself by dealing only with reliable houses, and that he require a bond from his seller, is often not feasible.[86]

---

[81] When it is considered that, "... most modern designs are taken from common sources open to all, usually in public museums, or in nature, and that on the question of substantial resemblance reasonable minds may differ, the dangers of injustice from the indulgence of such presumptions must be apparent." *Bar Ass'n Memo. supra* note 12, at 45.

[83] It is claimed that, "Every merchant of any size would be required to maintain centralized files of design registrations, the transfer of such registration and the names of producers licensed to manufacture under such registrations...." See Brief of the National Retail Dry Goods Ass'n, included in *House Hearings, supra* note 48 [*Hearings Held Before the Committee on Patents, House of Representatives* (71st Cong., 2d Sess.) on H. R. 7243], at 128.

[85] The retailer will be unable to shift his loss (a) if the plaintiff is insolvent, (b) if the plaintiff did not know or have reason to know that his copyright was invalid. § 18 (c).

[86] R. H. Macy does require bonds from the sellers of patented articles when the owner of the patent claims an infringement. But this device has not worked well. See *House Hearings, supra* note 48 [*Hearings Held Before the Committee on Patents, House of Representatives* (71st Cong., 2d Sess.) on H. R. 7243], at 107.

Opinions as to the probable effect of the Vestal Bill on the consuming public are conflicting. Proponents of the bill argue vigorously[87] that the public is being injured by the practice of copying good designs on inferior materials, and that the bill will remedy this situation. Such a statement would only be warranted by a careful study of the relative prices of the original and the copy, and the length of service each renders.[88]

It seems likely that legislation of the kind proposed will result in preventing the average consumer from gratifying his or her desires for attractive and fashionable clothing and other style articles.[89] It has long been one of the wonders of America, to the eyes of foreign visitors, that stenographers, shopgirls, and even factory workers dress in clothes scarcely distinguishable from the garments of those whose incomes are greatly disparate. The similarity of the American worker's car, shoes, hat, suit and tombstone to those of his employer is an important basis of

---

[87] See e.g., House Hearings, supra note 48 [Hearings Held Before the Committee on Patents, House of Representatives (71st Cong., 2d Sess.) on H. R. 7243], at 39.

[88] Unfortunately, such figures are not available. This whole problem is presented strikingly by a practice adopted by the Regal Shoe Co. and many other concerns in New York. This store displays in its window an original custom shoe produced by Nihleen, with a selling price of $50. Next to it is placed the Regal reproduction, sold at $6.60. The materials of the original are set forth; those of the copy stated to be identical. The great disparity in price is ascribed solely to mass production and machine methods. Even though the material employed by the reproducer is not identical with that used by the innovator, it is believed that $50 invested in Regal shoes will produce more satisfaction to the average person (whose monthly income in this country is somewhat less than that figure) than the same amount invested in Nihleen's. The fact that the material used by the "pirate" is inferior to, and cheaper than, that used by the originator catering to the "exclusive" is not a condemnation. A superior quality may not be the best buy, considering its high price.

"...when we see those other lines of merchandise come into the market, that those originators are pleased to call 'piracy' and 'inferior quality,' what they should say is that that other article is better value for the money than the original article, and that is why the American public buys it." House Hearings, supra note 48, [Hearings Held Before the Committee on Patents, House of Representatives (71st Cong., 2d Sess.) on H. R. 7243], at 73.

[89] "But the consumer is caught, coming and going, by this plan....

"The rich woman can either have her clothes made to order or buy the seasonal novelties at the high prices which will surely result from such a control, and she will discard these novelties when the styles are set and women who must wait until the styles are set are ready to buy. But if these two bills [Vestal and Capper-Kelly resale price maintenance bill] are passed, there will be no production of cheaper models in the season's style nor any reduction of prices until the end of the season.

"If these two ... bills are passed, the great middle and lower classes of our country may as well abandon themselves to the condition of the Middle Ages, when beauty of textiles and charm of design in clothing was the exclusive right of nobles and the rest of the world used clothing merely as a protection from the weather. We all have a right to the beauty as well as the utility of clothing." Letter of Hellena Weed, of the American Ass'n of University Women, included in Senate Hearings, supra note 12, at 178, 179.

"Thus, while copying and so-called style piracy are admittedly an evil to the individual manufacturing concern whose successful designs are stolen and reproduced in cheaper and cheaper models, it is copying that makes mass fashion possible." Nystrom, supra note 71, at 26.

American democracy. In view of the fact that the most distinctive innovations are commonly begun by the manufacturers of higher-priced garments, who depend more on satisfying the whims of the fashion-conscious, it is obvious that a tendency of a design copyright law will be to thwart the satisfaction of this desire for conformity. Supporters of the bill counter that protection will enable manufacturers to apply their designs to cheaper fabrics.[90] That this will be done to any appreciable extent during the height of the season is doubtful; style manufacturers naturally wish to maintain the exclusiveness of their wares.[91] Nor is it likely that protection of designs will enable the manufacturer to bring his prices within the reach of the average purse. The argument that the benefits of large scale production will make this possible[92] has two answers: first, style merchandise cannot be produced on too large a scale without losing its essential distinctiveness, and second, it is at least doubtful that the saving, if any, will be passed on to the consumer. And competition between manufacturers will not be of great assistance in keeping the owner of a distinctive design which has become a "rage" from demanding a high price. Finally, to be borne by the consumer, are the costs of litigation, and of investigation of existing copyrights, which will manifest themselves in a general rise in retail prices.[93]

It is likely, however, that the bill can never be very extensively enforced. Before effective relief can be given, the source of the copying of which the plaintiff is complaining in any given case must be unearthed. This will obviously be difficult, when the production of the copies occurs in the small loft of a nomadic, unscrupulous manufacturer. And if the culprit is not located until the damage has been done, an injunction will be worthless, a suit for damages often unprofitable. "Piracy" is still the chief problem of French manufacturers of women's wear, although "protection" has been afforded by a supposedly stringent statute for a century.[94]

---

[90] Senate Hearings, supra note 12, at 65.

[91] And compare the views of the wealthy. "The women who pay several hundred dollars for original gowns have the right to expect that their gowns will not appear on the $10.75 racks in the stores the next week." Mrs. Conde Nast, in the New York Evening Telegram, Dec. 6, 1930, at 24. Cf. Veblen, The Theory of the Leisure Class (1899) c. 6 (Pecuniary Standards of Taste).

[92] House Hearings, supra note 48, [Hearings Held Before the Committee on Patents, House of Representatives (71st Cong., 2d Sess.) on H. R. 7243], at 33, 37, 143.

[93] Supra note 83. Some backers of the bill have admitted the probable increase in retail prices, but justify it on ethical bases, with the usual analogy to the laws against larceny, House Hearings, supra note 48 [Hearings Held Before the Committee on Patents, House of Representatives (71st Cong., 2d Sess.) on H. R. 7243], at 43.

[94] "The protection of the industry against copying, or style piracy, as it is known, is perhaps the most difficult and at the same time the most engrossing problem before the Haut Couture of Paris. Every known device is used by the style creators to prevent their designs from going into the hands of imitators and copyists, particularly before the products of a design are offered for sale and become a part of the commerce of the country, but it seems that every possible method is employed by the

Difficult as is the enforcement of the statutory provision against infringement, even more difficult is the enforcement of the provision against improper assertions of copyright rights. It is necessary in an action for the statutory penalties to show that the defendant obtained his copyright unwarrantably, and proof must be adduced to show that he knew, or ought to have known, of the lack of originality.[95] In practice, this will probably mean that the unscrupulous manufacturer will hide behind his designer, and it will be impossible to prove the necessary *scienter*.

The constitutionality of the bill has been challenged on the ground that its effect is not

> To promote the progress of science and useful arts, by securing for limited times to authors and inventors the exclusive right to their respective writings and discoveries.[96]

It may be expected that the courts will attach enough weight to the presumption of legislative reasonableness to reject the argument that the actual effect of the bill will be to aid manufacturers rather than authors and inventors. Nor does it seem likely that greater weight will be attached to the "due process" objection, which has also been advanced by opponents of the bill. There are in Anglo-American legal history a pretty large number of statutes similar in ultimate effect.[97]

---

copyist to secure information about these designs, for copies are offered at about the same time that originals are displayed, and the copies are usually offered at half or less of the regular prices. Thus many retailers depend, for their business on French models, upon their purchases from the style pirates, the copyists....

"The leaders of the style field have tried, by systems of legal control, to prevent style piracy. There is a French law protecting design. Several of the leading houses pursue copyists systematically and ruthlessly, with all the means that the law provides. There are almost continuously lawsuits and prosecutions for infringements of design...." Nystrom, *supra* note 71, at 190-191. The commission appointed by the Secretary of Commerce, see *supra* note 64, also found "piracy" prevalent in France, but declared it was less so than here. *Report* at 23.

Almost all of the countries of the Union for the Protection of Industrial Property have special laws for the protection of designs and models. Ladas, *op. cit. supra* note 62 [*The International Protection of Industrial Property* (1930)], § § 57, 249.

Protection has existed longest in France and England. For a history of the English statutes, see Russell-Clarke, *op. cit. supra* note 62 [*Copyright in Industrial Designs* (1930)], 2 *et seq.* The present English statutes are the *Patents and Designs Acts*, 7 EDW. VII, c. 29 (1907); 9 & 10 GEO. V, c. 80 (1919); and the *Design Rules of 1920.* The present French statute is the Law of July 14, 1909, art. 2 (1909 *Bulletin des Lois*, I, 1231).

[95] Sec. 18 (a).

[96] U.S. Constitution, Art. I, § 8.

[97] For collections of English statutes intended to prevent the use by lower classes of the garments appropriate to superior wealth or dignity, see 3 *Co. Inst.* * 198; and F. E. Baldwin, *Sumptuary Legislation and Personal Regulation in England* (Johns Hopkins Studies in Historical and Political Sciences, Ser. 44, No. 1, 1926) 245-246 *et passim.* *Cf.* Instructions to Governor Wyatt (1621) 1 *Hening's Statutes at Large of Virginia* 114 (1809).

R. H. TAWNEY, THE ACQUISITIVE SOCIETY*

Chapter II. Rights and Functions

.   .   .   .   .

It is not surprising, therefore, that in the new industrial societies which arose on the ruins of the old regime the dominant note should have been the insistence upon individual rights, irrespective of any social purpose to which their exercise contributed. . . . [P. 9.]

.   .   .   .   .

. . . The essence of the change was the disappearance of the idea that social institutions and economic activities were related to common ends, which gave them their significance and which served as their criterion. In the eighteenth century both the State and the Church had abdicated that part of the sphere which had consisted in the maintenance of a common body of social ethics; what was left of it was repression of a class, not the discipline of a nation. Opinion ceased to regard social institutions and economic activity as amenable, like personal conduct, to moral criteria, because it was no longer influenced by the spectacle of institutions which, arbitrary, capricious, and often corrupt in their practical operation, had been the outward symbol and expression of the subordination of life to purposes transcending private interests. . . .

. . . The conception of men as united to each other, and of all mankind as united to God, by mutual obligations arising from their relation to a common end, which vaguely conceived and imperfectly realized, had been the keystone holding together the social fabric, ceased to be impressed upon men's minds, when Church and State withdrew from the center of social life to its circumference. What remained when the keystone of the arch was removed, was private rights and private interests, the materials of a society rather than a society itself. These rights and interests were the natural order which had been distorted by the ambitions of kings and priests, and which emerged when the artificial superstructure disappeared, because they were the creation, not of man, but of Nature herself. They had been regarded in the past as relative to some public end, whether religion or national welfare. Henceforward they were thought to be absolute and indefeasible, and to stand by their own virtue. They were the ultimate political and social reality; and since they were the ultimate reality, they were not subordinate to other aspects of society, but other aspects of society were subordinate to them.

The State could not encroach upon these rights, for the State existed

---

* [From *The Acquisitive Society*, by R. H. Tawney, copyright, 1920, by Harcourt, Brace and Company, Inc.]

for their maintenance.... The currents of social activity did not converge upon common ends, but were dispersed through a multitude of channels, created by the private interests of the individuals who composed society. But in their very variety and spontaneity, in the very absence of any attempt to relate them to a larger purpose than that of the individual, lay the best security of its attainment. There is a mysticism of reason as well as of emotion, and the eighteenth century found, in the beneficence of natural instincts, a substitute for the God whom it had expelled from contact with society, and did not hesitate to identify them.

> "Thus God and nature planned the general frame
> And bade self-love and social be the same."

The result of such ideas in the world of practice was a society which was ruled by law, not by the caprice of Governments, but which recognized no moral limitation on the pursuit by individuals of their economic self-interest. In the world of thought, it was a political philosophy which made rights the foundation of the social order, and which considered the discharge of obligations, when it considered it at all, as emerging by an inevitable process from their free exercise. The first famous exponent of this philosophy was Locke, in whom the dominant conception is the indefeasibility of private rights, not the pre-ordained harmony between private rights and public welfare. In the great French writers who prepared the way for the Revolution, while believing that they were the servants of an enlightened absolutism, there is an almost equal emphasis upon the sanctity of rights and upon the infallibility of the alchemy by which the pursuit of private ends is transmuted into the attainment of public good.... [Pp. 11-15.]

Chapter III. The Acquisitive Society

. . . . .

That conception is written large over the history of the nineteenth century, both in England and in America. The doctrine which it inherited was that property was held by an absolute right on an individual basis, and to this fundamental it added another, which can be traced in principle far back into history, but which grew to its full stature only after the rise of capitalist industry, that societies act both unfairly and unwisely when they limit opportunities of economic enterprise. Hence every attempt to impose obligations as a condition of the tenure of property or of the exercise of economic activity has been met by uncompromising resistance. The story of the struggle between humanitarian sentiment and the theory of property transmitted from the eighteenth century is familiar. No one has forgotten the opposition offered in the name of the rights of property to factory legislation, to housing reform, to interference with the adulteration of goods, even to the compulsory sanitation of private houses. "May I not do what I like with my own?" was the answer to the proposal to require a minimum standard of safety and sanitation from the owners of mills and houses. . . .

No one needs to be reminded, again, of the influence of the same doctrine in the sphere of taxation. Thus the income tax was excused as a temporary measure, because the normal society was conceived to be one in which the individual spent his whole income for himself and owed no obligations to society on account of it. The death duties were denounced as robbery, because they implied that the right to benefit by inheritance was conditional upon a social sanction. The Budget of 1909 created a storm, not because the taxation of land was heavy—in amount the land-taxes were trifling—but because it was felt to involve the doctrine that property is not an absolute right, but that it may properly be accompanied by special obligations, a doctrine which, if carried to its logical conclusion, would destroy its sanctity by making ownership no longer absolute but conditional.

Such an implication seems intolerable to an influential body of public opinion, because it has been accustomed to regard the free disposal of property, and the unlimited exploitation of economic opportunities, as rights which are absolute and unconditioned. On the whole, until recently, this opinion had few antagonists who could not be ignored. As a consequence the maintenance of property rights has not been seriously threatened even in those cases in which it is evident that no service is discharged, directly or indirectly, by their exercise. No one supposes, that the owner of urban land, performs *qua* owner, any function. He has a right of private taxation; that is all. But the private ownership of urban land is as secure to-day as it was a century ago; and Lord Hugh Cecil, in his interesting little book on Conservatism, declares that whether private property is mischievous or not, society cannot interfere with it, because to interfere with it is theft, and theft is wicked. No one supposes that it is for the public good that large areas of land should be used for parks and game. But our country gentlemen are still settled heavily upon their villages and still slay their thousands. No one can argue that a monopolist is impelled by "an invisible hand" to serve the public interest. But over a considerable field of industry competition, as the recent Report on Trusts shows, has been replaced by combination, and combinations are allowed the same unfettered freedom as individuals in the exploitation of economic opportunities. No one really believes that the production of coal depends upon the payment of mining royalties or that ships will not go to and fro unless ship-owners can earn fifty per cent. upon their capital. But coal mines, or rather the coal miner, still pay royalties, and ship-owners still make fortunes and are made Peers. [Pp. 21-24.]

. . . . . .

The enjoyment of property and the direction of industry are considered, in short, to require no social justification, because they are regarded as rights which stand by their own virtue, not functions to be judged by the success with which they contribute to a social purpose. . . . [P. 24.]

. . . . .

. . . The appeal of this conception must be powerful, for it has laid the whole modern world under its spell. Since England first revealed the possibilities of industrialism, it has gone from strength to strength, and as industrial civilization invades countries hitherto remote from it, as Russia and Japan and India and China are drawn into its orbit, each decade sees a fresh extension of its influence. The secret of its triumph is obvious. It is an invitation to men to use the powers with which they have been endowed by nature or society, by skill or energy or relentless egotism or mere good fortune, without inquiring whether there is any principle by which their exercise should be limited. It assumes the social organization which determines the opportunities which different classes shall in fact possess, and concentrates attention upon the right of those who possess or can acquire power to make the fullest use of it for their own self-advancement. By fixing men's minds, not upon the discharge of social obligations, which restricts their energy, because it defines the goal to which it should be directed, but upon the exercise of the right to pursue their own self-interest, it offers unlimited scope for the acquisition of riches, and therefore gives free play to one of the most powerful of human instincts. To the strong it promises unfettered freedom for the exercise of their strength; to the weak the hope that they too one day may be strong. Before the eyes of both it suspends a golden prize, which not all can attain, but for which each may strive, the enchanting vision of infinite expansion. It assures men that there are no ends other than their ends, no law other than their desires, no limit other than that which they think advisable. Thus it makes the individual the center of his own universe, and dissolves moral principles into a choice of expediences. And it immensely simplifies the problems of social life in complex communities. For it relieves them of the necessity of discriminating between different types of economic activity and different sources of wealth, between enterprise and avarice, energy and unscrupulous greed, property which is legitimate and property which is theft, the just enjoyment of the fruits of labor and the idle parasitism of birth or fortune, because it treats all economic activities as standing upon the same level, and suggests that excess or defect, waste or superfluity, require no conscious effort of the social will to avert them, but are corrected almost automatically by the mechanical play of economic forces.

Under the impulse of such ideas men do not become religious or wise or artistic; for religion and wisdom and art imply the acceptance of limitations. But they become powerful and rich. . . . [Pp. 29-31.]

Chapter IV. The Nemesis of Industrialism

. . . . .

Because rewards are divorced from services, so that what is prized most is not riches obtained in return for labor but riches the economic origin of which, being regarded as sordid, is concealed, two results follow. The first is the creation of a class of pensioners upon industry, who levy toll upon its product, but contribute nothing to its increase, and who are not merely tolerated, but applauded and admired and protected with assiduous care, as though the secret of prosperity resided in them. . . .

The second consequence is the degradation of those who labor, but who do not by their labor command large rewards; that is of the great majority of mankind. . . . But when the criterion of function is forgotten, the only criterion which remains is that of wealth, and an Acquisitive Society reverences the possession of wealth, as a Functional Society would honor, even in the person of the humblest and most laborious craftsman, the arts of creation. [Pp. 34-35.]

. . . . .

The rejection of the idea of purpose involves another consequence which every one laments, but which no one can prevent, except by abandoning the belief that the free exercise of rights is the main interest of society and the discharge of obligations a secondary and incidental consequence which may be left to take care of itself. It is that social life is turned into a scene of fierce antagonisms and that a considerable part of industry is carried on in the intervals of a disguised social war. The idea that industrial peace can be secured merely by the exercise of tact and forbearance is based on the idea that there is a fundamental identity of interest between the different groups engaged in it, which is occasionally interrupted by regrettable misunderstandings. Both the one idea and the other are an illusion. The disputes which matter are not caused by a misunderstanding of identity of interests, but by a better understanding of diversity of interests. Though a formal declaration of war is an episode, the conditions which issue in a declaration of war are permanent; and what makes them permanent is the conception of industry which also makes inequality and functionless incomes permanent. It is the denial that industry has any end or purpose other than the satisfaction of those engaged in it.

That motive produces industrial warfare, not as a regrettable incident, but as an inevitable result. It produces industrial war, because its teaching is that each individual or group has a right to what they can get, and denies that there is any principle, other than the mechanism of the market, which determines what they ought to get. For, since the income available for distribution is limited, and since, therefore, when certain limits have been passed, what one group gains another group must lose, it is evident that if the relative incomes of different groups are not to be determined by their functions, there is no method other than mutual self-assertion which is left to determine them.... [Pp. 40-41.]

. . . . .

... If miners demanded higher wages when every superfluous charge upon coal-getting had been eliminated, there would be a principle with which to meet their claim, the principle that one group of workers ought not to encroach upon the livelihood of others. But as long as mineral owners extract royalties, and exceptionally productive mines pay thirty per cent to absentee shareholders, there is no valid answer to a demand for higher wages. For if the community pays anything at all to those who do not work, it can afford to pay more to those who do. The naive complaint, that workmen are never satisfied, is, therefore, strictly true. It is true, not only of workmen, but of all classes in a society which conducts its affairs on the principle that wealth, instead of being proportioned to function, belongs to those who can get it. They are never satisfied, nor can they be satisfied. For as long as they make that principle the guide of their individual lives and of their social order, nothing short of infinity could bring them satisfaction.

... The possibility that one aspect of human life may be so exaggerated as to overshadow, and in time to atrophy, every other, has been made familiar to Englishmen by the example of "Prussian militarism.". . .

Militarism, as Englishmen see plainly enough is fetish worship. It is the prostration of men's souls before, and the laceration of their bodies to appease, an idol. What they do not see is that their reverence for economic activity and industry and what is called business is also fetish worship, and that in their devotion to that idol they torture themselves as needlessly and indulge in the same meaningless antics as the Prussians did in their worship of militarism. . . .

When a Cabinet Minister declares that the greatness of this country depends upon the volume of its exports, so that France, which exports comparatively little, and Elizabethan England, which exported next to nothing, are presumably to be pitied as altogether inferior civilizations, that is Industrialism. It is the confusion of one minor department of life with the whole of life. When manufacturers cry and cut themselves with knives, because it is proposed that boys and girls of fourteen shall attend school for eight hours a week, and the President of the Board of Education is so gravely impressed with their apprehensions, that he at once allows the hours to be reduced to seven, that is Industrialism. It is fetish worship. When the Government obtains money for a war, which cost $28,000,000 a day, by closing the Museums, which cost $80,000 a year, that is Industrialism. It is contempt for all interests which do not contribute obviously to economic activity. When the Press clamors that one thing needed to make this island an Arcadia is productivity, and more productivity, and yet more productivity, that is Industrialism. It is the confusion of means with ends.

Men will always confuse means with ends if they are without any clear conception that it is the ends, not the means, which matter—if they allow their minds to slip from the fact that it is the social purpose of industry which gives it meaning and makes it worth while to carry it on at all. And when they do that, they will turn their whole world upside down, because they do not see the poles upon which it ought to move. So when, like England, they are thoroughly industrialized, they behave like Germany, which was thoroughly militarized. They talk as though man existed for industry, instead of industry existing for man, as the Prussians talked of man existing for war. They resent any activity which is not colored by the predominant interest, because it seems a rival to it. So they destroy religion and art and morality, which cannot exist unless they are disinterested; and having destroyed those, which are the end, for the sake of industry, which is a means, they make their industry itself what they make their cities, a desert of unnatural dreariness, which only forgetfulness can make endurable, and which only excitement can enable them to forget. [Pp. 43-47.]

Chapter V. Property and Creative Work

.   .   .   .   .

...In modern industrial societies the great mass of property consists, as the annual review of wealth passing at death reveals, neither of personal acquisitions such as household furniture, nor of the owner's stock-in-trade, but of rights of various kinds, such as royalties, ground-rents, and, above all, of course shares in industrial undertakings which yield an income irrespective of any personal service rendered by their owners. Ownership and use are normally divorced. The greater part of modern property has been attenuated to a pecuniary lien or bond on the product of industry which carries with it a right to payment, but which is normally valued precisely because it relieves the owner from any obligation to perform a positive or constructive function.

Such property may be called passive property, or property for acquisition, for exploitation, or for power, to distinguish it from the property which is actively used by its owner for the conduct of his profession or the upkeep of his household. To the lawyer the first is, of course, as fully property as the second. It is questionable, however, whether economists shall call it "Property" at all, and not rather, as Mr. Hobson has suggested, "Improperty," since it is not identical with the rights which secure the owner the produce of his toil, but is opposite of them. A classification of proprietary rights based upon this difference would be instructive. If they were arranged according to the closeness with which they approximate to one or other of these two extremes, it would be found that they were spread along a line stretching from property which is obviously the payment for, and condition of, personal services, to property which is merely a right to payment from the services rendered by others, in fact a private tax. The rough order which would emerge, if all details and qualification were omitted, might be something as follows:

1. Property in payments made for personal services.
2. Property in personal possessions necessary to health and comfort.
3. Property in land and tools used by their owners.
4. Property in copyright and patent rights owned by authors and inventors.
5. Property in pure interest, including much agricultural rent.
6. Property in profits of luck and good fortune: "quasi-rents."
7. Property in monopoly profits.
8. Property in urban ground rents.
9. Property in royalties. [Pp. 62-64.]

LINDSAY, THE PRINCIPLE OF PRIVATE PROPERTY*

The principle of private property has the twofold character of all rights. It is a right vested in individuals thought of as set over against one another, and it requires the recognition and protection of society for its existence. Extreme views which neglect either of these aspects are too obviously wrong to need consideration. Differences of opinion about the right of property arise as too exclusive attention is paid to the claims of the solidarity of society or of the independent development of its individual members. The first attitude gives rise to the view that property is entirely the arbitrary creation of society, the second to the view that society must recognize the right of property but cannot modify or control it. The attempt to make the right of property inherent in the individual apart from society is false to the facts of the creation of wealth. Yet the denial of such rights often leads to mere political opportunism. The good of society is the criterion of rights, but that good can only be expressed in the good lives of individuals. Private property can only be defended as a condition of the good life.

Before such defence is attempted it must be noticed that the right of private property has taken the most diverse forms, and the same defence will not serve all forms.

---

* [*Essay in Property: Its Duties and Rights,* 2nd Ed., pp. 70-71. New York: The Macmillan Company, 1922.
    Alexander Dunlop Lindsay, 1st Baron of Kirkev since 1945 (b. 1879), Master of Balliol College, Oxford, previously had taught at Edinburgh, Glasgow and Victoria. His major writings include: *The Nature of Religious Truth* (1927); *The Essentials of Democracy* (1929); *Christianity and Economics* (1933); and *The Modern Democratic State* (1944).]

We might try to find a defense of private property in the necessary separation of men in some respects. If the production of wealth is co-operative, much consumption is necessarily separate. But property in things that are separately used, in so far as they are so used, is not the principle of private property but of Communism. Communism is an attempt to confine property to use. The disadvantages of such an attempt to distinguish property in matter not in use and in matter in use, and confine the first to the community, are that it is hardly compatible with the discovery of new uses and needs, that it gives enormous power to those who govern the community, and that it takes from the individual the necessity for deliberation and foresight. Private property is essential to the full development of the individual.

This, however, is not an objection to Socialism, which defends private property in goods to be consumed but attacks it in the means of production on the ground that the production of wealth is co-operative. Consideration of the difficulty of distinguishing between the means of consumption and of production shows that most property does not consist in things but in power over other men, and suggests that the real basis of the attacks on property is the evils of the irresponsible power it bestows.

Nevertheless something can be said for private property in the means of production. Although the production of wealth is co-operative it is not therefore impossible to distinguish between the different values of the work of different individuals, and it is essential to encourage in individuals originality and invention. Giving to certain individuals power to direct and organize the work of others is also essential. The principle of private property in the means of production may be defended as being but the carrying out of the principles of "tools to those who can use them."

On the other side the following considerations must be noted:

1. This defence does not apply to the rights of bequest and inheritance, which must be defended on very different grounds.
2. The amount of money earned by any individual may represent only very roughly his power to serve society.
3. The fact that the power given to individuals by private property tends to efficiency when rightly used, does not remove the evils produced by the irresponsible use of that power. We are still faced with the problem of how we can combine efficiency with control in the interests of society. But this is precisely the problem of the control of political power which has in the political sphere been largely solved. The political analogy should show us that no simple or ready-made solution of the problem of property is possible, but may also suggest the lines along which a solution is likely to be found. [Pp. 70-71.]

CHAPTER 2

CONTRACT

Contents

Introductory Note

"The law of contract," as Pollock and Maitland warned us, has, on occasion, "threatened to swallow up all public law.... If there is to be any law at all, contract must be taught to know its place."

Certainly there are few legal transactions that have not, at one time or another, been treated on a contract basis. At the hands of Locke, Kant, and Sutherland, government itself is a contractual affair; at least for Locke, and perhaps for Sutherland, property also is a matter of contract. To Hegel, even the crime of murder and its necessary punishment assume aspects of contract law.

"Contract" is indeed an "accordion" word. Its shape will depend, at any moment, upon the tune that society is playing. This means, to the practicing lawyer or judge, that surrounding currents of thought may illumine the daily problems of contract law. It also means, to those who wonder about the paths of historic destiny, that what happens in law courts and legislatures with relation to contract may throw in bold relief the profiles of our society and our generation.

Maine, Williston, Pound, Holdsworth, Llewellyn, and Kessler, in the studies from which the following chapter borrows its materials, are all primarily concerned with the interconnections between legal theories of contract and the economic, domestic, and scholastic folkways and thoughtways of human beings in various societies. And if the diversity of theories of contract is startling, one may find equal cause for wonder and reflection in the fact that thinkers and societies that are poles apart geographically, economically, and culturally, so often agree on specific rules of contract law. The excerpts from the Civil Code of Spain showing basic contract rules equally valid in France, Chile, Colombia, Germany, Holland, Italy, Mexico, Portugal, and many other lands, and equally honored across eighteen or more centuries, offer a substantial challenge to the view that law reflects all the changes of changing economies and all the diversities of diverse civilizations. The spectacle of Pollock describing English common law by quoting whole paragraphs from a German scholar's description of the law of ancient Rome raises a real problem for those who think, with Holmes, that the common law is "not a brooding omnipresence in the sky but the articulate voice of some sovereign or quasi-sovereign that can be identified." (*Infra,* Chapter 6.) Such reflections may lead to a better understanding of what has been said under the rubric of natural law on many legal problems.

Within the broader context to which these diverse writers point, there remain the central problems of contract law: What promises should be enforced? What nonpromissory relinquishments of privileges should be validated? What are the respective roles of formality, consideration, value received, injurious reliance, risk distribution, social policy, and public ideals, in answering such questions? The answers offered by Bentham, Kant, Hegel, Williston, Oliphant, Steele, Corbin, Gellhorn, Justices Sutherland, Holmes, and Hughes, and other contributors to the following pages, are bound to enrich our understanding of the law even if, in the end, we appraise each of these views as incomplete.

As in our dealings with the vocabulary of property law, we find that many men have meant many different things by the term "contract." For some, a realistic defintion of contract as a function of sovereignty, a *vinculum juris,* in the sturdy terms of the Roman realists, will parallel a similar definition of property; court decisions will then offer the only possible answer to the recurring question in Karl Llewellyn's "Ballade of the Class in Contracts" (quoted *infra*). For those who, like Locke or Kant or Sutherland, look to something more basic than government, by which governments themselves may be judged, a natural law or nonrealistic legal definition may be more useful. And within either the realistic or the nonrealistic families of definitions, one finds endless variations. For those who use the language of natural law, a contract may be a promise (Marshall, C.J., in *Sturges v. Crowinshield*) or an exchange of promises (Taney, C.J., in the *Charles River Bridge* case) or any self-limitation of freedom, promissory or nonpromissory (Locke, Kant, Hegel, and Marshall, C.J. at times, as in the *Dartmouth College* case, where a non-promissory charter was held to be obviously a contract). For the realists, the language of enforceable promises today holds the field, and the only important contemporary disagreement is over the question whether one such promise or two must be the starting point of the analysis. But this definition, like contemporary definitions of property, is more of a literary convention than a working rule. Even the American Law Institute still recognizes that a warranty deed, a deed poll, a bill of exchange, or a patent may be a contract without containing any promises whatever. The fact remains that in Anglo-American legal history a promise is an accidental and not an essential element in contracts; what is essential is that somehow a person has by his own act relinquished a privilege and assumed an obligation towards another person. The Roman phrasing "*Contrahitur Obligatio*" throws more light than volumes of exegesis: one contracts an obligation as one contracts pneumonia, or any other disability. Contract is that part of our legal burdens that we bring on ourselves. That this is a very large part of all our burdens is the teaching of much of contemporary history as well as of ancient philosophy.

---

1. The Nature and Types of Contract

THE INSTITUTES OF JUSTINIAN *

Preamble

In the Name of Our Lord
Jesus Christ

The Emperor Caesar Flavius Justinianus, vanquisher of the Alamani, Goths, Francs, Germans, Antes, Alani, Vandals, Africans, pious, happy, glorious, triumphant conqueror, ever August, to the youth desirous of studying the law, greeting. [P. 1.]

. . . . . .

3. When by the blessing of God this task was accomplished, we summoned the most eminent Tribonian, master and ex-quaestor of our palace, together with the illustrious Theophilus and Dorotheus, professors of law, all of whom have on many occasions proved to us their ability, legal knowledge, and obedience to our orders; and we have specially charged them to compose, under our authority and advice, Institutes, so that you may no more learn the first elements of law from old and erroneous sources, but apprehend them by the clear light of imperial wisdom; and that your minds and ears may receive nothing that is useless or misplaced,

---

* [8th ed. (1888). Sandars, ed. Italicized matter in brackets is the translator's. See footnote, *supra*, p. 50.]

but only what obtains in actual practice. So that, whereas, formerly, the junior students could scarcely, after three years' study, read the imperial constitutions, you may now commence your studies by reading them, you who have been thought worthy of an honour and a happiness so great as that the first and last lessons in the knowledge of the law should issue for you from the mouth of the emperor. [P. 2.]

. . . . .

7. Receive, therefore, with eagerness, and study with cheerful diligence, these our laws, and show yourselves persons of such learning that you may conceive the flattering hope of yourselves being able, when your course of legal study is completed, to govern our empire in the different portions that may be entrusted to your care.

Given at Constantinople on the eleventh day of the calends of December, in the third consulate of the Emperor Justinian, ever August (533). [P. 3.]

. . . . .

Liber III
Tit. XIII
De Obligationibus
[*On Obligations*]

Let us now pass to obligations, An obligation is a tie of law [*vinculum juris*], by which we are so constrained that of necessity we must render something according to the laws of our state. [*D. xliv. 7.3. pr.*] [P. 319.]

. . . . .

2. A further division separates them into four kinds, for they arise *ex contractu* or *quasi ex contractu, ex maleficio* or *quasi ex maleficio*. Let us first treat of those which arise from a contract: which again are divided into four kinds according as they are formed *re, verbis, litteris,* or *consensu*. Let us examine each kind separately. [*Gai. iii. 88, 89; D. xliv. 7.1. pr. and 1.*] [P. 319.]

. . . . .

Tit. XIV
Quibus Modis Re Contrahitur Obligatio
[*On the Ways in Which an Obligation is Contracted Through a Thing*]

An obligation is contracted *re*, as, for example, by giving a *mutuum*. This always consists of things which may be weighed, numbered, or measured, as wine, oil, corn, coin, brass, silver, or gold. In giving these things by number, measure, or weight, we so give them that they may become the property of those who receive them. And identical things lent are not returned, but only others of the same nature and quality; and hence the term *mutuum*, because what I give, from being mine, becomes yours. From this contract arises the action termed *condictio*. [*Gai. iii. 90; D. xii. 1. pr. 1, 2.*] [P. 327.]

. . . . .

Tit. XV
De Verborum Obligatione
[On the Obligation of Words]

An obligation *verbis* is contracted by means of a question and an answer, when we stipulate that anything shall be given to or done for us. . . . [*D. xliv. 7. 1.7; D. xii. 1.24.*] [P. 332.]

. . . . .

1. Formerly the words used in making this kind of contract were as follows—"*Spondes?* do you engage yourself? *Spondeo,* I do engage myself. *Promittis?* do you promise? *Promitto,* I do promise. *Fidepromittis?* do you promise on your good faith? *Fidepromitto,* I do promise on my good faith. *Fidejubes?* do you make yourself *fidejussor? Fidejubeo,* I do make myself *fidejussor. Dabis?* will you give? *Dabo,* I will give. *Facies?* will you do? *Faciam,* I will do." And it is immaterial whether the stipulation is in Latin or in Greek, or in any other language, so that the parties understand it; nor is it necessary that the same language should be used by each person, but it is sufficient if the answer agrees with the question. So two Greeks may contract in Latin. Anciently indeed it was necessary to use the formal words just mentioned, but the constitution of the Emperor Leo was afterwards enacted,* which, removing formalities of expression, requires only that the parties understand one another and mean the same thing, no matter what words they use. [*Gai. iii. 92, 93; D. xlv. 1.1.6; C. viii. 37.10.*] [Pp. 333-334.]

. . . . .

Tit. XXII
De Consensu Obligatione
[On Obligation Derived Through Consent]

Obligations are formed by the mere consent of the parties in the contracts of sale, of letting to hire, of partnership, and of mandate. An obligation is, in these cases, said to be made by the mere consent of the parties, because there is no necessity for any writing, nor even for the presence of the parties; nor is it requisite that anything should be given to make

---

* [This constitution of Leo was published A.D. 472 (C.viii. 37.10).]

the contract binding, but the mere consent of those between whom the transaction is carried on suffices. Thus these contracts may be entered into by those who are at a distance from each other by means of letters, for instance, or of messengers. In these contracts each party is bound to the other to render him all that equity demands, while in verbal obligations one party stipulates and the other promises. [*Gai. iii. 135-138.*] [P. 361.]

AMERICAN LAW INSTITUTE, RESTATEMENT OF CONTRACTS

Chapter 1.

Sec. 1. Contract Defined.

A contract is a promise or a set of promises for the breach of which the law gives a remedy, or the performance of which the law in some way recognizes as a duty.*

. . . . .

Sec. 7. Formal Contracts.

Formal contracts are

(a) Contracts under seal,

(b) Recognizances,

(c) Negotiable instruments.

. . . . .

Sec. 9. Recognizances.

A recognizance is an acknowledgment in court by the recognizor that he is bound to make a certain payment unless a specified condition is performed.†

---

* [*Cf.* the following standard definitions:

"A contract is an agreement in which a party undertakes to do or not to do a particular thing." Marshall, C.J., in Sturges v. Crowninshield, 4 Wheat. 122, 197 (1819).

"A contract is defined to be an agreement between two or more persons to do or not to do a particular thing." Taney, C.J., in Charles River Bridge v. Warren Bridge, 11 Pet. 420, 572 (1837).

And compare the position of Chief Justice Marshall in Dartmouth College v. Woodward, 4 Wheat. 518, 625 (1819) with respect to the character of Dartmouth College: "It can require no argument to prove that the circumstances of this case constitute a contract."]

† [*Cf.* the following definitions of early common law contract forms:

Statute Staple. "The statute of the staple 27 Ed. III Stat. 2 . . . authorized a security for money . . . to be taken by traders . . . effect to convey the lands of the debtor to the creditor till out of the rents and profits of them he should be satisfied. . . . It was a bond of record acknowledged before the mayor of the staple. A seal was required and that was all that was necessary to attest the contract." *Bouvier's Law Dictionary.*

Statute Merchant. "A security entered before the Mayor of London, or some chief

Sec. 10. Negotiable Instruments.

Negotiable instruments are such bills of exchange, promissory notes, and bonds as are payable to bearer, or to the order of a specified person. . . .

CIVIL CODE OF SPAIN *

Title II. Contracts

Chapter First. General Provisions

Article 1254. A contract exists from the moment when one or several persons consent to bind himself or themselves, in respect to another or others, to give something or to render some service.

Fr. Civ. 1101, Chile 1438, Col. 1495, Ger. 151, Holl. 1349, Ital. 1098, Mex. 1272, Port. 641.†

1255. The contracting parties may establish any pacts, clauses, and conditions which they deem convenient, provided they do not conflict with the laws, morals, or public order.

Fr. Civ. 1131, Chile 1467, Holl. 1371, Ital. 1119, Port. 659 et seq.

. . . . . .

1257. Contracts shall only be effectual between the parties by whom they are executed and their heirs, except, with respect to the latter, in the cases where the rights and obligations originating from the contract are not transmissible, either by their nature, or by pact, or by provision of law.

When the contract contains any stipulation in favor of a third party he can exact its fulfillment, whenever he has given notice of his acceptance to the person bound, before the said stipulation has been revoked.

Fr. Civ. 1119, 1121, Chile 1448 et seq., Ger. 328, Holl. 1351, Ital. 1128, Mex. 1277 et seq., Port. 645 et seq.

1258. Contracts are perfected by mere consent and from that time they are binding, not only in respect to the fulfillment of what has been expressly stipulated, but also in all the consequences which, according to their nature, are in accordance with good faith, use, and law.

---

warder of a city, in pursuance of 13 Ed. I Stat. 3, c. 1, whereby the lands of the debtor are conveyed to the creditor till out of the rents and profits of them his debt may be satisfied." *Bouvier's Law Dictionary.*

Deed Poll. "A deed made by one party only, as a sheriff, the edges of the instrument being 'polled' or shaven even." 2 Blackstone, *Commentaries,* 296.]

* [Book IV *(Obligations and Contracts).* The translation here given follows generally that found in Walton, *The Civil Law in Spain and Spanish America* (1900), pp. 352-356.]

† [References are to substantially identical provisions in the civil codes of other countries (taken in part from the edition of the Spanish Civil Code translated and edited by A. Leve, 2d Ed., Paris, 1904).]

Fr. Civ. 1134, Chile 1546, Ger. 152, Holl. 1375, Ital. 1124, Mex. 1276, Port. 702 et seq.

1259. No one can contract in the name of another without being authorized by him, or without lawfully having his legal representation.

A contract entered into in the name of another by one who has not either his authorization or legal representation, shall be null and void, unless it is ratified by the person in whose name it was executed, before it is revoked by the other contracting party.

Fr. Civ. 1119, Chile 1448, Col. 1505, Ger. 164, Holl. 1353, Ital. 1128, Mex. 1277, Port. 645.

1260. Oaths shall not be admitted in contracts. If admitted, they shall be considered as not existing.

Chapter Second. Essential Requirements for the Validity
of Contracts

Article 1261. There is no contract unless the following requirements are present:

1. The consent of the contracting parties.
2. A definite object which may be a matter of contract.
3. A cause for the obligation which is established therein.

Fr. Civ. 1108, Chile 1446, Ger. 151, Holl. 1365, Mex. 1282, Port. 644.

Section First. Consent

Article 1262. Consent is shown by the concurrence of the offer and of the acceptance of the thing and the cause which shall constitute the contract.

Acceptance made by letter only binds the person who made the offer when it came to his notice. The contract, in this case, is presumed as entered into at the place where the offer was made.

Ger. Civ. 151.

1263. The following persons cannot give their consent:

1. Minors who are not emancipated.
2. Lunatics or the insane, and the deaf and dumb who cannot write.
3. Married women, in the cases specified by law.

Fr. Civ. 1124, Chile 1446 et seq., Ger. 104, Holl. 1366 et seq., Ital. 1106, Mex. 420, Port. 98, 314, 340, 355, 1192.

1264. The incapacity, set forth in the preceding article, is subject to the modifications which are determined by law and is to be understood without prejudice to the special incapacities established by such law.

1265. Consent given by error, under violence, intimidation or by deceit shall be void.

Fr. Civ. 1109, Chile 1451, Col. 1508, Ger. 123, Holl. 1367, Ital. 1108, Mex. 1286, Port. 656.

1266. In order that the error may invalidate the consent, it must refer to the substance of the thing, object of the contract, or to those conditions of the same, which should have been principally the cause of its celebration.

An error as to the person shall invalidate a contract only when the consideration of the person should have been the principal cause of the contract.

A mere error of accounts shall only give cause of its correction.

Fr. Civ. 1110, Chile 1452, Col. 1510, Ger. 119, Holl. 1358, Ital. 1109, Mex. 1296, Port. 659.

1267. Violence exists when, to exact the consent, an irresistible force is used.

Intimidation exists when one of the contracting parties is inspired with a reasonable and well-grounded fear of suffering an imminent and serious injury to his person or property, or to the person or property of his consort, descendants or ascendants.

To qualify the intimidation, the age, sex, and status of the person must be considered.

Fear of displeasing the persons to whom obedience and respect is due shall not annul the contract.

Fr. Civ. 1112-1114, Chile 1456, Col. 1513, Holl. 1360, Ital. 1112, 1114, Mex. 1299, Port. 666.

1268. Violence or intimidation shall annul the obligation, even if they have been employed by a third person who did not intervene in the contract.

Chile Civ. 1457, Col. 1514.

1269. There is deceit, when by words or insidious contrivances on the part of one of the contracting parties, the other is induced to enter into a contract which he would not have done without the use of them.

Fr. Civ. 1116, Chile 1458, Col. 1515, Ger. 123, Holl. 1364, Ital. 1115, Mex. 1296 et seq., Port. 663.

1270. In order that deceit may cause the nullity of a contract, it should be grievous and must not have been employed by both of the contracting parties.

Incidental deceit renders only the party who employed it liable to indemnity for damages and injuries.

Fr. Civ. 1116, Chile 1460 et seq., Holl. 1368, Ital. 1116, Mex. 1304 et seq., Port. 671.

Section Second. Objects of Contracts

Article 1271. All things, even future ones, which are not out of the commerce of men, can be objects of contracts.

Notwithstanding, no contract can be entered into in respect to future inheritances, other than those whose object is to make a distribution *inter vivos* of the estate, according to article 1056.

All services not contrary to law or to good morals may also be the object of a contract.

Fr. Civ. 1128, 1180, Chile 1460 et seq., Col. 1518, Ger. 306, 312, Holl. 1368, 1370, Ital. 1116, 1118, Mex. 1304, 1306, Port. 671.

1272. Things or services which are impossible cannot be the object of a contract.

Fr. Civ. 1128, Col. 1518, Ital. 1116, Port. 671.

1273. The object of every contract must be a thing determined as to its kind. The indetermination of the sum cannot be an obstacle to the existence of the contract, provided it may be possible to determine it without necessity of a new agreement between the contracting parties.

Fr. Civ. 1128, Chile 1461, Col. 1518, Holl. 1369, Ital. 1117, Mex. 1306, Port. 671.

Section Third. "Cause" * [causa] for Contracts

Article 1274. In onerous contracts, the prestation or promise of a thing or services by the other party is understood as a "cause" for each contracting party; in remuneratory ones, the services or benefits remunerated, and in those of pure beneficence, the mere liberality of the benefactor.

Chile Civ. 1467, Col. 1524.

1275. Contracts without "cause" or with an illicit one are not effectual. A "cause" is illicit, when it is contrary to law and good morals.

Fr Civ. 1131, 1133, Chile 1467, Col. 1524, Holl. 1371, Ital. 1119.

1276 The statement of a false "cause" in contracts shall render them void, unless it is proven that they are based on another real and licit one.

1277. Although the "cause" is not expressed in the contract, it is presumed as existing and that it is licit, unless the debtor proves the contrary.†

Fr. Civ. 1132, Chile 1467, Col. 1524, Holl. 1372, Ital. 1120.

KANT. PHILOSOPHY OF LAW ‡

Second Section
Principles of Personal Right

§ 18. Nature and Acquisition of Personal Right

The possession of the active free-will of another person, as the power to determine it by my Will to a certain action, according to Laws of Free-

---

* [It has been thought better to translate the Spanish "causa" literally as "cause" rather than by the term "consideration," which, although filling a position in the common law similar to that filled by the Roman conception of *causa*. has entirely different historical and analytical connotations.]

† [The four following sections of the code deal with the form, interpretation, rescission, and voidability of contracts.]

‡ [Book II (*The Science of Right*), Part I, Chap. 2nd, Sec. 2d. Hastie, trans.]

dom, is a form of Right relating to the external Mine and Thine, as affected by the Causality of another. It is possible to have several such Rights in reference to the same Person or to different persons. The Principle of the System of Laws, according to which I can be in such possession, is that of Personal Right, and there is only one such principle.

The Acquisition of a Personal Right can never be primary or arbitrary, for such a mode of acquiring it would not be in accordance with the Principle of the harmony of the freedom of my will with the freedom of every other, and it would therefore be wrong. Nor can such a Right be acquired by means of any *unjust* act of another (*facto injusto alterius*), as being itself contrary to Right; for if such a wrong as it implies were perpetrated on me, and I could demand satisfaction from the other, in accordance with Right, yet in such a case I would only be entitled to maintain undiminished what was mine, and not to acquire anything more than what I formerly had.

Acquisition by means of the action of another, to which I determine his Will according to Laws of Right, is therefore always derived from what that other has as his own. This derivation, as a Juridical act, cannot be effected by a mere *negative relinquishment* or *renunciation* of what is his (*per derelictionem aut renunciationem*); because such a negative Act would only amount to a cessation of *his* Right, and not to the acquirement of a Right on the part of another. It is therefore only by positive TRANSFERENCE (*translatio*), or CONVEYANCE, that a Personal Right can be acquired; and this is only possible by means of a common Will, through which objects come into the power of one or other, so that as one renounces a particular thing which he holds under the common Right, the same object when accepted by another in consequence of a positive act of Will, becomes his. Such transference of the *Property* of one to another is termed its ALIENATION. The act of the united Wills of two Persons, by which what belonged to one passes to the other, constitutes CONTRACT. [Pp. 100-101.]

HEGEL, PHILOSOPHY OF RIGHT *

Contract

§ 72. In contract property is no longer viewed in the aspect of its external reality, as a mere thing, but rather as containing the elements of will, another's as well as my own. Contract is the process which presents and occasions the contradiction by which I, existing for myself and excluding another will, am and remain an owner in so far as I identify myself with the will of another, and cease to be an owner.

§ 73. Guided by the conception I must relinquish my property not

---

* [First Part, Second Section. See pp. 73-76 *supra* for earlier passages.]

merely as an external thing (§ 65), but as property, if my will is to become a genuine factor in reality. But by virtue of this procedure my will, when relinquished, is another's will. The necessary nature of the conception is thus realized in a unity of different wills, which, nevertheless, give up their differences and peculiarities. But this identity implies not that one will is identical with the other, but rather that each at this stage remains an independent and private will.

§ 74. This relationship, therefore, is the means by which two absolutely distinct and separate owners form one will. While each, in accordance with the common will of both, ceases to be an owner, he is and remains one. Each will gives up a particular property, and receives the particular property of another, adopting only that conclusion with which the other coincides.

§ 75. Since the two contracting parties appear as directly independent persons (a) contract proceeds from arbitrary choice; (β) the one will formed by the contract is the product merely of the two interested persons, and is thus a common, but not an absolutely universal will; (γ) the object of the contract is a single external thing, because only such a thing is subject to relinquishment at the mere option of the parties (§ 65 and fol.).

Note.—Marriage cannot be subsumed under the conception of contract. This view is, we must say it, in all its shamelessness, propounded by Kant (*Metaph. Anf. der Rechtslehre*, p. 106). Just as little does the nature of the state conform to contract, whether the contract be regarded as a compact of all with all, or of all with the prince or government.—The introduction of the relations of contract and private property into the functions of the state has produced the greatest confusion both in the law and in real life. In earlier times civil rights and duties were thought and maintained to be a directly private possession of particular individuals in opposition to the rights of prince and state. In more recent years, also, the rights of prince and state have been treated as objects of covenant. They are said to be based on contract, or the mere general consent of those who wish to form a state. Different as these two views of the state are, they agree in taking the phases of private property into another and a higher region. This will be referred to again when we come to speak of ethical observances and the state.

Addition.—It is a popular view in modern times that the state is a contract of all with all. All conclude, so the doctrine runs, a compact with the prince, and he in turn with the subjects. According to this superficial view, there is in contract only one unity of different wills; but in fact there are two identical wills, both of which are persons and wish to remain property-owners. Contract, besides, arises out of the spontaneous choice of the persons. Marriage, indeed, has that point in common with contract, but with the state it is different. An individual cannot enter or leave the social condition at his option, since every one is by his very nature a citizen of a state. The characteristic of man as rational is to live in a state; if there is no state, reason demands that one should be founded. Permission either to enter or to leave it must, it is true, be accorded by the state, but this permission is not given in deference to the arbitrary choice of the individual, nor is the state founded upon contract, which presupposes this arbitrary individual choice. It is false to say that it rests with the arbitrary will of all to establish a state, rather is it absolutely necessary for every one to be a citizen of a state. The great progress of the modern state is due to the fact that it has and keeps an absolute end, and no man is now at liberty to make private arrangements in connection with this end, as they did in the middle ages.

§ 76. Contract is formal when the two elements through which the common will arises, the negative disposal of the thing and the positive reception of it, are so divided, that one of the contracting parties makes one side of the agreement, and the other, the other. This is gift. Contract is real when each of the contractors performs both sides of the double agreement, and is and remains an owner. This is a contract of exchange.

Addition.—Contract involves two consenting parties and two things; I both give up and acquire a property. Real contract occurs, when each yields up and acquires property, and each party in giving up property remains an owner. Formal contract occurs when a person only gives up or acquires.

§ 77. In real contract every one both keeps the same property as he had when he undertook the contract, and also yields up his property. Hence it is necessary to distinguish the property, which in contract remains permanently mine, from the external objects which change hands. The universal and self-identical element in exchange, that with regard to which the objects to be exchanged are equal, is the value (§ 63).

Note.—By the very conception of contract a *laesio enormis* annuls the agreement, since the contractor, in disposing of his goods, must remain in possession of a quantitative equivalent. An injury (*laesio*) may fairly be called enormous, if it exceeds half of the value; but it is infinite, when a contract or any stipulation is entered into to dispose of an inalienable good (§ 66). A stipulation is only one single part or side of the whole contract, or a merely formal settlement, of which more hereafter. It contains only the formal phase of contract, the consent of one party to perform something, and the consent of the other party to accept the performance. It must, therefore, be classed amongst the so-called unilateral contracts. The division of contracts into unilateral and bilateral contracts, and many other divisions of the same kind in Roman law, are superficial combinations, arising from some particular and external consideration, as, for instance, the way in which they are made. They may also confuse characteristics intrinsic to contract itself with others which do not concern the nature of the contract, such as those which only arise later in connection with the administration of justice (*actiones*), and to the legal processes giving effect to positive laws, or such as may arise out of wholly external circumstances and contravene the conception of right.

POLLOCK, PRINCIPLES OF CONTRACT *

Chapter 1. Agreement, Proposal, and Acceptance

One always thinks of the consent of the parties as the main thing that goes to make a contract, as beyond question it is. A contract is before all things a transaction in which two or more persons consent. But this is a generic, not a specific description. Every contract involves consent, but many legal transactions involve consent without being contracts. For a generic name of all legal transactions in which consent is necessary we may provisionally, for want of any better word, use the term Agreement in the widest possible sense.[1] Let us now see how many things are included in the consent that makes a legal agreement. Consider a familiar and unquestionable instance, the contract of sale. The first thing we observe is that it takes not less than two persons to make it. In this and in most cases there are in fact not more; but others readily occur, such as partnership, where the number is not limited. The next thing is that these persons have a distinct intention, and the intention of both or all of them is the same. Without this one obviously cannot say there is an agreement. Next, they must be aware that their intentions agree: in other words, they must communicate them to one another, for it is again obvious that uncommunicated intentions, however exactly they correspond, do not make an agreement. Moreover the scope of the intention is material. If people make agreements to go out for a walk or to read a book together, that is no agreement in a legal sense. Why not? Because their intention is not directed to legal consequences, but merely to extralegal ones; no rights or duties are to be created. In the case of the sale the buyer and the seller intend to acquire new rights and undertake new duties. The buyer means to become the owner of the goods and the seller to become his creditor for the price, and this is what gives the

---

* [*The Principles of Contract* (1876), of *Sir Frederick Pollock* (1845–1937) represents one of the first major efforts to systematize the common law decisions in the contract field. Equally significant is Sir Frederick Pollock's volume on *Torts* (1st edition 1887). Pollock collaborated with F. W. Maitland to produce what is probably the most significant single work in English legal history, the *History of English Law* (1895). Pollock was a practicing lawyer for a number of years, became Corpus professor of jurisprudence at Oxford in 1883 and in 1911 became a Privy Councillor. In 1914 he became Judge in Admiralty. His correspondence with Justice Holmes, edited by Mark DeWolf Howe, was published in 1941.]

[1] *Vertrag* as used by Savigny, whose analysis (Syst. § 140, vol. 3, p. 307) we follow almost literally in this paragraph.

agreement its legal character.[2] The intention of the parties must therefore be an intention directed to legal consequences; and, finally, those consequences must be such as to confer rights or impose duties on the parties themselves. The judgment of a full Court, or the verdict of a jury, for example, expresses a common intention of several persons which has legal consequences for its immediate object, and yet it is not an agreement. Nobody would think of calling it so. Why not? Because the rights and duties determined by the judgment or verdict are not those of the judges or jurors. The result, then, comes out in this way:

When two or more persons concur in expressing a common intention so that rights or duties of those persons are thereby determined, this is an agreement.[3] [Pp. 1-2.]

. . . . .

Thus far, however, we are still on general ground. We have not yet got any specific mark of contract, as distinguished from agreement (*Vertrag*) in the wide sense. What distinguished the agreement in a contract from the agreement in any other of the transactions falling within the more general conception, such as for example a perfect conveyance? The distinction is this: in the case of a contract something remains to be done by one or by each of the parties, which the other has or will have a right to call upon him to do. Now, in the language of Roman law (which is often adopted by our own, but perhaps cannot strictly be called part of it), there is a technical and appropriate name for this state of things. When one man has a peculiar right (*i.e.*, not a merely public right, or a right incident to ownership or a permanent family relation) to control another man's actions by calling upon him to do or forbear some particular thing, there is said to be an obligation between them.[4] The person whose action is thus controlled is said to be obliged or bound. A contract accordingly is an agreement which produces an obligation.[5] In this case, therefore, the common intention expressed by the parties has this peculiar character, that it contemplates a future performance or performances to

---

[2] The difference is "*dass in diesem der Wille auf ein Rechtsverhältniss als Zweck gerichtet ist, in jenen Fallen auf andere Zwecke*": the want of an English equivalent for *Rechtsverhältniss* has made some circumlocution unavoidable in the text.

[3] The original words are subjoined, as a perfectly literal translation is not practicable: *Vertrag ist die Vereinigung Mehrer zu einer übereinstimmenden Willenserklärung, wodurch ihre Rechtsverhältnisse bestimmt werden.* Savigny, Syst., § 140 (3,309). This is one of the things which look very obvious when they are once stated, and the reader may be tempted to think it too obvious to be worth making so much of. But it is just these obvious things which remain hidden or unfruitful till a man of true scientific genius like Savigny sees the importance of bringing them distinctly into the light.

[4] Sav. Syst. 1, 338-9; *id. Obl.* 1. 4, seq.

[5] *Obligatorischer Vertrag*, or (expanding *Vertrag* according to its previous definition) thus: *Vereinigung Mehrer zu einer übereinstimmenden Willenserklärung, wordurch unter ihnen eine Obligation entstehen soll.* Sav. Obl. 2, 7, 8.

which one or each of them is to be bound. On the side of the party so bound, the expression of this intention is accordingly nothing else than an undertaking to perform the thing he is bound to—in other words, a promise. This is the specific mark of Contract which we sought. That which distinguishes it from the genus Agreement is that the expression of intention is not only constituted by proposal and acceptance, but includes the particular kind of expression which is called a promise. We have as the proper ground-work of contract a promise determined by the acceptance of a proposal.[P. 5.]

WILLISTON, THE LAW OF CONTRACTS *

§ 22. *Mutual Assent Must Be Manifested* [1]

It is customarily said that mutual assent is essential to the formation of informal contracts, but it should further be stated that the mutual assent must be manifested by one party to the other, and except as so manifested is unimportant.[2] In some branches of the law, especially in the criminal law, a person's secret intent is important, but in the formation of contracts it was long ago settled that secret intent was immaterial; only overt acts being considered in the determination of such mutual assent as that branch of the law requires.[3] During the first half of the nineteenth century there

---

* [Rev. ed. Vol. I, Part 1, Chap. 3, "Making of Offers," p. 40 *et seq*. New York: Baker, Voorhis & Co., 1936.

Samuel Williston, (b. 1861), Professor of Law at Harvard 1890–1938, as well as a practicing attorney since 1889, and a prolific author. Williston's works have exerted a profound influence in the field of commercial law, where his treatises on the law of contracts and of sales, respectively, have established themselves as authoritative.]

[1] *Acc.*, Rest., Contracts, § 20. See Ashley, Mutual Assent in Contract, (1903) 3 *Col. L. Rev.* 71 [*Selected Readings*, p. 114]; Williston, Mutual Assent in the Formation of Contracts, (1919) 14 *Ill. L. Rev.* 85, *Wigmore Celebration Essays*, p. 525 [*Selected Readings*, p. 119]; Corbin, Offer and Acceptance and Some of the Resulting Legal Relations, (1917) 26 *Yale L.J.* 169 [*Selected Readings*, p. 170]; Ferson, The Formation of Simple Contracts, (1924) 9 *Corn. L.Q.* 402 [*Selected Readings*, p. 128]; Costigan, Implied-in-Fact Contracts and Mutual Assent, (1920) 30 *Harv. L. Rev.* 376 [*Selected Readings*, p. 144]; Corbin, The Offer of an Act for a Promise, (1920) 29 *Yale L.J.* 767 [*Selected Readings*, p. 199]. Cf. Whittier, The Restatement of Contracts and Mutual Assent, (1929) 17 *Calif. L. Rev.* 441; The Restatement of Contracts Again, (1929) 15 *Ia. L. Rev.* 278.

[2] For the exceptional situations in which informal contracts may be formed without a manifestation of mutual assent, see *infra*, §§ 138 *et seq.*, and Rest., Contracts, Chap. 3, Topic 4, §§ 85 *et seq.* Also see obligations imposed by law distinguished, *infra*, § 32A.

[3] "It is trite learning that the thought of man is not triable, for the devil himself knows not the thought of man." Brian in Y.B., 17 Edw. IV, 1. The text is cited and Brian's dictum quoted in Verdery v. Withers, 30 Ga. App. 63, 72, 116 S.E. 894.... In O'Donnell v. Clinton, 145 Mass. 461, 463, 14 N.E. 747, Holmes, J., said: "Assent in the sense of the law is a matter of overt acts, not of inward unanimity in motives, design or the interpretation of words" and this was quoted by Cardozo, J., in Sokoloff v. National City Bank, 239 N.Y. 158, 145 N.E. 917, 920, 37 A.L.R. 712. *See also* ... Gross v. Yeskel, 100 N.J.Eq. 293, 134 A. 737:... See Rest., Contracts, §§ 71, 233, and *infra*, § 95.

are many expressions which seem to indicate the contrary, chief of which was the familiar rubric, still reëchoing in judicial dicta that a contract requires the meeting of the minds of the parties.[4] That the fundamental basis of contract in the common law is reliance on an outward act (that is a promise) is shown by the early development of the law of consideration as compared with that of mutual assent. Courts of equity indeed have not shown the same indifference to the undisclosed intent of the parties, as have courts of law; but equity makes its views effective not by denying or altering the rules of law governing the formation contracts but by subsequently reforming or rescinding legally valid contracts in cases coming within its own rules.[5]

Not only must assent to a contract be manifested by overt acts but promises in contracts must be made by a manifestation of agreement moving from the promisor to the promisee. The assent of the promisee to a unilateral contract may be indicated by an act requested by the promisor, but of which he has no knowledge, and is not likely to acquire knowledge unless he takes steps to inform himself;[6] but a promise necessarily implies either communication from the promisor to the promisee, or at least some action which will normally indicate to the promisee the intent of the promisor.[7] [Pp. 41-43.]

HOLMES, THE COMMON LAW *

Lecture VIII. Contract

II. Elements

An assurance that it shall rain to-morrow,[1] or that a third person shall paint a picture, may as well be a promise as one that the promisee shall receive from some source one hundred bales of cotton, or that the promisor will pay the promisee one hundred dollars. What is the difference in the cases? It is only in the degree of power possessed by the promisor over the event. He has none in the first case. He has equally little legal authority to make a man paint a picture, although he may have larger means of persuasion. He probably will be able to make sure that the promisee has the cotton. Being a rich man, he is certain to be able to pay the one hundred dollars, except in the event of some most improbable accident.

---

[4] Modern instances of this unfortunate survival may be seen in practically all jurisdictions, e.g., International Transp. Assn. v. Bylenga, 254 Mich. 236, 236 N.W. 771; 300 West End Ave. Corp. v. Warner, 250 N.Y. 221, 165 N.E. 271, noted (1929) 14 Corn. L.Q. 379;...

[5] See, for instance, Gross v. Yeskel, supra, n. 3.

* [(1881), pp. 298-303. Footnotes have been renumbered.]

[1] Canham v. Barry, 15 C.B. 597, 619; Jones v. How, 9 C.B. 1, 9; Com. Dig. Condition, D. 2; 1 Roll. Abr. 420 (D) pl. 1; Y.B. 22 Ed. IV. 26, pl. 6.

But the law does not inquire, as a general thing, how far the accomplishment of an assurance touching the future is within the power of the promisor. In the moral world it may be that the obligation of a promise is confined to what lies within reach of the will of the promisor (except so far as the limit is unknown on one side, and misrepresented on the other). But unless some consideration of public policy intervenes, I take it that a man may bind himself at law that any future event shall happen. He can therefore promise it in a legal sense. It may be said that when a man covenants that it shall rain tomorrow, or that *A* shall paint a picture, he only says, in a short form, I will pay if it does not rain, or if *A* does not paint a picture. But that is not necessarily so. A promise could easily be framed which would be broken by the happening of fair weather, or by *A* not painting. A promise then, is simply an accepted assurance that a certain event or state of things shall come to pass.

But if this be true, it has more important bearings than simply to enlarge the definition of the word *promise*. It concerns the theory of contract. The consequences of a binding promise at common law are not affected by the degree of power which the promisor possesses over the promised event. If the promised event does not come to pass, the plaintiff's property is sold to satisfy the damages, within certain limits, which the promisee has suffered by the failure. The consequences are the same in kind whether the promise is that it shall rain, or that another man shall paint a picture, or that the promisor will deliver a bale of cotton.

If the legal consequence is the same in all cases, it seems proper that all contracts should be considered from the same legal point of view. In the case of a binding promise that it shall rain to-morrow, the immediate legal effect of what the promisor does is, that he takes the risk of the event, within certain defined limits, as between himself and the promisee. He does no more when he promises to deliver a bale of cotton.

If it be proper to state the common-law meaning of promise and contract in this way, it has the advantage of freeing the subject from the superfluous theory that contract is a qualified subjection of one will to another, a kind of limited slavery. It might be so regarded if the law compelled men to perform their contracts, or if it allowed promises to exercise such compulsion. If, when a man promised to labor for another, the law made him do it, his relation to his promisee might be called a servitude *ad hoc* with some truth. But that is what the law never does. It never interferes until a promise has been broken, and therefore cannot possibly be performed according to its tenor. It is true that in some instances equity does what is called compelling specific performance. But, in the first place, I am speaking of the common law, and in the next, this only means that equity compels the performance of certain elements of the total promise which are still capable of performance. For instance, take a promise to convey land within a certain time, a court of equity is not in the habit of interfering until the time has gone by, so that the promise cannot be performed as made. But if the conveyance is more important than the time, and the promisee prefers to have it late rather than never, the law may compel the performance of that. Not literally compel even in that case, however, but put the promisor in prison unless he will convey. This remedy is an exceptional one. The only universal consequence of a legally binding promise is, that the law makes the promisor pay damages if the promised event does not come to pass. In every case it leaves him free from interference until the time for fulfillment has gone by, and therefore free to break his contract if he chooses.

A more practical advantage in looking at a contract as the taking of a risk is to be found in the light which it throws upon the measure of damages. If a breach of contract were regarded in the same light as a tort, it would seem that if, in the course of performance of the contract the promisor should be notified of any particular consequence which would result from its not being performed, he should be held liable for that consequence in the event of non-performance. Such a suggestion has been made.[2] But it has not been accepted as the law. On the contrary, according to the opinion of a very able judge, which seems to be generally followed, notice, even at the time of making the contract, of special circumstances out of which special damages would arise in case of breach, is not sufficient unless the assumption of that risk is to be taken as having fairly entered into the contract.[3] If a carrier should undertake to carry the machinery of a saw-mill from Liverpool to Vancouver's Island, and should fail to do so, he probably would not be held liable for the rate of hire of such machinery during the necessary delay, although he might know that it could not be replaced without sending to England, unless he was fairly understood to accept "the contract with the special condition attached to it."[4]

It is true that, when people make contracts, they usually contemplate the performance rather than the breach. The express language used does not generally go further than to define what will happen if the contract is fulfilled. A statutory requirement of a memorandum in writing would be satisfied by a written statement of the promise as made, because to require more would be to run counter to the ordinary habits of mankind, as well as because the statement that the effect of a contract is the assumption of the risk of a future event does not mean that there is a

---

[2] Gee v. Lancashire & Yorkshire Railway Co., 6 H.&N. 211, 218, Bramwell, B. *Cf.* Hydraulic Engineering Co. v. McHaffie, 4 Q.B.D. 670, 674, 676.

[3] British Columbia Saw-Mill Co. v. Nettleship, L.R. 3 C.P. 499, 509, Willes, J.; Horne v. Midland Railway Co., L.R. 7 C.P. 583, 591; s.c., L.R. 8 C.P. 131.

[4] British Columbia Saw-Mill Co. v. Nettleship, L.R. 3 C.P. 499, 509.

second subsidiary promise to assume that risk, but that the assumption follows as a consequence directly enforced by the law, without the promisor's co-operation. So parol evidence would be admissible, no doubt to enlarge or diminish the extent of the liability assumed for non-performance, where it would be inadmissible to affect the scope of the promise.

But these concessions do not affect the view here taken. As the relation of contractor and contractee is voluntary, the consequences attaching to the relation must be voluntary. What the event contemplated by the promise is, or in other words what will amount to a breach of contract, is a matter of interpretation and construction. What consequences of the breach are assumed is more remotely, in like manner, a matter of construction, having regard to the circumstances under which the contract is made. Knowledge of what is dependent upon performance is one of those circumstances. It is not necessarily conclusive, but it may have the effect of enlarging the risk assumed.

The very office of construction is to work out, from what is expressedly said and done, what would have been said with regard to events not definitely before the minds of the parties, if those events had been considered. The price paid in mercantile contracts generally excludes the construction that exceptional risks were intended to be assumed. The foregoing analysis is believed to show that the result which has been reached by the courts on grounds of practical good sense falls in with the true theory of contract under the common law.

HOLMES, THE PATH OF THE LAW *

Nowhere is the confusion between legal and moral ideas more manifest than in the law of contract. Among other things, here again the so-called primary rights and duties are invested with a mystic significance beyond what can be assigned and explained. The duty to keep a contract at common law means a prediction that you must pay damages if you do not keep it—and nothing else. If you commit a tort, you are liable to pay a compensatory sum. If you commit a contract, you are liable to pay a compensatory sum unless the promised event comes to pass, and that is all the difference. But such a mode of looking at the matter stinks in the nostrils of those who think it advantageous to get as much ethics into the law as they can.

---

* [From *Collected Legal Papers*, by Oliver Wendell Holmes, copyright, 1920, by Harcourt, Brace and Company, Inc., p. 167 *et seq.* Also printed in 10 *Harv. L. Rev.* 457 (1897).]

CORBIN, NON-BINDING PROMISES AS CONSIDERATION *

In thousands of cases it has been dogmatically stated that both parties to a contract must be bound or neither is bound. So convincing was this dictum that it has been a painfully slow process to re-introduce to the legal profession the unilateral contract—the only kind of contract that our ancestors knew a few centuries ago. It is still generally believed, even by those who well understand the unilateral contract, that the dictum is quite correct with respect to bilateral contracts; and the suggestion of Professor Oliphant that this may never be so came as a surprise. Everyone had known, indeed, that the dictum did not fully apply to contracts between an infant and an adult, contracts within the Statute of Frauds signed by one party only, and contracts induced by the fraud of one party; but it was loosely supposed that these cases could be harmonized with the dictum by use of the magic words "voidable" and "unenforceable". Both parties were "bound"; but one had the power of avoidance of the whole, upon the exercise of which neither was bound. It can easily be shown that this analysis is unsound in very many cases;[1] and we must admit that the dictum is subject to many clear exceptions. Have the exceptions, in this case as in so many others, come to occupy the whole field?

OLIPHANT, MUTUALITY OF OBLIGATION IN BILATERAL CONTRACTS AT LAW †

. . . . .

It is generally known and agreed that there are many cases in which only one of the two parties to a bilateral contract can maintain special assumpsit thereon. Among such cases are, those in which one party: (1) is an infant, (2) is insane, (3) has been guilty of fraud, (4) of duress, (5) of illegality, (6) is a corporation acting *ultra vires*, (7) has not complied with the Statute of Frauds. One party in such cases can maintain

---

* [26 *Col. L. Rev.* 550 (1926).
Arthur L. Corbin (b. 1874), author of many articles and other works in the field of contract law, taught at Yale for forty years, retiring in 1943.]
† [25 *Col. L. Rev.* 705 (1925).
Herman Oliphant (1884–1939), after beginning his academic career as a Professor of English, joined the faculty of the University of Chicago Law School in 1914, and that of Columbia Law School in 1921, finally assuming in 1929 a professorship at the short-lived Institute of Law at Johns Hopkins University. From 1933 until his death, Oliphant served as General Counsel to the U. S. Treasury Department. Oliphant is generally considered among the leading spirits of the "realist" movement in the law. His analysis of actual decisions in the field of contract law departs in important respects from the more traditional modes of analysis of Williston and others who rely more heavily on judicial opinions as distinguished from judicial decisions. The distinction is illuminated in Oliphant's classic article "A Return to *Stare Decisis*," quoted in Chapter 8, *infra.*]

an action upon the contract although the other cannot. Are these cases exceptions to an underlying general rule that, if either party to a bilateral contract is not subject to an action thereon, the other, in consequence, is not? Or, is the truth that there is no such underlying general rule, the supposed exceptions being merely examples of a contrary rule? [P. 706.]

. . . . .

Professor Williston says, "In view of the number of cases and the uniformity with which courts have spoken, it seems idle to try to show that the cases might have been decided on other ground, or that the judges did not know what they were talking about."[3] This statement conveys the impression that there are not only many dicta in support of the supposed rule, but also a large or substantial number of cases which actually *decide* that, in an exchange of promises, if one is not actionable the other similarly is not actionable.

First as to the dicta. It is true that there is an abundance of them in the cases. If to ignore them were thought to put one in the ungracious attitude of saying "that judges did not know what they were talking about," then it must be confessed that that is an embarrassment which students of few, if of any, branches of the law can always escape. Take for instance the very matter of the formation of simple contracts. Is it necessary that there be a "meeting of the minds" or that the parties "intend a legal obligation"? Courts have *said* so in hosts of cases. Students of the subject, and notably Professor Williston, have rejected such statements as true formulations of the law. And why? Because they found that the courts, while repeatedly *saying* that there must be a "meeting of the minds," regularly contradicted such statements by the results they reached in all cases whose facts put the truth of these statements to a test. [P. 998.]

. . . . .

There is a practical argument against this generalization, in addition to the practical argument against the predestination of any such super-generalization. For example, a state statute provides that the contracts of a foreign corporation which has not complied with certain statutory regulations shall be void. Under a statute so explicit as this, there are substantial practical reasons why the corporation should not be able to sue, but equally strong reasons why the other party should be. To clamp down upon our law any such universal as the alleged mutuality rule would deprive the courts of the power to attain both of these desirable ends. The corporation case is merely mentioned as an instance. Such liberty of judicial action is desirable in all cases. And the decisions testify in no uncertain terms that the courts actually have it.* [P. 1012.]

---

* [28 *Col. L. Rev.* 997 (1928).]

LLEWELLYN, BALLADE OF THE CLASS IN CONTRACTS *

Is there a contract? What the hell!
    Fever and night-mare cases raise:
A offers fondly, offers well,
    but B withholds reply for days,
    or, answering, rewords a phrase,
and A determines not to sell.
    A falls for fraud. B's eyeballs glaze.
Is there a contract? What the hell!

The Great Restatement casts its spell,
    yet some dissenting justice neighs—
Is there a contract? What the hell!
    Who knows, until the Court's ukase?
A owes it all, and part he pays,
While B relies on Schnell and Nell.
    Pea-soupish hangs the legal haze:
Is there a contract? What the hell!

My hand against your eye! Which shell?
    The nimble pea eludes the gaze—
Step up, step up, a child can tell,
    and guessing right results in A's!
Hawks, pepper corns, or roundelays—
    they move the Court like calomel.
The cases hold all fourteen ways—
Is there a contract? What the hell!

Prince—or Professor—why the maze?
    Cook on—the law will never jell,
and theories pass—like the moon's phase.
    Is there a contract? What the hell!

---

* [K. N. Llewellyn, *Put in His Thumb*, pp. 39-40. New York: Appleton-Century-Crofts, 1931. Copyright, 1931, by K. N. Llewellyn.

Karl N. Llewellyn (b. 1893), taught at Yale from 1922 until 1925, and thereafter, until 1951, at Columbia. An authority on the law of sales, Llewellyn is presently engaged in the preparation of a new and comprehensive commercial code, designed to encompass the entire field of business law. In the field of jurisprudence he has become known as a pioneer "legal realist." Among his more important works are: *Cases and Materials on the Law of Sales* (1929); *The Bramble Bush* (1930); "A Realistic Jurisprudence—The Next Step" 30 *Col. L. Rev.* 431 (1930); "Some Realism about Realism: Responding to Dean Pound" 44 *Harv. L. Rev.* 1222 (1931). In the field of legal anthropology Llewellyn has successfully applied the technique of realistic jurisprudence, centering on what happens in actual cases, to a field never before studied in that way. His most significant work in this field is the product of collaboration with the anthropologist A. E. Hoebel in the writing of a work on Cheyenne law, *The Cheyenne Way* (1941).]

2. The Social Roots of Contract

LORENZEN, CAUSA AND CONSIDERATION IN THE LAW OF CONTRACTS *

. . . . .

The fundamental question is, what agreements shall be enforced? What operative facts must exist before the law will say that a party must perform? From what precedes we find that the answer varies not only in the different systems of law that have reached the same degree of development but also in the different stages of the legal development of the same system. And this may be regarded as inevitable, because law is the expression of the *mores* of the times and must therefore to appear reasonable and just satisfy the sense of the particular community. In all primitive law a legal obligation arises only from the use of symbols and forms which because of their connection with religion or tradition are regarded as sacred. In Rome the principal formal contract was the stipulation; in English law it was the deed. With the progress of civilization society regards it as reasonable that a legal obligation should also under certain circumstances result from the delivery of an article. Thereupon the notion of a *real* contract develops. Ultimately the idea gains ground that the law ought to attach legal consequences to agreements as such. In Roman law this idea never found a logical and consistent development. We have seen that in theory only four contracts were recognized as based upon consent as such, but that at the time of Justinian by reason of the recognition of enforceable pacts this theory was actually breaking down.

Under the influence of scholasticism there arose during the Middle Ages the belief in the power of the human will to create law. In the field of private law the doctrine of the omnipotence of the human will became on the continent a veritable dogma. The notion arose, therefore, that all agreements should be enforceable without reference to any form, from the very fact that the parties intended such a result. The earlier continental codifications of the last century still require, however, as an additional element, the presence of a sufficient *causa*, while the Anglo-American law to this day insists that the agreement must be supported by a verbal consideration or be clothed in a solemn form, that is, embodied in a sealed instrument.

---

* [28 *Yale L.J.* 621 (1919).

Ernest Gustav Lorenzen (b. 1867), is best known for his writings on the conflict of laws, including *Cases on Conflicts* (1909, 5th ed. 1946); *Selected Articles on the Conflict of Laws* (1947); *The Conflict of Laws Relating to Bills and Notes* (1919). Lorenzen has taught at many American universities. Professor Emeritus at Yale since 1944, Lorenzen served on the law faculty of the University of California until his death in 1951.]

But the dogma of the omnipotence of the human will, the development of which was powerfully assisted by the natural law jurists, survived on the continent of Europe until the present time, in spite of a reaction against it which has arisen more recently. The entire conception of the juristic act which plays such an important role in the theory of the civil law of the present day, is based largely upon the above doctrine. It is not strange, then, that the most recent civil codes—those of Brazil, Germany, Japan and Switzerland—omit all reference to the requirement of a *causa* or a consideration for the validity of contracts. . . .

. . . To say that the presence of a *causa* distinguishes agreements that are enforceable by law from all non-legal agreements is to use a phrase which merely restates that some agreements will be so enforced and others not—a phrase which therefore has no legal significance. [Pp. 641-644.]

MAINE, ANCIENT LAW *

The movement of the progressive societies has been uniform in one respect. Through all its course it has been distinguished by the gradual dissolution of family dependency, and the growth of individual obligation in its place. The Individual is steadily substituted for the Family, as the unit of which civil laws take account. The advance has been accomplished at varying rates of celerity, and there are societies not absolutely stationary in which the collapse of the ancient organization can only be perceived by careful study of the phenomena they present. But, whatever its pace, the change has not been subject to reaction or recoil, and apparent retardations will be found to have been occasioned through the absorption of archaic ideas and customs from some entirely foreign source. Nor is it difficult to see what is the tie between man and man which replaces by degrees those forms of reciprocity in rights and duties which have their origin in the Family. It is Contract. Starting, as from one terminus of history, from a condition of society in which all the

---

* [6th ed., Chap. V, pp. 168-170.

Sir Henry James Sumner Maine (1822–1888), educated at Cambridge, was appointed Regius Professor of Civil Law in 1847, holding this chair until 1854. His lectures at the Inns of Court formed the basis for *Ancient Law* (1861), the work which made Maine's reputation, and by which he is most generally known today. From 1863 to 1869 Maine served as legal member of council in India; the legal reforms later adopted were largely based on Maine's suggestions.

In 1869 Maine returned to teaching, this time at Oxford, where a new chair of historical and comparative jurisprudence had been established. From 1877 he was again at Cambridge where he remained until shortly before his death.

His works, in addition to *Ancient Law*, include *Village Communities in the East and West* (1871); *Early History of Institutions* (1875); *Early Law and Custom* (1883); *Popular Government* (1885); and a treatise, *International Law* (1888 posth.). An illuminating and sympathetic account of Maine's significance in English jurisprudence is given in Julius Stone's *Scope and Province of Law* (1946).]

relations of Persons are summed up in the relations of Family, we seem to have steadily moved towards a phase of social order in which all these relations arise from the free agreement of Individuals. In Western Europe the progress achieved in this direction has been considerable. Thus the status of the Slave has disappeared—it has been superseded by the contractual relation of the servant to his master. The status of the Female under Tutelage, if the tutelage be understood of persons other than her husband, has also ceased to exist; from her coming of age to her marriage all the relations she may form are relations of contract. So too the status of the Son under Power has no true place in the law of modern European societies. If any civil obligation binds together the Parent and the child of full age, it is one to which only contract gives its legal validity. The apparent exceptions are exceptions of that stamp which illustrate the rule. The child before years of discretion, the orphan under guardianship, the adjudged lunatic, have all their capacities and incapacities regulated by the Law of Persons. But why? The reason is differently expressed in the conventional language of different systems, but in substance it is stated to the same effect by all. The great majority of Jurists are constant to the principle that the classes of persons just mentioned are subject to extrinsic control on the single ground that they do not possess the faculty of forming a judgment on their own interests; in other words, that they are wanting in the first essential of an engagement by Contract.

The word Status may be usefully employed to construct a formula expressing the law of progress thus indicated, which, whatever be its value, seems to me to be sufficiently ascertained. All the forms of Status taken notice of in the Law of Persons were derived from, and to some extent are still coloured by, the powers and privileges anciently residing in the Family. If then we employ Status, agreeably with the usage of the best writers, to signify these personal conditions only, and avoid applying the term to such conditions as are the immediate or remote result of agreement, we may say that the movement of the progressive societies has hitherto been a movement *from Status to Contract.**

M. R. COHEN, THE BASIS OF CONTRACT †

I. The Social Roots of Contract

One of the most influential of modern saws is Maine's famous dictum that the progress of the law has been from status to contract. It has generally been understood as stating not only a historical generalization but also a judgment of sound policy—that a legal system wherein rights

---

* [To what extent would such a generalization be true today?]

† [From Chapter II of *Law and the Social Order*, by M. R. Cohen, copyright, 1933, by Harcourt, Brace and Company, Inc. Originally published in 46 *Harv. L. Rev.* 553 (1933).]

and duties are determined by the agreement of the parties is preferable to a system wherein they are determind by "status."

This easy assumption, that whatever happens to be the outcome of history is necessarily for the best and cannot or ought not to be counteracted by any human effort, is typical not only of the historical school of jurisprudence since Savigny, but also of the general progressive or evolutionary philosophy of Maine's generation and largely of our own. Accordingly pleas that under present conditions we need certain limitations on the freedom of contract have encountered the objection that we must not go against history and thereby revert to barbarism.

1. Contract in History

Before considering the validity of the last argument let us briefly consider Maine's dictum from the point of view of the present state of historical learning. . . .

That Maine's generalization is not a universal and necessary law, he himself recognized in his treatment of feudal land tenure.[2] . . . [Pp. 69-70.]

. . . . .

Nevertheless there is enough truth in Maine's observation to warrant a more discriminating attitude to it than that of complete acceptance or complete rejection.

Looking at the matter macroscopically rather than microscopically, there can be little doubt that legally binding agreements or promises play a smaller part in the earlier history of all known peoples. The development of contract is largely an incident of commercial and industrial enterprises that involve a greater anticipation of the future than is necessary in a simpler or more primitive economy. [P. 71.]

. . . . .

The growth of the Hebrew law of contract in the Mishnah seems to have followed the expansion of commerce that came with the capture of their first seaport, Jaffa, by Simon Maccabaeus. The older Deuteronomic law, that in the Sabbatical year released all debtors, naturally discouraged credit transactions at certain times. This inconvenience was overcome in the time of King Herod by the institution of the *prosbul*, a contract of record by which loans became debts to the court unaffected

---

[2] Maine, *Ancient Law*, 6th ed., pp. 170, 305. In referring to the feudal centuries as the golden days of "free" if formal contract, Pollock and Maitland (*History of English Law*, Vol. II, p. 233) assert that in that period "the law of contract threatened to swallow up all public law. . . . The idea that men can fix their rights and duties by agreement is in its early days an unruly anarchical idea. If there is to be any law at all, contract must be taught its place."

by the older law.[3] In general Talmudic jurisprudence favoured contracts, even in cases where religious scruples might have led to restrictions.[4] It is interesting to note that the notion of individual responsibility, a point in which religion, commerce, and ideas of contract or covenant meet, was first vigorously put forth when the Jews were settled in Babylonia, where they were largely engaged in commerce. I refer to the prophet Ezekiel. The older view held the family, tribe, or nation responsible for the acts of any one individual, whether he was ruler like Saul or David or an ordinary rapacious soldier like Achan.[5] God visits the sins of the fathers upon the children to the third and the fourth generation. But the experience of transplantation to a foreign land led Ezekiel to the rejection of the older view that if the fathers eat sour grapes, the children's teeth are set on edge. *"The righteousness of the righteous shall be upon him, and the wickedness of the wicked shall be upon him."* [6] After this came the further reflection that sin is a voluntary act, an affair of the heart, and not something that can happen to you by involuntary contact with an object that is "unclean" or taboo, or even when with the most wor-. shipful intentions in the world you touch a holy object.[7] The significance for the law of contract of this notion of individual responsibility for voluntary acts is too obvious to need development.

The same expansion of the law of free contracts under a predominantly commercial regime can be seen in the history of Greece. The Hellenic laws of contract seem to have allowed as much freedom of business transactions as any legal system known to us. This is particularly clear in Athens after the change, under Cleisthenes, from tribal organization and after the rapid expansion of commerce that followed in the fifth century B.C. The effect of commerce on the Roman law of contract can be seen in the change from the old rigid rules of the *jus civile* to those of the *jus gentium* and praetor's edict. When, as a result of the Crusades and other influences, European trade began to expand, the law of contract was liberalized by the extensive use of the oath to bind verbal agreements[8]—a procedure to which the Church yielded support only after some reluctance in view of Christ's explicit prohibition: "Swear not at all." [Pp. 72-73.]

· · · · ·

---

[3] See Dr. Greenstone's article on "Prosbul" in the *Jewish Encyclopedia*, and Schurer's *History of the Jewish People in the Time of Jesus Christ*, 1898, Div. II, Vol. I, p. 362.

[4] See the tractate *Baba Metzia*, 94a, in which the prevailing opinion allows some stipulations as to money matters even contrary to the Torah.

[5] II Sam. 21, 24; Josh. 7.

[6] Ezek. 18:20.

[7] II Sam. 6:6-7.

[8] *Cf.* Esmein, *Le Serment promissoire dans le droit canonique*, 1888, pp. 1 *et seq.*; 37 *et seq.*

II. Excesses of Contractualism

As the result of the various forces that have thus supported the cult of contractualism there has been developed in all modern European countries (and in those which derive from them) a tendency to include within the categories of contract transactions in which there is no negotiation, bargain, or genuinely voluntary agreement. Let us consider a few typical situations. [P. 85.]

.   .   .   .   .

A more serious confusion of fact and fiction occurs when we speak of the "labour contract." There is, in fact, no real bargaining between the modern large employer (say the United States Steel Corporation) and its individual employees. The working man has no real power to negotiate or confer with the corporation as to the terms under which he will agree to work. He either decides to work under the conditions and schedule of wages fixed by the employer or else he is out of a job. If he is asked to sign any paper he does so generally without any knowledge of what it contains and without any real freedom to refuse. For we cannot freely change our crafts, and if a man is a weaver or shoe-laster, he is dependent on the local carpet or shoe factory for his livelihood, especially so if he has a family, which is not as mobile as money. The greater economic power of the employer exercises a compulsion as real *in fact* as any now recognized by law as duress. The extreme form of such duress, the highwayman's pistol, still leaves us with the freedom to accept the terms offered or else take the consequences. But such choice is surely the very opposite of what men value as freedom.

Clearly, then, the element of consent on the part of the employee may be a minor one in the relation of employment—a relation much more aptly and realistically described by the old law as that between master and servant. Down to the end of the eighteenth century this relation was in fact regulated by the government. Wages used to be regularly fixed by justices of the peace under the authority of parliamentary enactments, and even the beer that the master was to serve to the servant with his bread had its strength regulated by law. Any demand by workman for higher wages or any accession to such demands on the part of masters was a violation of the law. Yet courts now speak as if the effort on the part of the state to regulate wages were an unheard of interference with the eternal laws of nature. As a matter of fact, it was only after the Civil War that the United States Supreme Court invented the doctrine that the "right *to* contract" is property and is thus protected against real government regulation by the Fifth and Fourteenth Amendments of our Federal Constitution. But so widespread has this idea become that few have noticed its radical novelty.

The spread of contractualistic notions shows itself in the tendency to speak of marriage as itself a contract. Now there are, usually, solemn promises exchanged when the marriage ceremony is performed and there may be agreements as to dowry and other property rights. But the specific legal relations of husband and wife are by no means determined thereby. These relations are entirely fixed by law and the parties to it cannot vary its terms, just as they cannot vary the terms of their obligations to any children they may bring into the world. If there is no sense in speaking of the rights and duties between parents and minor children as contractual, neither is there in speaking of the relations of husband and wife as contractual. The fact that an act is more or less voluntary does not make its legal consequences contractual. [Pp. 86-87.]

WILLISTON, FREEDOM OF CONTRACT *

A gospel of freedom was preached by both metaphysical and political philosophers in the latter half of the eighteenth century. In political affairs the classical expression of this philosophy in the United States is found in the sweeping generalities of the Declaration of Independence....

In metaphysics, at the same time, philosophers were emphasizing the ego and the individual human will as the basic facts of life. Such philosophy inevitably tended to emphasize the cardinal importance of individual freedom. Economic writers adopted the same line of thought. Adam Smith, Ricardo, Bentham, and John Stuart Mill successively insisted on freedom of bargaining as the fundamental and indispensable requisite of progress; and imposed their theories on the educated thought of their times with a thoroughness not common in economic speculation....
[P. 366.]

.   .   .   .   .

In theories of education the same influence is observable. The earlier theory of education, as expressed by an opponent of the elective system, was to teach pupils to do difficult things easily, and disagreeable things cheerfully....

In revolt against such methods the kindergarten was established for little children, and the elective system and voluntary attendance at lectures or recitations for pupils of older growth....

...In the field of education, routine practice was not greatly affected by the new ideas until after the middle of the nineteenth century; and in that field these ideas are still often pushed to a degree which excludes consideration of inferences which might be drawn from concrete observation of concrete facts.

The theorizing in metaphysics, politics and economics could not fail

---

* [6 Cornell L.Q. 365 (1921).]

to have its effect on the law, and the law of contracts was a field in which its application was not difficult. Indeed it was a corollary of the philosophy of freedom and individualism that the law ought to extend the sphere and enforce the obligation of contract.

In this branch of the law, it is also to be observed, individualistic doctrines found earlier acceptance than would have probably been the case had they had a more fully developed established theory to contend with and dethrone. There had been little theoretical discussion prior to the *Commentaries* of Blackstone of any branches of private law other than those relating to real property and to crimes. It was comparatively easy, therefore, to adopt a new theory of contract, since any inconsistency with earlier notions was not obvious enough to be disturbing.

Two separate effects in the law of contracts, plainly traceable to the cause of which I am speaking, may be observed; the first relating to the requisites for the formation or discharge of contracts, and the second to the permissibility of making such contracts as the parties might choose.

It was a consequence of the emphasis laid on the ego and the individual will that the formation of a contract should seem impossible unless the wills of the parties concurred. Accordingly we find at the end of the eighteenth century, and the beginning of the nineteenth century, the prevalent idea that there must be a "meeting of minds" (a new phrase) in order to form a contract; that is, mental assent as distinguished from an expression of mutual assent was required. It was therefore assumed that if one who offered to sell specific goods sold the goods before his offer was accepted, the offer was necessarily revoked though the offeree knew nothing of the sale.[3] [Pp. 367-368.]

.   .   .   .   .

As it took the agreement of two parties to create a contract, so likewise, according to the doctrine of which we are speaking, it took the concurrence of wills of those parties to rescind or discharge it. Though Lord Mansfield, and courts following his time, had in effect decided that a material breach by one party to a bilateral contract excused the other party from continuing performance, and, therefore, in effect enabled him to regard the contract as discharged or rescinded, another idea gradually replaced this and became and is still the orthodox view of the English law. This theory is that one party to a bilateral contract cannot be freed from the obligation of the contract unless the other party has manifested an intent to repudiate it.[4]

---

[3] This was assumed in both Cooke v. Oxley, 3 T.R.(Eng.) 653 (1790); Adams v. Lindsell, 1 B. & Ald. 681 (1818).

[4] This was first clearly stated in Freeth v. Burr, L.R. 9 C.P. 208 (1874); and has since been repeated as a decisive test in several more recent cases. See 2 Williston, *Contracts*, sec. 865.

... The whole theory that the discharge of contracts by breach or repudiation is based on mutual assent is wrong. [Pp. 369-370.]

•   •   •   •   •

The same tendency to reduce to a rule of construction what should be a rule wholly exterior to the intentions of the parties is found in the law governing penalties and liquidated damages. A contract which provides for a penalty is invalid. A contract which provides for liquidation of damages is valid. It is obvious that the prohibition of penalties is a rule imposed in spite of the will of the parties, the plain purpose of the prohibition being to prevent the punishment of one who breaks his contract by the imposition of consequences disproportionate to the injury which he has inflicted, even though the parties had agreed that he should be so punished. For the same reason that a mortgagor is relieved of the literal terms of his bargain in spite of his own agreement, it is immaterial that a contractor agrees that disproportionate punishment shall be inflicted upon him if he fails to keep his promise. Yet both the House of Lords[6] and the Supreme Court of the United States,[7] not to mention a number of other courts,[8] have said that whether a provision in contract is penal or merely provides for liquidated damages, is a question of construction, and depends upon the intention of the parties.

If this statement in its literal sense were applied to the cases coming before the courts, the rule in regard to penalties would be practically abolished. [Pp. 371-372.]

•   •   •   •   •

As theories of individual freedom thus seemed to require that no obligations or defences to obligations should be allowed unless willed by the parties, so on the other hand the same theories led to opposition to restrictions being placed on the kind of contracts which they in fact did will. The English courts prior to the 19th century had no hesitation, when they deemed a particular kind of contract opposed to public policy, in refusing to enforce it. Obviously where a contract contemplated a tort or a crime this result was reached and no court has ever gone so far as to suggest a contrary rule. But it was not only contracts of this character that were refused enforcement. Perhaps the most striking examples, prior to the 19th century, of contracts which were held invalid as such, though performance of them would have been obnoxious to no law, were contracts in restraint of trade, and contracts involving a penalty or forfeiture. It was not illegal to refrain from trade or other

---

[6] Elphinstone v. Monkland Iron & Coal Co., 11 App. Cas. 332, 342, 345 (1886); Clydebank Engineering, &c. Co. v. Yzquierdo y Castaneda (1905), App. Cas. 6, 15.
[7] Sun Printing and Publishing Co. v. Moore, 183 U. S. 642, 662 (1902).
[8] See 2 Williston, *Contracts*, secs. 777, 778.

occupation to any degree, yet promises, if unreasonable, thus to refrain, were early held unenforceable. So, likewise, courts relieved mortgagors from provisions in their deeds or contracts providing for forfeiture of mortgaged property and refused to enforce provisions for unreasonable penalties which the parties agreed should be paid in case some act or performance was neglected or delayed.

It is interesting to see the effect of the 19th century upon these doctrines. They were too well established to be discarded, and yet there are clear indications of the indisposition of courts to carry them farther than they felt obliged to. I have already said something of the attempt made to avoid the admission that disallowance of penalties is a limitation of freedom of contract. The prohibition of contracts in restraint of trade could not similarly be reduced to a problem of construction but the scope of the prohibition could be kept as narrow as possible. The best expression of the disposition so to keep it is found in the often quoted words of Sir George Jessel:

"If there is one thing more than any other which public policy requires, it is that men of full age and competent understanding shall have the utmost liberty of contracting, and that contracts, when entered into freely and voluntarily, shall be held good and shall be enforced by courts of justice."[10] [P. 373.]

. . . . .

In recent years the tide has set strongly in the other direction. Observation of results has proved that unlimited freedom of contract, like unlimited freedom in other directions, does not necessarily lead to public or individual welfare and that the only ultimate test of proper limitations is that provided by experience. [P. 374.]

. . . . .

In the United States a difficulty has been experienced in graduating from extreme doctrines of freedom of contract which is due to our written constitutions. Many of our constitutions and bills of rights were framed when the theories of individualism and liberty were at their height, and later constitutions have naturally been based on the earlier ones. When legislatures, therefore, sought to impose restraints on freedom of contract their efforts were often nullified by decisions declaring their legislation unconstitutional. This tendency has been most marked with reference to various kinds of labor legislation, though observable also in other directions. [P. 375.]

---

[10] Printing Co. v. Sampson, 19 Eq. Cas. L. R. 462 (1875), quoted in Diamond Match Co. v. Roeber, 106 N. Y. 473, 482 (1887), and in other decisions. See also Hall Mfg. Co. v. Western Steel and Iron Works, 227 Fed. 588 (1915); Styles v. Lyon, 87 Conn. 23 (1913); Harbison-Walker Refractories Co. v. Stanton, 227 Pa. 55 (1910).

LLEWELLYN, WHAT PRICE CONTRACT?–AN ESSAY IN PERSPECTIVE * a

. . . . .

We have records, here and there, of explorations. Maine's famous dictum of "status to contract";[2] Isaac's hypothesis that status-to-contract-to-status runs in cycles or in pendular swinging;[3] Demogue's presentation in terms of major contracts with tails, appendages, adhesions, of various details;[4] Pound's development of "relation" as a status-like element constantly latent and now re-emergent in our order;[5] Ehrlich's inquiry into agreement as a constitution-making device of sub-groups within the state, and into the relation of legal to non-legal ways and norms;[6] Ely's attempt to place contract in relation to property;[7] Commons' more successful study of rent-bargain, price-bargain, and wage-bargain, as foci and levers for the adjustment of an economic system to new strains, and as im-

---

* [40 *Yale L.J.* 704 (1931).]

a This paper was first prepared, in much more compact form and without the notes, for use in the *Encyclopedia of Social Sciences*. The editors wisely felt it desirable for the article "Contract" to contain more Roman and comparative law material, and more material on the history of doctrine, than I had included. Collaboration with Dean Pound then became advisable, in order to insure to the *Encyclopedia* the benefit of a wide background in those fields. But our own society offers its peculiar unity and character, and it seemed worth while to expand and explore the bearings of my initial paper in the hope of gaining in sharpness of focus what is thereby sacrificed in comprehensiveness. It is a peculiar pleasure to be able to offer the result, as a study of the common law, in a number dedicated to the author of *The Common Law*, to the thinker whose work is the major foundation on which the realistic trends in jurisprudence rest.

[2] Maine, *Ancient Law* (Pollock's ed. 1930) 182. Maine, it will be remembered, very carefully uses "status" in this generalization "to signify these personal relations only" (those "derived from and to some extent still colored by the powers and privileges anciently residing in the family") and avoids "applying the term to such conditions as are the immediate or remote result of agreement." My usage here differs.

[3] Isaacs, The Standardizing of Contracts (1917) 27 *Yale L.J.* 34.

[4] Demogue, *Modern French Legal Philosophy* (1921) 472, 477. My phrasing is hardly fair to Demogue; it hits but one of his two phases of "adhesion," the other being the presentation to individuals of complete forms (railroad ticket, etc.) not subject to dicker, to take or leave.

[5] Pound, The End of Law as Developed in Juristic Thought (1917) 30 *Harv. L. Rev.* 201; *Spirit of the Common Law* (1912) c. I. Isaacs' criticism *op. cit. supra* note 3 of Pound's position that "status to contract" has "*no* foundation in our legal history" is obviously sound. Yet the curious assertion is repeated, without notice of the criticism, four years later. *Ibid.* 28.

"Norm" is used in this paper to mean a rule or standard of Oughtness, not a statistical norm. "Normal" is used loosely.

[6] Ehrlich, *Grundlegung der Soziologie des Rechts* (1913), esp. c. II-V, XVII. This whole paper builds at every point on Ehrlich, as any such paper must. And on Veblen. And, as always, on Max Weber. *Wirtschaft und Gesellschaft* (2d ed. 1925).

[7] Ely, *Contract and Property* (1914).

portant controlling factors in new development outside the law;[8] the economists at large, in their study of the effects of free contract and of specialization on the development of capitalism, on mobilization of capital, on the allocation of risks, and, finally, on the divorce of invest-ment from control.[9] So much, indeed, has been done that some hope offers of putting together a sketch of the whole. Chimerical such a sketch must be—compounded of parts strangers to each other, a dream-thing, and mayhap a monster; worse than chimerical in the gaping incom-pleteness of content and of form. Yet worth attempting. Rules, techni-calities, systematizations gain meaning, gain opalescence, gain vibrancy, when their fragile beauty is seen—though imperfectly—against the rich background of the Great Society.

I. Origins

"Contract" itself is an ambiguous concept, ambiguous particularly when more is concerned than unmixed legal doctrine. (1) The word is used especially to indicate business agreements-in-fact, as such, irrespective of their legal consequences—irrespective indeed of whether they have legal consequences. At times, on the fringes of discussion, this use may overlap into the non-business field. (2) Or the word is used to indicate agreements-in-fact *with* legal consequences. Not merely *pacta vestita* as distinct from *nuda pacta,* but barter and outright conveyance, and even—again on the fringes—any form of gift in which assent of the donee may be a matter of concern. This, roughly, was Ely's use. (3) Again, the word indicates the legal effects, if such there be, of *promises*—including those various incidents which, if I may twist Demogue's phrase, "adhere" to major promises of various kinds. This last, stricter concept Corbin has demon-strated to be singularly useful for the law; it will here be adopted. I shall endeavor to reserve "promise" for the promise-in-fact, "contract" for the legal effects of such a promise. (4) A fourth current meaning of the

---

[8] Commons, *Legal Foundations of Capitalism* (1924) c. VI-VIII—a book whose in-sight is too little noted because it is too legal for the layman, too lay to satisfy a meticulous legal critique. I have derived further suggestion from many quarters: Messrs. Alvin Johnson and William Seagle of the Encyclopedia of Social Sciences; and my colleague Patterson, in comments on this paper; Morris Cohen, especially Property and Sovereignty (1927) 13 *Corn. L.Q.* 8; Hale, especially Coercion and Distribution in a Supposedly Non-Coercive State (1923) 38 *Pol. Sci. Q.* 470; Underhill Moore; Samuel Klaus; Wigmore, especially The Pledge Idea (1897) 10 *Harv. L. Rev.* 321, 389; 11 *ibid* 18; and 5 *Evidence* (2d ed. 1923); Ames, *Lectures on Legal History* (1913) c. XII-XIV; Pound, *Introduction to the Philosophy of Law* (1924) c. VI, Liberty of Contract (1909) 18 *Yale L.J.* 454; Lorenzen, Causa and Consideration (1919) 28 *ibid.* 621; Wright, Opposition of Law to Business Usages (1926) 26 *Col. L. Rev.* 917. My own papers, The Effect of Legal Institutions on Economics (1925) 15 *Am. Ec. Rev.* 665 and (1928) *Proc. Conf. Social Work* 127 also bear on the problems raised.

word, the writing embodying an agreement (commonly assumed to be one with legal consequences) may here be disregarded. [Pp. 704, 705-708.]

· · · · ·

Primitive Form and Its Value

When observation first becomes possible we find the officials of primitive law limiting their aid in enforcement to single stereotyped classes of transaction recognizable by specific strictly formal or formulaic character. [P. 710.]

· · · · ·

Formal acts of the known type then signify openly definitive intent to change the existing situation—and to be relied on. Early or late, and in whatever culture, and whatever the form in vogue, this feature is common to all. The copper and scales, the ceremonial handclasp ("Shake on it!"), a magical ceremony like the establishment of blood-brotherhood, the solemn invocation of supernatural sanction by oath[19] or conditional curse, the promise or act before official witnesses, the delivery and acceptance of the unambiguous token (engagement ring, pledge button, King's shilling and the nosegay in the hat) or the ambiguous token (earnest money), sealing and delivery, indenture or broken shard or crooked sixpence, the speaking of the binding words, the known words which had power ("I warrant;" "*Spondesne? Spondeo;*" "Open, Sesame!")—whether sanctions other than legal be invoked in addition or not, and whether or not the form accomplishes additional purposes (identification of person, transaction, and terms), the common purpose of the form is clear. The overt sign of utter intent to assume obligation has been given. The other party has reason to rely. The consequence to be expected is both recognition by law officials, and—at least as soon as this has occurred—a strong tendency thereafter to limit the number of these recognized forms which will move either officials to act or laymen to feel justified in taking words as meaning obligation.

Legal v. Non-Legal Obligation

Yet as an economy changes, as it grows more complex, as bargains become more frequent, as new types of bargain appear, the ritual forms theretofore established on older models must prove inadequate to cover all engagements-in-fact, inadequate to protect all reliance-in-fact. [Pp. 711-712.]

II. Contract as an Adjustment Device

In such a survey as this, however, interest centers less immediately upon what society (including the lawyer) has done to contract than

---

[19] Still in use, as Holmes reminds us, on the assumption of public office, or of a public function such as testifying or serving as juror. Holmes, *The Common Law* 246.

on what contract may have done to society. As to agreement-in-fact, an influence is obvious. Viewing a status-organized society as a whole, it is trite that bargain is a tool of change and of growing individual self-determination, as is also any property regime which by increasing individual control increases the scope of experiment, the differentiation of holdings, and the factual effectiveness of the bargains of the wealthy....

Bargain is then the social and legal machinery appropriate to arranging affairs in any specialized economy which relies on exchange rather than tradition (the manor) or authority (the army, the U.S.S.R.) for apportionment of productive energy and of product. It is a machinery which like status, but in contrast to tort, makes it easy to insist on positive, affirmative action. *Contract* in the strict sense is the specifically legal machinery appropriate when such an economy moves into the phase of credit—meaning or connoting thereby future dealings in general; in which aspect the mutual reliance of two dealers on their respective promises comes of course into major importance. This machinery of contract applies in general to the market for land, goods, services, credit, or for any combination of these.[38] Or if one prefers to minimize the danger of reifying the abstraction he may put it: what we mean by contract is whatever the officials do about promises in these various fields [39]—and

---

[38] Holmes as early as *The Common Law*, with what seems to one unfamiliar with the then literature extraordinary grasp and originality, both states and develops the risk point of view as basic to contract.

[39] It is interesting to watch Holmes' thought on this grow sharper as a heterodox insight bores its way into his working kit. In 1881 he writes (my italics): "The statement that the effect of a promise is the assumption of a risk of a future event does not mean that there is a second subsidiary promise to assume that risk, but that the assumption follows *as a consequence* directly enforced by the law, without the promisor's cooperation." *The Common Law* 302. "The only universal consequence of a legally binding promise is, that the law makes the promisor pay damages if the promised event does not come to pass. In every case it leaves him free from interference until the time for fulfilment has gone by, and therefore free to *break his contract* if he chooses." *Ibid.* 301. "If we look at the law as it would be regarded by one who had no scruples against doing anything which he could do without incurring legal consequences, it is obvious that the main consequence *attached by the law to a contract* is a greater or less possibility of having to pay money. The only question from the purely legal point of view is whether the promisor will be compelled to pay." *Ibid.* 317. "Contract" is envisaged here as something pre-existing. Also: "*The substance of the law* at any given time pretty nearly corresponds, so far as it goes, with what is then understood to be convenient; *but its form and machinery*, and the degree to which it is able to work out desired results, depend very much upon its past." *Ibid.* 1-2. Now contrast this with the firm precision in 1897: "A legal duty so called is *nothing but* a prediction that *if a man does or omits certain things* he will be made to suffer *in this or that way* by judgment of the court; and so of a legal right." *Collected Legal Papers* 169. "If you commit a contract, you are liable to pay a compensatory sum unless the promised event comes to pass." *Ibid.* 175. That this does not deny the importance of rules but merely clarifies their relation to purposes of law, and to lay action-patterns consonant with such purposes, I have tried to develop in (1928) *Proc. Conf. Social Work* 129 ff., and A Realistic Jurisprudence—The Next Step (1930) 30 *Col. L. Rev.* 431. I have found no trace of this analysis in

curiously enough, there are similarities, some of them significant, to be found in what the officials do from time to time from field to field.

Is the Law of Contract Necessary?

All of which, however, begs the question of why there need be any *legal* machinery at all for the purposes mentioned, other than mere protection of the factual results of accomplished bargains, work, deliveries, and payments. The peace, and more dubiously the law of alienability and of ownership, at least as against persons entrusted with possession—what more is needed? As one puts such a question, one recalls first how seldom law touches *directly* any case in which a promise has been performed, or in which an inadequate performance has been received in satisfaction. Promise, performance and adjustment are in this sense primarily extralegal. It needs no argument that if they did not normally occur without law's intervention, no regime of future dealings would be possible. The lawyer's idea of "contract," applied to these normal cases, where performance and informal business adjustments proceed to occur, is thus a conceptual projection of trouble and the legal spawn of trouble upon the untroubled in fact.... [Pp. 716-718.]

. . . . .

Neither will it do to treat the mere presence of legal machinery in any particular field as of itself demonstrating a *need* for it there. For such presence may merely be an instance of unneeded or even of parasitic expansion of a going institution.... [P. 719.]

. . . . .

Whatever the need for legal enforcement of contract in current dealings, then, its place in an *investment* structure is obvious. It is essential to any approach to a market for capital, to any machinery for mobilizing funds or diversifying investments. Equally essential with contract itself is the transferability—which is to say, the depersonalization—of contract rights. The older view of "privity" as essential to legal action on a contract was connected partly with semi-magical aspects of legal form; partly with a conception of contract as an essentially peculiar, unusual thing; partly with a conception that contractual transactions had no proper importance for non-participants. None of these conceptions fits with an investment market; it is significant that the first free transferability, that of bills of exchange, developed among merchants *apart from law proper*. It is further significant that merchants found no trouble with the concept of suit by a third party beneficiary—which still gives trouble to some

---

the Holmes notes to the 12th edition of Kent (1873). But it is somewhat foreshadowed in Codes and the Arrangement of the Law (1870) 5 *Am. L. Rev.* 1., the paternity of which has been acknowleged in personal communication.

courts—and that they shaved the freely transferable contract right down to certain standardized essentials. In business essence, although not so strictly in law, a very similar standardizing and simplifying process occurs in the investment market today. The investor looks for six or seven familiar standard features in a stock or bond, irrespective of the length of mortgage indenture or articles of incorporation—six or seven features familiar and simple enough to be summed up conveniently in Poor or Moody. For business purposes, too, a distinction in kind between bonds and stocks tends definitely to disappear. Both, in the same way, are thought of as property—as is also any prospectively profitable contract, whether unilateral or bilateral. Both, in much the same way again, are conceived as in the nature of promises: anticipated performance by "the corporation" (which is factually viewed as centered in the managing personnel, plus some assets, plus the established management policies) is the essence of the picture; and legal sanction in both cases looms very large. ... Frequently enough no other sanction than the legal exists at all. Where other sanctions do exist (*e.g.*, desire for continued dealings, or for a business reputation) they show an unfortunate tendency to fail precisely where most needed, *i.e.*, when stress of loss (or gain: management manipulation of the market or merger of the debtor) is strong. Max Weber cogently remarks that expediency-founded ethics are less reliable factors in performance than are those founded in tradition. It results that even to some extent in short-run face-to-face dealings, and *a fortiori* and importantly in long-run ones, legal enforceability figures as an element of added security in credit matters; a partial insurance against the very case of need: when credit-judgment was misguided, or in case of death or assignment, or where supervening troubles disrupt either willingness or power to perform. [Pp. 721-722.]

.   .   .   .   .

Informal Promises

But more important to a commercial economy than the stiltedness of formality is the question of informal promises. It is commonly said that their enforcement is essential to a business world; the statement sounds too simple to be probable, unless by "informal" is meant simply "not involving elaborate ritual." The Romans did come to admit suits on book accounts. The Greeks developed actions on written promises (*synallagma*). Modern Continental law admits a suit—in general—on any promise with a proper *causa;* and *causa* seems to mean, very roughly, any justification in policy which warrants recognition by a court. All of this indicates that it would be hard for any business system to develop or to get on if legal enforcement were conditioned on the ceremony with the copper and the scales, or on procuring the three official old men to watch and witness the hand clasp, or—save such transactions as are more elephantine, perhaps, *e.g.*, those involving realty—on official recording of agreements made. But when we see the great exchanges devising means for exchanging written and signed memoranda of sales of grain and stocks—and, so far as an outsider can determine, profiting by the necessity—the notion that speed requires utter informality loses cogency. Indeed there would be no apparent loss in efficiency if all the memorandum slips used on exchanges had to carry in the lower right-hand corner a printed "seal," and if the business stationery now used for confirming oral deals between merchants were similarly ornamented. And the practice of immediate confirmation has sufficiently developed to make a case for the position that limiting enforceability to signed promises would do no violence to the *business* side of our economy—at least, as to the *initiation* of contract. Surface indications are that the effects as between solvent contractors might rather be healthy than otherwise. There would be some reduction in telephone dealings with persons lacking established reputation. There would be troubles, even in the case of established reputation and honesty, where death or insolvency of the one obligor supervened. Yet neither inconvenience would be so material as not to offer some hope of being outweighed by the gain in adequacy and unambiguity of proof. As a conclusion, then: a business economy demands a means of quick, not one of "informal" contracting. [Pp. 740-741.]

.   .   .   .   .   .

In Summa

One turns from contemplation of the work of contract as from the experience of Greek tragedy. Life struggling against form, or through form to its will—"pity and terror—." Law means so pitifully little to life. Life is so terrifyingly dependent on the law.

Marginal cases, hospital cases, most of our cases well may be. Much doctrine, however sweetly spun, serves chiefly to grow grey with dust against the rafters. Overwhelming is the certainty that any synthesis which is to match with the meaning of the law in life must expand beyond the futile limits set by present legal theory to include great blocks of what we know as property, and equity, and remedies, to cover as well the most significant parts of business associations, and who knows what besides. Overwhelming is the realization of how far a law still built in the ideology of Adam Smith has been meshed into the new order of mass-production, mass-relationships. Overwhelming in no less measure is the conviction that broad forms of words are chaos, that only in close study of the facts salvation lies.

Against these conclusions stand others. The *ad hoc* approach of case-law courts is sane, it cuts close to need, it lives, it grows. And the work of law and lawyers in the contract field, however little of the whole it constitutes, has vital meaning. It is both hinge and key of readjustment. And how, without it, shall the great gate swing open? [P. 751.]

KESSLER, CONTRACT AS A PRINCIPLE OF ORDER *

The triumph of capitalism during the 18th and 19th centuries with its unheard of increase in the productivity of labor was possible only because of a constant refinement of the division of labor. This development in turn presupposed that enterprisers could depend on a continuous flow of goods and services exchanged in a free market. And to be able to exploit the factors of production in the most efficient way, enterprisers had (and still have) to be able to bargain for goods and services to be delivered in the future and to rely on promises for future delivery. Thus, it became one of the main functions of our law of contracts to keep this flow running smoothly, making certain that bargains would be kept and that legitimate expectations created by contractual promises honored. "The foundation of contract," in the language of Adam Smith, "is the reasonable expectation, which the person who promises raises in the person to whom he binds himself; of which the satisfaction may be extorted by force."[3] In this sense, contract liability is promissory liability. In an industrial and commercial society, where wealth is largely made up of promises, the interest of society as a whole demands protection of the interest of the individual promisee.

Contract, to be really useful to the business enterpriser within the setting of a free enterprise economy, must be a tool of almost unlimited pliability. To accomplish this end, the legal system has to reduce the ceremony necessary to vouch for the deliberate nature of a contractual transaction to the indispensable minimum; it has to give freedom of contract as to form. Furthermore, since the law must keep pace with the constant widening of the market without being able to anticipate the content of an infinite number of transactions into which members of the community may need to enter, parties must be given freedom as to the content of their contractual arrangements. . . .

Within the framework of a free enterprise system the essential prerequisite of contractual liability is volition, that is, consent freely given

---

* [Extract from introduction to Kessler and Sharp, *Cases on Contract* (materials prepared for the private and confidential use of the students in the University of Chicago Law School and the Yale University School of Law; rev. ed. 1950), pp. iii-xvi.

Friedrich Kessler (b. 1901), member of the Illinois bar, professor of law at Yale Law School, former professor at University of Chicago Law School, has taught a wide range of subjects including jurisprudence, contracts, agency, bills and notes, commercial bank credit, and insurance. His article on "Contracts of Adhesion" in 43 *Col. L. Rev.* 629 (1943) is a major contribution to the theory of contract law.]

[3] *Lectures on Justice, Police, Revenue and Arms* 7 (Cannan ed., 1896).

and not coercion or status. Contract, in this view, is the "meeting place of the ideas of agreement and obligation."[4] As a matter of historical fact, the rise of contract within western civilization reflects the erosion of a status-organized society; contract became, at an ever increasing rate, a tool of change and of growing self-determination and self-assertion. Self-determination during the 19th century was regarded as the goal towards which society progressed; the movement of progressive societies, in the words of Sir Henry Maine, is a movement from Status to Contract. "It is through contract that man attains freedom. Although it appears to be the subordination of one man's will to another, the former gains more than he loses."[5]

Nineteenth century industrial society was a mobile society of small enterprisers, individual merchants and independent craftsmen. Its dominant current of belief was that individual and cooperative action left unrestrained in family, church and market would not lessen the freedom and dignity of the individual but would secure the highest possible social justice. The representatives of this school of thought were firmly convinced, to state it somewhat roughly, of the existence of a natural law according to which the individual serving his own interest was also serving the interest of the community.[6] Profits, under this system, could only be earned by supplying wanted commodities, and freedom of competition would prevent profits from rising unduly. The play of the market, if left to itself, would, therefore, maximize net satisfactions and afford the ideal conditions for the distribution of wealth....

Contract, in this view, is the principle of order par excellence and the only legitimate means of social integration in a free society. Translated into legal language this means that in a progressive society all law is ultimately based on contract.[9] And since contract as a social phenomenon is the result of a "coincidence of free choices" on the part of the members of the community, merging their egoistical and altruistic tendencies, a contractual society safeguards its own stability. Contract is an instrument of peace in society. It testifies to the "natural identity of interests" of the members of the community—all the more since, with increasing rationality, man becomes less rather than more egoistic.

This spirit of individualism and laissez faire, the dominant current of thought during the 19th century, gave birth to the ideal of freedom of contract. Freedom of contract, according to this liberal tradition, means that subject to narrow limits the law, in the field of contracts, has dele-

---

[4] Watt, *The Theory of Contract in Its Social Light* 2 (1897).

[5] The quotation is taken from Stone, *The Province and Function of the Law* 251 (1946).

[6] For the most thorough formulation of the beneficial operation of laissez faire, see Marshall, *Principles of Economics* (8th ed., 1938). See further Moos, Laissez-faire, Planning and Ethics, 55 *The Economic Journal* 17 (1947).

[9] See 1 Parsons, *The Law of Contracts* 3 (1855).

gated legislation to the contracting parties. As far as the parties are concerned, the law of contracts is of their own making; society merely lends its machinery on enforcement to the party injured by the breach. To be sure, society, in order to accommodate the members of the business community, has placed at their disposal a great variety of typical transactions whose consequences are regulated in advance, thus supplying "the short-sightedness of individuals, by doing for them what they should have done for themselves, if their imagination had anticipated the course of nature.[10] But these statutory provisions come into operation only in the absence of an agreement to the contrary.

Freedom of contract, as evolved in the spirit of laissez faire, has found repeated expression in Anglo-American case law. "[If] there is one thing which more than another public policy requires," Sir John Jessel, M.R., assures us, "it is that men of full age and competent understanding shall have the utmost liberty of contracting and that their contracts entered into *freely and voluntarily* shall be held sacred and shall be enforced by Courts of Justice."[11] True, fraud and force must be ruled out by the courts in the exercise of their function of making sure that the "rules of the game" will be adhered to. But this qualification was thought to be of no great moment due to the policing force of the competitive market. Except for according protection against force and fraud, it is not the function of courts to make contracts for the parties or to strike down or tamper with improvident bargains. Courts have only to interpret contracts made by the parties; they do not make them. This attitude is in keeping with liberal social and moral philosophy according to which it pertains to the dignity of man to lead his own life as a reasonable person and to accept responsibility for his own mistakes.

These pronouncements, however, are representative only of the main current of thought which deeply influenced freedom of contract. They fail to take into account that even during the period which is traditionally called the height of liberalism there was an undertow which gradually increased in strength. This development is foreshadowed by the conflicting scopes assigned to freedom of contract by Bentham and his contemporary, Ricardo, in the early part of the 19th century. Bentham, to whom we owe *The Defense of Usury*, in advocating the enforcement of private agreements, adds this significant qualification: "The reasons for declaring certain contracts invalid or unlawful, ought to be drawn from the nature of the contracts themselves, inasmuch as they are contrary to the public interest;—or to the interest of a third party, or to that

---

[10] Bentham, A General View of a Complete Code of Laws 3 *Works* 191 (Bowring ed., 1843). Bentham's statement does not do justice to the significance of statutory provisions. They are often attempts to reflect standardizations in existing patterns of behavior.

[11] Printing Numerical Registering Co. v. Sampson, L.R. 19 Eq. 462, 465 (1875).

of the contracting parties."[12] Ricardo's philosophy, on the other hand, is far less squeamish: "Like all other contracts, wages should be left to the fair and free competition of the market, and should never be controlled by the interference of the legislation."[13]

Dicey's famous *Lectures on Law and Public Opinion in England During the Nineteenth Century* (1907) have done much to popularize the idea that Ricardo's view gained unequivocal application not only in England but also in this country for a considerable period. But in the light of most recent studies it appears that Dicey and his followers may have misstated the origins and underestimated the strength of the countercurrent, represented both in England and the United States by social legislation, particularly in the interest of workers, dating back to the early 19th century.[14]

Furthermore, this countercurrent deeply affected the evolution of the consideration doctrine.[15] Originally, the doctrine was a judicial technique for distinguishing enforceable bargains from unenforceable gratuitous promises. Gradually, under the impact of the countercurrent, again and again common law courts, by refusing to reduce consideration to a mere form, seized upon the consideration doctrine as an instrument of control. For the same purpose, courts have utilized their prerogative of "interpreting" contracts, thus preserving the appearance of respecting freedom of volition while, in substance, controlling the intention of the parties.

.   .   .   .   .

This countercurrent of control, as reflected by the somewhat ambivalent attitudes of courts and legislatures towards freedom of contract, has been given impetus by increasingly strong movements of protest and reform which towards the end of the nineteenth century began everywhere to share political and social power, and profoundly to influence the formation of social policy. These movements gained strength during the great depressions of the late nineteenth century, and from the profound public reaction against railroad amalgamations and the pioneer trusts, against child labor, unregulated working conditions, social insecurity, and other emerging problems of contemporary industrial society. Experience in dealing with these issues strengthened the doubt as to the universal validity of the basic presuppositions of the belief in the success of unregulated individualism. Society, in granting freedom of contract,

---

[12] 3 *Works* 190 (Bowring ed., 1843).

[13] *Principles of Political Economy and Taxation* 57 (*Works*, McCulloch ed., 1852).

[14] See Stone, The Myths of Planning and Laissez Faire, 18 *Geo. Wash. L. Rev.* 1, 15-23 (1949).

[15] Reduced to its general terms, this doctrine means that common law requires for the validity of an informal contract not merely agreement, or deliberate intention, but bargain. Expectations created by a mere promise are not legitimate. They have to be paid for.

did not guarantee that all members of the community would be able to utilize it to the same extent. The free use that can be made of contract will depend on the system governing the distribution of property: to the extent that the law sanctions an unequal distribution of property, freedom of contract inevitably becomes a one-sided privilege. Society, by guaranteeing that it will not interfere with the exercise of power by contract, has enabled many an enterpriser to legislate by contract in a substantially authoritarian manner without using the appearance of authoritarian forms. According to a theory which has gained wide popular appeal, many an industrial empire, using contract as a weapon of industrial warfare, has strengthened its power.

American courts in the second half of the last century, and sometimes even as late as the 1920's, were slow in fully recognizing the dangers inherent in the inequality of bargaining power to the existing ways of life. Convinced of the justice of the system of property[16] upon which the justice of freedom of contract rests, they believed that the existence of large industrial empires was in the interest of society as a whole. Only the fittest were worthy of surviving, and the very fact that many enterprisers did not survive the competitive struggle was simply an indication that their services were not sufficiently beneficial to society as a whole. Small wonder that the courts, though they were aware of a limited common law disapproval of contracts in restraint of trade, and though they enforced Anti-Trust laws with reasonable vigor until 1920, balked

---

[16] The following excerpt from a lecture of the late President Hadley of Yale, delivered at the University of Berlin in 1908, contains the most honest formulation of the significance of the system of property. Discussing the Constitutional Position of Property in America, he said:

"When it is said, as it commonly is, that the fundamental division of powers in the modern State is into legislative, executive and judicial, the student of American institutions may fairly note an exception. The fundamental division of powers in the Constitution of the United States is between voters on the one hand and property owners on the other. The forces of democracy on one side, divided between the executive and the legislature, are set over against the forces of property on the other side, with the judiciary as arbiter between them; the Constitution itself not only forbidding the legislature and executive to trench upon the rights of property, but compelling the judiciary to define and uphold those rights in a manner provided by the Constitution itself.

"This theory of American politics has not often been stated. But it has been universally acted upon.... The voter was omnipotent—within a limited area. He could make what laws he pleased, as long as those laws did not trench upon property right. He could elect what officers he pleased, as long as those officers did not try to do certain duties confided by the Constitution to the property holders. Democracy was complete as far as it went, but constitutionally it was bound to stop short of social democracy. I will not go so far as to say that this set of limitations on the political power of the majority in favor of the political power of the property owner has been a necessary element in the success of universal suffrage in the United States. I will say unhesitatingly that it has been a decisive factor in determining the political character of the nation and the actual development of its industries and institutions." 64 *Independent* 837 (1908).

at extended antitrust enforcement against monopolies which were not characterized by business practices which the courts regarded as "predatory" or coercive. Similarly, state statutes attempting to protect the weaker contracting party against abuses of freedom of contract by fixing minimum wages and maximum hours in employment and attempting to outlaw discriminations against union members with the help of yellow dog contracts did not fare any better in the hands of American courts. The climate of opinion prevailing at the end of the last and well into this century is strikingly illustrated by the celebrated cases of *Lochner v. New York*, 198 U.S. 45 (1904), *Adair v. United States*, 208 U.S. 161 (1907) and *Coppage v. Kansas*, 286 U.S. 1 (1914). Declaring such statutes unconstitutional under the due process clause of the 14th Amendment, these decisions elevated liberty of contract to the status of a fundamental property right. Pitney, J., speaking for the majority of the court in *Coppage v. Kansas* which declared an anti-yellow-dog statute unconstitutional formulated the then prevailing philosophy of social Darwinism.

... The principle of control, which began as a countercurrent in the early days of the dominance of freedom of contract, finally swelled into a main current of thought in these areas. This is particularly true in the field of labor relations[19] where the constitutionality of social legislation, which might have been struck down as late as 1936, has since been upheld. In addition, under the protective cover of legislation, the bargain for individual terms of employment has been replaced in many fields by master contracts arrived at between labor unions and employers or groups of employers. But the law has not yet reached the stage of compulsory arbitration; it requires only collective bargaining on the part of both sides.

Furthermore, to protect the public against the danger of powerful suppliers dictating the terms of contracts or not contracting at all, statutes frequently prescribe, either wholly or partially, the terms of transactions of great social significance. The field of insurance contracts furnishes excellent illustrations. And, public utilities frequently have been required by statute to furnish their services and to comply with conditions and rates approved by public authority. "Compulsory" contracts have thus made their appearance. But again the law has not as yet reached the stage where any corporation which has achieved a substantial monopoly is held to the standards of a public utility and has to supply all comers.

To sum up, the individual member of the community, from the moment he arises in the morning to the time he retires at night, finds himself involved in a number of contractual obligations, the contents of which are often predetermined for him by statute, public authority or group action. The terms and conditions under which he obtains his supply of electricity and gas will in all likelihood be regulated by a public utility commission. So will be his fare, should he use a public conveyance going to work. The rent he will have to pay may be fixed by governmental authority. The price of his food will largely depend on the government's farm support program and not on the interplay of demand and supply in a free market. No longer will he be able to haggle for the price of many a standard brand used in daily consumption, since prices may well be fixed by arrangement between producer and distributor under price maintenance requirements with the blessing of statutory approval. The wages he will have to pay or will earn may have been fixed for him in advance.

Thus, in the evolution of the law of contracts, the basic assumption of the past that contract deals with the individual relations of men with each other has gradually given way to the realization that in large sectors of our social and economic life contract is no longer an individual and private affair, but a social institution affecting more than the interests of the two contracting parties. An analysis, therefore, of present-day contract exclusively in terms of volition and agreement does not do justice to contract as a social institution. Social control has become an integral part of contract itself, and cannot be omitted from any analysis of the modern law of contract.

---

3. What Promises Should Be Enforced

The Minimum Wage Case

ADKINS v. CHILDREN'S HOSPITAL
U.S. SUPREME COURT, 1923
261 U.S. 525

MR. JUSTICE SUTHERLAND delivered the opinion of the Court.

The question presented for determination by these appeals is the constitutionality of the Act of September 19, 1918, providing for the fixing of minimum wages for women and children in the District of Columbia ... [P. 539.]

. . . . .

The statute now under consideration is attacked upon the ground that it authorizes an unconstitutional interference with the freedom of contract included within the guaranties of the due process clause of the Fifth Amendment. That the right to contract about one's affairs is a part of the liberty of the individual protected by this clause, is settled by the decisions of this Court and is no longer open to question.... Within this liberty are contracts of employment of labor. In making such contracts, generally speaking, the parties have an equal right to obtain from each other the best terms they can as the result of private bargaining.

In *Adair v. United States*, 208 U.S. 161, Mr. Justice Harlan (pp. 174, 175), speaking for the Court, said:

The right of a person to sell his labor upon such terms as he deems proper is, in its essence, the same as the right of the purchaser of labor to prescribe the conditions upon which he will accept such labor from the person offering to sell.... In all such particulars the employer and employee have equality of right, and any legislation that disturbs that equality is an arbitrary interference with the liberty of contract which no government can legally justify in a free land. [P. 545.]

.   .   .   .   .

That this constituted the basis of the decision is emphasized by the subsequent decision in *Lochner v. New York*, 198 U.S. 45, reviewing a state statute which restricted the employment of all persons in bakeries to ten hours in any one day....

Mr. Justice Peckham, speaking for the Court (p. 56), said: [P. 548.]

.   .   .   .   .

Statutes of the nature of that under review, limiting the hours in which grown and intelligent men may labor to earn their living, are mere meddlesome interferences with the rights of the individual, and they are not saved from condemnation by the claim that they are passed in the exercise of the police power and upon the subject of the health of the individual whose rights are interfered with, unless there be some fair ground, reasonable in and of itself, to say that there is material danger to the public health or to the health of the employees, if the hours of labor are not curtailed. [P. 550.]

.   .   .   .   .

In the *Muller Case* the validity of an Oregon statute, forbidding the employment of any female in certain industries more than ten hours during any one day was upheld. The decision proceeded upon the theory that the difference between the sexes may justify a different rule respecting hours of labor in the case of women than in the case of men. It is pointed out that these consist in differences of physical structure, especially in respect of the maternal functions, and also in the fact that historically woman has always been dependent upon man, who has established his control by superior physical strength. The cases of *Riley, Miller* and *Bosley* follow in this respect the *Muller Case*. But the ancient inequality of the sexes, otherwise than physical, as suggested in the *Muller Case* (p. 421) has continued "with diminishing intensity." In view of the great—not to say revolutionary—changes which have taken place since that utterance, in the contractual, political and civil status of women, culminating in the Nineteenth Amendment, it is not unreasonable to say that these differences have now come almost, if not quite, to the vanishing point. In this aspect of the matter, while the physical differences must be recognized in appropriate cases, and legislation fixing hours or conditions of work may properly take them into account, we cannot accept the doctrine that women of mature age, *sui juris*, require or may be subjected to restrictions upon their liberty of contract which could not lawfully be imposed in the case of men under similar circumstances. [Pp. 552-553.]

. . . . .

The relation between earnings and morals is not capable of standardization. It cannot be shown that well paid women safeguard their morals more carefully than those who are poorly paid. Morality rests upon other considerations than wages; and there is, certainly, no such prevalent connection between the two as to justify a broad attempt to adjust the latter with reference to the former. As a means of safeguarding morals the attempted classification, in our opinion, is without reasonable basis. No distinction can be made between women who work for others and those who do not; nor is there ground for distinction between women and men, for, certainly, if women require a minimum wage to preserve their morals men require it to preserve their honesty. For these reasons, and others which might be stated, the inquiry in respect of the necessary cost of living and the income necessary to preserve health and morals, presents an individual and not a composite question, and must be answered for each individual considered by herself and not by a general formula prescribed by a statutory bureau. [P. 556.]

. . . . .

The moral requirement implicit in every contract of employment, viz, that the amount to be paid and the service to be rendered shall bear to each other some relation of just equivalence, is completely ignored. The necessities of the employee are alone considered and these arise outside of the employment, are the same when there is no employment, and as great in one occupation as in another. Certainly the employer by paying a fair equivalent for the service rendered, though not sufficient to support the employee, has neither caused nor contributed to her poverty. On the contrary, to the extent of what he pays he has relieved it. . . .

We are asked, upon the one hand, to consider the fact that several States have adopted similar statutes, and we are invited, upon the other hand, to give weight to the fact that three times as many States, presumably as well informed and as anxious to promote the health and morals of their people, have refrained from enacting such legislation. We have also been furnished with a large number of printed opinions approving the policy of the minimum wage, and our own reading has disclosed a large number to the contrary. These are all proper enough for the consideration of the lawmaking bodies, since their tendency is to establish the desirability or undesirability of the legislation; but they reflect no legitimate light upon the question of its validity, and that is what we are called upon to decide. The elucidation of that question cannot be aided by counting heads. [Pp. 558-560.]

.   .   .   .   .

To sustain the individual freedom of action contemplated by the Constitution, is not to strike down the common good but to exalt it; for surely the good of society as a whole cannot be better served than by the preservation against arbitrary restraint of the liberties of its constituent members.

It follows from what has been said that the act in question passes the limit prescribed by the Constitution, and, accordingly, the decrees of the court below are

Affirmed [Pp. 561-562.]

.   .   .   .   .

Mr. Justice Holmes, dissenting. [P. 567.]

.   .   .   .   .

... in the present instance the only objection that can be urged is found within the vague contours of the Fifth Amendment, prohibiting the depriving any person of liberty or property without due process of law. To that I turn.

The earlier decisions upon the same words in the Fourteenth Amendment began within our memory and went no farther than an unpretentious assertion of the liberty to follow the ordinary callings. Later that innocuous generality was expanded into the dogma, Liberty of Contract. Contract is not specially mentioned in the text that we have to construe. It is merely an example of doing what you want to do, embodied in the word liberty. But pretty much all law consists in forbidding men to do some things that they want to do, and contract is no more exempt from law than other acts. Without enumerating all the restrictive laws that have been upheld I will mention a few that seem to me to have interfered with liberty of contract quite as seriously and directly as the one before us. Usury laws prohibit contracts by which a man receives more than so much interest for the money that he lends. Statutes of frauds restrict many contracts to certain forms. Some Sunday laws prohibit practically all contracts during the one-seventh of our whole life. Insurance rates may be regulated. *German Alliance Insurance Co. v. Lewis*, 233 U.S. 389....

... *Muller v. Oregon*, I take it, is as good law today as it was in 1908. It will need more than the Nineteenth Amendment to convince me that there are no differences between men and women, or that legislation cannot take these differences into account. I should not hesitate to take them into account if I thought it necessary to sustain this act. . . . But after *Bunting v. Oregon*, 243 U.S. 426, I had supposed that it was not necessary and that *Lochner v. New York*, 198 U.S. 45, would be allowed a deserved repose. [Pp. 568-570.]

.   .   .   .   .

The criterion of constitutionality is not whether we believe the law to be for the public good. We certainly cannot be prepared to deny that a reasonable man reasonably might have that belief in view of the legislation of Great Britain, Victoria and a number of the States of this Union. The belief is fortified by a very remarkable collection of documents submitted on behalf of the appellants, material here, I conceive, only as showing that the belief reasonably may be held. In Australia the power to fix a minimum for wages in the case of industrial disputes extending beyond the limits of any one State was given to a Court, and its President wrote a most interesting account of its operation. 29 *Harv. Law Rev.* 13. If a legislature should adopt what he thinks the doctrine of modern economists of all schools, that "freedom of contract is a misnomer as applied to a contract between an employer and an ordinary individual employee," *ibid.* 25, I could not pronounce an opinion with which I agree impossible to be entertained by reasonable men. If the same legislature should accept his further opinion that industrial peace was best attained by the device of a Court having the above powers, I should not feel myself able to contradict it, or to deny that the end justified restrictive legislation quite as adequately as beliefs concerning Sunday or exploded theories about usury. I should have my doubts, as I have them about this statute—but they would be whether the bill that has to be paid for every gain, although hidden as interstitial detriments, was not greater than the gain was worth: a matter that it is not for me to decide.

I am of opinion that the statute is valid and that the decree should be reversed. [P. 571.]

Mortgage Moratoria and the Contract Clause

HOME BUILDING AND LOAN ASSOCIATION v. BLAISDELL ET AL.

U. S. Supreme Court, 1934
290 U.S. 398

Mr. Chief Justice Hughes delivered the opinion of the Court.

Appellant contests the validity of Chapter 339 of the Laws of Minnesota of 1933, p. 514, approved April 18, 1933, called the Minnesota Mortgage Moratorium Law, as being repugnant to the contract clause (Art. I, § 10) and the due process and equal protection clauses of the Fourteenth

Amendment, of the Federal Constitution. The statute was sustained by the Supreme Court of Minnesota, ... and the case comes here on appeal.

The Act provides that, during the emergency declared to exist, relief may be had through authorized judicial proceedings with respect to foreclosures of mortgages, and execution sales, of real estate; that sales may be postponed and periods of redemption may be extended. [Pp. 415-416.]

．　．　．　．　．

In determining whether the provision for this temporary and conditional relief exceeds the power of the State by reason of the clause in the Federal Constitution prohibiting impairment of the obligations of contracts, we must consider the relation of emergency to constitutional power, the historical setting of the contract clause, the development of the jurisprudence of this Court in the construction of that clause, and the principles of construction which we may consider to be established.

Emergency does not create power. Emergency does not increase granted power or remove or diminish the restrictions imposed upon power granted or reserved. The Constitution was adopted in a period of grave emergency. Its grants of power to the Federal Government and its limitations of the power of the States were determined in the light of emergency and they are not altered by emergency. What power was thus granted and what limitations were thus imposed are questions which have always been, and always will be, the subject of close examination under our constitutional system.

While emergency does not create power, emergency may furnish the occasion for the exercise of power. "Although an emergency may not call into life a power which has never lived, nevertheless emergency may afford a reason for the exertion of a living power already enjoyed." *Wilson v. New,* 243 U.S. 332, 348. The constitutional question presented in the light of an emergency is whether the power possessed embraces the particular exercise of it in response to particular conditions. [Pp. 425-426.]

．　．　．　．　．

The inescapable problems of construction have been: What is a contract?[8] What are the obligations of contract? What constitutes impairment of these obligations? What residuum of power is there still in the States in relation to the operation of contracts, to protect the vital inter-

---

[8] Contracts, within the meaning of the clause, have been held to embrace those that are executed, that is, grants, as well as those that are executory.... They embrace the charters of private corporations.... But not the marriage contract, so as to limit the general right to legislate on the subject of divorce.... Nor are judgments, though rendered upon contracts, deemed to be within the provision.... Nor does a general law, giving the consent of a State to be sued, constitute a contract....

ests of the community? Questions of this character, "of no small nicety and intricacy, have vexed the legislative halls, as well as the judicial tribunals, with an uncounted variety and frequency of litigation and speculation." Story on the Constitution, § 1375.

The obligation of a contract is "the law which binds the parties to perform their agreement." *Sturges v. Crowninshield*, 4 Wheat. 122, 197; Story, *op. cit.*, § 1378. This Court has said that "the laws which subsist at the time and place of the making of a contract, and where it is to be performed, enter into and form a part of it, as if they were expressly referred to or incorporated in its terms. This principle embraces alike these which affect its validity, construction, discharge and enforcement. ... Nothing can be more material to the obligation than the means of enforcement. ... The ideas of validity and remedy are inseparable, and both are parts of the obligation, which is guaranteed by the Constitution against invasion." *Von Hoffman v. City of Quincy*, 4 Wall. 535, 550, 552 ... But this broad language cannot be taken without qualification. Chief Justice Marshall pointed out the distinction between obligation and remedy. *Sturges v. Crowninshield, supra*, p. 200. Said he: "The distinction between the obligation of a contract, and the remedy given by the legislature to enforce that obligation, has been taken at the bar, and exists in the nature of things. Without impairing the obligation of the contract, the remedy may certainly be modified as the wisdom of the nation shall direct." And in *Von Hoffman v. City of Quincy, supra*, pp. 553, 554, the general statement above quoted was limited by the further observation that "It is competent for the States to change the form of the remedy, or to modify it otherwise, as they may see fit, provided no substantial right secured by the contract is thereby impaired. No attempt has been made to fix definitely the line between alterations of the remedy, which are to be deemed legitimate, and those which, under the form of modifying the remedy, impair substantial rights. Every case must be determined upon its own circumstances." And Chief Justice Waite, quoting this language in *Antoni v. Greenhow*, 107 U.S. 769, 775, added: "In all such cases the question becomes, therefore, one of reasonableness, and of that the legislature is primarily the judge." [Pp. 429-430.]

. . . . .

Not only are existing laws read into contracts in order to fix obligations as between the parties, but the reservation of essential attributes of sovereign power is also read into contracts as a postulate of the legal order. The policy of protecting contracts against impairment presupposes the maintenance of a government by virtue of which contractual relations are worth while,—a government which retains adequate authority to secure the peace and good order of society. [P. 435.]

. . . . .

It is manifest from this review of our decisions that there has been a growing appreciation of public needs and of the necessity of finding ground for a rational compromise between individual rights and public welfare. The settlement and consequent contraction of the public domain, the pressure of a constantly increasing density of population, the inter-relation of the activities of our people and the complexity of our economic interests, have inevitably led to an increased use of the organization of society in order to protect the very bases of individual opportunity. Where, in earlier days, it was thought that only the concerns of individuals or of classes were involved, and that those of the State itself were touched only remotely, it has later been found that the fundamental interests of the State are directly affected; and that the question is no longer merely that of one party to a contract as against another, but of the use of reasonable means to safeguard the economic structure upon which the good of all depends.

It is no answer to say that this public need was not apprehended a century ago, or to insist that what the provision of the Constitution meant to the vision of that day it must mean to the vision of our time. If by the statement that what the Constitution meant at the time of its adoption it means to-day, it is intended to say that the great clauses of the Constitution must be confined to the interpretation which the framers, with the conditions and outlook of their time, would have placed upon them, the statement carries its own refutation. It was to guard against such a narrow conception, that Chief Justice Marshall uttered the memorable warning—"We must never forget that it is *a constitution* we are expounding"... "a constitution intended to endure for ages to come, and consequently, to be adapted to the various *crises* of human affairs."... When we are dealing with the words of the Constitution, said this Court in *Missouri v. Holland*, 252 U.S. 416, 433, "we must realize that they have called into life a being the development of which could not have been foreseen completely by the most gifted of its begetters.... The case before us must be considered in the light of our whole experience and not merely in that of what was said a hundred years ago." [Pp. 442-443.]

· · · · ·

If it be determined, as it must be, that the contract clause is not an absolute and utterly unqualified restriction of the State's protective power, this legislation is clearly so reasonable as to be within the legislative competency. [P. 447.]

· · · · ·

We are of the opinion that the Minnesota statute as here applied does not violate the contract clause of the Federal Constitution. Whether the legislation is wise or unwise as a matter of policy is a question with which we are not concerned. [Pp. 447-448.]

• • • • •

Judgment affirmed.

MR. JUSTICE SUTHERLAND dissenting.

Few questions of greater moment than that just decided have been submitted for judicial inquiry during this generation. He simply closes his eyes to the necessary implications of the decision who fails to see in it the potentiality of future gradual but ever-advancing encroachments upon the sanctity of private and public contracts. The effect of the Minnesota legislation, though serious enough in itself, is of trivial significance compared with the far more serious and dangerous inroads upon the limitations of the Constitution which are almost certain to ensue as a consequence naturally following any step beyond the boundaries fixed by that instrument. And those of us who are thus apprehensive of the effect of this decision would, in a matter so important, be neglectful of our duty should we fail to spread upon the permanent records of the court the reasons which move us to the opposite view.

A provision of the Constitution, it is hardly necessary to say, does not admit of two distinctly opposite interpretations. It does not mean one thing at one time and an entirely different thing at another time. If the contract impairment clause, when framed and adopted, meant that the terms of a contract for the payment of money could not be altered *in invitum* by a state statute enacted for the relief of hardly pressed debtors to the end and with the effect of postponing payment or enforcement during and because of an economic or financial emergency, it is but to state the obvious to say that it means the same now. This view, at once so rational in its application to the written word, and so necessary to the stability of constitutional principles, though from time to time challenged, has never, unless recently, been put within the realm of doubt by the decisions of this court. The true rule was forcefully declared in *Ex parte Milligan*, 4 Wall. 2, 120-121, in the face of circumstances of national peril and public unrest and disturbance far greater than any that exist today. In that great case this court said that the provisions of the Constitution there under consideration had been expressed by our ancestors in such plain English words that it would seem the ingenuity of man could not evade them, but that after the lapse of more than seventy years they were sought to be avoided. "Those great and good men," the court said, "foresaw that troublous times would arise, when rulers and people would become restive under restraint, and seek by sharp and decisive measures to accomplish ends deemed just and proper; and that the principles of constitutional liberty would be in peril, unless established by irrepealable law. The history of the world had taught them that what was done in the past might be attempted in the future." And then, in words the power and truth of which have become increasingly evident with the lapse of time, there was laid down the rule without which the Constitution would cease to be the "supreme law of the land," binding equally upon governments and governed at all times and under all circumstances, and become a mere collection of political maxims to be adhered to or disregarded according to the prevailing sentiment or the legislative and judicial opinion in respect of the supposed necessities of the hour:

"The Constitution of the United States is a law for rulers and people, equally in war and in peace, and covers with the shield of its protection all classes of men, at all times, and under all circumstances. No doctrine, involving more pernicious consequences, was ever invented by the wit of man than that any of its provisions can be suspended during any of the great exigencies of government. Such a doctrine leads directly to anarchy or despotism, . . ." [Pp. 448-450.]

.   .   .   .   .

A candid consideration of the history and circumstances which led up to and accompanied the framing and adoption of this clause will demonstrate conclusively that it was framed and adopted with the specific and studied purpose of preventing legislation designed to relieve debtors *especially* in time of financial distress. [P. 453.]

.   .   .   .   .

The present exigency is nothing new. From the beginning of our existence as a nation, periods of depression, of industrial failure, of financial distress, of unpaid and unpayable indebtedness, have alternated with years of plenty. The vital lesson that expenditure beyond income begets poverty, that public or private extravagance, financed by promises to pay, either must end in complete or partial repudiation or the promises be fulfilled by self-denial and painful effort, though constantly taught by bitter experience, seems never to be learned; and the attempt by legislative devices to shift the misfortune of the debtor to the shoulders of the creditor without coming into conflict with the contract impairment clause has been persistent and oft-repeated.

The defense of the Minnesota law is made upon grounds which were discountenanced by the makers of the Constitution and have many times been rejected by this court. That defense should not now succeed, because it constitutes an effort to overthrow the constitutional provision by an appeal to facts and circumstances identical with those which brought it into existence. With due regard for the processes of logical thinking, it legitimately cannot be urged that conditions which produced the rule may now be invoked to destroy it. [Pp. 471-472.]

.   .   .   .   .

Being unable to reach any other conclusion than that the Minnesota statute infringes the constitutional restriction under review, I have no choice but to say so.

I am authorized to say that Mr. Justice Van Devanter, Mr. Justice McReynolds and Mr. Justice Butler concur in this opinion. [P. 472.]

WEST COAST HOTEL COMPANY v. PARRISH

U. S. Supreme Court, 1937
300 U.S. 379

Mr. Chief Justice Hughes delivered the opinion of the Court.

This case presents the question of the constitutional validity of the minimum wage law of the State of Washington. [P. 386.]

·   ·   ·   ·   ·

The state court has refused to regard the decision in the *Adkins Case* as determinative and has pointed to our decisions both before and since that case as justifying its position. We are of the opinion that this ruling of the state court demands on our part a reexamination of the *Adkins Case*. [Pp. 389-390.]

·   ·   ·   ·   ·

In *Nebbia v. New York*, 291 U.S. 502, 78 L. ed. 940, 54 S.Ct. 505, 89 A.L.R. 1469, dealing with the New York statute providing for minimum prices for milk, the general subject of the regulation of the use of private property and of the making of private contracts received an exhaustive examination and we again declared that if such laws "have a reasonable relation to a proper legislative purpose, and are neither arbitrary nor discriminatory, the requirements of due process are satisfied"; that "with the wisdom of the policy adopted, with the adequacy or practicability of the law enacted to forward it, the courts are both incompetent and unauthorized to deal"; that "times without number we have said that the legislature is primarily the judge of the necessity of such an enactment, that every possible presumption is in favor of its validity, and that though the court may hold views inconsistent with the wisdom of the law, it may not be annulled unless palpably in excess of legislative power." *Id.* pp. 537, 538.

With full recognition of the earnestness and vigor which characterize the prevailing opinion in the *Adkins Case*, we find it impossible to reconcile that ruling with these well-considered declarations. What can be closer to the public interest than the health of women and their protection from unscrupulous and overreaching employers? And if the protection of women is a legitimate end of the exercise of state power, how can it be said that the requirement of the payment of a minimum wage fairly fixed in order to meet the very necessities of existence is not an admissible means to that end? The legislature of the State was clearly entitled to consider the situation of women in employment, the fact that they are in the class receiving the least pay, that their bargaining power is relatively weak and that they are the ready victims of those who would take advantage of their necessitous circumstances. The legislature was entitled to adopt measures to reduce the evils of the "sweating system," the exploiting of workers at wages so low as to be insufficient to meet the bare cost of living, thus making their very helplessness the occasion of a most injurious competition. The legislature had the right to consider that its minimum wage requirements would be an important aid in carrying out its policy of protection. The adoption of similar requirements by many States evidences a deep-seated conviction both as to the presence of the evil and as to the means adapted to check it. Legislative response to that conviction cannot be regarded as arbitrary or capricious and that is all we have to decide. Even if the wisdom of the policy be regarded as debatable and its effects uncertain, still the legislature is entitled to its judgment.

There is an additional and compelling consideration which recent economic experience has brought into a strong light. The exploitation of a class of workers who are in an unequal position with respect to bargaining power and are thus relatively defenceless against the denial of a living wage is not only detrimental to their health and well-being but casts a direct burden for their support upon the community. What these workers lose in wages the taxpayers are called upon to pay. The bare cost of living must be met. We may take judicial notice of the unparalleled demands for relief which arose during the recent period of depression and still continue to an alarming extent despite the degree of economic recovery which has been achieved. It is unnecessary to cite official statistics to establish what is of common knowledge through the length and breadth of the land. While in the instant case no factual brief has been presented, there is no reason to doubt that the State of Washington has encountered the same social problem that is present elsewhere. The community is not bound to provide what is in effect a subsidy for unconscionable employers. [Pp. 397-400.]

.   .   .   .   .

Our conclusion is that the case of *Adkins v. Children's Hospital*, 261 U.S. 525, *supra*, should be, and it is, overruled.

The Judgment of the Supreme Court of the State of Washington is affirmed.

Mr. Justice Sutherland, dissenting:

Mr. Justice Van Devanter, Mr. Justice McReynolds, Mr. Justice

BUTLER and I think the judgment of the court below should be reversed. [P. 400.]

. . . . .

It is urged that the question involved should now receive fresh consideration, among other reasons, because of "the economic conditions which have supervened"; but the meaning of the Constitution does not change with the ebb and flow of economic events. We frequently are told in more general words that the Constitution must be construed in the light of the present. If by that it is meant that the Constitution is made up of living words that apply to every new condition which they include, the statement is quite true. But to say, if that be intended, that the words of the Constitution mean today what they did not mean when written—that is, that they do not apply to a situation now to which they would have applied then—is to rob that instrument of the essential element which continues it in force as the people have made it until they, and not their official agents, have made it otherwise. [Pp. 402-403.]

. . . . .

The judicial function is that of interpretation; it does not include the power of amendment under the guise of interpretation. To miss the point of difference between the two is to miss all that the phrase "supreme law of the land" stands for and to convert what was intended as inescapable and enduring mandates into mere moral reflections. [P. 404.]

. . . . .

In support of minimum-wage legislation it has been urged, on the one hand, that great benefits will result in favor of underpaid labor, and, on the other hand, that the danger of such legislation is that the minimum will tend to become the maximum and thus bring down the earnings of the more efficient toward the level of the less efficient employees. But with these speculations we have nothing to do. We are concerned only with the question of constitutionality. [Pp. 405-406.]

. . . . .

If, in the light of the facts, the state legislation, without reason or for reasons of mere expediency, excluded men from the provisions of the legislation, the power was exercised arbitrarily. On the other hand, if such legislation in respect of men was properly omitted on the ground that it would be unconstitutional, the same conclusion of unconstitutionality is inescapable in respect of similar legislative restraint in the case of women, 261 U.S. 553. [P. 413.]

STEELE, THE UNIFORM WRITTEN OBLIGATIONS
ACT—A CRITICISM* [a]

The Commissioners on Uniform State Laws have recommended for adoption "a Written Obligations Act."[†] Aside from the usual formal sections the Act reads as follows:

"Section I: A written release or promise hereafter made and signed by the person releasing or promising shall not be invalid or unenforcible for lack of consideration, if the writing also contains an additional express statement, in any form of language, that the signer intends to be legally bound."

The adoption of this act in a state in which seals have been abolished would, of course, in effect amount to a restoration of the sealed instrument doctrine, substituting a written expression for a mechanical or graphic device; and its adoption by those states in which the sealed instrument doctrine still obtains would merely affect the introduction of a new formality, analogous but additional to that of the seal.

That such is the purpose of the Act is indicated by the following statement of Mr. Williston, the drafter of it:

I am making the law, if this act is enacted, substantially the same as it was when seals were in force, so far as the doctrine of consideration is concerned, except that in lieu of the formality of a seal, the formality of this statement is substituted.[1]

The recommendation of the proposed Act presents, therefore, the question whether it is wise to attempt to check the modern tendency to subject all contracts, regardless of form, to the test of consideration, and to give to the formality of a written phrase identically the same effect that the Common law gave to a seal. [P. 185.]

.   .   .   .   .

Assuming that the recommendation is not merely the beginning of a general attack upon the whole doctrine of consideration, it yet may be

---

* [Reprinted by special permission of the *Illinois Law Review* (Northwestern University School of Law). 21 *Ill. L. Rev.* 185 (1926).]

[a] *Sherman Steele*, born in Lancaster, Ohio, 1878; Litt. B. Notre Dame 1897, LL.B. 1899. Practiced law Indianapolis 1899–1902. Taught history and economics in Notre Dame University 1902–04; Professor of Law, Notre Dame University 1904–08; Professor of Law, St. Louis University 1908–20; Professor of Law, Loyola University School of Law, Chicago, Ill., since 1920. Editor, *Cases on Equity*. Author, *Student's Text on Agency* and occasional contributions to legal periodicals.

[†] [*Uniform Written Obligations Act* (approved in 1925 by the National Conference of Commissioners on Uniform State Laws). It has since been adopted by two States, Pennsylvania (May 13, 1927, L. 1927 c. 985; 33 P.S. secs. 6-8) and Utah (July 1, 1929, L. 1929 c. 62).]

[1] *Handbook of Conference of Commissioners on Uniform Laws* (1925) p. 213.

seriously urged that the proposed modification of that doctrine is neither necessary nor advisable. The notion that legal obligations should be reciprocal or based on quid pro quo is innate, and finds expression in the development of our law of consideration. No one will gainsay that under ordinary circumstances a man should keep his word and ordinarily he intends to do so and usually does. Under other circumstances a man might be justified in revoking a gratuitous promise and where such is the case, there is no equity in preventing his doing so merely because he expressed an intention to be bound. . . .

Leaving the hypothetical, take, offhand, an actual case. In *Schnell v. Nell*,[6] it appears that appellant's wife was under the impression that her inchoate dower right constituted a vested interest in her husband's property. In any event, at her death, the old lady who had nothing, left a will in which she bequeathed substantial sums to three of her relatives who appeared on the scene to collect their legacies. Schnell, apparently sharing his wife's misapprehension of law, and presumably to avoid litigation, agreed in writing to pay each of the legatees the sum of two hundred dollars. Upon learning that there had never existed the shadow of a claim against his property, Schnell refused to perform his agreement. Let us assume—though the statement of facts doesn't disclose it—that Schnell had no interest in these relatives or had reason to strongly dislike them, and that furthermore he acted under belief that their claims were well founded. Upon learning his rights, he unquestionably would be justified in repudiating any obligation. Yet, in this case, the written agreement was formally drafted, probably by the claimants' lawyer; had the proposed Written Obligations Act been in force in Indiana its binding expression would undoubtedly have been incorporated in the instrument without objection by the signer. In such event, by virtue of the mere magic of a phrase, Schnell would have been forced by law to pay the money. [Pp. 187-188.]

. . . . . .

The proposed Written Obligations Act also covers releases and much importance seems to have been attached to that fact by proponents of the statute, some of whom apparently find in the inclusion of releases a justification of the entire proposal. . . .

In many cases hardship is imposed upon parties by an application of the sealed instrument doctrine to releases of meritorious claims. . . .

A similar application of the rule was made by the same court in the later case of *Woodbury v. U. S. Casualty Co.*[9] There Woodbury, who carried a large amount of accident insurance, "went out to a tool house in the rear

---

[6] 17 Indiana 29.
[9] 284 Ill. 227.

of his home and reached up for his rifle. It got away from his hand, struck the door, dropped muzzle down, and then fell over and was discharged, the bullet going transversely through his right leg three inches above the ankle." After an unsuccessful operation it was found necessary to amputate the lower part of his leg. While "still very much weakened in body and mind as a result of the operation," an adjuster for the insurance companies called upon him, expressed suspicions about the occurrence, "cited the case of a man in Buffalo who threw his arm under a street car, had it cut off, sued the company and they sent him to the penitentiary." The adjuster cited similar cases, warned Woodbury that the insurance companies were powerful and that if he refused to settle they would bankrupt him, possibly put him in the penitentiary and in any event would ruin his reputation. This talk greatly alarmed Woodbury and his wife who was herself worn out by lack of sleep and care of her husband; they but recently had left Chicago to establish themselves in the far west and were practically strangers in a strange land. These driving attacks were kept up, a day set by the adjuster for the execution of his threats and finally in desperation Woodbury accepted part of what was due him, executing releases. In an action upon the policies in the courts of Illinois it was held that as the releases were under seal they could not be attacked for want of consideration or for fraud unless the fraud went to the execution of the instrument, *i.e.*, "that they were signed upon representation that they were a different character of instrument." It is true that here, as in the earlier case, the court indicated that relief might be obtained in equity, but that fact offers slight excuse for retaining in our law the formality of the seal and less reason for inventing a new formality analogous to that of the seal.

Finally, as to the contention, which found expression in the Commissioners' discussions, that the doctrine of consideration is sordid and that a man should be permitted by law to bind himself by a gratuitous promise.[10] In the sense that the average men ordinarily demand a quid pro quo, most human transactions are sordid; but in any event, the law of consideration does not preclude the execution of altruistic impulses. Men may indulge in generosity and fully perform unenforceable agreements. But tested by practical average results, it seems a sound rule that purely gratuitous promises should find their enforcement in the tribunals of conscience and honor and that if a man intends to be legally bound by a gift, he should manifest such intention by execution of the gift. [Pp. 189-190.]

---

[10] *Handbook of Conference* p. 200.

HOLDSWORTH, HISTORY OF ENGLISH LAW *

Usury and the Usury Laws [1]

At no time can the state be wholly indifferent to the use which the owners of property make of their property. More especially must it interest itself in the actions of those who, having a sum of ready money at their disposal, seek, without risk to themselves, to exploit the needs of poorer or less fortunate men, and to exact from them a reward for the loan of this money. Thus, at all times, the relations of the lenders of money on onerous terms to those in need of pecuniary assistance, require to be watched carefully, lest the processes of the law be used for the purposes of the most grievous oppression. In this country a very short experience of the consequences of allowing lenders and borrowers to make what bargains they please has been sufficient to demonstrate this fact; [2] and this century has seen the state resume a control, which it had abandoned under the influence of the *a priori* theories of Bentham, and of the pseudo-scientific laws of the school of *laissez faire* economists.[3] In this, as in other cases, these so-called laws placed obstacles in the way of necessary legislative changes, some time after the purely temporary political and economic conditions, from which they were deduced, had ceased to exist.[4]

We have seen that in the Middle Ages the state, and the different communities through which the power of the state was exercised, considered that they were very much interested in seeing that property was used in accordance with the current notions of morality and justice.[5] And it is

---

* [2nd ed., Vol. VIII, Book IV, Part II, Chap. 4, §1. London: Methuen & Co., Ltd., 1937. Reprinted by permission. Footnotes have been renumbered.

The most famous work of *Sir William Searle Holdsworth* is the massive *History of English Law* in twelve volumes, which appeared over the course of three decades, beginning in 1903. Holdsworth was professor at London and Oxford, specializing in the law of real property and British Constitutional Law.]

[1] Much the best English account of the evolution of the mediaeval, and the growth of the modern ideas on this subject, will be found in Ashley, *Economic History* vol. i Pt. I chap. iii; Pt. II chap. vi; the introduction to Tawney's edition of *Wilson on Usury* gives a good account of the transition from the mediaeval ideas to those of the sixteenth and seventeenth centuries; for a good account of the whole subject, from the point of view of foreign law, see Brissaud, *Cours d'histoire générale du droit française* 1422-1434; see also Malynes, *Lex Mercatoria* Part II chaps. x-xv; Bl. Comm. ii 454-464; Stephen H. C. L. iii 194-199; Bellot, *Bargains with Money Lenders* (2nd ed.) 1-82.

[2] See the evidence of Mathew, J., given to the Select Committee on money-lending in 1898, cited Bellot, *op. cit.* 70, 71.

[3] Bentham's *Defence of Usury* was published in 1787; and Sir William Ashley has pointed out, in a review of Mr. Tawney's book, that Leslie Stephen has said that Bentham's tract "became one of the sacred books of the economists."

[4] The usury laws were repealed in 1854, 17, 18 Victoria c. 90; the Money-lenders Act was passed in 1900, 63, 64, Victoria c. 51.

[5] Vol. ii, 468-469; Vol. iv, 316-326.

clear that when trade was in its infancy, when, therefore, there was little opportunity for profitable investment, the relation of lender and borrower must be very strictly supervised. For, in such a state of society, borrowers of money were more often than not either the extravagant or the needy. The money was borrowed, as Sir William Ashley says, not for productive but for consumptive expenditure.[6] There was therefore some justification, both for Aristotle's view that all interest was unlawful because money did not breed money, and for the literal acceptance of the Scriptural prohibitions of usury.[7] If we remember these facts, we shall not be surprised that the church and the canon law [8] condemned all lending of money as a sin; that the civil law and the laws of the states of Western Europe endorsed and sanctioned this condemnation;[9] that all transactions were carefully sifted to see whether they were tainted with its presence; and that the prohibition of usury thus became, as Brissaud has said, the keystone of the political economy of the Middle Ages.[10]

From the earliest times the law of the English state was based upon these ideas.[11] Glanvil tells us that usury was both a sin and a crime. In the usurer's lifetime he was dealt with by the ecclesiastical courts as a sinner; but, if he died unrepentant, the king asserted a claim to his goods.[12] This was also the law in Bracton's day;[13] and it was restated in 1341. A statute passed in that year enacted that, "The king and his heirs should have the cognisance of the usurers dead; and that the Ordinaries of Holy Church have the cognisance of the usurers in life, as to them appertaineth, to make compulsion

---

6 "Where money was borrowed it was, in the vast majority of cases, not for what is called productive expenditure, but for consumptive; not to enlarge the area of tillage, or to invest in trade or industry, but to meet some sudden want due to the frequent famines, or to oppressive taxation, or to extravagance. The money that was lent was money for which it would otherwise have been exceedingly difficult to secure an investment. The alternative to lending was allowing it to remain idle," Ashley, *op. cit.* i. Pt. II 435; cp. Brissaud, *op. cit.* 1423-1424.

7 *Ethics v. Politics* 1. 10; Luke vi 35; Cunningham, *Industry and Commerce* i 252 n. 1; Malynes, *op cit.* chap. x.

8 See Clement v.'s Canon of 1311, cited Ashley, *op. cit.* i. Pt. I 150-151.

9 *Ibid* Pt. II 382-383; Brissaud, *op. cit.* 1425-1426.

10 *Op. cit.* 1424—"*Les casuistes cherchent à le proscrire partout; par suite de leur intransigeance, la défense de l'usure prend une extension invraisemblable, et devient comme la clef de voûte de l'économie politique du moyen-âge; vente, payement, dommages intérêts, société, banque, lettre de change, autant de matières où on s'en pré-occupe particulièrement.*"

11 The apocryphal laws of Edward the Confessor c. 37 (Lieberman, *Die Gesetze der Angelsachsen* i 668) treated usury as a crime—"*si aliquis inde probatus esset omnes possessiones suas perderet et pro ex lege haberetur.*"

12 Bk. vii 16—"*Usurarii vero omnes res, sive testatus sive intestatus decesserit, domini Regis sunt; vivus autem non solet aliquis de crimine usurae appellari nec convinci.... Si quis aliquo tempore usurarius fuerit in vita sua, et super hoc in patria publice defamatus; si tamen a delicto ipso ante mortem suam destiterit et penitentiam ejerit, post mortem ipsius ille vel res ejus lege usurarii minime censebuntur*"; cp. *Dialogus de Scaccario*, Stubbs, Sel. Ch. (6th ed.) 229.

13 At ff. 116b, 117.

by the censures of Holy Church for the sin, and to make restitution of the usuries taken against the laws of the Holy Church."[14]

As we might expect, the temptation to fall into this sin was felt most keenly in the great commercial towns. In 1363 the city of London, encouraged thereto by the king,[15] issued an ordinance against it; and in 1391 further provisions were made. [Pp. 101-102.]

. . . . .

At the latter part of the fifteenth and in the sixteenth centuries economic conditions were changing.[16] The growth of trade was making it clear that the traders could make a productive use of borrowed money, and that therefore a payment for the use of borrowed money might be advantageous both to the parties to the contract and to the state. The result was, not the repeal of the general prohibition of usury, but the growth of a large number of rules, which were designed to distinguish between those payments for the use of money which were usurious and illegal, from those which were permissible.

The basis of these rules was the distinction drawn, as early as the first half of the thirteenth century, between a mere payment for the use of money, and a payment made to compensate the lender for some loss actually occasioned by non-payment (*damnum emergens*), or for failure to realize some expected gain in consequence of his not having the money in hand (*lucrum cessans*).[17] A payment on account of *damnum emergens* was recognized as valid by Aquinas;[18] and, as opportunities for profitable investment increased, a payment on account of *lucrum cessans* gradually came to be regarded as lawful. Sir William Ashley says that in the fifteenth century its legality was generally accepted by the best theologians.[19] But it should be noted that the loss must actually be proved;[20] and it was necessary, that, in the first instance, the loan should have been gratuitous. Technically, the payment was made, not for the loan, but for non-payment of a gratuitous loan at the date promised.[21] Gradually, however, in the case of traders, the loss came to be presumed; and, with the shortening of the period of the gratuitous loan, the making of it gratuitously for a short period came to be a mere formality.[22] But this development did not take place till

---

[14] 15 Edward III. st. 1 c. 5.
[15] *Liber Albus* (R. S.) iii 142, 143; for the French text see *ibid* i 267, 268.
[16] Vol. iv 316-319.
[17] Ashley, *op. cit.*, i Pt. II. 399; Brissaud, *op. cit.* 1427.
[18] Ashley, *op. cit.* i Pt. II. 399.
[19] "Even some of the contemporaries of Aquinas among the canonists had held this opinion; so that during the following century, the fourteenth, it could hardly be regarded as distinctly under the ban of the Church; and in the fifteenth it was certainly very generally accepted by the best theologians," *ibid* 401.
[20] Straccha, *De Mercatura*, Pt. IV....
[21] Ashley, *op. cit.* i Pt. II. 401, 402.
[22] *Ibid* 402.

after the close of the mediaeval period; [23] and, by that time, the application of the strict mediaeval principle had been weakened by the manner in which this idea of compensation for loss had been applied to render legal many kinds of commercial contracts. [Pp. 103-104.]

. . . . .

If we look at these various methods by which in substance it had become possible to borrow money at interest; if we remember that many of the Italian states borrowed money and contracted to pay interest on their loans; that in many of the Italian commercial towns litigants were prohibited from invoking the aid of the laws against usury; that the Franciscans had in some of these states established, with the approval of the church, *montes pietatis*, or funds from which loans were made to the needy in return for a low rate of interest—we shall see that many inroads from many different sides had, at the close of the mediaeval period, been made on the general principle that all usury was sinful.

But the principle was still accepted. Usury was still denounced in the old terms; and those who wished to evade the law made use of various devices to cloak their real intentions. We shall see that when the legality of the contract of insurance was in doubt, recourse was had to the expedient of a sale and resale to cloak the real bargain; and that the machinery of the contract of exchange or cambium was largely used to effect the same object.[24] We are reminded of the various expedients which can be used at the present day to evade the laws which declare wagering contracts to be void. Such expedients are the best evidence of the existence of the general prohibition. But, it may be asked, why was it that this general prohibition was still maintained, seeing that the exceptions to, and the evasions of it, now covered so much ground? No doubt this was partly due to the authority of the church; but, as Sir William Ashley has pointed out, there was a substantial justification for this use of the church's authority. No doubt in the trading centres the modifications of the rule almost went to the length of repealing it; but the merchants were but a small fraction of the people who owned allegiance to and sought protection from the church. "By far the greater part of the population of Western Europe continued to be engaged

---

[23] *Ibid* 403; Malynes, *Lex Mercatoria* 243, clearly states the view of his own day on this matter—"A man may take a benefit for his money two manner of ways, which is *ex damno habito*, when he hath sustained a loss, or *ex lucro cessante*, when his benefit or profit hath been taken away or prevented for want of his money, which he might have bestowed in some wares to furnish his shop at convenient time, and in both these the party is not active but passive."

[24] Ashley, *op. cit.* i Pt. II. 426-427; cp. *Liber Albus* iii 147—a letter under the Privy Seal of 1366 says that, "many merchants and others dwelling in our city of London, colourably and subtly have made, and do make from day to day, divers exchanges of money and of other things that do not concern the dealings of lawful merchandise"; the practice under the name of "dry exchange" is alluded to in 3 Henry VII. c. 5; Tawney, *op. cit.* 73-74 . . .

in the old unchanging pursuits of agriculture: a declaration that payment could be taken for the loan of money would have meant the delivering them into the hands of the spoiler. The church, caring for the masses of the people, for the weak and stupid, might think it well to maintain a prohibition which imposed no restriction on the activity of the traders in the towns, who were well enough off to take care of themselves. The original prohibition had really aimed at preventing the oppression of the weak by the economically strong. The gradual exemption from the prohibition of methods of employing money which did not involve oppression, instead of obscuring the original principle, may be said to have brought it out more clearly." [25] [Pp. 106-107.]

．　　．　　．　　．　　．

But in Elizabeth's reign other counsels prevailed. Protestant opinion had wavered. Though Luther had supported the general prohibition, Melanchthon had seen that traders must be allowed to borrow at a moderate rate of interest; [26] and Calvin, though not perhaps prepared to go quite so far as Melanchthon, admitted that there might be circumstances in which the taking of interest was lawful.[27] Among both Protestants and Catholics, "the moral distinction was tending more and more to become one between excessive demand and moderate demand, rather than between gratuitous and non-gratuitous loan." [28] In 1571 [29] a statute was passed repealing the statute of Edward VI, and reviving that of Henry VIII. Usury was still

---

[25] Ashley, *op. cit.* i Pt. II. 438-439. These principles continued to be applied to the types of credit transactions entered into by peasants and small masters, Tawney, *op. cit.* 17-30 and by needy gentlemen, *ibid* 31-42; the former class of borrowers were protected till 1854 by the usury laws, and the latter class were also protected by the growth of the equitable doctrines as to mortgages, and as to catching bargains.

[26] *Ibid* 456-458.

[27] Among the conditions laid down by Calvin as justifying usury are the following;—"That usury should not be demanded from men in need; nor is it lawful to force any man to pay usury who is oppressed by need or calamity"; and that, "he who receives a loan on usury should make at least as much for himself by his labour and care as he obtains who gives the loan," cited *ibid* 459; as Mr. Tawney says, *op. cit.* III, Calvin approached the question from the standpoint of a man of affairs who assumed the existence of capital and credit, and wished to moralize the commercial institutions of his day; his "indulgence to moderate interest, like Adam Smith's individualism, was remembered when the qualifications surrounding it were forgotten," *ibid* 120.

[28] Ashley, *op. cit.* Pt. II. 451; cp. Grotius, *De jure belli et pacis* ii 12. 22 (cited Bl. Comm. ii 456)—"If the compensation allowed by law does not exceed the proportion of the hazard run, or the want felt, by the loan, it's allowance is neither repugnant to the revealed nor the natural law; but if it exceeds those bounds, it is then oppressive usury; and though municipal laws may give it impunity, they never can make it just."

[29] 13 Elizabeth c. 8, made perpetual 39 Elizabeth c. 18; for an attempt to legislate in this way in 1563, see Tawney, *op. cit.* 158; for some cases on the statute see Burton's Case (1592) 5 Co. Rep. 69a; Clayton's Case (1595) *ibid* 70a; cp. Cunningham, *op. cit.* ii 153, 154.

branded as a detestable sin punishable in the ecclesiastical courts; and in the temporal courts it was declared to be an offence which rendered those guilty of it liable to the penalties of a praemunire. But it was provided that no one should be liable to these punishments if the rate of interest did not exceed ten per cent.[30] [P. 109.]

.   .   .   .   .

An Act of Anne finally reduced the rate to 5 per cent; and this and subsequent Acts excepted certain transactions from the operation of the law. Subject to these modifications and exceptions, the scheme of the Elizabethan statute, supplemented by the rules of equity, was the basis upon which the law rested down to the repeal of the usury laws in 1854, under the influence of Bentham and the economists. When, in 1900, the Legislature saw fit to resume some control over the operations of moneylenders, it directed the courts to apply these equitable doctrines as to harsh and unconscionable dealings, when they were considering the question whether a borrower was entitled to relief.[31] By so doing it has again brought our modern law into touch with the policy which commended itself to the lawyers and statesmen of the sixteenth and seventeenth centuries, and with the elements of substantial truth and justice which underlay the mediaeval condemnation of usury. [P. 112.]

BENTHAM, THEORY OF LEGISLATION *

Chapter II. Title By Consent

It may happen that possessing a thing by a lawful title, we wish to dispossess ourselves of it, and to abandon its enjoyment to another. Shall such an arrangement be confirmed by the law? Doubtless it shall be. All the reasons which plead in favour of the old proprietor change sides with the transfer, and then plead in favour of the new one. Besides, the former proprietor must have had some motive for abandoning his property. *Motive* is *pleasure*, or equivalent; *pleasure of friendship* or of benevolence, if the thing was given for nothing; *pleasure of acquisition*, if it was a means of exchange; *pleasure of security*, if it was given to ward off some evil; *pleasure of reputation*, if the object was to acquire the esteem of others. It seems, then, that the transfer must increase the enjoyment of the parties interested in it. The acquirer stands in the place of the conferrer as to the

---

[30] That no distinction was drawn by the Act of Edward VI between different rates of interest was noted in 13 Elizabeth c. 8 as one of the reasons for repealing it.

[31] 63, 64 Victoria c. 51—The court must be satisfied (§1. 1) that "the transaction is harsh and unconscionable, or is otherwise such that a court of equity would give relief."

* ["Principles of the Civil Code," Part II (*Distribution of Property*). Dumont, ed., Hildreth, trans. (1864). Reprinted with introduction and notes by C. K. Ogden, London: Routledge and Kegan Paul, Ltd., 1931.]

old advantages, and the conferrer acquires a new advantage. We may then lay it down as a general maxim, that *every alienation imports advantage.* A good of some sort is always the result of it.

When the question is of an exchange, there are then two alienations, of which each has its separate advantages. The advantage for each of the contracting parties is, the difference to him between the value of the thing he gives, and that of the thing he acquires. In every transaction of this sort there are two new masses of enjoyment. In this the good of commerce consists.

In all the arts, there are many things which cannot be produced except by the concourse of a great number of workmen. In all these cases the labour of an individual would have no value, either for himself or for others, if it could not be exchanged.

II. Cases In Which Exchanges Should Be Invalid.—But there are cases in which the law ought not to sanction exchanges, and in which the interests of the parties ought to be regulated, as if the bargain had not taken place, because, instead of being advantageous, the exchange would be injurious to one of the parties, or to the public. We may arrange all the causes which invalidate exchanges under the nine following heads:

1. Concealment.
2. Fraud.
3. Coercion.
4. Subornation.
5. Erroneous idea of legal obligation.
6. Erroneous idea of value.
7. Incapacity.
8. Probable inconvenience to the public.
9. Want of right on the part of the conferrer. [Pp. 168-169.]

POUND, LIBERTY OF CONTRACT *

"The right of a person to sell his labor," says Mr. Justice Harlan, "upon such terms as he deems proper, is in its essence, the same as the right of the

---

* [The article on "Liberty of Contract" by *Roscoe Pound* (b. 1870), published in 18 *Yale L. J.* 454 (1909), represented one of the first and most powerful assaults on the extreme individualism underlying the cases which are noted and criticized in this essay. Most of these cases have since been over-ruled on the basis of the arguments here set forth. Other articles by Pound in a similar vein, criticizing the extreme individualism of American legal decisions during the half century from 1885 to 1935 are: "Common Law and Legislation" (1908) 21 *Harv. L. Rev.* 383 and "Mechanical Jurisprudence" (1908) 8 *Col. L. Rev.* 605. (See Chapters 7 and 8 *infra.*)

In the field of general jurisprudence Pound's most important studies are: "The Scope and Purpose of Sociological Jurisprudence" (1911–1912) 24 *Harv. L. Rev.* 591, 25 *Harv. L. Rev.* 140, 489; "Justice According to Law" (1913) 13 *Col. L. Rev.* 696, (1914) 14 *Col. L. Rev.* 1103; "The Limits of Effective Legal Action" (1917) 27 *Internat. Jour. of Ethics* 150; *The Spirit of the Common Law* (1921); *Introduction to the Philosophy of Law* (1922); *Interpretations of Legal History* (1923); "The

purchaser of labor to prescribe the conditions upon which he will accept such labor from the person offering to sell it. So the right of the employee to quit the service of the employer, for whatever reason, is the same as the right of the employer, for whatever reason, to dispense with the services of such employee. . . . In all such particulars the employer and the employee have equality of right, and any legislation that disturbs that equality is an arbitrary interference with the liberty of contract, which no government can legally justify in a free land." [1] With this positive declaration of a lawyer, the culmination of a line of decisions now nearly twenty-five years old, a statement which a recent writer on the science of jurisprudence has deemed so fundamental as to deserve quotation and exposition at an unusual length, as compared with his treatment of other points,[2] let us compare the equally positive statement of a sociologist.

"Much of the discussion about 'equal rights' is utterly hollow. All the ado made over the system of contract is surcharged with fallacy." [3]

To everyone acquainted at first hand with actual industrial conditions the latter statement goes without saying. Why, then, do courts persist in the fallacy? [P. 454.]

. . . . .

In my opinion, the causes to which we must attribute the course of American constitutional decisions upon liberty of contract are seven: (1) The currency in juristic thought of an individualist conception of justice, which exaggerates the importance of property and of contract, exaggerates private right at the expense of public right, and is hostile to legislation, taking a minimum of law-making to be the ideal; (2) what I have ventured to call on another occasion a condition of mechanical jurisprudence, a condition of juristic thought and judicial action in which deduction from conceptions has produced a cloud of rules that obscures the principles from which they were drawn, in which conceptions are developed logically at the expense of practical results and in which the artificiality characteristic of legal reasoning is exaggerated; (3) the survival of purely juristic notions of the state and of economics and politics as against the social conceptions of the present; (4) the train-

---

Theory of Judicial Decision" (1923) 36 *Harv. L. Rev.* 641, 802, 940; *Law and Morals* (1924); "The Call for a Realistic Jurisprudence" (1931) 44 *Harv. L. Rev.* 697.

Roscoe Pound has served in many public offices in addition to his long academic career, during which he has taught as professor of law at Northwestern and Chicago Universities, and as professor and dean at Nebraska and Harvard. Pound is considered the outstanding exponent of "sociological jurisprudence" in America.]

[1] Adair v. United States, 208 U.S. 161, 175.

[2] Taylor, *Science of Jurisprudence*, pp. 538-542.

[3] Ward, *Applied Sociology*, 281. See Wright, *Practical Sociology*, (5th Ed.) 226, Seager, *Introduction to Economics* (3rd Ed.), Sects. 234 ff. "For one who really understands the facts and forces involved, it is mere juggling with words and empty legal phrases." Ely, *Economic Theory and Labor Legislation*, 18.

ing of judges and lawyers in eighteenth century philosophy of law and the
pretended contempt for philosophy in law that keeps the legal profession
in the bonds of the philosophy of the past because it is to be found in law-
sheep bindings; (5) the circumstance that natural law is the theory of our
bills of rights and the impossibility of applying such a theory except when
all men are agreed in their moral and economic views and look to a single
authority to fix them; (6) the circumstance that our earlier labor legislation came before the public was prepared for it, so that the courts largely
voiced well-meant but unadvised protests of the old order against the new,
at a time when the public at large was by no means committed to the
new; [23] and (7) by no means least, the sharp line between law and fact in
our legal system which requires constitutionality, as a legal question, to be
tried by artificial criteria of general application and prevents effective judicial investigation or consideration of the situations of fact behind or bearing upon the statutes. [Pp. 457-458.]

.   .   .   .   .

The second cause, a condition of mechanical jurisprudence, I have discussed in its relation to the legal system generally in another place.[50] The
effect of all system is apt to be petrification of the subject systematized.
Legal science is not exempt from this tendency. Legal systems have their
periods in which system decays into technicality, in which a scientific jurisprudence becomes a mechanical jurisprudence. In a period of growth
through juristic speculation and judicial decision, there is little danger of
this.

But whenever such a period has come to an end, when its work has
been done and its legal theories have come to maturity, jurisprudence tends
to decay. Conceptions are fixed. The premises are no longer to be examined. Everything is reduced to simple deduction from them. Principles
cease to have importance. The law becomes a holy body of rules. This is
the condition Professor Henderson refers to when he speaks of the way of
social progress as barred by barricades of dead precedents.[51] Manifestations
of mechanical jurisprudence are conspicuous in the decisions as to liberty
of contract. A characteristic one is the rigorous logical deduction from
predetermined conceptions in disregard of and often in the teeth of the
actual facts, which was noted at the outset. Two courts, in passing on statutes abridging the power of free contract have noted the frequency of
such legislation in recent times, but have said that it was not necessary to
consider the reasons for it.[52] Another court has asked what right the legis-

---

[23] Professor Seager has made a similar suggestion. *Introduction to Economics*
(3rd Ed.), 417.
[50] "Mechanical Jurisprudence," 8 *Columbia Law Review*, 605.
[51] 11 *American Journal Sociology*, 847.
[52] See cases in note 48 *supra*. [Lowe v. Rees Printing Co., 41 Neb. 127, 135. State
v. Kreutzberg, 114 Wis. 530, 537.]

lature has to "*assume* that one class has the need of protection against another." [53] Another has said that the remedy for the company store evil "is in the hands of the employee," since he is not compelled to buy from the employer,[54] forgetting that there may be a compulsion in fact where there is none in law. Another says that "theoretically there is among our citizens no inferior class," [55] and, of course no facts can avail against that theory. Another tells us that man and woman have the same rights, and hence a woman must be allowed to contract to work as many hours a day as a man may.[56] We have already noted how Mr. Justice Harlan insists on a legal theory of equality of rights in the latest pronouncement of the Federal Supreme Court. Legislation designed to give laborers some measure of practical independence, which, if allowed to operate, would put them in a position of reasonable equality with their masters, is said by courts, because it infringes on a theoretical equality, to be insulting to their manhood [57] and degrading [58] to put them under guardianship,[59] to create a class of statutory laborers,[60] and to stamp them as imbeciles.[61] I know of nothing akin to this artificial reasoning in jurisprudence unless it be the explanation given by Pomponius for the transfer of legislative power from the Roman people during the Empire. "The *plebs* found, in course of time, that it was difficult for them to meet together, and the general body of the citizens, no doubt, found it more difficult still." [62] No doubt they did. Caesar or the praetorian prefect would have seen to that. [Pp. 462-464.]

.   .   .   .   .

---

[53] State v. Haun, 61 Kans. 146, 162.

[54] State v. Fire Creek Coal & Coke Co., 33 W.Va. 188, 190. Those who have studied the *actual* situation do not look at it in this way. "He is not free to make such a contract as might please him because, like every party to a contract, he must come to such conditions as can possibly be agreed upon. He is less free than the parties to most contracts, and, further, he cannot utilize his labor in many directions; he must contract for it within restricted lines." Wright, *Practical Sociology* (5th Ed.), 226.

[55] Frorer v. People, 141 Ill. 171, 186, holding against a statute prohibiting company stores and requiring miners to be paid weekly.

[56] Ritchie v. People, 155 Ill. 99, 111.

[57] Godcharles v. Wigeman, 113 Pa. St. 431, 437 (wages in iron mills to be paid in money).

[58] State v. Goodwill, 33 W.Va. 179, 186 (store orders).

[59] Braceville Coal Co. v. People, 147 Ill. 66, 74 (coal to be weighed for fixing wages); State v. Haun, 61 Kans. 146, 162 (wages to be paid in money).

[60] People v. Beck, 10 Misc. 77 (dissenting opinion of White, J.). The statute fixed hours of labor on municipal contracts.

[61] State v. Goodwill, *supra*; Frorer v. People, 141 Ill. 171, 187 (company stores).

[62] Dig. I, 2, 2, Sect. 9. Professor Seager says of these objections: "The opposition to such regulations...is based on the fear that they may serve to undermine the spirit of independence of the protected persons. Experience seems to indicate that they have in fact a directly contrary effect." *Introduction to Economics* (3rd ed.), 421. See also p. 423: "Those who advance it fail to consider that deadening and monotonous toil too long continued is much more inimical to the spirit of independence than any amount of legislation."

Turning now to the actual state of the decisions, let us look first at the cases in which the idea of liberty of contract has been invoked to defeat legislation. The fountain head of this line of decisions seems to be the opinion of Mr. Justice Field in *Butchers' Union Co. v. Crescent City Co.*,[81] in which he restates the views of the minority in the *Slaughter House Cases*.[82] This opinion has been one of the staple citations in causes involving liberty of contract.[83] In it he took a vigorous stand against legislative interference with the "right to follow lawful callings." Although it did not represent the views of the Federal Supreme Court, this opinion had a far-reaching influence in the State Courts. It produced a reactionary line of decisions in New York on liberty to pursue one's calling,[84] and through these cases its echoes are still ringing in the books. [P. 470.]

. . . . . .

In *Lochner v. New York*,[121] a bare majority of the Supreme Court of the United States took the reactionary view, as it had fairly become by this time, of a statute prescribing the hours of labor in bakeries. The view of the majority in this case, as usual, goes back to the restatement in the *Butchers' Union Company* case of the views of the minority in the *Slaughter House Cases*. Mr. Justice Peckham cites his own definition of liberty in *Allgeyer v. Louisiana*,[122] and that definition is admittedly based upon the views of Mr. Justice Field and Mr. Justice Bradley in the cases referred to. In the Allgeyer case he had said: "The liberty mentioned in that amendment means, not only the right of the citizen to be free from the mere physical restraint of his person, as by incarceration; but the term is deemed to embrace the right of the citizen to be free in the enjoyment of all his faculties; to be free to use them in all lawful ways; to live and work where he will; to earn his livelihood by any lawful calling; to pursue any livelihood or avocation, and for that purpose to enter into all contracts which may be proper, necessary and essential to his carrying out to a successful conclusion the purposes above mentioned."

One may grant this definition and yet deny the consequence which Mr. Justice Peckham derived from it in the Lochner case. His position was, in effect, that a baker had a constitutional right to contract to work as long as he pleased. He says (p. 57):

---

[81] 3 U.S. 746, 762.

[82] 16 Wall. 36.

[83] Cited and relied on particularly in State v. Goodwill, 33 W.Va. 179, 183, and, through this case and the New York cases, in nearly all the later decisions. It is interesting to note that the Supreme Court of Illinois, at least, has fallen into a settled practice of citing the opinion of the minority in the *Slaughter House Cases* as if it were that of the court.

[84] Matter of Jacobs, 98 N.Y. 98; People v. Marx, 99 N.Y. 377.

[121] (1905) 198 U.S. 45.

[122] 165 U.S. 578.

There is no contention that bakers as a class are not equal in intelligence and capacity to men in other trades or manual occupations, or that they are not able to assert their rights and care for themselves without the protecting arm of the State, interfering with their independence of judgment and of action. They are in no sense wards of the State. Viewed in the light of a purely labor law, with no reference whatever to the question of health, we think that a law like the one before us involves neither the safety, the morals nor the welfare of the public, and that the interest of the public is not in the slightest degree affected by such an act. The law must be upheld, if at all, as a law pertaining to the health of the individual engaged in the occupation of a baker. It does not affect any other portion of the public than those who are engaged in that occupation. Clean and wholesome bread does not depend upon whether the baker works but ten hours per day or only sixty hours a week.

It will be seen that this opinion assumes two propositions of fact: (1) That the public has no concern in how long a baker works, because the time he works has no effect on the product of his labor; (2) that there is nothing in the trade of baking, as carried on in large cities, inimical to the health of those who are employed in it for long hours at a stretch. Here again study of the facts has shown that the legislature was right and the court was wrong. Actual investigation has shown that the output of shops in which the only kind of men who can be had to work for unreasonable hours under unsanitary conditions are employed, is not at all what the public ought to eat, and that long hours in shops of the sort are distinctly injurious to health.[123] But the decisive objection to the position of the majority is put by Mr. Justice Holmes in a few sentences that deserve to become classical:

This case is decided upon an economic theory which a large part of the country does not entertain. If it were a question whether I agreed with that theory, I should desire to study it further and long before making up my mind. But I do not conceive that to be my duty because I strongly believe that *my agreement or disagreement has nothing to do with the right of a majority to embody their opinions in law....The fourteenth Amendment does not enact Mr. Herbert Spencer's Social Statics....A constitution is not intended to embody a particular economic theory*, whether of paternalism and the organic relation of the citizen to the State or of *laissez-faire....*

Finally, we have two cases, one in the Court of Appeals of New York,[124] and the other, the Adair case, in the Supreme Court of the United States,[125] in which the doctrine of the Julow case is adopted and legislation to pre-

---

[123] *City Club Bulletin,* Chicago, Vol. 2, No. 25 (Feb. 24, 1909). See also the authorities cited in the dissenting opinion of Harlan, J., pp. 70–71. Sir Frederick Pollock makes this very pertinent comment: "How can the Supreme Court at Washington have conclusive judicial knowledge of the conditions affecting bakeries in New York? If it has not such knowledge as matter of fact, can it be matter of law that no conditions can reasonably be supposed to exist which would make such an enactment...constitutional?" 21 *Law Quarterly Review,* 212.

[124] People v. Marcus (1906) 185 N.Y. 257.

[125] (1908) 208 U.S. 161.

vent employers from prohibiting employees from joining or requiring them to withdraw from labor unions is held unconstitutional, as infringing liberty of contract. In the former case, the court puts the matter thus:

The free and untrammeled right to contract is part of the liberty guaranteed to every citizen by the Federal and State Constitutions. Personal liberty is always subject to restraint when its exercise affects the safety, health or moral and general welfare of the public, but subject to such restraint, an employer and employee may make and enforce such contract relating to labor as they may agree on. (p. 255.)

In other words, the public have no interest in bringing about a real equality in labor-bargainings, even though thereby strikes and disorders may be obviated, and have no concern with contracts for labor except where the safety, health or morals of the public at large may be concerned! This is practically the position from which we found the courts starting twenty years before. [Pp. 479-481.]

. . . . .

Some of the statutes passed upon in the foregoing cases may have gone too far. Some of them involved bad or careless classifications. Some of them ran counter to local constitutional provisions, requiring general laws whenever possible. But one cannot read the cases in detail without feeling that the great majority of the decisions are simply wrong, not only in constitutional law, but from the standpoint of the common law, and even from that of a sane individualism. Looking at them upon common law principles, we must first of all recognize that there never has been at common law any such freedom of contract as they postulate. From the time that promises not under seal have been enforced at all, equity has interfered with contracts in the interests of weak, necessitous, or unfortunate promisors. One of the earliest cases of equitable interference was to prevent forfeitures to which promisors had agreed solemnly under seal. Not only did equity grant to a debtor a right of redemption for which he did not stipulate, but it would not and will not let him contract it away in advance or "clog" it by a collateral agreement that will operate to prevent a redemption.[126] In like manner, equity interfered to set aside contracts of sailors for the disposition of their wages or of prize money due them, where they appeared unfair, one-sided or inequitable.[127] It interfered also with contracts of heirs or reversioners in case of inadequacy of consideration, on the theory that they were peculiarly liable to be imposed on and subject to the danger of "sac-

---

[126] "A man will not be suffered in conscience to fetter himself with a limitation or restriction of his right of redemption." Lord Keeper Henley in Spurgeon v. Collier, I Eden 56, 59. "I take it to be an established rule that the mortgagee can never provide at the time of making the loan for any condition or event on which the equity of redemption shall be discharged and the conveyance absolute." Lord Northington in Vernon v. Bethell, 2 Eden 110, 113. See Rice v. Noakes (1900), 2 Ch. 445; Jarrah Timber, etc., Corporation v. Samuel (1903), 2 Ch. 1.

rificing their future interests in order to meet their present wants." [128] It refused and refuses to grant specific performance of hard bargains, simply because they are hard, leaving promisees to confessedly inadequate and nugatory actions for damages. ... It has been said that the common law will not help a fool. But equity exists to help and protect him. It is because there are fools to be defrauded and imposed upon, and unfortunates to meet with accidents and careless to make mistakes, that we have courts of equity. Surely what equity has done to abridge freedom of contract, legislation may do likewise.

Moreover, usury laws, despite all that has been said to the contrary, furnish a perfect analogy. ...

Rightly considered, even individualist and natural law principles lead to the same conclusion. The authorities are agreed upon the "natural" invalidity of a contract to become a slave.[132] But, as Sidgwick points out, any "serious approximation to the condition of slavery" comes to the same thing.[133] Mill, much more liberal than his followers, admits this, saying:

> Not only persons are not held to engagements which violate the rights of third parties, but it is sometimes considered a sufficient reason for releasing them from an engagement that is injurious to themselves.

Some of the writers on natural law had argued that there were cases where natural law justified sale of oneself into slavery. To this Mill says:

> He therefore defeats, in his own case, the very purpose which is the justification of allowing him to dispose of himself.[134]

The principle of this applies to any situation where a person by contract imposes substantial restraints upon his liberty. Freedom to impose these restraints, in the hands of the weak and necessitous, defeats the very end of liberty.[135] Liberty and equality *in fact* make for a rational individualism. Academic individualism defeats itself. [Pp. 478-484.]

ELY, PROPERTY AND CONTRACT IN THEIR RELATIONS TO THE DISTRIBUTION OF WEALTH *

Chapter V. Criticism of the Individualistic Theory of Contract and the Social Theory of Contract

. . . . .

B. *The Social Theory of Contract*

In opposition to the individualistic theory of contract, we place what we designate as the *social theory of contract: contract is established and main-*

---

[132] Spencer, *Justice* Sect. 70 "The Principle of freedom cannot require that he should be free not to be free. *It is not freedom to be allowed to alienate his freedom.*" Mill, *Liberty*, Chap. V.

[133] *Elements of Politics* (2nd Ed.), 93.

[134] *Liberty*, Chap. V.

[135] See a case in point in Dicey, *Law and Public Opinion in England*, 264-265.

* [Vol. II. New York: The Macmillan Company, 1914.]

tained for social purposes. All contracts find their logical origin in the social welfare and in this they find the grounds for their maintenance.[18] This theory of contract is analogous to the social theory of property. We may say in fact it is substantially the same thing if we take the view of American courts that the right to contract is a property right.* ...

Contract finds its limitations in the social welfare, and as time goes on less and less hesitation is felt in drawing the line beyond which contract must not go. With increasing frequency our legislatures and our courts establish metes and bounds of contract. Story says in his work on *Law of Contracts:* [19]

> The rule of law, applicable to this class of cases, is, that all agreements which contravene the public policy are void, whether they be in violation of law or of morals, or tend to interfere with those artificial rules which are supposed by the law to be beneficial to the interests of society, or obstruct the prospective objects flowing indirectly from some positive legal injunction or prohibition.

Nevertheless, on account of false ideas of freedom, courts are less advanced in recognising the social theory of contract than in recognising the social theory of property. The ideas of the judges are more rigid when it comes to the social control of contract. They allow the constitutionality of laws which impose a real burden on property but at times set aside laws which regulate contract as to hours of labour, the means of payments, etc. as shown elsewhere in the present work, although these laws impose slight burdens and often in the end, when allowed, promote the welfare of all, employer, employee and society at large. ...

The rapid progress even American courts are making in the recognition of the social theory of contract is illustrated by their treatment of assumption of risk as a defence where negligence is a breach of statutory duty. If a statute imposes a duty to provide safety appliances and makes the employer who fails to do so criminally liable, he cannot contract out of his liability.[22] ... But the chief point for the economist and the sociologist is that the courts recognize that society has the dominant interest; and thus they work away from that individualism which has done so much harm in the past. In conclusion it is not possible to do better than to quote from an excellent note on this subject which appeared in a recent issue of the *Harvard Law Review:*

---

[18] Mr. Justice Holmes has repeatedly pointed out that the historic origin of contract is to be found in different specific cases which would have led to different theories and between which there was a struggle for life. See 12 *Harvard Law Review*, pp. 447-449, 1899; 25 (Eng.) *Law Quarterly Review*, p. 413, 1909.

* [Cf. *Pound's* point that promises form the substance of modern wealth, *supra.*]

[19] Story, *Law of Contracts* (5th ed. by Melville M. Bigelow, 2 vols. Boston, 1874), Vol. 1, p. 649, § 674.

[22] Fitzwater v. Warren, 206 N.Y. 355 (1912).

If the right of the individual to recover involves only his personal interest he may consent to give it up. But if society has an interest in the right then the consent of the individual cannot destroy the right. Thus a householder cannot waive his exemption because of the social interest that he and his family be not reduced to poverty. An insurance company cannot waive a lack of insurable interest because of the danger to society in tempting the beneficiary to destroy the life or chattel in which he has no interest. The importance which the doctrine of assumption of risk acquired in the nineteeth century is an example of the individualistic theory of justice on which the common law of that period proceeded, allowing each man to work out his own salvation. But statutes prescribing criminal liability for failing to guard machinery are enacted to protect the interest which society has that its members be not maimed. The principal case, in overruling an earlier New York decision construing the same statute, illustrates the increasing inclination of the courts to-day to recognize this interest of society. The employee's consent by an assumption of the risk to give up a right involving such an interest should not be effective whether such consent be worked out contractually or otherwise.[23] [Pp. 615-618.]

Chapter VI. Contracts for Personal Services with Special Reference to the Labour Contract

·   ·   ·   ·   ·

Certain peculiar characteristics of labour manifest themselves in labour contracts and should be taken into account in legal decisions concerning these. Labour is inseparably connected with the personality of the worker; and from this condition spring the peculiar characteristics which we have just mentioned. The workman must give himself when he gives his work. Thus there is a great difference between labour and, let us say, wheat as a commodity. Wheat is sent from buyer to seller, but the man who sells the labour of his hands cannot dispose of this apart from himself.

This connection of labour power with the labourer gives the purchaser "power over vital functions which he does not buy." [3] The fact that the function of working is bound up with the rest of a human personality gives the purchaser control over other parts of the worker's life than those which he has directly bought. Mrs. Sidney Webb has said: "The wage-earner does not, like the shopkeeper, merely sell a piece of goods which is carried away; it is his whole life which, for the stated sum, he places at the disposal of his employer. What hours he shall work, when and where he shall get his meals, the sanitary conditions of his employment, the safety of the machinery and temperature to which he is subjected, the fatigues or strains which he endures, the risks of accident or disease which he has to incur,—all these are matters no less important to the workman than his wages. Yet about the majority of these vital conditions he cannot bargain at all." [4] Hobson adds to this statement, "The necrosis of

---

[3] Mrs. Sidney Webb, *Commonwealth*, February, 1896.

[4] Quoted by Hobson, *Economics of Distribution*, pp. 220–1.

the phosphorus match maker and the phthisis of the Belfast linen spinner are not part of any bargain and are not paid for."

Another consequence of this inseparable connection between labour power and the labourer is that, as the worker must sell his work where he happens to be, the employer at times attempts to prevent him from leaving one place in order that he may try to make a more advantageous bargain elsewhere. This was perhaps most systematically done by the English Poor Law under the Law of Settlement, which made it impossible for a workman to move into another parish unless he could give a guarantee that for a year and a day he would not be a burden on the poor rates. If he were unable to do so he was obliged to remain in the parish where his settlement was. Adam Smith said that there was hardly a workman in all England who had not suffered from this law.[5]

When labour power is bought and sold, the seller is generally weaker than the buyer. There are many reasons why this is so. In most cases the purchaser of labour power has relatively large resources, and the sale is more pressing than the purchase. Compare this with the sale of land or of goods. It is possible, and sometimes even desirable, to hold back land or goods for longer or shorter periods—sometimes even for years—but a man who offers labour for sale generally depends for his immediate subsistence upon the sale of that labour. A man who offers land has, in addition to this, his labour power. The labourer must sell his power of working; if he cannot get work, he will soon starve. But the man who owns land may withhold it from sale and make a living by working on it.[6] "This labour power," says Hobson, "must be sold continuously; it must be sold in small quantities, commonly measured by the day or by the week; finally it must be sold to a buyer who knows the necessity under which the seller stands to effect a sale. In a word, the labourer is selling his labour power under the conditions of a forced sale."[7] The inferiority of the seller is such that the buyer is usually able to dispense with "higgling" or bargaining. He fixes the price, and the seller has only the alternative of accepting or refusing outright. An employer knows that for every single job he has to offer, several applicants will frequently be found; whereas an employee does not even in prosperous times meet with several competitors for his labour.

When an employer has many employees, it is generally of small importance to him whether he gets a particular labourer or not; and this holds good more particularly with regard to tasks which require little or no special skill, so that a man who falls out can easily be replaced. On the other hand, it is much more frequently of the highest importance to a labourer, whether or not he gets a particular job.

---

[6] Modifications of this general statement must be made in case of pressing indebtedness and of need generally.

[7] Hobson *op. cit.*, pp. 218-9. The rest of the paragraph follows Hobson closely.

As the demand for labour decreases, the supply may increase. This happens because, when wages fall and employment slackens, the wives and children of the workers try to earn something in order to keep the home together. In such times of stagnation, when the demand for labour is falling off, each class of workers receives accessions from the class immediately above: on the other hand, when the demand for labour begins to grow stronger, the good effect of this is not always felt at once, because in many countries there is a reserve army of unemployed and wages will in many cases not begin to rise until these men have all been supplied with work.

It is also possible, unless this is prevented by legislation or otherwise, for an employer to withhold wages in order to promote dependence. Akin to this is the truck system of payment in kind, which is so obviously bad from the worker's point of view that in many countries it is forbidden by law.

A workman's associates are chosen for him. This plainly shows the influence of the employer over the intellectual and moral, sometimes even the religious life of his employees. It may be held a criminal act for a man to say he will not work with another. Blacklisting and the ironclad oath illustrate the inferiority of the worker in the labour bargain, for nothing like an ironclad contract has ever yet been forced upon an employer by employees. Workmen have rarely been in such a position that they could say to their employers, "We will not work with you unless you give up your membership in the federation of railways," etc.[8]

Again, the cumulative effect of a series of bad bargains may be noticed. One bad bargain in the labour market weakens the position of the worker and is apt to lead to others.

Adam Smith stated long ago that one reason why the labourer is at a disadvantage, in comparison with the employer, is that employers tacitly or openly combine together to keep down wages, whereas labourers compete with each other when unorganised. While the employer is to this extent exalted above the sphere of competition, even the comparatively well-off among the working class are affected by the competition of those who sell their labour under the direct pressure of necessity. Thus the necessities of the poor influence those who have resources.... [Pp. 627-631.]

Chapter VIII. Facts as to Impairment of Liberty. Deprivation of Property and Possibility of Individual Regulation of Contract as Opposed to Class Regulation. Law versus Trade Unions for Class Regulation

There can be little doubt as to the facts concerning the impairment of liberty under individualistic contract. Preceding chapters have made this clear. It is said we must not deprive the workman of his liberty to work in factories on Sunday. But that is not liberty. No workmen desire long hours and payment in kind: the claim that they desire this is either sophistry or claptrap. It is said that their liberty is impaired because they cannot contract to work thirty-six hours in succession nor to take payment in goods over the quality and price of which they have no adequate control; but they do not desire these evils if the evils can be obviated; and in collective action we find at least a partial remedy. All this is clearly illustrated by a quotation from an article by Professor John R. Commons concerning a decision of the Supreme Court of Illinois on the eight hour day for working women (*Ritchie v. People*, 155 Ill. 98 (1895), which has since then been reversed in *Ritchie & Co. v. Wayman*, 224 Ill. 509 in 1910—only five years later).

"The Supreme Court of Illinois has declared unconstitutional the factory and sweat shop act limiting the working day for women to eight hours. . . .

". . . Speaking of the decision the *Chicago Times-Herald* says:

"There is a ghastly sort of irony in the attempt of the supreme court to explain or excuse its decision upon the plea that it is protecting the rights of weak individuals with labor to sell. Of course, a judicial tribunal cannot be expected to take cognizance of the facts that working people, in so far as they are represented by labour organizations and earnest but unofficial friends of the laboring classes, urged the enactment of the law, and that millionaire firms attacked its constitutionality. . . . Dives demands protection. The court accedes to his demand, but pleads that it acts in the interests of Lazarus." [1]

If the court had not made the decision on the ground that they were trying to protect the freedom of the workingmen it would have been another matter. But especially irritating was the claim of the judges that they were carrying out the wishes and desires of the wage-earning class when they were really carrying out the schemes of the big firms behind them who had put up their money to defeat the few. [2] [Pp. 651-653.]

---

[1] By J. R. Commons in *The Kingdom*, April 12, 1895.

[2] Schmoller makes the point that the old labour contracts preceding the so-called freedom of labour contract were arranged in accordance with custom and law in certain fixed types; that is to say, the contracts were class contracts. This was the case, for example, with journeymen, with household servants, and with mine laborers. It was determined what payment they should receive, both in kind and in money, also what shares of profit they should receive, if any. It was thus determined when and how the work should be done, what free time the labourers should have, whether or not they should work on Sunday, etc. The labour conditions were regulated for the entire course of the labourer's life in accordance with economic conditions of production on the one hand, and on the other in accordance with certain moral and legal points of view corresponding to the needs of the family life, etc. Later it was thought that all limitations upon labour contracts should be removed and that each one should make his own individual contract. This was the eighteenth century philosophy. Schmoller also points out the fact that the so-called free labour contract may indicate deterioration in condition for the indolent and backward

GELLHORN, CONTRACTS AND PUBLIC POLICY *

.   .   .   .   .

From early times Anglo-American courts have refused to enforce illegal contracts, that is, those that are "opposed to public policy." As a rule, no substantial distinctions were made by the courts among situations where the contract bore an element of criminality, where the contract might prove to be a step in the commission of the crime (either by way of making its commission possible or by way of enjoying its fruits), and where the contract was merely shocking to the sense of justice and of the fitness of things. In each instance the judges, as representing the community conscience, declared that such contracts should not be executed with the court's assistance, because to assist in their enforcement would be to encourage conduct which was inimical to the public welfare. Until a relatively recent day, be it noted, too, criminal conduct was by definition largely limited to the common law crimes; the full bloom of penal statutes describing new offenses had not yet been attained,[2] and the courts were themselves largely the moulders of thought concerning what was criminal.[3]

When the simplicity of the law-making structure passed, however, and when judges were at least nominally relegated to the role of interstitialists, a web of complexity was cast over what had before seemed to be the easy application of a corollary rule. Now the legislature was the authoritative denouncer of conduct. Now the statutes, rather than judges' opinions, determined what acts were to be regarded as antisocial, that is, against public policy. And now the lawmakers, with a wide range of choice

---

labourers, for the immature (those who are not adults), and for women and children; that is, as compared with the former status. (Notes from the lectures of Professor Gustav Schmoller). But Schmoller has shown that even now the individual contract in labour relations plays a far smaller role than we are apt to think. Contracts are made for groups; they become type-contracts rather than individual contracts, and not only are substantially the same for great groups and classes, but they are increasingly regulated by social forces, including legislation and administration. This is clearly brought out in Schmoller's *Grundriss der allgemeinen Volkswirtschaftslehre* (1st ed., Pt. II, Bk. III, § § 205-208, pp. 268-292).

* [35 *Col. L. Rev.* 679 (1935).

Walter Gellhorn (b. 1906) is author of *Cases and Comments—Administrative Law* (2d ed. 1947) and of *Security, Loyalty and Science* (1950), and editor of several monographs on administrative procedure. He is now professor at Columbia Law School.]

[2] See R. Pound, *Criminal Justice in America* (1930) 15-20.

[3] Even today, when penal laws are codified, there are large areas in which judicial innovation is still contemplated. See, *e.g.,* N.Y. Penal Law (1909) § 43: "A person who wilfully and wrongfully commits any act which serious'y disturbs or endangers the public peace or health, or which openly outrages public decency, for which no other punishment is expressly prescribed by this chapter, is guilty of a misdemeanor;..." *Cf.* People v. Knapp, 206 N.Y. 373, 99 N.E. 841 (1912).

before them, could select the penalties they thought best suited to the proscribed conduct, and, by a generalization, lay down the rule to guide the judiciary in making appropriate disposition of the particular case that might later arise. Acts thought to be undesirable could be discouraged or desired results could be achieved (among other ways) by altering procedural rules,[4] by creating a tort liability [5] or by removing or establishing defenses against such a liability,[6] by imposing taxes,[7] by conditioning the enjoyment of a privilege upon the surrender of some other privilege or upon the performance of an affirmative act, by withdrawing the protection of legal process in the enforcement of claims, by various money impositions, by penalties in the form of fine and imprisonment or both, or by a combination of two or more of these methods.

But when the legislature selected only one sanction to enforce compliance with what it regarded as the public interest, the courts at once came face to face with the problem whether the selection of one negatived the desirability of also utilizing another. [Pp. 679-680.]

.   .   .   .   .

The judicial plowing of the soil in this field has led to the growth of patent inanities. Because a contract is part of an illegal transaction is no reason for disregarding its existence [25] or for declining to weigh the consequences of holding it to be void.[26] Nor should a court's disposition of a

---

[4] *E.g.*, changes in the law governing issuance of injunctions in labor disputes [Norris-La Guardia Act, 47 Stat. 70-73 (1932), 29 U.S.C.A. § § 101-115 (1933); N.Y.C.P.A. § 876-a, added by N.Y. Laws 1935, c. 477].

[5] *E.g.*, erection of a cause of action for invasion of the right of privacy [N.Y. Civil Rights Law (1909) Art. 5, § § 50-51].

[6] *E.g.*, the elimination of the fellow servant doctrine by the various employers' liability acts which preceded, and which have in some instances survived, the general adoption of workmen's compensation legislation; statutes exempting automobile drivers from liability to gratuitous guests [Conn. Gen. Stat. (1930) § 1628; The Liability of the Driver to His Gratuitous Guest (1932) 18 *Iowa L. Rev.* 78].

[7] *E.g.*, Wash. Gen. Stat. (Remington, 1932) § 8358-2, levying a tax of fifteen cents per pound on all butter substitutes sold within the state.

[25] *Cf.* People v. Steurnthal, 154 Misc. 130, 276 N.Y. Supp. 689 (Mag. Ct. 1935), holding that the failure of a stakeholder, who had lost a bet, to return the money deposited with him constituted larceny, though the bet was unquestionably illegal.

[26] It would of course be unfair to say that courts always fail to balance the considerations involved in treating an "illegal" contract. See, *e.g.*, Rideout v. Mars, 99 Miss. 199, 54 So. 801 (1911) (the contract there in question, relating to a rebate of an insurance premium, was affected by a prohibitory statute enforced by a one year revocation of license to do business); Duval v. Wellman, 124 N.Y. 156, 26 N.E. 343 (1891) (the contract related to marriage brokerage and was therefore, according to established non-statutory precedents, "void as against public policy"). On the other hand, the countenancing of shocking immorality is seen in some of the decisions. In Levy v. Kansas City, Kan., 168 Fed. 524 (C.C.A. 8th, 1909), the plaintiff sued to recover $5000 he had paid pursuant to an ordinance authorizing the licensing, upon payment of that sum, of the business of book making and pool selling. A state statute prohibited that business. Two days after plaintiff commenced business, he alleged, the city was instigated and induced by those who were conducting a rival

contract be dependent solely upon whether it purports to find the presence or absence of a purely imaginary legislative intent that a given result be reached.

To inject a rational basis of decision it is necessary to sweep aside the cliches and pseudo-scientific measures which now customarily accompany examination of the question whether courts should enforce contracts in this category. Some courts have already frankly reverted to the old position. They have refused to lend their aid to contracts which they deemed to be contrary to public policy. They have exercised their inherent power to avoid permitting their process to be used for antisocial ends—exercised this power not because legislatively directed to do so in a particular case, but because, in their own discretion, they deemed such an exercise necessary as a protection of the public welfare against noxious consequences.[27]

But the discarding of the present juggling with a nonexistent statutory intent must not carry with it the discarding of judicial dependence on the legislative judgment. Statutes denouncing conduct as criminal must continue to be, as they now are, the starting point of the judges' excursions into territory uncharted.

What does or does not represent the general interest is for the legislature to determine. Equipped to make factual investigations, constituted so that in greater or lesser degree it is responsive to the judgments and desires of that balance of interests known as the general public, the legislature must today be regarded as the court of last resort in resolving the clamorous claims for one policy or another. Less and less, even in the disposition of constitutional questions, do the courts seek to substitute for the legislative judgment their own convictions concerning what is wisdom.[28] With diminishing frequency does the student find contemporary counterparts of the frank declaration that "the paternalistic theory of government is to me odious. The utmost liberty to the individual... is both the limitation and duty of government," with which comment Justice Brewer once sought to justify his conclusion that a regulatory statute was unconstitutional.[29] Indulgence in subjectivism does still on occasion convert the United States Supreme Court into a super-legislature. But the occasions

business to revoke his license and thus to prevent him from carrying on his illegal business. Recovery of the $5000 was denied, the court being of opinion that the controlling issue was the righteousness of the plaintiff's acts; "those of the defendant have little materiality," though they were characterized as "despicable" and "abhorrent to the sense of fairness."

[27] Cf. Fidelity & Deposit Co. of Maryland v. Grand Nat. Bank, 2 F. Supp. 666, 668 (E.D.Mo. 1933): "The question of how close illegality must be woven into a transaction in order to taint it is often difficult to determine. The principle to be applied is one of general public policy, and the inquiry is not alone as to the effect of a particular transaction, but whether its tendency is in the direction of public detriment."

[28] Cf. R. A. Brown, Due Process of Law, Police Power, and the Supreme Court (1927) 40 Harv. L. Rev. 943.

[29] Dissenting in Budd v. New York, 143 U.S. 517, 551 (1892).

are happily becoming less numerous. In the complexities of modern life, prejudice and presupposition may no longer be permitted to guide constitutional judgments.[30] The former embarrassing confusions of functions is abating. In the usually less controversial matters which are the subjects of penal statutes [31] there is still smaller reason, or tendency, for the courts to question the definitiveness of the legislative conclusion that what has been proscribed is in fact something which, if not impeded, would operate to the public detriment. In short, every definition of a crime contains an implicit declaration that the results of the prohibited conduct are "against public policy," and there is no justification for the courts' hesitating (and slight disposition on their part to hesitate) in accepting that declaration as an appraisal conclusive for the moment, of what is in fact "against public policy."

Having accepted these determinations as embodying the value judgments they were themselves wont to make an earlier day, the courts must now be prepared to utilize them in weighing the question whether they will aid in enforcing contracts which, while not expressly banned by the legislature, have some tendency to bring about the results which have been officially stigmatized as undesirable. The penal statutes thus become significant not as controlling the disposition of a civil case, but as enlightening the judiciary concerning specific "public policies." [Pp. 684-686.]

. . . . .

This approach, if utilized by the courts, lends added significance to non-penal statutes which contain indications of what are "public policies." It also makes available in the decision of cases the statutes of states other than the state of jurisdiction. Where they employ this method of attack, the courts will refuse to enforce a contract not "because it is illegal" or because the legislature "intended that a person making such a contract should be punished," but because they have satisfied themselves that, in the light of what has been indicated to them by legislative bodies, at home or abroad, the contract is against public policy. Criminality is not a requisite element; punishment (in the sense of retribution for undesirable conduct) is not a primary purpose. No novelty is involved in a refusal to

---

[30] See, e.g. Borden's Farm Products Co. v. Baldwin, 293 U.S. 194, 210 (1934): "With the notable expansion of the scope of governmental regulation, and the consequent assertion of violation of constitutional rights, it is increasingly important that when it becomes necessary for the Court to deal with the facts relating to particular commercial or industrial conditions, they should be presented concretely with appropriate determinations upon evidence, so that conclusions shall not be reached without factual support."

[31] That is, "usually less controversial" in the sense that they do not typically evoke debate concerning basic economic and social theory; disagreement is constant as to the means, but the ends are customarily not in dispute.

enforce a contract which relieves against liability for negligence or which involves the commission of a tort, even though no statute requires that result. Similarly, the courts should frown upon contracts which, though not touching a penal statute, involve other conduct which has been inveighed against by the legislature. What is suggested is not an extension of the scope of judicial disapprobation of contracts, for at all times the courts have freely declared that non-criminal agreements might be against public policy and consequently unenforcible.[46] What is urged is, again, merely that legislative judgments should be used as indicators of the occasion for employment of the common law rule governing the validity of contracts. . . .

Similarly, where legislative materials are used as sources of information and as analogies, there need be no direct connection in terms between statutes and the contract under judicial consideration. James M. Landis, in addressing the Association of American Law Schools in 1934, suggested that the courts should with hesitancy enforce "yellow-dog contracts." In 1917, in the *Hitchman* case,[47] the Supreme Court thought that, as a matter of public policy, such contracts warranted judicial protection. But in 1930, the Senate, after thorough consideration, rejected the nomination of Judge John J. Parker to sit on the Supreme Court, largely because he had followed and applied the *Hitchman* case.[48] Later, when Congress adopted the Norris-La Guardia Act, not a single voice was raised in defense of yellow-dog contracts as such; even the opponents of the measure did not argue that such agreements deserved protection. In the event of a suit to enforce such a contract or to recover damages from one who induced its violation, these matters should be worthy of a court's consideration as important legal facts. They are more significant than prior inexpert judicial pronouncements that such contracts are not against public policy, and hence must be honored.

Again, the statutes of other jurisdictions may be useful as informing the court of considerations which it might otherwise ignore. In other fields the judges have shown more and more liberality in employing the laws of other states as aids in reaching sound results in cases not controlled

---

[46] See, *e.g.*, discussion in Diamond Match Co. v. Roeber, 106 N.Y. 473, 479 *et seq.*, 13 N.E. 419, 420 (1887). And see Holland v. Sheehan, 108 Minn. 362, 367, 122 N.W. 1, 3 (1909): "We are not required to look exclusively to statutory enactments in determining questions of public policy. Constitutions and statutes are evidence of the general policy of a state; but when confronted with questions of general public policy, as defined in the books, the courts go beyond express legislation and look to the whole body of the law—statutory, common, and judicial decisions. Public policy requires of courts of equity protection from unjust and unconscionable bargains, though no statutory authority be granted by legislation." See also Reiner v. North American Newspaper Alliance, 259 N.Y. 250, 181 N.E. 561 (1932).

[47] Hitchman Coal & Coke Co. v. Mitchell, 245 U.S. 229 (1917).

[48] In International Organization, U.M.W.A. v. Red Jacket Consolidated Coal & Coke Co., 18 F. (2d) 839 (C.C.A. 4th, 1927).

by any statute operative in the forum.[49] So long as its own legislature has not clearly directed a court to enforce or to ignore contracts of a given nature, the court is free to decide for itself whether or not such contracts are against public policy. It is clear that of most weight would be local statutes having some bearing upon the subject matter of the contract. But where such statutes are lacking, there is no reason why the scope of the search for information should not be widened to include examination of pertinent conclusions in other jurisdictions. Utilizations of judicial opinions are not uncommon and are accepted as an appropriate aid in making similar determinations,[50] legislative opinions upon the same matters should be employed with, if anything, more confidence in their helpfulness.

The method here urged warrants employment by the courts of administrative pronouncements, which are suggestive indications of what is "public policy." When a legislature has delegated to a body of experts the task of formulating rules for public guidance, those rules merit the dignity of being deemed authoritative and informed judgments upon the issues at stake. To be sure, unlike statutes, they are infrequently generally known or widely available for study by the public.[51] But this circumstance, while it may clearly be significant in particular cases, should not operate to induce disregard by the courts of this rich mine of information.[52] Again, the question is not whether a party to a contract deserves to be punished because he entered into the contract, but it is whether the

---

[49] See, e.g., Funk v. United States, 290 U.S. 371 (1933) (abolishing the common law rule that the wife of a defendant in a criminal trial is not a competent witness in his behalf); but cf. Sternlieb v. Normandie Securities Corp., 263 N.Y. 245, 188 N.E. 726 (1934) (false representation regarding age does not prevent rescission of contract entered into by infant—"well, the law is as it is, and the duty of this court is to give force and effect to the decisions as we find them").

[50] See Mendelson v. Gogolick, 243 App. Div. 115, 117, 276 N.Y. Supp. 158, 161 (2d Dept. 1934); Waychoff v. Waychoff, 309 Pa. 300, 163 Atl. 670 (1932).

[51] See E. N. Griswold, Government in Ignorance of the Law—A Plea for Better Publication of Executive Legislation (1934) 48 Harv. L. Rev. 198; W. W. Cook, Certainty in the Construction of the Law (1935) 21 A.B.A.J. 19.

[52] But cf. Freund, Administrative Powers Over Persons and Property (1928) 223: After approving Schumer v. Caplin, 241 N.Y. 346, 150 N.E. 139 (1925), which held that the disregard of an administrative rule does not constitute negligence as a matter of law, the author observes: "If violation of an administrative rule creates a civil liability, it would also be true that a contract made in disregard of such a rule is null and void. In either case the administrative rule affects civil relations, the control of which the legislature ought to keep in its own hands. It is true that municipal ordinances are permitted in this indirect way to determine civil rights; it is also true that some kinds of administrative determinations (e.g., rate orders) must necessarily operate civilly. It does not, however, follow that subordinate regulations should indiscriminately be given civil effect by current phrases of general import. The state of the statute law can be readily ascertained, and notice of it must be imputed to everyone; administrative regulations, on the other hand, are frequently confused, obscure, and difficult of ascertainment. To make them a source of peril in civil transactions (a form of enforcement withdrawn from administrative control) may therefore constitute grave injustice."

public deserves to be protected against harm that might result from execution of the contract. [Pp. 691-694.]

.   .   .   .   .

Conclusion

The obvious criticism of any suggestion that the validity of contracts should depend upon an independent judicial answer to the question whether they comport with public policy, is that too much uncertainty would thus be injected into contractual relationships. If "public policy" should be defined as something having no relationship to the judgments formulated by Constitutions, statutes, and prior judicial and non-judicial investigations, but as being ascertainable only by an unassisted judicial discovery of "what is naturally and inherently just and right between man and man," [55] there would be much to be said in favor of the criticism. But if a determination of the relevant public policy rests upon authoritative legislative pronouncement and upon intelligent effort to procure informative data, the criticism loses force. Of course it is true that in many situations neither courts nor the lawyers who argue before them have knowledge necessary to determine whether desirable public ends are to be attained by enforcement or refusal to enforce particular contracts. Just so, today, they have not the knowledge (nor do they very assiduously seek to acquire the knowledge) necessary to determine whether one decision or another will better serve the particular legislative purpose they discern in a penal statute. To make either determination, the good lawyer or the good judge must become adept in making essentially non-"legal" judgments based upon essentially non-"legal" materials. [P. 695.]

M. R. COHEN, THE BASIS OF CONTRACT *

1. The Social Roots of Contract

.   .   .   .   .

2. The Political Theory of Contractualism

Contractualism in the law, *i.e.*, the view that in an ideally desirable system of law all obligation would arise only out of the will of the individual contracting freely, rests not only on the will theory of the contract but also on the political doctrine that all restraint is evil and that the government is best which governs least. This in turn is connected with the classical economic optimism that there is a sort of preëstablished harmony

---

[55] *Cf.* Pittsburgh, C., C. & St. L. Ry. Co. v. Kinney, 95 Ohio St. 64, 68-69, 115 N.E. 505, 506 (1918); City of Leesburg v. Ware, 113 Fla. 760, 153 So. 87, 89 (1934).

* [From *Law and the Social Order*, by M. R. Cohen, copyright, 1933, by Harcourt, Brace and Company, Inc. Originally published in 46 *Harv. L. Rev.* 553 (1933).]

between the good of all and the pursuit by each of his own selfish economic gain. These politico-economic views involve the Benthamite hedonistic psychology, that happiness consists of individual states of pleasures and that each individual can best calculate what will please him most. Back of this faith of legal individualism is the modern metaphysical assumption that the atomic or individual mind is the supreme reality and the theologic view that sin is an act of individual free will, without which there can be no responsibility.

The argument that a regime of free contract assures the greatest amount of liberty for all is characteristic of the eighteenth century philosophy of the Enlightenment and is still essential to the faith of Jeffersonian democracy behind our bills of rights.... [Pp. 74-75.]

· · · · ·

3. The Economic Argument for Contractualism

When the political argument is closely pressed, it is found to rest on the economic one that a regime in which contracts are freely made and generally enforced gives greater scope to individual initiative and thus promotes the greatest wealth of a nation. [P. 79.]

· · · · ·

The clearest and most convincing statement of the case for the classical theory of free competition is that of Justice Holmes.[12] Let us, he urges, get behind the fact of ownership, and look at the processes of production and consumption of goods. The men who achieve great private fortunes do not consume very much of this social wealth. Their fortunes denote rather power to control the flow of goods. And who is better fitted to command this process of production and distribution than the man who wins it in the competition of the market? The assumption behind this is that the man who succeeds in winning a fortune (not, it should be noted, the man who receives it by inheritance) has succeeded because he has been able to anticipate the largest effective demand for goods and to organize the most economical way of producing them.

One weakness of this argument is that it ignores the frightful waste involved in competition. The community as a whole ultimately pays the cost, in labour and capital goods (including their extensive sales and advertising forces), of all the economic enterprises that are allowed to compete and fail. Moreover, the greatest profits do not always come with the greatest productivity. There are monopoly profits, like the unearned increment of land value, that clearly do not arise from productivity of the owners, and there are monopoly profits that are swelled by reducing the output, so that fishermen, wheat and cotton growers, and other

---

[12] *Collected Legal Papers* (1920) 279 *et seq.*, 293 *et seq.*

producers are often advised to do this. Neither can free competition prevent the paradoxical situation that our economic crises repeatedly show, *viz.*, an overstocked food market and general destitution from inability to buy. The latter is certainly in part due to the fact that, under unrestrained competition, wages and the return for the labour of the farmer are not sufficient to enable the vast majority of the people to buy enough of what they have produced. Thus, some of the supposedly greater efficiency of private over public business, to the extent that it involves lower real wages, is detrimental to the general welfare. The latter depends not only on the mass of production, but also on the kind of goods produced, on the conditions under which men work, and on the ways in which the product is distributed.

For these reasons it is rare nowadays to find any advocates of a regime of free competition except among certain lawyers and judges who use it to oppose regulation of the "labour contract" by the state. The general consensus among businessmen has demanded the organization of our Interstate Commerce Commission and Federal Trade Commission, our state railway and public service commissions, our state insurance and industrial commissions, and other administrative bodies that limit and regulate certain essential business contracts. Also the great captains of industry are everywhere trying to eliminate free competition. And those who talk about "keeping the government out of business" are the last to desire that the government shall not help or protect, by proper rules, the business in which they are involved. The differences that divide men in this respect concern the questions of what interests should be protected and who should control the government. [Pp. 80-82.]

.   .   .   .   .

III. The Justification of Contract Law

1. The Sanctity of Promises

Contract law is commonly supposed to enforce promises. Why should promises be enforced?

The simplest answer is that of the intuitionists, namely, that promises are sacred *per se*, that there is something inherently despicable about not keeping a promise, and that a properly organized society should not tolerate this. This may also be said to be the common man's theory. [Pp. 88-89.]

.   .   .   .   .

But while this intuitionist theory contains an element of truth, it is clearly inadequate. No legal system does or can attempt to enforce all promises. Not even the canon law held all promises to be sacred. And when we come to draw a distinction between those promises which should be and those which should not be enforced, the intuitionist theory, that all promises should be kept, gives us no light or guiding principle.

Similar to the intuitionist theory is the view of Kantians like Reinach [17] that the duty to keep one's promise is one without which rational society would be impossible. There can be no doubt that from an empirical or historical point of view, the ability to rely on the promises of others adds to the confidence necessary for social intercourse and enterprise. But as an absolute proposition this is untenable. The actual world, which assuredly is among the possible ones, is not one in which all promises are kept, and there are many people—not necessarily diplomats—who prefer a world in which they and others occasionally depart from the truth and go back on some promise. It is indeed very doubtful whether there are many who would prefer to live in an entirely rigid world in which one would be obliged to keep *all* one's promises instead of the present more viable system, in which a vaguely fair proportion is sufficient. Many of us indeed would shudder at the idea of being bound by every promise, no matter how foolish, without any chance of letting increased wisdom undo past foolishness. Certainly, some freedom to change one's mind is necessary for free intercourse between those who lack omniscience.

For this reason we cannot accept Dean Pound's theory [18] that all promises in the course of business should be enforced. He seems to me undoubtedly right in his insistence that promises constitute modern wealth and that their enforcement is thus a necessity of maintaining wealth as a basis of civilization. My bank's promise to pay the checks drawn to my account not only constitutes my wealth but puts it into a more manageable form than that of my personal possession of certain goods or even gold. Still, business men as a whole do not wish the law to enforce every promise. Many business transactions, such as those on a stock or produce exchange, could not be carried on unless we could rely on a mere verbal agreement or hasty memorandum. But other transactions, like those of real estate, are more complicated and would become too risky if we were bound by every chance promise that escapes us. Negotiations would be checked by such fear. In such cases men do not want to be bound until the final stage, when some formality like the signing of papers gives one the feeling of security, of having taken proper precautions. The issue obviously depends upon such factors as the relative simplicity of a given transaction, the speed with which it must be concluded, and the availability of necessary information. [Pp. 90-91.]

.   .   .   .   .

---

[17] Reinach, *Die apriorischen Grundlagen des bürgerlichen Rechts* 1922 § § 2-4. Kant himself derives the obligation of contract not from promises but from the union of free-wills to transfer rights.

[18] Pound, *Introduction to the Philosophy of Law* 1922, pp. 236, 276.

2. The Will Theory of Contract

According to the classical view, the law of contract gives expression to and protects the will of the parties, for the will is something inherently worthy of respect. Hence such authorities as Savigny, Windsheid, Pothier, Planiol, Pollock, Salmond, and Langdell hold that the first essential of a contract is the agreement of wills, or the meeting of minds. [P. 927.]

.   .   .   .   .

A more important objection to the theory that every contract expresses the consensus or agreed wills of the two parties is the fact that most litigation in this field arises precisely because of the advent of conditions that the two parties did not foresee when they entered into the transaction. Litigation usually reveals the absence of genuine agreement between the parties *ab initio*. If both parties had foreseen the difficulty, provision would have been made for it in the beginning when the contract was drawn up. When courts thus proceed to interpret the terms of the contract they are generally not merely seeking to discover the actual past meanings (though these may sometimes be investigated), but more generally they decide the "equities," the rights and obligations of the parties, in such circumstances; and these legal relations are determined by the courts and the jural system and not by the agreed will of the contesting parties. [Pp. 93-94.]

.   .   .   .   .

3. The Injurious-Reliance Theory

Though this seems the favourite theory today, it has not as yet been adequately formulated, and many of those who subscribe to it fall back on the will theory when they come to discuss special topics in the law of contract. The essence of the theory, however, is clear enough. Contractual liability arises (or should arise) only where (1) some one makes a promise explicitly in words or implicitly by some act, (2) some one else relies on it, and (3) suffers some loss thereby.

This theory appeals to the general moral feeling that not only ought promises to be kept, but that anyone innocently injured by relying on them is entitled to have his loss "made good" by the one who thus caused it. If, as Schopenhauer has maintained, the sense of wrong is the ultimate human source of the law, then to base the obligation of the promise on the injury of the one who has relied on it, is to appeal to something really fundamental.

This theory also appeals powerfully to modern legal theorists because it seems to be entirely objective and social. It does not ask the court to examine the intention of the promisor. Instead, the court is asked to consider whether what the defendant has said or done is such that reasonable people generally do rely on it under the circumstances. The resulting loss can be directly proved and, to some extent, even measured. In emphasizing the element of injury resulting from the breach, the whole question of contract is integrated in the larger realm of obligations, and this tends to put our issues in the right perspective and to correct the misleading artificial distinctions between breach of contract and other civil wrongs or torts.

Nevertheless, this theory is not entirely consistent with existing law, nor does it give an altogether satisfactory account of what the law should do. [Pp. 95-96.]

·   ·   ·   ·   ·

(1) ... Even clearer are those cases where someone advertises goods for sale or a position to be filled, and, when I come, tells me that he has changed his mind. The fact that I have suffered actual loss from relying on this public statement does not in this case give me a cause of action. The law does not help everyone who has relied on the word or act of another.

(2) In formal contracts, such as promises under seal, stipulation in court, and the like, it is clearly not necessary for the promisee to prove reliance and injury. Certain formalities are binding *per se*....

(3) Finally, the recovery that the law allows to the injured promisee is determined not by what he lost in relying on the promise, but rather by what he would have gained if the promise had been kept. There are obviously many cases where the injured party is substantially no worse after the breach than if the contract had never been made. He has thus not been in fact injured. And yet he may recover heavy damages if he would have gained heavily by the performance of the contract. The policy of the law, then, is not merely to redress injuries but also to protect certain kinds of expectation by making men live up to certain promises. [Pp. 96-97.]

·   ·   ·   ·   ·

5. Formalism in Contract

The recognition of the formal character of consideration may help us to recognize the historical myopia of those who speak of the seal as "importing" consideration. Promises under seal were binding (because of the formality) long before the doctrine of consideration was ever heard of. The history of forms and ceremonies in the law of contract offers an illuminating chapter in human psychology or anthropology. We are apt to dismiss the early Roman ceremonies of *mancipatio, nexum,* and *sponsio,* the Anglo-Saxon *wed* and *born,* or the Frankish ceremonies of *arramitic, wadiatic,* and of the *festuca,* as peculiar to primitive society. But reflection shows that our modern practices of shaking hands to close a bargain, signing papers, and protesting a note are, like the taking of an oath on assuming office, not only designed to make evidence secure, but are in large part also expression of the fundamental human need for formality and ceremony, to make sharp distinctions where otherwise lines of demarcation would not be so clearly apprehended.

Ceremonies are the channels that the stream of social life creates by its ceaseless flow through the sands of human circumstance. Psychologically, they are habits; socially, they are customary ways of doing things and ethically, they have what Jellinek has called the normative power of the actual, *i.e.,* they control what we do by creating a standard of respectability or a pattern to which we feel bound to conform. The daily obedience to the act of the government, which is the basis of all political and legal institutions, is thus largely a matter of conformity to established ritual or form of behaviour. . . .

6. Contract and the Distribution of Risks

Justice Holmes has suggested that a legal promise may be viewed as a wager: I assure you of a certain event (which may or may not be within my control) and I pay in case of failure. [Pp. 99-100.]

·   ·   ·   ·   ·

All human transactions are directed to a future that is never free from elements of uncertainty. Every one of our ventures, therefore, involves the taking of a risk. When I board a train to go home I am betting my life that I will get to my destination. Now a contract or agreement may be viewed as an agreement for the distribution of anticipated gains or losses. . . . Now the human power to foresee all the consequences of an agreement is limited, even if we suppose that the two parties understand each other's meaning to begin with. Disputes or disagreements are therefore bound to come up; and the law of contract may thus be viewed as an attempt to determine the rights and duties of the two parties under circumstances that were not anticipated exactly in the same way by the two contracting parties, or at any rate were not expressly provided for in an unambiguous way. One can therefore say that the court's adjudication supplements the original contract as a method of distributing gains and losses. [P. 101.]

·   ·   ·   ·   ·

In this latter respect for the law of contract is a way of enforcing some kind of distributive justice within the legal system. And technical doctrines of contract may thus be viewed as a set of rules that will systematize decisions in this field and thus give lawyers and their clients some guidance in the problem of anticipating future decisions.... [P. 102.]

IV. Contract and Sovereignty

. . . . .

The cardinal error of the traditional individualistic theories of contract is their way of speaking as if the law does nothing but put into effect what the contracting parties originally agreed on. The best that can be said for this is that it may sometimes be true. But even if that were more generally the case, we should still have to attach more importance to the factor of enforcement than the prevailing theories do. The fact that two people agree to do something not prohibited by the public criminal law and carry out their agreement, or fail to do so, does not of itself bring the law of contract into being. A large number of important agreements, even in business, as in social, political, and religious matters, are left to be directly regulated by other agencies, such as the prevailing sense of honor, individual conscience, or the like. It is an error, then, to speak of the law of contract as if it merely allows people to do things. The absence of criminal prohibition will do that much. The law of contract plays a more positive role in social life and this is seen when the organized force of the state is brought into play to compel the loser of a suit to pay or to do something.... The law of contract, then, through judges, sheriffs, or marshals puts the sovereign power of the state at the disposal of one party to be exercised over the other party. It thus grants a limited sovereignty to the former. In ancient times, indeed, this sovereignty was legally absolute. The creditor acquired dominion over the body of the debtor and could dispose of it as he pleased. But even now, when imprisonment for debt has been, for the most part, abolished, the ability to use the forces of the state to collect damages is still a real sovereign power and the one against whom it can be exercised is in that respect literally a subject.

From this point of view the law of contract may be viewed as a subsidiary branch of public law, as a body of rules according to which the sovereign power of the state will be exercised as between the parties to a more or less voluntary transaction. [Pp. 103-104.]

. . . . .

If, then, the law of contract confers sovereignty on one party over another (by putting the state's forces at the disposal of the former), the question naturally arises: For what purposes and under what circumstances shall that power be conferred? ... [P. 105.]

. . . . .

The notion that standardization is necessarily inimical to real freedom is a fallacy of the same type as the one that habits are necessarily hindrances to the achievements of our desires. There is doubtless the real possibility of developing bad social customs, as we develop bad individual habits. But in the main, customs and habits are necessary ways through which our aims can be realized. By standardizing contracts, the law increases the real security which is the necessary basis of initiative and the assumption of tolerable risks. . . .

Contracts are standardized not only by statutory enactments such as the New York legislation on life insurance, by orders of commissions such as the Interstate Commerce Commission and the like, but also by the process of interpretation that courts apply to human transactions and to their formulated agreements. All agreements, if they are to hold for any length of time, must be constantly revised or supplemented. When disputes arise and courts are appealed to, the latter, by the process of interpretation, do this work of supplementing the existing agreements, just as they generally engage in subsidiary legislation when they interpret statutes. When courts follow the same rules of interpretation in diverse cases, they are in effect enforcing uniformities of conduct.

We may thus view the law of contract not only as a branch of public law but also as having a function somewhat parallel to that of the criminal law. Both serve to standardize conduct by penalizing departures from the legal norm. [Pp. 106-107.]

. . . . .

A realization of the growth of standard forms suggests the introduction of a point of view in the study of contract similar to what has been called the institutional approach in the study of economics. The classical method in economics starts with a theory of free competition and then seeks to qualify that theory by taking note of the hindrances to the free mobility of capital or labour in actual conditions. While this is perfectly just as a scientific procedure, it postpones an adequate account of actual economic conditions. Recently economists have begun at the other end, i.e., with the existing organized social habits involved in economic institutions such as our currency, our technical methods of increasing production, the system of distributing and marketing goods, and the like. From this point of view competition is a real and important incident, but its limitations become more clear in this context. A similar change of approach in the study of the law of contract means beginning not with the bargaining between the two parties, but with the legal form or way of doing things, with the established institution within which negotiation is possible. [P. 108.]

CHAPTER 3

TORTS AND LIABILITY

Contents

1. DEFINITION OF TORT

Pollock, Law of Torts
Bishop, Non-Contract Law
Innes, Principles of Torts
Burdick, Law of Torts
Wigmore, The Tripartite Divison of Torts
Wigmore, Selected Cases on the Law of Torts

2. ANALYSIS OF TORT LIABILITY

Holmes, The Common Law
Winfield, The Foundation of Liability in Tort
Salmond, Law of Torts
Pollock, Law of Torts
Wigmore, The Tripartite Division of Torts
Pound, An Introduction to the Philosophy of Law
Radin, A Speculative Inquiry into the Nature of Torts

3. DAMAGE

Pound, Interests of Personality

4. CAUSATION

Section A. Legal Act.

Buch v. Amory Manufacturing Co.
Bohlen, The Moral Duty to Aid Others as a Basis of Tort Liability

Section B. Proximate Cause.

Brunner, History of Germanic Law
Pollock and Maitland, History of English Law
Bacon, Maxims of the Law
Palsgraf v. Long Island R.R. Co.
Laidlaw v. Sage
Edgerton, Legal Cause
F. S. Cohen, Field Theory and Judicial Logic

Section C. Culpable Cause.

Ives v. South Buffalo Ry. Co.
Charmont, The Changes in the Civil Law

Introductory Note

That the highest court of our largest industrial state should in 1911 have called workmen's compensation legislation "plainly revolutionary" tells us a good deal more about the court than it tells us about the statute. Historical scholarship, as exemplified in the writings here excerpted from Pollock and Maitland, Brunner, and Holmes, shows how far the historical views of the New York Court of Appeals lay from the facts but does not explain how such myths arise. How far judicial history is a result of value judgments born of philosophies and economic theories that prevailed in the college days of elderly judges, and how far it may be a product of economic forces, are questions to which some later chapters of these readings (especially Chapter 11, "Law and History") will return. A parallel problem of intellectual and economic determinants is raised by a series of cases, here excerpted, exhibiting the various ways in which a jury's (or a legislature's) determination to redress an injury may be reversed by a judicial theory of tort law. By imperceptible stages, concern over the linkage of events in the case before the court and in the other influences that affect court decisions brings us face to face with the whole philosophical problem of causation, with which several of the writings in this chapter deal.

The difficulties which these problems present may tempt those of us who still believe in torts to re-examine the two underlying assumptions: (1) that there is some common doctrine that unites cases in assault and battery, libel, conversion, negligent trespass to person or property, unfair competition, and false imprisonment; and (2) that this doctrine, whatever it may be, does not apply to contracts. The efforts of Pollock, Wigmore, Winfield, Salmond, Pound, Radin, and others to find such a comprehensive and yet distinctive doctrine are spread out in the pages that follow as the raw material from which there may develop, let us hope, some theory more persuasive than any thus far put forward.

If, as the great master of the law of torts suggests, no half-way measures will suffice and the whole idea of torts, indeed the very word itself, must be discarded, we then inevitably face the task of organizing our knowledge concerning liability generally. Recognizing that the lines conventionally drawn between contract and tort change from year to year and from court to court, that bailments, workmen's compensation, injuries to business guests, liabilities of innkeepers or public utilities, and assumpsit itself may be treated now under the rubric of tort and again under the rubric of contract, we have still to ask ourselves what are the values and possibilities of these situations that call for one solution or another, regardless of what Max Radin would undoubtedly term "the piffling particularity of the prevailing pigeon-hole." Roscoe Pound has acutely remarked (in his article on "Contracts" in the *Encyclopedia of the Social Sciences*):

As the civil law has been at its best in the law of contracts and has treated torts on a contract theory, the common law has been at its best in the law of torts and has treated contracts on a tort theory.

Roscoe Pound himself has offered some small beginnings towards a general theory of liability that may free us from enslavement to the postulate of "no liability without fault" and permit a cross-fertilization between fields of legal thought that have too long been kept distinct. Bentham, Radin, and James, and the Frenchmen, who never took our tort-contract distinctions very seriously, Charmont, Demogue, and Duguit, all help to provide the materials for such a general theory of liability, in which fault may take its proper and limited place in a wider plan of compensation for injuries.

---

1. Definition of Tort

POLLOCK, LAW OF TORTS *

. . . If the collection of rules which we call the law of torts is founded on any general principles of duty and liability, those principles have nowhere been stated with authority. And, what is yet more remarkable, the want of authoritative principles appears to have been felt as a want by hardly any one.[b]

We have no right, perhaps, to assume that by fair means we shall discover any general principles at all. The history of English usage holds out, in itself, no great encouragement. In the earlier period we find a current distinction between wrongs accompanied with violence and wrongs which are not violent; a distinction important for a state of society where open violence is common, but of little use for the arrangement of modern law, though it is still prominent in Blackstone's exposition.[c] Later we find a more consciously and carefully made distinction between contracts and causes of action which are not contracts. This is very significant in so far as it marks the ever gaining importance of contract in men's affairs. That which is of contract has come to fill so vast a bulk in the whole frame of modern law that it may, with a fair appearance of equality, be set over against everything which is independent of contract. But this unanalysed remainder is no more accounted for by the dichotomy of the Common Law Procedure Act than it was before. It may have elements of coherence within itself, or it may not. If it has, the law or torts is a body of law capable of being expressed in a systematic form and under appropriate general principles, whether any particular attempt so to express it be successful or not. If not, then there is no such thing as the law of torts in the sense in which there is a law of contracts, or of

---

* [1st ed. (1887), Chap. 1.]

[b] The first, or almost the first, writer who has clearly called attention to it is Dr. Markby. See the chapter on Liability in his *Elements of Law.*

[c] *Comm.* iii. 118.

real property, or of trusts, and when we make use of the name we mean nothing but a collection of miscellaneous topics which, through historical accidents, have never been brought into any real classification. [Pp. 4-6.]

.   .   .   .   .

We have, then, three main divisions of the law of torts. In one of them, which may be said to have a quasi-criminal character, there is a very strong ethical element. In another no such element is apparent. In the third such an element is present, though less manifestly so. Can we find any category of human duties that will approximately cover them all, and bring them into relation with any single principle? Let us turn to one of the best-known sentences in the introductory chapter of the Institutes, copied from a lost work of Ulpian. "*Iuris praecepta sunt haec: honeste vivere, alterum non laedere, suum cuique tribuere.*" *Honeste vivere* is a vague phrase enough; it may mean refraining from criminal offences, or possibly general good behaviour in social and family relations. *Suum cuique tribuere* seems to fit pretty well with the law of property and contract. And what of *alterum non laedere?* "Thou shalt do no hurt* to thy neighbor." Our law of torts, with all its irregularities, has for its main purpose nothing else than the development of this precept....[1] [Pp. 11-12.]

BISHOP, NON-CONTRACT LAW †

The word "tort" means nearly the same thing as the expression "civil wrong." It denotes an injury inflicted otherwise than by a mere ‡ breach of contract; or, to be more nicely accurate, a tort is one's disturbance of another in rights which the law has created either in the absence of a

---

* [In the later editions of his work, Pollock substitutes the translation "unlawful harm." He further adds the remark that "neither the Latin nor the English phrase is clear enough to bring out the real fundamental distinctions implied in the fact that we recognize Torts as forming an individual branch of the law."]

[1] Compare the statement of "duty towards my neighbor" in the Church Catechism, probably from the hand of Goodrich, Bishop of Ely, who was a learned civilian: "To hurt nobody by word nor deed: to be true and just in all my dealing...."

† [1st ed. (1889), Chap. 1.

The Commentaries on the Non-Contract Law ... or the Everyday Rights and Torts, from which the above excerpt is taken, published in 1889 by *Joel Prentiss Bishop* (1814–1901), as one of the pioneer efforts to piece together a "law of torts," won wide attention both in the United States and England. A practicing lawyer in Boston, beginning in 1844, Bishop produced a number of treatises on various branches of the law, many of which are still considered authoritative.]

‡ [Does not this word give rise to a vicious circle? How can we learn that something is a "mere" breach of contract unless we know it is not also a tort? Cf. Salmond's definition (*Law of Torts*): "a civil wrong for which the remedy is an action for damages, and which is not exclusively the breach of a contract or the breach of a trust or other merely equitable obligation."]

contract, or in consequence of a relation which a contract had established between the parties. [P. 3.]

．　　．　　．　　．　　．

The greater part of our law, when accurately considered, is seen to be contract law. Such, for example, is most of the law of real property; it is greatly tangled with technical rules, which limit the power of parties to bargain in relation thereto, but so also in a less degree is the law of contracts as respects personal property. [P. 3.]

INNES, PRINCIPLES OF TORTS *

§ 6.... A tort is usually said to be "A wrong independent of contract," *i.e.*, the violation of a right independent of contract; and it will be seen by this statement that the rights, of which a tort is a violation, are in fact, distinct from those arising out of contract. But they are also, as will be seen, distinct from a vast array of other rights; so that the usual definition is as defective as would be a definition of the horse as "a class of animal independent of horned cattle."

The following is a more accurate definition:

A tort is the unauthorized prejudicial interference of some person by act or omission with a right in rem of another person. The conduct which brings about the prejudicial interference is said to be tortious.

BURDICK, LAW OF TORTS †

Other writers have attempted to simplify this branch of the law by defining a tort as the violation of a right *in rem*,[11] and declaring that to avoid committing a tort one need only to forbear.[12] Such statements, admirable as they are for brevity and comprehensiveness, are inadequate, if not misleading.

Not every tort involves an affirmative act. Omission may be tortious as truly as commission.[13] An honest and respectable traveler enters an

---

* [From *The Principles of the Law of Torts* (1891), p. 5.]

† [1st ed., Chaps. 1-2.

Francis Marion Burdick (1845–1920) was well-known as a teacher of law. His *Law of Torts* appeared first in 1905 and won wide acceptance as a standard treatise. His *Cases on Torts*, first published in 1891, is still widely used as a classroom text in its various revised editions.]

[11] Innes, *Law of Torts*, § 6.

[12] Austin, *Jurisprudence*, Lect. XIV. [Lect. XIV: It should be noted that Austin does not declare that "to avoid committing a tort one need only forbear." He does say that "duties which correlate with rights in rem are always negative: that is to say, they are duties to forbear or abstain, "but not that torts are violations of rights in rem.]

[13] United Railways v. Deane, 93 Md. 619, 49 At. 923, 86 Am.St.R. 453 (1901); holding that the negligent failure or omission of railroad servants to protect a pas-

inn, calls for lodging and refreshment and tenders the proper price therefor. The innkeeper has unoccupied rooms and abundant supplies, but ignores the guest's demand. He takes no affirmative action. He does not eject the guest, nor does he say a word, nor pay any attention to him. He is simply passive. This omission is an actionable tort. The law imposed upon the innkeeper a duty towards guests, which he has violated. That duty was to receive, and furnish food and lodging at reasonable prices to, all travelers presenting themselves in proper condition, so long as he had room and supplies.[14] It was an affirmative duty; a duty that was violated by omitting to act. [Pp. 4-5.]

.   .   .   .   .

Equally unsound with the general proposition that we have just considered, is that other, (often linked with it) that a tort is a violation of a right *in rem.** Many, perhaps most, torts are of this character. On the other hand many a tort is a violation of a right *in personam.* †

Such it is submitted is the tort of the innkeeper in the case mentioned above. The traveler's right to entertainment is not a legal right available against all the world. . . . Nor is it an absolute right against every innkeeper. Whether the traveler has a legal right to be received and cared for as a guest, depends upon the plight of the inn when he presents himself. If it is full of guests, the innkeeper may ignore the traveler's request for entertainment, and may even turn him curtly away, without violating any right of the jaded and famished traveler. [Pp. 6-7.]

.   .   .   .   .

A tort is an act or omission which unlawfully violates a person's right, created by the law, and for which the appropriate remedy is a common law action for damages by the injured person.

It will be observed that the right violated is private not public. This differentiates tort from crime. Again, the right is created by the law, not

---

senger from the violence of a drunken fellow-passenger, was an actionable tort. "In such cases," said the court, "the negligence for which the company is liable is not the tort of the fellow-passenger, but the negligent omission of the carrier's servants."

[14] White's Case, Dyer 158b (1693); Commonwealth v. Mitchell, Parsons' Cases (Pa.) 431 (1850); Watson v. Cross, 2 Duvall (Ky.) 147 (1865). In the last case it is said: "Appellant, being an innkeeper, was legally bound to receive and entertain all guests apparently responsible and of good conduct, who might come to his house, and if he refused to do so, he was liable alike to an indictment and an action by the party aggrieved." Atwater v. Sawyer, 76 Me. 539 (1884). In this case, plaintiff applied for dinner at defendant's inn and was refused. He recovered eight dollars damages.

* [*Cf.* Austin, *op. cit.*, "Rights in rem are those which avail against persons generally: rights in personam are those which avail exclusively against certain or determinate persons."]

† [Burdick cites as rights in personam one's right against an innkeeper, common carrier, surgeon, attorney, etc. Is this correct?]

by the agreement of the parties. This is the broad distinction between tort and breach of contract. Still again, the violation of this legal right must be remediable by a common law action for damages.* [P. 11.]

WIGMORE, THE TRIPARTITE DIVISION OF TORTS †

Private law deals with the relations between members of the community regarded as being ultimately enforceable by the political power. Such a single relation may be termed a Nexus; it has a double aspect, for it is a Right at one end, and a Duty or Obligation at the other; every relation or Nexus necessarily having both these aspects.

In classifying them, we may of course rest the division on the nature of either the Rights involved or the Duties involved. For the first and broadest division it seems best to take the latter point of view, and to distinguish according as the Duty has inhered in the Obligor (1) without reference to his wish or assent, or (2) in consequence of some volition or intention of his to be clothed with it. The former we may term Irrecusable,—having reference to the immateriality of the attitude of the obligor in respect to consent or refusal; the latter, Recusable,—for the same reason. The latter sort includes Contracts (in the narrow sense), and some few varieties not here important. The former includes Torts (so called), Enrichment (a part of Quasi-Contracts as nowadays treated), and a few minor ones. The permanent justification for this division, it may be said, will be found in the deep-rooted instinct of the Anglo-American legal spirit, which is strikingly backward in imposing or enlarging an irrecusable nexus, but gives the freest scope for the voluntary assumption (Recusable) of nexus of any content.[1]

---

* [Is there any right which is not created by law? Is there not agreement of parties in tort actions based upon lack of professional skill in fulfilling an assumed undertaking? Are there not purely equitable torts? See Vane v. Lord Barnard, 2 Vern. 738 (1716).]

† [*Wigmore's* essay on "The Tripartite Division of Torts" was first published in 1894 in 8 *Harv. L. Rev.* 200 and exercised an important influence on the theoretical development of tort law. The essay is reprinted in Wigmore's illuminating but little-used book, *Selected Cases on the Law of Torts*, p. 6 et seq., Boston: Little, Brown and Company, 1911–1912. Another passage from this essay appears later in this chapter.

John Henry Wigmore (1863–1943) is chiefly known as the author of the standard American treatise on *The Law of Evidence*, 3d ed. (1940). Wigmore taught for three years in Japan, before coming to Northwestern University, where he was active until his retirement in 1933, as professor and dean of the School of Law.

Wigmore's writings, voluminous and on a variety of topics, include: *The Principles of Judicial Proof*, 1st ed. (1913); *Panorama of the World's Legal Systems* (1929); and *Select Essays in Anglo-American Legal History*, 1st ed. (1907).]

[1] Compare Holmes, *The Common Law*, 77: "The liabilities . . . arising from a tort are independent of any previous consent of the wrongdoer to bear the loss occasioned by his act. . . . He does a harm which he has never consented to bear, and if the law makes him pay for it, the reason for so doing must be found in some general view of the conduct which every one may fairly expect and demand from every other, whether that other has agreed to it or not."

Dividing further the former sort, we find (a) many imposed *universally*, *i.e.*, on all other members of the community in favor of myself; and (b) a few imposed on *particular classes of persons* by reason of special circumstances. Of the latter sort the duty of a child to support a parent, as recognized in Continental and other law, is an example; but the most important group is found in parts at least of the subject known in Roman law as *quasi-contractus*, in modern French and German jurisprudence as *enrichissement indu* and *Bereicherung*, and with us today as Quasi-Contract. As the feature which distinguishes this sort (b) from the former (a) is that the nexus is imposed in the one case on all persons whatever, but in the other on those particular persons only of whom special facts are true, the natural terms of distinction are, for the one, Universal Irrecusable Nexus; for the other, Particular Irrecusable Nexus.

The subject of Tort, then, deals with the large group of relations here termed Universal Irrecusable Nexus.*

WIGMORE, SELECTED CASES ON THE LAW OF TORTS †

Preface

The field of Torts (as none will doubt) stands in special need of a more exact and scientific treatment. The future should see an improvement in method. But it must begin with the present generation of students. By way of Preface, then, let a few Wishes here be recorded for their reflection. If the suggestions should seem radical, they can at least not be thought crude; for they proceed from a twenty years' study of the subject.

I. The first Wish is that we might proscribe, expel, and banish the obnoxious term "Torts," as the title of the subject. Never did a Name so obstruct a true understanding of the Thing. To such a plight has it brought us that a favorite mode of defining a Tort is to declare merely that it is not a Contract. As if a man were to define Chemistry by pointing out that it is not Physics nor Mathematics! No half-way measures will do; the name must go.

---

* [*Cf.* the criticism, *supra* (pp. 200-202), of the propositions (a) that all torts are violations of rights in rem, (b) that all torts are violations of rights imposed regardless of the consent of the obligor. Are all violations of rights in rem so imposed torts?]

† [P. vii. Boston: Little, Brown and Company, 1911-1912.]

2. Analysis of Tort Liability

HOLMES, THE COMMON LAW *

Lecture I. Early Forms of Liability †

.   .   .   .   .

In Massachusetts to-day, while, on the one hand, there are a great many rules which are quite sufficiently accounted for by their manifest good sense, on the other, there are some which can only be understood by reference to the infancy of procedure among the German tribes, or to the social condition of Rome under the Decemvirs.

I shall use the history of our law so far as it is necessary to explain a conception or to interpret a rule, but no further. In doing so there are two errors equally to be avoided both by writer and reader. One is that of supposing, because an idea seems very familiar and natural to us, that it has always been so. Many things which we take for granted have had to be laboriously fought out or thought out in past times. The other mistake is the opposite one of asking too much of history. We start with man full grown. It may be assumed that the earliest barbarian whose practices are to be considered, had a good many of the same feelings and passions as ourselves.

The first subject to be discussed is the general theory of liability civil and criminal. The Common Law has changed a good deal since the beginning of our series of reports, and the search after a theory which may now be said to prevail is very much a study of tendencies. I believe that it will be instructive to go back to the early forms of liability, and to start from them.

It is commonly known that the early forms of legal procedure were grounded in vengeance. Modern writers have thought that the Roman law started from the blood feud, and all the authorities agree that the German law began in that way. The feud led to the composition, at first optional, then compulsory, by which the feud was bought off. The gradual encroachment of the composition may be traced in the Anglo-Saxon laws,[1] and the feud was pretty well broken up, though not extinguished, by the time of William the Conqueror. The killings and house-burnings of an earlier day became the appeals of mayhem and arson. The appeals *de pace et plagis* and of mayhem became, or rather were in substance, the action of trespass which is still familiar to lawyers.[2] . . . [Pp. 1-3.]

---

* [1881. Other excerpts from this volume appear in Chapters 1, 2, and 8. Footnote numbers have been changed.]

† [The first paragraph of this chapter, here omitted, is printed in Chapter 8.]

[1] *E.g.* Ine, c. 74; Alfred, c. 42; Ethelred, IV. 4, Sec. 1.

[2] Bract., fol. 144, 145; Fleta, I. c. 40, 41; Co. Lit. 126 b; Hawkins, P.C., Bk. 2, ch. 23, Sec. 15.

Lecture IV. Fraud, Malice, and Intent—The Theory of Torts

.   .   .   .   .

Be the exceptions more or less numerous, the general purpose of the law of torts is to secure a man indemnity against certain forms of harm to person, reputation, or estate, at the hands of his neighbors, not because they are wrong, but because they are harms. The true explanation of the reference of liability to a moral standard, in the sense which has been explained, is not that it is for the purpose of improving men's hearts, but that it is to give a man a fair chance to avoid doing the harm before he is held responsible for it. It is intended to reconcile the policy of letting accidents lie where they fall, and the reasonable freedom of others with the protection of the individual from injury.

But the law does not even seek to indemnify a man from all harms. An unrestricted enjoyment of all his possibilities would interfere with other equally important enjoyments on the part of his neighbors. There are certain things which the law allows a man to do, notwithstanding the fact that he foresees that harm to another will follow from them. He may charge a man with crime if the charge is true. He may establish himself in business where he foresees that the effect of his competition will be to diminish the custom of another shopkeeper, perhaps to ruin him. He may erect a building which cuts another off from a beautiful prospect, or he may drain subterranean waters and thereby drain another's well; and many other cases might be put.

As any of these things may be done with foresight of their evil consequences, it would seem that they might be done with intent, and even with malevolent intent, to produce them. The whole argument of this Lecture and the preceding tends to this conclusion. If the aim of liability is simply to prevent or indemnify from harm so far as is consistent with avoiding the extreme of making a man answer for accident, when the law permits the harm to be knowingly inflicted it would be a strong thing if the presence of malice made any difference in its decisions. That might happen, to be sure, without affecting the general views maintained here, but it is not to be expected, and the weight of authority is against it.

As the law, on the one hand, allows certain harms to be inflicted irrespective of the moral condition of him who inflicts them, so, at the other extreme, it may on grounds of policy throw the absolute risk of certain transactions on the person engaging in them, irrespective of blameworthiness in any sense. Instances of this sort have been mentioned in the last Lecture,[1] and will be referred to again.

Most liabilities in tort lie between these two extremes, and are founded

---

[1] *Supra,* pp. 115 *et seq.*

on the infliction of harm which the defendant had a reasonable opportunity to avoid at the time of the acts or omissions which were its proximate cause. But as fast as specific rules are worked out in place of the vague reference to the conduct of the average man, they range themselves alongside of other specific rules based on public policy, and the grounds from which they spring cease to be manifest. So that, as will be seen directly, rules which seem to lie outside of culpability in any sense have sometimes been referred to remote fault, while others which started from the general notion of negligence may with equal ease be referred to some extrinsic ground of policy.

Apart from the extremes just mentioned, it is now easy to see how the point at which a man's conduct begins to be at his own peril is generally fixed. When the principle is understood on which that point is determined by the law of torts, we possess a common ground of classification, and a key to the whole subject, so far as tradition has not swerved the law from a consistent theory. It has been made pretty clear from what precedes, that I find that ground in knowledge of circumstances accompanying an act or conduct indifferent but for those circumstances. [Pp. 144-146.]

.   .   .   .   .

Taking knowledge, then, as the true starting-point, the next question is how to determine the circumstances necessary to be known in any given case in order to make a man liable for the consequences of his act. They must be such as would have led a prudent man to perceive danger, although not necessarily to foresee the specific harm. But this is a vague test. How is it decided what those circumstances are? The answer must be, by experience.

But there is one point which has been left ambiguous in the preceding Lecture and here, and which must be touched upon. It has been assumed that conduct which the man of ordinary intelligence would perceive to be dangerous under the circumstances, would be blameworthy if pursued by him. It might not be so, however. Suppose that, acting under the threats of twelve armed men, which put him in fear of his life, a man enters another's close and takes a horse. In such a case, he actually contemplates and chooses harm to another as the consequence of his act. Yet the act is neither blameworthy nor punishable. But it might be actionable, and Rolle, C. J. ruled that it was so in *Gilbert v. Stone*.[2] If this be law, it goes the full length of deciding that it is enough if the defendant has had a chance to avoid inflicting the harm complained of. And it may well be argued that, although he does wisely to ransom his life as he best may, there is no reason why he should be allowed to intentionally and permanently transfer his misfortunes to the shoulders of his neighbors.

---

[2] Aleyn, 35; Style, 72; A.D. 1648.

It cannot be inferred, from the mere circumstance that certain conduct is made actionable, that therefore the law regards it as wrong, or seeks to prevent it. Under our mill acts a man has to pay for flowing his neighbor's lands, in the same way that he has to pay in trover for converting his neighbor's goods. Yet the law approves and encourages the flowing of lands for the erection of mills.

Moral predilections must not be allowed to influence our minds in settling legal distinctions. If we accept the test of the liability alone, how do we distinguish between trover and the mill acts? or between conduct which is prohibited, and that which is merely taxed? The only distinction which I can see is in the difference of the collateral consequences attached to the two classes of conduct. In the one, the maxim *in pari delicto potior est conditio defendentis*, and the invalidity of contracts contemplating it, show that the conduct is outside the protection of the law. In the other, it is otherwise.[3] This opinion is confirmed by the fact, that almost the only cases in which the distinction between prohibition and taxation comes up concern the application of these maxims.

But if this be true, liability to an action does not necessarily import wrong-doing. And this may be admitted without at all impairing the force of the argument in the foregoing Lecture, which only requires that people should not be made to pay for accidents which they could not have avoided.

It is doubtful, however, whether the ruling of Chief Justice Rolle would now be followed. The squib case, *Scott v. Shepherd*, and the language of some text-books, are more or less opposed to it.[4] If the latter view is law, then an act must in general not only be dangerous, but one which would be blameworthy on the part of the average man, in order to make the actor liable. But, aside from such exceptional cases as *Gilbert v. Stone*, the two tests agree, and the difference need not be considered in what follows.

I therefore repeat, that experience is the test by which it is decided whether the degree of danger attending given conduct under certain known circumstances is sufficient to throw the risk upon the party pursuing it. [Pp. 147-149.]

. . . . .

The question what a prudent man would do under given circumstances is then equivalent to the question what are the teachings of experience as to the dangerous character of this or that conduct under these or those circumstances; and as the teachings of experience are matters of fact, it is easy to see why the jury should be consulted with regard to them. They

---

[3] 1 Kent (12th ed.), 467, n. 1; 6 *Am. Law Rev.* 723-725; 7 id. 652.

[4] 2 Wm. Bl. 892, A.D. 1773; *supra*, p. 92; *Addison on Torts* (4th ed.), 264, citing Y.B. 37 Hen. VI. 37, pl. 26, which hardly sustains the broad language of the text.

are, however, facts of a special and peculiar function. Their only bearing is on the question, what ought to have been done or omitted under the circumstances of the case, not on what was done. Their function is to suggest a rule of conduct. [P. 150.]

.   .   .   .   .

Another case of conduct which is at the risk of the party without further knowledge than it necessarily imports, is the keeping of a tiger or bear, or other animal of a species commonly known to be ferocious. If such an animal escapes and does damage, the owner is liable simply on proof that he kept it. In this instance the comparative remoteness of the moment of choice in the line of causation from the effect complained of, will be particularly noticed. Ordinary cases of liability arise out of a choice which was the proximate cause of the harm upon which the action is founded. But here there is usually no question of negligence in guarding the beast. It is enough in most, if not in all cases, that the owner has chosen to keep it. Experience has shown that tigers and bears are alert to find means of escape, and that, if they escape, they are very certain to do harm of a serious nature. The possibility of a great danger has the same effect as the probability of a less one, and the law throws the risk of the venture on the person who introduces the peril into the community. [Pp. 154-155.]

.   .   .   .   .

The theory of torts may be summed up very simply. At the two extremes of the law are rules determined by policy without reference of any kind to morality. Certain harms a man may inflict even wickedly; for certain others he must answer, although his conduct has been prudent and beneficial to the community.

But in the main the law started from those intentional wrongs which are the simplest and most pronounced cases, as well as the nearest to the feeling of revenge which leads to self-redress. It thus naturally adopted the vocabulary, and in some degree the tests, of morals. But as the law has grown, even when its standards have continued to model themselves upon those of morality, they have necessarily become external, because they have considered, not the actual condition of the particular defendant, but whether his conduct would have been wrong in the fair average member of the community, whom he is expected to equal at his peril.

In general, this question will be determined by considering the degree of danger attending the act or conduct under the known circumstances. If there is danger that harm to another will follow, the act is generally wrong in the sense of the law.

But in some cases the defendant's conduct may not have been morally wrong, and yet he may have chosen to inflict the harm, as where he has acted in fear of his life. In such cases he will be liable, or not, according as the law makes moral blameworthiness, within the limits explained above, the ground of liability, or deems it sufficient if the defendant has had reasonable warning of danger before acting. This distinction, however, is generally unimportant, and the known tendency of the act under the known circumstances to do harm may be accepted as the general test of conduct.

The tendency of a given act to cause harm under given circumstances must be determined by experience. And experience either at first hand or through the voice of the jury is continually working out concrete rules, which in form are still more external and still more remote from a reference to the moral condition of the defendant, than even the test of the prudent man which makes the first stage of the division between law and morals. It does this in the domain of wrongs described as intentional, as systematically as in those styled unintentional or negligent.

But while the law is thus continually adding to its specific rules, it does not adopt the coarse and impolitic principle that a man acts always at his peril. On the contrary, its concrete rules, as well as the general questions addressed to the jury, show that the defendant must have had at least a fair chance of avoiding the infliction of harm before he becomes answerable for such a consequence of his conduct. And it is certainly arguable that even a fair chance to avoid bringing harm to pass is not sufficient to throw upon a person the peril of his conduct, unless, judged by average standards, he is also to blame for what he does. [Pp. 161-163.]

WINFIELD, THE FOUNDATION OF LIABILITY IN TORT *

Is the English law of torts based on the principle that (1) all injuries done to another person are torts, unless there is some justification recognized by the law; or on the principle that (2) there is a definite number of torts outside which liability in tort does not exist? According to the first theory, if I injure my neighbour he can sue me in tort whether the wrong happens to have a particular name like assault, battery, deceit, slander, or whether it has no special title at all. According to the second theory, I can injure my neighbour as much as I like, without fear of his suing me in tort, provided my conduct does not fall under the rubric,

* [27 *Col. L. Rev.* 1 (1927).

Percy H. Winfield (b. 1878) is the author of numerous treatises and articles on law and legal history, among them the following: (with Sir J. W. Salmond) *Principles of the Law of Contracts* (1927); *Textbook of the Law of Tort*, 1st ed. (1937), 4th ed. (1948); *Casebook on the Law of Tort* (1938), 4th ed. (1948); *The Province of the Law of Tort* (1930 Tagore Lectures) (1931); *The Chief Sources of English Legal History* (1925); *The Foundations and the Future of International Law* (1941); *The History of Conspiracy and Abuse of Legal Procedure* (1921); *The Present Law of Abuse of Legal Procedure* (1921).]

assault, battery, deceit, slander, and so forth. If the first principle is the correct one, the courts have full power to create new torts, or (more consistently with judicial caution) to extend the law of torts without any baptismal ceremony for each extension. But the second principle presents us with a row of pigeonholes, each labelled with the name of a particular tort, and if an injury cannot be fitted into one of these, whatever the plaintiff's remedy may be, he has none in tort.

SALMOND, LAW OF TORTS *

§ 2. The General Conditions of Liability

1. In general, though subject to important exceptions, a tort consists in some act done by the defendant whereby he has wilfully or negligently caused some form of harm to the plaintiff. That is to say, liability for a tort is commonly based on the co-existence of two conditions: —

(a) Damage suffered by the plaintiff from the act of the defendant;
(b) Wrongful intent or culpable negligence on the part of the defendant.

2. *Damage.* The law of torts exists for the purpose of preventing men from hurting one another, whether in respect of their property, their persons, their reputations, or anything else which is theirs. The fundamental principle of this branch of the law is *Alterum non laedere*—to hurt nobody by word or deed. An action of tort, therefore, is usually a claim for pecuniary compensation in respect of damage so suffered.

3. *Damnum sine injuria.* Nevertheless there are many forms of harm of which the law takes no account. There are many acts which, though harmful, are not wrongful, and give no right of action to him who suffers their effects. Damage so done and suffered is called *damnum sine injuria,*e and the reasons for its permission by the law are various and not capable of exhaustive statement. For example, the harm done to the individual may be more than counterbalanced by the benefit accruing to the public at large: as in the case of the loss inflicted on individual traders by competition in trade,f or certain forms of harm done to one's neighbour in the exercise of one's rights of property.g Or the harm complained of may

---

* [6th ed., Chap. 1. London: Sweet & Maxwell, Ltd., 1924.

Sir John William Salmond (1862–1924), a noted English jurist in the tradition of Bentham and Austin, is chiefly known today as the author of: *First Principles of Jurisprudence* (1893); *Jurisprudence, or the Theory of the Law* (1902), 10th ed. (1947); and *The Law of Torts* (1907), from which the instant selection is excerpted.]

e The term *injuria* is here used in its original and proper sense of *wrong* (*in jus,* contrary to law). The modern use of injury as a synonym for damage is unfortunate but inveterate.

f Mogul Steamship Co. v. McGregor Gow & Co., [1892] A.C. 25.

g Mayor of Bradford v. Pickles, [1895] A.C. 587.

be too trivial, too indefinite, or too difficult of proof for the legal suppression of it to be expedient or effective. Thus no action, it seems, will lie to recover damages for mere mental suffering unaccompanied by physical harm, though caused by the wilful act of the negligence of the defendant.[h] "Mental pain or anxiety the law cannot value and does not pretend to redress."[i] So also the harm done may be of such a nature that the law considers it inexpedient to confer any right of pecuniary redress upon the individuals injured, but provides some other remedy, such as a criminal prosecution, as exclusively appropriate. Such is the case, for example, with the harm which an individual suffers in common with the public at large by reason of the existence of a public nuisance.[k]

Since, therefore, all harm is not actionable, it is necessary to ascertain whether liability for harm is the general rule, subject to specific exceptions based on definite grounds, or whether, on the contrary, the general rule is one of exemption from liability save in those specific instances in which the law declares that particular kinds of harm are wrongful. In other words: Does the law of torts consist of a fundamental general principle that it is wrongful to cause harm to other persons in the absence of some specific ground of justification or excuse, or does it consist of a number of specific rules prohibiting certain kinds of harmful activity, and leaving all the residue outside the sphere of legal responsibility? It is submitted that the second of these alternatives is that which has been accepted by our law. Just as the criminal law consists of a body of rules establishing specific offences, so the law of torts consists of a body of rules establishing specific injuries. Neither in the one case nor in the other is there any general principle of liability. Whether I am prosecuted for an alleged offence, or sued for an alleged tort, it is for my adversary to prove that the case falls within some specific and established rule of liability, and not for me to defend myself by proving that it is within some specific and established rule of justification or excuse.[i] [Pp. 8-10.]

· · · · ·

---

[h] Dulieu v. White [1901] 2 K.B. at p. 673, *per* Kennedy, J. Similarly, no *solatium* for wounded feelings is recoverable under the Fatal Accidents Act for the death of a relative. Blake v. Midland Rly. Co. (1852), 18 Q.B. 93.

[i] Lynch v. Knight (1861), 9 H.L.C. at p. 598.

[k] Winterbottom v. Lord Derby (1867), L.R. 2 Ex. 316.

[i] The contrary opinion, indeed, has in its favour the high authority of Sir Frederick Pollock (*Law of Torts*, p. 21, 9th ed.). His view that all harm is actionable unless it falls within some specific and recognized ground of justification or excuse is one which I should gladly accept as affording a comprehensive and logical basis for the law of torts; but it seems hard to reconcile it with the actual contents of our legal system. It is difficult to see that English law contains any reasoned and exhaustive list of the grounds of exemption from liability. The only adequate answer to many claims for damages is the mere *ipse dixit* of the law that no such cause of action is recognized.

4. *Injuria sine damno.* Just as there are cases in which damage is not actionable as a tort (*dammum sine injuria*), so conversely there are cases in which an act is actionable as a tort, although it has been the cause of no damage at all (*injuria sine damno*). Torts are of two kinds—namely, those which are actionable *per se*, and those which are actionable only on proof of actual damage resulting from them. The law sometimes says to a defendant: You will be held liable if you do such and such an act. At other times it says merely: You will be held liable if, in consequence of such and such an act, damage is inflicted on the plaintiff. Thus the act of trespassing upon another's land is wrongful and actionable, even though it has done the plaintiff not the slightest harm. "By the laws of England every invasion of private property, be it ever so minute, is a trespass. No man can set his foot upon my ground without my license but he is liable to an action, though the damage be nothing." [q] Similarly a libel is actionable *per se*, while slander, on the other hand (that is to say, verbal as opposed to written defamation), is in most cases not actionable without proof of actual damage.

The explanation of those cases in which a right of action is conferred on a person who has sustained no harm is to be found in the fact that certain acts are so likely to result in harm that the law prohibits them absolutely and irrespective of the actual issue. We may say that in such cases the law conclusively presumes damage, because of the mischievous tendency of the act; whereas in other cases there is no presumption, and actual harm must be proved as a fact. [P. 11.]

. . . . .

5. *Mens rea.* The second condition usually demanded by the law for liability in an action of tort is the existence of either wrongful intention or culpable negligence on the part of the defendant. These two different mental attitudes of the defendant towards his act and its consequences may be classed together under the name of *mens rea*—a guilty mind—and a fundamental principle of delictal liability is expressed in the maxim, *Actus non facit reum, nisi mens sit rea.* The act itself creates no guilt in the absence of a guilty mind.[r] The reason of this rule is that the ultimate purpose of the law in imposing liability on those who do harm to others is to prevent such harm by punishing the doer of it. He is punished by being compelled to make pecuniary compensation to the person injured. It is clear, however, that it is useless to punish any person, either civilly or criminally, unless he acted with a guilty mind in the sense already ex-

---

[q] Entick v. Carrington (1765), 19 St. Tr. 1066.

[r] In its application to the *criminal* law, *mens rea* is used in a narrower sense to include wrongful intention only, this being commonly the only form of it which is sufficient to create criminal liability. In the law of torts, however, the term must be taken to include negligence also.

plained. No one can be deterred by a threat of punishment from doing harm which he did not intend and which he did his best to avoid. All that the law can hope to effect by way of penal discipline is to make sure that men will not either wilfully or carelessly break the law and inflict injuries upon others.

Pecuniary compensation is not in itself the ultimate object or a sufficient justification of legal liability. It is simply the instrument by which the law fulfills its purpose of penal coercion. When one man does harm to another without any intent to do so and without any negligence, there is in general no reason why he should be compelled to make compensation. The damage done is not thereby in any degree diminished. It has been done, and cannot be undone. By compelling compensation the loss is merely shifted from the shoulders of one man to those of another, but it remains equally heavy. Reason demands that a loss shall lie where it falls, unless some good purpose is to be served by changing its incidence; and in general the only purpose so served is that of punishment for wrongful intent or negligence. There is no more reason why I should insure other persons against the harmful results of my own activities, in the absence of any *mens rea* on my part, than why I should insure them against the inevitable accidents which result to them from the forces of nature independent of human actions altogether.[8] [Pp. 11-13.]

.   .   .   .   .

§ 3. *Absolute Liability*

1. The rule that *mens rea* in one or other of its two forms—wrongful intent or negligence—is an essential condition of civil liability for a tort is subject to important exceptions. These exceptional cases in which liability is independent of intention or negligence may be conveniently distinguished as cases of *absolute* liability. They may be explained and justified (except so far as they are merely the outcome of historical accident) as being based on a conclusive presumption of negligence—a presumption established by the law on the ground that to require actual proof of the necessary *mens rea* would in these particular instances impose too great a burden upon the plaintiff and unduly limit the efficiency and the certainty of the administration of justice. [P. 13.]

POLLOCK, LAW OF TORTS *

Chapter 2. Principles of Liability

Down to our time it was difficult to find any definite authority for stating as a general proposition of English law that it is a wrong to do

---

[8] For a discussion of this matter, see Holmes' *Common Law*, pp. 81-96; Pollock's *Torts*, pp. 138-151, 9th ed.

* [14th edition (1939), pp. 15-16.]

wilful harm to one's neighbour without lawful justification or excuse. Neither is there any express authority for the general proposition that men must perform their contracts. Both principles are in this generality of form or conception modern, and there was a time when neither was true. Law begins not with authentic general principles, but with enumeration of particular remedies. There is no law of contracts in the modern lawyer's sense, only a list of certain kinds of agreements which may be enforced. Neither is there any law of delicts, but only a list of certain kinds of injury which have certain penalties assigned to them. Thus in the Anglo-Saxon and other early Germanic laws we find minute assessments of the compensation due for hurts to every member of the human body, but there is no general prohibition of personal violence; and a like state of things appears in the fragments of the Twelve Tables.[a] Whatever agreements are outside of the specified forms of obligation and modes of proof are incapable of enforcement; whatever injuries are not in the table of compensation must go without legal redress. The phrase *damnum sine injuria*, which for the modern law is at best insignificant, has meaning and substance enough in such a system. Only that harm which falls within one of the specified categories of wrong-doing entitles the person aggrieved to a legal remedy.

General Duty.—Such is not the modern way of regarding legal duties or remedies. It is not only certain favoured kinds of agreement that are protected, but all agreements that satisfy certain general conditions are valid and binding, subject to exceptions which are themselves assignable to general principles of justice and policy. So we can be no longer satisfied in the region of tort with a mere enumeration of actionable injuries. The whole modern law of negligence, with its many developments, enforces the duty of fellow-citizens to observe in varying circumstances an appropriate measure of prudence to avoid causing harm to one another. The situations in which we are under no such duty appear at this day not as normal, but as exceptional. A man cannot keep shop or walk into the street without being entitled to expect and bound to practice observance in this kind, as we shall more fully see hereafter. If there exists, then, a positive duty to avoid harm, much more must there exist the negative duty of not doing wilful harm, subject, as all general duties must be subject, to the necessary exceptions. The three main heads of duty with which the law of torts is concerned—namely, to abstain from wilful injury, to respect the property of others, and to use due diligence

---

[a] In Gaius, iii. 223, 224, the contrast between the ancient law of fixed penalties and the modern law of damages assessed by judicial authority is clearly shown. The student will remember that, as regards the stage of development attained, the law of Justinian, and often that of Gaius, is far more modern than the English law of the Year Books. Perhaps the historical contract holds only in Europe: see a note in L.Q.R. ix. 97, showing that among the Kachins on the Burmese frontier claims for unliquidated damages are not only known but freely assignable.

to avoid causing harm to others—are all alike of a comprehensive nature. As our law of contract has been generalized by the doctrine of consideration and the action of *assumpsit*, so has our law of civil wrongs by the wide and various applications of actions on the case. It is submitted, moreover, that any attempt, at this day, to maintain a narrower conception of civil duty can lead only to interminable difficulties.

WIGMORE, THE TRIPARTITE DIVISION OF TORTS *

There are, therefore, three distinct elements in every Tort, which may be conveniently termed the Primary, Secondary, and Tertiary limitations. The first class deals with the sort of harm to be recognized as the basis of the right; this may be called the *Damage* element. The second class deals with the circumstances fixing the connection of the obligor with this forbidden harm; this we may call the *Responsibility* element. The third class deals with the circumstances in which (assuming both the Damage and the Responsibility elements to be satisfied) the harm may be inflicted with impunity; this we may term the *Excuse* or *Justification* element. This analysis results in a tripartite division of the Tort-nexus. [P. 202.]

· · · · ·

I. *The Damage Element.*—The question is here, What sorts of harm is it that the law recognizes as the subject of a claim for its protection? We have here nothing to do with the question, Who is responsible? or, Is X responsible? nor with the question, Is X, though responsible, here excusable? We may and do determine the limitations of the Damage element without regard to these questions. Of course, after determining that the one exists, we may then determine that the other does not; and cases are frequent in which two or even all of the questions are disputable, and must be settled before a final determination can be reached as to the existence of a claim, *i.e.* a nexus. But, whenever there is a decision upon the Secondary or the Tertiary limitations, it necessarily involves, by assumption or otherwise, the sufficient existence of the other element or elements; nor can a claim be sanctioned by a favorable decision as to the Damage element without an assumption as to the existence of the other two.

Under the Damage element, of course, are to be considered physical injuries,—what sort of physical or corporal harm may be the subject of a claim. Mere touching of the person may be, while mere touching of personal property once was not. Physical illness of course is. Whether nervous derangement may be, when not brought about through corporal

---

* [8 *Harv. L. Rev.* 200 (1894). Reprinted in Wigmore, *Selected Cases on the Law of Torts*, p. 8. See p. 202 *supra* for another excerpt from this essay.]

violence, and whether mere fright, with or without corporal violence, may be, is still the subject of discussion. Forms of annoyance, such as disagreeable odors, sights, and sounds, are usually said to be the subject of recovery only in connection with the ownership of real property. There must in all such cases be a degree of inconvenience worth taking systematic notice of. The content of the right to land is also here concerned, including the right against mere intrusion upon the air space, against the cutting off of surface or subterranean water, etc. The nature of the harm known as conversion must also be treated here. The social relations must be enumerated with which interference is forbidden, and the words known as libel and the words deemed slanderous *per se* are to be discussed. The facts vesting the rights of patent and copyright, and the matters as to which we have a "right to privacy," and several other modes of harm, involve also some statement of the Damage element. [Pp. 203-204.]

II. *The Responsibility Element.*—Assuming that the kinds of harm to be avoided or to be protected against have been determined, we have next to consider the Responsibility element, by defining what connection must exist between the obligor and the harm done, in order to bring him within the scope of the nexus. The question is, in a concrete case of the specified harm, what person, if any, shall be looked to as bound to bear legal responsibility for it.

This is not the place to attempt to define the order and nature of the topics that belong under this head. The doctrine of "acting at peril," the phrasing and application of the tests of "proximate cause," "reasonable and probable consequences,"—these, with their attendant refinements and exceptions, form the substance of the general topic. But the important circumstance to call attention to is that this topic has an application in the domain of each one of the common so-called Torts,—conversion, defamation, loss of service, etc.,—no less than in case and trespass. It has been customary to treat the subject of Negligence as if it were a specific injury by itself, instead of merely a question of Responsibility liable to arise in connection with various kinds of harm; but this obscures the true situation. Speaking roughly, a man may be made responsible for a given harm by initiatory action of one of three sorts: by acting (1) designedly, with reference to the harm; (2) negligently, with reference to it; (3) at peril, in putting his hand to some nearly related deed or some unlawful act. A part of the law is occupied with determining whether or not this last and strictest standard shall be applied; and when it is, no resort is needed to the second standard, negligence. Thus it happens, that, as almost all direct dealing with personal property is done at peril, the question of negligence (or of knowledge) seldom arises in that connection. Yet it may arise; and thus, even though the treatment of the Responsibility element—mainly negligence and acting at peril—under the head of conversion is trifling in comparison with its place in injuries covered by trespass and trespass on the case, still it has its rightful place there as elsewhere. [Pp. 205-206.]

POUND, AN INTRODUCTION TO THE PHILOSOPHY OF LAW *

IV. Liability

. . . . .

One of the stock questions of the science of law is the nature and system and philosophical basis of situations in which one may exact from another that he "give or do or furnish something" (to use the Roman formula) for the advantage of the former. The classical Roman lawyer, thinking in terms of natural law, spoke of a bond or relation of right and law between them whereby the one might justly and legally exact and the other was bound in justice and law to perform. In modern times, thinking, whether he knows it or not, in terms of natural rights and by derivation of legal rights, the analytical jurist speaks of rights *in personam*. The Anglo-American lawyer, thinking in terms of procedure, speaks of contracts and torts, using the former term in a wide sense. If pressed, he may refer certain enforceable claims to exact and duties of answering to the exaction to a Romanist category of quasi-contract, satisfied to say "quasi" because on analysis they do not comport with his theory of contract, and to say "contract" because procedurally they are enforced *ex contractu*. Pressed further, he may be willing to add "quasi tort" for cases of common-law liability without fault and workmen's compensation—"quasi" because there is no fault, "tort" because procedurally the liability is given effect *ex delicto*. But cases of duties enforceable either *ex contractu* or *ex delicto* at the option of the pleader and cases where the most astute pleader is hard pushed to choose have driven us to seek something better. [Pp. 145-147.]

... In this lecture, I shall use the simple word "liability" for the situation whereby one may exact legally and the other is legally subjected to the exaction. Using the word in that sense, I shall inquire into the philosophical basis of liability and the system of the law on that subject as related to that basis. [P. 147.]

. . . . .

Roman law and English law begin with a set of what might be called nominate delicts or nominate torts. In Roman law there were *furtum* (conversion), *rapina* (forcible conversion) and *iniuria* (wilful aggression

---

* [New Haven: Yale University Press, 1922.]

upon personality). All these involved *dolus,* i.e. intentional aggression. [P. 158.]

.   .   .   .   .

Modern law has given up both the nominate delicts and quasi-delict, as things of any significance. The French civil code made the idea of Aquilian *culpa* into a general theory of delictual liability, saying, "Every act of man which causes damage to another obliges him through whose fault it happened to make reparation." In other words, liability is to be based on an act, and it must be a culpable act. Act, culpability, causation, damage, were the elements. This simple theory of liability for culpable causation of damage was accepted universally by civilians until late in the nineteenth century and is still orthodox. Taken up by text writers on torts in the last half of that century, it had much influence in Anglo-American law. But along with this generalization the French code preserved a liability without fault, developed out of the noxal actions, whereby parents and teachers may be held for injuries by minors under their charge, masters for injuries by their apprentices, employers for injuries by employees and those in charge of animals for injuries by such animals. [Pp. 161-162.]

.   .   .   .   .

In the common law, as has been said, we begin likewise with a set of nominate torts—assault, battery, imprisonment, trespass on lands, trespass on chattels, conversion, deceit, malicious prosecution, slander and libel— developed procedurally through the action of trespass and the action of trespass on the case. All of these, except trespass on lands, trespass upon possession of chattels and conversion, are cases of intentional injury. Trespass on lands, trespass on chattels and conversion involve more than the general security and must be considered in connection with ideas of property. The social interest in security of acquisitions demands that we be able to rely on others keeping off of our lands and not molesting our chattels; that they find out for themselves and at their own risk where they are or with whose chattels they are meddling. But even here there must be an act. If there is no act, there is no liability. To these nominate torts each with its own special rules, coming down from the strict law, we added a new ground of liability, namely, negligence, going on a principle, not of duty to answer for aggression, but of duty to answer for injuries resulting from falling short of a legal standard of conduct governing affirmative courses of action. Some, indeed, sought to give us a "tort of negligence" as a nominate tort. But it was soon recognized that in negligence we have a principle of liability dependent upon a standard, not a tort to be ranged alongside of assault or imprisonment. Later, with the rise of doctrines as to injury to advantageous relations and the failure of negligence to account for all unintended harms of which the law actually was taking note, we developed an indefinite number of innominate torts. To-day with the obsolescence of procedural difficulties, there is no reason why we should not generalize, as the civil law did at the beginning of the last century; and such a generalization was attempted in the last third of the nineteenth century. It became orthodox common law that liability was a corollary of fault. So far as established common-law rules imposed a liability without fault, they were said to be historical exceptions, and some of our courts, under the influence of this theory, were willing to go a long way in abrogating them. [Pp. 164-166.]

.   .   .   .   .

It is a practical question of the first importance, as well as a theoretical question of interest, whether we are to generalize our whole system of tort liability by means of one principle of liability for fault and for fault only, as the French sought to do and as we later sought to do largely under their influence, or, on the other hand, are to admit another source of delictual liability alongside of fault, as the French law does in fact and is coming to do in theory, and as our law has always done in fact. For in our law as it stands one may perceive readily three types of delictual liability: (1) Liability for intentional harm, (2) liability for unintentional culpable harm, (3) liability in certain cases for unintended non-culpable harm. The first two comport with the doctrine of no liability without fault. The third cannot be fitted thereto. We must either brand cases of the third type as historical anomalies, of which we are gradually to rid ourselves, or else revise our notions of tort liability. [Pp. 167-168.]

Suppose that instead of beginning with the individual free will we begin with the wants or claims involved in civilized society—as it has been put, with the jural postulates of civilized society. One such postulate, I think we should agree, is that in civilized society men must be able to assume that others will do them no intended injury—that others will commit no intentional aggressions upon them. The savage must move stealth-ily, avoid the sky-line and go armed. The civilized man assumes that no one will attack him and so moves among his fellow men openly and unarmed, going about his business in a minute division of labor. [P. 169.]

Is it not another such postulate that in civilized society men must be able to assume that their fellow men, when they act affirmatively, will do so with due care, that is with the care which the ordinary understand-ing and moral sense of the community exacts, with respect to conse-quences that may reasonably be anticipated? Such a postulate is the basis of delictual *culpa*, using *culpa* in the narrower sense, and of our doctrine of negligence. In Roman law and at one time in our law attempts were made to develop this postulate contractually. If in a transaction involving good faith—that is an informal legal transaction—one's conduct fell short of action to which the other party was justified by the understanding of upright men in expecting him to adhere, there was contractual *culpa*; there was a violation of a promise implied in the transaction and consequent liability. We borrowed something of this mode of thought from the Romans in our law of bailments and hence think indifferently in terms of tort or contract in that connection, although historically our action for such cases is delictual. In other connections also our law for a time sought to develop this postulate contractually by means of an "implied undertaking to use skill" for which one must answer if his skill fell short of that which the legal standard of affirmative conduct called for under the circumstances. Also in the Year Books an undertaking implied in certain relations or callings to use the skill or diligence which the relation or calling demanded is often made the basis of liability. But here the basis of liability must be found in a relation. The fiction of an undertaking to use the skill or diligence involved in a relation or calling is a juristic way of saying that one who deals with another in such a relation or with another who professes such a calling is justified in assuming the skill and diligence ordinarily involved therein, so that the law holds those in the relation or engaged in the calling to that standard in order to maintain the general security. In other words another, though closely related, postulate of civilized society is involved.

It is worth a moment's digression to suggest that such things show how little the historical categories of delict and contract represent any essential or inherent need of legal thinking. Austin thought that "the distinction of obligations (or of duties corresponding to rights against persons specifically determined) into obligations which arise from contracts, obligations which arise from injuries, and obligations which arise from incidents which are neither contracts nor injuries," was a "necessary distinction," without which a "system of law evolved in a refined community" could not be conceived. This "necessary" systematic scheme, which must be "a constituent part" of any imaginable developed legal system, is but the Roman division into obligations *ex contractu,* obligations *ex delicto* and obligations *ex uariis causarum figuris,* in which the third category is obviously a catch-all. In trying to fit our law into this necessary scheme, we find three types of cases must go in the third: (a) Duties or liabilities attached by law to a relation, (b) duties imposed by law to prevent unjust enrichment, (c) duties involved in an office or calling. In the third of these our Anglo-American procedure allows recovery either *ex delicto* or *ex contractu.* In the second our law sometimes goes on a property theory of constructive trust. In the first duties are sometimes sanctioned affirmatively by conferring legal powers or negatively by legal non-restraint of natural powers, as in the law of domestic relations, where the wife has a power to pledge the husband's credit for necessaries and the law does not interfere with the parent's administering reasonable "correction" to the child. Are we to say that these dogmatic departures of our law from the Roman scheme are inconceivable or that because of them our law is not matured or was not "evolved in a refined community"? Or are we to say that Austin derived his systematic ideas, not from scientific study of English law, but from scientific study of Roman law in a German university? Are we to say that we cannot "imagine coherently" a system of law which enforces warranties indifferently *ex contractu* or *ex delicto* as our law does, or which goes further and applies the contract measure of damage *ex delicto* as does the law of Massachusetts? But enough of this. What we have here is not any necessary distinction. It is rather what Austin calls a "pervading notion," to be found generally in the systematic ideas of developed legal systems by derivation from the Roman books. Roman law may have a contractual conception of obligation *ex delicto*—thinking of the delict as giving rise to a debt—and the common law a delictual conception of liability upon contract—thinking in terms of recovery of damages for the wrong of breaking a promise—without much difference in the ultimate results. The fundamental things are not tort and contract but justifiable assumptions as to the mode in which one's fellow men will act in civilized society in many different situations of which aggression and undertaking are but two common types. [Pp. 170-174.]

·   ·   ·   ·   ·

Must we not recognize also a third postulate, namely, that men must be able to assume that others, who keep things or maintain conditions or employ agencies that are likely to get out of hand or escape and do damage, will restrain them or keep them within proper bounds? Just as we may not go effectively about our several businesses in a society dependent on a minute division of labor if we must constantly be on guard against the aggressions or the want of forethought of our neighbor, so our complex social order based on division of labor may not function effectively if each of us must stay his activities through fear of the breaking loose or getting out of hand of something which his neighbor harbors or maintains.... Looked at in this way, the ultimate basis of delictual liability is the social interest in the general security. This interest is threatened or infringed in three ways: (1) Intentional aggression, (2) negligent action, (3) failure to restrain potentially dangerous things which one maintains or potentially dangerous agencies which one employs. Accordingly these three are the immediate bases of delictual liability. [Pp. 175-177.]

·   ·   ·   ·   ·

Another type of common-law liability without fault, the so-called liability of the carrier as an insurer and the liability of the innkeeper, is relational and depends upon a different postulate. Nineteenth-century courts in the United States endeavored to hold down the former, restricting it because of its inconsistency with the doctrine of liability as a corollary of fault. But it has proved to have abundant vitality, has been extended by legislation in some states to carriers of passengers and has been upheld by recent legislation everywhere.

Two other types of liability, contractual and relational, must receive brief notice. The former has long done valiant service for the will theory. Not only liability arising from legal transactions but liability attached to an office or calling, liability attached to relations and liability to restitution in case of unjust enrichment have been referred to express or implied undertaking and hence to the will of the person held. But beneath the surface the so-called contract by estoppel, the cases of acceptance of a wrongly transmitted offer, the doctrine that a public utility has no general power of contract as to facilities or rates except to liquidate the terms of its relational duties in certain doubtful cases, and cases of imposition of duties on husband or wife after marriage by change of law, have caused persistent and recurring difficulties and call everywhere for a revision of our ideas. Also the objective theory of contract has undermined the very citadel of the will theory. May we not refer these phenomena, not to the will of the person bound, but to another postulate of civilized society and its corollaries? May we not say that in civilized society men must be able to assume that those with whom they deal in the general intercourse of society will act in good faith? If so, four corollaries will serve as the bases of four types of liability. For it will follow that they must be able to assume (a) that their fellow men will make good reasonable expectations created by their promises or other conduct, (b) that they will carry out their undertakings according to the expectation which the moral sentiment of the community attaches thereto, (c) that they will conduct themselves with zeal and fidelity in relations, offices and callings, and (d) that they will restore in specie or by equivalent what comes to them by mistake or unanticipated situation whereby they receive what they could not have expected reasonably to receive under such circumstances. Thus we come back to the idea of good faith, the idea of the classical Roman jurists and of the philosophical jurists of the seventeenth century, out of which the will theory was but a metaphysical development. Only we give it a basis in social philosophy where they sought a basis in theories of the nature of transactions or of the nature of man as a moral creature.

Looking back over the whole subject, shall we not explain more phenomena and explain them better by saying that the law enforces the reasonable expectations arising out of conduct, relations and situations, instead of that it proceeds upon willed action and willed action only, enforcing the willed consequences of declared intention, enforcing reparation for willed aggression and enforcing reparation for culpable carrying on of willed conduct? If we explain more and explain it more completely by saying that the ultimate thing in the theory of liability is justifiable reliance under the conditions of civilized society than by saying that it is free will, we shall have done all that we may hope to do by any theory. [Pp. 186-190.]

RADIN, A SPECULATIVE INQUIRY INTO THE NATURE OF TORTS *

What is a tort?¹ [P. 697.]

. . . . .

While the common lawyer of an older day and the Roman lawyer might well dispense with a definition of a tort, since he generally knew whether he had a cause of action or not, the modern lawyer is not in so simple a case. He can, of course, begin with the assurance that nearly everything that was actionable at common law is actionable now. But many of the actions at common law in which a plea of "not guilty" was necessary to raise the general issue are considered contract actions now. And, secondly, there are a great many situations which create a cause of action which would not have done so at all at the common law.

The common lawyer of today must in some way that is a little less definite than that offered his older predecessor convince himself that he has before him a situation that will justify a claim for some sort of legal redress. He can do it much as it was done before, by examining cases in which such redress has been permitted. But he may quickly exhaust the old categories of fraud, assault, libel, nuisance, trespass and the like, and still find that the situation confronting him, is as obviously one that demands redress as any of these, and yet will not fit into their forms.

Can he meet new situations without some sort of an understanding of what a tort is? It would be difficult. It would be of little value to say that a tort is something that is actionable but is neither a contract nor a quasi-

---

* [21 *Texas L. Rev.* 697 (1943).

Max Radin (1880–1950), professor of law, philologist, and historian, taught at the College of the City of New York, Columbia, Stanford, Northwestern, Yale, and Pacific University. He became a member of the faculty of the University of California in 1919. Radin was the author of many legal works and is particularly well known for his historical works, especially in the field of the Roman law. His viewpoint in jurisprudence is set forth in *Law as Logic and Experience* (1940), quoted in Chapter 8 *infra*, and, more briefly, in his contribution to the symposium volume *My Philosophy of Law: Credos of Sixteen American Scholars* (1941). See also his article "Case Law and Stare Decisis: Concerning *Prajudizienrecht in Amerika*," 23 *Col. L. Rev.* 609 (1923).]

¹ This article both in its character and title was stimulated by recent articles of Professor Warren Seavey of Harvard. I have omitted confirming footnotes, and especially those which refer the reader to discussions of the thousands of special questions involved. The tort-literature forest is amply supplied with trees which range from ancient oaks to last year's saplings. Each of them is quite capable of obscuring the view of those who would observe the forest itself. They are almost exhaustively enumerated in Professor William Prosser's *Handbook of the Law of Torts* (1941), which in fullness and critical acuteness leaves nothing to be desired.

contract. That is an obvious begging of the question. The point is to know why the situation presented creates a cause of action, at all, if it is not a contract or a quasi-contract. [Pp. 697-699.]

.　.　.　.　.

In order therefore, to understand the nature of a tort, lawyers will have to come to grips with a question which they have persistently evaded. That question deals with the relation between law and morals. Lawyers have evaded it because they are afraid of being called moralizers and sentimentalists. They like to think of themselves as technical experts, and morals is apparently not a technique. Besides, morals sounds soft and lawyers like to think of themselves as hard. They are, however, sensitive to the moral censure of legal results and compensate by pretending a lofty indifference to it. They are prone to think of morals as a vague and nebulous set of standards sharply in contrast with the precision and definiteness claimed for the law.

Far be it from me to decide so ancient a debate and one so likely to arouse petulance. But the law itself injects the word "wrongful" and "fault" into many of the situations on which it predicates liability. Most of the definitions which are offered for torts stress this element, and assume that we shall be able to recognize an act as "wrongful" when we see it. It is hard to see what standards we are to use, unless they are those of current and traditional morality.

Once we are agreed that an act is wrongful, it does not immediately follow that a court or some similar public body will or can take cognizance of it. But if it does, what it will do depends on the special development of its legal procedure. If, as at the common law, criminal procedure is wholly divorced from civil, the wrongful act will be punished, if it is to be punished, in one way, and an obligation to make reparation for the wrong will be enforced in a wholly different way. Crime and tort, that is to say, are quite separated.

The law in the matter of wrongs has continually oscillated between punishment and reparation, and this oscillation is merely the reflection of popular feeling in the matter. There is no difficulty in getting popular support for the doctrine that a man who has caused injury to another should be compelled to do something about it. But it has never been altogether clear whether what he is to do is by way of punishment or by way of making whole the person injured.

The Roman law—and the Greek as well—differentiated crime and tort but never completely separated them. The prosecutor of the crime was regularly the victim of the tort, and reparation, generally in the form of some multiple of the damage caused, or of a sum fixed more or less arbitrarily, was taken to be primarily punishment and only secondarily a matter of making the victim whole. But the Roman law finally developed the concept of reparation through a wrong or delict which became the basic type of such obligations in the later civil law. This was done by an ancient statute, the Aquilian law—probably as early as the third century B.C.— which required the payment of money for property damaged by a "wrongful" act, an *iniuria*. A limited penal quality remained. This Aquilian action, made abstract and general, became the foundation for claims in torts in modern civil law and received classic formulation in the famous section of French Civil Code, § 1382.

"Every act whatsoever of an individual which causes injury to another obliges the one by whose fault [*faute*] it has occurred to make reparation for it."

This section has been translated and copied into a great many modern codes including most of the countries of Latin-America, as well as Spain and Italy in Europe.

A later attempt at a generalized definition of tort is that of the Swiss Code of Obligations of 1911. Section 41 runs as follows:

"Whoever wrongfully [*widerrechtlich, d'une manière illicite*] causes damage to another, either deliberately or negligently, owes reparation to him.

"In the same way whoever deliberately causes injury to another in a way contrary to morality [*die guten Sitten, moeurs*] owes reparation to him."

The German Civil Code of 1900 did not venture on a general definition. But after specific torts are defined (§ § 823, 824, 825), a much interpreted section (§ 826) provides:

"A person who wilfully causes damage to another in manner contrary to morality [*die gutten Sitten*] is bound to compensate the other for the damage."

The common law never formulated a general definition of tort. If a claim for reparatory damages could not be brought within one of the list of nominate torts, no recovery could be had, but the list was large and in the course of centuries so many approximations had been permitted for the typical examples under these torts, that few concededly wrongful situations escaped legal remedies.

In both systems what determined the wrongful, tortious, delictual character of the act was in the first instance a social and moral tradition, old enough to be practically unquestioned, and enforced at first by those who possessed religious as well as moral authority. At the common law, however, when procedure became fixed and the forms of action had attained a certain independence of anything but their own legal framework, a wrong was whatever could be the basis of an action. While analogy stretched these boundaries somewhat and changes in moral valuations seeped into the formalized law, there was a limit to which this process could go. The maxim that the law will not suffer a wrong to be without a remedy is a logical tautology. It really means that if in some fashion an act had been legally recognized as wrongful, the absence of a specific precedent which would fit it into a definite form of action would not exclude a legal remedy.

In all these instances, both at Roman law and at the common law, it was the wrongful act that was emphasized. [Pp. 703-705.]

. . . . .

The common law had early come to regard the *damnum* element as an effective constituent of a cause of action, if not its exclusive basis. Some wrongful acts were not actionable at all unless damages were pleaded and proved. In a great many, the absence of any real harmful consequence would result at best in a verdict for nominal damages, a verdict which was very nearly the equivalent of losing the suit. In a very few cases, the penal element is fully recognized.

These two bases of popular feeling about wrongs, first that a wrongdoer should be made to pay because he has done wrong and, second, that an innocent person damaged should be made whole because he has been damaged, are often enough in conflict. Both have roots that go deep enough in a general sense of justice and the law historically has not quite been able to keep an even course between them, much less decide for one to the exclusion of the other.

There are two situations in which the damage notion has outweighed the notion of wrong-doing. One is the case of a mentally irresponsible tortfeasor and the other is that of vicarious liability. [Pp. 705-706.]

. . . . .

It is clear that if we begin with damage we have at least a concrete fact. And we have something more. We have a slight prima facie assumption—a popular assumption, not a legal presumption in any sense—that a man damaged has some claim to be made whole. This popular assumption has also some popular conditions. The first is that the person damaged has been innocent. The second is that the cause of the damage must not be an unavoidable accident. If there is a damage-feasor, i.e., a man who by any act of his caused or increased or occasioned the damage, there is, in popular conception, a wrongdoer. We may say that generally a man is under a moral obligation not to inflict damage on his neighbor by any act which he could have avoided doing. [P. 710.]

. . . . .

The notion that an innocent sufferer should be made whole by the man who caused the suffering—except in the case of wholly unavoidable accidents—has deep roots in popular feeling and has made extensive strides toward legal recognition. Against it must be placed the resistance that the law has offered to any cause of action that is not based on fault. If nuisance leads us to an increasing valuation in law of the moral duty of neighborliness, there are other common-law doctrines which stress the fact that generally more than mere loss suffered is necessary to make an actionable wrong between neighbors. There are many losses due to preventable causes that are none the less *damnum absque iniuria*. Sinking a well on one's ground that sucks up all your neighbor's water, lowering a head of water for your own purposes that cuts off a neighbor's supply, the fairly destructive privileges of upper riparian owners, spite-fences, obstruction of lights in the absence of an easement—all these indicate a theory that runs counter to inferences which might be drawn from an overextension of the doctrine of *Rylands v. Fletcher;* and gives a large range of self-regarding actions and even malicious actions which are not torts even if they cause damage.

Is the foundation of this common-law attitude to be sought less in a desire to attach liability only to fault than in a tendency to give owners a free hand over their property? If that is the case, it is something that developed in the seventeenth century when the Roman notion of dominion with its *ius abutendi* was encroaching on the common law's feudal doctrine of tenure with its reciprocity of obligation and its abhorrence of waste. In any case it is clear that *sic utere tuo* and *ex damno absque iniuria non oritur actio* are conflicting lines of doctrine and make a single line of development impossible. [Pp. 712-713.]

* * * * *

There is further a large field of relations which by their very nature implied that damage must result to one or the other of the persons involved. This is the field of commercial competition, and commercial competition is an essential part of our economic system. Evidently the purpose of competition is to gain at the expense of some one else, and all devices used for that purpose have until recently been regarded as legitimate—if they avoid force or fraud—no matter how much damage was done. In this case clearly the emphasis is, or was, wholly on the wrongdoing of a competitor and not on the damage done.

Newer concepts in the fields of commercial relations have resulted in rules of unfair competition which have been, to some extent, embodied in statutes. In the main, the determination of whether the competition was in fact "unfair" has been left to courts and to administrative tribunals. But the extension of the rules of unfair competition so that they will include not only force or fraud, but many acts that are in other situations not illegal, does not change the tort-concept in this field. It still emphasizes wrongdoing rather than harm suffered.

At the same time it must be noticed that to include among wrongful acts situations which are wrong in a less obvious sense than acts formerly called so, to make acts wrongful which would normally be called merely "unfair" or "improper," is a method which can be used to whittle the concept of wrong-doing away until its characteristic element is the harm inflicted. [Pp. 713-714.]

. . . . .

We have, therefore, in the concept of tort at common law a complex aggregation of motivating ideas. Moral and social valuations create a standard of conduct and to violate it is a wrong. Originally the punishment of this wrong was left to the injured party. Now, in many cases—it is assumed always in sharply defined cases—communal authorities will inflict punishment. But to some extent even when the communal authorities intervene, the injured party is permitted to cumulate a penalty on it for his own benefit, generally in addition to strict compensation, but often without reference to compensation.

And on the other hand, there are cases in which the wrong—a conceded wrong—does not create a claim for anything either by way of penalty or as formal compensation, because no actual harm was inflicted. The wrong-doer escapes by the lucky accident that through no fault of his, his prospective or possible victim has escaped loss. [P. 715.]

. . . . .

Is it necessary to put some of these heterogeneous elements into a single formula in order to obtain something that will satisfy the law?

When all is said and done, the facts of social and commercial life involve collisions that do damage. Most of them are preventable. We are not yet ready to establish a society in which every man is his brother's keeper and under an active duty to protect him from harm. Since we are not, we must put up with preventable harm done that carries no legal liability. Much of it can be alleviated by an extension of the principle of insurance in which ultimately it may be the burden of such preventable harm will be borne by the community.

But the converse of this, that wilful or negligent wrongdoing may escape liability is one that modern society tends to restrict. New types of wrong-doing need, it is true, a certain intermediate period in which they are recognized by the moral sense before the law will do anything about them. But once the recognition is established there is little reason why calculable harm should be made a test of liability.

We may take the development of copyright protection as a model. Originally only calculable damages were permitted even if the violation was admitted. At present, by statute, a penal sum is recoverable for each case of infringement whether it actually caused loss or not.

The extension of the active duty to prevent harm so long as it is not exaggerated into an impracticable degree of social solidarity coupled with the revival of a moderate penalty usually recoverable as damages for most instances of wrongdoing that only by accident escape causing loss, will still leave a no-man's land within which there is no liability either for harm inflicted or moral duty disregarded. It is not likely that in human societies this margin will ever be completely eliminated.

If we were formulating a law of torts for a new jurisdiction, we might set up the following propositions.

1. Any act which renders the actor punishable by public authority and which causes damage to any person other than an accomplice or accessory, creates an absolute liability to pay that person compensation.

2. Any other act which causes damage to a person creates a prima facie liability to pay compensation.

3. The liability does not exist under 2, if the damage-feasor has done all that could reasonably be expected of him to avoid the damage or had no opportunity to prevent it.

4. He is not reasonably expected to prevent damage under 2 if he is doing no more than is necessary to protect himself or protect some property interest or some legitimate interest in the safety and rights of another person.

5. The liability does not exist under 2 if the person damaged has substantially contributed to the act which caused the damage.

6. A person is prima facie liable for damage caused to another, if the damage is caused:

a. by an agent acting under his orders or while conducting his business;

b. by an irresponsible person whose conduct he had the physical power and the legal right to control;

c. by an inanimate object which he had the physical power and legal right to control.

7. The liability does not exist under 6, if it would not have existed had the person charged been himself the damage-feasor.

8. Damage consists in a bodily attack or the threat of a bodily attack; an attack on reputation or the threat of such an attack; the destruction or impairment of property or the threat of such destruction or impairment; the deprivation or the impairment of an interest in property or in a chose in action, or the threat of such deprivation or impairment; the deprivation or impairment of a family relationship or the threat of such deprivation or impairment.

9. In case of a threat as described under 8, if the threat is of an imminent act and if money damages are likely to be inadequate, the threatened person may enjoin the act.

A brief commentary may add little to this quite speculative determination. If, as I have attempted to set forth, we must have some basis for calling an action wrongful, we can surely not avoid including in that classification,

acts which a public statute has rendered punishable by fine or imprisonment. Mr. Lowndes [6] finds that it is excessive to predicate tort liability on
every violation of criminal legislation, and in this he is supported by Mr.
Prosser.[7]

I cannot find their reasoning convincing. The fact that the legislature did
not expressly add tort liability to the criminal penalty is surely not conclusive. Very few torts were established by statute. Nor do we need to presume that the legislature had anything about it in mind. The tort liability
follows from the wrongful character of the act, overwhelmingly established by the fact that the act is made a crime.

The only other comment that seems clearly necessary is that which concerns Sections 3 and 4. I suggest that any harm caused by one person to
another throws upon the damage-feasor the burden of proving that the
harm was accidental or unpreventable or justified self-protection. That, I
think, is the popular view and it seems to me the reasonable view as well.
It is not the accepted view of the courts in most cases, but I am strongly
of the opinion that it plays a part both in determining even in courts
whether liability exists and what reparation is to be demanded. [Pp. 715-
718.]

---

3. Damage

POUND, INTERESTS OF PERSONALITY *

A legal system attains its end by recognizing certain interests,—individual,
public, and social,—by defining the limits within which these interests shall
be recognized legally and given effect through the force of the state, and
by endeavoring to secure the interests so recognized within the defined
limits. It does not create these interests. There is so much truth in the old
theories of natural rights. Undoubtedly the progress of society and the development of government increase the demands which individuals may
make, and so increase the number and variety of these interests.[2] But they
arise, apart from the law, through the competition of individuals with each
other, the competition of groups or societies with each other, and the competition of individuals with such groups or societies. The law does not
create them, it only recognizes them. Yet it does not have for its sole func-

---

[6] Lowndes, Civil Liability and Private Action (1914) 27 *Harv. L. Rev.* 317.

[7] *Handbook of the Law of Torts* 265-266.

* [28 *Harv. L. Rev.* 343 (1915). Reprinted in *Selected Essays on the Law of Torts*,
p. 87. Pagination of excerpts follows former source.]

[2] "A man's rights multiply as his opportunities and capacities develop.... The more
civilized the nation, the richer he is in rights." Miraglia, *Comparative Legal Philosophy*
(Lisle's trans.), 324. The idea here is that interests,—that is, demands of the individual,—increase with increasing civilization, and hence the pressure upon the law
to meet these interests increases the scope and character of legal rights.

tion to recognize interests which exist independently. It must determine which it will recognize, it must define the extent to which it will give effect to them in view of other interests,—individual, public, or social,—and the possibilities of effective interference by law, and it must devise the means by which they are to be secured. Hence in determining the scope and subject-matter of a legal system we have to consider (1) the interests which it may be asserted the law ought to recognize and to secure; (2) the principles upon which interests are to be selected for such recognition and securing; (3) the principles upon which such interests should be defined and limited for the purposes of legal recognition, or, in other words, the principles upon which conflicting interests should be weighed or balanced in order to determine the extent to which the respective interests are to be given effect; (4) the means by which the law may secure the interests which it recognizes; and (5) the limitations upon effective legal action which preclude complete recognition or complete securing of all these interests to the full extent which ethical considerations might require. [Pp. 343-344.]

.   .   .   .   .

Individual interests which it is conceived the law ought to secure are usually called "natural rights" because they are not the creatures of the state and it is held that the pressure of these interests has brought about the state. In the stage of equity or natural law, when what ought to be law is made the test of what is, it is natural to confuse the interests which the law does secure, the interests it ought to secure, and the means of securing them under the one name of "rights." Those which are secured and the means whereby they are secured are called legal rights; those which ought to be secured are called natural rights. [P. 346.]

.   .   .   .   .

Individual interests may be classified as (a) interests of personality,—the individual physical and spiritual existence; (b) domestic interests,—"the expanded individual life"; [16] and (c) interests of substance,—the individual economic life. [P. 349.]

.   .   .   .   .

Inviolability of the physical person is universally put first among the demands which the individual may make. [P. 355.]

.   .   .   .   .

Injury to the nervous system, mental injury, and injury to sensibilities, where there is no physical impact or no injury to substance or to any relation, is a new problem of modern law. Here also development has been

---

[16] Paulsen, *Ethics* (Thilly's trans.), 634.

slow and cautious, partly because the law on this subject has had to be made in a period of legal stability, but partly also because of practical limitations upon the enforcement of legal rules and hence upon the securing of interests thereby. A nervous derangement manifested objectively is like any bodily illness. But our law does not protect against purely subjective mental suffering except as it accompanies or is incident to some other form of injury and within certain disputed limits.[51] There are obvious difficulties of proof in such cases, so that false testimony as to mental suffering may be adduced easily and is very hard to detect. Hence this individual interest has to be balanced carefully with a social interest against the use of the law to further imposture. For these reasons courts, thinking more of the practical problem of proof than of the logical situation, have looked to see whether there has been some bodily impact or some wrong infringing some other interest, which is objectively demonstrable, and have put nervous injuries which leave no physical record and purely mental injuries in the same category. In case of nervous injury or mental suffering along with other injury as a result of bodily impact, considerations of what would naturally happen to persons of normal sensibilities enable the law to meet the practical difficulties. This is true also where there has been an infringement of some other interest in itself raising a right of action. But if there is no physical impact and there is no independent right of action for a coincident injury, the practical difficulties weigh heavily.... So long as the margin for imposture and the scope of pure expert conjecture remain as large as they are at present, this phase of the interest of personality must remain in some measure insufficiently secured.* [Pp. 359-360, 362.]

---

[51] "A factor which we may for the sake of convenience refer to as the parasitic element of damage. The idea which is meant to be brought out by the use of this expression is that in certain situations the law permits elements of harm to be considered in assessing the recoverable damage which cannot be taken into account in determining the primary question of liability. It is only under this head that such factors as insult, disgrace, and anguish of feeling can get legal recognition at all." Street, *Foundations of Legal Liability*, I, 461. A striking instance may be seen in Floyd v. Atlantic Coast Line R. Co., 83 S.E. 12 (N.C., 1914), where a mother sued for mental anguish caused by the negligent mutilation of the dead body of her boy. As the right to possession of the body for the purposes of burial was in her husband as next of kin, and hence there was no infringement of any interest of the mother other than that involved in the injury to feelings and sensibilities, recovery was denied.

*[For a statement of developments toward a broader recognition of rights to recover for injuries not resulting from contact, see Magruder, "Mental and Emotional Disturbances in the Law of Torts" 49 *Harv. L. Rev.* 1033 (1936), and see Warren and Brandeis, "The Right of Privacy," 4 *Harv. L. Rev.* 193 (1890), reprinted in *Selected Essays on the Law of Torts*, p. 122.]

4. Causation

A. Legal act

BUCH v. AMORY MANUFACTURING CO.

SUPREME COURT OF NEW HAMPSHIRE, 1897
69 N.H. 257

CARPENTER, C.J. On the evidence, the jury could not properly find that the plaintiff was upon the premises of the defendants with their consent or permission. Although there was evidence tending to show that other back-boys had taken their brothers into the room for the purpose of instructing them in the business, there was no sufficient evidence that the fact that they did so was known to the defendants, and there was evidence that on the first occasion brought to their knowledge they objected. Upon this state of the evidence, a license by the defendants—whether material or immaterial—for the plaintiff's presence in the room could not legitimately be inferred. The plaintiff was a trespasser.

The defendants' machinery was in perfect order and properly managed. They were conducting their lawful business in a lawful way and in the usual and ordinary manner. During the plaintiff's presence they made no change in the operation of their works or in their method of doing business. No immediate or active intervention on their part caused the injury. It resulted from the joint operation of the plaintiff's conduct and the ordinary and usual condition of the premises. Under these circumstances, an adult in full possession of his faculties, or an infant capable of exercising the measure of care necessary to protect himself from the dangers of the situation, whether he was on the premises by permission or as a trespasser, could not recover. [Pp. 258-259.]

. . . . .

Assuming, then, that the plaintiff was incapable either of appreciating the danger or of exercising the care necessary to avoid it, is he, upon the facts stated, entitled to recover? He was a trespasser in a place dangerous to children of his age. In the conduct of their business and management of their machinery the defendants were without fault. The only negligence charged upon or attributed to them is that, inasmuch as they could not make the plaintiff understand a command to leave the premises and ought to have known that they could not, they did not forcibly eject him.

Actionable negligence is the neglect of a legal duty. The defendants are not liable unless they owed to the plaintiff a legal duty which they neglected to perform. With purely moral obligations the law does not deal. For example, the priest and Levite who passed by on the other side were not, it is supposed, liable at law for the continued suffering of the man who fell among thieves, which they might and morally ought to have prevented or relieved. Suppose A, standing close by a railroad, sees a two-year-old babe on the track and a car approaching. He can easily rescue the child with entire safety to himself, and the instincts of humanity require him to do so. If he does not, he may, perhaps, justly be styled a ruthless savage and a moral monster; but he is not liable in damages for the child's injury, or indictable under the statute for its death. P.S., c. 278, § 8. [Pp. 259-260.]

.   .   .   .   .

There is a wide difference—a broad gulf—both in reason and in law, between causing and preventing an injury; between doing by negligence or otherwise a wrong to one's neighbor, and preventing him from injuring himself; between protecting him against injury by another and guarding him from injury that may accrue to him from the condition of the premises which he has unlawfully invaded. The duty to do no wrong is a legal duty. The duty to protect against wrong is, generally speaking and excepting certain intimate relations in the nature of a trust, a moral obligation only, not recognized or enforced by law. Is a spectator liable if he sees an intelligent man or an unintelligent infant running into danger and does not warn or forcibly restrain him? What difference does it make whether the danger is on another's land, or upon his own, in case the man or infant is not there by his express or implied invitation? If A sees an eight-year-old boy beginning to climb into his garden over a wall stuck with spikes and does not warn him or drive him off, is he liable in damages if the boy meets with injury from the spikes? *Degg v. Railway*, 1 H. & N. 773, 777. I see my neighbor's two-year-old babe in dangerous proximity to the machinery of his windmill in his yard, and easily might, but do not, rescue him. I am not liable in damages to the child for his injuries, nor, if the child is killed, punishable for manslaughter by the common law or under the statute. (P.S., c.278, § 8), because the child and I are strangers, and I am under no legal duty to protect him. Now suppose I see the same child trespassing in my own yard and meddling in like manner with the dangerous machinery of my own windmill. What additional obligation is cast upon me by reason of the child's trespass? The mere fact that the child is unable to take care of himself does not impose on me the legal duty of protecting him in the one case more than in the other. Upon what principle of law can an infant by coming unlawfully upon my premises impose upon me the legal duty of a guardian? None has been suggested, and we know of none. [Pp. 261-262.]

.   .   .   .   .

There was no evidence tending to show that the defendants neglected to perform any legal duty to the plaintiff. *McGuiness v. Butler*, 159 Mass. 233, 236, 238; *Grindley v. McKechnie*, 163 Mass. 494; *Holbrook v. Aldrich*, 168 Mass. 15, 17, and cases cited.

Verdict set aside: judgment for the defendants. [P. 262.]

BOHLEN, THE MORAL DUTY TO AID OTHERS AS A BASIS OF TORT LIABILITY *

There is no distinction more deeply rooted in the common law and more fundamental than that between misfeasance and non-feasance, between active misconduct working positive injury to others and passive inaction, a failure to take positive steps to benefit others, or to protect them from harm not created by any wrongful act of the defendant. This distinction is founded on that attitude of extreme individualism so typical of Anglo-Saxon legal thought.† Misfeasance differs from non-feasance in two respects; in the character of the conduct complained of, and second, in the nature of the detriment suffered in consequence thereof. The difference between the nature of the alleged misconduct is in theory obvious,‡ but in practice is it not always easy to say whether an alleged misconduct is active or passive. There is a borderland in which the act is of a mixed character, partaking of the nature of both.

The difference between the results of non-feasance and misfeasance, while quite as fundamental, is much less obvious. The final physical injury to the plaintiff may be the same whether defendant's alleged misconduct is an act of violence or a failure to protect him from the violence of others. But, there is a point intermediate between the plaintiff's actual harm and the defendant's misconduct, where its consequences are substantially different. In the case of active misfeasance the victim is positively worse off as a result of the wrongful act. In cases of passive inaction plaintiff is in reality no worse off at all.§ His situation is unchanged; he is merely deprived of a protection which, had it been afforded him, would have benefited him.

B. Proximate cause

BRUNNER, HISTORY OF GERMANIC LAW ‖

The ancient law was harsh. A man was liable not only for harm caused unintentionally, but also for any harm which came about through him; and

---

* [56 *U. of Pa. L. Rev.* 217. Reprinted in Bohlen, *Studies in the Law of Torts*, p. 291.

Francis Hermann Bohlen (b. 1868). Authority on the law of torts, professor at Harvard and University of Pennsylvania Law Schools, Reporter for the American Law Institute on the *Restatement of the Law of Torts*, is the author of *Studies in the Law of Torts* (1926) and *Cases on Torts* (1st ed. 1909).]

† [A contrary view is set forth by Bentham in his *Theory of Legislation* (Hildreth, ed., 1864) pp. 65-66.]

‡ [What is this theoretical difference?]

§ [In what "reality" was the plaintiff in the preceding case no worse off at all after the period during which the accident might have been prevented?]

‖ [1st ed. (1892) Vol. II, § 125. Reprinted in Wigmore, *Selected Cases on the Law of Torts* (1911-12), Vol. I, 768.

The quoted passage is from section 125 of Volume II of the *History of Germanic*

the liability extended to persons who would in our modern view seem to have had little or no connection with the harm. Excusable accident was not recognized. The law sought to hold somebody liable, and laid hold of him by principles of causal connection which are to us nowadays scarcely comprehensible. The scope of liability was so broadly bounded that it made a man liable for any misfortune which in its origin was somewhere traceable to his region of existence. Certain liabilities were fixed on him by virtue of his class-relationships, or of his status as guardian, or as householder with a body of free retainers, or as lord of the manor, or as a member of the hundred or the township, irrespective of his privity to the wrongful act. But more than this, the owner of property was responsible for harm done by his menials, by his domestic animals, and even by his inanimate chattels. And still further as a tradesman and a master he was under an extensive liability for injuries received by his hired workmen in the course of their service to him. The master paid the "head-money" of a workman who was killed in his service, as well as the damages (at the usual tariff) for lesser injuries, except only when the injury was attributable to some third person, so as to exonerate the master; and the master was also liable for wrongs done by his servants. For example, if a person lost his life accidentally, by fire or water or tree, while in another's service, the master was responsible for the "*homicidium*"; and if a person was sent away or sent for, in the service of another, and lost his life on the errand, the employer was regarded as the "*causa mortis*."

POLLOCK AND MAITLAND, HISTORY OF
ENGLISH LAW *

Guesswork perhaps would have taught us that barbarians will not trace the chain of causation beyond its nearest link, and that, for example, they will not impute one man's death to another unless that other has struck a blow which laid a corpse at his feet. All the evidence however points the other way:—I have slain a man if but for some act of mine he might perhaps be yet alive. Very instructive is a formula which was still in use in the England of the thirteenth century; one who was accused of homicide and was going to battle was expected to swear that he had done nothing whereby the dead man was "further from life or nearer to death." [42] Dam-

---

Law by *Heinrich Brunner* (1840–1915). Professor at various Central European universities, Brunner achieved distinction as an historian of the law, particularly Germanic law. His works also include books treating of Roman, French, and English law and their sources.]

* [2nd ed., Vol. II, p. 470. Boston: Little, Brown & Co., 1899.]

[42] Leg. Hen. 90, § 11: "*Quod per eum non fuerit vitae remotior morti propinquior.*" Bracton, f. 141 b: "*per quod remotior esse debeat a vita et morti propinquior.*" Note Book, pl. 1460: "*Nec per ipsum fuit morti appropiatus nec a vita elongatus.*" Munim. Gildh. i. 105: "*Iuravit ... quod numquam ipsam Isabellam verberavit, unde puer, de*

ages which the modern English lawyer would assuredly describe as "too remote," were not too remote for the author of the *Leges Henrici*. At your request I accompany you when you are about your own affairs; my enemies fall upon and kill me; you must pay for my death.[43] You take me to see a wild-beast-show or that interesting spectacle, a madman; beast or madman kills me; you must pay. You hang up your sword; some one else knocks it down so that it cuts me; you must pay. In none of these cases can you honestly swear that you did nothing that helped to bring about death or wound.[44] [Pp. 470-471.]

·   ·   ·   ·   ·

But the most primitive laws that have reached us seem to point to a time when a man was responsible, not only for all harm done by his own acts, but also for that done by the acts of his slaves, his beasts, or—for even this we must add—the inanimate things that belonged to him.[45] ...

Our English law of deodands gives us a glimpse into a far off past. In 1846 [46] we still in theory maintained the rule that any animate or inanimate thing which caused the death of a human being should be handed over to the king and devoted by his almoner to pious uses, "for the appeasing" says Coke "of God's wrath." ... Horses, oxen, carts, boats, millwheels and cauldrons were the commonest of deodands. ...

The deodand may warn us that in ancient criminal law there was a sacral element which Christianity could not wholly suppress, especially when what might otherwise have been esteemed a heathenery was in harmony with some of those strange old dooms that lie embedded in the holy books of the Christian. Also it is hard for us to acquit ancient law of that unreasoning instinct that impels the civilised man to kick, or consign to eternal perdition, the chair over which he has stumbled. [Pp. 472-474.]

BACON, MAXIMS OF THE LAW *

Regula I: *"In jure non remota causa, sed proxima spectatur."* It were infinite for the law to judge the causes of causes, and their impulsions

---

quo fecit absorsum, propinquior fuit morti et remotior a vita." Brunner, *Forschungen*, p. 495, gives a similar formula from the Icelandic Grágás.

[43] *Leg. Hen.* 88, § 9.

[44] *Leg. Hen.* 90, § 11.

[45] Brunner, *op. cit.* 507-523.

[46] Stat. 9-10 Vic. c. 62. For the law of deodands, see Bracton, f. 122; Fleta, p. 37; Britton, i. 14, 13, 39; Staundford, P.C. f. 20; Coke, *Third Inst.* 57; Hale, P.C. i. 419; Stephen, *Hist. Crim. Law*, iii. 77.

* [*Sir Francis Bacon* (1561–1626), became Lord Chancellor of England in 1618. He was removed from this position two years later, when he admitted accepting bribes from litigants. Although the sentence meted out to Bacon was not executed except in part, he retired from public life and devoted himself to writing. Bacon's best known works include the *Essays*, the *Advancement of Learning* and the *Novum*

one of another; therefore it contenteth itself with the immediate cause, and judgeth of acts by that, without looking to any further degree. . . . This rule faileth in covinous acts, which though they be conveyed through many degrees and reaches, yet the law taketh heed to the corrupt beginning, and counteth all as one corrupt act. . . . In like manner, this rule holdeth not in criminal acts, except they have full interruption; because when the intention is matter of substance and that which the law doth principally behold, there the first motive will be principally regarded, and not the last impulsion.

HELEN PALSGRAF v. LONG ISLAND R.R. CO.
N.Y. COURT OF APPEALS, 1928
248 N.Y. 339

APPEAL from a judgment of the Appellate Division of the Supreme Court in the second judicial department, entered December 16, 1927, affirming a judgment in favor of plaintiff entered upon a verdict.

. . . . .

CARDOZO, Ch. J. Plaintiff was standing on a platform of defendant's railroad after buying a ticket to go to Rockaway Beach. A train stopped at the station, bound for another place. Two men ran forward to catch it. One of the men reached the platform of the car without mishap, though the train was already moving. The other man, carrying a package, jumped aboard the car, but seemed unsteady as if about to fall. A guard on the car, who had held the door open, reached forward to help him in, and another guard on the platform pushed him from behind. In this act, the package was dislodged, and fell upon the rails. It was a package of small size, about fifteen inches long, and was covered by a newspaper. In fact it contained fireworks, but there was nothing in its appearance to give notice of its contents. The fireworks when they fell exploded. The shock of the explosion threw down some scales at the other end of the platform, many feet away. The scales struck the plaintiff, causing injuries for which she sues.

The conduct of the defendant's guard, if a wrong in its relation to the holder of the package, was not a wrong in its relation to the plaintiff, standing far away. Relatively to her it was not negligence at all. Nothing in the situation gave notice that the falling package had in it the potency

---

Organum. A sympathetic and comprehensive account of Bacon's thinking on general problems of jurisprudence will be found in Cairns, *Legal Philosophy from Plato to Hegel* (1949). For a dissent from the common opinion, which regards Bacon as the founder of modern science, see "Bacon and the Inductive Method" in M. R. Cohen, *Studies in Philosophy and Science* (1941), pp. 99-106.]

of peril to persons thus removed. Negligence is not actionable unless it involves the invasion of a legally protected interest, the violation of a right. "Proof of negligence in the air, so to speak, will not do" (Pollock, *Torts* [11th ed.], p. 455; *Martin v. Herzog*, 228 N.Y. 164, 170; cf. Salmond, *Torts* [6th ed.], p. 24).... The plaintiff as she stood upon the platform of the station might claim to be protected against intentional invasion of her bodily security. Such invasion is not charged. She might claim to be protected against unintentional invasion by conduct involving in the thought of reasonable men an unreasonable hazard that such invasion would ensue. These, from the point of view of the law, were the bounds of her immunity, with perhaps some rare exceptions, survivals for the most part of ancient forms of liability, where conduct is held to be at the peril of the actor (*Sullivan v. Dunham*, 161 N.Y. 290). If no hazard was apparent to the eye of ordinary vigilance, an act innocent and harmless, at least to outward seeming, with reference to her, did not take to itself the quality of a tort because it happened to be a wrong, though apparently not one involving the risk of bodily insecurity, with reference to someone else.... The plaintiff sues in her own right for a wrong personal to her, and not as the vicarious beneficiary of a breach of duty to another. [Pp. 340-341.]

. . . . .

...In this case, the rights that are said to have been violated, the interests said to have been invaded, are not even of the same order. The man was not injured in his person nor even put in danger. The purpose of the act, as well as its effect, was to make his person safe. If there was a wrong to him at all, which may very well be doubted, it was a wrong to a property interest only, the safety of his package. Out of this wrong to property, which threatened injury to nothing else, there has passed, we are told, to the plaintiff by derivation or succession a right of action for the invasion of an interest of another order, the right to bodily security. The diversity of interests emphasizes the futility of the effort to build the plaintiff's right upon the basis of a wrong to some one else. The gain is one of emphasis, for a like result would follow if the interests were the same. Even then, the orbit of the danger as disclosed to the eye of reasonable vigilance would be the orbit of the duty.... [P. 343.]

. . . . .

The law of causation, remote or proximate, is thus foreign to the case before us. The question of liability is always anterior to the question of the measure of the consequences that go with liability. If there is no tort to be redressed, there is no occasion to consider what damage might be recovered if there were a finding of a tort. We may assume, without deciding, that negligence, not at large or in the abstract, but in relation to the plaintiff, would entail liability for any and all consequences, however novel or extraordinary (*Bird v. St. Paul F. & M. Ins. Co.*, 224 N.Y. 47, 54; *Ehrgott v. Mayor, etc. of N.Y.*, 96 N.Y. 264; *Smith v. London & S.W. Ry. Co.*, L.R. 6 C.P. 14; 1 Beven, *Negligence*, 106; Street, *op. cit.* vol. 1, p. 90; Green, *Rationale of Proximate Cause*, pp. 88, 118; cf. *Matter of Polemis*, L.R. 1921, 3 K.B. 560; 44 *Law Quarterly Review*, 142). There is room for argument that a distinction is to be drawn according to the diversity of interests invaded by the act, as where conduct negligent in that it threatens an insignificant invasion of an interest in property results in an unforeseeable invasion of an interest of another order, as, *e.g.*, one of bodily security. Perhaps other distinctions may be necessary. We do not go into the question now. The consequences to be followed must first be rooted in a wrong.

The judgment of the Appellate Division and that of the Trial Term should be reversed, and the complaint dismissed, with costs in all courts.

ANDREWS, J. (dissenting). [After restating the facts.]

Upon these facts may she recover the damages she has suffered in an action brought against the master? The result we shall reach depends upon our theory as to the nature of negligence. Is it a relative concept—the breach of some duty owing to a particular person or to particular persons? Or where there is an act which unreasonably threatens the safety of others, is the doer liable for all its proximate consequences, even where they result in injury to one who would generally be thought to be outside the radius of danger? This is not a mere dispute as to words. We might not believe that to the average mind the dropping of the bundle would seem to involve the probability of harm to the plaintiff standing many feet away whatever might be the case as to the owner or to one so near as to be likely to be struck by its fall. If, however, we adopt the second hypothesis we have to inquire only as to the relation between cause and effect. We deal in terms of proximate cause, not of negligence. [Pp. 346-348.]

· · · ·

The proposition is this. Every one owes to the world at large the duty of refraining from those acts that may unreasonably threaten the safety of others. Such an act occurs. Not only is he wronged to whom harm might reasonably be expected to result, but he also who is in fact injured, even if he be outside what would generally be thought the danger zone. There needs be duty due to the one complaining but this is not a duty to a particular individual because as to him harm might be expected. Harm to some one being the natural result of the act, not only that one alone, but all those in fact injured may complain. . . . [P. 350.]

· · · ·

... But there is one limitation. The damages must be so connected with the negligence that the latter may be said to be the proximate cause of the former.

These two words have never been given an inclusive definition. What is a cause in a legal sense, still more what is a proximate cause, depend in each case upon many considerations, as does the existence of negligence itself. Any philosophical doctrine of causation does not help us. A boy throws a stone into a pond. The ripples spread. The water level rises. The history of that pond is altered to all eternity. It will be altered by other causes also. Yet it will be forever the resultant of all causes combined. Each one will have an influence. How great only omniscience can say. You may speak of a chain, or if you please, a net. An analogy is of little aid. Each cause brings about future events. Without each the future would not be the same. Each is proximate in the sense it is essential. But that is not what we mean by the word. Nor on the other hand do we mean sole cause. There is no such thing.

Should analogy be thought helpful, however, I prefer that of a stream. The spring, starting on its journey, is joined by tributary after tributary. The river, reaching the ocean, comes from a hundred sources. No man may say whence any drop of water is derived. Yet for a time distinction may be possible. Into the clear creek, brown swamp water flows from the left. Later, from the right comes water stained by its clay bed. The three may remain for a space, sharply divided. But at last, inevitably no trace of separation remains. They are so commingled that all distinction is lost.

As we have said, we cannot trace the effect of an act to the end, if end there is. Again, however, we may trace it part of the way. A murder at Serajevo may be the necessary antecedent to an assassination in London twenty years hence. An overturned lantern may burn all Chicago. We may follow the fire from the shed to the last building. We rightly say the fire started by the lantern caused its destruction.

A cause, but not the proximate cause. What we do mean by the word "proximate" is, that because of convenience, of public policy, of a rough sense of justice, the law arbitrarily declines to trace a series of events beyond a certain point. This is not logic. It is practical politics. Take our rule as to fires. Sparks from my burning haystack set on fire my house and my neighbor's. I may recover from a negligent railroad. He may not. Yet the wrongful act as directly harmed the one as the other. We may regret that the line was drawn just where it was, but drawn somewhere it had to be. We said the act of the railroad was not the proximate cause of our neighbor's fire. Cause it surely was. The words we used were simply indicative of our notions of public policy. Other courts think differently. But somewhere they reach the point where they cannot say the stream comes from any one source. [Pp. 351-353.]

·   ·   ·   ·   ·

It is all a question of expediency. There are no fixed rules to govern our judgment. There are simply matters of which we may take account. We have in a somewhat different connection spoken of "the stream of events." We have asked whether that stream was deflected—whether it was forced into new and unexpected channels. (*Donnelly v. Piercy Contracting Co.*, 222 N.Y. 210). This is rather rhetoric than law. There is in truth little to guide us other than common sense.

There are some hints that may help us. The proximate cause, involved as it may be with many other causes, must be, at the least, something without which the event would not happen. The court must ask itself whether there was a natural and continuous sequence between cause and effect. Was the one a substantial factor in producing the other? Was there a direct connection between them, without too many intervening causes? Is the effect of cause on result not too attenuated? Is the cause likely, in the usual judgment of mankind, to produce the result? Or by the exercise of prudent foresight could the result be foreseen? Is the result too remote from the cause, and here we consider remoteness in time and space. (*Bird v. St. Paul F. & M. Ins. Co.*, 224 N.Y. 47, where we passed upon the construction of a contract—but something was also said on this subject.) Clearly we must so consider, for the greater the distance either in time or space, the more surely do other causes intervene to affect the result.... [P. 354.]

. . . . . .

... The act upon which defendant's liability rests is knocking an apparently harmless package onto the platform. The act was negligent. For its proximate consequences the defendant is liable. If its contents were broken, to the owner; if it fell upon and crushed a passenger's foot, then to him. If it exploded and injured one in the immediate vicinity, to him also as to A in the illustration. Mrs. Palsgraf was standing some distance away. How far cannot be told from the record—apparently twenty-five or thirty feet. Perhaps less. Except for the explosion, she would not have been injured. We are told by the appellant in his brief "it cannot be denied that the explosion was the direct cause of the plaintiff's injuries." So it was a substantial factor in producing the result—there was here a natural and continuous sequence—direct connection. The only intervening cause was that instead of blowing her to the ground the concussion smashed the weighing machine which in turn fell upon her. There was no remoteness in time, little in space. And surely, given such an explosion as here it needed no great foresight to predict that the natural result would be to injure one on the platform at no greater distance from its scene than was the plaintiff. Just how no one might be able to predict. Whether by flying fragments, by broken glass, by wreckage of machines or structures no one could say. But injury in some form was most probable.

Under these circumstances I cannot say as a matter of law that the plaintiff's injuries were not the proximate result of the negligence. That is all we have before us. The court refused to so charge. No request was made to submit the matter to the jury as a question of fact, even would that have been proper upon the record before us.

The judgment appealed from should be affirmed, with costs.

POUND, LEHMAN and KELLOGG, J.J., concur with CARDOZO, Ch.J.; ANDREWS, J., dissents in opinion in which CRANE and O'BRIEN, J.J., concur.

*Judgment reversed, etc.** [Pp. 355-356.]

LAIDLAW v. SAGE
N. Y. COURT OF APPEALS
158 N.Y. 73

On the morning of December 4, 1891, the plaintiff, William R. Laidlaw, Jr., went to call on the defendant, Russell Sage. Upon entering his office he found Mr. Sage and a person with a satchel in his hand standing by the entrance to the anteroom, talking. It later appeared that Mr. Sage had received from the third party a note reading as follows: "This carpet bag I hold in my hand contains 10 pounds of dynamite and, if I drop this bag on the floor, it will destroy this building in ruins and kill every human being in it. I demand $1,200,000, or I will drop it. Will you give it,—yes or no?" Mr. Sage, taking hold of Mr. Laidlaw, used him as a shield. The uninvited guest dropped the satchel. The plaintiff was severely injured by the explosion, and this action was brought to recover damages claimed to have been sustained by reason of the alleged wrongful act of the defendant in using the plaintiff's body to protect himself from the effect of the anticipated explosion.

·   ·   ·   ·   ·

MARTIN, J.: ... When we apply to the undisputed fact of this case these rules relating to proximate cause, it becomes quite manifest that the judgment in this action cannot be upheld. All the injuries which the plaintiff sustained were caused directly and immediately by the act of Norcross in exploding the dynamite. That was clearly the proximate, and we think the only, cause of the plaintiff's injury. It was the only efficient cause, as, confessedly, without the explosion the plaintiff would not have been injured; and under no circumstances can it be properly said that the act of the defendant in changing the plaintiff's position a few inches to the

---

* [For a typical interpretation of "proximate" consequence as a result reasonably foreseeable, see Hoag v. Lake Shore and Mich. So. Ry. Co., 85 Pa. 293. A fourth method of limiting liability along the causal chain more consonant with Cardozo's approach, is outlined in Green: *Rationale of Proximate Cause*.]

left of where he previously stood caused the explosion or occasioned a catastrophe. Surely that was not an act without which the explosion would not have occurred; nor can it be held to have been the proximate cause of the explosion. . . . There was no evidence in the case of any necessary relation of cause and effect between the act of which the plaintiff complains and the explosion which caused his injury. . . . The court erred in not directing a verdict for the defendant on that ground.

EDGERTON, LEGAL CAUSE *

A wrongful act or omission has occurred, a harm has been suffered. Will the law treat the one as the cause of the other? My thesis is that it neither is nor should be possible to extract from the cases rules which cover the subject and are definite enough to solve cases; that the solution of cases depends upon a balancing of considerations which tend to show that it is, or is not, reasonable or just to treat the act as the cause of the harm—that is, upon a balancing of conflicting interests, individual and social; that these considerations are indefinite in number and value, and incommensurable; that legal cause is justly attachable cause. I believe that, while logic is useful in the premises it is inadequate; that intuition is necessary and certainty impossible. [P. 211.]

· · · · ·

The fact that the rules of legal cause are intended to produce a just result, rather than to save time or avoid uncertainty, is emphasized by the attitude of the law toward what may be called alternative causes; *i.e.*, causes each of which, without the concurrence of the other, would have been sufficient to produce the result. In general, "a defendant's tort cannot be considered a legal cause of plaintiff's damage, if that damage would have occurred just the same even though the defendant's tort had not been committed.[128] But, by exception "where two tort-feasors are simultaneously operating independently of each other, and the separate tortious act of each is sufficient in and of itself to produce the damaging result," each is liable.[129] It would be shocking to our sense of justice to relieve two wrongdoers of liability on the ground that both are responsible. [P. 346.]

---

* [72 *U. of Pa. L. Rev.* 211, 343 (March, May, 1924).

Judge Henry W. Edgerton (b. 1888), since 1938 a Circuit Judge of the United States Court of Appeals for the District of Columbia Circuit, has distinguished himself as a consistent champion of civil liberties. Prior to his appointment to the Federal bench, Edgerton had engaged in private practice and had served on the faculties of Cornell and George Washington law schools.]

128 Prof. Smith, 25 *Harv. L. Rev.* 312.

129 *Ibid.*

F. S. COHEN, FIELD THEORY AND JUDICIAL LOGIC *

.   .   .   .   .

Causation: Physics and Practical Politics

Some form of causation is involved in every law suit. For every plaintiff claims that somehow the defendant has caused him to suffer and for that reason should be subjected to the strong arm of the law. One might expect, therefore, that after so many centuries of litigation jurists would have a pretty clear idea of what causation really is. The fact remains, however, that jurists have ordinarily conceived of "causation" as a problem of natural science and have therefore studiously refrained from inquiry as to its significance.

On the other hand, natural scientists have decided in recent years that causation has no proper place in their studies, that in fact "cause," its Latin progenitor *"causa,"* and its Greek prototype αἰτία, are all words borrowed from the law courts, which crept into physics on the coat tails of the dignified Stoic theory that the physical world is run like a legal system, under "laws of nature." [17] Today physicists are pretty generally agreed in rejecting as invalid the explanation that gravitation is the "cause" of an apple's downfalling. Gravitation is nothing but a highly abstract way of stating the fact that apples and many other things *do* fall. Insofar as the idea of "cause" carries with it an anthropomorphic or animistic sense of pushing and pulling, it has no proper place in modern physics. Functions and equations have displaced "cause and effect" as the basic terms of physical explanation. The trend of scientific physics is being reflected today, more or less promptly, in every other science.

Where does this leave the jurist? If "cause" is banished from law, will lawsuits be banished also? Or can we refine the concept of causation and hold on to it in the law even though all other sciences reject it?

According to the orthodox view, whether event *A* is the cause of event *B* is a question of objective fact to which all value judgments are irrelevant. What, then, we may ask, is the cause of the injury when a plaintiff and his car have been smashed up by defendant's car? The location and speed of the defendant's car certainly contributed to the accident. So, too, did the location and speed of the plaintiff's car; if plaintiff had stayed in bed instead of driving, he would not have been hurt. Relevant also are the durability and tensile strength of the two cars, the width of the road, the character of the road-surface, the weather, and a host of other more or less important facts. How can we possibly pick out one of these facts,

---

* [59 *Yale L. J.* 238, 251-259 (1950).]
[17] See M. R. Cohen, *The Meaning of Human History* 95 (1947).

or any combination of them, and say: "This was the cause of the accident?" Certainly there is no rule of physics, no rule of engineering, and no rule of logic that will enable us to reach such a result.

What do we actually do? If it turns out that plaintiff was driving on the right side of the road and that the defendant was driving on the left side of the road, we say that the defendant's driving on the left side was the cause of the accident, unless the case arises in England, in which case we say that the plaintiff's driving on the right side was the cause of the accident. From the standpoint of logic or physics the physical collision of the cars had exactly the same physical antecedents whether the collision occurred in England or in America. But from the standpoint of the law, the judgment of "wrongness" or "carelessness" is an essential part of the judgment that attributes the cause of the accident to some human act. Without such standards, we should find in every accident only the intersection of an infinity of strands of occurrences reaching back into the past without end.

What we actually do when we look for a legal cause is to pick out of this infinity of intersecting strands a useful point at which public pressure can be placed.[18] We pick one point rather than another because we think the imposition of pressure at that point will tend to bring about either a better course of conduct on the part of defendants or a fair measure of relief for plaintiffs. What we will take to be the cause of an accident, then, is not determined entirely by the objective facts. The standards of conduct applied to the situation are an integral part of any judgment of legal causation.

In this, the law does not differ essentially from other social fields. When one man finds the cause of high prices in high profits, another in high wages, and a third in high taxes, we recognize that three different value patterns are being applied to the same set of facts. That, perhaps, is why statistical facts and figures seldom sway anybody's viewpoint in such a controversy. When we meet a man who feels that all his efforts are constantly being thwarted by the connivings and conspiracies of other people, we recognize that such a person's ascriptions of causal efficacy may be powerfully affected by a private system of values. If he tells us that all his failures are the result of Catholic conspiracies, or a conspiracy of publishers not to publish his works, we learn a little more about his own set of value judgments, even though we may learn very little about Catholics or publishers. So, too, if a writer tells us in May of 1941 that the cause of World War II is British imperialism and tells us, a few weeks later, that the cause of World War II is Nazi aggression, we may not learn much about World War II, but we do learn something about the "line" of our writer. Indeed we generally learn a good deal more about other peoples' value standards from the statements they make about causal relations than we do from their explicit formulations of value standards. The acquisition of similar knowledge about our own unavowed value standards is a more painful process.[19]

The intimate dependence of causality judgments upon value standards is evident in the work of those historians whose value judgments differ from our own. As Morris R. Cohen points out in *The Meaning of Human History*,

> In effect [most historians] select from the vast conglomerate of determinants which form the necessary and sufficient conditions of a given event some element or elements to which they attach special importance and this they call "the cause," classifying all other elements as "conditions."

> .   .   .   .   .

> Now, though it is perhaps inevitable that historians, like other human beings, should see causal relationships through a screen of human values that gives importance to some antecedents and relegates others to obscurity, it is not inevitable that historians should fail to recognize that this is what they are doing. Indeed if the role which value judgments play in determining our opinions as to historical causation were more clearly understood, we should have less difficulty in understanding how historians who agree on measurable facts so often disagree in tracing the causal relations between them; how, for instance, the decline of Rome can be attributed by equally conscientious and intelligent historians working from a common fund of historical data to such diverse factors as the exhaustion of soil, the corruption of rulers, the rise of Christianity, spots on the sun, and population movements in central Asia. At the same time we might be more cautiously skeptical of the moral lessons drawn from history by historians who fail to disclose the moral presuppositions with which they embarked on the task of historical explanation. For few historians have recognized, as did Darwin, that facts which do not fit into our theories make less of an impression on us than those that do, or have made a sustained effort, as Darwin did, to give special note to those facts that fail to fit into preconceived patterns. Indeed the field of history is so much more complex than that of biology that it is doubtful whether any efforts to make allowances for our own value systems in the writing of history can ever be completely successful. But the historian can make a contribution to intelligent understanding and to the scientific objectivity that transcends national boundaries, racial loyalties, and class interests, by setting forth, as a good map-maker does, his own magnetic deviations and perspectives.[20]

That judgments of causality vary with the standpoint of the observer has come to be widely recognized during recent decades, in scientific, legal, and philosophical circles.[21] Consider, for example, the very practical question: What is the cause of malaria? In the history of science, various answers have been given to this question:

---

[19] "We may often find it easy to indicate approximately on what properties of an object our liking or disliking is founded. But we do not realize with the same clearness on what characteristics of our own self these attitudes depend. For this reason it is, and often remains, so difficult to understand certain valuations of others, for example in the field of art or in that of sex." W. Kohler, *The Place of Value in a World of Facts* 339 (1938).

The ancients found a correlation between exposure to damp air, especially at night, and malaria. It was an essential task of biology and medical science to ask why these two should be thus connected. An intermediate term was found in the bite of certain mosquitoes. But why should the bite of the mosquito produce the given result? Again an intermediate term is found in the virus that is injected into the organism by the bite. But why should that virus destroy the red blood corpuscles? It is obvious that no matter how many middle terms are thus interpolated we still have a discrete series, and the question why two terms should be causally connected remains. This is, of course, no objection to a process which extends our knowledge even though it never can be absolutely completed.[22]

Clearly, for the sanitary engineer, the existence of untreated swamps is the cause of malaria. For the king's attendant with the palm-leaf fans, the bite of the mosquito is the only relevant cause. For the pathologist, the effect of the malaria virus upon red blood corpuscles is the cause. In each case the cause is the point at which effort can be usefully applied.

At least two great American judges, Benjamin Cardozo and Henry Edgerton, have clearly recognized that in law, as elsewhere, judgments of causation are essentially relative and purposive. Thus Justice Cardozo, after noting the infinity of antecedents that come together in any event we seek to explain, observes:

From this complex web the law picks out now this cause and now that one. Thus the same event may have one jural cause when it is considered as giving rise to a cause of action upon contract, and another when it is considered as giving rise to a cause of action for a tort. The law accepts or rejects one or another as it measures its own ends and the social benefits or evils of rejection or acceptance.

A case will point my meaning. A fire occurred at Big Tom, New Jersey. The fire exploded dynamite. The explosion by its vibrations caused damage to a vessel standing out in the river half a mile way. A policy of insurance secured the owner of the vessel against loss proximately caused by fire. The court assumed that by the law in most jurisdictions the fire would be the jural cause if the action were in tort against a wrongdoer who had negligently spread the flames. Indisputably it would if he had acted with intent to cause the very damage that resulted. On the other hand, the court refused to find that the fire was the jural cause within the meaning of the contract.

The reasoning that led to this conclusion is in close approach to Lord Haldane's, though rendition of the judgment preceded by some years the publication of his book. "In last analysis," we said, "it is something in the minds of men, in the will of the contracting parties, and not merely in the physical bond of union between events, which solves, at least for the jurist, this problem of causation. In all this, there is nothing anomalous. Everything in nature is cause and effect by turns. For the physicist, one thing is the cause; for the jurist, another. Even for the jurist, the same cause is alternately proximate and remote as the parties choose to view it. A policy provides that the insurer shall not be liable for damage caused by the explosion of a boiler. The explosion causes a fire. If it were not for the exception in the policy, the fire would be the proxi-

---

[22] M. R. Cohen, *The Meaning of Human History* 105-6 (1947).

mate cause of the loss and the explosion the remote one. By force of the contract, the explosion becomes proximate. A collision occurs at sea and fire supervenes. The fire may be the proximate cause and the collision the remote one for the purpose of an action on the policy. The collision remains proximate for the purpose of suit against the colliding vessel. There is nothing absolute in the legal estimate of causation. Proximity and remoteness are relative and changing concepts." [23]

Probably the most precise formulation of the value-orientation that is implicit in every judgment of causation is that given by Judge Edgerton in his epochal article on "Legal Cause." [24] The painstaking analysis of cases and materials in that article exposes the emptiness of all efforts to define "cause" or "proximate cause" in terms simply of time, space, and mechanics and without reference to values. Judge Edgerton's thesis is best summarized in his own words:* [Pp. 251-256.]

. . . . .

Today it is perhaps no longer necessary to argue that judgments of causation in the law are relative and changing. The real question is how they change. Can we plot out the ways in which changing judgments of purpose and value will lead courts to shift the directions in which they seek to trace chains of causation?

It is when we face the problem of *how* judgments of causality vary that the physical analogy of a field of forces becomes helpful. Such an analogy may indicate that just as precedents shift in direction when they enter a neighborhood of high value tension, so judgments of causality will undergo a similar shift in direction. Generally, the direction shift, whether of precedent connection or of causal connection, will be such as strengthens and reinforces the basic valuations in the field. Precedents which support our objectives grow; precedents that appear to others to be against us drop away. Causal connections which support our objectives are strengthened; those that threaten them drop away. Thus, increasing sympathy for the victims of industrial accidents will bring about a broadening of the field within which causation for such accidents is found in some act of an employer who is able to provide some measure of compensation.[25] Similarly, increasing fear of Communism (or, in a Communist society, of anti-Communism) will expand the field in which responsibility for industrial stoppages and breakdowns is ascribed to Communist (or anti-Communist) propaganda.

All of us, in everyday life, when we attribute causality to anybody or anything, do so through a highly selective value-screen. Most of us, for example, in thinking about accomplishments of which we are particu-

---

[23] Cardozo, *Paradoxes of Legal Science* 83-5 (1928).

[24] 72 *U. of Pa. L. Rev.* 211, 343 (1924).

* [See p. 244 *supra*.]

[25] See Charmont, *Les Transformations du Droit Civil*, c. 15 (1912).

larly proud, attribute the cause of our success to our foresight, perseverance, hard work, or other admirable qualities. Even if we are too modest to talk aloud in these terms, these are the terms in which we generally think. On the other hand, in thinking about our failures, we commonly find that they were brought about by some action of third parties, some accident of the weather, or something else external to ourselves. When we view the works of others, we are more likely to attribute their successes to external circumstances such as inherited wealth, parental care, educational opportunities, and good fortune in health, unless those we are judging are persons whom we particularly love or respect. So, too, we are more skeptical towards others than we are towards ourselves or our dear friends when it comes to excusing failures and misdeeds by attributing them to the intervention of external causes. Concisely, we may say that "causality" is a value-weighted term. The person we admire is viewed as active in the events we admire and as external or passive in events we condemn, which are then viewed as the product of external circumstance. With persons we despise or hate, success is normally attributed to environmental factors for which they can claim no credit, and failure is traced to the person judged.[26] [Pp. 257-258.]

· · · · ·

When two people in a law court blame each other for an accident they are simply behaving like human beings. The function of a law court is not to eliminate all the personal value-tones that lead individuals to draw causal lines one way or another but rather to apply a more comprehensive set of values and to achieve a more comprehensive view of the facts as a guide for social action.

From this analysis a number of inferences can be drawn concerning the disposition of actual cases, and by testing such inferences against the facts we can hope to illumine the validity of this analysis. Such a task must lie beyond the limits of the present essay. But perhaps it is significant to formulate the following hypotheses:

1. The more reprehensible the conduct, the more readily will judges find a causal connection between the conduct and the injury complained of.[27]
2. The more hateful the defendant, the more readily will judges find a causal connection between the defendant and the injury complained of.[28]
3. A judgment against a highly respected citizen has a larger precedent value than a judgment against a despised person; conversely, a judgment in favor of a despised person has a larger precedent value than one for a pillar of society.[29]

---

[26] The shifting lines we draw between an individual and his environment mark the outlines of the problem of civil and criminal responsibility. See F. S. Cohen, "The Socialization of Morality" in Kallen & Hook, *American Philosophy Today and Tomorrow* (1935).

4. A value differential in attitude of judge and jury towards a given class will be reflected in differences of judgment as to whether individuals of the given class are responsible for the wrongs complained of.[30] [Pp. 258-259.]

C. Culpable cause

EARL IVES v. THE SOUTH BUFFALO RY. CO.
N.Y. COURT OF APPEALS, 1911
201 N.Y. 271

WERNER, J.: . . . The statute [Workmen's Compensation Law of 1910], judged by our common-law standards, is plainly revolutionary. Its central and controlling feature is that every employer who is engaged in any of the classified industries shall be liable for any injury to a workman arising out of and in the course of the employment by "a necessary risk or danger of the employment or one inherent in the nature thereof; . . . provided that the employer shall not be liable in respect of any injury to the workman which is caused in whole or in part by the serious and willful misconduct of the workman." This rule of liability, stated in another form, is that the employer is responsible to the employee for every accident in the course of the employment, whether the employer is at fault or not, and whether the employee is at fault or not, except when the fault of the employee is so grave as to constitute serious and willful misconduct on his part. The radical character of this legislation is at once revealed by contrasting it with the rule of the common law, under which the employer is liable for injuries to his employee only when the employer is guilty of some act or acts of negligence which caused the occurrence out of which the injuries arise, and then only when the employee is shown to be free from any negligence which contributes to the occurrence. The several judicial and statutory modifications of this broad rule of the common law we shall further on have occasion to mention. Just now our purpose is to present in sharp juxtaposition the fundamentals of these two opposing rules, namely, that under the common law an employer is liable to his injured employee only when the employer is at fault and the employee is free from fault; while under the new statute the employer is liable, although not at fault, even when the employee is at fault, unless this latter fault amounts to serious and willful misconduct. The reasons for this departure from our long-established law and usage are summarized in the language of the commission as follows:

First, that the present system in New York rests on a basis that is economically unwise and unfair, and that in operation it is wasteful, uncertain and productive of antagonism between workmen and employers.

Second, that it is satisfactory to none and tolerable only to those employers and workmen who practically disregard their legal rights and obligations, and fairly share the burden of accidents in industries.

Third, that the evils of the system are most marked in hazardous employments, where the trade risk is high and serious accidents frequent.

Fourth, that, as a matter of fact, workmen in the dangerous trades do not, and practically cannot, provide for themselves adequate accident insurance, and, therefore, the burden of serious accidents falls on the workmen least able to bear it, and brings many of them and their families to want.

This indictment of the old system is followed by a statement of the anticipated benefits under the new statute as follows: "Those results can, we think, be best avoided by compelling the employer to share the accident burden in intrinsically dangerous trades, since by fixing the price of his product the shock of the accident may be borne by the community. In those employments which have not so great an element of danger, in which, speaking generally, there is no such imperative demand for the exercise of the police power of the state for the safeguarding of its workers from destitution and its consequences, we recommend, as the first step in this change of system, such amendment of the present law as will do away with some of its unfairness in theory and practice, and increase the workman's chance of recovery under the law. With such changes in the law we couple an elective plan of compensation which, if generally adopted, will do away with many of the evils of the present system. Its adoption will, we believe, be profitable to both employer and employee, and prove to be the simplest way for the State to change its system of liability without disturbance of industrial conditions. Not the least of the motives moving us is the hope that by these means a source of antagonism between employer and employed, pregnant with danger for the State, may be eliminated."

This quoted summary of the report of the commission to the legislature, which clearly and fairly epitomizes what is more fully set forth in the body of the report, is based upon a most voluminous array of statistical tables, extracts from the works of philosophical writers and the industrial laws of many countries, all of which are designed to show that our own system of dealing with industrial accidents is economically, morally and legally unsound. Under our form of government, however, courts must regard all economic, philosophical and moral theories, attractive and desirable though they may be, as subordinate to the primary question whether they can be moulded into statutes without infringing upon the letter or spirit of our written constitutions. In that respect we are unlike any of the countries whose industrial laws are referred to as models for our guidance. Practically all of these countries are so called constitutional monarchies in which, as in England, there is no written constitution, and the Parliament or law-making body is supreme. In our country the Federal and State Constitutions are the charters which demark the extent and the limitations of legislative power; and while it is true that the rigidity of a written constitution may at times prove to be a hindrance to the march of progress, yet more often its stability protects the people against the frequent and violent fluctuations of that which, for want of a better name, we call public opinion. [Pp. 285-287.]

.   .   .   .   .

This legislation is challenged as void under the fourteenth amendment to the Federal Constitution and under section 6, article 1 of our State Constitution, which guarantee all persons against deprivation of life, liberty or property without due process of law. We shall not stop to dwell at length upon definitions of "life," "liberty," "property" and "due process of law." They are simple and comprehensive in themselves and have been so often judicially defined that there can be no misunderstanding as to their meaning. Process of law in its broad sense means law in its regular course of administration through courts of justice, and that is but another way of saying that every man's right to life, liberty and property is to be disposed of in accordance with those ancient and fundamental principles which were in existence when our Constitutions were adopted. . . . One of the inalienable rights of every citizen is to hold and enjoy his property until it is taken from him by due process of law. When our Constitutions were adopted it was the law of the land that no man who was without fault or negligence could be held liable in damages for injuries sustained by another. . . . The right of property rests not upon philosophical or scientific speculations nor upon the commendable impulses of benevolence or charity, nor yet upon the dictates of natural justice. The right has its foundation in the fundamental law. That can be changed by the people, but not by legislatures. In a government like ours theories of public good or necessity are often so plausible or sound as to command popular approval, but courts are not permitted to forget that the law is the only chart by which the ship of state is to be guided. Law as used in this sense means the basic law and not the very act of legislation which deprives the citizen of his rights, privileges or property. Any other view would lead to the absurdity that the Constitutions protect only those rights which the legislatures do not take away. If such economic and sociologic arguments as are here advanced in support of this statute can be allowed to subvert the fundamental idea of property, then there is no private right entirely safe, because there is no limitation upon the absolute discretion of legislatures, and the guarantees of the Constitution are a mere waste of words. . . . [Pp. 292-295.]

CHARMONT, THE CHANGES IN THE CIVIL LAW *

Chapter 15. The Idea of Fault and the Idea of Risk: The Theory of Risk

. . . . .

According to the traditional doctrine, delictual liability presupposes two conditions: (1) a connection of cause and effect between the person liable and the fact from which damage results; (2) a fault of this person, which implies at once an act of intelligent volition that is illicit, or contrary to law.

It is necessary in the first place that there be a detrimental occurrence and that this occurrence have been caused by the person of whom reparation is demanded. The nature of the detriment is of little importance: it is admitted that a non-physical detriment can, as well as a physical, require reparation. Likewise the mode of causation is of little importance; what is needed is that the judge perceive a connection between the accident and the act of a party.

Of course, it is upon the injured person that the burden of furnishing proof of the existence and the cause of the injury devolves. It is the application of the principle: *actori incumbit probatio.* We are assuming that the victim and the author of the injury are not connected by any contract. The situation would be modified if the injury resulted from the failure to execute an agreement; the promisee would only have to prove the existence of the contract and the promisor who attempted to escape from the consequences of failure of execution would have to establish that this failure is not imputable to him, that it has as its cause a pure accident.

The material fact of detriment and of the participation of another person does not suffice to engender liability; there is needed, in addition, an element more difficult to define, which is termed *fault*, and which implies in order that the author of the detriment be reproachable for something (1) that he has committed an illicit act, (2) that he had had conciousness of this act. M. Geny has noted the fact [1] that the treatises on civil law have a tendency to confuse these two characteristics, designating them both under the same term; it is not useless, however, to distinguish them; their existence is a condition of delict. In the classical doctrine there is no fault, and consequently no liability, if one of these two elements is missing.

* [*Joseph Charmont* (1859–1922), professor of civil law at the University of Montpellier from 1885 until his death, was active in the attempt to harmonize the apparent conflicts amongst the teachings of the individualists, the sociological jurists, and the exponents of natural law. *Les Transformations du droit civil*, from which the above passage is translated, appeared in 1912, after the publication of *Le Droit et l'esprit démocratique* (1908) and *La Renaissance du droit naturel* (1910), most of which is translated in *Modern French Legal Philosophy* (1916), Volume VII of the Modern Legal Philosophy Series. Footnotes in this extract have been renumbered.]
[1] "*Risques et responsabilité*" (*Revue de droit civil*, 1902, p. 820).

If one who confines himself to the exercise of a right causes a detriment to another, this is of little importance; he is not bound to compensate this; *neminem laedit qui jure suo utitur.* [Pp. 233-237.]

.   .   .   .   .

Under the pressure of events and resulting change of opinion, this traditional conception was imperceptibly modified: in the first place, there was a tendency to take account of a superior interest of equity and human welfare in granting compensation for detriment caused by irresponsible persons. Thus, article 829 of the German Civil Code accords an indemnity to the victim of a detriment caused by one who is insane, provided that the author of the detriment can pay this compensation without himself being reduced to indigence.[2] In the second place, the law has thought it possible to distinguish between the exercise and the abuse of a right. It has admitted the liability of the author of detriment in cases where his acts cannot be considered illicit.[3] There is no need of invoking any new principle in order to justify these solutions; they are indistinctly connected with the idea of fault.

II.

Let us see now how there has developed the theory of risk which has appeared to offer an antithesis to that of responsibility but which is much more a complement.

The old notion of risk relates exclusively to patrimonial detriment resulting from fortuitous accident. The owner of anything which has been destroyed is compelled to bear the loss of this thing, and since this loss is accidental he cannot fix it upon any one else. By parity of reasoning, the same principle can be applied to an accident occasioned by chance. Whoever is the victim of an accident occasioned by chance bears the consequences alone. No one owes him compensation, unless this compensation has been stipulated for by a contract, for instance, by a contract of insurance. It is apparent what the consequences of these principles can be in the matter of industrial accidents. It is shown by statistics prepared by the Imperial German Bureau of Insurance, taken from 15,970 cases, that the cause of accidents sustained in industry can be summed up as follows: in every 100 accidents, 19.76 are imputable to the employer,—25.64 to the worker,—4.45 to the concurrent negligence of employer and worker,—3.28 to the fault of other workers,—46.87 to dangers inherent in work, chance, and unknown causes. Simplifying the figures, one can say that the fortuitous cases are accounted for by one half,—the fault of employer and that of worker, each by one quarter. In the traditional doctrine, the worker obviously bears the loss caused by his fault; he can claim nothing even in the case of mischance. He has an action against the employer only if the accident has happened through the fault of the latter; what is more, he has to prove this, and the burden of this proof is exceptionally severe.

Then too, what mistakes may not one make when in such a case he thinks it within his power to individualize the responsibilities and find the cause of an accident in the negligence or imprudence of this or that person! One forgets that statistics permits us to tell in advance how many victims each sort of industry will produce in a given time. We know, for instance, that the construction and maintenance of a railway line entails a certain average of accidents. It is hardly necessary to observe that we are, in almost every case, faced with a problem of risk and not with a problem of fault, and that risks ought equitably to be placed to the charge of the entrepreneur who reserved to himself the management and the profit.

III.

Before arriving at this point, law and legal theory underwent certain modifications and made certain tentative changes. Although the change and the hesitations have only a historical interest, one may not neglect to speak of them when studying the modifications of law.

The civil law remained faithful to the traditional doctrine: it condemns the employer only if his fault is proved, but this fault is understood in a singularly wide sense; one loses sight of the causal relation, and comes to consider as fault any irregular fact charged against the employer even though nothing is shown between such fact and the accident which establishes a relation of cause and effect.... This fault, purely collateral, without direct bearing upon the accident, is near to being fortuitous mischance; however, the line which binds the conclusions of such law to the traditional doctrine is not broken.

IV.

Bolder and more independent is the attitude of administrative jurisprudence....

Civil law is not applicable to questions of the liability of the State. The administrative judge, in the absence of a text, must examine whether such liability is justly enlisted. The State, which carries through an industrial operation in the public service must take to its charge risks inherent in the work....

Thus, in the front rank administrative law was moving towards its objective and considering risk inherent in the work as chargeable to the State.

V.

It remains for us to show what has been attempted in the way of modifying the civil law; during the period when a legislative reform was slowly being worked out, an important current of juristic theory sought to bring the courts to a solution of the question. A first theory, that of contractual liability, represents an effort almost sterile; the moment that this effort appeared to be rejected, the course of judicial decisions seemed suddenly disposed to enter upon a new path; it might be thought that it was going to accept the idea of liability in objects for their effects, which had been adopted and developed by certain writers, notably by Saleilles and Josserand.

The doctrine of contractual liability consists in pretending that the course of judicial decisions was mistaken when it derived the liability of the employer from Article 1382. The basis of this liability is to be found in the contract of the hiring of service which has been formed between the two parties. By the effect of the contract the employer has the right of using for a certain time the activity of the worker; but he is not freed from his obligation to the other party by the mere payment of wages; he owes him security. According to the expression of M. Sauzet, he ought to be able to restore him, to give him back to himself in as good a condition as when he received him; he is then in the position of a bailee of a particular body. If the worker, in these circumstances, is the victim of an accident, the employer who cannot repair the damage is presumed to be in fault; the worker has nothing to prove.

M. Sauzet [4] in 1883 and a Belgian, M. Sainctelette,[5] independently offered this conception at almost the same time. [Pp. 237-244.]

.   .   .   .   .

Above all, this theory presented a double disadvantage; it left an uncertainty concerning the object and the extent of this obligation of warranty. [P. 244.]

.   .   .   .   .

This uncertainty as to the extent of the liability was neither the sole nor the most severe disadvantage of contractual liability. The weak point of the system, says Saleilles, is that this liability can be overcome by a clause of exoneration. . . . Certain adherents of this theory, notably M. Labbe, refused to admit unrestrictedly the validity of clauses of exoneration.[6]

It is not then to be too much regretted that the course of decisions refused to enter upon this path. . . .

. . . In Belgium, where the course of decisions did adopt the theory of contractual fault . . . . by an error of logic they refused to draw from the system its characteristic consequence, the shifting of proof, or to admit

---

[4] *Revue critique. Responsabilité des patrons.*
[5] *Responsabilité et garantie,* 1884.
[6] *Revue critique de legislation,* 1886, p. 448.

that the fault of the employer should be presumed by the mere fact that this obligation was not executed.

VI

Legal theory had been left discouraged by the failure of these efforts, when, in 1896, a judgment of the Court of Appeals [*Cour de cassation*] gave new hopes to some writers who favored a judicial solution of the problem of labor accidents. One of the pipes in the steam-engine of a tug-boat had exploded, on the Loire near Nantes; the accident had resulted in the death of a mechanic. The trial judge, accepting the conclusion of a commission for the supervision of steamships, had attributed the explosion to a defect in the soldering of the pipe. The defect consisted, undeniably, in a fault of construction. Accordingly it had to be recognized that the owner of the tug-boat had not known of the defect and could not have learned of it. The widow of the victim demanded compensation; the Court of Paris awarded her the decision, applying by analogy Article 1386 of the Civil Code, which declares the owner liable for the fall of a building. An appeal was taken before the Court of Appeals for erroneous application of the law; it was claimed that Article 1386 was inapplicable; a machine is not, in fact, a building. The appeal was dismissed. The Civil Chamber declared that in default of Article 1386 one might invoke Article 1384 which had a general application and according to which one is responsible for things that one has under his control.

Some months later, the same question presented itself in circumstances hardly different before the Chamber of Appeals [*Chambre des requêtes*]. It arose again out of an accident caused by the explosion of a steam-engine; only the cause of the accident had remained unknown. The widow of one of the victims claimed damages and submitted that she had no proof to make, the company being liable as a matter of law. The tribunal of Marseille and the court of Aix had dismissed her complaint; the Chamber of Appeals in its turn rejected the appeal. [Pp. 245-248.]

.   .   .   .   .

These decisions ... had a certain permanency. They were the point of departure for a doctrinal movement. M. Saleilles took up again[9] in this development a position that he had maintained for some years before[10] this view, defended as well by Josserand[11] looks upon liability in the matter of industrial accidents as a consequence of the more general principle of liability for things which one has under his control. It is maintained that the line of judicial decisions, in extending the notion of fault

---

[9] *Les accidents du travail et la responsabilité civile.* Paris, 1897.
[10] *Revue bourguignonne de l'enseignement supérieur*, 1894, p. 660.
[11] *De la responsabilité du fait des choses inanimées*, 1897.

in a more and more liberal manner, is coming to consider the use of machines and tools as a fault. Thus there is gradually substituted for the old notion the idea of risk: "Let us call things by their names; let us lay aside this idea of fault; and let us say in all simplicity what will be more equitable from the point of view of society and more in conformity with the idea of individual dignity, that each person, in acting, incurs risks, and that when a misfortune thus happens in consequence of a free and voluntary act, the author of the act shall pay for the risks.[12]

It is proper to note, however, that the liability for the effects of objects, even understood as it appeared to have been by the Civil Chamber, does not lay the totality of industrial risks to the charge of the employer. The employer could exonerate himself by declaring that the accident happened by a fortuitous mischance or by *force majeure,* and indeed, after the judgment of the Chamber of Appeals, it was enough for him to establish that he had committed no fault. Thus many classes of accidents continued to be burdens of the worker; those which resulted from his fault; from a fortuitous mischance, or from an unknown cause. [Pp. 249-250.]

· · · · ·

VII

Juristic theory and the course of judicial decisions had been powerless expediently and plainly to secure reform; an intervention by the legislature was indispensable. This intervention came about in 1898. The law of April 9, 1898, framed to take effect from July 1, 1899, voted and applied with much difficulty, modified by several amendments, borrowed from the German laws the theory of professional risk. It is summed up in the idea that the employer is to compensate the victim of an accident occurring in the course of or by reason of the employment, leaving no place, in principle, for an investigation into the cause. In return, the compensation is not a full reparation of the damage caused. It is fixed by a tariff of forfeitures. [Pp. 251-252.]

· · · · ·

DEMOGUE, FAULT, RISK, AND APPORTIONMENT OF LOSS *

The development of machinery and, in a more general manner, the increasing importance of the applied sciences have rendered more frequent

---

[12] Saleilles, *Les accidents du travail,* p. 74.

* [Reprinted by special permission of the *Illinois Law Review* (Northwestern University School of Law). 13 *Ill. L. Rev.* 297. The translation of this article by Edward Matthews, appearing in 15 *Ill. L. Rev.* 369, has been generally followed; page references are to 13 *Ill. L. Rev.*

A statement of Demogue's views on the general theory of liability, and particularly the conflict between the demands of static security (*e.g.,* security of ownership) and

certain installations, certain uses of substances, of instruments, of motors which we could ill dispense with, which increase the comfort or the conveniences of life and which have the common character of being dangerous. Not only do they demand certain precautions for their manipulation, but even when all measures of prudence at present known have been taken, accidents may still take place quite easily. It is sufficient to cite among these causes of damages, explosives, inflammable liquids, stationary motor machines, automobiles, gas, electricity, acetylene.

When they appeared successively and when the diffusion of their employment revealed at the same time with their advantages the ill consequences which they could produce for others, it had been universally maintained that, in this case as in the others, the victim should prove that a fault was committed. Still, being vaguely conscious that this solution was not very satisfying, the tribunals have taxed their ingenuity to discover in the employer of the dangerous instrument a fault even slight so as to make it the basis of a responsibility. [P. 307.]

. . . . .

We are nevertheless favorable to the responsibility, apart from all imprudence or negligence, of him who employs a dangerous engine. First and foremost, this person cannot complain of supporting the weight of the loss which he has caused. He utilizes this engine for a personal advantage; he cannot complain of suffering its ill consequences. He cannot object that this responsibility finally renders the employment of this engine onerous to him. Socially this employment is useful only if the profit which comes principally to him who utilizes the engine exceeds the loss caused to others. An industrial establishment by its smoke, by the gases which it exhales, renders uninhabitable a neighboring house and thereby causes a depreciation in the value of the land of 50,000 francs. This factory economically is usfeul to the country only if the profits which are drawn from it permit of the payment without difficulty of the loss sustained by the neighboring proprietor. Undoubtedly exceptional cases may be shown where a factory working only with small returns may be of great benefit from the point of view of the city or the nation. Certain machinery is manufactured there for a neighboring port, an industry is exploited there which must not be allowed to fall into the hands of foreign manufacturers. But it is then the public authorities that should take the steps necessary to ensure that the industry does not operate at a loss. The manufacturer who in order to exploit his industry violates the rights of others and devotes himself to a real dispossession for

---

the demands of dynamic security (*e.g.*, security of acquisition in the open market) will be found in the passages from his *Les Notions fondamentales de droit privé: essai critique pour servir d'introduction à l'étude des obligations* (1911), translated by Joseph P. Chamberlain in *Modern French Legal Philosophy* (1921) at pp. 347-572.]

cause of private utility must be responsible for that act. But it is especially by taking the point of view of the facility to support the loss, as the preceding idea already indicates, that we may discover grounds for the solution of our difficulty.

We may in the first place make this general remark that the instrumentalities which modern civilization has multiplied are generally costly. He who uses them is then often able to support the loss which they cause. Belonging to the possessing classes, it will more frequently happen that he is insured. The mechanism of insurances moreover often adapts itself better here to the insurance by the author of the harm than by the victim.

In fact, when the holder of a right insures it against accidents which threaten it, insurance is not practiced as a general mode of perpetuating in a property its pecuniary value in spite of all perils which threaten it. It functions only as security against a fixed category of accidents to the exclusion of others: fire, theft. More frequently, the insurances of responsibility permit him who makes use of a thing to arrange that the actions which will be brought against him will not be onerous to him. They have then a more general character. If, on the other hand, we consider him who makes use of the dangerous engine, which almost always has a permanent position, and him who fortuitously is its victim, we see that the first having his attention much more drawn to possible accidents will be more driven to protect himself with an insurance. He who makes use of gas will think more of insuring himself than the passer-by who walking alongside the property at the moment of the explosion suffers a physical harm.

If we thus admit the responsibility of him who utilizes the engine, we should nevertheless be forced to admit that the victim should bear a small fraction of responsibility. It is not necessary that a person be without interest to avoid a harm which can reach him. He must always be urged to show himself prudent on his side to avoid an accident which is always a destruction of wealth.

What would the dangerous engines be whose use would thus involve full responsibility? It would be for the legislator to give the list of them. That would spare him, the principle being once stated, from being lost, in every case of responsibility, in the complications of special legislation.

Even without the employment of dangerous instrumentalities, an accident may happen without any fault on one side or the other. The classic theory of responsibility here refuses all indemnity to the victim. On the contrary, the partisans of responsibility without fault, saying that it is sufficient that loss is caused, to owe an indemnity, admit there again full liability of the author. A solution of compromise, consisting of dividing the loss to be borne between the author and the victim seems preferable to us. We can no longer speak here of a machinery from which a profit is drawn, which justifies the full responsibility of the author. It should be remarked, moreover, that chance may have alone determined the party who stands the damage. In an obscure street two persons violently collide for want of having seen each other. Chance will often dispose that one person rather than the other is thrown down.

Divided responsibility causes each to have an interest in order to avoid harm, a part of the consequences of which he will bear. At the same time, in all the cases where the exact conditions, culpable or fortuitous, in which the harm produced cannot be determined, we arrive at an acceptable solution, as well for the author as for the victim; the responsibility being divided between them will be more easy to support. Insofar as the presumption controls, unless the victim proves that the case is one where the author is completely responsible, this solution is much more in accord than any other with the reality of the facts. If the exact conditions under which the harm has taken place have remained unknown, it is more reasonable to suppose that there has been some little fault on the part of each, rather than to think that the author has nothing wherewith to reproach himself.

This solution of compromise has such force that the tribunals recognize willingly enough that the author is in fault whilst estimating the indemnity sufficiently low, or they admit that the author and the victim are both faulty and divide the responsibility between them. The division of responsibility being thus the common rule and having for basis not an idea of fault, but the facility with which the loss may be borne, this principle may receive a very broad application; it may be extended to the case where the author of the harm does not enjoy the plenitude of his mental faculties, being an insane person or a minor. We are indeed in the presence of one of those mitigated solutions which life, being unable to achieve the ideal, readily accepts.* [Pp. 308-310.]

DUGUIT, GENERAL CHANGES IN PRIVATE LAW SINCE THE CODE NAPOLEON †

V. The New Conception of Liability for an Injurious Act

. . . . .

§ 39. The Individualistic Principle of Liability.

. . . . .

The individualistic principle of liability is expressed in Article 1382 of the Napoleonic Code: "Any act by which a person causes damage to

---

* [For a general consideration of the opposing elements of static security and dynamic security and of the compromises or reconciliations which the law of tort and contract may effect, see Demogue, *Les Notions fondamentales du droit prive*, Chaps. 2-4. (Trans. in Modern Legal Philosophy Series, Vol. VII, *Modern French Legal Philosophy*, pp. 418-479.)]

† [Originally delivered as a course of lectures at the Argentine University Law School of Buenos Aires in 1911. Translated from *Les Transformations générales du*

another binds the person by whose fault the damage occurred to repair such damage." Almost the same words are found in Article 1109 of the Argentine Code: "Whoever does an act, which by his fault or negligence causes damage to another, is bound to repair the damage. . . . "

§ 40. *Subjective Liability for an Injurious Act and Objective Liability for Risk.*—The rule is very simple and very consistent with the whole structure of the individualistic system.

In the relations between two subjects of right an obligation can only arise out of contract. But if a wrongful or negligent act can be imputed to a party, this imputation raises an obligation in him to repair the injury which he has caused to the subject of right. The party who alleges the injury must, therefore, prove the wrong or negligence of the actor. In the last analysis it is still the will of the subject of the right which is the generating cause of the legal relation between the parties. In this system it is invariably the principle of moral imputation that is the sole basis of both the civil and the criminal liability of the subject of right. Hence the system has been named that of subjective liability.

I do not pretend that the subjective liability has disappeared or should disappear completely; in the relations between individuals it continues and no doubt will continue for a long time to come. I do claim that the domain of subjective liability is narrowing and that imputation can no longer be the criterion of liability where the question is not one arising between individuals, but between groups or between groups and individuals. And it is not to be denied that there very often does exist in fact a relation between groups or between groups and individuals when there appear to be only isolated relations between individuals. In that case it is not a question of imputation, but simply a question of risk. The problem is to determine what interests should ultimately support the risks attached to the activity of the group under consideration. When the problem is so viewed there can arise an objective responsibility, something distinct from subjective responsibility. To determine whether liability exists, we no longer inquire whether a wrongful or negligent act has been committed, but simply which group must eventually support the risk. The only proof is the damage caused; once this is established, liability results, automatically, as it were.

§ 41. *Objective Liability attaches only to Groups.*—It is easy to see how this sort of liability has been a consequence of the socialization of law. When those acts of a man's life to which legal results attached were

---

droit depuis le Code Napoléon (1912) in *The Progress of Continental Law in the Nineteenth Century*, pp. 65, 124-128. Ass'n of American Law Schools, ed. Boston: Little, Brown & Company, 1918.

Leon Duguit (1859–1922) was professor of constitutional law at the University of Bordeaux for a long service dating from the turn of the century, and author of a number of important works of legal philosophy and French constitutional law.]

viewed simply as relations between individual and individual, and when all acts interesting society were derived from the autonomy of the individual will, it was impossible to imagine the rise of an obligation save as the produce of the will. The bearer of subject of right wills conformably to law: he, thereby, becomes a creditor or a debtor; he wills contrary to law; he is made liable and becomes a debtor to the extent of the damage caused.

But to-day the life of the community and, therefore, life as it is reflected in the law, is the product of a division of labor into activities of the individual and activities of groups. Groups are not, as we have seen, subjects of will; liability cannot be imputed to them. But group activity is none the less an important element of social activity. The labor which the group performs no doubt benefits society as a whole, but its more immediate benefit redounds to the members of the group. If the latter reaps the proximate benefit, it is fair that it support the risk to which the exercise of that activity subjects individuals and other groups.

This is the very simple conception upon which hang all the cases of objective liability.

It would be interesting to study in detail the examples of objective liability to be found in modern statutes and cases. I cannot do more than refer to the two most important instances, those of liability for accidents to workmen and of liability for injury in a public service.

§ 42. *Liability for Injuries to Workman.*—The Act of April 9, 1898, relating to accidents to workmen, as completed and expanded by the Act of April 12, 1906, is the first law in France to create an express instance of objective liability. It already existed in certain countries, notably England and Germany. Before the passing of this law, an effort had been made in France by text writers and Courts to prepare the ground for the Act by shifting the burden of proof. The employer was declared to be always liable for the accident unless he proved that fault was imputable to the workman. They tried to justify their doctrine by torturing the sense of several provisions of the Napoleonic Code, especially Articles 1384 and following.[1] Finally, the Act of 1898 created a complete system of objective liability. . . .

The individualistic school is still active in its criticism of the system. Obviously it is wholly repugnant to individualistic principles. But the spread of the system is one of the best proofs of the defeat of individualism. If we consider in industrial concerns only the isolated relation between employer and employee, evidently there can arise against the employer merely a subjective liability for a wrongful act. The only question that might, perhaps, be raised would be whether the liability

---

[1] *Cf.* particularly Josserand, "*De la responsabilité du fait des choses inanimées*" (1897); Saleilles, "*Les accidents du travail et la responsabilité civile*," from the "*Revue bourguignonne de l'enseignement superieur*" (1894), pp. 655 *et seq.*

were "ex contractu" or "ex delicto." But in modern industrial communities this is no longer the situation. Industrial establishments have acquired a social importance; the employer exercises truly a social function. In reality two social elements are brought face to face: capital and labor. The whole problem is to determine which of these two elements ought to support the risks of the enterprise or whether it ought to be supported by them both; and lastly, whether an accident to an employee, or his death, constitutes a part of that risk. As the element of capital, apparently at least, enjoys all the profits of the enterprise, the conclusion has followed that this is the element which ought to support all the risks and which consequently is liable for accidents. But this liability is one in which the element of imputation is entirely foreign. [Pp. 125-127.]

.   .   .   .   .

§ 43. *Liability for Injury in Public Service.*—Lastly, objective liability appears very clearly in what I call, by way of abbreviation, liability for injury in a public service. It should be called the liability of the public treasury by reason of facts arising in the operation of a public service. The decisions of the French Council of State have established a doctrine in this matter that is essentially protective of the public who enjoy the service and which is certainly more progressive than any existing in foreign countries. It is impossible for me to go into it here; I would have to develop the whole theory of a public service, and that would be outside my program. It must suffice to say that the French doctrine is based entirely upon the idea that the public treasury must support the risks to the individual which attend the operation of a public service; that the Council of State no longer obliges the individual to prove that actual fault is chargeable to the agents of the public service, that liability attaches, no matter what the class of public service, since the old distinction between a public service that was responsible for its management and a public service that was not, has been definitely abandoned; and lastly, that the Council of State admits of liability to-day even for police acts.[2] [P. 128.]

WU, THE ART OF LAW *

It is interesting to note that what is merely a tendency in juristic doctrine in the common law countries has actually been accomplished in the modern Chinese law, at least in two connections.

---

[2] *Cf.* Duguit, *"Traité de droit constitutionnel,"* Vol. I, pp. 253 *et seq.*...

* [Shanghai: The Commercial Press, Ltd., 1936.

John Chin Hsung Wu (b. 1899), a contemporary Chinese writer on jurisprudence, for many years judge at Shanghai, studied in the United States, particularly at Harvard where he worked with Roscoe Pound. *The Art of Law* appeared in 1936 in Shanghai and was followed two years later by an excellent anthology of *Essays in Jurisprudence and Legal Philosophy,* which Wu edited together with M. C. Liang.]

As we have seen, an employer is responsible for any damage which his employee unlawfully causes to a third party in the performance of his work but the theory of fault requires that if the employer is free from any negligence in the selection and supervision of the employ[ee], he shall be able to exonerate himself from liability. In fact, the German Civil Code stops here. The Chinese Civil Code, however, goes a step further and proceeds to provide that, even though the employer may be entirely free of fault, the court may still consider the relative economic conditions of the injured party and the employer, and, when justice requires, award the whole or a part of the damages. While in its results this rule comes near to the common law, yet the basis of liability is different. At common law, the liability springs from a relation irrespectively of fault, but in the Chinese law it arises *ex aequo et bono*, and its scope is extremely elastic. Corresponding to the individualization of punishment in the criminal law, we have here an example of the individualization of civil liability. [Pp. 68-69.]

. . . . .

Now, with what name shall we baptize this newborn form of liability? I would suggest the name of quasi-tort. . . .

To my mind, "tort" should be reserved for liability because of fault. Fault is to tort what agreement is to contract; and just as a quasi-contract is a juridical situation where there is avowedly no agreement but justice requires that consequences ordinarily arising *ex contractu* shall also be attached to that type of juridical situation, so a quasi-tort is a juridical situation where there is avowedly no fault but justice requires that consequences ordinarily arising *ex delicto* shall be attached to it. [Pp. 70-71.]

JAMES, ACCIDENT LIABILITY RECONSIDERED: THE IMPACT OF LIABILITY INSURANCE *

I

During the formative period of most of the current doctrines of negligence law, liability in tort was looked on as shifting a loss that had already occurred from one individual to another—generally from the person who suffered the loss to the person who caused it. It is against the background of this way of looking at things that nearly all of our conventional reasoning about the objectives of tort law has developed and that nearly all of our conclusions have been drawn and our rules formulated. But society has no interest in the mere shifting of a loss between individuals *just for the sake of shifting it.* The loss, by hypothesis, has already happened. A has been killed, or his leg broken or his automobile smashed up. If the

---

* [57 *Yale L.J.* 549-551 (1947-48).]

only question is whether B shall be made to pay for this loss, any good that may come to society from having compensation made to *one* of its members is exactly offset by the harm caused by taking that amount away from *another* of its members. In that view of the problem there had to be some additional reason for a defendant to compensate a plaintiff for his injury before society would compel compensation. These reasons might be (a) a feeling of what is fair or just; (b) a desire to discourage dangerous conduct, or of course a combination of both.

To a very considerable extent this last-named desire was tempered by a strong counter-desire not unduly to discourage enterprising affirmative activity—even when it was dangerous—because people were very much imbued with the idea that unfettered enterprise and activity in nearly all directions worked out through the laws of competition to promote the general good. And again, these matters of fairness and deterrence were all considered on the assumptions that plaintiff and defendant were alone involved and that what happened between them was the real issue—that tort liability was paid for out of the defendant's own pocketbook. This focussed attention on the moral quality of the conduct of the individual participants in the accident. The net result was the general principle of no liability without fault.

There is however an altogether different approach to tort law. Human failures in a machine age cause a large and fairly regular—though probably reducible—toll of life, limb, and property. As a class the victims of these accidents can ill afford the loss they entail. The problem of decreasing this toll can best be solved through the pressure of safety regulations with penal and licensing sanctions, and of self-interest in avoiding the host of non-legal disadvantages that flow from accidents. But when this is all done, human losses remain. It is the principal job of tort law today to deal with these losses. The best and most efficient way to do this is to assure accident victims of compensation, and to distribute the losses involved over society as a whole or some very large segment of it. Such a basis for administering losses may be called social insurance.

This at once brings in an important new element. For while no social good may come from the mere shifting of a loss, society does benefit from the wide and regular distribution of losses, taken alone.[1] The administration of losses in this way may entirely change evaluations of what is fair. If a certain type of loss is the more or less inevitable by-product of a desirable but dangerous form of activity it may well be just to distribute such losses among all the beneficiaries of the activity though it would be unjust to visit them severally upon those individuals who had happened to be the faultless instruments causing them.[2]

---

[2] Surely there is here at least as much of a moral point of view as in the "fault" basis of liability, "but it is social morality, and not personal blame which is involved." Prosser, *Torts* 21 (1941); Pound, The End of Law as Developed in Legal Rules and

What I have termed the principle of social insurance has been openly accepted in one important branch of what used to be tort law—the field of industrial accident. For the rest, the older principles of tort liability based on fault remain on the surface and, as they are reflected in legal reasoning, remain pretty much the same although there have been peripheral extensions. But this lack of formal change in the main body of accident law is really misleading. Great changes are going on under the surface which have profoundly affected the operation and incidence of tort liability and the assurance of compensation.

Chief among the factors which have brought about this change is the prevalence of liability insurance—a device which was unknown until practically the end of the last century. Legally, liability insurance was at first (and still largely is) regarded as an altogether irrelevant fact in the consideration of tort liability. It was a private contract of indemnity between the defendant and an outsider, by which the latter undertook to protect the insured from loss on account of his individual legal liability. As to the injured person it was *res inter alios acta*—or as the non-classically trained layman would put it, "none of his business." But whatever the orthodox legal notion, the fact of widely held assurance and the form and development of insurance policies and insurance practices have very greatly changed the way tort law actually works. What these things have done, in effect, is to introduce into our present system some of the aspects of a scheme of social insurance.

---

5. Compensation

BENTHAM, THEORY OF LEGISLATION *

Chapter VI. Nature of Satisfaction

Satisfaction is a good received, in consideration of a damage suffered. If the question relates to an offence, satisfaction is an equivalent given to the party injured on account of the damage he has sustained.

Satisfaction is *complete*, whenever the good conferred is equal to the amount of evil suffered; so that if the injury should be repeated and the same reparation should follow, the event would appear indifferent to the injured party. If something is wanting to raise the value of the good to an equality with the evil, the satisfaction is partial and imperfect.

Satisfaction has two aspects or two branches, the past and the future. Satisfaction for the past is what is called *indemnity;* satisfaction for the

---

Doctrines, 27 *Harv. L. Rev.* 195, 233 (1914). See James, Contribution Among Joint Tortfeasors: A Pragmatic Criticism, 54 *Harv. L. Rev.* 1156, 1158 (1941).

* [(1864) "Principles of the Penal Code," Part II ("Political Remedies against the Evil of Offences"), pp. 280-321. Dumont, ed., Hildreth, trans. Reprinted with introduction and notes by C. K. Ogden, London: Routledge and Kegan Paul, Ltd., 1931.]

future consists in putting a stop to the evil of the offence. If the evil ceases of itself, nature has performed the functions of justice, and in this respect the tribunals have nothing more to do.

If a sum of money has been stolen, from the moment it is restored to the owner the satisfaction for the future is complete. It only remains to indemnify him for the past, for the temporary loss which he experienced while the offence continued.

But if the question is of a thing spoiled or destroyed, satisfaction for the future can only take place by giving to the party injured a similar or equivalent article. Satisfaction for the past would consist in an indemnity for the temporary privation.

Chapter VII. Reasons on Which the Necessity of Satisfaction is Founded

Satisfaction is necessary to put a stop to the evil of the first order, to re-establish things in the state in which they were before the offence was committed, and to restore the sufferer to the condition in which he would have been if the law had not been violated.

Satisfaction is yet more necessary to put a stop to the evil of the second order. Punishment alone is not sufficient for that purpose. It tends, without doubt, to diminish the number of offenders; but this number, though diminished, can never be considered as nothing. Examples of the commission of offences, as they are more or less known, excite more or less of apprehension. Every observer sees in them the chance of suffering in his turn. If it be desired to dissipate this sentiment of fear, it is necessary that the offence should be as constantly followed by satisfaction as by punishment. If it were followed by punishment without satisfaction, as many offenders as were punished, so many proofs there would be of the inefficacy of punishment; and consequently so much alarm weighing upon society.

But here needs to be made an essential observation. To take away the alarm, it is enough that the satisfaction is complete in the eyes of observers, although not complete to the persons interested. How can we determine whether the satisfaction is complete for him who receives it? The balance, in the hands of passion, would always incline to the side of interest; to the greedy it would be impossible to give enough; the vindictive never would think his adversary sufficiently humbled. We must suppose, then, an impartial observer, and regard that satisfaction as sufficient which he would estimate as equivalent to the evil endured.

Chapter VIII. The Different Kinds of Satisfaction

We may distinguish six kinds:—

1st. *Pecuniary Satisfaction.*—As money is a pledge for the greater part of pleasures, it is an efficacious compensation for a multitude of evils.

But it is not always in the offender's power to pay it, nor always proper that the offended party should receive it. To offer a man, whose honour has been outraged, a compensation in money for the insult is a new affront.

2nd. *Restitution in Nature.*—This satisfaction consists either in returning the thing taken away or in giving a thing similar or equivalent to that taken away or destroyed.

3rd. *Attestatory Satisfaction.*—If the evil results from a falsehood, a statement false in point of fact, satisfaction is complete by a legal attestation of the truth.

4th. *Honorary Satisfaction.*—An operation which has for its end either to maintain or to re-establish in favour of an individual a portion of honour, of which the offence had deprived him, or threatened to deprive him.

5th. *Vindictive Satisfaction.*—Everything which implies a manifest pain to the offender implies a pleasure of vengeance to the party injured.

6th. *Substitutive Satisfaction,* or satisfaction at the expense of a third party; when a person not a party to the offence is held responsible in his fortune for the person who committed it.

To determine our choice as to the kind of satisfaction, three things must be considered,—the *ease* of furnishing it; the *nature* of the evil to be compensated; and the probable *sentiments* of the party injured. These different heads will presently be taken up, and more fully considered.

Chapter IX. The Quantity of Satisfaction

As much as the satisfaction fails of being complete, to the same degree the evil remains without a remedy.

We may fix, by two rules, what is necessary to prevent a deficit in this respect.

1st. *Follow the evil of the offence in all its ramifications, and among all parties to it, and proportion the satisfaction accordingly.*

If the question relates to irreparable corporal injuries, two things must be considered; a means of enjoyment and a means of subsistence taken away forever. There cannot be a compensation of the same nature, but there ought to be applied to the evil a perpetual periodical remedy.

If the question relates to a homicide, it is proper to consider the loss experienced by the heirs of the deceased, and to make it up by a gratification paid at once, or periodically for a longer or shorter term.

If the question relates to an offence against property, we shall see, under the head of Pecuniary Satisfaction, what is required to put the reparation on a level with the offence.

2nd. *In doubtful cases, the balance ought to incline in his favour who has suffered the injury, rather than in favour of him who committed it.*

All accidents ought to be at the risk of the offender. All satisfaction ought rather to be superabundant than defective. If superabundant, the excess being in the nature of a punishment, cannot but serve to prevent like offences. If defective, that deficit always leaves a certain degree of alarm; and in vindictive offences, all the unsatisfied evil is a matter of triumph to the offender.

Laws are everywhere very imperfect upon this point. On the side of punishments there has been little fear of excess; on the side of satisfaction, a deficit has caused little concern. Punishment, which, if it goes beyond the limit of necessity, is a pure evil, has been scattered with a prodigal hand. Satisfaction, which is purely a good, has been dealt out with the most evident parsimony.

Chapter X. The Certainty of Satisfaction

Certainty of satisfaction is an essential branch of security; and in proportion as this certainty is wanting, in the same proportion security is diminished.

What shall be thought of those laws which, to the natural causes of uncertainty, add other factitious and voluntary causes? To obviate this defect the following rules are necessary:—

1st. *The obligation to satisfy ought not to be extinguished by the death of the injured party. The satisfaction due to the deceased is due to his heirs.*

To make the right of receiving satisfaction dependent upon the life of an individual, is to take away from that right a part of its value. It is like reducing a perpetual annuity into an annuity for life. Satisfaction is not to be obtained except by a process which may last a long time. If the claimant is an aged or infirm person, the value of his right fluctuates with his health; if the claimant is on his death-bed, his right is worth nothing.

Moreover, if you diminish on one side the certainty of satisfaction, you increase on the other the hope of impunity. You show in perspective to the offender a time when he may hope quietly to enjoy the fruit of his offence. You give him a motive to retard, by a thousand impediments, the judgment of the court, and even to hasten the death of the injured party. At all events you put out of the protection of the law those persons who have the greatest need of it,—the dying and the sick.

It is true that, although the obligation of satisfaction be extinguished by the death of the injured party, the offender may still be subjected to another punishment; but what other punishment can be so fit and proper? *

---

* [For an account of the changes effected in the common law by legislation along

2nd. *The right of the injured party ought not to be extinguished by the death of the offender, the author of the wrong. The satisfaction due from him is due from his heirs.*

To determine otherwise would be to diminish the value of the right and to encourage offences. A man conscious that death was near, might commit an injustice with no other object except to advance the fortune of his children,—a case more common than is generally supposed.

Is it said that if satisfaction be given to the injured party, after the death of the delinquent, it is only by an equivalent suffering imposed upon his heirs? But there is a great difference between the two cases. The expectation of the injured party is a clear, precise, decided expectation, firm in proportion to his confidence in the protection of the laws. The expectation of the heir is but a vague hope. The object of it is not the entire succession, but a certain, unknown, net produce, after all lawful deductions. That which the deceased might have spent in pleasures he has spent upon injustice. [Pp. 280-285.]

---

the lines proposed by Bentham, see: Dillon, *Law and Jurisprudence of England and America,* Vol. 1, p. 316, reprinted as "Influence of Bentham" in Association of American Law Schools, *Select Essays in Anglo-American Legal History,* Vol. 1, p. 492; and Leslie Stephen, *The English Utilitarians.* See also Holdsworth, "The Origin of the Rule in Baker v. Bolton," 32 *L. Q. Rev.* 431 (1916).

Prior to enactment of such legislation it was commonly said, among railroad men, that it was cheaper to kill passengers than to injure them. The unfriendly attitude of courts towards the reform legislation is illustrated in the 5-to-4 decision of the Supreme Court in Panama R. Co. v. Rock, 266 U.S. 209 (1924), in which the majority reversed a judgment of the District Court for the Canal Zone allowing damages for wrongful death. The majority opinion, *per* Sutherland, J., declared:

> ...under the principles of the common law, it has required specific statutes to fix civil liability for death by wrongful act; and it is this requirement, rather than the construction put upon the statute in civil-law countries, that the inhabitants of the Canal Zone are presumed to be familiar with, and which affords the rule by which the meaning and scope of the statute in question are to be determined. (P. 215.)

The dissenting opinion, *per* Holmes, J. (concurred in by White, C. J., McKenna, and Brandeis) commented:

> ...it seems to me that courts, in dealing with statutes, sometimes have been too slow to recognize that statutes, even when in terms covering only particular cases, may imply a policy different from that of the common law, and therefore may exclude a reference to the common law for the purpose of limiting their scope. Johnson v. United States, 18 L.R.A.(N.S.) 1194, 89 C.C.A. 508, 163 Fed. 30, 32. Without going into the reasons for the notion that an action (other than an appeal) does not lie for causing the death of a human being, it is enough to say that they have disappeared. The policy that forbade such an action, if it was more profound than the absence of a remedy when a man's body was hanged and his goods confiscated for the felony, has been shown not to be the policy of present law by statutes of the United States and of most, if not all, of the states. In such circumstances it seems to me that we should not be astute to deprive the words of the Panama Code of their natural effect. (P. 216.)]

Chapter XI. Pecuniary Satisfaction

．　　．　　．　　．　　．

Pecuniary satisfaction is at its highest point of propriety in cases where the damage experienced by the injured party, and the advantages obtained by the delinquent, are alike of a pecuniary nature; as in theft, peculation, and extortion. The remedy and the evil are homogeneous; the compensation may be exactly measured by the loss, and the punishment by the profit of the offence.

This kind of satisfaction is not so well founded when there is a pecuniary loss upon one side, without any pecuniary profit upon the other; as in the case of offences committed through hostility, negligence, or accident.

It has still less foundation in those cases in which it is not possible to value in money either the evil of the party injured, or the advantage of the offender; as in case of injuries to honour. [P. 286.]

．　　．　　．　　．　　．

There is still in existence an English law, which is a true relic of barbarous times. A daughter is considered as the servant of her father; if she is seduced, the father cannot obtain any other satisfaction than a sum of money, the price of the domestic services which he is supposed to have lost by the pregnancy of his daughter.

As respects injuries to the person, a pecuniary indemnity may be proper or not, according to the respective wealth of the parties. . . .

The expense of satisfaction ought to be shared among the offenders in proportion to their wealth, or according to circumstances, in proportion to their respective degrees of criminality. For, in fact, the obligation to satisfy is a punishment, and it would be in the highest degree unequal if co-delinquents of unequal wealth were mulcted in the same sum. [P. 287.]

．　　．　　．　　．　　．

Chapter XVI. Vindictive Satisfaction

This subject does not require many particular rules. Every kind of satisfaction, as it is a punishment to the offender, naturally produces a pleasure of vengeance to the injured party.

That pleasure is a gain; it calls to mind Samson's riddle—it is the sweet coming out of the terrible, it is honey dropping from the lion's mouth. Produced without expense, a clear gain resulting from an operation necessary on other accounts, it is an enjoyment to be cultivated, like any other; for the pleasure of vengeance, abstractly considered, is, like every other pleasure, a good in itself. It is innocent while restrained within the limits of the law; it only becomes criminal at the moment when it breaks those limits. It is not vengeance which is to be regarded as the most malignant and dangerous passion of the human heart; it is antipathy, it is intoler-ance—the hatreds of pride, of prejudice, of religion, of politics. The enmity which is dangerous is not that which is well founded, but that which springs up without any substantial cause.

Useful to the individual, this motive is also useful to the public; indeed, it is necessary. It is this vindictive satisfaction which sets tongues of wit-nesses in motion; it is this which animates the accuser and engages him in the public service, in spite of the embarrassments, the expenses, the enmities to which it exposes him; it is this, too, which surmounts the public pity in the punishment of criminals. Take away this resource, and the power of the laws will be very limited; or, at all events, the tribunals will not obtain assistance, except for money—a means not only burden-some to society, but exposed to other very serious objections.

Common moralists, always duped by words, are not able to comprehend the truth. The spirit of vengeance is odious; all satisfaction drawn from that source is faulty; forgiveness of injuries is the first of virtues. No doubt those implacable characters which no satisfaction can soften are odious, and ought to be so. Forgetfulness of injuries is a virtue necessary to humanity; but it becomes a virtue only after justice has done its work, when it has furnished or denied a satisfaction. Before that, to forget injuries is to invite their repetition; it is not being the friend, it is being the enemy of society. What more can crime desire than an arrangement by which offences shall be always pardoned?

What ought to be done to afford this vindictive satisfaction? Every-thing which justice requires for the sake of satisfactions of other kinds and for the punishment of the offence, but nothing more. The least excess consecrated to the sole object of vengeance would be a pure evil. Inflict the proper punishment, and let the injured party derive from it such a degree of satisfaction as comports with his situation, and of which his nature is susceptible.

But though nothing should be added to the severity of punishment with this particular end in view, the punishment may be modified for the accomplishment of this end, according to what may be supposed to be the sentiments of the injured party, from his position or from the nature of the offence. . . .

Chapter XVII. Substitutive Satisfaction; or, Satisfaction at the Charge of a Third Party

In ordinary cases, the expense of satisfaction ought to fall upon the author of the evil; because, falling in that way, it tends in quality of punishment to prevent the evil—that is, to diminish the frequency of the offence. Where it falls upon another person, it has no such tendency.

Where this reason does not exist, with regard to the first respondent, the law of responsibility must be modified in consequence; or, in other terms, a third person must be called in to pay, instead of the author of the damage, when he cannot himself furnish the satisfaction, and when such an obligation imposed upon a third person tends to prevent the offence.

This may happen in the following cases:—1st. The responsibility of a master for his servant. 2nd. The responsibility of a guardian for his ward. 3rd. The responsibility of a father for his children. 4th. The responsibility of a mother for her children, in her character of guardian. 5th. The responsibility of a husband for his wife. 6th. The responsibility of an innocent person who profits by the offence.

I. *Responsibility of a Master.*—This responsibility is founded upon two reasons, the one of security, the other of equality. This obligation imposed upon the master acts like a punishment, and diminishes the chance of like mishaps. He is interested to know the character, and to watch over the conduct of those for whom he is responsible. By making him accountable for neglect of this duty, the law appoints him a police inspector and a domestic magistrate.

Besides, the condition of a master almost necessarily supposes a certain fortune, the quality of being an injured party supposes nothing of that sort. Since an inevitable evil lies between two parties, it is best to throw the weight of it upon him who has most means of sustaining it. [Pp. 309-311.]

·   ·   ·   ·   ·

Such are the presumptions which serve as a basis to responsibility; presumption of negligence on the part of the master; presumption of his superiority in wealth. But it is not to be forgotten that presumptions are nothing when belied by facts. For example, an accident has happened by the overturn of a vehicle. Nothing is known of the injured party. It is presumed that he stands in need of an indemnity from the owner of the vehicle, who offers himself to the imagination as being well able to support the loss. But what becomes of this presumption, when it is known that this owner is a poor farmer, and the injured party an opulent landlord; that the first would be ruined if obliged to pay an indemnity, hardly of the slightest consequence to the other? Presumptions ought to guide, but not to govern us. The legislator ought to consult them in establishing general rules; he should leave it to the magistrate to modify their application according to individual cases.

The general rule would establish the responsibility of the master; but the magistrate, according to circumstances, might change this arrangement, and make the weight of the loss fall upon the true author of the evil.

The greatest abuse which can result from leaving to the magistrate the utmost latitude in this distribution will be to produce, in certain cases, the same inconvenience which must necessarily result from a general and inflexible rule. Should the magistrate on one occasion favour the author of the evil, and the master on another? He who suffers wrong will suffer no more from this partiality than he might have suffered from the inflexibility of the law.

In our systems of law, no attention has been given to these modifications. The entire burden of the loss has been thrown sometimes upon the servant who has caused the damage, and sometimes upon the master; whence it follows that sometimes security and sometimes equality have been neglected, both of which ought alternately to have the preference, according to the nature of the case.

Chapter XVIII. Subsidiary Satisfaction at the Public Expense

The best fund whence satisfaction can be drawn is the property of the delinquent,—since it then performs, as we have seen, with superior convenience the functions both of satisfaction and of punishment.

But if the offender is without property, ought the injured person to remain without satisfaction? No; for, according to the reasons already laid down, satisfaction is almost as necessary as punishment. It ought to be furnished out of the public treasury, because it is an object of public good, and the security of all is interested in it. This obligation of the public to furnish satisfaction is founded upon a reason which has the evidence of an axiom. A pecuniary charge divided among the mass of individuals is nothing to each contributor, in comparison with what it would be to an individual or a small number.

If *insurance* is useful in enterprises of commerce, it is not less so in the great social enterprise in which the associates find themselves united as partners, in consequence of a train of chances, without knowledge or choice on their part, without the power of separation, or of securing themselves by any prudential means from a multitude of snares which they mutually spread for each other. The calamities which spring from offences are evils not less real than those which result from accidents of nature. If the owner of a house sleeps sounder because it is insured against fire, his sleep will be sounder yet if he is also insured against robbery. Putting out of sight the abuses to which it is liable, it seems impossible to give too much extension to a means so ingenious, which renders real losses so slight, and which gives so much security against eventual evils.

But all kinds of *insurances* are exposed to great abuse from fraud or negligence; fraud on the part of those who feign or exaggerate losses for the sake of obtaining indemnities not due; negligence on the part of the assurers in not taking necessary precautions, or on the part of the assured, who use less diligence in protecting themselves against losses which are certain to be made up.

In a system of satisfactions at the public expense we have, then, to fear—

1st. A secret connivance between a party pretending to be injured and the author of a pretended offence to obtain an indemnity not due.

2nd. Too great security on the part of individuals, who, not having the same consequences to fear, will no longer make the same efforts for the prevention of offences.

This second danger is little to be dreaded. Nobody will neglect an actual possession certain and present in the hope of recovering, in case of loss, an equivalent for the thing lost, even a perfect equivalent; and when we consider that an indemnity cannot be obtained without trouble and expense, that there is a temporary privation, that the vexations of a claim and its pursuit are to be encountered, and the disagreeable part of an accuser to be played; and that, after all, under the best system of procedure, success is always doubtful;—these things considered, it is plain that every man will still have motives enough to watch over his property, and not to encourage offences by negligence.

On the side of fraud the danger is much greater. It can only be prevented by detailed precautions, which will be explained elsewhere. It will here suffice to point out, as examples, two opposite cases, one in which the utility of the remedy surpasses the danger of abuse, the other in which the danger of abuse is greater than the utility of the remedy.

Whenever the damage is occasioned by an offence of which the punishment is severe, and the author of which must be juridically ascertained, and also the fact of an offence committed, fraud is very difficult. The only method an impostor, who pretends to be injured, can employ to procure an accomplice, is to give him a part of the profits of the fraud; but, provided there has not been a neglect of the clearest principles of proportion between offences and punishments, the punishment which such an accomplice must encounter would be more than equivalent to the total profit of the fraud.

Observe, that the offender must be judicially convicted before the satisfaction is granted; without that precaution the public treasure would be exposed to pillage. Nothing would be more common than stories of imaginary robberies, of pretended thefts committed by unknown persons who had taken to flight, in a manner the most secret, and in nights the darkest. But when it is necessary to bring the offenders into court, a secret understanding is not easy. This is not a part which can be readily filled; for besides the certainty of punishment for the alleged offence encountered by the person who charges himself with it, in case the imposture be discovered, there will be still a particular and additional punishment to be shared by both accomplices; and if it be recollected how difficult it is to fabricate a probable history of an offence absolutely imaginary, it is likely that these kinds of frauds will be very rare, if they ever happen at all.

The danger most to be apprehended is the exaggeration of a loss resulting from a real offence. But then it is necessary that the offence be susceptible of such sort of falsehood,—a case sufficiently rare.

It would seem, then, that it may be regarded as a general maxim, that in all cases in which the punishment of the offence is severe, there is no occasion for apprehending that an imaginary offender will charge himself with the offence for the sake of a doubtful gain.

But, for the opposite reason, when the damage results from an offence of which the punishment is slight or nothing, if the public treasure were responsible in such cases, the danger of abuse would be at its highest point. Insolvency is an example of this sort. Who so poor that he would not be trusted, if the public were his security? What treasure would suffice to pay the creditors, whose debtors were really deficient, and how easy it would be to get up false debts?

Not only would such an indemnity be liable to abuse, it would be unreasonable; for, in the transactions of commerce, the risk of loss makes a part of the price of merchandise and of the interest of money. Let the merchant be sure of losing nothing, and he would sell cheaper; so that, to demand an indemnity from the public for a loss thus made up for beforehand, would be asking to be paid twice over.

There are still other cases in which satisfaction ought to be a public charge.

1st. The case of physical calamities, such as inundations and fires. Aids furnished by the state to sufferers in that way are not solely founded on the principle that an evil divided among many becomes light; they rest also upon this other principle—that the state, as protector of the national wealth, is interested to prevent the deterioration of its domain, and to re-establish the means of reproduction in places which have suffered. Such were the liberalities, so called, of the great Frederic towards provinces desolated by some scourge; they were acts of prudence and conservation.

2nd. Losses and misfortunes in consequence of hostilities. Those who have been exposed to the invasions of a public enemy have so much the clearer right to a public indemnity, since they may be considered as having sustained a shock which threatened all the citizens, and as having been by their situation the most exposed points of the public defense.

3rd. Evils resulting from unintentional mistakes of the ministers of justice. An error of justice is always of itself a subject of lamentation; but that such an error, when known, should not be repaired by proportional indemnities, is an overthrow of social order. Ought not the public to follow the same rule of equity which it imposes upon individuals? Is it not an odious thing that the government should exert its power to exact severely all that is due to it, and should avail itself of the same means to refuse the payment of its own debts? But this obligation is so evident, that no attempt to demonstrate it can make it clearer.

4th. Responsibility of a community for a high-handed offence committed in a public part of its territory. It is not properly the public which is responsible in this case; it is the district or the province which should be taxed for the reparation of an offence resulting from negligence of police.

In cases of competition, the interests of an individual ought to take precedence over those of the treasury. What is due to an injured party under the title of satisfaction ought to be paid in preference to what is due to the public by way of fine. This is not the decision of vulgar jurisprudence, but it is the decision of reason. The loss to an individual is an evil that is felt; the gain to the public is a good felt by nobody. What the offender pays in quality of fine is a punishment, and nothing more; what he pays in quality of satisfaction is also a punishment, and a severer one; it is, beside, a satisfaction to the injured party, and so far a good. What I pay to the state, a creature of reason with which I have no quarrel, affects me only with the sort of chagrin I should feel if I dropped the same money into a well; what I pay to my adversary, the satisfaction which I am forced to make, at my own expense, to him I wished to injure, is a degree of humiliation which gives to punishment its most appropriate character. [Pp. 313-321.]

CHAPTER 4

CRIME AND PUNISHMENT

Contents

Introductory Note

A passage in the *Protagoras* of Plato reminds us that there is nothing very new about the dispute between those who find reason for punishment simply in the past acts of the offender and those who would justify punishment as a means of diminishing future offenses. The great debate between the philosophical idealists like Kant and Hegel, on the one hand, and the social utilitarians like Beccaria and Bentham, on the other, is still with us, although today few criminologists will be found in the antiutilitarian camp.

Indeed the most insistent problems of modern criminology have to do with the alternative ways of looking at the future consequences of crime and punishment. Those who focus their attention on the effects of punishment upon the criminal himself are likely to stress the need of individualization, along lines discussed in the writings of Pound, Saleilles, and The Venerable Bede. Others, like Bentham, look primarily to the deterrent effects of punishment on the marginal criminal. Still others, like Tarde, Saleilles, and Tourtoulon, stress the effect of punishment upon those who inflict it, who are generally the great majority of society and worth more attention than most theorists of the criminal law have yet conferred upon them.

The changes in the substance and spirit of our criminal law recounted in the essays by Pound and Poland point to the practical consequences of the modern emphasis upon a utilitarian appraisal of crime and punishment. This emphasis raises to a critical point the problem: "What causes crime?" For certainly we cannot treat a social disease without knowing something about its causes. And here we face serious difficulties. For the subject of crime unlocks such powerful emotions that it is most difficult to obtain objective or scientific data on the incidence of crime and on the circumstances under which the crime rate rises and falls. More basic, if more subtle, is the difficulty that most of those who search for the causes of crime have a very vague idea of the nature of crime. We are all apt to think of crime in "lump concept" terms and to overlook the fact that crime is a relational affair involving victims and societies as well as criminals. Those who look for the fundamental causes of crime within the body or the soul of the criminal therefore do less than justice to the complexity of the criminal situation. Crime, like property and contract, must be viewed socially as a function of sovereignty or government, if we are to treat intelligently of its causes and of the ways in which a society may rationally act to decrease crime.

Such a conception of crime and society must take account of the anthropological views of Ferri and Lombroso, the economic interpretation of Bonger, the sociological interpretation of criminal statistics offered by A. C. Hall, and the "duet frame" of crime portrayed by Von Hentig. All these varying perspectives may help to clarify the social context in which we search for answers to our questions about the cause of crime. To help the student unravel the ambiguities that cluster around the concept of causation, a brief passage from Aristotle's *Metaphysics* is included in this chapter.

1. Crime

A. Nature of crime

VON BAR, A HISTORY OF CONTINENTAL CRIMINAL LAW *

§ 109.—*Tort and Crime.*—The distinction between civil wrongs (*i.e.,* torts) and wrongs punishable criminally is now apparent. A civil wrong represents a condition at variance with a right regardless of whether it is founded upon an action contrary to morality. Wrong punishable criminally is an act specially characterized as being contrary to morality; and it is generally but not necessarily a violation or at least a jeopardizing of a subjective right.† It is not possible "a priori" to go further in fixing the distinction between civil wrongs and wrongs punishable criminally, since, according to the premises, the conception of crime cannot "a priori" be completely determined for a definite positive law and a definite period of time.

Hegel's Distinction.—Especially is it incorrect to hold with Hegel that the distinction consists in crime being intentional wrong and in tort being unintentional or innocent wrong. The positive law shows us that there are acts of negligence which are punished criminally, and that on the other hand there are cases of wrong committed quite intentionally which nevertheless remain merely torts; for example, when a person, openly and with knowledge of its illegality, but without other violence to person or thing occupies a piece of ground belonging to another, or when one shamelessly refuses to discharge an obligation of debt unequivocally entered into. [Pp. 524-525.]

. . . . . .

---

* [Bell, trans. Vol. 6, Continental Legal History Series; Boston: Little, Brown & Co., 1916.

Karl Ludwig Von Bar (1836–1913), a well-known German jurist, taught at a number of German universities and served on the Hague Tribunal as well. Among his works, which have attracted wide attention, are: *Die Grundlagen des Strafrechts* (1869) (*i.e., Foundations of Criminal Law*); *Die Lehre vom Kausalzusammenhang im Rechte* (1871) (*i.e., The Doctrine of Causal Connection in the Law*); and *Lehrbuch des Internationalen Privat- und Strafrechts* (1892) (*i.e., Manual of Criminal and Private International Law*).

The present passages from Von Bar are drawn from the first part of his *Handbuch des Strafrechts,* published in 1882 and translated as *History of Continental Criminal Law.* The sequel volume, *Theorie und Praxis des internationalen Privatrechts* (*Theory and Practice of Private International Law*) appeared in 1892 and has not as yet been put into English.]

† [A right is, in Continental legal phraseology, termed "subjective," as contrasted with law, which is "objective right."]

Hälschner's Distinction.—Hälschner's distinction is even less tenable than that of Hegel.[3] According to Hälschner, crime should be an attack upon the general legal system, a violation of law in principle, while a tort is merely a violation of a concrete right, the law as a principle being recognized.[4] But this conception is undoubtedly incorrect in the vast majority of cases, from the standpoint of the one committing the act. The thief in stealing does not absolutely reject the right of property;[5] on the contrary, he desires to be the owner or at least to actually occupy the position of the owner. What he rejects, from his standpoint, is merely the concrete right of the party whose property is stolen. To be sure, the *objective* law regards the theft as in principle irreconcilable with the theory of ownership. Yet as a matter of fact this also applies to other violations of property which are not punished. [Pp. 526-527.]

. . . . .

Relation of Tort and Crime.—Moreover, one may not, as Binding has done, draw the general conclusion that the distinction between tort and crime is purely a creation of positive law,—that there is no fixed principle nor even a general basis for this distinction, and that every crime contains the essential element of tort. However, every wrong, even the most insignificant, entailing only a civil sanction, contains *one* element which might possibly qualify it as a crime, although often only one: and Merkel is really correct to the extent that *in certain cases* the obligation to pay damages can tend towards the repression of wrong, just as punishment.[12] The legislator who would subject every wrong to criminal punishment would work a hardship upon humanity and do violence to his own authority. Such freedom of action and omnipotence do not belong to him. Where gentler means would accomplish the same end, the legislator commits a grave wrong by inflicting punishment. Therefore it is absolutely correct to say that where the civil sanction is sufficient, there is no meaning to punishment. [Pp. 528-529.]

. . . . .

---

[3] *"Die Lehre vom Unrechte und seinen verschiedenen Formen"* in *"Gerichtssaal"* (1869), pp. 1-36, 81-114 (also published separately). To the contrary *cf.* Merkel, *"Zeitschrift"* (1881), pp. 586 *et seq.*

[4] Stahl, *"Die Philosophie des Rechts"*, II, 2, § 185, had already advanced a similar view,—acts which violate the legal system are crimes only if they challenge the authority and respect due to the State. However, Stahl's conception is more true to life and its results are more readily perceived. In the emphasis which he lays upon the *positive* nature of crime, his insistence that the act must manifest itself "in thesi" (thus under all circumstances) as contrary to law, there lies the principle that crimes must be readily distinguishable from acts that are not punishable.

[5] *Cf.* also *"Das gemeine deutsche Strafrecht"*, I, pp. 33 *et seq.*

[12] It must be admitted, however, that a strict obligation to make indemnity can exercise a deterring and disciplinary influence. *Cf.* Zink, *"Die Ermittlung des Sachverhalts im französischen Civilprocesse"*, I (1860), pp. 591 *et seq.;* Von Bar, *"Recht und Beweis im Civilprocesse"* (1867), pp. 24 *et seq.*

It is more in accord with actual relations, if one place the nature and purpose of private justice simply in the adjustment and arrangement of the actual or alleged confusion of the spheres of rights of two or more possessors of rights. While the element of guilt is of very considerable importance in private law, yet it plays only a secondary part. It is only by an artificial and therefore defective argument that the duty to indemnify is based upon guilt.... [P. 530.]

.   .   .   .   .

...According to our conception, an act is in principle punishable not because it violates a subjective right, but rather because it is contrary to morality....

...In a theory which founds criminal law directly upon morality, the civil sanction receives attention simply as a "factum," a "factum" which may have the possible consequence that the State may omit punishment. [Pp. 531-533.]

SAVIGNY, SYSTEM OF THE MODERN ROMAN LAW *

I do not desire to narrow the state to the purposes of law; indeed theory will not presume to desire to limit the freedom of development by the assertion of exclusive aims for the activity of the state. Nevertheless its first and most inevitable task is to make the idea of law dominant in the visible world. To this object leads a double activity of the state. First it has to protect the individual who is injured in his right against that injury; we call the rules to which this activity is subject, civil process. Secondly it has to defend and re-establish the injured right, without reference to the individual interest. This is done by punishment, through which the human will, in the narrower field of law, imitates the law of moral retribution prevailing in the higher system of the world.[a] We call the rules to which this activity is subject, criminal law of which criminal procedure forms merely a part.[b] Civil procedure, criminal law and criminal procedure are hence parts of state's-law and were so regarded by the Romans.

JEROME HALL, GENERAL PRINCIPLES OF CRIMINAL LAW †

*Chapter Seven. Interrelations of Criminal Law and Torts—
Intentional Wrongs*

American legal scholarship, beginning particularly with the publication of Holmes' *Common Law*, has stressed the prospects of important scientific

* [Pp. 20-21. Holloway, trans. Madras: J. Higginbotham, 1867. First published in 1840. On the significance of Savigny, generally, see *infra*, Chap. 5.]

[a] Thus far one may say that the general moral ordinance of retribution in a limited way, assumes the nature of an institution of law and as such ought to be brought into practice by the state. See Hegel *Naturrecht*, pp. 102, 103, 120. Klenze *Lehrbuch des Strafrechts*, pp. 10-17.

† [Indianapolis: The Bobbs-Merrill Company, Inc. Copyright, 1947.

Jerome Hall (b. 1901) is the author of: *Theft, Law and Society* (1935); *Readings*

development by implying an underlying unity in the law of crimes and torts. Holmes' chief interest in that regard was to establish a theory of objective liability common to both fields, which was the basis for his assertion that "the general principles of criminal and civil liability are the same." [1] Terry discussed both fields of law under the head of Wrongs; [2] and Beale's casebook on Legal Liability likewise joined what he regarded as common doctrines.

A formal view of the rules strongly supports the position that the two fields are more or less arbitrary divisions of what is actually a single discipline. At the very outset one encounters many terms which are employed in both fields, *e.g.*, those designating specific torts and crimes, such as assault, battery, conspiracy, fraud, libel, slander, false imprisonment or arrest, nuisance, seduction, etc. Other common terms such as act, omission, cause, consent, mistake and motive refer to apparently identical doctrines. Finally, the fundamental principles of culpability are expressed in identical words in both fields. The suggested possibilities for unification are that the rules of torts and criminal law may be interrelated as species to genus, *i.e.*, one may be merely a specific instance of the other; or, that the two sets of prescriptions may be co-ordinate species of other, broader doctrines. The hypothesis that the above terms represent identical doctrines and that they subsume identical fact-situations has been strongly implemented through being frequently intermingled in criminal and tort cases by courts and treatise writers. [Pp. 188-189.]

· · · · ·

That scholars of logical bent—the early Holmes, Beale and Terry—thought in such terms is not surprising; indeed such thinking is still characteristic of legal positivists. But the results have been negative. The difficulties on the logical side, alone, have been numerous and involved. Thus the challenge to various fundamental principles, *e.g.*, that concerning *mens rea*, has unsettled a relatively well-organized body of law. [P. 190.]

· · · · ·

---

in *Jurisprudence* (1938); *General Principles of Criminal Law* (1947); *Cases and Readings on Criminal Law and Procedure* (1949); *Living Law of Democratic Society* (1949). He has contributed to *20th Century Sociology* (1945) and *Interpretations of Modern Legal Philosophies* (1947).

Currently professor of law at Indiana University, he has also taught or lectured at the University of North Dakota, Louisiana State University, and Pacific University. He is the chairman of the editorial committee of the 20th Century Legal Philosophy Series.]

[1] *The Common Law* (1881) 44.

[2] Terry's analytical bent was not hampered by moral or sociological curiosity. For him, "There is no general principle determining whether a given act or omission shall be a crime or not. Each State makes such acts or omissions crimes as it thinks proper." *Some Leading Principles of Anglo-American Law* (1884) 538.

Substantive and Formal Distinctions

At least since Plato, compensation has been distinguished from punishment [4] just as the respective harms were themselves later differentiated with reference to moral culpability.[5] The unvarying corollaries of traditional philosophy were that "the law of nature has it that the evil-doer should be punished," [6] and that "the natural law requires that each should . . . repair the injury which he occasioned by his tort." [7] The long history of the traditional interpretation may be conveniently regarded as having culminated in Mansfield's dictum that "there is no distinction better known, than the distinction between civil and criminal law." [8] [Pp. 191-192.]

.   .   .   .   .

The significance of the principles enunciated above (that the individual harm can be rationally evaluated in terms of money whereas this is impossible as to the social harm, and that morally culpable conduct is essential to the crime but not for the tort) depends on their verification in the positive law of both fields and on the range of their application. The first supporting data, it will be recalled, were such crimes as sedition, possession of burglars' tools, and the like, i.e., situations that represent social harms but have no individual incidence whatever. The converse, representing the basic tort principle, may be most readily induced by reference to the negligent invasions; they are not social harms, in the sense employed above, because moral culpability is lacking.

We come to closer grips with the crucial testing of the above principles in the field of intentional invasions of individual interests. Here, in both fields, the conduct of the actor is morally culpable, the same terms are employed, and common ideas are generally intermingled in the decisions. If we carefully examine the relevant phenomena, however, we note important differentiae that support the theory suggested above. Thus obtaining property by false pretenses is committed even though the complainant has sustained no financial loss,[41] but a civil suit for misrepresentation can not

---

[4] *Laws*, bk. IX, 445.

[5] 3 Wigmore, Responsibility for Tortious Acts: Its History, in *Select Essays in Anglo-American Legal History* (1907) 479, also 2 Holdsworth, *History of English Law* (3d ed. 1937) 259; 3 *id.* at 372-3. 1 Hale, *Pleas of the Crown* (1736) 16, 38; Rede, J., in 1506, cited by Holmes, *The Common Law* 87, and T. Raymond in Bessey v. Olliot at 467 (1682) cited by Holmes, *The Common Law* 88; *cf.* Foyer, *Exposé du Droit Pénal Norman au xiii Siècle* (1931) 46-47.

[6] Aquinas, *Summa*, II-I, Q. 95, A. 2.

[7] Pothier, *Treatise on Obligations* (1802 trans.) 76. *Cf.* Grotius, *The Rights of War and Peace* (ed. Campbell 1925) 195; St. Thomas devotes eight articles to Restitution. See Q. 62, II-II; and Pufendorf wrote practically a modern treatise on the subject. See his *Law of Nature and Nations* (Kennett ed. 1703) bk. 3, c. 1.

[8] Atcheson v. Everitt, 1 Cowp. 391 (K. B. 1775); *cf.* 2 James Wilson, *Works* (Andrews ed. 1896) 376.

[41] Miller, *Criminal Law* (1934) 389.

succeed in such circumstances.[42] In libel, too, the distinction between the social and the individual harms is registered in the tort requirement that there be publication to a third person whereas prosecution lies if the communication was sent only to the one defamed. This is also the rationale of decisions holding that whereas truth is a defense to the suit for damages, it is necessary in the criminal law that publication, in addition, be for the public benefit. Although it is arguable whether the circulation of such matter is harmful if it is true and, also, whether a true publication does not damage the individual concerned, the consistency of the questionable premises implicit in the above holdings with the underlying principles of torts and criminal law, respectively, is apparent.... [Pp. 206-208.]

.   .   .   .   .

Even in the most difficult of all situations for testing the suggested thesis, battery or assault with a loaded gun, *i.e.*, where identical terms are employed in both fields to denote identical behavior, the tort is distinguishable from the social harm, comprising the crime. The difference is clear regarding such wrongs as conversion of chattels contrasted with larceny and as to conduct by an insane person or a child which is tortious but not criminal. But the same principle obtains even when moral culpability is also, as in the above illustrations, a material component of the tort. The tort rules integrate the culpable conduct with the injury to the individual whereas the criminal law fuses that conduct in the pecuniarily non-commensurable harm to the community.... [Pp. 209-210.]

.   .   .   .   .

Although the function of tort law generally, as the vehicle of a just distribution of economic losses and the logic of the theory that could serve as the best available unifying principle require restriction of the field to harms that actually damage, the traditional classification of torts includes a number of wrongs where damage is not essential. It is this area of *injuria sine damno* which opposes the sweep of the theory presented above. These torts invite careful attention because they reveal the pervading influence of experience and expediency as perennial obstacles to generalization. They comprise two types of situation. Trespass to land is perhaps the most representative of of one of these and most indicative of the sort of influence that restricts the march of logic. The action functions as a defense of the right to possession. Invasion of water rights, nuisance, and infringement of trade-marks seem to involve the same principle of invoking tort law to establish a property right. In these instances, equitable relief is frequently available to secure the desired results; in any event some expansion of other remedies would eliminate the need for suit at law in the above torts where damage is non-existent.

---

[42] See Harper, *Law of Torts* (1933) § 226.

The other type of these exceptional wrongs [46] is represented by the minimal definition of assault. Mere apprehension, not fear, is all that is required. Battery is closely related, for though some contact is required, it need not cause substantial harm. False imprisonment, libel, the special forms of slander, criminal conversation and malicious prosecution are likewise actionable without proof of actual damage sustained. In contrast to the first group of harms, those involving authoritative determination of property rights, the damages awarded in this latter group are usually substantial. In some of them, *e.g.*, in defamation actionable *per se* and in false imprisonment, the difficulty of proving damage coupled with the high probability that substantial harm was sustained, supports the prevailing rules. Apart from that, *i.e.*, where there probably is no actual damage, the salient fact is that most of those torts are intentional aggressions which usually stimulate much resentment. As Holt put it: "If such an action [against one denying a vote] comes to be tried before me, I will direct the jury to make him pay well for it; it is denying him his English right." [47] In this type of harm, the law of torts frequently functions as a punitive apparatus—the "fine" going to the injured victim of the aggression. Thus many of the cases that defy explanation on other grounds can be understood as preferences to impose substantial money-judgments rather than the nominal penalties provided by the criminal law.

This sort of phenomenon, distressing to an aesthetic appreciation of the logic of the general principle of tort law, is nonetheless, persuasive to common sense.[48] The civil judgment is an authoritative vindication of the injured person's rights. He is here not dependent on the public authorities for prosecution and he remains master of the proceedings. Moreover, as in England, the assessment of costs alone may be no trifling matter. Thus the tort law, by the above combination of circumstances, sometimes serves as a more drastic and effective agency than does the penal law.[49] But the punitive function is here rarely exclusive for it frequently coalesces with compensation for the indignity suffered by the victim of the aggression. This is apparent, also, as regards punitive damages, the merits of which have been widely argued.[50] They have been defended by a distinguished French

---

[46] For citations on all of these harms, see McCormick, *Law of Damages* (1935) 89-91.

[47] Ashby v. White, 2 Ld.Raym. 958 (K.B. 1701-2). *Cf.* Kennedy v. Davis, 171 Ala. 609, 55 So. 104 (1911) and Pratt, C. J. in Wilkes v. Wood, 19 How.St.Tr. 1167 (1763).

[48] *Cf.* Bentham's proposal to indemnify the victim of any crime. Here the common law reflects indifference as compared with the French and other systems that provide for the *partie civile*.

[49] *Cf.* Note, Restitution and the Criminal Law (1939) 39 *Col. L. Rev.* 1185.

[50] *Cf.* Willis, Measure of Damages when Property is Wrongfully Taken by a Private Individual (1909) 22 *Harv. L. Rev.* 419 and Morris, Punitive Damages in Tort Cases (1931) 44 *Harv. L. Rev.* 1173; 1 Street, *Foundations of Legal Liability* (1906) 479-482.

scholar,[51] but his suggestion that they be regarded as occupying an intermediate zone between torts and criminal law seems to confuse important established distinctions rather than to clarify the problems involved.

Related to the above are the special problems raised by penal actions—the *bête noire* of all the systematizers since Austin. Penal actions antedate professional police. They have been severely criticized [52] and, assuredly, reliance on informers and pecuniary rewards for discharge of the duties of a citizen are hardly to be encouraged. They limit systematization; whether the tests be formal or substantive, these actions are hybrids which can hardly be ignored as "freaks." [53] They are made of that same larger cloth which includes the intentional torts noted above,[54] especially those where punitive damages are awarded. On the other hand, these wrongs also fall within the province of the penal law—the procedural variations and disposition of the "fines" being of secondary importance. A practical arrangement may be justifiable on grounds of social policy, but the analyst must try to pierce the veils of historical contingency, practical utility and traditional vocabulary, and to construct his theory on the actualities—the nature of the harms and of the sanctions. After he has done all that, he must be willing to recognize that at the periphery of his subject-matter there may be phenomena which evade his general theory—just as the biologist knows organisms that in some ways are "animal," in others, "plant." The only immediate comfort is that these exceptional concatenations sometimes provide the chief stimuli to discovery of more inclusive knowledge.

But, for the most part, even in the field of intentional aggressions, the theory suggested above seems to have been validated—penal law is concerned with social harms which include moral culpability as an essential element whereas torts deal with individual damage which need not have been affected by morally culpable conduct. [Pp. 210-213.]

M. R. COHEN, MORAL ASPECTS OF THE CRIMINAL LAW *

Jurists often distinguish the criminal from the civil law on the ground that the former is concerned with punishments for violation of these rules of public order to which normal people naturally conform, while the civil law is concerned only with determining the rights of the parties in private

---

[51] Demogue, Validity of the Theory of Compensatory Damages (1918) 27 *Yale L.J.* 594.

[52] Freund, *Standards of American Legislation* (1917) 268.

[53] Allen, *Legal Duties* (1931) 226.

[54] See Note, Statutory Penalties—A Legal Hybrid (1938) 51 *Harv. L. Rev.* 1092, and Note (1909) 27 L.R.A. (N.S.) 739.

* [49 *Yale L.J.* 987, 988-990 (1940).]

The article was originally delivered as one of the Fenton Lectures at Buffalo Law School. It constitutes the second chapter of the author's *Reason and Law* (Glencoe, Ill.: The Free Press, 1950).]

transactions. In fact, however, not only does the criminal law today regulate all sorts of private business, but *all* legal provisions (at least in a modern state) have at their back an enforcing machinery that operates through some system of penalties. Consider for instance such requirements as that certain agreements must be in writing or involve a "consideration," that a will must have two or three witnesses, that a valid protest of a note must be within a certain time, or that one may legally charge an interest rate of six per cent. Anyone who ignores these provisions exposes himself to the penalty of losing certain advantages—a loss which may be far more severe than many of the fines for public disorder or for various misdemeanors. A law permitting a man to transfer his property by a will is significant only when the beneficiary legatee or devisee can invoke the penal machinery of the state against those who would deprive him of possession. All laws as to property, contract or personal rights may thus be viewed as specifications within the criminal law, specifications as to when the public force will be brought into play to punish non-obedience to its prescriptions. [P. 988.]

．　．　．　．　．

In the United States today, it seems very easy to distinguish between criminal and civil procedure on the ground that in the former some state official is in duty bound to prosecute, whereas a civil action is brought by a private individual acting at his pleasure. We must add however that state officials are also bound to bring certain civil suits, and in England the attorney general may intervene in tort cases between private parties. This is not to deny that there are today some differences between civil and criminal procedure, *e.g.*, the one in regard to the burden of proof. But it is well to remember that these differences are far from prevailing in all legal systems and are apt to appear more important in theory than in the actual practice of our jury trials. In any case, up to the second decade of the nineteenth century the common law allowed a private action or "appeal" for murder and other injuries.

These considerations are not intended to deny that legislatures and courts can, do, and should call certain acts criminal and provide some distinctive procedures for dealing with them. The general desire for security demands that everyone know, with a fair degree of certainty, what is and what is not criminal. The fear that some innocent act may be branded as criminal is as horrible as the older paralyzing fear of unconscious unintentional sin. What I wish to insist on is that the criminal law is an integral part of the legal system and is subject to the same considerations which do and should influence the whole. More specifically, the criminal law cannot be distinguished from the rest by any difference of moral principle. Some crimes, to be sure, are shocking; but there are many crimes that are felt to be much less reprehensible than many outrageous forms of injustice, cruelty or fraud, which the law does not punish at all, or else makes their perpetrator liable to money damages in a civil suit. It is well to remember that Moses murdered an Egyptian and fled the country, that Socrates was, by a majority of his fellow citizens that voted, found guilty of a crime, and that George Washington and others would have been treated as criminals if the American Revolution had been as unsuccessful as was the Scotch rebellion under Sir William Wallace. Those who, like Kant, regard obedience to the law as an absolute duty, must logically deny the moral right of any revolution. But this cannot be carried out consistently, since most, if not all, established governments, even the Constitution of the United States, have arisen out of revolutions and military conquest. Some dim, uncomfortable perception of this may be responsible for Kant's remarkable prohibition of any inquiry as to how the existing government acquired its authority.

An adequate discussion of justice in the criminal law must therefore deal with all the ethical issues of the law generally, such as the principle of equality, the adjustment of conflicting interests, or the relation between respect for personality and the demands of social responsibility and solidarity. [Pp. 989-990.]

B. Causes of crime

FERRI, CRIMINAL SOCIOLOGY *

Introduction. The Positive School of Criminal Law

§ 7. *The Application of the Positive Method to Criminal Law*

Indeed, who does not see how much analogy there is between this happy and useful transformation in the medical sciences and that which the new school represents in criminal law, which indeed should be a social pathology and a clinic? Criminal law, also, has until now consisted in the study of crimes considered as abstract entities. Until now the criminologist has studied robbery, homicide, and forgery, in and for themselves, as "juridical entities,"—as abstractions. He studied them with the sole aid of abstract logic and sentiments suitable to an honest man, which were wrongfully believed to be imputable to criminals. For each crime (as the result of a calculation, which several of the best-advised criminologists proclaim a scientific impossibility) there has been established a punishment fixed in ad-

---

* [Pp. 1, 12-13. Kelly, trans. Vol. 5, Modern Criminal Science Series; Boston: Little, Brown & Company, 1917.

Enrico Ferri (1856–1929), after completing his studies in Italy and France, became professor of criminal law, teaching successively at universities in Italy, France, Belgium, and South America. He is considered a great exponent of positivism in criminal law and is reckoned one of the founders of modern criminal sociology. Ferri's most significant contribution is contained in *Sociologia Criminale*, a work which was constantly being revised and supplemented from 1881 until the year of his death, when the fifth edition was published.]

vance, in the same way that a remedy was determined in advance, strictly prescribed and dosed for each disease. To the classical criminologist, the person of the criminal is an entirely secondary element, as the patient formerly was to the physician: he is only a subject to whom theoretical formulae, theoretically conceived, are applied; he is an animated manikin, on the back of which the judge places the number of a section of the penal code, and the prisoner himself becomes a number by the execution of the sentence. The criminologist, like the physician of the old school, was, of course, obliged in spite of all, to consider the transgressor, by reason of certain personal conditions, too evident to be neglected, which modified, it was claimed, the moral responsibility of the man.

With respect to all else—organic and psychic conditions surrounding the delinquent, except for a small number of manifest circumstances, expressly enumerated (minority, deaf-mutism, insanity, intoxication, uncontrollable outbreak of passion) influences of heredity and family, conditions of physical and social environment, which constitute the inseparable antecedents of the person of the criminal, and consequently of his acts—to these the criminologist remained an entire stranger. He was concerned with the crime and not with the criminal, and conducted himself exactly in the manner of the physicians of the past. I do not maintain that all this study of crime in itself, considered as a juridical being, has been futile; nor do I contend that medicine, even after its transformation, has not derived some advantage from the nosological studies of former days; but I do maintain that this abstract study of crime, considered independently of the person of the dilinquent, does not suffice to-day. In consequence, one can understand the reason of this evolution in criminal science, wherein crime in itself assuredly continues to be studied, but only after first studying the criminal with the aid of all of the means which the positive method can properly afford us.[7]

LOMBROSO, CRIME, ITS CAUSES AND REMEDIES *

§ 248. *Symbiosis*

. . . . .

There exists, it is true, a group of criminals, born for evil, against whom all social cures break as against a rock—a fact which compels us to eliminate

---

* [Pp. 446-451. Horton, trans. Vol. 3, Modern Criminal Science Series; Boston: Little, Brown & Company, 1911.

Cesare Lombroso (1836–1909), after studying at Padua, Vienna, and Paris, became professor of psychiatry at Pavia, then director of the Pesaro asylum, and again professor, first of forensic medicine, then of psychiatry, and finally of criminal anthropology, at Turin.

Although his theories as to the biological causes of mental conditions are no longer highly regarded, Lombroso's researches were valuable in their time, wide in scope,

them completely, even by death. But we comprehénd that this deplorable necessity will end by disappearing,—at least for the less dangerous criminals, the criminaloids,—and that the means of adapting them to social life will become more and more frequent, thanks to medical cure and to their utilization in occupations suited to their atavistic tendencies. Such would be war or surgery for homicides, the police or journalism for swindlers, etc., and finally colonization in wild and unhealthy countries for vagabonds, where they would be at least subjected to a fixed abode.

If, on the one hand, natural history has shown us the existence of murderous organs even in plants (carnivorous plants),[1] it shows us also, almost as a symbol of human charity, numerous cases of symbiosis, *i.e.*, instances where plants, harmful in themselves, become useful and beneficial when united together, while increasing their own vigor. . . . If science has shown us that the fusion of two useless or harmful plants may be useful, as when the fungi and the algae together produce the lichens, the time is not far distant when society will find the means, with an appropriate symbiotic culture, to acclimate the criminaloid to the environment of the most fully developed civilization, not only tolerating him but also utilizing him to its own advantage. The time is doubtless not far distant when we shall see in human civilization the carnivorous plants being eliminated, while the symbiotic plants go on increasing.

But we shall attain this end completely only upon the basis of the new science of anthropology, which, by individualizing its work, can give us powerful aid in discovering the special tendencies of criminals, in order to direct them and utilize the less anti-social of them.

Nino Bixio * is a striking example of the possibility of this reform. Criminal and impulsive from his childhood, he was the terror of his companions, whom he struck on all occasions. A vagabond and deserter, he seemed entirely incorrigible; yet he became a famous man when he was brought into the navy, where he could expend his excess of activity. In the same way men are not rare whom Garibaldi transformed from vagabonds into heroes. Very often in prisons I have heard thieves and assassins declare that they had committed their crimes only in order to get the means to become comedians or bicyclists; protesting, with that accent that does not admit of doubt, that if they had been able to attain their ideal they would have become famous and forever escaped from crime. I am the more convinced that they were right, since I have observed born criminals occupying high positions in the world, who satisfied their evil propensities in the exercise

---

and systematic. His works include a number of books on genius and insanity (a favorite topic of Lombroso's) and several on delinquency and crime.]

[1] *"Home Criminel"*, Vol. I, Pt. 1.

* [*Nino Bixio* (1821–1873), famous for his military exploits, was active in the long struggle for Italian independence. His political career followed his election as deputy in 1861, whereupon he sought to reconcile Cavour and Garibaldi. Created Senator in 1870, Bixio took part in the march on Rome in that year.]

of their profession, becoming very often, instead of the anti-social beings they once were, useful members of society. There is a certain celebrated surgeon who presents upon his face and skull and even in his talk all the marks of congenital criminality, of which he has also the aetiology. He has found an outlet for his cruel energy in surgical operations which, while doubtless sometimes dangerous, have nevertheless always the signs of genius. I have also known a certain Trinis, an athletic workman, who was well-behaved as long as he could spend his energy upon his work, but became dangerous as soon as sickness kept him idle. This is the type of the murderer from superabundance of force, which he discharges against someone else, especially against the police. I have known another criminal, analgesic and afflicted with vertigo from birth, who remained honest as long as he could satisfy his fondness for the sight of blood in his trade of butcher. When he became a corporal, however, he beat the soldiers to whom he had to teach the manual of arms. Out of work he became a swindler, thief, and murderer. Tolu, the Sardinian brigand, many times a murderer, was in the last years of his life very useful for the public safety in Sardinia against certain bands organized to steal cattle, whom he kept in order by the terror of his name alone, while soldiers and gendarmes could do nothing against them. . . .

I have shown in my previous studies [2] that genius, like moral insanity, has its basis in epilepsy. It is not absurd, then, to see moral insanity united with genius, and by that very union made not only harmless but sometimes even useful to society. This occurs in the case of great conquerors and leaders of revolutions, so that the criminal marks escape notice, even with contemporaries, although they may be even more striking than the marks of genius. When we study the lives of the great pioneers in Australia and America we see that they were almost all born criminals, pirates, or assassins, whose excessive fondness for action, strife, carnage, and novelty, which would have been an immense danger for their country, found a useful outlet in the midst of tribes of savages. All this proves that we must profit by the change which epileptic insanity sometimes brings on, impelling born criminals to excessive altruism and even saintliness, which, in its turn, draws along not only individuals but whole masses in an epidemic of virtue. Such were the cases of Lazzaretti, of Loyola, and of St. John of Ciodad. Their insensibility to pain and their recklessness make heroes of them in the face of danger, as we have seen in the case of Hollen, Fieschi, and Mottini, who had gained medals for valor in war, and the Clephtes, who were the first heroes of the Greek war of independence. . . .

It is for this reason that the state, instead of using repressive measures, ought to attempt to direct to great altruistic works that energy, that passion for the good, the just, and the new, which animates the criminal by

---

[2] *Man of Genius*, Pt. III.

passion and the political criminal. A great people ought to aim at the utilization of these forces, which, left to themselves, would certainly become dangerous; for they can be utilized, and may even succeed in transforming the apathetic masses. . . . In a nation like Russia, exhausted by an all-powerful bureaucracy, we have seen the energy of persecuted sectaries transform almost uninhabitable regions into fruitful fields with prosperous and populous cities.

Here are the results of symbiosis. This is the sublime goal which the great Redeemer and the prophets foresaw when they prophesied, "The wolf and the lamb shall feed together, and the lion shall eat straw like the bullock. . . . They shall not hurt nor destroy in all my holy mountain, saith the Lord"; and it is what Madame de Stael, that saint of a newer time, divined when she declared: "To understand is to pardon."

LINDNER, REBEL WITHOUT A CAUSE *

The Problem: Criminal Psychopathy

. . . Those searchers of the soul—psychiatrists and psychologists—have wasted much fine paper in vain attempts to attach a single group of signs to the disorder [psychopathic personality] unfortunately neglecting to extend their scientific objectivity to the proposition that psychopathic behavior is relative to the culture in which it flourishes and can be measured by no other rule than that of the prevailing ethic and morality. So in a society where total abstinence is mandatory—as among the Brahmins of India— a sign of psychopathy would be inebriation: and, among the prostitute priestesses of Astarte, the persistent continence of a beauteous devotee consecrated to the distribution of erotic favors would indicate a psychopathic trend. In short, psychopathy is a disorder of behavior which affects the relationship of an individual to the social setting.

Symptomatologically, then, the description of psychopathy derives from the consideration of the culture in which it appears and to which it is relative. Considered in this light, the psychopath, like Johnstone's rogue-elephant, is a rebel, a religious dis-obeyer of prevailing codes and standards. Moreover, clinical experience with such individuals makes it appear that the psychopath is a rebel without a cause, an agitator without a slogan, a revolutionary without a program; in other words, his rebelliousness is aimed to achieve goals satisfactory to himself alone; he is incapable of exertions for the sake of others. All his efforts, hidden under no matter what guise, represent investments designed to satisfy his immediate wishes and desires.

---

* [Pp. 1-2. New York: Grune & Stratton, 1944.
Rebel Without a Cause, by Robert M. Lindner (b. 1914), is a case study of a psychopathic criminal, secured by the technique of "hypnoanalysis."]

BONGER, CRIMINALITY AND ECONOMIC CONDITIONS *

Chapter 7. Conclusions

What are the conclusions to be drawn from what has gone before? When we sum up the results that we have obtained it becomes plain that economic conditions occupy a much more important place in the etiology of crime than most authors have given them.

First we have seen that the present economic system and its consequences weaken the social feelings. The basis of the economic system of our day being exchange, the economic interests of men are necessarily found to be in opposition. This is a trait that capitalism has in common with other modes of production. But its principal characteristic is that the means of production are in the hands of a few, and most men are altogether deprived of them. Consequently, persons who do not possess the means of production are forced to sell their labor to those who do, and these, in consequence of their economic preponderance, force them to make the exchange for the mere necessaries of life, and to work as much as their strength permits.

This state of things especially stifles men's social instincts; it develops, on the part of those with power, the spirit of domination, and of insensibility to the ills of others, while it awakens jealousy and servility on the part of those who depend upon them. Further the contrary interests of those who have property, and the idle and luxurious life of some of them, also contribute to the weakening of the social instincts.

The material condition, and consequently the intellectual condition, of the proletariat are also a reason why the moral plane of that class is not high. The work of children brings them into contact with persons to associate with whom is fatal to their morals. Long working hours and monotonous labor brutalize those who are forced into them; bad housing conditions contribute also to debase the moral sense, as do the uncertainty of existence, and finally absolute poverty, the frequent consequence of sickness and unemployment. Ignorance and lack of training of any kind also contribute their quota. Most demoralizing of all is the status of the lower proletariat.

The economic position of woman contributes also to the weakening of the social instincts.

The present organization of the family has great importance as regards criminality. It charges the legitimate parents with the care of the education

---

* [Pp. 667-672. Horton, trans. Vol. 7, Modern Criminal Science Series; Boston: Little, Brown & Company, 1916.

Willem Adriaan Bonger (1876–1940) was a well-known Dutch criminologist. Several of Bonger's works are available in English. His *Criminality and Economic Conditions* (1905), the source of the present excerpt, was translated in 1916. His *Introduction to Criminology* and *Race and Crime* appeared in English versions in 1936 and 1939 respectively.]

of the child; the community concerns itself with the matter very little. It follows that a great number of children are brought up by persons who are totally incapable of doing it properly. As regards the children of the proletariat, there can be no question of the education properly so-called, on account of the lack of means and the forced absence of one or both of the parents. The school tends to remedy this state of things, but the results do not go far enough. The harmful consequences of the present organization of the family make themselves felt especially in the case of the children of the lower proletariat, orphans, and illegitimate children. For these the community does but little, though their need of adequate help is the greatest.

Prostitution, alcoholism, and militarism, which result, in the last analysis, from the present social order, are phenomena that have demoralizing consequences.

As to the different kinds of crime, we have shown that the very important group of economic criminality finds its origin on the one side in the absolute poverty and the cupidity brought about by the present economic environment, and on the other in the moral abandonment and bad education of the children of the poorer classes. Then, professional criminals are principally recruited from the class of occasional criminals, who, finding themselves rejected everywhere after their liberation, fall lower and lower. The last group of economic crimes (fraudulent bankruptcy, etc.) is so intimately connected with our present mode of production, that it would not be possible to commit it under another.

The relation between sexual crimes and economic conditions is less direct; nevertheless these also give evidence of the decisive influence of these conditions. We have called attention to the four following points.

First, there is a direct connection between the crime of adultery and the present organization of society, which requires that the legal dissolution of a marriage should be impossible or very difficult.

Second, sexual crimes upon adults are committed especially by unmarried men; and since the number of marriages depends in its turn upon the economic situation, the connection is clear; and those who commit these crimes are further almost exclusively illiterate, coarse, raised in an environment almost without sexual morality, and regard the sexual life from the wholly animal side.

Third, the causes of sexual crime upon children are partly the same as those of which we have been speaking, with the addition of prostitution.

Fourth, alcoholism greatly encourages sexual assaults.

As to the relation between crimes of vengeance and the present constitution of society, we have noted that it produces conflicts without number; statistics have shown that those who commit them are almost without exception poor and uncivilized, and that alcoholism is among the most important causes of these crimes.

Infanticide is caused in part by poverty, and in part by the opprobrium incurred by the unmarried mother (an opprobrium resulting from the social utility of marriage).

Political criminality comes solely from the economic system and its consequences.

Finally, economic and social conditions are also important factors in the etiology of degeneracy, which is in its turn a cause of crime.

Upon the basis of what has gone before, we have a right to say that the part played by economic conditions in criminality is preponderant, even decisive.

This conclusion is of the highest importance for the prevention of crime. If it were principally the consequence of innate human qualities (atavism, for example), the pessimistic conclusion that crime is a phenomenon inseparably bound up with the social life would be well founded. But the facts show that it is rather the optimistic conclusion that we must draw, that where crime is the consequence of economic and social conditions, we can combat it by changing those conditions.

However important crime may be as a social phenomenon, however terrible may be the injuries and the evil that it brings upon humanity, the development of society will not depend upon the question as to what are the conditions which could restrain crime or make it disappear, if possible; the evolution of society will proceed independently of this question.

What is the direction that society will take under these continual modifications? This is not the place to treat fully of this subject. In my opinion the facts indicate quite clearly what the direction will be. The productivity of labor has increased to an unheard of degree, and will assuredly increase in the future. The concentration of the means of production into the hands of a few progresses continually; in many branches it has reached such a degree that the fundamental principle of the present economic system, competition, is excluded, and has been replaced by monopoly. On the other hand the working class is becoming more and more organized, and the opinion is very generally held among working-men that the causes of material and intellectual poverty can be eliminated only by having the means of production held in common.

Supposing that this were actually realized, what would be the consequences as regards criminality? Let us take up this question for a moment. Although we can give only personal opinions as to the details of such a society, the general outlines can be traced with certainty.

The chief difference between a society based upon the community of the means of production and our own is that material poverty would be no longer known. Thus one great part of economic criminality (as also one part of infanticide) would be rendered impossible, and one of the greatest demoralizing forces of our present society would be eliminated. And then, in this way those social phenomena so productive of crime, prostitution and alcoholism, would lose one of their principal factors. Child labor and overdriving would no longer take place, and bad housing, the source of much physical and moral evil, would no longer exist.

With material poverty there would disappear also that intellectual poverty which weighs so heavily upon the proletariat; culture would no longer be the privilege of some, but a possession common to all. The consequences of this upon criminality would be very important, for we have seen that even in our present society with its numerous conflicts, the members of the propertied classes, who have often but a veneer of civilization, are almost never guilty of crimes of vengeance. There is the more reason to admit that in a society where interests were not opposed, and where civilization was universal, these crimes would be no longer present, especially since alcoholism also proceeds in large part from the intellectual poverty of the poorer classes. And what is true of crimes of vengeance, is equally true of sexual crimes in so far as they have the same etiology.

A large part of the economic criminality (and also prostitution to a certain extent) has its origin in the cupidity excited by the present economic environment. In a society based upon the community of the means of production, great contrasts of fortune would, like commercial capital, be lacking, and thus cupidity would find no food. These crimes will not totally disappear so long as there has not been a redistribution of property according to the maxim, "to each according to his needs," something that will probably be realized, but not in the immediate future.

The changes in the position of woman which are taking place in our present society, will lead, under this future mode of production, to her economic independence, and consequently to her social independence as well. It is accordingly probable that the criminality of woman will increase in comparison with that of man during the transition period. But the final result will be the disappearance of the harmful effects of the economic and social preponderance of man.

As to the education of children under these new conditions it is difficult to be definite. However, it is certain that the community will concern itself seriously with their welfare. It will see to it that the children whose parents cannot or will not be responsible for them, are well cared for. By acting in this way it will remove one of the most important causes of crime. There is no doubt that the community will exercise also a strict control over the education of children; it cannot be affirmed, however, that the time will come when the children of a number of parents will be brought up together by capable persons; this will depend principally upon the intensity that the social sentiments may attain.

As soon as the interests of all are no longer opposed to each other, as they are in our present society, there will no longer be a question either of politics ("a fortiori" of political *crimes*) or of militarism.

Such a society will not only remove the causes which now make men egotistic, but will awaken, on the contrary, a strong feeling of altruism. We have seen that this was already the case with the primitive peoples, where their economic interests were not in opposition. In a larger measure this will be realized under a mode of production in common, the interest of all being the same.

In such a society there can be no question of crime properly so called. The eminent criminologist, Manouvrier, in treating of the prevention of crime expresses himself thus: "The maxim to apply is, act so that every man shall always have more interest in being useful to his fellows than in harming them." It is precisely in a society where the community of the means of production has been realized that this maxim will obtain its complete application. There will be crimes committed by pathological individuals, but this will come rather within the sphere of the physician than that of the judge. And then we may even reach a state where these cases will decrease in large measure, since the social causes of degeneracy will disappear, and procreation by degenerates be checked through the increased knowledge of the laws of heredity and the increasing sense of moral responsibility.

"It is society that prepares the crime," says the true adage of Quetelet. For all those who have reached this conclusion, and are not insensible to the suffering of humanity, this statement is sad, but contains a ground of hope. It is sad, because society punishes severely those who commit the crime which she has herself prepared. It contains a ground of hope, since it promises to humanity the possibility of some day delivering itself from one of its most terrible scourges.*

M. R. COHEN, MORAL ASPECTS OF THE CRIMINAL LAW †

The Economic Cause of Crime

. . . . .

That crime has its sole cause in a given economic system is a proposition which has been fanatically maintained and fanatically denied. But if we abandon the monistic prejudice of trying to explain everything as due to one cause, the question is not a difficult one. Crime is certainly not unrelated to economic conditions but there is no simple ratio between crime and poverty. There are many crimes of passion which affect the prosperous as well as the needy. But it must be admitted that men of wealth have

---

* [Alternative theories, (1) that the criminal is a peculiar physical type, (2) that the criminal is a madman, (3) that the criminal is an atavism, (4) that the criminal is a degenerate, (5) that the criminal is an epileptic, and (6) that criminal stigmata are the peculiarities of a professional type, are discussed by Tarde, *Penal Philosophy*, Chap. 5.]

† [From *Reason and Law*, pp. 15, 36-38. Glencoe, Ill.: The Free Press, 1950. Reprinted from 49 *Yale L. J.* 987, 1005-1007 (1940).]

a greater opportunity of escaping imprisonment. They have more means for securing witnesses and documents, hiring more skillful lawyers, etc.[7] It has been argued that a relatively small number of prisoners have committed crimes because of actual lack of food. But who supposes that economic need ends where the line of actual starvation is passed? Moreover, it is a fact that men and women are demoralized by extreme poverty to the extent that they cannot bring up their children properly. Morrison mentions in this connection that the number of female beggars is less than the number of male beggars though the former are more often in need. But the obvious answer to this is that successful mendicancy requires a certain energy, and that women not only cling more to ideas of respectability but that when they go in for mendicancy, many of them soon drift into prostitution. Many writers have urged that mendicancy cannot be due to extreme poverty because there have been instances of able bodied beggars who are offered opportunities to work at fair remuneration.[8] This argument seems to me to show a singular lack of social imagination. In the first place, it ignores the fact that none of us find it easy to change our occupation, even though originally we may have made great efforts to avoid it. How many of those engaged in the kind of soliciting that is regarded as respectable, e.g., for subscriptions to periodicals or to new stock companies, would change their occupation if offered the kind of work and pay which Monot and the others offered? We must also remember that the granting of alms was regarded as a virtue long before begging for alms (when not done by organized groups) became a crime.

But while there is no simple proportionality between economic distress and criminality, the causal relation between the two cannot be ignored. The inmates of our jails and prisons are, in overwhelming proportions, poor people. Of course, we must take into account that the poor are also in the great majority outside of prison. But even allowing for this, the wealthy certainly have the advantage of attaining their ends by legal ways which are not open to the poor. In the business world, it is common for certain powerful financial interests to demand that they be allowed a liberal share in certain profitable undertakings, for their ill will is very dangerous. This was notoriously the case a few years ago in the tobacco trade. Railroads also have been compelled to engage in certain deals in order to give controlling bankers an opportunity to make commissions on the flotation of certain loans. In the same way, politically powerful individuals extort money from business men by compelling them to contribute to party funds which they control. But the man without wealth or political power has no such lever. He has to use the threat of physical force or blackmail. This does not deny the great evil

---

[7] Ettinger, *The Problem of Crime* (1932) 149.

[8] Morrison, *Crime and its Causes* (1891) 105; Leroy-Beaulieu, *L'Etat moderne* (1900) 30.

of the latter. But though the poor are more numerous and more needy, they are not inherently more criminal or even more ruthless in attaining their ends.

We may conclude then that economic conditions are a very important cause of crime. But it is obvious that not every one in a given economic situation will be equally tempted or will as readily yield to temptation. Psychic dispositions and previous habits and associations enter into the situation. On the whole it can safely be asserted that the greatest resistance to criminal temptation is steady employment. If, then, a crime curve be plotted along the line of income, we shall not find the former straight. We shall, I think, find the maximum in the classes that have the lowest income, with a lower rate for peasants who continue to live on their family lands even if on a rather low income level. There seems to be an increase in criminality when boys and girls try to improve their lot by going to the cities where the opportunity for crime is greater and settled custom exerts less force. The influence, however, of past tradition may last for a considerable time. Thus, the smaller criminality among the foreign born is to be explained not only by their age distribution but by the persistence of their old home training, while the increased criminality of their more Americanized children is due to the fact that those accustomed to the old world discipline have difficulty in transmitting it to their children who are living under new conditions.

Does the existence of economic causes remove the necessity of punishment? The fact that some conditions leading to crime are removable does not prove that all are so. But what is even more important is to be on guard against the assumption that the elimination of social conditions can be effected at once. If, as human experience indicates, this is not so easy, we may well ask of our reformers: what do you propose to do with those guilty of rape, incendiary murder or the like? Abolish the cause? Admirable, when feasible. But so long as these offenses do occur, do you propose to do nothing to the offender? Even if you propose to reform him, must you not detain him against his will? And is not such detention a punishment?

While these counter questions are legitimate, they do not go sufficiently to the root of the matter. For back of all the arguments against the right or duty of punishment is the natural and just, if inadequately formulated, resentment against the stupid and ineffective cruelty of our whole penal system. It was the conservative President Taft, later Chief Justice of the Supreme Court, who characterized our criminal law as a disgrace to civilization.

LUNDEN, STATISTICS ON CRIME AND CRIMINALS *

All available data indicate that (1) more criminals are born in urban centers, (2) more criminals live in the cities, (3) more crimes occur in the metropolitan areas, and (4) as cities become larger rates of crime tend to rise.

How may these differences be explained?

(1) The city family is unstable and divorce rates are higher in the city. This shatters familial control of individuals.

(2) Urban populations are more heterogeneous racially, culturally and occupationally. This increases social distance and isolation.

(3) The religious life of the city is not integrated in the life of the people. Life becomes mechanistic and less sacred.

(4) There is much greater horizontal and vertical mobility in urban centers. Generally mobility is positively correlated with criminality.

(5) The cities are densely populated. Density of itself is not important but density implies increased social interaction and a greater number of social conflicts. More conflicts bring about more crime.

(6) The artificiality and shallow character of urban life creates an urge for thrills and the desire to "go places and do things."

(7) Criminals and lawless persons "hideout" in larger cities much easier than in rural areas.

(8) Gambling houses, saloons and houses of vice concentrate in the city. [P. 74.]

·   ·   ·   ·   ·   ·

Social Mobility and Social Stability

Excessive social mobility is a process that disrupts the lives of persons and shatters the cohesive bonds which maintain and control a well ordered society. The average man needs a fixed residence and occupation to develop a sense of security and stability of character. Torn loose from natal community and traditional vocation most men become relativistic in standards and lose their sense of moral values. People who change their residence often possess no ties of place or of groups and correspondingly are outside the sphere of the social solidarity and the control of a community. Families who migrate from country to country encounter a number of conflicting situations and their children suffer from the clash of old and new cultures.† For this reason the native born children of for-

---

* [Pittsburgh: Stevenson & Foster, 1942.]

† [Cf. J. L. Gillen, *Criminology and Penology* (3d ed., p. 57. New York: Appleton-Century-Crofts, 1945): "On the basis of arrests reported to the FBI in 1940, as shown in the preceding table, foreign-born whites were arrested less than one-third as fre-

eign born parents in America have always displayed a much higher crime rate than other nativity groups. In addition sections of a city composed chiefly of migrants and "suit-case folks" always show higher rates of crime than areas where people own their homes. The generality and intensity of social mobility is, therefore, a very important factor in the amount and character of crime in a society. [P. 134.]

VON HENTIG, THE CRIMINAL AND HIS VICTIM *

Chapter XII. The Contribution of the Victim to the Genesis of Crime

> I am a man
> More sinn'd against than sinning.
> —*King Lear*

1. The Duet Frame of Crime

Crime, for the most part, is injury inflicted on another person. Setting aside felonies directed against fictitious victims, the state, order, health, and so forth, there are always two partners: the perpetrator and the victim. [P. 383.]

. . . . .

In a sense the victim shapes and moulds the criminal.[4] The poor and ignorant immigrant has bred a peculiar kind of fraud. Depressions and wars are responsible for new forms of crimes because new types of potential victims are brought into being.[5] ... [P. 384.]

. . . . .

The victim is the injured party, and because he has been despoiled or harmed he is at the same time a claimant for punishment, for harm to be inflicted on the injurer. It is therefore of the utmost importance to the perpetrator that this capacity to be an informant and prosecutor should be eliminated or reduced. The criminal accordingly prefers victims who, for peculiar reasons, after suffering damage cannot breathe a word of it. Why should any victim set silence above retaliation? Criminal prosecution entails publicity. This publicity may be unwelcome for two reasons. Either it would do harm to the social status, marital security, or other vital condition of the victim, or the victim is a criminal or a

---

quently as native-born whites relative to their numbers in the population fifteen years of age and over (201.7 compared with 619.9 per 100,000 of the population). It is clear that the old assumption that foreigners are responsible for more than their share of crime is quite incorrect."]

* [New Haven: Yale University Press, 1948.

The Criminal and His Victim by *Hans von Hentig* (b. 1887), is a study of the personality and environmental factors incident to crime. Professor von Hentig is the author of several volumes in the field of criminal law and of the essay on "Punishment" in the *Encyclopedia of Social Sciences.*]

delinquent himself and thus unable to set the mechanisms of the state in operation without himself coming too close to the crime-repressing agencies. [P. 386.]

   . . . . .

Since it would be hard and wearisome to wait for situations in which the victim is practically defenseless,[8] many criminal games aim at giving the prospect a lift. The wanted combination of circumstances is brought about. Some sort of temptation is dangled before the strongest human urges; the victim takes the bait and the crime is committed in the ensuing discrediting situation.[9] [P. 387.]

3. Victim Statistics

   . . . . .

Whenever the problem of culture areas and crime comes up we speak not of the criminal but of the area in which some individual has been victimized.[45] Clifford Shaw has shown that sections of Chicago have high crime rates and that delinquency fades with distance from the city center.[46] The assumption is that criminals are herded together in areas adjacent to the central business district, and that the slum produces criminals. The suggestion is offered herewith that slums attract both potential victims and potential criminals, the preyer and the prey, and that out of their contact originates what we call crime, or vice, or unlabeled exploitation.

These people do not by any means live entirely in the slums or areas adjacent to railroad tracks, canals, or the districts of heavy industry. They come from all parts of the city to meet as brokers convene at Wall Street, and then scatter again. This rendezvous is assisted and promoted by powerful economically interested parties who have built up convenient meeting places in the guise of amusement establishments, night clubs, gambling houses, and so forth. Here victims present themselves or are presented by the owners of countless places of entertainment and "fun." [Pp. 399-400.]

   . . . . .

---

[8] Only fools or psychotics might report the offense. For these reasons drug addicts are avoided.

[9] On such shakedowns see Sutherland, *Professional Thief*, pp. 78-81. The popularity of Europe for indulging in all sorts of foibles rests on the reduced danger of extortions in another hemisphere.

[45] See Sutherland, *Principles of Criminology*, pp. 131 ff.; Wood and Waite, *Crime and Its Treatment*, pp. 95 ff.; Lunden, *op. cit.* [*Statistics on Crime and Criminals*], pp. 114 ff. (with a good chart of murder areas in Pittsburgh); Brearley, *op. cit.* [*Homicide in the United States*], pp. 6 ff.

[46] *Delinquency Areas* (Chicago, University of Chicago Press, 1929).

4. *General Classes of Victims*

.   .   .   .   .

Immigrants, Minorities, Dull Normals

Three other groups of typical victims may be mentioned. An artificial disadvantage is imposed on the immigrant, the minority race, and the large class of what the psychological testers call the "dull normals." This handicap extends from the social sphere to everyday conflicts. All are easily and frequently victimized.

We have already considered the immigrant status, or the situation of being a foreigner, from the point of view of criminality. There is a tendency all over the world to make the foreigner bear blame for others. Their different appearance,[94] their poverty, the life in slums, the disturbed balance of sexes, their competitive efficiency, all render them suspect. In America for a long time the idea prevailed that these aliens must be highly criminal, till careful statistical studies gave evidence of their low delinquency. In European countries foreigners coming from the West—the United States and the Dominions—are supposed by contrast to be rich people; they are regarded as wealthy—noncriminal, but good victims.[95] Immigrants from the East, again, are poor, highly competitive, and thus received with distrust. [Pp. 414-415.]

.   .   .   .   .

Racial minorities do not receive the same protection of the law as is given to the dominating class. This attitude makes it easier to victimize them. . . . [Pp. 416-417.]

.   .   .   .   .

6. *The Activating Sufferer—Some Broader Aspects*

.   .   .   .   .

In suggesting that increased attention should be paid to the crime-provocative function of the victim, whether individual or community, I have had certain practical consequences in mind. In most crimes the perpetrator is hidden, the victim—dead or alive—available. With a thorough knowledge of the interrelations between doer and sufferer new approaches to the detection of crime will be opened. The potentialities

---

[94] In fathoming the "Middletown spirit" the Lynds run into the tenet that "only foreigners and long-haired troublemakers are radicals" and that "most foreigners are 'inferior.'" Robert S. and Helen Merrell Lynd, *Middletown in Transition* (New York, Harcourt, Brace & Co., 1937), pp. 414, 407. "In Italy a drunkard is called a Frenchman, a beggar a Spaniard, a card-sharper a Greek." Ellis, *The Criminal*, p. 168.

of crime prevention will experience a vast expansion. Crime will become a problem of dynamics, and we will build our systems of treatment and prevention around the most seizable and workable of the causative forces. [P. 450.]

A. C. HALL, CRIME AND ITS RELATION TO SOCIAL PROGRESS *

Germany and Spain. The judicial statistics of Germany and Spain relate only to offences punished under the criminal code, and, in Germany, to a few other crimes recently created by special laws. Later chapters of this book will show the radical difference in the nature of the crimes most prevalent in these two countries. Meanwhile, a glance at the following table will reveal the enormous increase of delinquency in modern Germany—a state that has been advancing so very rapidly to the proud position of political, educational and industrial leadership upon the continent of Europe—and the almost stationary condition of criminality in Spain, where political disaster, economic distress, and the burden of uneducated ignorance and blind superstition have made of a once great nation an almost unprogressive, if not a degenerating people.

... Do not the most civilized and progressive states have the most crime, and more crime as civilization increases? † [Pp. 299-301.]

.   .   .   .   .

Is not crime clearly a social product, and has it not been increasing with giant strides in this enlightened and humane nineteenth century? Is not this increase due to growth of intelligence and social morality, realizing the new needs of a rapidly progressing civilization, causing the enactment of new social prohibitions, and by the enforcement of these prohibitions increasing crime and making criminals? Doubtless society does not wish offenders against her laws; she would much prefer that all men prove obedient; but the times are in the future, far distant, more Christian centuries, when a new criminal law will find none to break it. Meanwhile, the most civilized and progressive nations have the most criminals, and more abundant crime as they ascend higher in the scale of social development.

The increase of social prohibitions and of offenders against them in

---

* [*Crime and Its Relation to Social Progress* (New York: Columbia University Press, 1901–2) by *A. C. Hall* (1865–1910) embodies an original philosophic effort at understanding the significance of criminal statistics.]

† [See Hall *op. cit.,* pp. 279-301 for statistics on crime in European countries. And see Chapters 3-4 for a presentation of the classical view as to the absence of crime among primitive peoples. But *cf.* Malinowski, *Crime and Custom in Savage Societies* (1926), Part I, Chap. 1, and Part II, Chaps. 1-2.]

England, is but a type of what is happening in all the leading nations of the world. In the United States of America, the most highly developed, most progressive, best educated, most moral states have in general the largest percentage of criminals, while the smallest percentage must be sought for in the unprogressive and illiterate regions of the south, or in lately settled territories of the west.* [Pp. 274-275.]

ARISTOTLE, METAPHYSICS †

.   .   .   .   .

'Cause' means (1) that from which, as immanent material, a thing comes into being, e.g. the bronze is the cause of the statue and the silver of the saucer, and so are the classes which include these. (2) The form or pattern, i.e. the definition of the essence, and the classes which include this (e.g. the ratio 2:1 and number in general are causes of the octave), and the parts included in the definition. (3) That from which the change or the resting from change first begins; e.g. the adviser is a cause of the action, and the father a cause of the child, and in general the maker a cause of the thing made and the change-producing of the changing. (4) The end, i.e. that for the sake of which a thing is; e.g. health is the cause of walking. For 'Why does one walk?' we say; 'that one may be healthy'; and in speaking thus we think we have given the cause. The same is true of all the means that intervene before the end, when something else has put the process in motion, as e.g. thinning or purging or drugs or instruments intervene before health is reached; for all these are for the sake of the end, though they differ from one another in that some are instruments and others are actions.

These, then, are practically all the senses in which causes are spoken of, and as they are spoken of in several senses it follows both that there are several causes of the same thing, and in no accidental sense (e.g. both the art of sculpture and the bronze are causes of the statue not in respect of anything else but qua statue; not, however, in the same way, but the one as matter and the other as source of the movement), and that things can be causes of one another (e.g. exercise of good condition, and the latter of exercise; not, however, in the same way, but the one as end and the other as source of movement).—Again, the same thing is the cause of contraries; for that which when present causes a particular thing, we sometimes charge, when absent, with the contrary, e.g. we impute the

---

* [See Hall, op. cit., pp. 275-276 for statistics on this point.]

† [Book V, Chap. 2. The text follows that given in the Basic Works of Aristotle, pp. 752-753. McKeon, ed. Oxford: The Clarendon Press, 1941. See Chapters 5, 6, 7, and 14 infra for other passages from Aristotle.]

shipwreck to the absence of the steersman, whose presence was the cause of safety; and both—the presence and the privation—are causes as sources of movement.

C. Criminal Procedure

POUND, THE FUTURE OF THE CRIMINAL LAW *

In the middle of the sixteenth century, so Maitland tells us, "in criminal causes that were of any political importance, an examination by one or two doctors of the civil law threatened to become a normal part of our procedure."[1] For a time, indeed, judicial criminal justice, dispensed in the king's courts of common law, seemed to be giving way before executive criminal justice dispensed or dispensed with in administrative tribunals.[2] In like manner today, in a period that has much in common with Tudor and Stuart England, the function of securing social interests through punitive justice seems to be insensibly slipping away from courts and hence from law and in substance, if not in form, to be coming more and more into the hands of administrative agencies. For example, the current of modern legislation is reducing the sentence of the court in all important prosecutions to a mere form, and is committing determination of the actual nature and duration of penal treatment of offenders to boards of probation and parole. In a growing number of jurisdictions, a preliminary report by alienists or psychiatrists, before prosecution, may determine a crucial issue for practical purposes. In case of factory acts, housing laws, pure food laws, laws for protection against fire and sanitary laws, to-day we commonly remove the whole subject in substance from the domain of judicial prosecution and turn it over to boards and commissions, to be dealt with by inspectors and secretaries and agents. In more than one jurisdiction today, after an administrative board has in effect convicted the citizen, it has only to conduct the empty form of a prosecution in a court to conform to the exigencies of constitutional guarantees.

So rapid and so continual is the growth of administrative justice to-day, that we may well ask, what is to be the future of the criminal law as lawyers have known it? And this is more than an academic question. For our common law of crimes is a characteristic part of our Anglo-American polity, as well as of Anglo-American law. It cannot decay without accompanying or occasioning far-reaching decay in our legal and political institutions. Hence it behooves the thoughtful lawyer to inquire into

---

* [21 *Col. L. Rev.* 1 (1921).]

[1] *English Law and the Renaissance* (1901) 22.

[2] Note, for example, the Star Chamber, the Court of the President and Council of the North, and the Court of the High Commission, as their jurisdiction is defined by one who was hostile to them, in Coke's Fourth Institute.

the basis of the present tendency and of the conditions that make for it. It behooves him to consider whether the phenomenon is permanent or fleeting. It behooves him to ask what may be done to make our traditional materials for the administration of punitive justice more effective in action for the social ends they are charged to serve or in the alternative to consider whether decadence of our traditional system of criminal justice is inevitable and the struggle to maintain common-law institutions in this instance is destined to be a losing fight. [Pp. 1-2.]

.   .   .   .   .

What we need to observe it that legal history shows a continual movement back and forth between an extreme solicitude for the general security and the security of social institutions, leading to a minimum of regard for the interests of the individual accused and reliance upon summary, unhampered, arbitrary administrative punitive justice; and at the other extreme excessive solicitude for the social interest in the individual life, leading to a minimum of regard for the general security and security of social institutions and reliance upon strictly regulated judicial punitive justice, hampered at all points by checks and balances and technical obstacles. At Rome, when archaic modes of social control did not secure paramount social interests, they are followed by development of the disciplinary power of the military commander into an arbitrary and summary power of the magistrate to deal with crime.[47] So later, when the over-mild criminal law of the republic did not sufficiently secure paramount social interests, it was followed by the rise of imperial exercise of the whole magisterial power. Likewise in England, the medieval legal checks upon punitive justice were followed by the rise of the Star Chamber and other forms of executive criminal administration. The exaggerated legalism of nineteenth-century administration of the criminal law is being followed hard today by the rise of administrative justice through boards and commissions. The over-technical tenderness for the offender in the nineteenth century is giving way to an over-callousness, to violation of the constitutional rights of accused persons in the supposed interest of efficient enforcement of the penal laws. American prosecutions today are coming to be conducted with a ferocity without parallel in common-law trials since the Stuarts. The reports are coming to be filled with speeches of prosecutors for which we can only find a parallel in the harangues of Jeffreys and his colleagues.[48] The spectacle of a federal court committing witnesses for contempt during the course of a state trial, because they could not swear up to the mark on behalf of the prosecution, requires us to turn back to Jeffreys at the trial of Alice Lisle in

---

[47] Mommsen, *Römisches Strafrecht*, (1899) 39, n. 4, 135, 475.
[48] See note Lawless Enforcement of Law (1920) 33 *Harvard Law Rev.* 956; Sir Frederick Pollock's observations in (1920) 36 *Law Quarterly Rev.* 335-336.

order to find another example.[49] Excessive securing of the technical rights of accused persons in the nineteenth century produced the third degree just as the excessive zeal of prosecutors, browbeating of witnesses and unreasonable searches of the seventeenth and eighteenth centuries produced the criminal procedure of the nineteenth century. No one who has reflected on the history of the criminal law can doubt that these things in their turn will be followed by some such reaction as that which superseded the executive justice of the Star Chamber by the system of excessive limitations upon prosecutions which became classical in our polity. [P. 9.]

· · · · ·

The condition of internal opposition, which has produced this continual movement from wide magisterial power to narrowly limited formal procedure beset with checks and then back to summary and arbitrary administrative action, is inherent in criminal law. Criminal law exists to maintain social interests as such. But the social interest in the general security and the social interest in the individual life continually come into conflict and in criminal law, as everywhere else in law, the problem is one of compromise, of balancing conflicting interests and of securing as many as may be and as completely as may be with the least sacrifice of other interests. . . .

Unhappily instead of intelligent compromise, our juristic theory of the past has sought to proceed on the basis of one of the two contending elements exclusively. Seventeenth and eighteenth century theories of natural rights exalted the social interest in the individual life at the expense of the social interest in the general security. They thought of the criminal law as an infringement of natural rights, which were fundamental and universal qualities of human beings. As such it had to be justified by deriving its rules, its sanctions and its authority in some fashion from the free will of the offender himself.[52] In the nineteenth century, the fashion of juristic thinking sought to make the individual free will, as an ultimate metaphysical *datum*, the starting point of all legal obligation.[53] As our present-day theories of criminal law took form when such ideas were dominant, it was inevitable that the second of the two

---

[49] Ex parte Hudgings (1919) 249 U.S. 378; Rutherford v. United States (C.C.A. 1919) 258 Fed. 855.

[52] "The social treaty has as its end the preservation of the contracting parties. He who desires the end desires also the means, and some risks, even some losses, are inseparable from these means." Rousseau, *Contrat Social* (1762) liv. 2 chap. 5.

[53] "The injury which the criminal experiences is inherently just because it expresses his own inherent will; is a visible proof of his freedom." Hegel, *Philosophy of Right* (Dyde's transl. 1896) 97. "I define liberty as being the permission or power to do what one pleases to do without any external restraint." "Every abridgment of it demands an excuse, and the only good excuse is the necessity of preserving it." Carter, *Law: Its Origin, Growth and Function*, (1907) 133, 337.

elements that make up the criminal law historically—namely, limitations on magisterial enforcement of the prohibitions imposed to maintain the general security—that this second element should receive the whole emphasis. Thus the entire philosophical and theoretical equipment of the American lawyer with respect to the nature and the basis of the criminal law ignored an element that is at least half of the subject and became so at variance with the exigencies of the social interest in the general security as to be felt by sociologists to be anti-social.[54] [Pp. 11-12.]

---

2. Punishment

A. Responsibility

TARDE, PENAL PHILOSOPHY *

Chapter II. The Positivist School

§ 9. (1) What is Responsibility?

The criminal, had he so wished, external or internal circumstances remaining the same, could have not committed his crime; he himself was aware of this possibility; therefore he is guilty of having committed it. Such is the postulate of the old school. This is completely overthrown by the general spirit of modern science, which has for guiding principle the belief in the necessary repetition of similar phenomena under similar circumstances, and especially by the discoveries of experimental psychology (not to mention hypnotism). There are thus so many contradictions of the illusion of the inner sense on this point that, in a number of cases which are daily increasing, the demonstration of its falseness becomes palpable. From this there arises a real social danger: the lawyer finds in the alienist a more and more extensive and firm support, and, as the latter conclusively shows that the accused was unable to will not to commit the crime, he insures immunity to this criminal. This is logical because the foundation of responsibility is freedom of will.... [Pp. 55-56.]

.   .   .   .   .

---

[54] For a recent discussion from this standpoint, with some significant statistics, see Fosdick, *American Police Systems* (1920) 29-34. See also Train, *The Prisoner at the Bar* (1906) c. 17.

* [Howell, trans. Vol. 6, Modern Criminal Science Series; Boston: Little, Brown & Company, 1912. Footnotes are omitted.

Gabriel de Tarde (1843–1904) was a distinguished original thinker who contributed much to the modern understanding of the influence of group environment on individual behavior. Tarde served as chief of the Statistical Service of the French Ministry of Justice before his appointment as professor of modern philosophy at the Collège de France. Available in English translation are three of his works: *Social Laws* (1899); *The Laws of Imitation* (1903); and *Penal Philosophy* (1912), from which last the present excerpt is drawn.]

§ 13. Preliminary Remarks

. . . . .

Does it follow from all this that it is impossible to find a rational foundation for an idea which is plainly visible to all of humanity, which enlightens every man coming into the social world, and which is no superstition in process of receding before the advance of civilization, but an exact conception, spreading as civilization increases and expands? We do not believe so. The best means, as we look at it, by which to combat or to acquire control over the various theories hereinbefore set forth, is to oppose to them some theory which has in it nothing scholastic, but which evolves itself and ought to formulate itself, if one closely scrutinizes what men in fact have always meant when they say that in their opinion one of themselves is responsible, either civilly or criminally. Have they thought that he was responsible for some action because in carrying it out he, through his voluntary decision, through his freedom of choice, made necessary a mere possibility which, previous to this decision born "*ex nihilo*," would have had not one of the characteristics of a necessity? Never has human common sense entered into such subtleties. From all time a being has been adjudged to be responsible for an act when it was thought that he and no one else was the author, the willing and conscious author, be it understood, of this very act. The problem solved by means of this judgment is one dealing with causality and identity and not with freedom. Just as soon as free will shall be a truth and not a hypothesis, the fact alone that its existence is denied almost universally by the learned men of our time and an ever increasing proportion of educated people should make us feel the urgency of seeking elsewhere for the support of responsibility. In fact, when consulted by justice on the point of whether an accused is responsible in the classical interpretation of the word, the medico-legal expert ought always to reply, and as a matter of fact does more and more reply in the negative; and from this arise acquittals as scandalous as they are logical. Our utilitarians have indeed felt this danger and they have endeavored to avert it. But they have not been successful in doing so. By reason of the obligation which they believe to be imposed upon them after having denied the existence of free will, of defining responsibility as being a thing apart from any idea of morality, that is to say of decapitating and destroying it, they appear to justify this pretension, so often advanced by the partisans of free will, that, their principle having been destroyed, morality falls to the ground. There is in this a prejudice so dear to the spiritual conscience, and so eloquently propagated and supported by the noblest minds, that we cannot hope to see broken up this association of ideas entirely opposed to morality, as long as we limit ourselves to the undermining of the pretended foundation of the latter without having carved out or unearthed some new foundation on which to rest it. The importance of and the opportunity for this attempt should be an excuse for its very boldness. So we are going to take the liberty of outlining in the following pages, in a theoretical way, our way of looking at the matter; after which we shall endeavor to show that it is in accord with the historical evolution of responsibility and enables us for the first time to establish a connection, and for the first time to avoid any hiatus between the older conception, which is fading out, and the new positivist conception, which has a tendency to triumph.

§ 14. (1) Moral Responsibility Founded on Personal Identity and Social Similarity

The problem of responsibility is connected with the philosophical search for causes and is but an application of the latter, but a very arduous one, to the study of the facts relative to man living in society.

It is just because of this slim connection between the two problems that the conception of free will came into existence. In fact it came into existence, and it must logically have come into existence, at a time when the idea of the unlimited and absolute guilt of the sinner was the rule. If being guilty of an act means primarily being the cause of the same, it follows that being guilty of it absolutely and without limit, in the opinion of everybody and without any restriction, as is necessary in order to justify the notion of eternal damnation, must indeed mean being its absolute and first cause, in other words, the free cause, beyond which it is impossible for us to go back along the chain of the series of causes. Liberty used in this sense is an "*ex nihilo*" creative power, a divine attribute conferred upon man. The free agent resists and is able to check God; he is in reality a little god opposed to a great one. To refuse to man this creative power, this privilege of suspending the divine laws by means of a sort of incomprehensible *veto*, and at the same time to judge him to be deserving of punishments without end for having placed an obstacle in the path of the will of God, would unquestionably be to contradict oneself. But if, instead of an absolute and unlimited liability, henceforth left out of the discussion, the only question is one of a relative and limited liability similar to every real and positive thing, a causality itself relative and limited, a *secondary* causality, so to speak, will suffice. Consequently liberty becomes a useless postulate. We have arrived at that point. The question is to know finally whether, in order to be simply a stitch of the tissue bound about by phenomena and woven by necessity, the "myself" has lost all right to be called a cause, and whether there is no true cause excepting the first cause which is hypothetical and imperceptible. The question is to find out whether, instead of being founded upon the supposed indeterminateness of the act, responsibility will not be conditioned upon the special nature of its very determination, its internal determinism.

Let us suppose that we are looking at it from the point of view of the determinist. Do I any the less exist because I must of necessity exist? Am I any the less myself because from all time it has been ordained that I should exist, because billions and billions of chains of causes, rivers, and streams of force have converged in my direction, unknown to themselves, but inevitably, since the world has been in existence? This is not all; it will not even suffice to say that I have been from all time the inevitable flowing together of so many evolutions in the past; we must go so far as to say that an immense fan of causal evolutions, extending into the infinite future, emanates from me. I am the point of intersection of this double infinity, I am the focal point of this double convergence. For in truth why could you not say, *if necessity is the universal rule*, that my true cause is in the future, which is not yet, as well as in the past, which is no more? Is it not because of an entirely subjective illusion, and because of a remnant of unconscious, but deeply imbedded belief in *the contingency of the future*, that we refuse to account to ourselves for the actual fact, the existing phase of an evolution, by means of its later phases, and that we insist upon explaining it, always insufficiently, by means of its previous phases? There is no more reason for saying of a man who resembles his ancestors, by virtue of the laws of heredity, "it is his ancestors acting through him," than there would be to say, "it is his sons, his grandsons, or, if he is to have none, his social descendants, his future imitators, who are acting through him." If one only thinks of speaking of one's ancestors, it is because one knows only them, it is because man's imperfect intelligence is in general deprived of the faculty of seeing into the future—unless it be with reference to astronomical phenomena of a certain kind,—and is reduced to the faculty of remembering. Thus, *I must always have existed, I must exist forever*, and I will not truly be—I am. Now, if I am and as long as I am, it is but a farce to seek any cause for my acts other than myself.

However, we must recognize the fact that there is nothing more obscure than the idea of a cause and the relation of causality, nothing has given rise to more discussion among the philosophers. Hume and Kant, the positivists, and the critical philosophers, scarcely agree on this subject; and if the question had to remain unsolved until they had reached some agreement thereon, one might look upon it as impossible of solution. But human consciousness is not engaged in this debate; it has never here asked itself, what is the cause? Taking this word in its most obvious and practical meaning, it has merely asked itself, *where* is the cause? It has replied, in various ways according to the period of time, by circumscribing the more or less narrow circle of reality judged to be indivisible, within which the cause should be found inclosed. We say when we see an assassin who has just committed a crime, it is in this brain, in this soul that the cause of this homicide lies. A few centuries ago we would have said in a more vague way, it is within this individual, and at a time still more remote, when the individual was bound to his family as the member is to the body, we would rather have said, it is within this family. The essential thing is not to mistake one family for another, one individual for another, one soul, one brain for another; let us now add, for this progress continues, one "myself" for another. A family changes during the course of time and is renewed, an organism is transformed, a "soul" is modified, a "myself" is altered; but as long as the family, the body, or the person endures, the transformations taking place in them are variations upon a theme which remains more or less identical and whose identity, attenuated but not destroyed, gives us the right to look upon these circles of reality as always inclosing the cause of an act previously committed, the same cause or very nearly the same. Psychologists have attached far too great an importance to the feeling which we have of our liberty and not enough to the feeling, firm in every other respect, which we have of our identity. Moralists have expended treasures of analysis as a loss simply, in setting up the scale of the degrees of liberty; and the degrees of identity have escaped their vigilance. It is, however, easy enough to say at a certain moment of time, when one scrutinizes a person very closely, to what extent that person has remained the same as at a previous date; but no one can say just to what extent that person was a free agent. Let us admit free will, be it so; but at least we ought to recognize the fact that there is a most incontestable practical advantage in making responsibility rest upon identity which is a patent fact, rather than upon liberty which is a latent force.

Is that as much as to say that the idea of *individual identity* alone is sufficient?

No, we must add to it that of *social similarity*, as we shall see, and it is only in combining these two notions that we can find the plausible solution of the problem. In order for me to judge an individual to be responsible for a criminal action committed a year, ten years ago, is it enough for me to believe that he is the identical author of this action? No, for though I might have brought the same judgment of identity to bear in the case of a murder committed on a European by a savage of a newly discovered isle, yet I would not have the same feeling of moral indignation and of virtuous hatred as a similar act carried out by one European on another, or by one islander on another, would inspire within me. Therefore one indispensable condition for the arousing of the feeling of moral and penal responsibility is that the perpetrator and the victim of a deed should be and should feel themselves to be more or less fellow-countrymen from a social standpoint, that they should present a sufficient number of resemblances, of social, that is to say, of imitative origin. This condition is not fulfilled when the incriminating act emanates from someone who is insane, or from an epileptic at the moment he is seized with a paroxysm, or even from one addicted to alcoholism in certain cases. This sort of people, at the very moment when they have acted, have not belonged to the society of which they are reputed to be members. But when the two conditions pointed out above are met with and are together developed to a high degree, the feeling of responsibility bursts forth with remarkable strength.... [Pp. 84-89.]

.   .   .   .   .

§ 16. (III) Comparison with the Collective Responsibility of a Nation. Its Numerous Analogies to Individual Responsibility

A comparison which is not a comparison merely will make the preceding statements more readily understood.

Let us ask ourselves under what conditions the collective responsibility of a nation as a nation is fully and undeniably brought into play. Here the equivalent of memory and habit, foundation of individual identity, is tradition and custom, foundation of national identity. [P. 93.]

.   .   .   .   .

Responsibility, I repeat, implies a social tie, a collection of similarities in nature which are not organic merely, between the great and the small, the States or the individuals judged to be responsible; and the responsibility implies, furthermore, a psychological tie between the former state during which the being adjudged to be responsible acted or contracted and the later state during which he called upon to answer for his act or to carry out his contract. Is it also necessary that there should be a psychological connection between the former and the later state of the one who makes the claim himself? Yes I believe so. When, following a conquest or a revolution, a people has been thrown into disorder from top to bottom, it is hardly the time to invoke against another people rights based upon an insult to the flag of its former government which has been overthrown, or even upon an agreement made with the leaders of this former State, whose name is all that is left of it. In Europe the French Revolution itself did not result in any such confusion as the cancellation of every diplomatic treaty previous to 1789 could have brought about; but assuredly the social transformation which resulted therefrom brought to bear on these treaties an effect at least equally far reaching. Similarly, I do not feel that I am obliged to carry out a promise made to someone who has become insane since my obligation was incurred, unless it be when it relates to the discharge of a debt the amount of which the guardian of this lunatic, or his heir after his death can collect. As a matter of fact, in such a case the law establishes the fiction of a legal person who never dies and who continues to exist without change. I will add that neither do I feel myself bound to discharge a debt which I contracted when I was five or six years old, before the absolute determining of my person, no matter with whom. . . .

It is worth while observing, in following our analogy, that whether it be in the relations of one people with another, or in the relations of one person with another, the slightest degree of identity or of similarity is sufficient to give birth to the feeling of civil responsibility only in order that it may arouse that of criminal or quasi-criminal responsibility. Such a State, after passing through a revolutionary crisis, believes itself to be exempted by reason of its metamorphosis from any reparation to another State arising from some offense to the latter before the revolution on the part of the displaced government, but it nevertheless believes it ought to honor the signature of this former government by conforming itself to the clauses of a former diplomatic agreement. Such a civilized people recalls without the slightest remorse having carried on the slave-trade with Guinea, having poisoned Chinamen or massacred Indians, but would feel some scruples about not conforming to the terms of a bargain struck with these inferior races, who, after all, are a part of the human race.

In the same way a private individual would laugh if reparations were asked of him by a duel-challenge for an insult dating back ten years, or two years even, especially when, during the interim a great illness or a disaster of some sort had greatly changed his character; but he would take seriously the demanding of a sum borrowed by himself without any right and at a period even more remote. He gaily recalls the annoyances which he caused Asiatics or Africans, providing they do not amount to real crimes (in this he is better than a nation would be in his place), but he would deem himself to be disgraced were he to fail to pay these foreigners what he owed them. It is perhaps because of a vague realization of this truth that the periods of limitation in criminal cases are much shorter under all legislation than are those of limitations in civil cases. . . .
[Pp. 93-98.]

.   .   .   .   .

§ 28. (1) *Family Solidarity of Primitive Times; Vendetta, Survivals of These Past Times, Reprisals.*

.   .   .   .   .

In England, it is only from the ninth or tenth century on that the woman ceased to be beaten for the crimes of her husband; but under Edward the Confessor again, each guild was responsible as a whole for the offense committed by one of its members. Moreover, even among the more or less civilized peoples who have for a long time admitted the individual character of offenses and of punishments on principle, the old principle survives or is resuscitated in certain particular cases, for example, on the occasion of crimes of a religious or of a political nature. In Egypt "the mother, the children, the whole family of the conspirator was given over to the executioner." In Mexico under the Aztecs, not only was the vestal guilty of having broken her vow condemned—just as in Rome, singular coincidence—to be buried alive, but even her relatives were banished and her native town destroyed. . . .

Is there any necessity of recalling that in France, in the case of crimes of high treason, this fearful archaism of family responsibility survived until the eighteenth century? The relatives of Damien were banished as had been those of Ravaillac. But even in our own day does there not remain something of this old historical prejudice in the fiction which makes us consider the members of a ministerial cabinet as mutually responsible for the misdeed committed by one of them? The immunity of parliament, by virtue of which a deputy or a senator may not be prosecuted without the authorization of the assembly of which he is a member, as though the latter judged itself to be in a measure responsible for his honor, is derived from the same source. Moreover, among the illiterate classes the old prejudice is still alive. A few years ago, for example, according to Ferri, an Italian stabbed a soldier whom he did not know, because another soldier had offended him some time before this.

What does this ancient custom signify? It means simply that in the eyes of primitive communities all the members of the same natural group, be it tribe or patriarchal family, went to make up an indivisible, and indissoluble whole, a truly identical and immortal person.* In vain might they be aware that the perpetrator of a crime was such and such an individual and not his brothers, they struck at all his brothers along with him, just as nowadays, though we may believe that the cause of a crime resides only in one portion of the brain of its perpetrator, we sometimes make his entire head fall under the blade of the guillotine. . . . [Pp. 135-139.]

. . . . . .

§ 31. (IV) Review and Completion

. . . . .

Let us now add that, after having led us gradually to affirm the individuality of every fault, social progress ought to go still further and be carried on under new forms. How can this be? By means of the development of mental pathology, or, if you will, of criminal anthropology, which will allow us to pick out from this very complex being called the individual the distinct elements, though they may not be severable, of which he is composed, to take them to one side and to apply to the special

---

* [Cf. Lee, "Corporate Criminal Liability," 28 Col. L. Rev. 1 (1928).]

treatment, of each one of them the appropriate remedies. So, in occupying ourselves in the chapter which follows, with the limitations or with the suppression of penal responsibility under the sway of certain abnormal states, such as madness and drunkenness, we will only be applying to these exceptional cases the general ideas which are set forth above, and engaged along the lines to which the historical evolution of the punishment of crime has forced existing societies.* [Pp. 147-148.]

B. Purpose of Punishment

KANT, PHILOSOPHY OF LAW †

§ 49. Distinct Functions of the Three Powers. Autonomy of the State.

E. The Right of Punishing and of Pardoning

Judicial or Juridical Punishment (*poena forensis*) is to be distinguished from Natural Punishment (*poena naturalis*), in which Crime as Vice punishes itself, and does not as such come within the cognizance of the Legislator. Juridical Punishment can never be administered merely as a means for promoting another Good either with regard to the Criminal himself or to Civil Society, but must in all cases be imposed only because the individual on whom it is inflicted *has committed a Crime*. For one man ought never to be dealt with merely as a means subservient to the purpose of another, ‡ nor be classified with the objects of the law of property. Against such treatment his inherent Personality has a Right to protect him, even although he may be condemned to lose his Civil Personality. He must first be found guilty and *punishable*, before there can be any thought of drawing from his Punishment any benefit for himself or his fellow citizens. The Penal Law is a Categorical Imperative; and woe to him who creeps through the serpent-windings of Utilitarianism to discover some advantage that may discharge him from the Justice of Punishment, or even from the due measure of it, according to the Pharisaic maxim: 'It is better that *one* man should die than that the whole people should perish.' For if Justice and Righteousness perish, human life would no longer have any value in the world. What, then, is to be said of such a proposal as to keep a Criminal alive who has been condemned to death, on his being given to understand that if he agreed to certain dangerous experiments being performed upon him, he would be

---

* [For a discussion of the traditional treatment of responsibility in the common law, see Kenny, *Outlines of Criminal Law* (Am. Ed. 1907), Chaps. 3, 4. *Cf.* Josserand, *Les Mobiles dans les actes juridiques du droit privé* (1928) § 7.]

† ["The Science of Right," Part II ("Public Right"). Hastie, trans. Minor revisions have been made in the translation.]

‡ [For a criticism of this view, see Holmes, *The Common Law*, 43-45 (1881).]

allowed to survive if he came happily through them? It is argued that Physicians might thus obtain new information that would be of value to the Commonweal. But a Court of Justice would repudiate with scorn any proposal of this kind if made to it by the Medical Faculty; for Justice would cease to be Justice, if it were bartered away for any consideration whatever.

But what is the mode and measure of Punishment which Public Justice takes as its Principle and Standard? It is just the Principle of Equality, by which the pointer of the Scale of Justice is made to incline no more to the one side than the other. It may be rendered by saying that the undeserved evil which any one commits on another, is to be regarded as perpetrated on himself. Hence, it may be said: 'If you slander another, you slander yourself; if you steal from another, you steal from yourself; if you strike another, you strike yourself; if you kill another, you kill yourself.' * This is the Right of RETALIATION (*jus talionis*); and properly understood, it is the only Principle which in regulating a Public Court, as distinguished from mere private judgment, can definitely assign both the quality and the quantity of a just penalty. All other standards are wavering and uncertain; and on account of other considerations involved in them, they contain no principle conformable to the sentence of pure and strict Justice. It may appear, however, that difference of social status would not admit the application of the Principle of Retaliation, which is that of 'Like with Like.' But although the application may not in all cases be possible according to the letter, yet as regards the effect it may always be attained in practice, by due regard being given to the disposition and sentiment of the parties in the higher social sphere. Thus a pecuniary penalty on account of a verbal injury, may have no direct proportion to the injustices of slander; for one who is wealthy may be able to indulge himself in this offence for his own gratification. Yet the attack committed on the honour of the party aggrieved may have its equivalent in the pain inflicted upon the pride of the aggressor, especially if he is condemned by the judgment of the Court, not only to retract and apologize, but to submit to some meaner ordeal, as kissing the hand of the injured person. In like manner, if a man of the highest rank has violently assaulted an innocent citizen of the lower orders, he may be condemned not only to apologize but to undergo a solitary and painful imprisonment, whereby, in addition to the discomfort endured, the vanity of the offender would be painfully affected, and the very shame of his position would constitute an adequate Retaliation after the principle of 'Like with Like.' But how then would we render the statement: 'If you *steal* from another, you steal from yourself'? In this way, that whoever steals anything makes the property of all insecure; he therefore robs himself of all security in

---

* [Kant later admits reservations on the *lex talionis*, with regard to rape.]

property, according to the Right of Retaliation. Such a one has nothing, and can acquire nothing, but he has the Will to live; and this is only possible by others supporting him. But as the State should not do this gratuitously, he must for this purpose yield his powers to the State to be used in penal labour; and thus he falls for a time, or it may be for life, into a condition of slavery.—But whoever has committed Murder, must *die*. There is, in this case, no juridical substitute or surrogate, that can be given or taken for the satisfaction of Justice. There is no Likeness or proportion between Life, however painful, and Death; and therefore there is no Equality between the crime of Murder and the retaliation of it but what is judicially accomplished by the execution of the Criminal. His death, however, must be kept free from all maltreatment that would make the humanity suffering in his Person loathsome or abominable. Even if a Civil Society resolved to dissolve itself with the consent of all its members—as might be supposed in the case of a People inhabiting an island resolving to separate and scatter themselves throughout the whole world—the last Murderer lying in the prison ought to be executed before the resolution was carried out. This ought to be done in order that every one may realize the desert of his deeds, and that bloodguiltiness may not remain upon the people; for otherwise they might all be regarded as participators in the murder as a public violation of Justice.* [Pp. 194-198.]

．　　．　　．　　．　　．

Against these doctrines, the Marquis BECCARIA has given forth a different view. Moved by the compassionate sentimentality of a humane feeling, he has asserted that all Capital Punishment is wrong in itself and unjust. He has put forward this view on the ground that the penalty of death could not be contained in the original Civil Contract; for in that case, every one of the People would have had to consent to lose his life if he murdered any of his fellow citizens. But, it is argued, such a consent is impossible, because no one can thus dispose of his own life.—All this is mere sophistry, and perversion of Right.

No one undergoes Punishment because he has willed to be punished, but because he has willed a *punishable Action*; for it is in fact no Punishment when any one experiences what he wills, and it is impossible for any one to will to be punished. To say, 'I *will* to be punished, if I murder any one,' can mean nothing more than, 'I submit myself along with all the other citizens to the Laws'; and if there are any Criminals among the People, these Laws will include Penal Laws. The individual who, as a

---

* [Holmes, *The Common Law*, p. 45 suggests that the feeling of fitness upon which the lex talionis is sometimes supported is experienced only in respect of crimes committed by others. Ethical criticisms of Kant's theory may be found in Willoughby, *Social Justice* (1900), pp. 326 *et seq.*; McConnell, *Criminal Responsibility and Social Constraint*, Chap. 2 (1912).]

Co-legislator, enacts *Penal Law*, cannot possibly be the same Person who, as a Subject, is punished according to the Law; for, qua Criminal, he cannot possibly be regarded as having a voice in the Legislation. The Legislator is holy.... [P. 201.]

HEGEL, PHILOSOPHY OF RIGHT *

92. Since it is only in so far as the will has visible existence that it is the idea and so really free, and its realized existence is the embodiment of freedom, force or violence destroys itself forthwith in its very conception. It is a manifestation of will which cancels and supersedes a manifestation or visible expression of will. Force or violence, therefore, is, according to this abstract treatment of it, devoid of right.

93. Since it in its very conception destroys itself, its principle is that it must be cancelled by violence. Hence it is not only right but necessary that a second exercise of force should annul and supersede the first. [P. 85.]

. . . . . .

99.... *Note.*—The theory of punishment is one of the matters, which in the modern positive science of right has fared worst. The attempt is made to base this theory upon the understanding, and not, as should be done, upon the conception. If crime and its removal, or, more definitely, punishment, are regarded merely as evil, it might indeed be thought unreasonable to will a second evil merely because one already existed. (Klein, "*Grunds. des peinlichen Rechts*," § 9 fol.) In the different theories of punishment, that it is preventive, deterrent, reformatory, etc., this superficial notion is taken to be fundamental. In the same superficial way the result of punishment is set down as a good. But here we are not dealing with an evil, and this or that good, but with wrong and justice. In these superficial theories the consideration of justice is set aside, and the moral aspect, the subjective side of crime, is made the essential. Also with the moral view are mingled trivial psychological notions about temptation, and the strength of sensual impulses opposing reason, about psychological compulsion also, and the influences affecting the imagination; it being forgotten that the subject may freely abase itself to something contingent and unreal. The treatment of punishment in its character as a phenomenon, of its relation to the particular consciousness, of the effect of threats upon the imagination, and of the possibility of reform is of great importance in its proper place, when the method of punishment is to be decided on. But such treatment must assume that punishment is absolutely just. Hence everything turns on the point that in crime it is not the production of evil but the injury of right as right, which must

---

* [From *Grundlinien der Philosophie des Rechts* (Leipzig, 1911).]

be set aside and overcome. We must ask what that is in crime, whose existence has to be removed. That is the only evil to be set aside, and the essential thing is to determine wherein that evil lies. So long as conceptions are not clear on this point, confusion must reign in the theory of punishment.

Addition.—Feuerbach, in his theory of punishment, considers punishment as a menace, and thinks that if any one disregards the threat and commits a crime, the punishment must follow, since it was already known to the criminal. But is it right to make threats? A threat assumes that a man is not free, and will compel him by vividly presenting a possible evil. Right and justice, however, must have their seat in freedom and in the will, and not in the restriction implied in menace. In this view of punishment it is much the same as when one raises a cane against a dog; a man is not treated in accordance with his dignity and honour, but as a dog. A menace may incite a man to rebellion in order that he may demonstrate his freedom, and therefore sets justice wholly aside. Psychological compulsion may refer to distinctions of quality or quantity in crime, but not to the very nature of crime. Books of law, written in accordance with the principle that punishment is a threat, lack their proper basis.

100. The injury which the criminal experiences is inherently just because it expresses his own inherent will, is a visible proof of his freedom and is his right. But more than that, the injury is a right of the criminal himself, and is implied in his realized will or act. In his act, the act of a rational being, is involved a universal element, which by the act is set up as a law. This law he has recognized in his act, and has consented to be placed under it as under his right.

Note.—Beccaria, as is well known, has denied to the state the right of exacting the death penalty, on the ground that the social contract cannot be supposed to contain the consent of the individual to his own death; rather, as he thought, must the opposite be assumed. To this it must be replied that the state is not a contract (§ 75), nor, moreover, are the protection and security of the life and property of individuals in their capacity as separate persons, the unconditioned object of the state's existence. On the contrary, the state is the higher existence, which lays claim to the life and property of the individual, and demands the sacrifice of them.

Not only has the conception of crime, the reasonable essence of it, to be upheld by the state, with or without the consent of the individual, but rationality on its formal side, the side of the individual will, is contained in the act of the criminal. The criminal is honoured as reasonable, because the punishment is regarded as containing his own right. The honour would not be shared by him, if the conception and measure of his punishment were not deduced from his very act. Just as little is he honoured when he is regarded as a hurtful animal, which must be made harmless, or as one who must be terrified or reformed.—Moreover, punishment is not the only embodiment of justice in the state, nor is the state merely the condition or possibility of justice.

Addition.—The desire of Beccaria that men should consent to their own punishment is reasonable, but the criminal has already yielded consent through his act. . . .

101. The doing away with crime is retribution, in so far as retribution is in its conception injury of an injury, implying that as crime has a definite qualitative and quantitative context, its negation should be similarly definite. This identity, involved in the very nature of the case, is not literal equality, but equality in the inherent nature of the injury, namely, its value. [Pp. 88-90.]

. . . . .

. . . To adhere obstinately to the equalization of punishment and crime in every case would reduce retribution to an absurdity. It would be necessary to institute a theft in return for theft, robbery for robbery, and to demand an eye for an eye and a tooth for a tooth, although the criminal, as we can easily fancy, might have only one eye or be toothless. For these absurdities, however, the conception is not responsible. They are due to the attempt to equate crime and punishment throughout their minute details. Value, as the inner identity of things specifically different, has already been made use of in connection with contract, and occurs again in the civil prosecution of crime (§ 95). By it the imagination is transferred from the direct attributes of the object to its universal nature. Since the essential character of crime lies in its infinitude, *i.e.*, in the breach of its own right, mere external details vanish. Equality becomes only a general rule for determining the essential, namely, a man's real desert, not for deciding the special external penalty. . . .

Addition.—Retribution is the inner connection and identity of two things which in outward appearance and in external reality are different. Requital seems to be something foreign, and not of right to belong to the criminal. But punishment is only the manifestation of crime, the other half which is necessarily presupposed in the first. Retribution looks like something immoral, like revenge, and may therefore seem to be something personal. But it is the conception, not the personal element, which carries out retribution. Revenge is mine, says God in the Bible, and, when some find in the word re-tribution the idea of a special pleasure for the subjective will, it must be replied that it signifies only the turning back of crime against itself. The Eumenides sleep, but crime wakes them. So it is the criminal's own deed which judges itself. Although in requital we cannot venture upon equality of details, the case is different with murder, to which death is necessarily due. Life is the total context of one's existence, and cannot be measured by value. Its punishment, therefore, cannot be measured by value, but must consist in the taking of another life.* [Pp. 91-92.]

SALEILLES, THE INDIVIDUALIZATION OF PUNISHMENT †

Chapter 1. The Statement of the Problem

. . . . .

§ 3. The Purpose of Punishment: "Zweckstrafe"

Opposed to this fundamentally legal view another has gradually gained ground and may, in its development, itself become classic. It holds that punishment is to be determined not by the material gravity of the crime, not by the injury done, but by the nature of the criminal. It would indeed be a violation of justice if under pretext of justice useless suffering should be inflicted. The legitimate purpose of punishment is to make of the criminal an honest man if that be possible; or, if not, to deprive him of the chance of doing further harm. For the view that punishment is an infliction of injury for injury there is substituted the view that punishment is a moral instrument, a means of regeneration for the individual as well as of protection for society. Punishment has thus a social end directed to the future, while hitherto it was regarded only as the necessary consequence of a past act. It was appraised and described in terms of the crime committed without reference to future issues; and this attitude resulted in making habitual criminals.

Where formerly only the accomplished deed was considered, the purpose of punishment is now taken into account. Such purpose is not to inflict a punishment for what has been done, as if in satisfaction of a sentiment of individual or collective vengeance, but to bring about a certain result. The Germans call this aspect of punishment (in contrast to the "*Vergeltungsstrafe*," which in the classic view was a punishment by way of compensation or retribution) the "*Zweckstrafe*" [1] which we can hardly

---

* [For a criticism of the expiative theory of punishment, see McConnell, *Criminal Responsibility and Social Restraint* (1912), Chap. 1.]

† [Pp. 8-10. Jastrow, trans. Vol. 4, Modern Criminal Science Series; Boston: Little, Brown & Company, 1911.]

Sébastien Félix Raymond Saleilles (1855–1912), noted French legal scholar, was professor at the universities of Dijon and Paris. In his works, he sought to bring legal thought into closer contact with contemporary social and philosophical ideas. He emphasized further and broader study of comparative law and legal history. Saleilles believed that it is not enough for a judge to seek so-called "legislative intent," but that he must adapt permanent texts to the changing requirements of the social milieu.

The present selection is from *The Individualization of Punishment*, an English translation of the second French edition of *L'individualisation de la peine: Etude de criminalité sociale* (1st ed. 1898; 3d ed. 1927).

See *infra*, p. 359 for a further selection from this volume.]

[1] For bibliography see *Von Liszt, "Lehrbuch des Deutschen Strafrechts"* (edition 1905, § 15).

render more closely than by the phrase "punishment for a purpose." Yet the term does scant justice to the important movement inspired by Ihering, and to the significance therein attached to the conception of the final purpose ("*Zweck*"), the consideration of which was to reanimate the dead bones of the law. The vital principle of every organic function is this same "*Zweck*" or final purpose; and this is equally true of the law. The function of punishment must accordingly be directed to its social purpose and adapted to that purpose as an instrument is adapted to the operation in view. Accordingly it is the future and not the past, not the crime committed, that sets the goal and the purpose sought.

Consequently punishment for each individual case should be so adjusted to its purpose as to produce the largest possible return. It cannot be strictly and rigidly determined in advance, nor inflexibly regulated by the law. The purpose of punishment is an individual one and is to be attained through a policy appropriate to the circumstances of the case, not by the application of an abstract law, that ignores the varieties of the cases considered. Such is the "*Zweckstrafe*," a punishment characterized by its purpose, as opposed to the "*Vergeltungstrafe*," a punishment crystallized as a mechanical and exact retribution, ineffective in regard to the past and without influence upon the future. If this conception of punishment, which looks to the future for the realization of a definite purpose, be accepted, it necessarily follows that the punishment must be adapted to the nature of the individual to whom it is applied. If the criminal is not fundamentally a pervert, the punishment should not contribute to his further perversion. It should serve for his regeneration and his rehabilitation. If the criminal is an incorrigible, the interests of society demand his punishment as a measure of protection and of radical prevention. Such adaptation of punishment to the individual is now known as the individualization of punishment. As in medicine, it has been maintained that there are no diseases but only patients, so one is tempted to say that, strictly speaking, there are no crimes but only criminals.*

TOURTOULON, PHILOSOPHY IN THE DEVELOPMENT OF LAW †

Chapter 4. Selection in and Through Law

. . . . .

3. *Selection and Criminal Law.* This branch of the law seems more especially charged with the work of selection. According to definition, is

---

* [See McConnell, *Criminal Responsibility and Social Constraint*, Chap. 4, for a criticism of the reformative theory of punishment.]

† [Read, trans. Vol. 13, Modern Legal Philosophy Series; New York: The Macmillan Company, 1922. There is an editorial preface by Morris R. Cohen, from which an excerpt appears *infra*, Chapter 11. *Pierre de Tourtoulon* (1867–1932), a leading

it not purifying society, to put to death, imprison, or transport murderers, robbers and other individuals who form the dregs of the population,—to suppress the bad elements and, up to a certain point, their descendants, and to select with the precise intention of obtaining a better humanity just as the breeder discards defective animals in order to improve the race?

This operation may be more or less well conducted. Well conducted, it will produce the proper selection; poorly conducted, an incomplete, insufficient, perhaps, insignificant selection. In every instance, to remove a malefactor from society is to better the social group from a moral point of view. This is a rather naive truth; but we must not conclude from it that criminal law is always a more or less effective instrument of selection. To rid us of harmful beings is one of its functions, but it is not its only function. [Pp. 120-121.]

.   .   .   .   .

Finally, when repression is exercised entirely by the State, criminal law favors, according to the time and circumstances, the families of the guilty as well as those of the victims. . . .

. . . We see in criminal law only the State prosecuting a malefactor, and we ignore the other side of the picture, the State tying our hands to prevent our taking revenge for the wrongs we have suffered. One of Courteline's characters who has been beaten is very much astonished that his assailant clears himself by the payment of a fine of sixteen francs. He criticizes this sentence and receives two years in prison. That man had seen both sides of the picture and had experienced this truth (with which treatises on Criminal Law have but little familiarized the people), that the protection accorded by the State to the guilty party against his victim is more vigorous and effective than that accorded the victim against the guilty party.

This is said, be it understood, without meaning to criticize anyone. We state without blaming a condition of affairs which is perhaps satisfactory; we draw from it this theoretical principle that criminal law cannot select, that crime and its suppression can only be favorable to the development of criminal tendencies, if we suppose them hereditary. Fortunately, they are not always or necessarily so. Every class of individuals occasionally is criminal. It is almost certain that the most moral and consistent man might, under certain circumstances, commit a crime. It is not positive that there are any born-criminals, those who could be recognized by physiological stigmata. This is not equivalent to saying that certain individuals cannot inherit a tendency to crime. But does this tendency to crime persist after several generations? This cannot be affirmed with certainty. Normal and fairly moral peoples have sprung from colonies of blackguards. So that if

French jurist, published the volume from which these excerpts are taken (*Les Principes philosophiques de l'histoire du droit*) in 1908.]

criminal law does not select, it is perhaps not indispensable that it should do so. [Pp. 124-126.]

BENTHAM, THEORY OF LEGISLATION *

Part II. Political Remedies Against the Evil of Offences

Chapter I. Subject of This Part

Having considered offences as *diseases* of the body politic, we are led by analogy to regard as *remedies* the means of prevention or redress.

These remedies may be arranged in four classes:

1. Preventive Remedies.
2. Suppressive Remedies.
3. Satisfactory Remedies.
4. Penal Remedies, or Punishments.

Preventive Remedies are means which tend to prevent offences. They are two kinds: direct means, which have an immediate application to such or such an offence in particular; indirect means, which consist in general precautions against an entire class of offences.

Suppressive Remedies are means which tend to put a stop to an offence already begun, an offence in progress, but not completed, and so to prevent the evil, or at least a part of it.

Satisfactory Remedies consist of reparations or indemnities, secured to those who have suffered from offences.

Penal Remedies or *Punishments* are also useful; for after a stop has been put to the evil, after the party injured has been indemnified, it still remains to prevent like offences, whether on the part of the same offender or of others. There are two ways of arriving at the end; one to correct the will, the other to take away the physical power. To take away the inclination to repeat the act, is reformation; to take away the power, is incapacitation. A remedy which operates by fear is called a punishment, whether or not it produces a physical incapacity depends upon its nature.

The principal end of punishments is to prevent like offences. What is past is but one act; the future is infinite. The offence already committed concerns only a single individual; similar offences may affect all. In many cases it is impossible to redress the evil that is done; but it is always possible to take away the will to repeat it; for however great may be the advantage of the offence, the evil of the punishment may be always made to outweigh it.

---

* [(1864), "Principles of the Penal Code." Dumont, ed., Hildreth, trans. Reprinted with introduction and notes by C. K. Ogden (London: Routledge and Kegan Paul, Ltd., 1931).]

These four kinds of remedies sometimes require as many separate operations; sometimes the same operation suffices for the whole.

In this part I shall treat of direct preventive remedies, suppressive remedies, and satisfactory remedies; the third part will treat of punishments; in the fourth part will be considered the indirect means of preventing offences. [Pp. 271-272.]

. . . . .

Part III. Of Punishments

Chapter I. Punishments Which Ought Not to be Inflicted

The cases in which punishment ought not to be inflicted may be reduced to four heads: when punishment would be—1st, Mis-applied; 2nd, Inefficacious; 3rd, Superfluous; 4th, Too expensive.

I. PUNISHMENTS MISAPPLIED.—Punishments are misapplied wherever there is no real offence, no evil of the first order or of the second order *; or where the evil is more than compensated by an attendant good, as in the exercise of political or domestic authority, in the repulsion of a weightier evil, in self-defense, etc.

If the idea of what constitutes a real offence has been clearly apprehended,† it will be easy to distinguish real from imaginary offences—from those acts, innocent in themselves, which have been arranged among offences by prejudice, antipathy, mistakes of government, the ascetic principle, in the same way that several wholesome kinds of food are considered among certain nations as poisonous or unclean. Heresy and witchcraft are offences of this class.

II. INEFFICACIOUS PUNISHMENTS.—I call those punishments *inefficacious* which have no power to produce an effect upon the will, and which, in consequence, have no tendency towards the prevention of like acts.

Punishments are inefficacious when directed against individuals who could not know the law, who have acted without intention, who have done the evil innocently, under an erroneous supposition, or by irresistible constraint. Children, imbeciles, idiots, though they may be influenced, to a certain extent, by rewards and threats, have not a sufficient idea of futurity to be restrained by punishments. In their case laws have no efficacy.

If a man is determined to act by a fear superior to that of the heaviest legal punishment, or by the hope of a preponderant good, it is plain that the law can have little influence over him. We have seen laws against duelling disregarded, because men of honour are more afraid of shame than of

---

* ["Evil of the second Order" consists in the alarm which an offence inspires.]
† [See Bentham, *Theory of Legislation*, Part I, for an analysis and classification of offences.]

punishment. Punishments directed against religious opinions generally fail to be effectual, because the idea of everlasting reward triumphs over the fear of death. According as these opinions have more or less influence, punishment, in such cases, is more or less efficacious.

III. SUPERFLUOUS PUNISHMENTS.—Punishments are superfluous in cases where the same end may be obtained by means more mild—instruction, example, invitations, delays, rewards. A man spreads abroad pernicious opinions; shall the magistrate therefore seize the sword and punish him? No; if it is the interest of one individual to give currency to bad maxims, it is the interest of a thousand others to refute him.

IV. PUNISHMENTS TOO EXPENSIVE.—If the evil of the punishment exceeds the evil of the offence, the legislator will produce more suffering than he prevents. He will purchase exemption from a lesser evil at the expense of a greater evil.

Two tables should be kept in view—one representing the evil of offences, the other the evil of punishments.

The following evils are produced by every penal law:—1st. *Evil of co-ercion.* It imposes a privation more or less painful according to the degree of pleasure with the thing forbidden has the power of conferring. 2nd. *The sufferings caused by the punishment,* whenever it is actually carried into execution. 3rd. *Evil of apprehension* suffered by those who have violated the law, or who fear a prosecution in consequence. 4th. *Evil of false prosecutions.* This inconvenience appertains to all penal laws, but particularly to laws which are obscure and to imaginary offences. A general antipathy often produces a frightful disposition to prosecute and to condemn upon suspicions or appearances. 5th. *Derivative evil* suffered by the parents or friends of those who are exposed to the rigour of the law.

Such is the table of evils or of *expenses* which the legislator ought to consider every time he establishes a punishment.

It is from this source that the principal reason is drawn for general amnesties, in case of those complicated offences which spring from a spirit of party. In such cases it may happen that the law envelopes a great multitude, sometimes half the total number of citizens, and perhaps more than half. Will you punish all the guilty? Will you only decimate them? In either case the evil of the punishment is greater than the evil of the offence.

If a delinquent is loved by the people, so that his punishment will cause national discontent; if he is protected by a foreign power whose good-will it is necessary to conciliate; if he is able to render the nation some extraordinary service;—in these particular cases the grant of pardon is founded upon a calculation of prudence. It is apprehended that punishment of the offence will cost society too dear.

Chapter II

Adsit

Regula, peccatis quae poenas irroget aequas:
Ne scutica dignum, horribile sectere flagello.

Hor. I. i. Sat. iii

Let's have a rule
Which deals to crimes an equal punishment:
Nor tortures with the horrid lash for faults
Worthy a birchen twig.

Proportion Between Offences and Punishments

Montesquieu perceived the necessity of a proportion between offences and punishments. Beccaria insists upon its importance. But they rather recommend than explain it; they do not tell in what that proportion consists. Let us endeavour to supply this defect, and to give the principal rules of this moral arithmetic.

FIRST RULE.—*The evil of the punishment must be made to exceed the advantage of the offence.*

The Anglo-Saxon laws, which established a price for the lives of men, two hundred shillings for the murder of a peasant, six times as much for that of a noble, and thirty-six times as much for that of the king, notwithstanding this show of pecuniary proportion, were evidently deficient in moral proportion. The punishment might appear as nothing compared to the advantage of the offence.

The same error is committed whenever a punishment is decreed which can only reach a certain point, while the advantage of the offence may go much beyond.

Some celebrated authors have attempted to establish a contrary maxim. They say that punishment ought to be diminished in proportion to the strength of temptation; that temptation diminishes the fault; and that the more potent seduction is, the less evidence we have of the offender's depravity.

This may be true; but it does not contravene the rule above laid down: for to prevent an offence, it is necessary that the repressive motive should be stronger than the seductive motive. The punishment must be more an object of dread than the offence is an object of desire. An insufficient punishment is a greater evil than an excess of rigour; for an insufficient punishment is an evil wholly thrown away. No good results from it, either to the public, who are left exposed to like offences, nor to the offender, whom it makes no better. What would be said of a surgeon, who to spare a sick man a degree of pain should leave the cure unfinished? Would it be a piece of enlightened humanity to add to the pains of the disorder the torment of a useless operation?

SECOND RULE.—*The more deficient in certainty a punishment is, the severer it should be.*

No man engages in a career of crime, except in the hope of impunity. If punishment consisted merely in taking from the guilty the fruits of his offence, and if that punishment were inevitable, no offence would ever be committed; for what man is so foolish as to run the risk of committing an offence with certainty of nothing but the shame of an unsuccessful attempt? In all cases of offence there is a calculation of the chances for and against; and it is necessary to give a much greater weight to the punishment, in order to counterbalance the chances of impunity.

It is true, then, that the more certain punishment is, the less severe it need be. Such is the advantage that results from simplicity of laws, and a good method of procedure.

For the same reason it is desirable that punishment should follow offence as closely as possible: For its impression upon the minds of men is weakened by distance, and besides, distance adds to the uncertainty of punishment, by affording new chances of escape.

THIRD RULE.—*Where two offences are in conjunction, the greater offence ought to be subjected to severer punishment, in order that the delinquent may have a motive to stop at the lesser.*

Two offences may be said to be in conjunction when a man has the power and the will to commit both of them. A highwayman may content himself with robbing, or he may begin with murder, and finish with robbery. The murder should be punished more severely than the robbery, in order to deter him from the greater offence.

This rule would be perfectly carried out if it could be so ordered that for each portion of evil committed there should be a corresponding portion of punishment. Let a man who has stolen ten crowns be punished as severely as if he had stolen twenty, and he will be a fool to take the less sum in preference to the greater. Equal punishment for unequal offences is often a motive for committing the greater offence.

FOURTH RULE.—*The greater an offence is, the greater reason there is to hazard a severe punishment for the chance of preventing it.*

We must not forget that the infliction of punishment is a certain expense for the purpose of an uncertain advantage. To apply great punishments to small offences is to pay very dearly for the chance of escaping a slight evil.

The English law which condemned women to be burnt for passing counterfeit coin, was a direct invasion of this rule of proportion. If burning were a punishment ever to be adopted, it ought to be confined to the single case of incendiary homicides.

FIFTH RULE.—*The same punishment for the same offence ought not to be inflicted upon all delinquents. It is necessary to pay some regard to the circumstances which affect sensibility.*

The same nominal punishments are not the same real punishments. Age, sex, rank, fortune, and many other circumstances, ought to modify the punishments inflicted for the same offence. If the offence is a corporal injury, the same pecuniary punishment would be a trifle to the rich, and oppressive to the poor. The same punishment which would brand with ignominy a man of a certain rank, would not produce even the slightest stain in case the offender belonged to an inferior class. The same imprisonment would be ruin to a man of business, death to an infirm old man, and eternal disgrace to a woman, while it would be next to nothing to an individual placed under other circumstances.

Let it be observed, however, that the proportion between punishments and offences ought not to be so mathematically followed upon as to render the laws subtle, complicated, and obscure. Brevity and simplicity are a superior good. Something of exact proportion may also be sacrificed to render the punishment more striking, more fit to inspire the people with a sentiment of aversion for those vices which prepare the way for crimes. [Pp. 322-327.]

TARDE, PENAL PHILOSOPHY *

... To see in the criminal only a dangerous being and not a guilty man, an invalid or a sick man and not a sinner, and in the punishment only a process of elimination or repair and not a stigma, is the same thing as wishing that criminologists, and following them the entire public, should bring to bear upon crime and the penalty an intellectual judgment, free from every emotion and all blame.

But the very school which proposes all these reforms is the one which excels in bringing to light this truth, that intelligence by itself is inert, and that sentiment alone is the motive power of people and of societies. When we shall cease to hate and stigmatize the criminal, crime will multiply. Besides, I repeat, for what reason should we deem it necessary, were it possible to do so, to remove from hatred and indignation their most natural object, crime, at the risk of causing them to overflow upon other objects, and of dangerously deflecting towards other ends, in our political or religious controversies, for example, those eternal sentiments of the heart? I am willing to admit that crime, being subject to the universal determinism, is as natural a fact as any other. But the anger which possesses us at the sight of a criminal action and the desire of revenge with which we are at once filled against its perpetrator are entirely natural phenomena as well. Why should they be deemed irrational? Why should they be blamed when it is thought that crime itself is not to be blamed? If it be claimed that these sentiments imply a mistake, the mistake of believing in the freedom of the

---

* [Chap. VIII ("The Penalty"), § 91 ("Rational Basis"), (1) "Penal Law Based upon Utility or Opinion?"), pp. 502, 505-507. Howell, trans. Vol. 6, Modern Criminal Science Series; Boston: Little, Brown & Company, 1912.]

criminal agent, then our theory of responsibility proves the contrary. Does a man suppress a sensation, an optical or acoustic illusion by proving that it is deceptive? The best taught color-blind man sees green and red as one color, although he knows that these colors are different. Similarly the most determinist of husbands heaps his scorn and rage upon his unfaithful wife, although he may know that she could not help deceiving him.

However, let us draw a distinction. If the irresistible cause of this in-fidelity appears to him to lie in the very nature of his wife, in her temperament and character combined, no argument will be able to have any effect upon his indignation and his thirst for revenge. If, on the other hand, it can be proved to him that the misconduct of his wife is the result of an attack of temporary madness, his contempt might be changed to pity or to sorrow. Similarly again, if one could prove to the victims of certain crimes and to the onlooking crowd that the perpetrators of these crimes are poor unfortunates, attacked with masked epilepsy, with imperfect nutrition of the brain, it might be that in time the public conscience would cease to demand a dishonoring of these luckless creatures. But, in admitting that the feelings of reprobation and of the necessity of purification, with which we are here dealing, can be weakened and converted into charitable compassion, is it a good thing once again thus to cut down the strongest dike which stands in the path of the progress of social evil? From a utilitarian point of view we must answer no. Why, on the other hand, should we answer yes, were it not for the fact that there is an aestheticism, a hidden idealism at the base of utilitarianism?

The conception of a penal law free from all vengeance and all hatred is a very old one in the history of spiritualism. As early as the third century, Gregory of Nazianzus affirms that, "God does not take vengeance by punishing the wicked. He calls them to Him and wakens them from the sleep of death." To Gregory of Nyassa, also, the thought of an eternal hell is intolerable. He dreams of a final and immense amnesty. "At the end of time," according to him, "every penalty will be expiated, every soul will be justified. The devil himself will be included within the work of universal salvation." This same generous inspiration has been continued down to our day, as we have seen, to Fouillée and Guyau. The utilitarians have breathed it in with the surrounding air; and it is as being contrary to this ideal, it is as stained with moral ugliness, that they hate hatred, even when it is useful. They, more than they think, resemble the Egyptians who abhorred the embalmer, the French who execrated the executioner, while at the same time appreciating the fact that both the embalmer and the executioner were the persons most indispensable to the State.

From this I draw the conclusion, not that the utilitarian doctrine ought to get rid as quickly as possible of the aesthetic and moral elements which have found their way into it,—for the conception of the useful cannot stand alone and is dependent upon the conception of the beautiful, the physically beautiful and the morally beautiful,—but that it is illogical apparently to proscribe moral ideas when in reality and unknowingly the inspiration is drawn from them and that it is impossible not to be inspired by them. It is a strange thing that while the positivist innovators in the matter of penal law are unwilling, they say, to hear any mention of right, duty, guilt, merit, and unworthiness, even when these words are filled with a new meaning; and when these old organs are employed in the fulfillment of new functions according to the processes of life, the innovators, who are no less positivists in political economy, the socialists of the body, give as the essential characteristic of their innovations the introduction of moral ideas in the order of economic phenomena. The latter have over the former the advantage of having a consciousness of their tendencies.*

M. R. COHEN, MORAL ASPECTS OF THE CRIMINAL LAW †

The Reform Theory

The most popular theory today is that the proper aim of criminal procedure is to reform the criminal so that he may become adjusted to the social order. A mixture of sentimental and utilitarian motives gives this view its great vogue. With the spread of humane feeling and the waning of faith in the old conception of the necessity for inflicting pain in the treatment of children and those suffering from mental disease, there has come a revulsion at the hard-heartedness of the old retributive theory. The growing belief in education and in the healing powers of medicine encourages people to suppose that the delinquent may be re-educated to become a useful member of society. Even from the strictest economic point of view, individual men and women are the most valuable assets of any society. Is it not better to save them for a life of usefulness rather than punish them by imprisonment, which generally makes them worse after they leave than before they entered?

There are, however, a number of highly questionable assumptions back of this theory which need to be critically examined.

We have already had occasion to question the assumption that crime is a physical or mental disease. We may now raise the question whether it is curable and if so at what cost to society? Benevolent social reformers are apt to ignore the amount of cold calculating business shrewdness among criminals. Some hot-blooded ones may respond to emotional appeal; but they are also likely to backslide when opportunity or temptation comes along. Human beings are not putty that can be remolded at will by benevo-

---

* [A more complete presentation of the view that the chief function of punishment is to strengthen the moral fibre of *those who punish* will be found in Von Bar, *History of Continental Criminal Law*, § 104.]

† [49 *Yale L.J.* 987, 1012-1016 (1940); reprinted in *Reason and Law*, pp. 15, 44-50 (Glencoe, Ill.: The Free Press, 1950).]

lent intentions. The overwhelming majority of our criminals have been exposed to the influence of our school system which we have at great cost tried to make as efficient as possible. Most criminals are also religious, as prison chaplains can testify. Yet with all our efforts school education and religion do not eliminate crime. It has not even been demonstrated that they are progressively minimizing it. Nor does the record of our special reformatories for young offenders prove that it is always possible to reform even young people so that they will stay reformed for any length of time. The analogy of the criminal law to medicine breaks down. The surgeon can determine with a fair degree of accuracy when there is an inflamed appendix or cancerous growth, so that by cutting it out he can remove a definite cause of distress. Is there in the complex of our social system any one cause of crime which any social physician can as readily remove on the basis of similarly verifiable knowledge?

Let us abandon the light-hearted pretention that any of us know how all cases of criminality can be readily cured, and ask the more modest and serious question: to what extent *can* criminals be re-educated or re-conditioned so that they can live useful lives? It would indeed be illiberal dogmatism to deny all possibility and desirability of effort along this line. Yet we must keep in mind our human limitations.

If the causes of crime are determined by the life of certain groups, it is foolish to deal with the individual as if he were a self-sufficient and self-determining system. We must deal with the whole group to which he naturally belongs or gravitates and which determines his morale. Otherwise we have to adapt him completely to some other group or social condition, which is indeed a very difficult problem in social engineering.

And here we must not neglect the question of cost. When we refer to any measure as impracticable, we generally mean that the cost is too great. There is doubtless a tremendous expense in maintaining our present system of punishment. But this expense is not unlimited. Suppose that fiendish perpetrators of horrible crimes on children could be reformed by being sent first for several years to a special hospital. Will people vote large funds for such purposes when honest law-abiding citizens so often cannot get adequate hospital facilities? Suppose that we find that a certain social environment or that an elaborate college course will reform a burglar or gunman, would our community stand for the expense when so many worthy young people cannot afford to go to college because they have to go to work? We certainly should not give even the appearance of reward for criminality. Let us not forget that there is always a natural resentment in any society against those who have attacked it. Will people be satisfied to see one who is guilty of horrible crimes simply reformed, and not give vent to the social horror and resentment against the miscreant? It is difficult to believe that any such course would not result in a return to personal vengeance on the part of the relatives or friends of the victim.

A crucial instance of the inadequacy of the reform theory is the case of a man who we are fairly certain will not commit the given offense again. A burglar, for instance, in trying to enter a house breaks his leg so that he can never again engage in that enterprise. A man in desperation kills one who has ruined his family life and it becomes obvious that he will never again have a chance to be in a similar situation. Or take the case of one who can for any reason convince us that the criminal act itself has sobered him so that never again will he commit such an act. What more can reform achieve in these cases? Shall we then close the account and let the guilty one off? That not only would arouse general resentment but would open the gates to all sorts of abuses and would certainly so encourage crime that the suffering of innocent people would increase.

It has been argued that on the theory of protection to society there should be no punishment for one who is no longer capable of doing harm. But this ignores the fact that the law contemplates not only the individual at the bar but all others who might be tempted to commit similar offenses even under conditions not quite the same.

Punishment as a Means of Preventing Crime

If we look at the criminal as one who assails or endangers the proper life of the community, it is not only our right but our duty to defend, if not ourselves, at least our dependents. Primitive communities effect this by getting rid of the unruly member through death or outlawry. In the course of time, this is largely replaced by fine or imprisonment. Societies, however, never abandon the effort to minimize crime by punishing the offenders. We do this by incapacitating the criminal either through death or detention, and by deterring him and others through the example of the painful consequences of crime to the criminal.

Few have ever argued against the right of society to protect itself and prevent crime by detaining the criminal at least so long as there is some reason to suppose that it would be dangerous to set him free. But the right to punish anyone to deter him or others from future acts, has been widely challenged on grounds of (1) justice and (2) utility.

1. Kant and others have urged that it cannot be just to punish anyone except for a wrong actually committed; and much less can it be just to punish Peter in order to prevent Paul from attempting any crime. This is an appeal to a principle so seemingly self-evident that most writers on the criminal law have preferred to ignore the objection rather than to meet it. But modern science has made enormous progress by learning to distrust self-evident principles. We need not, therefore, hesitate to challenge Kant's assumption in this case. Why should we not inflict pain on A if that is the only way of securing the safety of the society of which he is a part, or preserving the general conditions of desirable life on which he depends for

all his goods? We tax an old bachelor for the support of the education of other men's children and we conscript our youth and put them in positions where they will be killed in order that others shall be able to live. Consider the case of the typhoid carrier Mary who spreads the germs of that dreadful disease wherever she goes. Do we not by detaining her and limiting her freedom in effect punish her for her misfortune rather than for her fault? We are at all times inflicting pains on innocent people in order to promote the common good, in time of peace, as well as in war. When we need a road or bridge, do we not order a family to abandon the house which has been its home from time immemorial, and for which there can be no equivalent restitution or compensation? The fact is, that the lives of individuals are not independent atoms which can be treated in isolation. We are all members of a common body and the health of the entire body may demand inflicting pain or even the cutting off of some member.

This does not mean the complete abandonment of the principle that one should be responsible only for his own voluntary act. That would be opening the floodgates to the most extreme and outrageous injustice. But our principle may be viewed not as an isolated independent absolute, but as the statement of a general condition of the social order necessary for the good life. Certainly nothing would be more detrimental to the effective enforcement of the law than the feeling in any community that some may commit crimes for which others will be punished.

This approach comes closer to the actual conscience of humanity and cuts the ground from the Kantian objection. A state has as much right to reform a criminal, even against his will, as to educate a child or to compel one with a contagious disease to be quarantined or to undergo curative treatment. And while it would destroy the basis of all that we hold dear in civilized life to make one man suffer merely that another be advantaged thereby, no society under present conditions can achieve the good of the whole without causing more suffering to some than to others. One need only add that we cannot be too critical in determining whether the good of the whole *is* promoted when the innocent suffer. For if we realize that our means are always part of the total end, we can see reason to doubt the goodness of an end which involves evil means. Unfortunately, however, the actual choice that life presents to any society is seldom a clear issue between absolute good and absolute evil but generally a choice between alternatives, all of which are imperfect embodiments of justice or of the highest good. Wisdom consists in such a balancing of rival considerations, that the total amount of evil is minimized.

2. We come now to the much more common objection that punishment does not in fact deter either the one punished, or others. Criminals who are tempted will not, we are told, desist from taking a risk just as wolves who attack a wild horse on the Russian steppes will not abandon their effort after one or two of them are killed or crushed by the horse's hoof. There

are more dangerous occupations than crime; yet people are not deterred from taking the risk.

Those who urge this objection illustrate the abuse of absolutism in the discussion of practical issues. To prove the utility of medicine it is not necessary to prove that it always prevents death and cures all instances of disease. It is enough if life is often prolonged and suffering sometimes diminished by its wise use. And to justify punishment it is not necessary to prove that it *always* prevents crime by its deterrent quality. It is enough to indicate that there would be more crime if all punishment were abolished. Now we may ignore the positivistic dogma that punishment cannot possibly have any deterrent effect, that criminals are bound to commit crimes. That kind of fatalism is not only opposed by human experience, but it is not even consistent with scientific determinism which it professes to follow. All experiments on animals as well as the historic observations of human experience indicate that fear of painful consequences is as effective a force in life as is the prospect of pleasant rewards. We are living at a time when terror on a large scale has succeeded in removing the effective temptation to rebellion. When in 1920 the police of Boston struck and left their posts, many young men broke store windows and possessed themselves of goods which they tried to sell at prices which no trained or professional criminal would demand. Sir James F. Stephen has suggested the following query: Suppose a burglar feels that he might catch a cold that would incapacitate him for as long a period as the usual prison term for burglary. Would that not deter him? Of course that largely depends on the exercise of the imagination. And the law, if wisely administered, should dramatize its punishment. It is a fact that all men live more or less in their imagination, and any imaginative realization that one will be hissed off the social stage or suffer pain is bound to act as a strong deterrent. In this connection, it is well to repeat the frequently-made, but still just, observation that not only the severity but the certainty of punishment is a factor in the case. Men will risk their lives if they think that there is some chance of winning something. And while many will take very "long" chances, as in lotteries, it is a fact that professional crime, like any other business, ceases to grow in extent when the chances of failure rise. That is why bandits do not try to rob the United States Treasury, or the Mint.

In general we know that just as certain factors will tend to increase crime, so certain factors will tend to diminish the amount of it; and that the penalties of the law, if enforced, constitute one of these minimizing causes. There is no doubt that the abolition of the police force, or the lessening of their vigilance or competence to detect the crime and to apprehend the criminal will tend to increase the amount of crime. Thus not only the specific penalty but the question of the procedure or mechanism of its enforcement, the ease of its proof, and the likelihood of finding proper witnesses are all determinants.

MICHAEL AND WECHSLER, CRIMINAL LAW AND
ITS ADMINISTRATION *

.   .   .   .   .

The major problems of the criminal law [6] are two: what behavior should be made criminal, and what should be done with persons who commit crimes. For reasons already stated, the analysis of these problems should begin with a consideration of ends; and the initial question properly concerns ultimate ends. In this dimension, it has been argued that the ultimate end of the criminal law should be retribution—the punishment of those who will to inflict undeserved evil on others by penalties proportioned to their offenses. This contention has far-reaching implications and its validity must be appraised.

That the retributive position is an ancient one cannot be doubted and it may be that, as Bradley has said, it represents the unstudied belief of most men.[7] Its first systematic development is, however, to be found in the ethi-

---

* [These passages are taken from the introduction to Michael and Wechsler's *Criminal Law and Its Administration: Cases, Statutes and Commentaries.* New York: The Foundation Press, Inc., 1940.

Jerome Michael (b. 1890) and *Herbert Wechsler* (b. 1909) are both professors at Columbia Law School. Michael is the author of *The Elements of Legal Controversy,* and is co-author with M. J. Adler of *Crime, Law, and Social Science.* Wechsler served as law secretary to Justice Harlan F. Stone, as assistant Attorney General of the United States in charge of the War Division, and is a member of the committee on rules of criminal procedure of the U.S. Supreme Court. He is also the author of several articles dealing with criminal law.]

[6] There are difficulties in defining precisely the scope of the criminal as opposed to the civil law. If we look at the law as it is, it is obviously difficult to maintain any of the traditional positions: that the criminal law deals with behavior which is offensive to society as a whole rather than that which is offensive only to individuals; that the criminal law deals with acts that involve great moral turpitude rather than those that involve slight moral turpitude or are morally indifferent; that the criminal law determines who shall be punished and the civil law who shall make restitution or pay damages; that the criminal law determines what proceedings shall be brought by the state rather than what proceedings may be instituted by private citizens at their option. See, in this connection, Kenny, *Outlines of Criminal Law* (15 ed., 1936), c. 1; M. R. Cohen, "On Absolutisms in Legal Thought" (1936) 84 *U. of Pa. L.Rev.* 681, 686-687, "Moral Aspects of the Criminal Law" (1940) 49 *Yale L.J.* 987, 988-990.

[7] Bradley, *Ethical Studies* (2d ed., 1927) 1-41. "If there is any opinion to which the man of uncultivated morals is attached, it is the belief in the necessary connexion of punishment and guilt. Punishment is punishment only where it is deserved. We pay the penalty, because we owe it, and for no other reason; and if punishment is inflicted for any other reason whatever than because it is merited by wrong, it is a gross immorality, a crying injustice, an abominable crime, and not what it pretends to be. ... Having once the right to punish, we may modify the punishment according to the useful and the pleasant; but these are external to the matter, they can not give us a right to punish, and nothing can do that but criminal desert.... Yes, in despite of sophistry, and in the face of sentimentalism with well nigh the whole body of our self-styled enlightenment against them, our people believe to this day that *punishment is inflicted for the sake of punishment....*" *Id.* at pp. 26-27, 28 But *cf.* Holmes, *The Common Law* (1881) 45, quoted *infra* note 17; see also Sharp and Otto, "A Study of

cal writings of Kant [8] and Hegel [9] and their followers, Stammler and Kohler. ... [Pp. 6-7.]

.   .   .   .   .

The critics of the retributive position deny that it is self-evident that retribution is just, whether one believes in free will (in the sense that purposive behavior is uncaused by antecedent physical, mental and environmental conditions but is the product of the will which is itself a first cause) or in determinism (in the sense of the rule of cause and effect in the behavior of human beings).[15] They ask what intuitive necessity there is, apart from a concern for future actions, that evil be repaid with punishment rather than ignored. "If we give up all utilitarian ideas of social welfare, what necessity is there that the universe should be organized like a penitentiary on the basis of rewards and punishments?" [16] Holmes contended that "it will be seen on self-inspection that this feeling of fitness [of punishment following wrong-doing] is absolute and unconditional only in the case of our neighbors" and that then it is "only vengeance in disguise." [17] Throughout the history of thought it has been argued in various ways that human punishment is a creature of human law and human law an instrument of the state; that the ultimate end of the state should be the welfare of its members and that both law and legal penalties should serve the same end; and that they are just precisely to the extent that they do serve that end. Since punishment consists in the infliction of pain it is, apart from its consequences, an evil; consequently, it is good and, therefore, just only if and to the degree that it serves the common good by advancing the welfare of the person punished or of the rest of the population. This is the position taken by Plato,[18] Aristotle, Cicero, St. Thomas Aquinas, and the

---

the Popular Attitude Toward Retributive Punishment" (1910) 20 *Int. J. of Ethics* 341, "Retribution and Deterrence in the Moral Judgments of Common Sense" *id.* at 438.

[8] See *The Science of Right*, Part 2, sec. 49; *Philosophy of Law* (Hastie tr., 1887) 194-204.

[9] *The Philosophy of Right* (Dyde tr., 1896) 90-103.

[16] M. R. Cohen, *Law and the Social Order*, 310.

[17] *The Common Law*, 45: "It does not seem to me that anyone who has satisfied himself that an act of his was wrong and that he will never do it again, would feel the least need or propriety, as between himself and an earthly punishing power alone, of his being made to suffer for what he has done, although when third persons were introduced, he might, as a philosopher, admit the necessity of hurting him to frighten others. But when our neighbors do wrong, we sometimes feel the fitness of making them smart for it, whether they have repented or not."

[18] See *Protagoras*, 324: "... No one punishes the evil-doer under the notion, or for the reason, that he has done wrong,—only the unreasonable fury of a beast acts in that manner. But he who desires to inflict rational punishment does not retaliate for a past wrong which cannot be undone; he has regard to the future, and is desirous that the man who is punished, and he who sees him punished, may be deterred from doing wrong again. He punishes for the sake of prevention. ..." See also *Gorgias*, 525; *Republic*, 380, 615; *Phaedo*, 113; *Laws*, 854, 862, 934, 957.

medieval Church,[19] as well as by Hobbes,[20] Baccaria,[21] Bentham,[22] and many others in more modern times.[23] According to this view retribution is itself unjust since it requires some human beings to inflict pain upon others, regardless of its effect upon them or upon the social welfare. In any event, it is urged, the retributive theory is incapable of practical application. How can men lacking omniscience measure degrees of guilt in individual cases and apportion pain thereto? How is it possible, moreover, to inflict pain upon the guilty without also inflicting pain upon their innocent relatives and friends? Since the retributive theory requires not only that the guilty be punished but also that the guiltless be not, how, as Ewing has asked, is it possible to avoid doing more retributive injustice than justice in any given case? [24]

These considerations seem to us not only to refute the retributive position but also to establish that the criminal law, like the rest of the law, should serve the end of promoting the common good; and that its specific capacity for serving this end inheres in its power to prevent or control socially undesirable behavior....

In order to determine the kinds of behavior which it is desirable to deter, the probable results, both good and bad, of behavior of various sorts must be discovered and then estimated as being on the whole socially desirable or socially undesirable. In making behavior criminal three questions must therefore be answered: (1) What consequences of human activity are socially undesirable; (2) what sorts of behavior tend to produce such results;

---

[19] See Michael and Adler, *op. cit. supra* note 1, at 342-352.

[20] *Leviathan* (1651), Part II, c. 30.

[21] *Crimes and Punishments* (1764), *passim*, especially cc. I, II, VII.

[22] "The general object which all laws have, or ought to have, in common, is to augment the total happiness of the community; and therefore in the first place, to exclude, as far as may be, everything that tends to subtract from that happiness; in other words, to exclude mischief....But all punishment is mischief; all punishment in itself is evil. Upon the principle utility, if it ought at all to be admitted, it ought only to be admitted in as far as it promises to exclude some greater evil." *Principles of Morals and Legislation* (Oxford ed., 1879) 170.

[23] See, in addition to the works cited above, Ewing, *The Morality of Punishment* (1929) 13-45; Holmes, *The Common Law*, 42-46; Willoughby, *Social Justice* (1900) 316 *et seq.*; McConnell, *Criminal Responsibility and Social Constraint* (1912) 6-59; Saleilles *op. cit. supra* note 15 [*The Individualization of Punishment* (ed. 1911), Chap. VI]; Aschaffenburg, *Crime and Its Repression* (Mod. Cr. Sci. ed., 1913) 250 *et seq.*; Oppenheimer, *The Rationale of Punishment* (1913) 234 *et seq.*

[24] Ewing, *op. cit. supra* note 23, at 39-40; see also Aschaffenburg, *loc. cit. supra* note 23. But *Cf.* M. R. Cohen, *op. cit. supra* note 10 ["Moral Aspects of the Criminal Law," 49 *Yale L.J.*, 987, 992-994, 1009-1012 (1940)], at 1007: "Few readers of the Bible, I imagine, have felt outraged at the fact that when Achan sins, his innocent children are also killed....Furthermore, as a result of the last war, Germany was made to pay reparations, and the burden fell upon the innocent children who had no part and could in no way prevent the invasion of Belgium and all the destruction which it involved. Was this unjust? By no means, if we recognize collective responsibility. It is obvious that in many relations the family of the nation rather than the individual is regarded as the moral unit."

(3) which of the sorts having that tendency are nevertheless socially desirable because their socially beneficial potentialities are greater than their socially dangerous tendencies. . . . [Pp. 8-12.]

．　　．　　．　　．　　．

That behavior is of a sort which it is desirable and possible to deter or which is indicative of the dangerousness of individuals who engage in it, does not necessarily establish that it should be made criminal. The consequences of making it criminal may be more undesirable than the consequences of the behavior itself. We desire to prevent anti-social behavior in order to improve the conditions of social life; we must take care, therefore, that social life is not made worse by the medicine than by the disease.[33]

When we turn to the problems of treatment we find that they are no less complex or difficult. We can be reasonably certain that no methods of treatment can be devised which will deter all potential offenders or reform all actual offenders or, what is even more difficult, do both at once. We do know, of course, that death and life imprisonment are effective methods of incapacitation. We do not know and may never know with certainty what methods of treatment are most efficacious as deterrents or as reformatives or how efficacious any method of treatment is.[34] Common sense tells us that most men fear punishment to an indeterminate and inconstant degree and that the more certain and severe punishment is, the more intensely it is likely to be feared.[35] But the law must rely for its enforcement upon ordinary men acting as complainants, as witnesses, as jurors, and as officials. Common sense also warns us that to varying and uncertain degrees the widespread imposition of drastically severe penalties arouses in many such men a sympathy for the accused which leads them to refuse to participate in inflicting them. When this result occurs nullification ensues, and the effect of the severity of punishment is greatly to magnify its uncertainty and to provoke a general hatred of the law which in a democratic society must inevitably culminate in its change. Accordingly, penalties must be mitigated in most cases to avoid nullification. Common sense further warns us that the infliction of severe punishment short of total incapacitation is likely to result in the return to society of men utterly unfit for a non-criminal life, embittered, and determined to exact their revenge. It cautions

---

[33] See Bentham, *Principles of Morals and Legislation*, 175-177; Michael and Adler, *Crime, Law and Social Science* (1933), at 353; F. S. Cohen, *Ethical Systems and Legal Ideals*, 249-285.

[34] To be able to answer these questions with certainty, we should have to know the causes of crime; to know the causes of crime we need a complete etiology of human behavior. For an evaluation of the most important impirical studies of causation, treatment, and prevention, see Michael and Adler, *Crime, Law and Social Science* (1933), at 44-225.

[35] For Bentham's elaborate discussion of the implications of this point, see his *Principles of Penal Law*, Part II, Book I, c. III in *Works* (1843), i. Compare Von Hentig, "Punishment," *Encyc. Soc. Sci.*, xii, 712-715, "The Limits of Deterrence" (1938) 29 *J. Crim. L. 555*.

us, too, that, to some extent at least, cruelty or bloodshed inflicted in the name of the law is likely to have the same deleterious effect upon public morals as cruelty or bloodshed inflicted in the name of anything else.[40] Moreover, prisons are relatively few in number and expensive to build and maintain; the government of any considerable number of persons sentenced to life imprisonment is inordinatedly difficult; and it may be doubted whether any widespread extension of the death penalty would be politically feasible, even if it were wise. There is an additional reason for the mitigation of punishment whenever criminal behavior can be attributed to some grave injustice done the criminal either by some other person or by society as a whole as, for example, when many people are near starvation and men are driven to steal by hunger. As T. H. Green has pointed out,[41] the mitigation of penalties on that ground serves to direct attention to and to increase popular awareness of the original injustice and, thus, may lead to its correction.

On the other hand, while common sense may suggest that lenient or non-punitive methods of treatment are, in general, better adapted to reformation than severe methods, not all men are corrigible; and the separation of the corrigible from the incorrigible requires psychological judgments which are difficult or impossible to make with any assurance on the basis of the psychological knowledge that we now have;[42] reluctance to delegate to officials the power to make them may, accordingly, be wise. Moreover, the desire for revenge, the belief that retributive punishment is just, and the feeling that examples must be made of those guilty of shocking crimes are to a very considerable degree entrenched in the general population. Too lenient treatment of offenders, however well adapted to reforming them, may therefore lead to lynching, self-help or indifference about prosecution which may be far worse in their social consequences than the utilization of more severe methods of treatment which satisfy the popular desire for severity though they have no reformative efficacy. This may be what Stephen meant by his famous remark that the criminal law stands to the passion for vengeance in much the same relation as marriage to the sexual appetite.[43] But, on the other hand, it is urged that the desires for revenge and for retribution are themselves anti-social and, therefore, ought not to be encouraged by law; [44] that if the public mind is unprepared to

---

[42] See note 34, *supra*; *cf.* Dession, "Psychiatry and The Conditioning of Criminal Justice" (1938) 47 *Yale L.J.* 319.

[43] *General View of the Criminal Law of England* (1863) 99; see also Holmes, *The Common Law*, 41-42; Ewing, *op. cit. supra* note 23, at 71.

[44] *Cf.* Holmes, *The Common Law*, 41-42: "If people would gratify the passion of revenge outside of the law, if the law did not help them, the law has no choice but to satisfy the craving itself, and thus avoid the greater evil of private retribution. At the same time, this passion is not one which we wish to encourage, either as private individuals or as law makers."

Consider, however, Tarde's hedonistic argument that since people as they are

view the problems of social control dispassionately, it ought to be educated
to do so; and that the legal devices adopted by society can and ought to be
employed to that end. Apart from these considerations, Bentham believed,
and not without reason, that unless punishments are graded in proportion
to the social harmfulness of behavior, there is no incentive to the potential
offender to engage in less rather than more undesirable behavior.[45] And
Beccaria insisted that it is important, not only for the prevention of crime
but for social relations in general, that the community should properly
evaluate the relative significance of anti-social conduct of various sorts, the
degree to which various types of behavior are inimical to the general welfare; and that very lenient treatment of those who engage in exceedingly
harmful behavior may lead the community to regard it as less harmful than
it is.[46] [Pp. 12-17.]

C. *Types of punishment*

BECCARIA, ESSAY ON CRIMES AND PUNISHMENTS *

Chapter IV. Of the Interpretation of Laws

. . . . .

There is nothing more dangerous than the common axiom: *the spirit of
the laws is to be considered*. To adopt it is to give way to the torrent of

---

take pleasure in the infliction of pain upon those who have offended, the legal system
ought to do its share to provide that pleasure as a means to the happiness of the
citizen. *Penal Philosophy* (Howell tr., 1912) 34-36. See also Bentham, *op. cit. supra*
note 22, 170-171, n. 1; Ewing, *op. cit. supra* note 23, at 69-71. Compare the following
rigorous passages in Stephen, *History of the Criminal Law*, i, 478: "In cases which
outrage the moral feelings of the community to a great degree, the feeling of indignation and desire for revenge which is excited in the minds of decent people is, I
think, deserving of legitimate satisfaction"; and ii, 81-82: "I think it highly desirable
that criminals should be hated, that the punishment inflicted on them should be so
construed as to give expression to that hatred, and to justify it so far as the public
provision of means for expressing and gratifying a healthy natural sentiment can
justify and encourage it."

[45] See Bentham, *The Theory of Legislation*, Principles of the Penal Code, Part
Third, c. ii.

[46] *Crimes and Punishments*, c. 23; *cf.* Ewing, *op. cit. supra* note 23, at 104.

* [The foregoing translation generally follows that by Edward D. Ingraham (2nd
American edition, 1819) from the French edition with Voltaire's commentary.

Beccaria's essay *On Crimes and Punishments* (*Dei delitti e delle pene*) is probably the most influential essay ever written on the subject. An economist and mathematician, the Marchese de Beccaria (1738–1794) served as consultant to the Austrian
Government, becoming professor of law and economy at Milan in 1768, then was
appointed Councillor of State and Magistrate. In 1790 Beccaria was appointed to the
commission for the reform of civil and criminal jurisprudence in Lombardy. The
essay was widely read and was translated into 22 languages shortly after its publication in 1764. Beccaria's plea for prevention rather than punishment was taken to
heart by several enlightened monarchs and strongly influenced the revolutionary
code of law in France. In England, Bentham and his follower, Sir Samuel Romilly,
developed and applied Beccaria's ideas to the reform of the English criminal law.
See Chapter 4 of B. L. Shientag, *Moulders of Legal Thought* (1943).]

opinions. This may seem a paradox to vulgar minds, which are more strongly affected by the smallest disorder before their eyes, than by the most pernicious though remote consequences produced by one safe principle adopted by a nation.

Our knowledge is in proportion to the number of our ideas. The more complex these are, the greater is the variety of positions in which they may be considered. Every man hath his own particular point of view, and at different times sees the same objects in very different lights. The spirit of the laws will then be the result of the good or bad logic of the judge; and this will depend on his good or bad digestion, on the violence of his passions, on the rank or condition of the accused, or on his connections with the judge, and on all those circumstances which change the appearance of objects in the fluctuating mind of man. Hence we see the fate of a delinquent changed many times in passing through the different courts of judicature, and his life and liberty victims to the safe ideas or ill humour of the judge, who mistakes the vague result of his own confused reasoning for the just interpretation of the laws. We see the same crimes punished in a different manner at different times in the same tribunals; the consequence of not having consulted the constant and invariable voice of the laws, but the erring instability of arbitrary interpretation.

The disorders that may arise from a rigorous observance of the letter of penal laws, are not to be compared with those produced by the interpretation of them. The first are temporary inconveniences, which will oblige the legislator to correct the letter of the law, the want of preciseness and uncertainty of which has occasioned these disorders; and this will put a stop to the fatal liberty of explaining; the source of arbitrary and venal declamations. When the code of laws is once fixed, it should be observed in the literal sense, and nothing more is left to the judge than to determine, whether an action be, or be not, conformable to the written law. . . .

These are the means by which security of person and property is best obtained; which is just, as it is the purpose of uniting in society; and it is useful, as each person may calculate exactly the inconveniences attending every crime. By these means subjects will acquire a spirit of independence and liberty; however it may appear to those who dare to call the weakness of submitting blindly to their capricious and interested opinions by the sacred name of virtue.

These principles will displease those who have made it a rule with themselves, to transmit to their inferiors the tyranny they suffer from their superiors. I should have everything to fear, if tyrants were to read my book; but tyrants never read. [Pp. 22-26.]

·   ·   ·   ·   ·

Chapter VI. Of the Proportion Between Crimes and Punishments

It is not only the common interest of mankind that crimes should not be committed, but that crimes of every kind should be less frequent, in proportion to the evil they produce to society. Therefore the means made use of by the legislature to prevent crimes should be more powerful, in proportion as they are destructive of the public safety and happiness, and as the inducements to commit them are stronger. Therefore there ought to be a fixed proportion between crimes and punishments.

It is impossible to prevent entirely all the disorders which the passions of mankind cause in society. These disorders increase in proportion to the number of people and the opposition of private interests. If we consult history, we shall find them increasing, in every state, with the extent of dominion. In political arithmetic, it is necessary to substitute a calculation of probabilities to mathematical exactness. That force which continually impels us to our own private interest, like gravity, acts incessantly, unless it meets with an obstacle to oppose it. The effects of this force are the confused series of human actions. Punishments, which I would call political obstacles, prevent the fatal effects of private interest, without destroying the impelling cause, which is that sensibility inseparable from man. The legislator acts, in this case, like a skilful architect, who endeavors to counteract the force of gravity by combining the circumstances which may contribute to the strength of his edifice. [Pp. 28-29.]

. . . . .

Chapter XII. Of the Intent of Punishments

From the foregoing considerations it is evident that the intent of punishments is not to torment a sensible being, nor to undo a crime already committed. Is it possible that torments and useless cruelty, the instruments of furious fanaticism or the impotency of tyrants, can be authorised by a political body, which, so far from being influenced by passion, should be the cool moderator of the passions of individuals. Can the groans of a tortured wretch recall the time past, or reverse the crime he has committed?

The end of punishment, therefore, is no other than to prevent the criminal from doing further injury to society, and to prevent others from committing the like offence. Such punishments, therefore, and such a mode of inflicting them, ought to be chosen, as will make the strongest and most lasting impressions on the minds of others, with the least torment to the body of the criminal. [P. 47.]

. . . . .

Chapter XIX. Of the Advantage of Immediate Punishment

.   .   .   .   .

It is, then, of the greatest importance that the punishment should succeed the crime as immediately as possible, if we intend that, in the rude minds of the multitude, the seducing picture of the advantage arising from the crime should instantly awake the attendant idea of punishment. Delaying the punishment serves only to separate these two ideas, and thus affects the minds of the spectators rather as being a terrible sight than the necessary consequence of a crime, the horror of which should contribute to heighten the idea of the punishment.

There is another excellent method of strengthening this important connection between the ideas of crime and punishment; that is, to make the punishment as analogous as possible to the nature of the crime, in order that the punishment may lead the mind to consider the crime in a different point of view, from that in which it was placed by the flattering idea of promised advantages. [Pp. 74-77.]

.   .   .   .   .

Chapter XXVII. Of the Mildness of Punishments

The course of my ideas has carried me away from my subject, to the elucidation of which I now return. Crimes are more effectually prevented by the *certainty* than the *severity* of punishment. Hence in a magistrate the necessity of vigilance, and in a judge of implacability, which, that it may become an useful virtue, should be jointed to a mild legislation. The certainty of a small punishment will make a stronger impression than the fear of one more severe, if attended with the hopes of escaping; for it is the nature of mankind to be terrified at the approach of the smallest inevitable evil, whilst hope, the best gift of Heaven, hath the power of dispelling the apprehension of a greater, especially if supported by examples of impunity, which weakness or avarice too frequently afford.

If punishments be very severe, men are naturally led to the perpetration of other crimes, to avoid the punishment due to the first. The countries and times most notorious for severity of punishments, were always those in which the most bloody and inhuman actions and the most atrocious crimes were committed; for the hand of the legislator and the assassin were directed by the same spirit of ferocity; which, on the throne, dictated laws of iron to slaves and savages, and in private instigated the subject to sacrifice one tyrant to make room for another. [Pp. 93-94.]

.   .   .   .   .

Chapter XXVIII. Of the Punishment of Death

The useless profusion of punishments, which has never made men better, induces me to inquire, whether the punishment of *death* be really just or useful in a well-governed state? What *right*, I ask, have men to cut the throats of their fellow-creatures? Certainly not that on which the sovereignty and laws are founded. The laws, as I have said before, are only the sum of the smallest portions of the private liberty of each individual, and represent the general will, which is the aggregate of that of each individual. Did any one ever give to others the right of taking away his life? Is it possible that, in the smallest portions of the liberty of each, sacrificed to the good of the public, can be contained the greatest of all good, life? If it were so, how shall it be reconciled to the maxim which tells us, that a man has no right to kill himself, which he certainly must have, if he could give it away to another.*

But the punishment of death is not authorised by any right; for I have demonstrated that no such right exists. It is therefore a war of a whole nation against a citizen whose destruction they consider as necessary or useful to the general good. But if I can further demonstrate that it is neither necessary nor useful, I shall have gained the cause of humanity. [P. 97.]

. . . . .

It is not the intenseness of the pain that has the greatest effect on the mind, but its continuance; for our sensibility is more easily and more powerfully affected by weak but repeated impressions, than by a violent but momentary impulse. The power of habit is universal over every sensible being. As it is by that we learn to speak, to walk, and to satisfy our necessities, so the ideas of morality are stamped on our minds by repeated impressions. The death of a criminal is a terrible but momentary spectacle, and therefore a less efficacious method of deterring others than the continued example of a man deprived of his liberty, condemned, as a beast of burden, to repair, by his labour, the injury he has done to society. *If I commit such a crime*, says the spectator to himself, *I shall be reduced to that miserable condition for the rest of my life.* A much more powerful preventive than the fear of death which men always behold in distant obscurity. [P. 99.]

. . . . .

The execution of a criminal is to the multitude a spectacle which in some excites compassion mixed with indignation. These sentiments

---

* [The unstated premise is provided by the maxim of Roman law. *No one can transfer to another a right which he himself does not possess (Digest L. xvii. 54).*]

occupy the mind much more than that salutary terror which the laws endeavour to inspire; but, in the contemplation of continued suffering, terror is the only, or at least predominant sensation. The severity of a punishment should be just sufficient to excite compassion in the spectators, as it is intended more for them than for the criminal.

A punishment, to be just, should have only that degree of severity which is sufficient to deter others. Now there is no man who, upon the least reflection, would put in competition the total and perpetual loss of his liberty, with the greatest advantage he could possibly obtain in consequence of a crime.....

In all nations, where death is used as punishment, every example supposes a new crime committed; whereas, in perpetual slavery, every criminal affords a frequent and lasting example; and if it be necessary that men should often be witnesses of the power of the laws, criminals should often be put to death; but this supposes a frequency of crimes; and from hence this punishment will cease to have its effect, so that it must be useful and useless at the same time. [Pp. 101-102.]

.   .   .   .   .

The punishment of death is pernicious to society, from the example of barbarity it affords. If the passions, or the necessity of war, have taught men to shed the blood of their fellow creatures, the laws, which are intended to moderate the ferocity of mankind, should not increase it by examples of barbarity, the more horrible as this punishment is usually attended with formal pageantry. Is it not absurd, that the laws, which detect and punish homicide, should, in order to prevent murder, publicly commit murder themselves? What are the true and most useful laws? Those compacts and conditions which all would propose and observe in those moments when private interest is silent, or combined with that of the public. What are the natural sentiments of every person concerning the punishment of death? We may read them in the contempt and indignation with which every one looks on the executioner, who is nevertheless an innocent executor of the public will, a good citizen, who contributes to the advantage of society, the instrument of the general security within, as good soldiers are without. What then is the origin of this contradiction? Why is this sentiment of mankind indelible to the scandal of reason? It is, that, in a secret corner of the mind, in which the original impressions of nature are still preserved, men discover a sentiment which tells them, that their lives are not lawfully in the power of any one, but of that necessity only which with its iron sceptre rules the universe. [Pp. 104-105.]

BENTHAM, THEORY OF LEGISLATION *

Chapter VI. The Choice of Punishment

In order that a punishment may adapt itself to the rules of proportion above laid down, it should have the following qualities:

1st. *It ought to be susceptible of more or less, or divisible,* in order to conform itself to variations in the gravity of offences. Chronic punishments, such as imprisonment and banishment, possess this quality in an eminent degree. They are divisible into portions of any requisite magnitude. It is the same with pecuniary punishments.

2nd. *Equal to Itself.*—It ought, to a certain extent, to be the same for all individuals guilty of the same offence, being made to correspond to their different measures of sensibility. This demands attention to age, sex, condition, fortune, individual habits, and many other circumstances; otherwise the same nominal punishment, being often found too severe for some persons, too mild for others, will overshoot the mark, or will fail to reach it. A fine fixed by law will never be a punishment equal to itself, on account of difference of fortune. Banishment has the same inconvenience; too severe for one, to another it is nothing.

3rd. *Commeasurable.*—If a man has two offences before his eyes, the law ought to give him a motive to abstain from the greater. He will have that motive, if he can see that the greater offence will draw upon him a greater punishment. It ought, then, to be in his power to compare these punishments, to measure their different degrees.

There are two methods of fulfilling this object. 1st. By adding to a given punishment another quantity of punishment of the same kind; for example, to five years' imprisonment for such an offence, two years' additional for such an aggravation. 2nd. By adding a punishment of a different kind; for example, to five years' imprisonment for such an offence, public ignominy for such an aggravation.

4th. *Analogous to the Offence.*—The punishment will more easily engrave itself on the memory, it will present itself more strongly to the imagination, if it has a resemblance, an analogy to the offence, a common character with it. The *lex talionis* is admirable in this respect— *An eye for an eye, a tooth for a tooth.* The most imperfect understanding is capable of connecting these ideas. But these sort of punishments are rarely practicable, and in most cases would be too expensive.

There are other means of analogy. Search out, for example, the motives of offences, and generally you will recognize the dominant passion of the offender, and you may punish him, according to the proverbial saying, with the instrument of his sin. Offences of cupidity will best be

---

* ["Principles of the Penal Code," Part III ("Of Punishments") pp. 336-340. Dumont, ed., Hildreth, trans. (1864). Reprinted with introduction and notes by C. K. Ogden, London: Routledge and Kegan Paul Ltd., 1931.]

punished by pecuniary fines, when the wealth of the offender admits it; offences of insolence, by humiliation; offences of idleness, by compulsory labour, or forced rest.

5th. *Exemplary.*—A real punishment which should not be apparent would be lost upon the public. The great art consists in augmenting the apparent punishment without augmenting the real punishment. This may be accomplished, either in the selection of the punishments themselves, or by accompanying their execution with striking solemnities.

The *auto-da-fé* would be one of the most useful inventions of jurisprudence, if instead of being an act of faith it were an act of justice. What is it but a public execution, a solemn tragedy which the legislator presents to the assembled people; a tragedy truly important, truly pathetic by the sad reality of its catastrophe, and by the greatness of its object. The preparations, the scenery, the ornaments, cannot be too studied, since upon them the effect principally depends. The tribunal, the scaffold, the dresses of the officers of justice, the habiliments of the criminals, the religious service, the procession, all the accompaniments, ought to bear a grave and mournful character. Why should not the executioners be covered with a mourning crape? The terror of the scene would be increased by it, and at the same time these useful servants of the state would be concealed from the unjust hatred of the people. Were it possible to keep up the illusion, all might pass in effigy. The reality of punishment is only necessary to maintain the appearance of it.

6th. *Economical.*—That is, punishments should have only that degree of severity absolutely necessary to answer their end. All beyond is not only so much superfluous evil, but produces a multitude of inconveniences, which intercept the ends of justice.

Pecuniary punishments are highly economical, since all the evil felt by him who pays turns into an advantage for him who receives.

7th. *Remissible or Revokable.*—It is necessary that the damage inflicted should not be absolutely irreparable, since unfortunately cases may occur in which the infliction may be subsequently discovered to have been without lawful cause. As long as testimony is susceptible of imperfection, as long as appearances may be deceitful, as long as men have no certain criterion whereby to distinguish truth from falsehood, one of the most important precautions which mutual security requires is, not to admit of punishments absolutely irreparable, except upon the clearest evidence of their necessity. Have we not seen all the appearances of crime accumulated upon the head of a culprit whose innocence was demonstrated, when nothing remained but to lament over the mistake of an arrogant precipitation? Weak and inconsistent that we are! We judge like fallible creatures; we punish as if we could not be deceived!

To these important qualities of punishment three others may be added, of less extensive utility, but to be aimed at when it is possible to procure them without detracting from the great object of example.

1st. It is a great merit in a punishment to contribute to the *reformation of the offender*, not only through fear of being punished again, but by a change in his character and habits. This end may be attained by studying the motive which produced the offence, and by applying a punishment which tends to weaken that motive. A house of correction, to fulfill this object, ought to admit a separation of the delinquents, in order that different means of treatment may be adapted to the diversity of their moral condition.

2nd. *Taking away the power of doing Injury.*—It is much easier to obtain this end than the preceding. Mutilations and perpetual imprisonment possess this quality. But the spirit of this maxim leads to an excessive rigour. It is this which has rendered the punishment of death so frequent.

If there are cases in which it is possible to deprive the offender of the power of doing injury only by taking away his life, it is upon very extraordinary occasions; for example, in civil wars, where the name of a leader, as long as he lives, is enough to inflame the passions of a multitude. And even in such cases death inflicted upon actions of a character so equivocal ought rather to be looked upon as an act of hostility than as a punishment.

3rd. *To furnish an indemnity to the injured party* is another useful quality in a punishment. It is a means of accomplishing two objects at once,—punishing an offence, and repairing it: removing the evil of the first order, and putting a stop to alarm. This is a characteristic advantage of pecuniary punishments.

I conclude this chapter by a general observation of the highest importance. *The legislator, in the choice of punishments, ought carefully to avoid such as shock established prejudices.* If there has been formed in the minds of the people a decided aversion to a given kind of punishment, though it has all the other requisite qualities, it ought not to be admitted into the penal code, because it would do more harm than good. In the first place, it is an evil to inspire the public with a painful feeling by the establishment of an unpopular punishment. It is no longer the guilty alone who are punished. It is the most innocent and tenderhearted persons upon whom is inflicted a punishment very real, though it has no particular name, by wounding their sensibility, braving their opinion, and presenting to them the image of violence and of tyranny. What can be expected from conduct so injudicious? The legislator, by despising public sentiment, imperceptibly turns it against himself. He loses the voluntary assistance which individuals lend to the execution of the law when they are content with it; the people, instead of being his assistants, are his enemies. Some endeavour to facilitate the escape of the guilty; others feel a scruple at denouncing them; witnesses hesitate to testify;

there is formed insensibly a fatal prejudice, which attaches a kind of shame and of reproach to the service of the law. This general discontent may go further; it sometimes bursts out into open resistance to the officers of justice, or to the execution of sentences. A success against authority is regarded by the people as a victory; and the unpunished delinquent triumphs over the weakness of the laws.

What renders punishments unpopular is almost always their bad selection. The more the penal code is conformed to the rules we have laid down, the more it will secure the enlightened esteem of the wise, and an approbation of feeling on the part of the multitude. Such punishments will be thought just and moderate. Everybody will be struck with their propriety, their analogy to offences, and with that scale of gradation by which aggravation of punishment is made to correspond to aggravation of offence, and mildness of punishment to smallness of offence. This kind of merit, founded upon domestic and familiar notions, is level to the comprehension of every kind. Nothing is more fit to give the idea of a paternal government, to inspire confidence, to make public opinion act in concert with authority. When the people are on the side of the laws, the chances of escape are reduced to their lowest term.

POLAND, CHANGES IN THE CRIMINAL LAW AND PROCEDURE SINCE 1800 *

To go back to the beginning of the century is to go back, as far as the Criminal Law is concerned, to an age of barbarism. Look at the punishments which were inflicted on convicted prisoners.

The sentence on a traitor was that he must be drawn on a hurdle from the gaol to the place of execution, and when he came there he must be hanged by the neck, but *not till he be dead*, for he must be *cut down alive*, then his bowels must be taken out and burnt before his face, then his head must be severed from his body, and his body divided into four quarters, and these must be at the king's disposal.

If you would like to see the way in which that sentence was carried out you should refer to Townley's case, 18 State Trials, 350 and 351, in 1746. It was not until 1814 that this sentence was altered, and the traitor was hanged by the neck until he was dead, and disembowelling

---

* [*A Century of Law Reform*, Chap. II. New York: The Macmillan Company, 1901.
The lecture from which these excerpts are taken was one of a series of "Twelve Lectures on the Changes in the Law of England During the Nineteenth Century" delivered at Lincoln's Inn under the auspices of the Council of Legal Education. In addition to Sir Harry B. Poland, Q.C., Treasurer of the Inner Temple, who delivered the lecture on criminal law, the roster of lecturers included W. Blake Odgers, John Pawley Bate, A. T. Carter, Augustine Birrell, Alfred Henry Ruegg, Arthur Underhill, Montague Lush, and T. B. Napier.]

and burning were abolished, but the drawing on a hurdle, the beheading and quartering still remained part of the sentence. [Pp. 43-44.]

. . . . .

A murderer after being hanged had to be dissected, or hung in chains in sight and view of the public, whichever of the two the Court should order. In 1832 the dissection of the bodies of murderers was abolished, and in 1834 the hanging in chains was prohibited. It was the practice before the body was hung in chains to shave the head of the body, and to tar it in order to preserve it from the action of the weather. It was a common practice to hang the bodies of executed criminals in chains near the site where their crimes were committed. The bodies of pirates were generally hung in chains on the banks of rivers.

At the beginning of the century most felonies were capital. Down to 1808 the crime of stealing from the person above the value of a shilling was punishable with death. In 1810 Lord Eldon was alarmed by a Bill of Sir S. Romilly's, which had passed the Commons, to abolish the punishment of death for the offence of privately stealing in a shop to the value of 5s.; and in the debate in the Lords he prided himself on having left a man, who was convicted before him for stealing a horse of the value of 7s. 6d., for execution, on the ground that he was a regular horse-stealer. Up to 1811 stealing from bleaching-grounds was capital. In 1811 Lord Eldon again opposed "a dangerous Bill to take away the punishment of death from the offence of stealing in a dwelling-house to the value of forty shillings." Both Bills were of course thrown out in the Lords, and the result was that juries used to find that goods of the clear value of say 50 pounds and upwards were under the value of 5s., so as to save prisoners from the punishment of death.[1]

Up to 1812 it was a capital crime for soldiers or seamen to be found vagrant without their passes, and up to 1823 it was also a capital crime for a man to fraudulently personate an out-pensioner of Greenwich Hospital or assume the name and character of one; and up to 1821 a fraudulent bankrupt was liable to be sentenced to death. About 1817 or 1818 hanging for forging bank-notes was discontinued. This reform was to some extent helped forward by a caricature by George Cruikshank, a copy of which you will find in that excellent book, Old-Time Punishments, by William Andrews. The last execution for attempted murder was at Chester in August, 1861.

Over 200 cases were capital at the beginning of the century, though many of these had fallen into desuetude. You will find further information on this subject in that valuable work, Walpole's History of England, vol. ii, page 58 and vol. iii, page 55. Now the only capital crimes are high

---

[1] See Lord Campbell's "Life of Lord Eldon" in his Lives of the Chancellors, vol. 7, p. 238.

treason, murder, piracy with violence, and setting fire to the Queen's ships, dockyards, arsenals, naval and military stores. Judgment of death may be recorded instead of being passed in all capital cases except treason and murder, and in such a case the prisoner is liable to be kept in penal servitude for life. [Pp. 44-46.]

.   .   .   .   .

The principal Evidence Acts of the century must now be referred to. The rules of evidence in civil and criminal cases were the same, and such rules were established by our ancestors as the most suitable for arriving at the truth. No one who had been convicted of crime, or who had any pecuniary interest in the result of a trial, could give evidence, and constant failures of justice took place in consequence of the incompetency of such persons. In 1828 the first blow was struck at this absurd rule. It was then enacted that the person whose name was forged should be a competent witness in prosecutions for forgery and uttering forged documents, notwithstanding that such person had an interest in the deed, writing, etc., alleged to be forged. Afterwards, in 1843, Lord Denman's Act rendered competent as witnesses all persons who had an interest in the trial or who had been convicted of crime, leaving the jury to judge as to their credibility. He had advocated this reform first in an article in the *Edinburgh Review* of 1824. The Evidence Acts of 1851, 1853 (Brougham's Acts), and of 1869, rendering parties to suits and their husbands and wives competent witnesses, did not apply to criminal cases. I will therefore leave Mr. Blake Odgers to deal with them in his lecture next term.

From 1872 to 1897 about twenty-six Acts were passed enabling accused persons in certain cases to give evidence: but at last came Lord Halsbury's important Act of 1898, which made an accused person and the husband and wife of such person *competent* witnesses, and which regulated the procedure as to their examination. That Act is so plain and clear that I need not detain you by enlarging on its provisions. I will only say that all the predictions of its opponents have been falsified, and that it works admirably. [P. 54.]

.   .   .   .   .

Appeals of murder and trial by battle were abolished in 1819, and, strange to relate, Lord Eldon concurred in this reform. Thornton's case in 1818, reported in Woodall's "Celebrated Trials," is the last case of this remnant of Gothic jurisprudence. Benefit of Clergy was abolished in 1827. [P. 60.]

.   .   .   .   .

I have pointed out to you the severity of our law at the beginning of the century, and I need not refer to its mildness at the end. We have at last learnt the great lesson which Dr. Paley taught more than a hundred years ago, that the certainty of punishment is more effective than severity.

We have now no gagging laws, we possess the right of free speech and the right of holding public meetings, and the press is absolutely free. We are enjoying what I hope it is not a boast to call British civilisation and British liberty, and we are protected by impartial laws and the purest administration of justice. [P. 66.]

.   .   .   .   .

D. Individualization of punishment

BEDE, ECCLESIASTICAL HISTORY OF THE ENGLISH NATION *

.   .   .   .   .

Augustine's Third Question.—I beseech you to inform me what punishment must be inflicted, if any one shall take anything by stealth from the Church?

Gregory answers: You may judge, my brother, by the person of the thief, in what manner he is to be corrected. For there are some, who, having substance, commit theft; and there are others, who transgress in this point through want. Wherefore it is requisite, that some be punished in their purses, others with stripes; some with more severity, and some more mildly. And when the severity is more, it is to proceed from charity, not from passion. . . . For it behooves us to maintain discipline among the faithful, as good parents do with their children after the flesh, whom they punish with stripes for their faults, and yet design to make those their heirs whom they chastise. . . . This charity is, therefore, to be kept in mind, and it dictates the measure of the punishment, so that the mind may do nothing beyond the rule of reason. You may add, that they ought to restore those things which they have stolen from the Church. But, God forbid, that the Church should make profit from those earthly things which it seems to lose, or seek to gain out of such vanities.

---

* [Book I, Chap. 27.

Little is known of *The Venerable Bede* (672 or 673–735), author of the *Ecclesiastical History* (written in 731) except that his life was spent almost entirely in religious study and meditation at the monasteries of Wearmouth and Jarrow. His works include books on historical and theological topics, as well as grammar, natural phenomena, and the calendar. It has been said that the writings of the Venerable Bede practically sum up the learning of Western Europe in his time. A convenient edition of the *Ecclesiastical History* appears in the series of Temple Classics (New York: E. P. Dutton & Co., Inc., 1903).]

SALEILLES, THE INDIVIDUALIZATION OF PUNISHMENT *

Chapter 1. The Statement of the Problem

§ 5. Types of Individualization

.   .   .   .   .

... On what basis shall the individualization of punishment proceed? This question, in turn, implied a second, closely allied to it: By whom shall the individualization of punishment be made? Shall it be done in advance by the law? If so, it proceeds upon presumption, in ignorance of the individuals concerned, and upon the judgment of them through their actions. It groups them according to prescribed classes, and undertakes approximately to set the punishment and to adjust it to the individual criminal. This would be a system of legal individualization.

On the other hand the judge is confronted not by an abstract and nameless individual, but by an actual criminal conscious of his crime and its significance. Shall the judge then undertake the adjustment of the punishment to the measure of surviving morality still available for reform and moral reinstatement? This would be a system of judicial individualization.

Or shall we go farther still and leave the individualization to the prison authorities, on the ground that they can observe the prisoner in confinement, carefully adjust the punishment to the progress made, and in due course omit it when they consider the reform established and rehabilitation secure? For it may be found that the judge is not in a favorable position to appreciate the criminal, because he knows nothing of him but the single fact of the crime committed; and though he knows this with all its accompanying circumstances, he has not the basis for anticipating the probable effect of punishment. This would be a system of administrative individualization.

§ 6. Queries and Objections: the Schools

Such are the important issues; yet there is another, more important than any such question of application, which is beset with conscientious doubts. The classic conception sets forth an important truth, or to speak more accurately, two truths, which should be clearly grasped. The first is that in itself and independently of the personality of the criminal the evil done carries an actual injury to the community which is the victim of the crime. This injury, quite apart from an expiation in any religious or philosophical sense, requires a satisfaction demanded by the public conscience. Now if the consideration of the individual prevails above

---

* [Pp. 12-14. Jastrow, trans. Vol. 4, Modern Criminal Science Series; Boston: Little, Brown & Company, 1911. Other excerpts from this volume appear *supra*, pp. 326-327.]

the reparation, will not the policy encourage others to continue in a criminal career? And for society, will this not produce a moral disorder which, like a contagious disease, tends to spread? An additional query or objection applies; namely, the difficulty of divesting the ordinary conception of justice from a kind of abstract mathematical equality. Accordingly, if two individuals receive different punishments for the same offence or are differently treated, it would seem as though equity had been disregarded, and that caprice had replaced justice. How shall these exacting requirements demanded by society be reconciled to the equally indispensable necessity of taking account of the individual? How shall they be reconciled to the like requirements of proportioning the punishment, not to the objective crime committed or to the material injury done, but to the inherent criminality of the criminal, to such latent or real criminality as makes him dangerous to his fellowmen? How, in brief, shall they be adjusted to the degree of morality, or if we may say so, of normality, and to the prospects of regeneration which it holds out? Such are the several aspects of this very large problem of the individualization of punishment.

M. R. COHEN, MORAL ASPECTS OF THE CRIMINAL LAW *

The Individualization of Punishment

.　.　.　.　.

Any plausible attempt to reform something that has worked as horribly as our prison system should have its frailties viewed with benevolent patience. Given time and experience, the new movement may overcome many of the evils which it has already manifested, such as the abuse of discretion by judges and parole boards, and the number of paroled prisoners who commit new crimes. But it is always helpful to clarify the issue by critically examining fundamental ideas.

1. The advocates of individualization of punishment should beware of overworking the analogy between crime and disease. Crime is not the direct result of physiologic factors, but depends directly on social institutions. It is foolish to talk glibly of treating the criminal according to his individual nature, when in fact we have no means of adequately knowing it. The physician does not need to know all about a man's individual character. In his diagnosis he looks for very definite facts of a recurrent character, and once that is determined the treatment moves along a limited number of alternatives. But can any judge be honestly said to know the character of a person convicted sufficiently to deter-

---

* [49 *Yale L.J.* 987, 1021-1022 (1940); reprinted in *Reason and Law*, pp. 15, 55-56 (Glencoe, Ill.: The Free Press, 1950). Other excerpts from this essay appear *supra* pp. 289, 300, 336.]

mine what precise treatment is needed? Similarly with parole boards. A man's conduct in prison is not always the best indication of what he will do when released. And in point of fact prison officials can be and have been influenced by political and social pressure.

2. The ideology of individualization tends to an extremely nominalistic position. That is, it tends to forget the logical fact that we are apt to have more reliable knowledge about classes than about individuals and that for certain purposes classes rather than individuals are relevant. If our country is invaded, we try to take measures against the invading army or armies. The treatment of individual soldiers is determined by these general policies. Of course, we may avoid the false ideology criticized here by admitting all this, and saying that the law needs more individualization of treatment than exists at present. But it is of the utmost importance not to forget that the abuse of discretion was one of the principal causes which led to the revolt expressed in the classical views on penology—a revolt that has undoubtedly done much for the humanization of the criminal law and its administration. And it would be a great calamity if this gain were frittered away by hastily conceived novelties.

E. Alternatives to Punishment

BENTHAM, THEORY OF LEGISLATION *

Part IV. Indirect Means of Preventing Offences

Introduction

In all the sciences there are branches which have been cultivated more tardily than others, because they demand a longer series of observations and meditations more profound. It is thus that mathematics have their transcendental or higher branch—that is, a new science, as it were, above ordinary science.

The same distinction, to a certain extent, may be applied to the art of legislation. What means shall be adopted to prevent injurious actions? The first answer, which presents itself to everybody, is this: "Forbid those actions; punish them." This method of combating offences being the most simple and the first adopted, every other method of arriving at the same end is, so to speak, a refinement of the art, and its transcendental branch.

That branch consists in devising a course of legislative acts adapted to prevent offences—in acting principally upon the inclinations of men,

---

* ["Principles of the Penal Code." Dumont, ed., Hildreth, trans. (1864). Reprinted with introduction and notes by C. K. Ogden, London: Routledge and Kegan Paul Ltd., 1931.]

in order to turn them from evil and to impress upon them the direction most useful to themselves and to others.

The first method—that of combating offences by punishments—constitutes *direct legislation*.

The second method—that of combatting offences by *preventive means* —constitutes a branch of legislation which may be called *indirect*.

The sovereign acts *directly* against offences when he prohibits them individually under special penalties. He acts *indirectly* when he takes precautions to prevent them.

By direct legislation the evil is attacked in front. Indirect legislation attacks it obliquely. In the first case, the legislator declares open war against the enemy, points him out, pursues him, meets him foot to foot, and carries his defences sword in hand. In the second case, he does not announce his whole design; he works underground, he procures intelligence, he seeks to prevent hostile enterprises, and to keep still in his alliance those who may have formed secret intentions against him.

Speculative writers upon politics have had glimpses of this art; but in speaking of this second branch of legislation they do not evince any clear idea of it. The first branch has been a long time reduced to system, the good part of it as well as the bad. The second branch has never been thoroughly examined; nobody has undertaken to treat it with method, to arrange it, to classify it—in one word, to master it in its whole extent. It is yet a new subject.

Writers who have composed political romances tolerate direct legislation as a necessary evil; it is a choice of evils to which they submit, but as to which they never express a very lively interest. But when they come to speak about the means of preventing offences, of rendering men better, of perfecting morals, their imagination grows warm, their hopes are excited; one would suppose they were about to produce the great secret, and that the human race was going to receive a new form. It is because we have a more magnificent idea of objects in proportion as they are less familiar, and because the imagination has a loftier flight amid vague projects which have never been subjected to the limits of analysis. *Major e longinquo reverentia*—the greater distance, the greater reverence—this is a saying as applicable to ideas as to persons. A detailed examination will reduce all these indefinite hopes to the just dimensions of the possible; and if in the process we lose fictitious treasures, we shall be well indemnified by the certainty of what remains.

To distinguish exactly what appertains to these two branches, it is necessary to begin by forming a just idea of direct legislation. It proceeds, or ought to proceed, in this way:

1st. The choice of acts to be erected into offences.

2nd. The description of each offence, as murder, theft, peculation, etc.

3rd. An exposition of the reasons for attributing to these acts the quality of offences—reasons which ought to be deduced from the single principle of utility, and consequently to be consistent with themselves.

4th. The assigning of a competent punishment for each offence.

5th. An exposition of the reasons which justify these punishments.

The penal system, though it be made as perfect as possible is defective in several respects:—1st. The evil must exist before the remedy can be applied. The remedy consists in the application of punishment, and punishment cannot be applied till offence is committed. Every new instance of punishment inflicted is an additional proof that punishment lacks efficacy and leaves behind it a certain degree of danger and alarm. 2nd. Punishment itself is an evil, though necessary to prevent greater evils. Penal justice, in the whole course of its operation, can only be a series of evils—evils arising from the threats and constraint of the law, evils arising from the prosecution of the accused before it is possible to distinguish innocence from guilt, evils growing out of the inflictions of judicial sentences, evils from the unavoidable consequences which result to the innocent. 3rd. The penal system is not able to reach many injurious actions, which escape justice either by their frequency, the facility of concealing them, by the difficulty of defining them, or finally by some vicious turn of public opinion by which they are favoured. Penal law can operate only within certain limits, and its power extends only to palpable acts, susceptible of manifest proof.

This imperfection of the penal system has caused new expedients to be sought for to supply its deficiencies. These expedients have for their object the prevention of offences, either by preventing the acquisition of the *knowledge* necessary to their commission or by taking away the *power* or the *will* to commit them. The most numerous class of these means relates to the art of directing the inclinations by weakening the seductive motives which excite to evil, and by strengthening the tutelary motives which impel to good.

Indirect means, then, are those which, without having the character of punishments, act upon man physically or morally, to dispose him to obey the laws, to shield him from temptations, to govern him by his inclinations and his knowledge. [Pp. 358-360.]

.   .   .   .   .

Chapter I. Means of Taking Away the Physical Power to do Harm

When the will, the knowledge, and the power necessary to the performance of an act concur, that act is of necessity performed. *Inclination, knowledge, power,*—these then, are the three points at which it is necessary to apply the influence of law, in order to determine the conduct of men. These three words contain in the abstract the sum and substance of all that can be done by legislation, direct or indirect.

I begin with *power*, because means in this respect are more simple and limited, and because, in those cases in which we can succeed in taking away the power to do harm, we have accomplished everything. Success is certain.

Power may be distinguished into two kinds. 1st. *Internal* power, that which depends upon the intrinsic faculties of the individual; 2nd. *External* power, that which depends upon persons and things external to the individual, but the aid of which he must have, in order to act.

As to internal power, that which depends upon the faculties of the individual, it is scarcely possible to deprive a man of it with advantage. The power of doing evil is inseparable from the power of doing good. With his hands cut off, a man cannot steal, but neither can he work.

Besides, these privative means are so severe that they cannot be employed except upon criminals already convicted. Imprisonment is the only one of them that can be justified, in certain cases, to prevent an apprehended offence.

The legislator will find greater resources for the prevention of offences by turning his attention to the material objects which aid their commission.

There are cases in which the power of doing harm may be taken away, by excluding what Tacitus calls *irritamenta malorum*, irritations to evil,— the subjects, the instruments of offence. In such cases, the policy of the legislator may be compared to that of a nurse; iron bars at the windows, grates around the fire, the care of keeping sharp and dangerous instruments from the hands of children, are means of the same kind as the prohibition to sell and to make tools for the fabrication of false money, venerific drugs, arms easy to be concealed, dice, or other instruments of prohibited games, and the prohibition to make or to have certain nets for the chase, or other instruments for trapping wild game.

Mahomet, not trusting to the restraining power of reason, wished to take away from men the power of abusing strong drinks; and if we consider the climate of warm countries, where wine renders men furious rather than stupid, we shall find perhaps that the total prohibition is a milder method of procedure than a permission which produces a numerous class of offences, and consequently of punishments.

Imposts upon spirituous liquors fulfill, in part, the same end. In proportion as the price is raised above the capacity of the most numerous class to purchase, they are deprived of the means of giving themselves up to intemperance. [Pp. 362-364.]

.　　.　　.　　.　　.　　.

Chapter II. Prohibition of Acquiring Knowledge Which May be Turned to a Bad Purpose

I mention this kind of policy only to condemn it. It has produced the censorship of the press; it has produced the inquisition; and wherever it is employed it will always produce the brutalization of mankind.

I propose here to show,—1st, that the diffusion of knowledge is not injurious on the whole, the offences of refinement being less fatal than those of ignorance; 2nd, that the most advantageous method of combatting the evil which may result from a limited degree of knowledge is to augment its quantity. [P. 366.]

. . . . . .

Chapter III. Indirect Means of Preventing the Wish to Commit Offences

We have seen that legislation can only operate by influencing the power, the knowledge, and the will. We have spoken of the indirect means of taking away the power to do injury; we have shown that the policy of preventing men from acquiring information, does more harm than good. All the indirect means, then, which we can use with advantage, must be employed in directing the inclinations of men, in putting into operation the rules of a logic hitherto but little known, *the logic of the will*—a logic which, as Ovid* has so well expressed it, seems often to be in opposition to that of the *understanding*:—

Video meliora proboque, deteriora sequor.

I see the better and approve it; the worse I follow.

The means about to be presented are of a nature to put a stop in many cases to this interior discord; to diminish that contrariety among motives, which often owes its existence to want of address on the part of the legislator, to an opposition which he has himself created between the natural sanction and the political sanction, between the moral sanction and the religious sanction. If he could make all these powers concur towards the same end, all the faculties of man would be in harmony, and the will to do evil would not exist. In cases where this end cannot be attained, it is necessary, at all events, that the force of the tutelary motives should exceed that of the seductive motives.

The indirect means by which the will can be influenced, may be illustrated under the form of political or moral problems, of which the solution may be shown by various examples:

---

* [*Metamorphoses*, Book VII, 1. 17.]

Problem First.—To change the course of dangerous desires, and to direct the inclinations towards amusements conformable to the public interest.

Second.—To arrange so that a given desire may be satisfied without injury, or with the least possible injury.

Third.—To avoid furnishing encouragements to crime.

Fourth.—To increase responsibility in proportion as temptation increases.

Fifth.—To diminish the sensibility to temptation.

Sixth.—To strengthen the impression of punishments upon the imagination.

Seventh.—To facilitate knowledge of the fact of an offence.

Eighth.—To prevent an offence by giving to many persons an immediate interest to prevent it.

Ninth.—To facilitate the means of recognizing and finding individuals.

Tenth.—To increase the difficulty of escape.

Eleventh.—To diminish the uncertainty of prosecutions and punishments.

Twelfth.—To prohibit accessory offences, in order to prevent the principal offence.

After these means, of which the object is special, others more general will be pointed out, such as the culture of benevolence, the culture of honour, the employment of the impulse of religion, and the use to be made of the power of instruction, and of education. [Pp. 371-372.]

Part II

THE GENERAL THEORY OF LAW

THE NATURE OF LAW

Contents

Introductory Note

A survey of the important theories that have been presented during the past 2500 years concerning the nature of law provides the subject matter for most courses and treatises in jurisprudence. Such a survey may be carried through in at least two ways. In the first place, our instructor may attempt to show the mistakes that were made by his various predecessors; an explanation of how they came to make these mistakes is helpful in buttressing the assumption that our teacher has been fortunate enough to avoid similar errors. If to this process is appended a careful pigeonholing of competing views under labels that stress "schools" and "isms," the unsuspecting reader or listener may easily be led to conclude that jurisprudence is a museum of intellectual horrors from which only a few modern *illuminati* have escaped.

The present volume of readings is an attempt to elaborate a different conception, a view of jurisprudence as a great adventure in intellectual cooperation stretching across many lands and many centuries, an exploration of possible perspectives through which the many-faceted problems that link life to law may be viewed.

From such a standpoint it becomes important to recognize that different people who use the word "law" are not necessarily talking about the same thing or answering the same questions. The house of jurisprudence has many mansions. Those who are chiefly concerned with legal history, men like Savigny and Maine, may offer us important answers to historical questions. Those who are concerned with analyzing and observing the contemporary ways of judges may offer us equally important analyses and predictions. Those who are concerned with the social context and effects of law can illumine our understanding without obscuring the importance of either legal history or legal anatomy. And those who write about the ideals that should light the legal paths of our society may serve up their wisdom or their foolishness and yet leave room for other courses. The fact that these four sorts of questions are often answered in terms of a definition of law is unfortunate but not fatal. By recognizing the relativity of definition to purpose and the possibility of translation from one system of definition to another, we may render our minds capable of receiving illumination from many directions and may come to see as complementary what to a narrower view appear as hopeless inconsistencies and meaningless mistakes.

The following chapter seeks to show the progression of realistic jurisprudence through Aristotle, Hobbes, Bentham, Austin, Gray, and Holmes, noting the qualifications and clarifications that are still emerging in the thought of men like Demogue and Frank.

It may be that Cicero, St. Thomas, St. Germain, Victoria, Grotius, Coke, Lorimer, and others who have used the language of natural law and natural rights to express their ethical insights and reflections have a better right to include Aristotle in their company than do the legal realists. But that is a question that may perhaps be left to historians and philologists. What is important for our purpose is that Aristotle has something worth-while to say to both realists and idealists. And if that be so, it may even be the case that realists and idealists have worth-while things to say to each other.

Slightly apart from these two main traditions run the stream of historical thought in which Savigny and Maine are the heroic figures and the stream of legal sociology in which Ehrlich is still recognized as the great craftsman, although the names of Brandeis and Pound will be more familiar to most American lawyers and law students.

That these traditions have diverse and competing utilities is made plain by the struggle over codification and the larger struggle between judiciaries and legislatures to which a good deal of the material in this chapter refers. The two chapters that follow, dealing more specifically with the judicial and the legislative process, may help to clarify these practical overtones and consequences.

ARISTOTLE, BASIC WORKS *

I †

Of political justice part is natural, part legal—natural, that which everywhere has the same force and does not exist by people's thinking this or that; legal, that which is originally indifferent, but when it has been laid down is not indifferent, *e.g.* that a prisoner's ransom shall be a mina, or that a goat and not two sheep shall be sacrificed, and again all the laws that are passed for particular cases, *e.g.* that sacrifice shall be made in honour of Brasidas, and the provisions of decrees. Now some think that all justice is of this sort, because that which is by nature is unchangeable and has everywhere the same force (as fire burns both here and in Persia), while they see change in the things recognized as just. This, however, is not true in this unqualified way, but is true in a sense; or rather, with the gods it is perhaps not true at all, while with us there is something that is just even by nature, yet all of it is changeable; but still some is by nature, some not by nature. It is evident which sort of thing, among things capable of being otherwise, is by nature; and which is not but is legal and conventional, assuming that both are equally changeable. And in all other things the same distinction will apply; by nature the right hand is stronger, yet it is possible that all men should come to be ambidextrous. The things which are just by virtue of convention and expediency are like measures; for wine and corn

---

* [Selections from *Aristotle* (384 B.C.–322 B.C.) are taken from the convenient one-volume collection of Aristotle's *Basic Works* edited by Richard McKeon (1941). To speak of the influence of Aristotle on later thinkers is almost to speak of the intellectual influence of Greece, since Aristotle as the most capable student of Plato (under whom he studied from about 368 B.C. to about 348 B.C.), as the spiritual heir of Socrates, and as founder and head of the leading scientific institution of the ancient world (the Athenian Lyceum) was in a unique position to systematize Greek scientific and philosophic thought. Much of the influence of Aristotle upon later, and even modern, thought has taken form not through conscious imitation but through unconscious adoption of concepts, distinctions, forms of speech, modes of argument, and basic assumptions to which Aristotle gave definitive formulation. In the law such Aristotelian concepts as "natural justice" and "legal" or "conventional" justice, the nature of man as a "political animal," the distinction between freedom and slavery, the political forms of democracy, aristocracy, oligarchy, and tyranny, the "state of nature," the corrupting force of political power, the distinction between government by law and government by men, and the standards of the "reasonable man," have continued to offer basic tools and insights in political and legal thinking for more than 20 centuries.

An excellent introduction to the life, thought, and influence of Aristotle will be found in the McKeon edition of Aristotle's *Basic Works* from which the excerpts in this volume are taken. For an account of Aristotle's legal philosophy, see Cairns, *Legal Philosophy from Plato to Hegel* (1949).]

† [Nichomachean Ethics, V, 7; McKeon, *Basic Works of Aristotle*, p. 1014. Oxford: The Clarendon Press, 1941. Compare Aristotle's conception of natural justice with the conception of natural law in passages from Justinian, Grotius and Locke on the origin of property, at pp. 50, 55, and 58 *supra*.]

measures are not everywhere equal, but larger in wholesale and smaller in retail markets. Similarly, the things which are just not by nature but by human enactment are not everywhere the same, since constitutions also are not the same, though there is but one which is everywhere by nature the best.

II *

... the words slavery and slave are used in two senses. There is a slave or slavery by law as well as by nature. The law of which I speak is a sort of convention—the law by which whatever is taken in war is supposed to belong to the victors. But this right many jurists impeach, as they would an orator who brought forward an unconstitutional measure: they detest the notion that, because one man has the power of doing violence and is superior in brute strength, another shall be his slave and subject. Even among philosophers there is a difference of opinion. The origin of the dispute, and what makes the views invade each other's territory, is as follows: in some sense virtue, when furnished with means, has actually the greatest power of exercising force: and as superior power is only found where there is superior excellence of some kind, power seems to imply virtue, and the dispute to be simply one about justice (for it is due to one party identifying justice with goodwill, while the other identifies it with the mere rule of the stronger).

III †

When several villages are united in a single complete community, large enough to be nearly or quite self-sufficing, the state comes into existence, originating in the bare needs of life, and continuing in existence for the sake of a good life. And therefore, if the earlier forms of society are natural, so is the state, for it is the end of them, and the nature of a thing is its end. For what each thing is when fully developed, we call its nature, whether we are speaking of a man, a horse, or a family. Besides, the final cause and end of a thing is the best, and to be self-sufficing is the end and the best.

Hence it is evident that the state is a creation of nature, and that man is by nature a political animal. And he who by nature and not by mere accident is without a state, is either a bad man or above humanity; he is like the

"Tribeless, lawless, hearthless one,"

---

* [Politics, I, 5; McKeon, p. 1133.

If superior power implies superior excellence or virtue, what is the difference between the rule of goodwill, on the one hand, and the "mere rule of the stronger"?]

† [Politics, I, 2; McKeon, pp. 1129-1130.

Does Aristotle's explanation of the natural origin of the state do away with his distinction between what is just by nature and what is just by law or convention? Or is the latter a special phase or development of the former?]

whom Homer[4] denounces—the natural outcast is forthwith a lover of war; he may be compared to an isolated piece at draughts.

Now, that man is more of a political animal than bees or any other gregarious animal, is evident. Nature, as we often say, makes nothing in vain,[5] and man is the only animal whom she has endowed with the gift of speech.[6] And whereas mere voice is but an indication of pleasure or pain, and is therefore found in other animals (for their nature attains to the perception of pleasure and pain and the intimation of them to one another, and no further), the power of speech is intended to set forth the expedient and inexpedient, and therefore likewise the just and the unjust. And it is a characteristic of man that he alone has any sense of good and evil, of just and the unjust, and the like, and the association of living beings who have this sense makes a family and a state.

Further, the state is by nature clearly prior * to the family and to the individual, since the whole is of necessity prior to the part; for example, if the whole body be destroyed, there will be no foot or hand, except in an equivocal sense, as we might speak of a stone hand; for when destroyed the hand will be no better than that. But things are defined by their working and power; and we ought not to say that they are the same when they no longer have their proper quality, but only that they have the same name. The proof that the state is a creation of nature and prior to the individual is that the individual, when isolated, is not self-sufficing; and therefore he is like a part in relation to the whole. But he who is unable to live in society, or who has no need because he is sufficient for himself, must be either a beast or a god: he is no part of a state. A social instinct is implanted in all men by nature, and yet he who first founded the state was the greatest of benefactors. For man, when perfected, is the best of animals, but, when separated from law and justice, he is the worst of all; since armed injustice is the more dangerous, and he is equipped at birth with arms, meant to be used by intelligence and virtue, which he may use for the worst ends. Wherefore, if he have not virtue, he is the most unholy and the most savage of animals, and the most full of lust and gluttony. But justice is the bond of men in states, for the administration of justice, which is the determination of what is just,[7] is the principle of order in political society.

---

[4] Il. ix. 63.

[5] Cp. 1256^b 20.

[6] Cp. vii. 1332^b 5.

* [Note that Aristotle uses the term "prior" not to designate a time relationship but rather to designate a relationship of value or dependence.]

[7] Cp. N. Eth. v. 1134^a 31.

IV *

... Now the laws in their enactments on all subjects aim at the common advantage either of all or of the best or of those who hold power, or something of the sort; so that in one sense we call those acts just that tend to produce and preserve happiness and its components for the political society. And the law bids us do both the acts of a brave man (*e.g.* not to desert our post nor take to flight nor throw away our arms), and those of a temperate man (*e.g.* not to commit adultery nor to gratify one's lust), and those of a good tempered man (*e.g.* not to strike another nor to speak evil), and similarly with regard to the other virtues and forms of wickedness, commanding some acts and forbidding others; and the rightly-framed law does this rightly, and the hastily conceived one less well.

V †

Now we have previously stated how the reciprocal is related to the just;[10] but we must not forget that what we are looking for is not only what is just without qualification but also political justice. This is found among men who share their life with a view to self-sufficiency, men who are free and either proportionately or arithmetically equal, so that between those who do not fulfil this condition there is no political justice but justice in a special sense and by analogy. For justice exists only between men whose material relations are governed by law; and law exists for men between whom there is injustice; for legal justice is the discrimination of the just and the unjust. And between men between whom there is injustice there is also unjust action (though there is not injustice between all between whom there is unjust action), and this is assigning too much to oneself of things good in themselves and too little of things evil in themselves. This is why we do not allow a *man* to rule, but *rational principle*, because a man behaves thus in his own interests and becomes a tyrant. The magistrate on the other hand is the guardian of justice, and, if of justice, then of equality also. And since he is assumed to have no more that his share, if he is just (for he does not assign to himself more of what is good in itself, unless such a share is proportional to his merits—so that it is for others that he labours, and it is for this reason that men, as we stated previously,[11] say that justice is "another's good"), therefore a reward must be given him, and this is honour and

---

* [Nichomachean Ethics V, 1; McKeon, p. 1003.]

† [Nichomachean Ethics V, 6; McKeon, p. 1013. What light, if any, does the distinction drawn in this and the succeeding passage between a "government of men" and "a government of laws" throw upon contemporary issues of administrative law, administrative discretion, and dictatorship?]

[10] 1132b 21-1133b 28.

[11] 1130a 3.

privilege; but those for whom such things are not enough become tyrants.

VI *

At this place in the discussion there impends the inquiry respecting the king who acts solely according to his own will; he has now to be considered. The so-called limited monarchy, or kingship according to law, as I have already remarked,[65] is not a distinct form of government, for under all governments, as, for example, in a democracy or aristocracy, there may be a general holding office for life, and one person is often made supreme over the administration of a state. . . . Now, absolute monarchy, or the arbitrary rule of a sovereign over all the citizens, in a city which consists of equals, is thought by some to be quite contrary to nature; it is argued that those who are by nature equals must have the same natural right and worth, and that for unequals to have an equal share, or for equals to have an unequal share, in the offices of state, is as bad as for different bodily constitutions to have the same food and clothing. Wherefore it is thought to be just that among equals every one be ruled as well as rule, and therefore that all should have their turn. We thus arrive at law; for an order of succession implies law. And the rule of the law, it is argued, is preferable to that of any individual.† On the same principle, even if it be better for certain individuals to govern, they should be made only guardians and ministers of the law. For magistrates there must be—this is admitted; but then men say that to give authority to any one man when all are equal is unjust. Nay, there may indeed be cases which the law seems unable to de-

---

* [Politics, I, 5; McKeon, p. 1201. Consider the development of the idea of law as "reason unaffected by desire" in the succeeding materials of this chapter.]

[65] 1286ª 2.

† [Aristotle, of course, was familiar with Plato's thesis on this point: "When there has been a contest for power, those who gain the upper hand so entirely monopolize the government, as to refuse all share to the defeated party and their descendants—they live watching one another, the ruling class being in perpetual fear that some one who has a recollection of former wrongs will come into power and rise up against them. Now, according to our view, such governments are not politics at all, nor are laws right which are passed for the good of particular classes and not for the good of the whole state. States which have such laws are not politics but parties, and their notions of justice are simply unmeaning . . . We must not entrust the government in your state to any one because he is rich, or because he possesses any other advantage, such as strength, or stature, or again birth; but he who is most obedient to the laws of the state, he shall win the palm; and to him who is victorious in the first degree shall be given the highest office and chief ministry of the gods; and the second to him who bears the second palm; and on a similar principle shall the other offices be assigned to those who come next in order. And when I call the rulers servants or ministers of the law, I give them this name not for the sake of novelty, but because I certainly believe that upon such service or ministry depends the well- or ill-being of the state. For that state in which the law is subject and has no authority, I perceive to be on the highway to ruin; but I see that the state in which the law is above the rulers, and the rulers are the inferiors of the law, has salvation, and every blessing which the Gods can confer." Plato, Laws, IV.]

termine, but in such cases can a man? Nay, it will be replied, the law trains officers for this express purpose, and appoints them to determine matters which are left undecided by it, to the best of their judgment. Further, it permits them to make any amendment of the existing laws which experience suggests. Therefore he who bids the law rule may be deemed to bid God and Reason alone rule, but he who bids man rule adds an element of the beast; for desire is a wild beast, and passion perverts the minds of rulers, even when they are the best of men. The law is reason * unaffected by desire.

CICERO, DE LEGIBUS †

[Marcus.] So it is that the most learned men have thought it best to begin with law, and it would seem that they are right, if, as they define law, it is the highest reason, implanted in nature, which commands what ought to be done and forbids the opposite. This reason, when firmly fixed and fully developed in the human mind, is law. And so they believe that law is practical wisdom, whose natural function it is to command right conduct and forbid wrongdoing. They think that this quality has derived its name in Greek from the idea of granting to every man his own, and in our language I believe it has been named from the idea of choosing. For as they have attributed the idea of fairness to the word law, so we have given it that of choice, though both ideas properly belong to law. Now if this is correct, as I think it to be in general, then the origin of justice is to be found in law, for law is a natural force; it is the mind and reason of the intelligent man, the standard by which justice (*Ius*) and injustice are measured. But since our whole discussion has to do with the reasoning of the populace, it will sometimes be necessary to speak in the popular manner, and give the name of law to that which in written form decrees whatever it wishes, either by command or prohibition. For such is the crowd's definition of law. But in determining what justice is, let us begin with that supreme law which had its origin ages before any written law existed or any state at all had been established. [Book I, VI.]

· · · · ·

---

* [Note the distinction drawn by St. Thomas (p. 377) between pure reason and practical reason. Since Aristotle clearly includes human purposes and the achievement of happiness in the idea of (practical) reason, the distinction between "desire" (as an individual emotion) and "purpose" (as a social or long-range objective) should not be overlooked.]

† [*Marcus Tullius Cicero* (106–43 B.C.) achieved fame as lawyer, statesman, and orator. One of Cicero's numerous works, the treatise entitled *De Legibus*, an imitation of Plato's *Laws*, is drawn largely from the doctrines of Chrysippus, the Greek stoic of the third century B.C. An illuminating and sympathetic account of Cicero's legal philosophy is given in Cairns, *Legal Philosophy from Plato to Hegel* (1949).]

M. What of the many deadly, the many pestilential statutes which are imposed on peoples? These no more deserve to be called laws than the rules a band of robbers might pass in their assembly. For if ignorant and unskilful men have prescribed deadly poisons instead of healing drugs, these cannot possibly be called physicians' prescriptions; neither in a nation can anything be called law, even though the nation, in spite of its being a ruinous regulation, has accepted it. Therefore law is the distinction between things just and unjust, made in agreement with that primal and most ancient of all things, nature; and in conformity to nature's standard are framed those human laws which inflict punishment upon the wicked but defend and protect the good. [Book II, V.]

ST. THOMAS AQUINAS, SUMMA THEOLOGICA *

Question 90. Concerning Laws

My reply is: It must be said that law is a rule and measure of acts, whereby any one is induced to act or is restrained from acting: for *lex* (law) is derived from *ligare* (to bind) because it binds one to act. Now the rule and measure of human acts is the reason, which is the first principle of human acts, as is evident from what has been stated above; since it belongs to the reason to direct towards the end, "which is the first principle in all matters of action," according to the Philosopher (*Phys.* ii.). Now that which is the principle in any genus, is the measure and rule of that genus: for instance, unity in the genus of numbers, and primary movement in the genus of movements. Consequently it follows that law is something pertaining to reason.

.   .   .   .   .

It must be said that reason has its power of moving from the will, as stated above: for it is because one wills the end, that the reason issues its commands concerning things that lead to the end. But in order that the volition of what is commanded may have the nature of law, it needs to be in accord with some rule of reason. And in this sense is to be understood the saying that the will of the sovereign has the force of law; otherwise the sovereign's will would be wickedness rather than law.

.   .   .   .   .

---

* [Part II, First Part (*Prima Secundae*), Question 90.
   The *Summa Theologica* (*c.* 1274) of *St. Thomas Aquinas* (1225 or 1226–1274) is regarded as the most comprehensive statement of scholastic philosophy, and is still considered authoritative by a large circle of neo-Thomists today. St. Thomas, a member of the Dominican order, was a student of the distinguished Aristotelian scholar Albertus Magnus at Cologne. His two major works, the *Summa Theologica* and the much shorter *Summa Contra Gentiles,* represent a combination of Aristotelian philosophy and science with Christian ethics and theology. A good survey of the Thomistic view of law will be found in the chapter on Thomas Aquinas in Cairns, *Legal Philosophy from Plato to Hegel* (1949).]

My reply is: It must be said that, as stated above, the law belongs to that which is a principle of human acts, because it is their rule and measure. Now as reason is a principle of human acts, so in reason itself there is something which is the principle in respect of all the rest: wherefore to this principle chiefly and mainly law must needs be referred. . . . Now the first principle in practical matters, which are the object of practical reason, is the final end: and the final end of human life is happiness or bliss, as stated above. Consequently the law must needs regard principally the relationship to happiness. Moreover, since every part is related to the whole, as imperfect to perfect; and since one man is a part of the perfect community, the law must needs regard properly the relationship to the common happiness. Wherefore the Philosopher, in the above definition of legal matters mentions both happiness and the political community: for he says (*Ethic*, v. 1) that we call those legal matters *just, which are adapted to produce and preserve happiness and its parts for the political community:* since the state is a perfect community, as is said in *Polit*. i. 1.

· · · · ·

It must be said that actions are always concerned with particular matters: but those particular matters are referable to the common good, not as to a common genus or species, but as to a common final cause, according as the common good is said to be the common end.

It must be said that just as nothing stands firm with regard to the speculative reason except that which is traced back to the first indemonstrable principles, so nothing stands firm with regard to the practical reason [*ratio practica*], unless it be directed to the final end which is the common good: and whatever stands to reason in this sense, has the reason that pertains to law.

· · · · ·

My reply is: It must be said that a law, properly speaking, regards first and foremost the relationship to the common good. Now to determine anything to the common good, belongs either to the whole people, or to someone who is the representative of the whole people. And therefore the making of law belongs either to the whole people or to a public personage who has care of the whole people: since in all other matters the relating of anything to an end is the function of the person whose end is involved.

· · · · ·

. . . Thus from the four preceding articles, the definition of law may be gathered; and it is nothing else than an ordinance of reason for the common good, made and promulgated by him who has care of the community.

ST. GERMAIN, A DOCTOR AND A STUDENT; OR DIALOGUES BETWEEN A DOCTOR OF DIVINITY AND A STUDENT IN THE LAWS OF ENGLAND *

Chapter II. Of the law of reason, the which by doctors is called the law of nature of reasonable creatures

... The law of nature specially considered: which is also called the law of reason, pertaineth only to creatures reasonable, that is, man, which is created to the image of God.

And this law ought to be kept as well among Jews and Gentiles, as among Christian men: and this law is alway good and righteous, stirring and inclining a man to good, and abhorring evil. And as to the ordering of the deeds of man, it is preferred before the law of God, and it is written in the heart of every man, teaching him what is to be done, and what is to be fled; and because it is written in the heart, therefore it may not be put away, ne it is never changeable by no diversity of place, ne time: and therefore against this law, prescription, statute nor custom may not prevail: and if any be brought in against it, they be not prescriptions, statutes nor customs, but things void and against justice. And all other laws, as well the laws of God as to the acts of men, as other, be grounded thereupon. [P. 4.]

·   ·   ·   ·   ·

Doct. Though the law of reason may not be changed, nor wholly put away; nevertheless, before the law written, it was greatly lett and blinded by evil customs, and by many sins of the people, beside our original sin; insomuch that it might hardly be discerned what was righteous, and what was unrighteous, and what was good, and what evil. Wherefore it is necessary, for the good order of the people, to have many things added to the law of reason, as well by the church as by secular princes, according to the manners of the country and of the people where such additions should be exercised. [P. 4.]

Chapter V. Of the first ground of the law of England

[*Stud.*] The first ground of the law of England is the *law of reason,* whereof thou hast treated before in the second chapter, the which is kept in this realm, as it is in all other realms, and as of necessity it must needs be, (as thou hast said before).

---

* [*A Doctor and a Student; or Dialogues Between a Doctor of Divinity and a Student in the Laws of England,* 1607 ed. (first published in 1518, ed. W. Muchall), written by *Christopher St. Germain* (1460-1540), embodies an exchange of views between the academic legal world, which at the time concerned itself only with canon law and other forms of Roman law, and the non-academic and nativist world of legal practice, which revolved about the common law courts and the Inns of Court.]

Doct. But I would know what is called the *law of nature* after the laws of England.

Stud. It is not used among them that be learned in the laws of England to reason what thing is commanded or prohibited by the law of nature, and what not, but all the reasoning in that behalf is under this manner. As when any thing is grounded upon the law of nature, they say, that reason will that such a thing be done; and if it be prohibited by the law of nature, they say it is against reason, or that reason will not suffer that to be done. [Pp. 8-9.]

COKE, CONFERENCE BETWEEN KING JAMES I AND THE JUDGES OF ENGLAND *

Note, upon Sunday the 10th of November in this same term, the King, upon complaint made to him by Bancroft, Archbishop of Canterbury, concerning prohibitions, the King was informed, that when the question was made of what matters the ecclesiastical Judges have cognizance, either upon the exposition of the statutes concerning tithes, or any other thing ecclesiastical, or upon the statute 1 El. concerning the high commission, or in any other case in which there is not express authority in law, the King himself may decide it in his royal person; and that the Judges are but the delegates of the King, and that the King may take what causes he shall please to determine, from the determination of the Judges, and may determine them himself. And the Archbishop said, that this was clear in divinity, that such authority belongs to the King by the word of God in the Scripture. To which it was answered by me, in the presence, and with the clear consent of all the Judges of England, and Barons of the Exchequer, that the King in his own person cannot adjudge any case, either criminal, as treason, felony, &c. or betwixt party and party, concerning his inheritance, chattels, or goods, &c. but this ought to be determined and adjudged in some court of justice, according to the law and custom of England; and always judgments are given, *ideo consideratum est per curiam*, so that the Court gives the judgment: and the King hath his Court, *viz.* in the upper house of Parliament, in which he with his Lords is the supreme Judge over

---

* [6 Coke's *Reports* 63 (1612).

Coke's report of the *Conference Between King James I and the Judges of England in 1612* must be read as an interested party's version of the argument. Sir Edward Coke (1552–1634), upon his appointment to the King's Bench in 1606, entered upon a bitter struggle over jurisdiction with various other courts, as a result of which his judicial career was terminated in 1616. It was in the midst of that struggle that he participated in the conference reported in the text.

Lord Coke's most important work is the four-volume treatise published under the traditional Roman title for a comprehensive legal text-book, *Institutes.*

Prior to his judicial career, Coke studied at Cambridge and at the Inner Temple and, after a period of private practice, served as Attorney General of England. Following his removal from the bench, Coke served in Parliament, where his defense of the powers of Parliament against the crown resulted in his imprisonment for a time.]

all other Judges; for if error be in the Common Pleas, that may be reversed in the King's Bench: and if the Court of King's Bench err, that may be reversed in the upper house of Parliament, by the King, with the assent of the Lords spiritual and temporal, without the Commons: and in this respect the King is called the Chief Justice, 20 H. 7.7 a. by Brudnell: and it appears in our books, that the King may sit in the Star-chamber; but this was to consult with the Justices, upon certain questions proposed to them, and not *in judicio:* so in the King's Bench he may sit, but the Court gives the judgment: and it is commonly said in our books, that the King is always present in Court in the judgment of law; and upon this he cannot be nonsuit: but the judgments are always given *per curiam;* and the Judges are sworn to execute justice according to law and the custom of England. And it appears by the act of Parliament of 2 Ed. 3. cap. 9. 2 Ed. 3. cap. 1. that neither by the great seal, nor by the little seal, justice shall be delayed; *ergo,* the King cannot take any cause out of any of his Courts, and give judgment upon it himself, but in his own cause he may stay it, as it doth appear 11 H.4. 8. And the Judges informed the King, that no King after the Conquest assumed to himself to give any judgment in any cause whatsoever which concerned the administration of justice within this realm, but these were solely determined in the courts of justice: and the King cannot arrest any man, as the book is in 1 H.7. 4. for the party cannot have remedy against the King; so if the King give any judgment, what remedy can the party have.

．　　．　　．　　．　　．

... [T]hen the King said, that he thought the law was founded upon reason, and that he and others had reason, as well as the judges: to which it was answered by me, that true it was, that God had endowed his Majesty with excellent science, and great endowments of nature; but His Majesty was not learned in the laws of his realm of England, and causes which concern the life, or inheritance, or goods, or fortunes of his subjects, are not to be decided by natural reason but by the artificial reason and judgment of law, which law is an art which requires long study and experience, before that a man can attain to the cognizance of it: and that the law was the golden met-wand and measure to try the causes of the subjects; and which protected his Majesty in safety and peace: with which the King was greatly offended, and said, that then he should be under the law, which was treason to affirm, as he said; to which I said, that Bracton saith, *quod Rex non debet esse sub homine, sed sub Deo et lege.*

HOBBES, LEVIATHAN *

. . . . .

To this warre of every man against every man, this also is consequent; that nothing can be Unjust. The notions of Right and Wrong, Justice and Injustice have there no place. Where there is no common Power, there is no Law; where no Law, no Injustice. Force, and Fraud, are in warre, the two Cardinall vertues. Justice, and Injustice are none of the Faculties neither of the Body, nor Mind. If they were, they might be in a man that were alone in the world, as well as his Senses, and Passions. They are Qualities, that relate to men in Society, not in Solitude. It is consequent also to the same condition, that there be no Propriety, no Dominion, no *Mine* and *Thine* distinct; but onely that to be every mans, that he can get; and for so long, as he can keep it. And thus much for the ill condition, which man be meer Nature is actually placed in; though with a possibility to come out of it, consisting partly in the Passions, partly in his Reason.

The Passions that encline men to Peace, are Feare of Death; Desire of such things as are necessary to commodious living; and a hope by their Industry to obtain them. And Reason suggesteth convenient Articles of Peace, upon which men may be drawn to agreement. These Articles, are they, which otherwise are called the Lawes of Nature. . . .

From that law of Nature, by which we are obliged to transferre to another, such Rights, as being retained, hinder the peace of Mankind, there followeth a Third; which is this, *That men performe their Covenants made;* without which, Covenants are in vain, and but Empty words; and

---

* [This was first published in 1651. The following text and page numbering follow generally the edition of A. R. Waller.

The *Leviathan* of *Thomas Hobbes* (1588–1679) represents the first comprehensive application of the realistic approach to the field of law. Locke, in part, and, to a much greater degree, Bentham, Austin, Holmes, Gray, and the later American realists have pursued and developed the Hobbesian approach. Hobbes' views on the evils of civil strife in the absence of generally acknowledged authority were based upon considerable personal experience.

In 1640, alarmed at political developments in England, Hobbes fled to France where he remained in the company of English refugee aristocrats, serving even as tutor to the future Charles II for two years. *De Cive* (Concerning the State), although published in 1647, was actually written ten years before the appearance of the *Leviathan*, Hobbes' most famous work. The latter book, having aroused the opposition of the French because of its attacks on the Catholic Church, forced Hobbes to return to London to make what peace he could with Cromwell. In spite of his notoriety as a materialist and suspected atheist, Hobbes was awarded a pension after the Restoration, although in fact it was never paid. After an investigation of atheistic writings by a committee of the House of Commons, Hobbes was forced to publish his works abroad in Amsterdam, a great centre of publishing in the 17th and 18th centuries because of its tradition of freedom of the press. There appeared the *Behemoth*, a less controversial work than the *Leviathan*, in 1668 and twenty years later, a century after Hobbes' birth but only nine after his death, the first collected edition appeared. Cairns' *Legal Philosophy from Plato to Hegel* contains an instructive chapter on Hobbes' legal views.]

the Right of all men to all things remaining, wee are still in the condition of Warre.

And in this law of Nature, consisteth the fountain and Originall of JUSTICE. For where no Covenant hath preceeded, there hath no Right been transferred, and every man has right to every thing; and consequently, no action can be Unjust. But when a Covenant is made, then to break it is *Unjust:* And the definition of INJUSTICE, is no other than *the not Performance of Covenant.* And whatsoever is not Unjust, is *Just.*

But because Covenants of mutuall trust, where there is a feare of not performance on either part (as hath been said in the former Chapter,) are invalid; though the Originall of Justice be the making of Covenants; yet Injustice actually there can be none, till the cause of such feare be taken away; which while men are in the naturall condition of Warre, cannot be done. Therefore before the names of Just, and Unjust can have place, there must be some coercive Power, to compell men equally to the performance of their Covenants, by the terrour of some punishment, greater than the benefit they expect by the breach of their Covenant; and to make good that propriety, which by mutuall contract men acquire, in recompense of the universall Right thay abandon: and such power there is none before the erection of a Common-wealth. And this is also to be gathered out of the ordinary definition of Justice in the Schooles: For they say, that *Justice is the constant Will of giving to every man his own.* And therefore where there is no *Own,* that is, no Propriety, there is no Injustice; and where there is no coercive power erected, that is, where there is no Common-wealth, there is no Propriety; all men having Right to all things: Therefore where there is no Common-wealth, there nothing is Unjust. So that the nature of Justice, consisteth in keeping of valid Covenants: but the Validity of Covenants begins not but with the Constitution of a Civill Power, sufficient to compell men to keep them: And then it is also that Propriety begins. . . .

. . . In a condition of Warre, wherein every man to every man, for want of a common Power to keep them all in awe, is an Enemy, there is no man can hope by his own strength, or wit, to defend himselfe from destruction, without the help of Confederates; where every one expects the same defence by the Confederation, that any one else does: and therefore he which declares he thinks it reason to deceive those that help him, can in reason expect no other means of safety, than what can be had from his own single Power. He therefore that breaketh his Covenant, and consequently declareth that he thinks he may with reason do so, cannot be received into any Society, that unite themselves for Peace and Defense, but by the errour of them that receive him; nor when he is received, be retayned in it, without seeing the danger of their errour; which errours a man cannot reasonably reckon upon as the means of his security: and therefore if he be left, or cast out of Society, he perisheth; and if he live in Society, it is by the errours of other men, which he could not foresee, nor reckon upon; and consequently against the reason of his preservation; and so, as all men that contribute not to his destruction, forbear him onely out of ignorance of what is good for themselves. [Pp. 97-100.]

.   .   .   .   .

And consequently all men agree on this, that Peace is Good, and therefore also the way, or means of Peace, which (as I have shewed before) are *Justice, Gratitude, Modesty, Equity, Mercy* & the rest of the Laws of Nature, are good; that is to say, *Morall Vertues;* and their contrarie Vices, Evill. Now the science of Vertue and Vice, is Morall Philosophie; and therefore the true Doctrine of the Lawes of Nature, is the true Morall Philosophie. But the Writers of Morall Philosophie, though they acknowledge the same Vertues and Vices; Yet not seeing wherein consisted their Goodnesse; nor that they come to be praised, as the meanes of peaceable, sociable, and comfortable living; place them in a mediocrity of passions: as if not the Cause, but the Degree of daring, made Fortitude; or not the cause, but the Quantity of a gift, made Liberality.

These dictates of Reason, men used to call by the name of Lawes; but improperly: for they are but Conclusions, or Theoremes concerning what conduceth to the conservation and defence of themselves; whereas Law, properly is the word of him, that by right hath command over others. But yet if we consider the same Theoremes, as delivered in the word of God, that by right commandeth all things; then are they properly called Lawes. [Pp. 109, 110.]

BLACKSTONE, COMMENTARIES *

Municipal law, thus understood, is properly defined to be "a rule of civil conduct prescribed by the supreme power in a state, commanding what is right and prohibiting what is wrong." Let us endeavor to explain its several properties as they arise out of this definition. And, first, it is a

---

* [I, 44-46 (1758).

Educated at the Charterhouse and Oxford, *Sir William Blackstone* (1723–1780) entered the Middle Temple in 1741, being called to the bar in 1746. Meanwhile in 1744 he had been elected a fellow of All Souls College, so that from that year until 1753, Blackstone divided his time between his practice in London and his academic life.

His lectures, later embodied in his famous *Commentaries on the Laws of England,* were probably not intended for publication. But many pirated "editions" having been published, Blackstone felt constrained to issue a correct version of the *Commentaries,* which appeared from 1765 through 1769.

Having attained great fame through his writings, Blackstone returned to London where, in addition to a successful practice, he also enjoyed a political career, and finally served a scant decade as a judge.

Probably no other English legal treatise reigned for so long a time as an authoritative exposition of Anglo-American jurisprudence as did Blackstone's *Commentaries,* notwithstanding that they were intended by their author as a guide for laymen, rather than as an authoritative presentation of the laws of England in technically accurate and detailed form. For many American judges on the bench today the reading of Blackstone was the sum and substance of a legal education.]

rule: not a transient sudden order from a superior to or concerning a particular person; but something permanent, uniform, and universal. Therefore a particular act of the legislature to confiscate the goods of Titius or to attaint him of high treason, does not enter into the idea of a municipal law: for the operation of this act is spent upon Titius only, and has no relation to the community in general; it is rather a sentence than a law. But an act to declare that the crime of which Titius is accused shall be deemed high treason; this has permanency, uniformity, and universality, and therefore is properly a rule. It is also called a rule, to distinguish it from advice or counsel, which we are at liberty to follow or not, as we see proper, and to judge upon the reasonableness or unreasonableness of the thing advised; whereas our obedience to the law depends not upon our approbation, but upon the maker's will. Counsel is only a matter of persuasion, law is matter of injunction; counsel acts only upon the willing, law upon the unwilling also.

It is also called a rule to distinguish it from a compact or agreement; for a compact is a promise proceeding from us, law is a command directed to us. The language of a compact is, "I will, or will not, do this"; that of a law is, "thou shalt, or shalt not, do it." It is true there is an obligation which a compact carries with it, equal in point of conscience to that of a law; but then the original of the obligation is different. In compacts we ourselves determine and promise what shall be done, before we are obliged to do it; in laws, we are obliged to act without ourselves determining or promising anything at all. Upon these accounts law is defined to be "a rule."

Municipal law is also "a rule of civil conduct." This distinguishes municipal law from the natural, or revealed; the former of which is the rule of moral conduct, and the latter not only the rule of moral conduct, but also the rule of faith. These regard man as a creature, and point out his duty to God, to himself, and to his neighbor, considered in the light of an individual. But municipal or civil law regards him also as a citizen, and bound to other duties towards his neighbor than those of mere nature and religion: duties which he has engaged in by enjoying the benefits of the common union; and which amount to no more than that he do contribute, on his part, to the subsistence and the peace of the society.

It is likewise "a rule prescribed." Because a bare resolution, confined in the breast of the legislator, without manifesting itself by some external sign, can never be properly a law. It is requisite that this resolution be notified to the people who are to obey it. But the manner in which this notification is to be made, is matter of very great indifference. It may be notified by universal tradition and long practice, which supposes a previous publication, as is the case of the common law of England. It may be notified viva voce, by officers appointed for that purpose, as is done with regard to proclamations, and such acts of parliament as are appointed to be publicly read in churches and other assemblies. It may lastly be notified by writing, printing, or the like; which is the general course taken with all our acts of parliament.... But when this rule is in the usual manner notified, or prescribed, it is then the subject's business to be thoroughly acquainted therewith; for if ignorance of what he might know were admitted as a legitimate excuse, the laws would be of no effect, but might always be eluded with impunity.

But farther: municipal law is "a rule of civil conduct prescribed by the supreme power in a state." For legislature, as was before observed, is the greatest act of superiority that can be exercised by one being over another. Wherefore it is requisite to the very essence of a law, that it be made by the supreme power. Sovereignty and legislature are indeed convertible terms; one can not subsist without the other.

From what has been advanced, the truth of the former branch of our definition, is (I trust) sufficiently evident; that *"municipal law is a rule of civil conduct prescribed by the supreme power in a state."* I proceed now to the latter branch of it; that it is a rule so prescribed, "commanding what is right, and prohibiting what is wrong."

Now in order to do this completely, it is first of all necessary that the boundaries of right and wrong be established and ascertained by law. And when this is once done, it will follow of course that it is likewise the business of the law, considered as a rule of civil conduct to enforce these rights, and to restrain or redress these wrongs.

SAVIGNY, OF THE VOCATION OF OUR AGE FOR LEGISLATION AND JURISPRUDENCE *

Preface to the Second Edition

The first edition of the present work appeared in 1814, at a time which can never be forgotten by any, who with full consciousness, have lived

---

* [The first edition of Friedrich Carl von Savigny's famous tract against codification, *Vom Beruf unsrer Zeit für Gesetzgebung und Rechtswissenschaft,* was published in 1814. It was written in reply to a pamphlet by Thibaut, *Über die Nothwendigkeit eines allgemeinen bürgerlichen Rechts für Deutschland* (1814). The translation here given follows generally the translation by Hayward (1831).

Friedrich Carl von Savigny (1779–1861) published his first treatise, *Das Recht des Besitzes* (*The Law of Possession*) in 1803. In 1810 Savigny became Professor of Roman Law at the new University of Berlin, where he also served as tutor to the Crown Prince and lectured on government. His protest against the demand for codification in 1814 served as a model for similar protests in other lands against the movement for codification to which Bentham had given great impetus. In 1815 the first volume of Savigny's *Geschichte des römischen Rechts im Mittelalter* came out; the final volume in 1831. Savigny's famous work on the contemporary Roman law, *System des heutigen römischen Rechts* (1840–1849, 8 volumes) was supplemented in 1853 by a treatise on Contracts (*Das Obligationrecht*). Meanwhile Savigny had served from 1842 to 1848 as head of the Prussian legal system, which afforded the opportunity of recasting the law of commercial paper and the divorce statutes. After 1848 Savigny devoted himself entirely to theoretical jurisprudence.]

through it. For years the fetters which bound our country to the arbitrary rule of a foreigner had been drawing tighter and tighter, and it was plain that, when the designs of the oppressor came to be fully developed, our destiny must end in the annihilation of our nationality. The momentous events by which the foreign yoke was broken, averted this hard lot from our country; and the feeling of grateful joy, universally excited by this deliverance from the greatest of all dangers, might well be cherished as a sacred recollection by the whole nation. . . .

. . . . .

II. Origin of Positive Law

We first inquire of history, how law has actually developed amongst nations of the nobler races; the question—What may be good, or necessary, or, on the contrary, censurable herein,—will be not at all prejudiced by this method of proceeding.

In the earliest times to which authentic history extends, the law will be found to have already attained a fixed character, peculiar to the people, like their language, manners and constitutions. Nay, these phenomena have no separate existence, they are but the particular faculties and tendencies of an individual people, inseparably united in nature, and only wearing the semblance of distinct attributes to our view. That which binds them into one whole is the common conviction of the people, the kindred consciousness of an inward necessity, excluding all notion of an accidental and arbitrary origin.

In modern times the view has come to prevail that all life was at first of an animal character, passing through evolution step by step to a tolerable existence, until at length the height on which we now stand has been attained. . . .

. . . . .

But this organic connection of law with the being and character of the people, is also manifested in the progress of the times; and here, again, it may be compared with language. For law, as for language, there is no moment of absolute rest; it is subject to the same movement and development as every other popular tendency; and this very development remains under the same law of inward necessity, as in its earliest stages. Law grows with the growth, and strengthens with the strength of the people, and finally dies away as the nation loses its nationality.

. . . . .

. . . With the progress of civilization, national tendencies become more and more distinct, and what otherwise would have remained common, becomes appropriated to particular classes. The jurists now become more and more a distinct class of the kind. Law perfects its language, takes a scientific direction, and, as formerly it existed in the consciousness of the community, it now devolves upon the jurists, who thus, in this respect, represent the community.

.   .   .   .   .

... The sum, therefore, of this view is, that all law is originally formed in the manner in which, in ordinary but not quite correct language, customary law is said to have been formed: *i.e.* that it is first developed by custom and popular faith, next by jurisprudence,—everywhere, therefore, by internal silently-operating powers, not by the arbitrary will of a law-giver.

.   .   .   .   .

III. Laws and Law Books

Legislation, properly so called, not infrequently exercises an influence upon particular portions of the law; but the causes of this influence vary greatly. In the first place, the legislator, in altering the existing law, may be influenced by high political purposes. When, in our time, unprofessional men speak of the necessity of new legislation, they commonly mean only that of which the settlement of the rights of land-owners is one of the most striking examples.[1] The history of the Roman law, also, supplies examples of this kind,—a few in the free times of the republic,—the important *Lex Julia et Papia Poppaea,* in the time of Augustus,—and a great number since the Christian emperors. That enactments of this kind easily become a baneful corruption of the law, and that they should be most sparingly employed, must strike any one who consults history.

.   .   .   .   .

Putting together what has been said above concerning the requisites of a really good code, it is clear that very few ages will be found qualified for it. Young nations, it is true, have the clearest perception of their law, but their codes are defective in language and logical skill, and they are generally incapable of expressing what is best, so that they frequently produce no individual image, whilst their matter is in the highest degree individual. The laws of the middle ages, already quoted, are examples of this; and had we the twelve tables complete before us, we should probably find something of the sort, only in a less degree. In declining ages, on the other hand, almost everything is wanting—knowledge of the matter, as well as language. There thus remains only a middle period; that which (as regards the law, although not necessarily in any other respect,) may be accounted the summit of civilization. But such an age has no need of a code for itself: it would merely compose one for a succeeding and less fortunate age, as we lay up provisions for winter. But an age is seldom disposed to be so provident for children and grandchildren.

---

[1] The author, I believe, alludes to the law of 1810, enacting that all hereditary tenants of lands in Prussia might, by giving up a certain proportion of them to the landlord, become free proprietors of the rest.—Transl.

SAVIGNY, SYSTEM OF THE MODERN ROMAN LAW *
§7. The General Origin of Law

What then are the origins of law in general, or where are the sources of law to be found?

As to this, one might wish to maintain that law arises in quite diverse ways, according to the influence of circumstances, or even according to the will, reflection and wisdom of human beings. But this assumption is contradicted by the indubitable fact that wherever a legal relationship comes into question and into consciousness, there is a rule for it already at hand, so that it is neither necessary nor possible to invent such a rule then for the first time. In consideration of this property of law in general according to which, in every given situation in which it can be sought for, it already has a given actual existence, we call it *positive* law.

If we inquire further for the subject in which and for which this positive law has its existence, we find this to be the people. It is in the common consciousness of the people that the positive law lives, and we have to call this therefore Folk-Law (*Volksrecht*). But one is not to interpret this as though it were the individual members of a people through whose arbitrary will the law is brought forth; for this will of individuals could perhaps accidentally choose this law, but might instead and more probably would, choose something diversified and heterogeneous. Rather it is the spirit of a people (*Volksgeist*) living and working alike in all individuals that brings forth the positive law, which is therefore necessarily and not merely by accident one and the same law to the consciousness of every individual. Inasmuch as we thus postulate an invisible origin of positive law, we must accordingly renounce every docmentary evidence of this origin. But this deficiency in our view of that origin is common to every other view, since we find in all peoples which have ever entered the bounds of documentary history a positive law already existent, whose primitive production must therefore lie outside of those bounds. But as to evidence of another sort, fitted to the nature of the object studied, there is no lack. One such form of evidence is found in the general, uniform recognition of positive law, and in the feeling of inner necessity by which the representation of this law is accompanied. This feeling expresses itself most definitely in the ancient assertion of a divine origin of law or of statutes (*Gesetze*), for a more decisive antithesis to the origin of law through accident or arbitrary human will cannot be conceived. A second form of evidence is found in the analogy of other characteristics of peoples which equally have an invisible origin reaching back beyond documentary history, as for instance the customs of social life, but above all, language. In this there is found the same independence from accident and free choice of individuals,

---

* [(1840), Vol. I, Chap. 2. The translation follows generally Wm. Holloway, 1867 ed.]

and so the same production out of the activity of the spirit of the people working uniformly in all individuals; in language, however, because of its sensuous nature, this whole is more plain and unmistakable than it is in law. Indeed the individual nature of a single people is determined and recognized only through these common tendencies and activities, among which language, as the most evident, takes first place.

The form, however, in which law lives in the common consciousness of a people is not that of abstract rules, but rather the living intuition of legal institutions in their organic connection, so that where the necessity arises of having rules known in their logical form these must be developed by an artificial process out of that total intuition. This form exhibits itself in symbolic acts, which present pictorially the essence of legal relations and in which the basic law of a people usually expresses itself more clearly and fundamentally than in particular rules of law.

On this view of the origin of positive law one would next turn to examine the past life of a people. If we consider its influence upon law, we must recognize in it primarily a fortifying power; the longer the conviction of law lives in a people, the deeper becomes its roots. Further, law is developed through usage and what was originally present merely in the germ will through application come in determinate form into consciousness. But change of law is also produced in this manner. For just as in the life of the individual man no moment of complete standstill is found, but on the contrary an ever-present organic development, so it is in the life of peoples, and in every single element of which this common life consists. So we find in language continuous development and evolution and the same is true of law. And even this further development stands under the same law of generation out of inner force and necessity, independent of accident and individual choice, as does the primitive origin. But the people experiences in this natural process of evolution not simply change in general, but rather change according to a definite, regular succession of stages, and in these stages every one has his peculiar relation to the particular utterance of the spirit of the people through which law is produced. Most freely and powerfully does this appear in the youth of a people, when the national coherence is more intimate and the awareness of it more general and where it is less obscured by diversity of individual training. But in the same measure in which the education of individuals becomes diversified and of predominating importance, and in which arises a sharper differentiation of activities, of knowledge, and of stations determined thereby, generation of law, which rests upon the community of consciousness, becomes more difficult; indeed it would finally vanish almost entirely if it did not produce for itself through the influence of these new conditions themselves, new peculiar organs, legislation and jurisprudence, whose nature will be set forth below.

For the rest, this development of law can have a very diversified relationship to the originally existent law. It may be the means of producing new legal institutions, or even of changing those already formed; indeed these may vanish utterly if they become foreign to the sense and needs of the time.

· · · · ·

§12. Customary Law

The legal creation represented by the term Folk-Law, which develops along invisible lines and therefore cannot be traced back to any external event or any determinate point of time, has of course been recognized in all ages. But for two reasons this recognition has been, in large measure, sterile. Its authority has been under-rated and its essential nature has been misconceived. The first of these points may be clarified later in connection with the subject of legislation. The second is related to the popular term customary law (*Gewohnheitsrecht*).

This term can easily mislead us into the following course of thinking. If in a given legal situation it was necessary that something be done, it was originally quite immaterial what was done. Accident and caprice forced a choice. If, then, the situation recurred, it would be easier to repeat this choice than to think of another, and with every repetition this course of action would appear easier and more natural. Thus after some time such a rule would come to be law, though originally it had no more claim to validity than its alternative, and the source of this law would be simply custom.

If one looks to the true basis, to the firm core, of any positive law he finds the true relation of cause and effect to be quite the reverse of this picture. That basis has its existence and reality in the common consciousness of the people. This existence is something invisible. How then can we recognize it? We recognize it in so far as it reveals itself in external activity, in so far as it comes to the fore in usage, *mores*, custom. In the uniformity of a continued, enduring type of activity, we recognize a common origin (something incompatible with mere chance), the belief of a people. Custom is thus the badge of positive law, not its source. Nevertheless even the misconception which makes custom a source has an element of truth which must be given its just weight. That is to say, there are, besides the grounds of positive law generally recognized in the national consciousness, and indubitable, many individual determinants, which have a less certain existence; these determinants may by means of repeated usage be brought into a more definite recognition in the consciousness of the people.[a] Such cases will occur more frequently to the extent that the ability to shape law is foreign to the outstanding traits of a people's nature. Then too, there is a relative indifference in the nature of many determina-

---

[a] Puchta, *Das Gewohnheitsrecht*, II, pp. 8-9: "And for a people, usage, which proceeds from its legal beliefs, serves as a mirror in which that people recognizes itself."

tions; in these situations it is only necessary that some fixed rule prevail, and that it be recognized as such, whatever it may be. To this category belong the many cases in which a rule of law involves a number, and for which, within fixed limits, there is a large amount of room for arbitrary choice, as is the case with periods of prescription; of this type too are the rules of law which have as their subject merely the external form of some legal transaction. In all cases of this sort we become, by means of our earlier thought and will, an authority for ourselves in every later instance, and thus custom can have a general influence over the generation of law. The rule of continuity in human opinions, activities, and circumstances is applicable here,—a rule which is of extraordinary influence in many particular legal institutions.[a] This assumption of a custom which acts upon law itself is degrading only if one thinks of repeated activity as something irrational, determined by accidental external pressure; if it be conceived, on the other hand, as something considered, proceeding from the energy of the spirit, then the dignity of law is not endangered by this origin. Although the term customary law can thus be clarified in two respects and in a manner justified, nevertheless a less narrow use of the term is desirable, since it brings with it a heritage of so many misconceptions which have traditionally attached themselves to it.

In both relations, then, in which legal custom is important, as a means of recognizing positive law and as an auxiliary ground of its origin, there are two categories of activity which exhibit themselves as pre-eminently fruitful and efficacious, the symbolic forms of legal transactions and the judgments of popular courts.[b] The former bring to our view the meaning of legal institutions as a whole; the latter, called forth by the opposition of conflicting claims, are made necessary by their end, the cognition and representation of a legal relationship in sharply defined bounds.

---

[a] The same rule is to be seen at work in burden of proof (as the prerequisite to a change in hitherto prevailing conditions), in possession, in adverse possession, in the limitation of actions, and finally in judicial precedent, everywhere with special twists and developments. Here we can only call attention to this common aspect. Its demonstration must be reserved for the discussion of the specified institutions.

[b] If I lay special stress upon the nature of the popular courts, this is done to distinguish them from the trained courts of our modern times, which consist of permanent bodies. The former character is seen unmistakably in the German *Schoeffengerichten;* but not less in the Roman *res judicatae,* and indeed in the latter not so much, as might easily be supposed, because the *judices* were private persons and thus in this sense taken from the people (for the legal rule, upon which everything depends here, proceeded from the Praetor and not from the *judex*); but rather because the Praetor himself changed every year, and did not belong to the class of trained jurists, so that he was representative of the popular legal beliefs. Thus the Romans themselves viewed the *res judicatae* as sources of law and the Praetor as its author. *Auctor ad Herenn.* II. 13. All this however relates only to the ordinary judges who were nominated singly or in small groups by the Praetor specially for each case. In the centumviral cases, on the other hand, it was the judges themselves who laid down the rule of law (since no *formula* was prescribed for them) and in this way the *querula inofficiosi* was developed.

For the rest, if it is here maintained that legal custom which exhibits itself in observed cases must be regarded as a means of recognizing the Folk-Law, this can be marked out as an indirect means of recognition necessary for those individuals who look upon this law indifferently from the outside without themselves belonging to the organs of the society in which this Folk-Law has arisen and in which it leads an enduring existence (§78). For to individuals of the latter type, such a process of inference from particular instances of social custom is not necessary, since their recognition is something immediate, based upon intuition.*

J. C. CARTER, THE PROPOSED CODIFICATION OF OUR COMMON LAW †

.   .   .   .   .

5. *The arrest of the self-development of private law—its true method of growth.*—This is, as I conceive, perhaps the gravest mischief with which codification is pregnant. It cannot too often be repeated that the practical business of administering private law consists in the application by the courts of the national standard of justice to the business and dealings of men. This national standard of justice is something which cannot be embodied in written rules, or set down in any form of words. It is the product of the combined operation of the thought, the morality, the intellectual and moral culture of the time. Under our present unwritten system of law it is ascertained and made effective by the judges, who know it and feel it because they are a part of the community. They cannot but recognize it and yield to it, because their judgments are subject to the instant and close scrutiny of keen professional observers, not to mention the oversight of the press and the general public. This national standard or ideal of justice grows and develops with the moral and intellectual growth of the community, and through the operation of judicial decision is transferred to the province of the law. Hence a gradual change, unperceived and unfelt in its progress, is continually going on in the jurisprudence of every progressive State. The natural agency through which this healthy progress is effected is that of the devoted students and authoritative interpreters of the law. In Rome it was the private jurisconsults. In England and with us it is the judiciary. The question is, shall this growth, development and improvement of the law remain under the guidance of men se-

---

* [*Cf.* M. R. Cohen, "The Process of Judicial Legislation" 48 *Am. L. Rev.* 161, 173-174 (1941).]

† ["A Paper Prepared at the Request of the Committee of the Bar Association of the City of New York, Appointed to Oppose the Measure," (1884) p. 86 *et seq.*

James Coolidge Carter (1827–1905) led the successful fight against the adoption in New York of the Civil Code of Substantive Law drafted by David Dudley Field. In this fight he utilized a good part of Savigny's argument against codification. His best-known work, *Law: Its Origin, Growth, and Function,* appeared posthumously in 1907.]

lected by the people on account of their special qualifications for the work, or be transferred to a numerous legislative body, disqualified by the nature of their duties for the discharge of this supreme function. There ought not, as I conceive, to be a difference of opinion among men who are willing to give this consideration the attention it deserves.

The point now under notice can be summed up in a very narrow compass, and I cannot help thinking that it is decisive of the whole question of codification.

(1) It is agreed on all hands that private jurisprudence is a science; whence it follows that it can be cultivated, developed and advanced only by the masters of that science.

(2) It is also agreed that a legislative body consisting principally of laymen, possesses no single qualification which enables it to prosecute the cultivation and improvement of this science, and its adaptation to human affairs.

(3) The mode of effecting the improvement of private law and adapting it to the ever-varying wants of men, which the recent advocates in England of codification suggest, is the creation by the Legislature of a Committee composed of eminent jurists, whose duty it shall be to observe the operation of the Code, and to report at intervals—say, of ten years— what improvements, changes and additions should be made. But what comparison can such a mode of amending, improving and adapting the law bear to that which is now in actual operation, in which the whole machinery of administering justice, embracing, upon the Bench, tenfold the ability and learning which could be arrayed upon a Committee, and all the ability of the Bar, is silently, slowly, and without violent change, performing, as a subsidiary function, this very task? * ...

---

* [This is the fifth and probably the fundamental objection raised by Mr. Carter against the proposed New York Civil Code. The others may be summed up as follows:

(1) "*The necessary introduction into the laws of a great mass of error.*" Statutory provisions by reason of their generality must unavoidably embrace unforeseen cases, "and the result necessarily is that such cases must be disposed of by a statute framed without reference to them, and consequently such disposition is as likely to be wrong as right, depending as it does wholly upon chance."

(2) "*A great increase of uncertainty in the administration of the law.*" "Human language is, at the best, so inaccurate a instrument, there being often numerous different senses in which the same word is understood that there are, and always will be, a multitude of doubts concerning the meaning of the best drawn statutes.... *This* source of doubt does not exist in unwritten law." The inevitable violent interpretation of statutes when they lead to unjust results adds to this uncertainty.

(3) "*Incessant, frequent, sharp and often ill-conceived changes in the law....* Whenever a statute is found to work injustice it must be changed.... the Legislature must be appealed to. The appeals will and must be frequent. The habit of changing the law necessarily tends to destroy that sense of the necessity of stability, which is now (although unfortunately diminishing) one of the greatest safeguards for property, business and liberty."

(4) "*The substitution in forensic debates of controversies concerning words in place of controversies concerning principles.*" Instead of searching for the just rule

LIVINGSTON, A SYSTEM OF PENAL LAW FOR THE STATE OF LOUISIANA*

...I propose to show the *necessity of a reform, from a view of the actual state of our penal laws*, and to answer the objections that have been made to the establishment of a written system.

---

as is done at present when the law is disputed, we should have to argue the meaning of words.

(6) "*The loss of another distinct instrumentality for the improvement of the law, viz.: that furnished by the writings of private jurists*.... Such minds will lend their efforts only while the law remains, as now, a science unimprisoned in the rigid language of a statute...."

(7) "*The enforced abandonment of all hope of bringing the private law of all English speaking States to a unity*.... The popular standards of justice in different States and nations, though in most particulars alike, are yet in many respects different, and lead to the adoption of different rules. Right, reason and justice are, however, everywhere the same; and in proportion as the popular standards are cultivated and made to approach perfection, they are brought more and more into unison. The progress of civilization acting upon the courts under our present system is continually aiding this approach to unity. The opinions of the courts appealing, as they now appeal, to the same principles, are not only cited as authorities in the jurisdictions where they are pronounced, but are listened to with respect in all others.... What more desirable condition, what more impressive spectacle can there be, than that of fifty States of a great continent, and Empires beyond the seas, all appealing to the same law, and aiming to drown all dissent in one concurring voice?"

The first half of Carter's essay is devoted to a proof of the thesis that written law is historically and necessarily connected with despotism, unwritten law with democracy.

For attacks upon Carter's philosophical premises and practical conclusions see R. L. Fowler, *Codification in the State of New York*, 2d ed. (1884). The subjects to which, in Carter's view, legislation should be restricted are enumerated in his volume, *Law: Its Origin, Growth, and Function* (1907), p. 203. For Field's defense of his code proposals, see the following articles, reprinted in *Speeches, Arguments and Miscellaneous Papers of David Dudley Field* (1884): "Codification of Our Common Law. A Short Reply to a Long Essay, Feb. 18, 1844. An answer to Mr. James C. Carter's Pamphlet on the Proposed Codification of Our Common Law," Vol. II, p. 494; "Codification," Vol. III, p. 238; "Codification Once More," Vol. III, p. 411.

Carter's pamphlet is very largely a development of the views presented by Savigny in an essay *Of the Vocation of our Age for Legislation and Jurisprudence*, translated by Hayward (1831) from the German, *Vom Beruf unsrer Zeit für Gesetzgebung und Rechtswissenschaft* (1814), written to meet the agitation for codification of German law. See Thibaut, *On the Necessity of a General Civil Law for Germany* (*Ueber die Nothwendigkeit eines allgemeinen bürgerlichen Rechts für Deutschland*), reprinted in Thibaut, *Civilistische Abhandlungen* (1814), p. 404.)

On the source of Carter's views, Pound has made the observation that the doctrines of the German historical school appear to have been taught first in this country in a course of lectures given by Luther S. Cushing at the Harvard Law School in 1849 and published in 1854. Pound notes that the late James C. Carter was a law student at Harvard the last year that this course was given and comments that "unless the effect of early training is borne in mind, it is hard to understand how a jurist of his caliber could dogmatically assent to Savigny's views in 1905." *The Spirit of the Common Law* (1921), p. 154.]

* [(1833), pp. 54-57. On Livingston and his activities as a law reformer, see M. Franklin, Concerning the Historical Importance of Edward Livingston, 11 *Tulane L. Rev.* 163 (1937). See also J. Hall, Edward Livingston and His Louisiana Penal Code, 22 *A.B.A.J.* 191 (1936).]

The objects of penal law are, to define offences, to prevent their commission, and to designate and direct the mode of inflicting the penalty, when they are committed. To effect these objects, there must be rules established by legislative authority. Those rules must be known; and to be known they must be promulgated. But the rule can neither be made, nor be known, nor promulgated, unless it be clothed in words. Are those words to be oral or written, is the first question. A strange one, it would seem, in our state of society, yet seriously made; seriously answered in favour of traditional against written law—made and answered by lawyers, by judges, by men whose situation gives influence, and whose opinions have weight. Such are the advocates for retaining the reference to that part of the English common law which forms a part of our criminal jurisprudence. That part is not inconsiderable: it pervades the whole mass of our legislation on this subject; and it is necessary to understand this, that we may know how to value the argument which asserts that our statutes, not the English common law, defines offences and imposes the penalties. This is not the fact. The groundwork of our penal law is the territorial statute of 1805. It enumerates the offences and indicates the penalties; but it does not define. Theft, burglary, murder, and other crimes, are made punishable. But if we want to know what theft, or murder, or any other offence on the list is; if we wish to know what means we may use to prevent either of these crimes; how the offender is to be arrested, how confined, how bailed, how tried, what evidence can be admitted, what is required for conviction; for all these, and an hundred other questions equally important, we are referred to the *common law of England;* that is to say, what one of its greatest panegyrists [Blackstone] styles, "the *unwritten* or common law," consisting of *"general customs"*—of *particular customs*—and of "certain particular laws, which *by custom are adopted and used by some particular courts.*" The whole resting, as we see, upon *custom:* and when we come to inquire, how these "customs" are to be known, the same author gives the answer, "by the judges"—who, he says, "are the depositaries of the laws, the living oracles who must decide in all cases of doubt," &c. Here, then, we see what is our law. It is "the unwritten customs of England," which, from the same authority, we are told, it requires twenty years of close study for a judge to understand; and which, without fear of incurring the charge of presumption, I will add, no man ever did or can understand—for this plain reason, that, in many instances, it does not exist, until the case arises which calls for its application; then it is pronounced, not by the legislative authority, but by one of these living oracles. It is a maxim with English lawyers, that the common law is the perfection of human reason. No case, therefore, can be supposed to be unprovided for by it, and consequently, whenever any new case occurs, and no preceding response has been given that will fit it, the judge must create one; and although it has never before been spoken, or written, or applied, we must believe it, from time immemorial, to have been a part of the common law; that is to say, as we have just seen, the *custom* of England; which involves the absurdity of supposing that to have been immemorial usage, which we know was never before practised or heard of.

But this is not the only difficulty or absurdity attending a reference to the common law. These oracles, it must be remembered, are not given like those of the sybil, in writing—but like most of those of antiquity, orally. The judge seldom or never writes his decision. The words of inspiration are caught by the reporter, and he publishes them. Here, it would be supposed, an opportunity is afforded of knowing, with some certainty, what the law is. To the people? No! The size, the number, the price, and the disgusting verbosity of the volumes, forbid it. To the lawyers, then, at least? Not even to them! The same causes operate to prevent many of them from examining more than an index or an abridgment; but even the few who are rich enough to buy, and have had leisure to examine, those repositories of the law, with reference to a single point, for a general study of them would consume the longest life, even on that single point will find themselves sadly mistaken if they look for a certainty. Hear what Blackstone—I take my authority only from professed admirers of this system—hear what he says of the credit that is to be given to these reports:—"From the reign of Henry the eighth to the present time, this task (that of reporting) has been executed by many private and contemporary hands; who sometimes through haste and inaccuracy, sometimes through mistake and want of skill, have published very *crude and imperfect,* perhaps *contradictory,* accounts of one and the same determination."

Admit, then, that the judge pronounces the true precept of the law, we can have no security that it is truly recorded; and a word omitted or transposed, may alter the whole sense of the rule. But this is not all. Let us suppose the record to be faithfully made, what is to be its effect? Is it binding on future judges, in similar cases? In other words, is it law? What say our oracles on this important question? Blackstone tells us, "it is an established rule to abide by former precedents, but with some exceptions: which are, first, when the precedent is evidently contrary to *reason;* secondly, when it is clearly contrary to the *divine law;* thirdly, which seems to be included in the first, when it is *flatly absurd* or *unjust.*" This is the doctrine of the text. Christian, the able commentator on this justly distinguished book, says, on the contrary, "precedents and rules must be followed even when they are *flatly absurd and unjust,* if they are agreeable to ancient principles:" and he gives an example which places the justice of this admired system in a most striking point of view. It is a maxim of the common law, that all statutes, whenever passed, refer to, and take effect from, the first day of the session of parliament. Now, to exemplify this rule, he says, if a statute should have been passed on the last day of the session, making an act a capital offence which before was innocent, any one who had done that act between the first and the last day of the session, that is to say, perhaps six months before it was made an offence, would have been condemned and executed under the law. "This," he adds, and every body must agree with him, "was flatly absurd and unjust;" but yet no judge could declare that it was not law, and this absurdity and tyranny, worthy of a Nero or Caligula, continued to form a part of the "perfection of human reason" until the year 1793, when one step in the road to common sense was made by enacting that the statute should not be in force before it was made, but gave it effect, when it contained no special provision on the subject, from the day on which it *passed*, without any attention to the time in which it was known by promulgation; so that even at this day, in England, according to the common law, a man at a distance from the seat of government may be punished for doing an act which, in the nature of things, he could not know to be illegal.

Thus the general assembly may form some idea of the nature of that law, to which our present system of criminal proceedings refers us for the definition of certain offences, and for the rules for preventing, trying, and punishing them. We see that it consists of unwritten rules, promulgated by the judges by precedents often incorrectly reported; of uncertain authority when known; to be followed, according to some writers, however unjust or absurd; and, according to others, to be modified by the principles of *reason* and the *divine law*, that is to say, by the caprice, or the bigotry, or the enthusiasm of the judge. What more uncertain rules can be referred to than *human reason* and the dogmas of religion? What may appear reason to one, is folly to another; and on no one subject does the mind of man take so wide a range as in imagination respecting the divine will.

But if no other objection existed, that which is contained in its very definition, would, it appears, be sufficient to ask for the substitution of some other;—it is *unwritten*. If we like its other provisions (and very many of them are excellent) let us, at least, destroy that characteristic, by reducing them to writing.

Two contradictory objections are commonly raised to this most important operation: the one, that the task is impracticable—that the body of the common law can never be reduced to writing; the other, that its rules are already written, and that a reference to the reporters and commentators will give a sufficient knowledge of its provisions. Now, of these two opinions, one only can be true; and if either be true, it presents a state of things that no reasonable being can wish to see continued. If all the precepts of the common law cannot be reduced to writing then a part of them are not contained either in the reporters or other writers, to which we are usually referred. Where are we, then, to find this unrecorded part?—in the unexplored mind of the judge. When is it to be promulgated?—for the first time after the case has occurred to which it is about to be applied. And who is to record or remember it—what is to be its effect and authority—in our state, which of the seven independent judges is to be considered as pronouncing the true oracle when they differ? Can principle be more completely abandoned; can common sense and common justice be more effectually lost sight of; can confusion be worse confounded than by this state of things? Take the other alternative. The precepts and principles of the common law are already reduced to writing. But where are they to be found? In voluminous reports which it requires great diligence to collect, very large sums of money to purchase, a long life to read, and a superhuman intellect to understand and reconcile with each other when they are read! They are to be found in commentaries on, and abridgments of, these reports, scarcely less voluminous; in which precedents and arguments may be found for almost every position that may be taken by sophistry, or required for an indiscriminate defence of right and wrong; add to this, that these sources of information are inaccessible to three-fourths of the inhabitants of this state, being written in a language which they cannot understand; and that of the other fourth, a very few only have the time or means of applying to them; and you have a state approaching to that which has been justly designated as a badge of the most abject slavery, one governed by unknown and uncertain laws.

SWIFT v. TYSON

U. S. SUPREME COURT, 1842

41 U.S. (16 Pet.) 1

MR. JUSTICE STORY delivered the opinion of the Court.

.		.		.		.		.

But, admitting the doctrine [that a pre-existent debt is not a sufficient consideration to shut out the equities of the original parties in favor of the holders of a bill of exchange] to be fully settled in New York, it remains to be considered, whether it is obligatory upon this Court, if it differs from the principles established in the general commercial law. It is observable that the Courts of New York do not found their decisions upon this point upon any local statute, or positive, fixed, or ancient local usage: but they deduce the doctrine from the general principles of commercial law. It is, however, contended, that the thirty-fourth section of the judiciary act of 1789, ch. 20, furnishes a rule obligatory upon this Court to follow the decisions of the state tribunals in all cases to which they apply. That section provides "that the laws of the several states, except where the construction, treaties, or statutes of the United States shall otherwise require or provide, shall be regarded as rules of decision in trials at common law in the Courts of the United States, in cases where they apply." In order to maintain the argument, it is essential, therefore, to hold, that the word "laws," in this section, includes within the scope of its meaning the decisions of the local tribunals. In the ordinary use of language it will hardly be contended that the decisions of Courts constitute laws. They are, at most, only evidence of what the laws are; and are not of themselves laws. They are often reexamined, reversed, and qualified by the Courts themselves, whenever they are found to be either defective, or ill-founded, or otherwise incorrect. The laws of a state are more usually understood to mean the rules and enactments promulgated by the legislative authority thereof, or long established local customs having the force of laws. In all the various cases which have hitherto come before us for decision, this Court have uniformly supposed, that the true interpretation of the thirty-fourth section limited its application to state laws strictly local, that is to say, to the positive statutes of the state, and the construction thereof adopted by the local tribunals, and to rights and titles to things having a permanent locality, such as the rights and titles to real estate, and other matters immovable and intra-territorial in their nature and character. It never has been supposed by us, that the section did apply, or was designed to apply, to questions of a more general nature, not at all dependent upon local statutes or local usages of a fixed and permanent operation, as, for example, to the construction of ordinary contracts or other written instruments, and especially to questions of general commercial law, where the state tribunals are called upon to perform the like functions as ourselves, that is, to ascertain upon general reasoning and legal analogies, what is the true exposition of the contract or instrument, or what is the just rule furnished by the principles of commercial law to govern the case. And we have not now the slightest difficulty in holding, that this section, upon its true intendment and construction, is strictly limited to local statutes and local usages of the character before stated, and does not extend to contracts and other instruments of a commercial nature, the true interpretation and effect whereof are to be sought, not in the decisions of the local tribunals but in the general principles and doctrines of commercial jurisprudence.

[The court found "no hesitation in saying, that a pre-existing debt does constitute a valuable consideration in the sense of the general rule already stated, as applicable to negotiable instruments."] *

---

* [For attacks upon Story's theory of a state law distinct from the course of judicial decisions, see Gray, *The Nature and Sources of Law*, (1909) §§ 528-550, and the dissenting opinions of Holmes in Kuhn v. Fairmont Coal Co., 215 U. S. 349, 30 Sup.

LORIMER, INSTITUTES OF LAW *

Chapter VIII. How We Become Cognizant of Law in General

. . . . .

There is probably no way in which the absolute and necessary character of positive law in all its branches, and the fact of jurisprudence being a science of nature, even in its minutest details, can be better illustrated than by remarking the close analogy which subsists between it and the sciences of external nature on the one hand, and the wide gulf which, on the other, separates it from any system of rules logically deduced from premises which have been arbitrarily assumed. As an example of the latter, let us take the so-called science of heraldry. A witty writer, in reviewing an heraldic book, claimed for the "noble science" a foundation in nature, on the ground that "man is a blazoning animal." But though the nature of man may impel him to blazon, it leaves him to blazon as he chooses, at least in so far as his actions are free at all. There might be fifty sciences of heraldry, each as good as the other, and this, not in different circumstances, but in circumstances absolutely identical. At any time it would be possible to put a sponge over such a "science," and to construct another diametrically opposed to it in every particular, and yet not inferior to it in any respect. The second would be just as true to nature as the first, just as true absolutely, because neither of them would have any basis in nature, any absolute truth. The premises in both cases being entirely arbitrary, so arbitrary that they might have been determined by the casting of a die, if the rules were adhered to and the conclusions logically deduced, that is all that could be demanded in order to place them on a footing of perfect equality. Both would be systems, neither would be sciences; and in place of two such systems coinciding, it would be quite wonderful if they bore the slightest resemblance to each other, even if the circumstances out of which they arose exhibited the closest analogy. But with the sciences which have nature for their object, and with the arts which rest upon these sciences, the very reverse is the case. . . . if the Chinese had a science of geometry different from ours it

---

Ct. 140 (1910); Southern Pacific Company v. Jensen, 244 U.S. 205, 37 Sup. Ct. 524 (1917); Black & White Taxi Co. v. Brown & Yellow Taxi Co., 276 U.S. 518, 48 Sup. Ct. 404 (1928), which were eventually adopted by a majority of the Supreme Court in Erie R. R. Co. v. Tompkins, 304 U.S. 64 (1938).]

* [*James Lorimer* (1818–1890), one of the ablest advocates of the Tory viewpoint in the 19th century, was Professor at Edinburgh from 1862 until his death. Trained on the Continent, he was instrumental in bringing Scottish legal thought into closer contact with the thought of the civil law countries of the Continent. He strenuously opposed the spread of Bentham's influence. His *Institutes of Law: A Treatise of the Principles of Jurisprudence as Determined by Nature* appeared first in 1872; a second edition was published in 1880.]

would be no science at all. . . . Now it is the same with their jurisprudence. Their positive law differs from ours, no doubt, very widely in its special provisions; but these differences arise wholly from two causes, *viz.,* (a) Error or imperfection in their conceptions of natural law, or in ours— for though natural law be infallible, all human interpretations of it are subject to many errors; and (b) difference of circumstances, which necessarily varies the means by which the same principles, or natural laws, are realizable in different places or at different times. . . . [Pp. 251-252.]

Chapter IX. Of The Laws of Nature, or Principles of Jurisprudence Which Result From the Human Rights and Duties Which Nature Reveals As Facts

(a) *All human laws are declaratory.*

The first great principle of jurisprudence, and that to which it owes at once its sacred and its scientific character, is determined by the necessity under which we have seen that our nature lies to accept itself as right and to seek its own realization. I cannot state it better than in the golden maxim of the greatest of our own statesmen, which I have adopted as a motto to this work.

The passage, as a whole, is so instructive that I shall quote it at length. "It would be hard," says Burke, "to point out any error more truly subversive of all the order and beauty, of all the peace and happiness of human society, than the position that any body of men have a right to make what laws they please; or that laws can derive any authority whatever from their institution merely, and independent of the quality of their subject-matter. . . . *All human laws are, properly speaking, only declaratory.* They may alter the mode and application, but have no power over the substance of original justice." (Tracts on the Popery Laws, cap. iii, part i). . . .

As laws are inferences from powers and rights, existing in wider or narrower spheres, it is obvious that powers and rights cannot owe their origin to laws. . . .

Keeping this fundamental principle in view, you will at once perceive the absurdity of the popular belief—of the prevalence of which even in professional minds too many instances might be given—that rights are "conferred," "constituted," "modified," "limited," "adapted," and even "altered" by law. Formally, or rather nominally, of course, the thing may be done; because anything may be enacted. But the effect of such an enactment is not to change rights, but to outrage them; not to declare new truths, but proclaim falsehoods. The *nomo kalon, nomo kakon* is an aspiration not only after the unjust, but the impossible.

AUSTIN, JURISPRUDENCE *

.   .   .   .   .

A law, in the most general and comprehensive acceptation in which
the term, in its literal meaning, is employed, may be said to be a rule
laid down for the guidance of an intelligent being by an intelligent being
having power over him. . . . In the comprehensive sense above indicated,
or in the largest meaning which it has, without extension by metaphor
or analogy, the term *law* embraces the following objects:—Laws set by
God to his human creatures, and laws set by men to men.

. . . . but rejecting the appellation Law of Nature as ambiguous and
misleading, I name those laws or rules, as considered collectively or in
a mass, the *Divine law*, or the *law of God*.

Laws set by men to men are of two leading or principal classes:
classes which are often blended, although they differ extremely; and
which, for that reason, should be severed precisely, and opposed distinctly and conspicuously.

Of the laws or rules set by men to men, some are established by
political superiors, sovereign and subject: by persons exercising supreme
and subordinate *government*, in independent nations, or independent
political societies. . . . To the aggregate of the rules thus established, or to
some aggregate forming a portion of that aggregate, the term *law*, as used
simply and strictly, is exclusively applied. But, as contradistinguished to
natural law, or to the law *of nature* (meaning, by those expressions, the
law of God), the aggregate of the rules, established by political superiors,
is frequently styled *positive* law, or law existing *by position*. . . .

Though *some* of the laws or rules, which are set by men to men, are
established by political superiors, *others* are *not* established by political
superiors, or are *not* established by political superiors, in that capacity
or character.

Closely analogous to human laws of this second class, are a set of
objects frequently but *improperly* termed *laws*, being rules set and enforced by *mere opinion*, that is, by the opinions or sentiments held or
felt by an indeterminate body of men in regard to human conduct. In-

---

* [3d ed. (1869), Vol. I, pp. 88-106.

Austin's Province of Jurisprudence (1832, 2d ed. 1861, 3d ed. 1869) set a pattern in
Anglo-American jurisprudence which has been closely followed, ever since, by
most Anglo-American teachers and treatises in this field. Gray and Holmes in the
United States, and Holland, Pollock, and Salmond in the British Empire were faithful
followers of Austin's analytical approach. For John Austin (1790–1859), as for his
teacher Bentham, clear objective analysis of law was not an end in itself but a necessary prelude to intelligent ethical criticism of actual rules.

In recent years Kelsen has been responsible for a somewhat similar development
of analytical jurisprudence on the Continent. See the extract from Kelsen in Chapter 9
of this volume.]

stances of such a use of the term *law* are the expressions—'The law of honour;' 'The law set by fashion;' and rules of this species constitute much of what is usually termed 'International law.'

The aggregate of human laws properly so called belonging to the second of the classes above mentioned, with the aggregate of objects *improperly* but by *close analogy* termed laws, I place together in a common class, and denote them by the term *positive morality*. The name *morality* severs them from *positive law*, while the epithet *positive* disjoins them from the *law of God*. And to the end of obviating confusion, it is necessary or expedient that they *should* be disjoined from the latter by that distinguishing epithet. For the name *morality (or morals)*, when standing unqualified or alone, denotes indifferently either of the following objects: namely, positive morality *as it is*, or without regard to its merits; and positive morality as it would be, if it conformed to the law of God, and were, therefore, deserving of *approbation*. [Pp. 88-90.]

.   .   .   .   .

Every *law* or *rule* (taken with the largest signification which can be given to the term *properly*) is a command.... [P. 90.]

.   .   .   .   .

It appears, then, from what has been premised, that the ideas or notions comprehended by the term *command* are the following. 1. A wish or desire conceived by a rational being, that another rational being shall do or forbear. 2. An evil to proceed from the former, and to be incurred by the latter, in case the latter comply not with the wish. 3. An expression or intimation of the wish by words or other signs. [P. 94.]

.   .   .   .   .

Commands are of two species. Some are *laws* or *rules*....

Now where it obliges *generally* to acts or forbearances of a *class*, a command is a law or rule. But where it obliges to a *specific* act of forbearance, or to acts or forbearances which it determines *specifically* or *individually*, a command is occasional or particular.... [Pp. 94-95.]

.   .   .   .   .

To conclude with an example which best illustrates the distinction, and which shows the importance of the distinction most conspicuously, *judicial commands* are commonly occasional or particular, although the commands, which they are calculated to enforce, are commonly laws or rules. [P. 96.]

.   .   .   .   .

Like most of the leading terms in the sciences of jurisprudence and morals, the term *laws* is extremely ambiguous....

Accordingly, the proposition 'that laws are commands' must be taken with limitations. Or, rather, we must distinguish the various meanings of the term *laws;* and must restrict the proposition to that class of objects which is embraced by the largest signification that can be given to the term *properly....* [P. 100.]

.   .   .   .   .

According to an opinion which I must notice *incidentally* here, though the subject to which it relates will be treated *directly* hereafter, *customary laws* must be excepted from the proposition 'that laws are a species of commands.'

By many of the admirers of customary laws (and, especially, of their German admirers), they are thought to oblige legally (independently of the sovereign or state), *because* the citizens or subjects have observed or kept them. Agreeably to this opinion, they are not the *creatures* of the sovereign or state, although the sovereign or state may abolish them at pleasure. Agreeably to this opinion, they are positive law (or law, strictly so called), inasmuch as they are enforced by the courts of justice: But, that notwithstanding, they exist *as positive law* by the spontaneous adoption of the governed, and not by position or establishment on the part of political superiors. Consequently, customary laws, considered as positive law, are not commands. And, consequently, customary laws, considered as positive law, are not laws or rules properly so called.

An opinion less mysterious, but somewhat allied to this, is not uncommonly held by the adverse party: by the party which is strongly opposed to customary law; and to all law made judicially, or in the way of judicial legislation. According to the latter opinion, all judge-made law, or all judge-made law established by *subject* judges, is purely the creature of the judges by whom it is established immediately. To impute it to the sovereign legislature, or to suppose that it speaks the will of the sovereign legislature, is one of the foolish or *knavish* fictions with which lawyers, in every age and nation, have perplexed and darkened the simplest and clearest truths.

I think it will appear, on a moment's reflection, that each of these opinions is groundless: that customary law is *imperative,* in the proper signification of the term; and that all judge-made law is the creature of the sovereign or state.

At its origin, a custom is a rule of conduct which the governed observe spontaneously, or not in pursuance of a law set by a political superior. The custom is transmuted into positive law, when it is adopted as such by the courts of justice, and when the judicial decisions fashioned upon it are enforced by the power of the state. But before it is adopted by the courts, and clothed with the legal sanction, it is merely a rule of positive morality: a rule generally observed by the citizens or subjects;

but deriving the only force, which it can be said to possess, from the general disapprobation falling on those who transgress it.

Now when judges transmute a custom into a legal rule (or make a legal rule not suggested by a custom), the legal rule which they establish is established by the sovereign legislature. A subordinate or subject judge is merely a minister. The portion of the sovereign power which lies at his disposition is merely delegated. The rules which he makes derive their legal force from authority given by the state: and authority which the state may confer expressly, but which it commonly imparts in the way of acquiescence. For, since the state may reverse the rules which he makes, and yet permits him to enforce them by the power of the political community, its sovereign will 'that his rules shall obtain as law' is clearly evinced by its conduct, though not by its express declaration.

The admirers of customary law love to trick out their idol with mysterious and imposing attributes. But to those who can see the difference between positive law and morality, there is nothing of mystery about it. Considered as rules of positive morality, customary laws arise from the consent of the governed, and not from the position or establishment of political superiors. But, considered as moral rules turned into positive laws, customary laws are established by the state: established by the state directly, when the customs are promulgated in its statutes; established by the state circuitously, when the customs are adopted by its tribunals.

The opinion of the party which abhors judge-made law, springs from their inadequate conception of the nature of commands.

Like other significations of desire, a command is express or tacit. If the desire be signified by *words* (written or spoken), the command is express. If the desire be signified by conduct (or by any signs of desire which are *not* words), the command is tacit.

Now when customs are turned into legal rules by decisions of subject judges, the legal rules which emerge from the customs are *tacit* commands of the sovereign legislature. The state, which is able to abolish, permits its ministers to enforce them: and it, therefore, signifies its pleasure, by that its voluntary acquiescence, 'That they shall serve as a law to the governed.'

My present purpose is merely this: to prove that the positive law styled *customary* (and all positive law made judicially) is established by the state directly or circuitously, and, therefore, is *imperative*. I am far from disputing, that law made judicially (or in the way of improper legislation) and law made by statute (or in the properly legislative manner) are distinguished by weighty differences. I shall inquire, in future lectures, what those differences are; and why subject judges, who are properly ministers of the law, have commonly shared with the sovereign in the business of making it.

I assume, then, that the only laws which are not imperative, and which belong to the subject-matter of jurisprudence are the following:—1. Declaratory laws, or laws explaining the import of existing positive law. 2. Laws abrogating or repealing existing positive law. 3. Imperfect laws, or laws of imperfect obligation (with the sense wherein the expression is used by the Roman jurists).*

But the space occupied in the science by these improper laws is comparatively narrow and insignificant. Accordingly, although I shall take them into account so often as I refer to them directly, I shall throw them out of account on other occasions. Or (changing the expression) I shall limit the term *law* to laws which are imperative, unless I extend it expressly to laws which are not. [Pp. 103-106.]

GRAY, NATURE AND SOURCES OF THE LAW †

Chapter IV. The Law

Sec. 191. The Law of the State or of any organized body of men is composed of the rules which the courts, that is, the judicial organs of that body, lay down for the determination of legal rights and duties. The difference in this matter between contending schools of Jurisprudence arises largely from not distinguishing between the Law and the Sources of the Law. On the one hand, to affirm the existence of *nicht positivisches Recht*, that is, of Law which the courts do not follow, is declared to be an absurdity; and on the other hand, it is declared to be an absurdity to say that the Law of a great nation means the opinions of half-a-dozen old gentlemen, some of them, conceivably, of very limited intelligence. The truth is, each party is looking at but one side of the shield. If those half-a-dozen old gentlemen form the highest judicial tribunal of a country, then no rule or principle which they refuse to follow is Law in that country. However desirable, for instance, it may be that a man should be obliged to make gifts which he has promised to make, yet if the courts of a country will not compel him to keep his promise, it is not the Law of that country that promises to make a gift are binding. On the other hand, those six men seek the rules which they follow not in their own whims, but they derive them from sources often

---

* [Note the treatment of so-called non-imperative laws as fragments of, or footnotes to, imperatives in the essay of M. R. Cohen in *Moral Aspects of the Criminal Law, supra*, pp. 289-290.]

† [First ed. (Carpentier Lectures for 1908, Columbia University). New York: Columbia University Press, 1909. Reprinted by permission of Roland Gray.

John Chipman Gray (1839–1915) was a fellow soldier with Holmes in the Union forces, a fellow student at Harvard Law School, and a fellow practitioner in Boston. Gray became a law professor at Harvard and served until 1913. A leading advocate of the "case method," Gray won wide repute in the field of real property, both his treatises (*Restraints on the Alienation of Property*, 1883, and *The Rule Against Perpetuities*, 1886) becoming the standard American works of their type.]

of the most general and permanent character, to which they are directed, by the organized body to which they belong, to apply themselves. I believe the definition of Law that I have given to be correct; but let us consider some other definitions of the Law which have prevailed and which still prevail.

Sec. 192. Of the many definitions of the Law which have been given at various times and places, some are absolutely meaningless, and in others a spark of truth is distorted by a mist of rhetoric. But there are three theories which have commended themselves to accurate thinkers, which have had and which still have great acceptance, and which deserve examination. In all of them it is denied that the courts are the real authors of the Law, and it is contended that they are merely the mouthpieces which give it expression.

Sec. 193. The *first* of these theories is that Law is made up of the commands of the sovereign. This is Austin's view. "Every positive law," he says, "obtaining in any community, is a creature of the Sovereign or State; having been established immediately by the monarch or supreme body, as exercising legislative or judicial functions; or having been established immediately by a subject individual or body, as exercising rights or powers of direct or judicial legislation, which the monarch or supreme body has expressly or tacitly conferred."[1]

Sec. 194. In a sense, this is true; the State can restrain its courts from following this or that rule, but it often leaves them free to follow what they think right; and it is certainly a forced expression to say that one commands things to be done, because he has power (which he does not exercise) to forbid their being done.

. . . . .

Sec. 196. When an agent, servant, or official does acts as to which he has received no express orders from his principal, he may aim, or may be expected to aim, *directly* at the satisfaction of the principal, or he may not. Take an instance of the first,—a cook, in roasting meat or boiling eggs, has, or at any rate the ideal cook is expected to have, *directly* in view the wishes and tastes of her master. On the other hand, when a great painter is employed to cover a church wall with a picture, he is not expected to keep constantly in mind what will please the wardens and vestry; they are not to be in all his thoughts; if they are men of ordinary sense, they will not wish to be; he is to seek his inspiration elsewhere, and the picture when done is not the "creature" of the wardens and vestry; whereas, if the painter adopted an opposite course, and had bent his whole energies to divining what he thought would please them best, he would have been their "tool," and the picture might not unfairly be described as their creature.

---

[1] 2 Jur. (4th ed.) 550, 551.

Sec. 197. Now it is clear into which of these classes a judge falls. Where he has not received direct commands from the State, he does not consider, he is not expected to consider, *directly* what would please the State; his thoughts are directed to the question—What have other judges held? What does Ulpian or Lord Coke say about the matter? What decision does *elegantia juris* or sound morals require?

.   .   .   .   .

Sec. 200. In this connection, the meaning of "Law," when preceded by the indefinite, is to be distinguished from that which it bears when preceded by the definite, article. Austin, indeed, defines the Law as being the aggregate of the rules established by political superiors,[2] and Bentham says, "*Law*, or *the Law*, taken indefinitely, is an abstract and collective term; which, when it means anything, can mean neither more nor less than the sum total of a number of individual laws taken together."[3] But this is not, I think, the ordinary meaning given to "the Law." A law ordinarily means a statute passed by the legislature of a state. "*The* Law" is the whole system of rules applied by the courts. The resemblance of the terms suggests the inference that the body of rules applied by the courts is composed wholly of the commands of the State, but to erect this suggestion into a demonstration, and say,—The system administered by the courts is "the Law," "the Law" consists of nothing but an aggregate of single laws, and all single laws are commands of the State—is not justifiable.*

.   .   .   .   .

Sec. 202. Austin's theory was a natural reaction against the views which he found in possession of the field. Law had been defined as "the art of what is good and equitable"; "that which reason in such sort defines to be good that it must be done"; "the abstract expression of the general will existing in and for itself"; "the organic whole of the external conditions of the intellectual life." If Austin went too far in considering the Law as always proceeding from the State, he conferred a great benefit on Jurisprudence by bringing out clearly that the Law is at the mercy of the State.

Sec. 203. The *second* theory on the nature of Law is that the courts, in deciding cases, are, in truth, applying what has previously existed in the common consciousness of the people. Savigny is the ablest expounder of this theory....

---

[2] 1 Jur. (4th ed.) 89.

[3] 1 Benth. Works, 148.

* [*Cf.* Jethro Brown, *The Austinian Theory of Law* (1912), Excursus E: A Consideration of Some Objections to the Conception of Positive Law as State Command, pp. 331 *et seq.*]

Sec. 204. Savigny is careful to discriminate between the common consciousness of the people and custom: "The foundation of the Law," he says, "has its existence, its reality, in the common consciousness of the people. This existence is invisible. How can we become acquainted with it? We become acquainted with it as it manifests itself in external acts, as it appears in practice, manners, and custom. By the uniformity of a continuous and continuing mode of action, we recognize that the belief of the people is its common root, and not mere chance. Thus, custom is the sign of positive law, not its foundation."[4]

Sec. 205. Savigny is confronted by a difficulty of the same kind as confronted Austin. The great bulk of the Law as it exists in any community is unknown to its rulers, and it is only by aid of the doctrine that what the sovereign permits he commands, that the Law can be considered as emanating from him; but equally, the great bulk of the Law is unknown to the people; how, then, can it be the product of their "common consciousness"? How can it be that of which they "feel the necessity as law"?

Sec. 206. Take a simple instance, one out of thousands. By the law of Massachusetts, a contract by letter is not complete until the answer of acceptance is received.[5] By the law of New York, it is complete when the answer is mailed. Is the common consciousness of the people of Massachusetts different on this point from that of the people of New York? Do the people of Massachusetts feel the necessity of one thing as law, and the people of New York feel the necessity of the precise opposite? In truth, not one in a hundred of the people of either State has the dimmest notion on the matter. If one of them has a notion, it is as likely as not to be contrary to the law of his State.

. . . . . .

Sec. 209. The jurists set forth the opinions of the people no more and no less than any other specially educated or trained class in a community sets forth the opinions of that community, each in its own sphere. They in no other way set forth the *Volksgeist* in the domain of Law than educated physicians set forth the *Volksgeist* in the matter of medicine. It might be very desirable that the conceptions of the *Volksgeist* should be those of the most skillful of the community, but however desirable this might be, it is not the case. The *Volksgeist* carries a piece of sulphur in its waistcoat pocket to keep off rheumatism, and thinks that butchers cannot sit on juries.

Sec. 210. Not only is popular opinion apart from professional opinion in Law as in other matters, but it has been at times positively hostile. Those who hold that jurists are the mouthpieces of the popular convictions in matters of law have never been able to deal satisfactorily with

---

[4] 1 *Heut. roem. Recht,* § 12. p. 35.
[5] This used to be the Law in Massachusetts. I am not so sure that it is now.

the reception of the Roman Law in Germany, for that Law was brought in not only without the wishes, but against the wishes, of the great mass of the people.[6]

Sec. 211. A *third* theory of the Law remains to consider. That theory is to this effect: The rules followed by the courts in deciding questions are not the expression of the State's commands, nor are they the expression of the common consciousness of the people, but, although what the judges rule is the Law, it is putting the cart before the horse to say that the Law is what the judges rule. The Law, indeed, is identical with the rules laid down by the judges, but those rules are laid down by the judges because they are the Law, they are not the Law because they are laid down by the judges, or, as the late Mr. James C. Carter puts it, the judges are the discoverers, not the creators, of the Law. And this is the way that judges themselves are apt to speak of their functions.

Sec. 212. This theory concedes that the rules laid down by the judges correctly state the Law, but it denies that it is Law because they state it. . . .

.   .   .   .   .

Sec. 215. To come, then, to the question whether the judges discover preëxisting Law, or whether the body of rules that they lay down is not the expression of preëxisting Law, but the Law itself. Let us take a concrete instance: On many matters which have come in question in various jurisdictions, there is no doctrine received *semper, ubique, et ab omnibus.* For instance, Henry Pitt has built a reservoir on his land, and has filled it with water; and, without any negligence on his part, either in the care or construction of his reservoir, it bursts, and the water pouring forth, floods and damages the land of Pitt's neighbor, Thomas Underhill. Has Underhill a right to recover compensation from Pitt? In England, in the leading case of *Rylands v. Fletcher*, it was held that he could recover, and this decision has been followed in some of the United States—for instance, in Massachusetts; but in others, as, I believe, in New Jersey, the contrary is held.

Sec. 216. Now, suppose that Pitt's reservoir is in one of the newer States, say Utah, and suppose, further, that the question has never arisen there before; that there is no statute, no decision, no custom on the subject; the court has to decide the case somehow; suppose it should follow *Rylands v. Fletcher* and should rule that in such cases the party injured can recover. The State, then, through its judicial organ, backed by the executive power of the State, would be recognizing the rights of persons injured by such accidents, and, therefore, the doctrine of *Rylands v. Fletcher* would be undoubtedly the present Law in Utah.

Sec. 217. Suppose, again, that a similar state of facts arises in the adjoining State of Nevada, and that there also the question is presented for the first time, and that there is no statute, decision, or custom on the point; the Nevada court has to decide the case somehow; suppose it should decline to follow *Rylands v. Fletcher,* and should rule that in such cases the party injured is without remedy. Here the State of Nevada would refuse to recognize any right in the injured party and, therefore, it would unquestionably be the present Law in Nevada that a person injured by such an accident would have no right to compensation.

Sec. 218. Let us now assume that the conditions and habits of life are the same in these two adjoining States; that being so, these contradictory doctrines cannot both conform to an ideal rule of Law, and let us, therefore, assume that an all-wise and all-good intelligence, considering the question, would think that one of these doctrines was right and the other wrong, according to the true standard of morality, whatever that may be. It matters not, for the purpose of the discussion, which of the two doctrines it is, but let us suppose that the intelligence aforesaid would approve *Rylands v. Fletcher;* that is, it would think the Law as established in Nevada by the decision of its court did not conform to the eternal principles of right.

Sec. 219. The fact that the ideal theory of Law disapproved the Law as established in Nevada would not affect the present existence of that Law. However wrong intellectually or morally it might be, it would be the Law of that State to-day. But what was the Law in Nevada a week before a rule for decision of such questions was adopted by the courts of that State? Three views seem possible: *first,* that the Law was then ideally right, and contrary to the rule now declared and practiced on; *second,* that the Law was then the same as is now declared and practiced; *third,* that there was then no Law on the matter.

Sec. 220. The first theory seems untenable on any notion of discovery. A discoverer is a discoverer of that which is,—not of that which is not. The result of such a theory would be that when Underhill received the injury and brought his suit, he had in interest which would be protected by the State, and that it now turns out that he did not have it,—a contradiction in terms.

Sec. 221. We have thus to choose between the theory that the Law was at that time what it now is, and the theory that there was then no law at all on the subject. The latter is certainly the view of reason and of common sense alike. There was, at the time in question, *ex hypothesi,* no statute, no precedent, no custom on the subject; of the inhabitants of the State not one out of a hundred had an opinion on the matter or had ever thought of it; of the few, if any, to whom the question had ever occurred, the opinions were, as likely as not, conflicting. To say that on this subject there was really Law existing in Nevada, seems only to show how strong a root legal fictions can strike into our mental processes.

. . . . .

Sec. 223. The difficulty of believing in preëxisting Law is still greater when there is a change in the decision of the courts. In Massachusetts it was held in 1849, by the Supreme Judicial Court, that if a man hired a horse in Boston on a Sunday to drive to Nahant, and drove instead to Nantasket, the keeper of the livery stable had no right to sue him in trover for the conversion of the horse. But in 1871 this decision was overruled and the right was given to the stable-keeper. Now, did stable-keepers have such rights, say, in 1845? If they did, then the court in 1849 did not discover the Law. If they did not, then the court in 1871 did not discover the Law.

·   ·   ·   ·   ·

Chapter V. The Courts

·   ·   ·   ·   ·

Sec. 266. The Limits of Judicial Power. Thus far we have seen that the Law is made up of the rules for decision which the courts lay down; that all such rules are Law; that rules for conduct which the courts do not apply are not Law; that the fact that the courts apply rules is what makes them Law; that there is no mysterious entity "The Law" apart from these rules; and that the judges are rather the creators than the discoverers of the Law.

Sec. 267. Is the power of the judges, then, absolute? Can the comparatively few individuals who fill judicial position in the State, for instance, lay down rules for the government of human intercourse at their bare pleasure or whim? Not so; the judges are but organs of the State; they have only such power as the organization of the State gives them; and what that organization is, is determined by the wills of the real rulers of the State.

Sec. 268. Who are the rulers of a State, is a question of fact and not of form. In a nominal autocracy, the real rulers may be a number of court favorites or the priests of a religion; and in a democracy, the real ruler may be a demagogue or political boss.

Sec. 269. It is conceivable that a body of judges may be the ruling wills of a community, and then they hold their powers by virtue of dominating other wills, but this, except in a very primitive community, can hardly ever be the case. The half-a-dozen elderly men sitting on a platform behind a green or red cloth, with very probably not commanding wills or powerful physique, can exercise their functions only within those limits which the real rulers of the State allow for the exercise; for the State and the court as an organ thereof are the product of the wills of those rulers.

Sec. 270. Who is to determine whether the judges are acting within those limits? In all the less important matters, the rulers intrust the determination of this question to the judges themselves; thus the judges are allowed to say what are the details of the organization of a State and the distribution of its powers among its organs; but, on the most vital matters, the rulers themselves determine what the organization of the body is and within what limits its organs shall work; and the acts and declarations of persons, being its organs, which are inconsistent with the very nature of the organization, are not acts and declarations of the State—are not its Law.

Sec. 271. How can it be told whether a rule laid down by a court is to be deemed not the Law, either because such a rule is inconsistent with the organization of the State as established by its rulers, or because it is beyond the limits of the power of the court as fixed by those rulers? The principal evidence that declarations of judges are inconsistent with the organization of the State, or beyond the limits fixed by it for their action, is the opinions of the members of the community to that effect. To determine whether such opinions are so strong and universal that they must be taken for the judgment of the rulers of the State, or whether the declarations, though much disregarded, are still to be deemed Law,[7] there seems to be no general definite rule, applicable to all cases.

Sec. 272. It should be observed that the unexpressed, and, in formal shape, inexpressible, opinion of the rulers of society lies behind the Law none the less in those countries which possess written constitutions than in those which do not. The organization and powers of the ordinary legislative bodies may be indeed defined in a constitution, but whether there was power in any one to bring into effect the constitution, the constitution itself cannot determine, any more than a book can prove its own inspiration, or a man lift himself up by his boots. For instance, What are the geographical limits for which the constitution is to be in force? Who are to vote upon it,—men, women, or children? Can paupers, slaves, aliens, vote? By what collections of individuals, such as towns or boroughs, must representatives to frame a constitution be chosen? These are questions that the rulers of the State must determine; their decision is a prerequisite for the constitution coming into existence. The elephant may rest on the tortoise, but in the last result we have to go back to the wills of those who rule the society.

Sec. 273. The power of the rulers of the State or other community in reference to its judicial organs or courts is exercised in a twofold way,—first, by creating them, and secondly, in laying down limits for their action, or, in other words, indicating the sources from which they are to derive the rules which make up the Law. From what *sources* does the State or other community direct its judges to obtain the Law? These sources are defined for the most part in a very vague and general way, but one rule is clear and precise. The State requires that the acts of its legislative organ shall bind the courts, and so far as they go, shall be

paramount to all other sources. This may be said to be a necessary consequence from the very conception of an organized community of men.

Sec. 274. The other sources from which courts may draw their general rules are fourfold,—judicial precedents, opinions of experts, customs,
and principles of morality (using morality as including public policy).
Whether there is any precedent, expert opinion, custom, or principle
from which a rule can be drawn, and whether a rule shall be drawn
accordingly, are questions which, in most communities, are left to the
courts themselves, and yet there are probably in every community limits
within or beyond which courts may, or, on the other hand, cannot, seek
for rules from the sources mentioned, although the limits are not precisely defined. Take, for instance, a country where the English Common
Law has prevailed. If a court in such a country should, in matters not
governed by statute, absolutely refuse to follow any judicial precedents,
it is not likely that the rulers of the country would recognize the doctrine of that court as Law; or, if a court should frame a rule based upon
the principle that infanticide was not immoral, that rule would not be
the Law.

Sec. 275. Though the commands by the rulers of a community as to
the limits within which these last four classes of sources are to be sought
by the courts are indefinite, while the command that legislative acts
must be followed by the courts is precise and peremptory, the fact is
that this latter rule, in its working, is almost as indefinite as those which
are imposed on the courts with reference to the other sources; for, after
all, it is only words that the legislature utters; it is for the courts to say
what those words mean; that is, it is for them to interpret legislative
acts; undoubtedly there are limits upon their power of interpretation,
but these limits are almost as undefined as those which govern them in
their dealing with the other sources.

Sec. 276. And this is the reason why legislative acts, statutes, are to
be dealt with as sources of Law, and not as part of the Law itself, why
they are to be coordinated with the other sources which I have mentioned. It has been sometimes said that the Law is composed of two parts,
legislative law and judge-made law, but, in truth, all the Law is judge-
made law. The shape in which a statute is imposed on the community as
a guide for conduct is that statute as interpreted by the courts. The
courts put life into the dead words of the statute. To quote again from
Bishop Hoadly, a sentence which I have before given: "Nay, whoever
hath an *absolute authority* to *interpret* any written or spoken law, it is
He who is truly the Law Giver to all intents and purposes, and not the
Person who first wrote and spoke them." [8] I will return to this later.*

---

[8] Sermon preached before the King, 1717 (15 ed.), 12.
* [See M. R. Cohen, "The Process of Judicial Legislation," 48 *Am. L. Rev.* 11,
passim (1914).]

HOLMES, THE PATH OF THE LAW *

When we study law we are not studying a mystery but a well-known profession. We are studying what we shall want in order to appear before judges, or to advise people in such a way as to keep them out of court. The reason why it is a profession, why people will pay lawyers to argue for them or to advise them, is that in societies like ours the command of the public force is intrusted to the judges in certain cases, and the whole power of the state will be put forth, if necessary, to carry out their judgments and decrees. People want to know under what circumstances and how far they will run the risk of coming against what is so much stronger than themselves, and hence it becomes a business to find out when this danger is to be feared. The object of our study, then, is prediction, the prediction of the incidence of the public force through the instrumentality of the courts.

The means of the study are a body of reports, of treatises, and of statutes, in this country and in England, extending back for six hundred years, and now increasing annually by hundreds. In these sibylline leaves are gathered the scattered prophecies of the past upon the cases in which the axe will fall. These are what properly have been called the oracles of the law. Far the most important and pretty nearly the whole meaning of every new effort of legal thought is to make these prophecies more precise, and to generalize them into a thoroughly connected system. The process is one, from a lawyer's statement of a case, eliminating as it does all the dramatic elements with which his client's story has clothed it, and retaining only the facts of legal import, up to the final analyses and abstract universals of theoretic jurisprudence. The reason why a lawyer does not mention that his client wore a white hat when he made a contract, while Mrs. Quickly would be sure to dwell upon it along with the parcel gilt goblet and the sea-coal fire, is that he foresees that the public force will act in the same way whatever his client had upon his head. It is to make the prophecies easier to be remembered and to be understood that the teachings of the decisions of the past are put into general propositions and gathered into text-books, or that statutes are passed in a general form. The primary rights and duties with which jurisprudence busies itself again are nothing but prophecies. One of the many evil effects of the confusion between legal and moral ideas, about which I shall have something to say in a moment, is that theory is apt to get the cart before the horse, and to consider the right or the duty as something existing apart from and independent of the consequences of its breach, to which certain sanctions are added afterward. But, as I

---

* [From *Collected Legal Papers*, by Oliver Wendell Holmes, copyright, 1920, by Harcourt, Brace and Company, Inc. Also printed in 10 *Harv. L. Rev.* 457-462 (1897).]

shall try to show, a legal duty so called is nothing but a prediction that if a man does or omits certain things he will be made to suffer in this or that way by judgment of the court; and so of a legal right. [Pp. 167-169.]

.   .   .   .   .

...If you want to know the law and nothing else, you must look at it as a bad man, who cares only for the material consequences which such knowledge enables him to predict, not as a good one, who finds his reasons for conduct, whether inside the law or outside of it, in the vaguer sanctions of conscience. The theoretical importance of the distinction is no less, if you would reason on your subject aright. The law is full of phraseology drawn from morals, and by the mere force of language continually invites us to pass from one domain to the other without perceiving it, as we are sure to do unless we have the boundary constantly before our minds. The law talks about rights, and duties, and malice, and intent, and negligence, and so forth, and nothing is easier, or, I may say, more common in legal reasoning, than to take these words in their moral sense, at some stage of the argument, and so to drop into fallacy. For instance, when we speak of the rights of man in a moral sense, we mean to mark the limits of interference with individual freedom which we think are prescribed by conscience, or by our ideal, however reached. Yet it is certain that many laws have been enforced in the past, and it is likely that some are enforced now, which are condemned by the most enlightened opinion of the time, or which at all events pass the limit of interference as many consciences would draw it. Manifestly, therefore, nothing but confusion of thought can result from assuming that the rights of man in a moral sense are equally rights in the sense of the Constitution and the law....

The confusion with which I am dealing besets confessedly legal conceptions. Take the fundamental question, What constitutes the law? You will find some text writers telling you that it is something different from what is decided by the courts of Massachusetts or England, that it is a system of reason, that it is a deduction from principles of ethics or admitted axioms or what not, which may or may not coincide with the decisions. But if we take the view of our friend the bad man we shall find that he does not care two straws for the axioms or deductions, but that he does want to know what the Massachusetts or English courts are likely to do in fact. I am much of his mind. The prophecies of what the court will do in fact, and nothing more pretentious, are what I mean by the law.

Take again a notion which as popularly understood is the widest conception which the law contains—the notion of legal duty, to which already I have referred. We fill the word with all the content which we draw from morals. But what does it mean to a bad man? Mainly, and in the first place, a prophecy that if he does certain things he will be subjected to disagreeable consequences by way of imprisonment or compulsory payment of money. But from his point of view, what is the difference between being fined and being taxed a certain sum for doing a certain thing? That his point of view is the test of legal principles is shown by the many discussions which have arisen in the courts on the very question whether a given statutory liability is a penalty or a tax. On the answer to this question depends the decision whether conduct is legally wrong or right, and also whether a man is under compulsion or free. Leaving the criminal law on one side, what is the difference between the liability under the mill acts or statutes authorizing a taking by eminent domain and the liability for what we call a wrongful conversion of property where restoration is out of the question. In both cases the party taking another man's property has to pay its fair value as assessed by a jury, and no more. What significance is there in calling one taking right and another wrong from the point of view of the law? It does not matter, so far as the given consequence, the compulsory payment, is concerned, whether the act to which it is attached is described in terms of praise or in terms of blame, or whether the law purports to prohibit it or to allow it. If it matters at all, still speaking from the bad man's point of view, it must be because in one case and not in the other some further disadvantages, or at least some further consequences, are attached to the act by the law. The only other disadvantages thus attached to it which I ever have been able to think of are to be found in two somewhat insignificant legal doctrines, both of which might be abolished without disturbance. One is, that a contract to do a prohibited act is unlawful, and the other, that, if one of two or more joint wrongdoers has to pay all the damages, he cannot recover contribution from his fellows. And that I believe is all. You see how the vague circumference of the notion of duty shrinks and at the same time grows more precise when we wash it with cynical acid and expel everything except the object of our study, the operations of the law.

Nowhere is the confusion between legal and moral ideas more manifest than in the law of contract. Among other things, here again the so called primary rights and duties are invested with a mystic significance beyond what can be assigned and explained. The duty to keep a contract at common law means a prediction that you must pay damages if you do not keep it—and nothing else. If you commit a tort, you are liable to pay a compensatory sum. If you commit a contract, you are liable to pay a compensatory sum unless the promised event comes to pass, and and that is all the difference. But such a mode of looking at the matter stinks in the nostrils of those who think it advantageous to get as much ethics into the law as they can. It was good enough for Lord Coke, however, and here, as in many other cases, I am content to abide with him. In *Bromage v. Genning*,[1] a prohibition was sought in the King's Bench against a suit in the marches of Wales for the specific performance of a covenant to grant a lease, and Coke said that it would subvert the intention of the covenantor, since he intends it to be at his election either to lose the damages or to make the lease. Sergeant Harris for the plaintiff confessed that he moved the matter against his conscience, and a prohibition was granted. This goes further than we should go now, but it shows what I venture to say has been the common law point of view from the beginning, although Mr. Harriman, in his very able little book upon Contracts has been misled, as I humbly think, to a different conclusion. [Pp. 171-175.]

POUND, LAW IN BOOKS AND LAW IN ACTION *

When Tom Sawyer and Huck Finn had determined to rescue Jim by digging under the cabin where he was confined, it seemed to the uninformed lay mind of Huck Finn that some old picks the boys had found were the proper implements to use. But Tom knew better. From reading he knew what was the right course in such cases, and he called for case-knives. "It don't make no difference," said Tom, "how foolish it is, it's the *right way*—and it's the regular way. And there ain't no other way that ever I heard of, and I've read all the books that gives any information about these things. They always dig out with a case-knife." So, in deference to the books and the proprieties, the boys set to work with case-knives. But after they had dug till nearly midnight and they were tired and their hands were blistered, and they had made little progress, a light came to Tom's legal mind. He dropped his knife and, turning to Huck, said firmly, "Gimme a case-knife." Let Huck tell the rest:

He had his own by him, but I handed him mine. He flung it down and says, "Gimme a *case-knife*."

I didn't know just what to do—but then I thought. I scratched around amongst the old tools and got a pickaxe and give it to him, and he took it and went to work and never said a word.

He was always just that particular. *Full of principle.*

Tom had made over again one of the earliest discoveries of the law. When tradition prescribed case-knives for tasks for which pickaxes were better adapted, it seemed better to our forefathers, after a little vain struggle with case-knives, to adhere to principle—but use the pickaxe. They granted that law ought not to change. Changes in law were full of danger. But, on the other hand, it was highly inconvenient to use case-knives. And so the law has always managed to get a pickaxe in its hands, though it steadfastly demanded a case-knife, and to wield it in the virtuous belief that it was using the approved instrument.

---

[1] Roll. Rep. 368.
* [44 *Am. L. Rev.* 12 (1910).]

It is worth while to recall some of the commonplaces of legal history by way of illustration.... [Pp. 12-13.]

.   .   .   .   .

...When wager of law had made the action of debt a worthless remedy upon simple contracts, wager of law was not abolished, but the courts found a trespass and a breach of the king's peace in failure to perform a promise, if only something had been given presently in exchange for it, and thus imposed upon our law of contracts the formality of a consideration. When the delay and formalism of real actions and the incident of trial by battle made them inadequate remedies, a fictitious lease and fictitious ejectment were resorted to in order to make another remedy meet the situation. When the hard and fast form of writ and declaration failed to provide for new cases of conversion of a plaintiff's property, the form was not altered, but the loss and finding were assumed from the conversion; so that we are able to read in an American report of the nineteenth century that the plaintiff casually lost one hundred freight cars and the defendant casually found them and converted them to its own use, as if it were a watch or a pocket book that had been lost.

We are by no means so much wiser than our fathers as we sometimes assume. While we have few of the old fictions of procedure left, we can make new ones of our own upon occasion in the like spirit.... [P. 14.]

.   .   .   .   .

Let us take a few examples. It is a settled dogma of the books that all doubts are to be resolved in favor of the constitutionality of a statute—that the courts will not declare it in conflict with the constitution unless clearly and indubitably driven to that conclusion. But it can not be maintained that such is the actual practice, especially with respect to social legislation claimed to be in conflict with constitutional guaranties of liberty and property. The mere fact that the Court of Appeals of New York and the Supreme Court of the United States differed on such questions as the power to regulate hours of labor on municipal and public contracts, and the power to regulate the hours of labor of bakers, the former holding adversely to the one[1] and upholding the other,[2] while the latter court had already ruled the opposite on the first question[3] and then reversed the ruling of the New York court on the second,[4] speaks for itself. Many more instances might be noted. But it is enough to say that any one who studies critically the course of decision upon constitutional questions in a majority of our state courts in recent

---

[1] People v. Coler, 116 N.Y. 1.
[2] People v. Lochner, 177 N.Y. 145.
[3] U.S. v. Martin, 94 U.S. 400.
[4] Lochner v. N.Y., 198 U.S. 45.

years must agree with Professor Freund that the courts in practice tend to overturn all legislation which they deem unwise,[5] and must admit the truth of Professor Dodd's statement:

The courts have now definitely invaded the field of public policy and are quick to declare unconstitutional almost any laws of which they disapprove, particularly in the fields of social and industrial legislation. The statement still repeated by the courts that laws will not be declared unconstitutional unless their repugnance to the constitution is clear beyond a reasonable doubt, seems now to have become "a mere courteous and smoothly transmitted platitude."[6] [Pp. 15-16.]

．　　．　　．　　．　　．

More striking still is the divergence between legal theory and current practice in the handling of persons suspected of crime. The "third degree" has become an every day feature of police investigation of crime. What is our law according to the books? "The prisoner," says Sir James Stephen, "is absolutely protected against all judicial questioning before or at the trial." "This," he adds, "contributes greatly to the dignity and apparent humanity of a criminal trial. It effectually avoids the appearance of harshness, not to say cruelty, which often shocks an English spectator in a French court of justice."[8] Such is the legal rule. But prosecuting attorneys and police officers and police detectives do not hesitate to conduct the most searching, rigid and often brutal examinations of accused or suspected persons, with all the appearance of legality and of having the power of the state behind them. It is true, no rich man is ever subjected to this process to obtain proof of violation of anti-trust or rebate legislation and no powerful politician is thus dealt with in order to obtain proof of bribery and graft. The malefactor of means, the rogue who has an organization of rogues behind him to provide a lawyer and a writ of *habeas corpus* has the benefit of the law in the books. But the ordinary malefactor is bullied and even sometimes starved and tortured into confession by officers of the law. It is no doubt a sound instinct that makes us hesitate to give any such examinations the sanction of legality. We may agree with Sir James Stephen's informant that there is a deal of laziness behind it, that, to use his words, "it is far pleasanter to sit comfortably in the shade rubbing red pepper into a poor devil's eyes than to go about in the sun hunting up evidence."[9] The fact remains, however, that the attempt of the books to compel prosecutors to use only a case-knife is failing. They will use the pick-axe in practice, and until the law has evolved some device by which they may use it in all cases the weak and friendless and lowly will be at a practical disadvantage, despite the legal theory. [Pp. 16-17.]

．　　．　　．　　．　　．

---

[5] Green Bag. XVII, 416.
[6] The Growth of Judicial Power, *Pol. Sci. Quarterly*, XXIV, 193, 194.

Another attempt at adjusting the letter of the law to the demands of administration in concrete cases, while apparently preserving the law unaltered, is to be seen in our American ritual, for in many jurisdictions it is little else, of written opinions, discussing and deducing from the precedents with great elaboration. As one reads the reports critically the conclusion is forced upon him that this ritual covers a deal of personal government by judges, a deal of "raw equity," or, as the Germans call it, of equitable application of law, and leaves many a soft spot in what is superficially a hard and fast rule, by means of which concrete causes are decided in practice as the good sense or feelings of fair play of the tribunal may dictate. One instance of this, in constitutional law, has been spoken of. Many others might be adduced from almost any department of private law. Let one suffice. In the law as to easements it is laid down that a right may be acquired by adverse user, although the known use was not objected to, if it was in fact, adverse. But the same courts say properly that a permissive user will give no right. When, however, one turns to the cases themselves and endeavors to fit each case in the scheme, not according to what the court said was the rule, but according to the facts of that case, he soon finds that the apparent rules to a great extent are no rules, and that where to allow the right would work a hardship the courts have discussed the decisions as to permissive user, and where, in the concrete cause, it seemed fair to grant the right they have insisted on the adverse character of the claimant's conduct.... [Pp. 19-20.]

.   .   .   .   .

Settled habits of juristic thought are characteristic of American legal science. Our legal scholarship is historical and analytical. In either event it begins and ends substantially in Anglo-American case law. But the fundamental conceptions of that case law are by no means those of popular thought today. Nor is this condition in any way unique. "All sciences," wrote Ulrich Zäsius in 1520, "have put off their dirty clothes, only jurisprudence remains in her rags."[12]... [P. 25.]

.   .   .   .   .

Sometime in the future when a philosophical jurist writes upon the spirit of the common law, we may have a worthy account of the relation between Puritan theology and the common law.... [P. 31.]

.   .   .   .   .

The fundamental proposition from which the Puritan proceeded was the doctrine that man was a free moral agent, with power to choose what he would do and a responsibility coincident with that power. He put individual conscience and individual judgment in the first place.

No authority must be permitted to coerce them, but every one must assume and abide the consequences of the choice he was free to make. In its application this led to a regime of "consociation, but not subordination."[21] "We are not over one another," said Robinson, "but with one another."[22] Hence law was a device to secure liberty, its only justification was that it preserved individual liberty, and its sole basis was the free agreement of the individual to be bound by it. The early history of New England abounds in examples of attempts to make this a practical political doctrine.[23] The good side of all this we know well. On the side of politics, the conception of the people—not as a mass, but as an aggregate of individuals—the precise ascription of rights to each of these individuals, the evolution of the legal rights of Englishmen into the natural rights of man, have their immediate origin in the religious phase of the Puritan revolution.[24] But on the side of law it has given us the conception of liberty of contract, which is the bane of all labor legislation, the rooted objection to all power of application of rules to individual cases which has produced a decadence of equity in so many of our state courts, the insistence upon and faith in the mere machinery of justice which makes American legal procedure almost impossible of toleration in the business world of today, the notion of punishing the vicious will and of the necessary connection between wrongdoing and retribution which make it so difficult for our criminal law to deal with anti-social actions and to adjust itself in its application to the exigencies of concrete criminality.

Finally, our interpretation of jurisprudence and of legal history is either idealistic or political. Brooks Adams is the only American writer to insist upon the economic and social interpretation. But until we come to look at our legal history in this way, history on which our jurists rely chiefly is not unlikely to prove a blind guide. The history of juristic thought tells us nothing unless we know the social forces that lay behind it. [Pp. 32-34.]

DEMOGUE, ANALYSIS OF FUNDAMENTAL NOTIONS *

.   .   .   .   .

§ 200. *The Notion of Law Bound up with the Idea of a Continuous Protection of Varying Interests.* Whether a person has or has not a given right, is an idea which evidently has to do with a concern for the future. He who puts this question to himself, is interested in knowing

---

* [Vol. 6 of the Modern Legal Philosophy Series. Scott and Chamberlain, trans. New York: The Macmillan Company, 1916.

René Demogue (b. 1872) gained international recognition after the publication in 1911 of his *Les Notions fondamentales du droit privé: Essai critique pour servir d'introduction à l'étude des obligations.* Footnotes have been renumbered.]

what will happen, in case he does or does not do a certain act, and whether the consequences of his action or abstention will be advantageous to him. . . . [P. 352.]

.   .   .   .   .

. . . If a given territory is usually devastated by storms or hail, if a certain business house is solidly established in a district in which it seems likely to hold its customers, if bands of evil-doers continually infest a particular region and are not molested, if public officials seek to injure one sort of enterprise and to aid another,—these are lasting facts of great importance. . . .

Among these probabilities which it is important to know should be classed the actions of strong, organized authorities. Composed of groups of men, they are stronger than isolated individuals, and more apt, also, to maintain their decisions, or those which have been made by their agents or representatives in their name. They have at once power and continuity. For the protection of interests, it is important to know the habits of these authorities, the result of which cannot be avoided. These habits may be expressed in different way, as simple usages, as customs, or as rules which they have established for the future and which they observe.

When such a state of fact exists, when there is such a probably permanent situation, whether it is a result of the action of a powerful organized band, of a State, of force or of guile, of menace, ill-will, or the corruption of individuals, it produces a certain sequence in events which cannot be neglected.

In this zone of facts capable of arising because there are strong probabilities for them, lies the law,—that vague and fugitive notion which we are about to try to fix from the point of view of observation, then from that of the ideal. [Pp. 354-355.]

.   .   .   .   .

§ 201. *Realistically Defined, Law is that which is Imposed without Recourse by an Organized Force.* What must be understood by law from the point of view of observation alone? When does law exist? Law is that which is imposed by an organized force from which there is no appeal. Law is practically a synonym for social fact imposed if need be by coercion.[1] When a judgment regular in form and unappealable settles a point, it is law; so also when an administrative authority makes a decision which is unattackable or which has been fruitlessly attacked,

---

[1] *Cf.* Picard, "*Le Droit Pur*," p. 40 and Alessandro Lévi, "*La Société et l'Ordre Juridique*" pp. 250 *ff.* Schatz very accurately says that where there is no force there is no law. "*L'Individualisme Economique et Social*," p. 318. See in Mill the same idea, "Utilitarianism," Chap. V.

or when a point is settled by a statute, which cannot be questioned according to our French notion, to the contrary of the American notion. This is the simple and most realistic idea of the law, that resulting from observation.... [Pp. 355-356.]

.   .   .   .   .

§ 203. The ideas which we are here defending may be supported by the great authority of Jhering. "Law," says he, "exists for self-realization. Practical application is the life and the reality of law, it is law itself. That which does not find expression in real life, that which exists only in the statute books or on paper, is only a phantom of law—no more than words. On the contrary, that which takes effect as law is law, even if it is not on the statute book and the people and legal science have not yet recognized it as such."[2] [P. 360.]

§ 204. *Law and Not-Law.* These statements, taken solely from observation, present to us the law in a somewhat different light from that in which it is usually shown. Obedient to the tendency of the human mind, which inclines toward simple categories, well marked frontiers, which unconsciously seeks security with a force of which we shall later have more to say, we are willing to believe that there are two distinct classes, one of illegal, one of legal, acts,[3] but we have a great deal of trouble in deciding in which class to put this or that act, and frequently end in doubt.

If we content ourselves with observing the facts, if we are interested less in simply following the tendencies of our minds than in presenting something more objective, our impressions are very different. Actual or possible facts appear as if ranged in an unbroken line between two extremes, legality and illegality. They are nearer to the limit of illegality in proportion to the interest taken by the organized forces in preventing or arresting them or in destroying the effect of their performance. They approach that of legality in proportion as the organized forces put in their way fewer obstacles, or afford more facilities for their accomplishment, consequently making individual resistance harder, and as these organized forces are directed by more stable wills, which are capable of more perseverance, of greater steadiness in conceptions, whose execution they are thus able to assure for a longer period.

The facts thus bring us to the conclusion that these two extremes, law and not-law, are of almost less importance from the point of view of the number of acts which can be directly classed under them, than are

---

[2] "*Geist des Römischen Rechts*," French ed., vol. iii. p. 15. (For this work see "Law as a Means to an End" in this Series, p. 455, Footnote.—Ed.) See in the same sense vol. i of this work, pp. 30 *ff.*, where Jhering perhaps adds the embryo of a subjective idea by saying that law should be carried out as law.

[3] In this sense see particularly Alessandro Lévi, "*La Société et l'Ordre Juridique*," p. 100.

the intermediate situations.[4] If persons in authority change their minds, if written law or custom is modified, existing rights will be affected so far as they fall within the scope of the new order. Consequently, the law is a somewhat weak support for acts which are to continue over a long period such as are concerned in rights of property, companies, endowments, etc.; it can more be depended on for those which are to last but a short time, and which disappear almost as soon as they are done, for in such cases law is supported by the power force of inertia. Organized force is halted by the impossibility of reviewing all past acts, by the disorder which would ensue if it should be attempted by the difficulties which would be met with, and thus makes use of such expressions as limitations and the various other bars to actions. It thus accepts without question facts which have been accomplished in the past, though it would not tolerate the same thing at present, and this has always been so except for rare exceptions in periods frankly revolutionary. The force of circumstances, or better, the disproportion between effort and result, is, therefore, the strongest support of the principle of the non-retroactivity of laws.

We have thus explained that we have the law in our favor when our interest has received from an organized force, or, if it be preferred, a constituted authority, a guaranty on which it can depend as lasting. [Pp. 360-362.]

EHRLICH, THE FUNDAMENTAL PRINCIPLES OF THE SOCIOLOGY OF LAW *

... Jurisprudence knows no scientific conception of law. Just as the structural engineer who deals with iron, if he speaks of iron, means not the chemically pure substance that the chemist or mineralogist so characterizes, but rather the very impure iron that is used in building, so the

---

[4] Pascal certainly exaggerated when he said: "Force is easy to recognize and indisputable." This is not wholly, but very largely true; enough so for practical life, which must be contented with probabilities.

* [Chap. 1, pp. 6-17. Reprinted by permission of the publishers from Ehrlich: *Grundlegung der Soziologie des Rechts,* trans. by Walter L. Moll. Cambridge, Mass.: Harvard University Press, 1936.

Eugen Ehrlich (1862–1922), a distinguished Austrian jurist, taught at a number of Central European universities. He sought to establish a "sociology of law" based on the findings of the German historical jurists of the nineteenth century. Ehrlich envisioned a system in which the norms of "living law," rather than the codes, would furnish the primary material of judicial reference. The work from which the present excerpt is taken was originally published in 1913 as *Die Grundlegung der Soziologie des Rechts.* Other works of Ehrlich's include: *Freie Rechtsfindung und freie Rechtswissenschaft* (1903), which has been translated by E. Bruncken in part in *The Science of Legal Method* (Vol. 9, Modern Legal Philosophy Series, 1917); *Die Rechtsfähigkeit* (1909), (*i.e.,* Legal Capacity); and *Die juristische Logik* (1918) (*i.e.,* Juristic Logic). The substance of the passage here translated appears in the Moll translation at pp. 9-23.]

jurist understands by law not that which lives and functions in human society as law but only (except for a few domains of public law) that which comes into view as law for the judge in his administration of justice.

From the judicial standpoint law is a rule according to which the judge has to decide the law-suits that are brought before him. . . . According to the definition which has prevailed in science especially in Germany, law would be a rule of human behavior. A rule of human behavior and a rule according to which a judge decides law-suits may be two very different things, for men certainly do not always behave in accordance with the same rules that are applied for the decision of their suits. The legal historian certainly conceives of law as a rule of human behavior; he portrays the rules according to which, in ancient times or in the middle ages, marriages were concluded, husband and wife, parent and child lived in the family, whether property was held individually or in common, whether the land of the owners was worked by rent-paying tenants or by serfs, and how bargains were concluded and goods inherited. One has the same experience if he requests a traveler who comes from a strange land to describe the law of the peoples that he has come to know. He will then relate how people there marry, live in the family, conclude transactions, but he will hardly come to tell how the rules sound according to which law-suits are decided.

This concept of law, which the jurist accepts quite automatically when he investigates the law of a strange people or a remote time with the interest of a pure scientist, he straightway renounces when he turns to the law in force in his own land and his own time. Quite unconsciously, underhandedly, so to say, the rule according to which men behave is turned into a rule according to which the behavior of men is judged by courts and magistrates. This is still a rule of behavior, but one only for a small section of the people, for the magistrates called upon to apply law, not, as formerly, for the broad general class. Instead of a scientific view there comes to the front simply the practical view fitted for those who hold judicial posts, and the official will still learn to know primarily the rules according to which he himself is to proceed. To be sure, the jurists still consider these rules to be rules of behavior, but there is manifestly a mental jump behind this. That is, they think that the rules according to which courts come to decisions are the rules according to which men *ought* to behave; and there is associated with this the dim thought that men will in time govern themselves by those rules according to which courts decide cases. Now a rule of behavior is self evidently a rule to which behavior not only conforms but also ought to conform, but the assumption that courts determine cases exclusively or even mainly upon the basis of this *Ought* is quite inadmissible; everyday experience teaches the contrary. That judicial decisions are of influence upon the actual behavior of men will certainly not be disputed, but one would still have to discover how far this is applicable and upon what circumstances it depends.

Every page of a juristic work, every juristic lecture affirms what has just been said. Almost every word shows that to the jurist, who deals with a jural relation, there is always but one question to be considered, namely how the conflicts which arise out of this jural relation are to be decided, and not the quite distinct question of how men conduct themselves and must conduct themselves in this relation. Even a man of the greatness of Maitland could say that to write the history of English actions was to write the history of English law.... [Pp. 6-8.]

.   .   .   .   .

... For one, however, who sees in law primarily a rule of conduct, the coercion involved in punishment as well as that in the execution of judgments necessarily falls into the background. For him, human life is not enacted before courts. A moment's observation teaches him that every man stands in countless legal relationships and that with very few exceptions he does quite of his own accord what is obligatory upon him in these relationships; he fulfills his duties as father and son, as husband or wife, he refrains from disturbing his neighbor in the latter's enjoyment of his property, he pays his debts, delivers what he has sold, performs that for which he has bound himself to his employer. The jurist always has the reply ready that men do their duty only because they know that in any case they could be forced to do it by the courts. But if he would only take the unfamiliar trouble of observing men in their activities he would easily convince himself that for the most part they do not think at all of the coercion of courts. So far as they do not do what is naturally according to the rule of the situation, they give quite different reasons for their decisions: they might, if they acted differently, fall out with their dependents, lose their positions and trade, and get the reputation of a quarrelsome, dishonorable, unreliable man. But this fact, at least, even the jurist ought not to have ignored, namely that what men do as their legal duties in this sense of the word is often something quite different from, and sometimes something much more than, what they can be compelled by the authorities to do. Not infrequently the rule of conduct is entirely distinct from the enforceable rule. [Pp. 15-16.]

.   .   .   .   .

... Order in human society rests upon the fact that obligations in general are fulfilled, not on the fact that they are actionable. [P. 17.]

F. S. COHEN, TRANSCENDENTAL NONSENSE AND THE FUNCTIONAL APPROACH *

1. The Definition of Law

The starting point of functional analysis in American jurisprudence is found in Justice Holmes' definition of law as "prophecies of what the courts will do in fact." It is in "The Path of the Law," [71] that this realistic conception of law is first clearly formulated:

> If you want to know the law and nothing else, you must look at it as a bad man, who cares only for the material consequences which such knowledge enables him to predict, not as a good one, who finds his reasons for conduct, whether inside the law or outside of it, in the vaguer sanctions of conscience.... Take the fundamental question, What constitutes the law? You will find some text writers telling you that it is something different from what is decided by the courts of Massachusetts or England, that it is a system of reason, that it is a deduction from principles of ethics or admitted axioms or what not, which may or may not coincide with the decisions. But if we take the view of our friend the bad man we shall find that he does not care two straws for the axioms or deductions, but that he does want to know what the Massachusetts or English courts are likely to do in fact. I am much of his mind. The prophecies of what the courts will do in fact, and nothing more pretentious, are what I mean by the law.

A good deal of fruitless controversy has arisen out of attempts to show that this definition of law as the way courts actually decide cases is either true or false. [72] A definition of law is *useful* or *useless*. It is not *true* or *false*,

---

* [35 *Col. L. Rev.* 809, 835-842 (1935).]

[71] Holmes, Path of the Law (1897) 10 *Harv. L. Rev.* 457, 459-461; *Collected Legal Papers* (1921) p. 167, 171-173. A more precise definition, following Holmes, is given in C. J. Keyser, On the Study of Legal Science (1929) 38 *Yale L.J.* 413.

[72] For examples of such argument see Dickinson, Legal Rules: Their Function in the Process of Decision (1931) 79 *U. of Pa. Law Rev.* 833; H. Kantorowicz, Some Rationalism about Realism (1934) 43 *Yale L.J.* 1240; Frank, *Law and The Modern Mind* (1930) 127-128. The vicious circle in Dickinson's attempted refutation of the realistic definition of law I have elsewhere analyzed. See F. S. Cohen, *Ethical Systems and Legal Ideals* (1933) 12, n. 16. Kantorowicz repeats the same argument, emphasizing the charge that a definition of law in terms of court decisions "puts the cart before the horse" and is as ridiculous as a definition of medicine in terms of the behavior of doctors. The parallel, though witty, is inapt: The correct analogy to a definition of the science of law as description of the behavior of judges would be a definition of the science of medicine as a description of the behavior of certain parasites, etc. Kantorowicz accepts uncritically the metaphysical assumption that definition is a one-way passage from the more general to the less general. But modern logic has demonstrated the hollowness of this assumption. It is useful for certain purposes to define points as functions of lines. For other purposes it is useful to define lines as functions of points. It is just as logical to define law in terms of courts as the other way about. The choice is a matter of convenience, not of logic or truth.

The same metaphysical fallacy vitiates the opposite argument of Frank, namely, that "primary" reality is particular and concrete, so that a definition of law must necessarily be in terms of actual decisions. To the eyes of modern logic, the world contains things *and* relations, neither of which can claim a superior grade of reality. One can start a fight or a scientific inquiry *either* with a concrete fact *or* with a general principle.

any more than a New Year's resolution or an insurance policy. A definition is in fact a type of insurance against certain risks of confusion. It cannot, any more than can a commercial insurance policy, eliminate all risks.
Absolute certainty is as foreign to language as to life. There is no final
insurance against an insurer's insolvency. And the words of a definition
always carry their own aura of ambiguity. But a definition is useful if it
insures against risks of confusion more serious than any that the definition
itself contains.

"What courts do" is not entirely devoid of ambiguity. There is room
for disagreement as to what a *court* is, whether, for instance, the Interstate
Commerce Commission or the Hague Tribunal or the Council of Tesuque
Pueblo is a court, and whether a judge acting in excess of those powers
which the executive arm of the government will recognize acts as a court.
There may even be disagreement as to the line of distinction between what
courts *do* and what courts *say*, in view of the fact that most judicial behavior is verbal. But these sources of ambiguity in Holmes' definition of
law are peripheral rather than central, and easily remedied. They are,
therefore, far less dangerous sources of confusion than the basic ambiguity
inherent in classical definitions of law which involve a confusion between
what is and what ought to be.

The classical confusion against which realistic jurisprudence is a protest
is exemplified in Blackstone's classical definition of law as "a rule of civil
conduct, prescribed by the supreme power in a State, commanding what
is right, and prohibiting what is wrong." [73]

In this definition we have an attempt to unite two incompatible ideas
which, in the tradition of English jurisprudence, are most closely associated with the names of Hobbes and Coke, respectively.

Hobbes, the grandfather of realistic jurisprudence, saw in law the commands of a body to whom private individuals have surrendered their force.
In a state of nature there is war of all against all. In order to achieve peace
and security, each individual gives up something of his freedom, something
of his power, and the commands of the collective power, that is the state,
constitute law.

Hobbes' theory of law has been very unpopular with respectable citizens, but I venture to think that most of the criticism directed against it,
in the last two and a half centuries, has been based upon a misconception
of what Hobbes meant by a state of nature. So far as I know, Hobbes
never refers to the state of nature as an actual historical era, at the end of
which men came together and signed a social contract. The state of nature
is a stage in analysis rather than a stage of history. It exists today and has
always existed, to a greater or lesser degree, in various realms of human
affairs. To the extent that any social relationship is exempt from governmental control it presents what Hobbes calls a state of nature.

In international relations today, at least to the extent that nations have

---

[73] *Bl. Comm.* * 44.

not effectively surrendered their power through compacts establishing such rudimentary agencies of international government as the League of Nations or the Universal Postal Union, there is in fact a state of nature and a war of all against all. This war, as Hobbes insists, is present potentially before actual hostilities break out. Not only in international relations, but in industrial relations today do we find war of all against all, in regions to which governmental control has not been extended, or from which it has been withdrawn—if it existed.

Mutual concessions and delegations of power involved in an arbitration contract, an international treaty, an industrial "code," a corporate merger, or a collective labor agreement, are steps in the creation of government, and call into operation new rules of law and new agencies of law enforcement. Governments do not arise once and for all. Government is arising today in many regions of social existence, and it arises wherever individuals find the conflicts inherent in a state of nature unendurable. The process by which government is created and its commands formulated is a process of human bargaining, based upon actual consent but weighted by the relative power of conflicting individuals or groups.

In all this conception of law, there is no appeal to reason or goodness. Law commands obedience not because of its goodness, or its justice, or its rationality, but because of the power behind it. While this power does rest to a real extent upon popular beliefs about the value of certain legal ideals, it remains true today, as Hobbes says in his *Dialogue on the Common Law,* "In matter of government, when nothing else is turned up, clubs are trump." [74]

Quite different from this realistic conception of law is the theory made famous by Coke that law is only the perfection of reason.[75] This is a notion which has had considerable force in American constitutional history, having served first as a basis for popular revolution against tyrannical violations of "natural law" and the "natural rights" of Englishmen, and serving more recently as a judicial ground for denying legality to statutes that judges consider "unreasonable." It would be absurd to deny the importance of this concept of natural law or justice as a standard by which to judge the acts of rulers, legislative, executive or judicial. It is clear, however, that the validity of this concept of law lies in a realm of values, which is not identical with the realm of social actualities.

The confusion and ambiguity which infest the classical conception of law, as formulated by Blackstone and implicitly accepted by most modern legal writers, arise from the attempt to throw together two inconsistent ideas. Blackstone attempts in effect to superimpose the picture of law drawn by the tender-minded hypocrite, Coke, upon the picture executed by the tough-minded cynic, Hobbes, and to give us a composite photo-

---

[74] Hobbes, *Dialogue Between a Philosopher and a Student of the Common Laws of England* (1681), Of Punishments.
[75] *Co.Litt.* * 976.

graph. Law, says Blackstone, is "a rule of civil conduct prescribed by the supreme power in a State (Hobbes speaking) commanding what is right and prohibiting what is wrong (Coke speaking)" [76] Putting these two ideas together, we have a fertile source of confusion, which many important legal scholars since Blackstone have found about as useful in legal polemics as the ink with which a cuttlefish befuddles his enemies.

Those theorists who adhere to the Blackstonian definition of law are able to spin legal theories to the heart's content without fear of refutation. If legislatures or courts disagree with a given theory, it is a simple matter to show that this disagreement is unjust, unreasonable, monstrous and, therefore, not "sound law." On the other hand, the intruding moralist who objects to a legal doctrine on the ground that it is unjust or undesirable can be told to go back to the realm of morality he came from, since the law is the command of the sovereign and not a matter of moral theory. Perhaps the chief usefulness of the Blackstonian theory is the gag it places upon legal criticism. Obviously, if the law is something that commands what is right and prohibits what is wrong, it is impossible to argue about the goodness or badness of any law, and any definition that deters people from criticism of the law is very useful to legal apologists for the existing order of society. As a modern authority on legal reason declares, "Thus all things made legal are at the same time legally ethical because it is law, and the law must be deemed ethical or the system itself must perish." [77]

2. The Nature of Legal Rules and Concepts

If the functionalists are correct, the meaning of a definition is found in its consequences. The definition of a general term like "law" is significant only because it affects all our definitions of specific legal concepts.

The consequence of defining law as a function of concrete judicial decisions is that we may proceed to define such concepts as "contract," "property," "title," "corporate personality," "right," and "duty," similarly as functions of concrete judicial decisions.

The consequence of defining law as a hodge-podge of political force and ethical value ambiguously amalgamated is that every legal concept, rule or question will present a similar ambiguity.

Consider the elementary legal question: "Is there a contract?"

When the realist asks this question, he is concerned with the actual behavior of courts. For the realist, the contractual relationship, like law in general, is a function of legal decisions. The question of what courts *ought* to do is irrelevant here. Where there is a promise that will be legally enforced there is a contract. So conceived, any answer to the question "Is

---

[76] That "right" and "wrong" are used in this definition as ethical, rather than strictly legal, terms is made clear in Blackstone's own exegesis upon his definition. *Comm.* * 54-55.

[77] Brumbaugh, *Legal Reasoning and Briefing* (1917), 7.

there a contract" must be in the nature of a prophecy, based, like other prophecies, upon past and present facts. So conceived, the question "Is there a contract?" or for that matter any other legal question, may be broken up into a number of subordinate questions, each of which refers to the actual behavior of courts: (1) What courts are likely to pass upon a given transaction and its consequences? (2) What elements in this transaction will be viewed as relevant and important by these courts? (3) How have these courts dealt with transactions in the past which are *similar* to the given transaction, that is, *identical in those respects which the court will regard as important?* (4) What forces will tend to compel judicial conformity to the precedents that appear to be in point (*e.g.* inertia, conservatism, knowledge of the past, or intelligence sufficient to acquire such knowledge, respect for predecessors, superiors or brothers on the bench, a habit of deference to the established expectations of the bar or the public) and how strong are these forces? (5) What factors will tend to evoke new judicial treatment for the transaction in question (*e.g.* changing public opinion, judicial idiosyncrasies and prejudices, newly accepted theories of law, society or economics, or the changing social context of the case) and how powerful are these factors?

These are the questions which a successful practical lawyer faces and answers in any case. The law, as the realistic lawyer uses the term, is the body of answers to such questions. The task of prediction involves, in itself, no judgment of ethical value. Of course, even the most cynical practitioner will recognize that the positively existing ethical beliefs of judges are material facts in any case because they determine what facts the judge will view as important and what past rules he will regard as reasonable or unreasonable and worthy of being extended or restricted. But judicial beliefs about the values of life and the ideals of society are *facts*, just as the religious beliefs of the Andaman Islanders are facts, and the truth or falsity of such moral beliefs is a matter of complete unconcern to the practical lawyer, as to the scientific observer.

Washed in cynical acid, every legal problem can thus be interpreted as a question concerning the positive behavior of judges.

There is a second and radically different meaning which can be given to our type question, "Is there a contract?" When a judge puts this question, in the course of writing his opinion, he is not attempting to predict his own behavior. He is in effect raising the question, in an obscure way, of whether or not liability *should* be attached to certain acts. This is inescapably an ethical question. What a judge ought to do in a given case is quite as much a moral issue as any of the traditional problems of Sunday School morality.[78]

It is difficult for those who still conceive of morality in other-worldly terms to recognize that every case presents a moral question to the court.

[78] *Cf.* F. S. Cohen, *Modern Ethics and the Law* (1934) 4 *Brooklyn L. Rev.* 33 on the conception of "Sunday School morality."

But this notion has no terrors for those who think of morality in earthly terms. Morality, so conceived, is vitally concerned with such facts as human expectations based upon past decisions, the stability of economic transactions, and even the maintenance of order and simplicity in our legal system. If ethical values are inherent in all realms of human conduct, the ethical appraisal of a legal situation is not to be found in the spontaneous outpourings of a sensitive conscience unfamiliar with the social context, the background of precedent, and the practices and expectations, legal and extra-legal, which have grown up around a given type of transaction.

It is the great disservice of the classical conception of law that it hides from judicial eyes the ethical character of every judicial question, and thus serves to perpetuate class prejudices and uncritical moral assumptions which could not survive the sunlight of free ethical controversy.

The Blackstonian conception of law as half-mortal and half-divine gives us a mythical conception of contract. When a master of classical jurisprudence like Williston asks the question "Is there a contract?", he has in mind neither the question of scientific prediction which the practical lawyer faces, nor the question of values which the conscientious judge faces. If he had in mind the former question, his studies would no doubt reveal the extent to which courts actually enforce various types of contractual obligation.[79] His conclusions would be in terms of probability and statistics. On the other hand, if Professor Williston were interested in the ethical aspects of contractual liability, he would undoubtedly offer a significant account of the human values and social costs involved in different types of agreements and in the means of their enforcement. In fact, however, the discussions of a Williston will oscillate between a theory of what courts actually do and a theory of what courts ought to do, without coming to rest either on the plane of social actualities or on the plane of values long enough to come to grips with significant problems. This confused wandering between the world of fact and the world of justice vitiates every argument and every analysis.

Intellectual clarity requires that we carefully distinguish between the two problems of (1) objective description, and (2) critical judgment, which classical jurisprudence lumps under the same phrase. Such a distinction realistic jurisprudence offers with the double-barreled thesis: (1) that every legal rule or concept is simply a function of judicial decisions to which all questions of value are irrelevant, and (2) that the problem of the judge is not whether a legal rule or concept actually exists but whether it

---

[79] So hallowed is the juristic tradition of ignoring the actual facts of cases that a distinguished jurist, Professor Goodheart, can argue in all seriousness that the practice adopted by some American law libraries of putting the records of cases on file is very dangerous. Students might be distracted from the official *ratio decidendi* of the case, and might try to discover what the actual facts of the case were, which would be a death-blow to traditional jurisprudence. See Goodheart, Determining *Ratio Decidendi* of a Case (1930) 40 *Yale L.J.* 161, 172.

ought to exist. Clarity on two fronts is the result. Description of legal facts becomes more objective, and legal criticism becomes more critical.

The realistic lawyer, when he attempts to discover how courts are actually dealing with certain situations, will seek to rise above his own moral bias and to discount the moral bias of the legal author whose treatise he consults.

The realistic author of textbooks will not muddy his descriptions of judicial behavior with wishful thinking; if he dislikes a decision or line of decisions, he will refrain from saying, "This cannot be the law because it is contrary to sound principle," and say instead, "This is the law, but I don't like it," or more usefully, "This rule leads to the following results, which are socially undesirable for the following reasons. . . ."

The realistic advocate, if he continues to use ritual language in addressing an unrealistic court, will at least not be fooled by his own words: he will use his "patter" to induce favorable judicial attitudes and at the same time to distract judicial attention from precedents and facts that look the wrong way (as the professional magician uses his "patter" to distract the attention of his audience from certain facts). Recognizing the circularity of conceptual argument, the realistic advocate will contrive to bring before the court the human values that favor his cause, and since the rules of evidence often stand in the way, he will perforce bring his materials to judicial attention by sleight-of-hand—through the appeal of a "sociological brief" to "judicial notice," through discussion of the background and consequences of past cases cited as precedents, through elaboration and exegesis upon admissible evidence, or even through a political speech or a lecture on economics in the summation of his case or argument.

The realistic judge, finally, will not fool himself or anyone else by basing decisions upon circular reasoning from the presence or absence of corporations, conspiracies, property rights, titles, contracts, proximate causes, or other legal derivatives of the judicial decision itself. Rather, he will frankly assess the conflicting human values that are opposed in every controversy, appraise the social importance of the precedents to which each claim appeals, open the courtroom to all evidence that will bring light to this delicate practical task of social adjustment, and consign to Von Jhering's heaven of legal concepts all attorneys whose only skill is that of the conceptual acrobat.

M. R. COHEN, ON ABSOLUTISMS IN LEGAL THOUGHT *

I. Logical Phase of Legal Absolutism

Absolutism in Definition

Let us begin by considering the vices of legal absolutism from the point of view of logic. The first manifestation of absolutism that suggests itself

---

* [From *Reason and Law*, Chap. 3. Glencoe, Ill.: The Free Press, 1950. The substance of this article appeared in 84 *U. of Pa. L. Rev.* 681 (1936), under the title "On Absolutisms in Legal Thought."]

is the complacent assumption that there can be only one true or correct
definition of any object. This assumption underlies the traditional controversies as to the nature of law and Kant's [1] famous reproach to jurists on
this score. Yet on consulting any scholarly dictionary we can readily see
that few words in common use have only one meaning. This should warn
us that in controversies as to the proper definition of a term, the contestants, while using the same word (*definiendum*) may be really concerned
with different things (*definiens*). Consider, for instance, Maine's [1a] criticism of Austin's [2] definition of law as an imperative or command of the
sovereign. In substance Maine's objection is that there are communities in
which there is no one who habitually issues commands that are generally
obeyed, and yet conduct in them is governed by some law. Now the word
law is, doubtless, used to denote the customs according to which the members of certain primitive communities generally conduct their lives. But
this is no objection at all to Austin's analysis of the law found in classical
Rome and in modern civilized states. In the latter we certainly do find law-
making bodies which abrogate certain customs, such as rebating or over-
certification, and create new ones, such as those connected with income
tax returns. It is not necessary for my present purpose to defend the complete adequacy of Austin's theory, but merely to note that Maine does not
really refute the given definition when he shows that the word *law* is also
used in another sense than that employed by Austin. Of course, the objects
of these two senses are connected, and one may well contend that law in
Austin's sense could not exist without law in Maine's sense, that is, that
there could be no sovereign whose orders are generally obeyed unless
there were certain more general customs actually prevailing, so that the
phenomenon to which Austin refers is thus sociologically derivative and
not primary. But while this statement may be true, those who make it are
generally guilty of the genetic fallacy of the identification of a thing with
its cause or condition. Law may be derived from custom but is obviously
not identical with it. The law which is studied in our law schools, administered in our courts and about which men consult lawyers or agitate in
the political forum for legislative changes is not the same as custom. The
late Mr. Carter, who identified law and custom,[3] had the courage of his
confusion and argued that judges are experts in the customs of the various
subjects on which they have to rule. But no one else has taken that consequence of the theory seriously. Yet, the failure to distinguish clearly between law and custom underlies all the assumptions of Ehrlich's *Living
Law*.[4] There are obviously many practices which actually prevail but are

---

[1] *Kritik der reinen Vernunft* (5th ed. 1797) 759A note.
[1a] Maine, *Lectures on Early History of Institutions* (1875), lectures 12 and 13.
[2] 1 Austin, *Lectures on Jurisprudence* (2d ed. 1869) 15, 118, 120.
[3] Carter, *Law: Its Origin, Growth and Function* (1907) 79.
[4] Ehrlich, *Grundlegung der Soziologie des Rechts*, c. 21.

not recognized or enforced by the legal machinery, *e.g.*, the practice of tipping waiters; and there are, on the other hand, laws regulating acts which are in no significant sense customary, *e.g.*, the rules governing testamentary dispositions or equitable conversion. Indeed legal prescriptions through legislation are necessary precisely because custom proves inadequate to regulate our social relations satisfactorily.

Following Ehrlich, my friend Professor Llewellyn has argued with great force that court litigation represents only the pathology of law, the divergence from the normal practice. The converse of that proposition, however, cannot well be denied. Modern business practice is undoubtedly moulded by past and expected court litigation, by legislative enactments and by administrative orders. That is what gives point to political struggles to control the organs of government.

Law as custom and law through deliberate legislation are thus both realities and we cannot by an arbitrary definition disprove the existence of one or of the other. The important thing is rather to unravel their actual interrelations, and that cannot be done by a mere definition.

It may seem trite, but it is important to insist that while there is an arbitrary element in all definitions, the question of their truth or correctness cannot be altogether dismissed. If we ignore the facts of actual historic usage, a definition is a resolution to use a word as a sign or symbol for a certain object and involves no necessary assumption that the object exists in nature. If we do not like a word in common use we can always invent a new one to denote the particular object we have in mind. In organizing a theoretic system such as geometry we are also free to choose our indefinables and our definitions will then vary according to this choice. We cannot, however, safely ignore the question of consistency in our use of words and this involves (1) attention to the meanings which our words in fact actually convey to our public and to ourselves and (2) the fact that definitions must serve a definite function in any scientific system.

(1) There can be no doubt that departures from general usage do lead to inconsistencies and confusion. For common usage is a habit and the resolution to use a word in a new sense is, like any other resolution, more easily made than kept. In point of fact, therefore, whenever we define a word like law, crime, marriage, person, or the like, in a manner that departs from current customary usage, we sooner or later unwittingly fall back on the common use and thus confuse the meaning of our terms. Regard, therefore, for common usage is a counsel of prudence or practical wisdom. [Pp. 65-67.]

·   ·   ·   ·   ·

(2) Definitions, while not absolutely necessary in pure mathematics, are practically indispensable in all sciences or responsible discourse. They can help us to grasp more clearly the fundamental ideas or patterns in any field

of study and thus serve to create a definite point of view or perspective for the organization of our subject matter. In this respect some definitions are certainly more helpful than others.

From this point of view we must condemn all definitions of law (or of parts of it, *e.g.*, the criminal law) as that which is right, just, expresses the will of the majority, safeguards the social welfare or security, etc. For the historic complaints so bitterly and persistently made against the law raise issues of fact which cannot be properly disposed of by a mere definition. When any one says that an unjust law is not a law, that a legislative enactment is not a law unless it is the will of the majority, or that a provision of the criminal code is not a law if it does not in fact promote the safety of the community, he is resorting to a violent use of words to escape the problem of considering the factual elements in the case.

The law about which we shall be concerned in what follows is that with which judges, lawyers and law schools are concerned, *i.e.*, with rules of conduct determinable by courts. That is what we commonly have in mind when we speak of the law of bankruptcy, divorce, etc., in any state; and our discussion of what is involved in a definition of law is thus only an illustration or paradigm of what is involved in the definition of any legal institution of property, contract, and the like, on which actual decisions depend.* [P. 68.]

---

* [To what extent do the various definitions of law given in the preceding pages represent mutually incompatible beliefs as to the characteristics of an agreed entity? To what extent are the authors listed simply talking about different things under the same term, "law," as Ehrlich suggests? Do such differences in the use of terms reflect any significant conflicts of valuation or interest?

Under which, if any, of the definitions of law given *supra* would the following provide a rule of law?

1. The provision in the federal constitution (Art. I, § 3) requiring Congress to reapportion representatives every decade.

2. The provision in the Clayton Act (38 Stat. 730, c. 323, § 8, 1914) forbidding interlocking directorates but providing no penalties for infraction.

3. A criminal statute the infringers of which are beyond the reach of the law (*e.g.*, against successful suicide).

4. A criminal statute under which juries regularly refuse to convict, but according to which judicial instructions are framed.

5. A criminal statute under which no prosecutions are attempted.

6. A custom of juries to assess damages in negligence cases upon due consideration of the defendant's wealth.

7. A judicial custom of issuing injunction against defamation only when defendants are labor unions.

8. The rule that legal malice is a condition of liability for libel.

9. The rule that a man's real property extends to the center of the earth.

10. A practice in the lower courts of a state to enjoin peaceful picketing, regularly held lawful by the highest court.]

CHAPTER 6

THE NATURE OF THE JUDICIAL PROCESS

Contents

Introductory Note

The true confessions of Judges Bridlegoose, Holmes, Cardozo, Hutcheson, and Frank which form the bulk of this chapter may serve as a good jumping-off point for at least *five* of the problems in the forefront of contemporary jurisprudence.

(1) What is the relationship between rules and concrete decisions? The answer given to this question by the great Roman jurist Paulus that law ought not to be put together out of rules but that rules are derived from the actual administration of justice [*"Non ex regula jus sumatur sed ex jure quod est regula fit"*],—and parallel answers of such modern disciples of Paulus as Holmes, Ehrlich, and Frank—are worth more thought, practical and philosophical, than they have yet received.

(2) How far does the "phonograph" theory of the judicial process (Cf., *infra*, p. 503) serve to degrade judicial law-making by removing it from the plane of conscious criticism?

(3) How far can the gap between rules and decisions be filled in by a more conscious treatment of ethical values, as Holmes urges?

(4) How far can the gap be filled by reliance on expertise, as Ehrlich and Frank suggest, and what merit, if any, still attaches to the warning of Aristotle (renewed by Haines, Myers, Boudin, and many others in our own day) that every increase of judicial power is likely to be followed by an increase of corruption or despotism?

(5) What is the significance or value attached to the ancient ideal of uniform law not dependent, in Beccaria's words, upon the digestion and humor of judges?

ARISTOTLE, BASIC WORKS *

Our next subject is equity and the equitable (*to epieikes*), and their respective relations to justice and the just. . . .

. . . What creates the problem is that the equitable is just, but not the legally just but a correction of legal justice. The reason is that all law is universal but about some things it is not possible to make a universal statement which shall be correct. In those cases, then, in which it is necessary to speak universally, but not possible to do so correctly, the law takes the usual case, though it is not ignorant of the possibility of error. And it is none the less correct; for the error is not in the law nor in the legislator but in the nature of the thing, since the matter of practical affairs is of this kind from the start. When the law speaks universally, then, and a case arises on it which is not covered by the universal statement, then it is right, where the legislator fails us and has erred by over-simplicity, to correct the omission—to say what the legislator himself would have said had he been present, and would have put into his law if he had known. Hence the equitable is just, and better than one kind of justice—not better than absolute justice but better than the error that arises from the absoluteness of the statement. And this is the nature of the equitable, a correction of law where it is defective owing to its universality. In fact this is the reason why all things are not determined by law, *viz.* that about some things it is impossible to lay down a law, so that a decree is needed.

RABELAIS, GARGANTUA †

Chapter X. How Pantagruel was present at the trial of Judge Bridlegoose, who decided causes and controversies in law by the chance and fortune of the dice

.   .   .   .   .

But how is it that you do these things? asked Trinquamelle. I very briefly, quoth Bridlegoose, shall answer you, according to the doctrine and

---

* [Nichomachean Ethics, Bk. V, Ch. 9, pp. 1019-1020. McKeon, ed. Oxford: The Clarendon Press, 1941.]

† [(1550), Book III. Urquhart and Motteux, trans.

François Rabelais (*c.* 1495–1553), cleric, physician, and author, is remembered today for his *Gargantua et Pantagruel* (published in 1533 and following years), a fantastic and lusty narrative in five books, containing an incisive but essentially good-natured satire on the world of the Renaissance. The colorful English version, begun by Urquhart in 1653 and completed (with a commentary by Motteux in 1694, is still considered standard, although a number of other translations, notably one by Samuel Putnam, have appeared in recent years.]

instructions of *Leg. ampliorem* §. *in refutatoriis. c. de appel.*, which is conform to what is said in *Gloss. 1. 1. ff. quod met. causa. Gaudent brevitate moderni.* My practice is therein the same with that of your other worships, and as the custom of the judicatory requires, unto which our law commandeth us to have regard, and by the rule thereof still to direct and regulate our actions and procedures; *ut not. extra. de consuet. in c. ex. litertis et ibi innoc.* For having well and exactly seen, surveyed, overlooked, reviewed, recognized, read, and read over again, turned and tossed over, seriously perused and examined the bills of complaint, accusations, impeachments, indictments, warnings, citations, summonings, comparitions, appearances, mandates, commissions, delegations, instructions, informations, inquests, preparatories, productions, evidences, proofs, allegations, depositions, cross speeches, contradictions, supplications, requests, petitions, inquiries, instruments of the deposition of witnesses, rejoinders, replies, confirmations of former assertions, duplies, triplies, answers to rejoinders, writings, deeds, reproaches, disabling of exceptions taken, grievances, salvation bills, re-examination of witnesses, confronting of them together, declarations, denunciations, libels, certificates, royal missives, letters of appeal, letters of attorney, instruments of compulsion, delineatories, anticipatories, evocations, messages, dimissions, issues, exceptions, dilatory pleas, demurs, compositions, injunctions, reliefs, reports, returns, confessions, acknowledgements, exploits, executions, and other such-like confects and spiceries, both at the one and the other side, as a good judge ought to do, conform to what hath been noted thereupon. *Spec. de ordination, Paragr. 3 et Tit. de Offi. omn. jud. paragr. fin. et de rescriptis praesentat parag. I.—* I posit on the end of a table in my closet all the pokes and bags of the defendant, and then allow unto him the first hazard of the dice according to the usual manner of your other worships. And it is mentioned, 1. *favorabiliores. ff. de reg. jur. et in cap. cum sunt eod. tit. lib.* 6, which saith, *Quum sunt partium jura obscura, reo potius favendum est quam actori.* That being done, I thereafter lay down upon the other end of the same table the bags and satchels of the plaintiff, as your other worships are accustomed to do, *visum visu,* just over against one another; for *Opposita juxta se posita clarius elucescunt: ut not. in lib. I. parag. Videamus. ff. de his qui sunt sui vel alieni juris, et in 1. munerum.* § *mixta. ff. de mun. et hon.* Then do I likewise and sembably throw the dice for him, and forthwith livre him his chance. . . .*

---

* [Compare the use of lots in selection of juries, as discussed in Bonner and Smith, *The Administration of Justice from Homer to Aristotle* (1930), Vol. 1, p. 375 *ff.*]

Chapter XL. How Bridlegoose giveth reasons why he looked upon those law-actions which he decided by the chance of the dice

Yea but, quoth Trinquamelle, my friend, seeing it is by the lot, chance, and throw of the dice that you award your judgments and sentences, why do not you livre up these fair throws and chances at the very same day and hour, without any further procrastination or delay, that the controverting party-pleaders appear before you? To what use can those writings serve you, those papers and other procedures contained in the bags and pokes of the law-suitors? To the very same use, quoth Bridlegoose, that they serve your other worships. They are behooveful unto me, and serve my turn in three things very exquisite, requisite, and authentical. First, for formality sake, the omission whereof, that it maketh all, whatever is done, to be of no force or value, is excellently well proved, by Spec. I, *tit. de instr. edit. et tit. de rescript. praesent.* . . .

Secondly, they are useful and steadable to me, even as unto your other worships, in lieu of some other honest and healthful exercise. The late Master Othoman Vadet [Vadere], a prime physician, as you would say, *Cod. de Comit. et Archi. lib.* 12 hath frequently told me that the lack and default of bodily exercise is the chief, if not the sole and only cause of the little health and short lives of all offices of justice. such as your worships and I am. . . .

Now, *resolutorie loquendo*, I should say, according to the style and phrase of your other worships, that there is no exercise, sport, game, play, no recreation in all this palatine, palatial, or parliamentary world, more aromatizing and fragrant than to empty and void bags and purses, turn over papers and writings, quote margins and backs of scrolls and rolls, fill panniers, and take inspection of causes, *Ex. Bart. et Joan. de Pra. in 1 falsa. de condit. et deomonst. ff.*

Thirdly, I consider, as your own worships use to do, that time ripeneth and bringeth all things to maturity, that by time everything cometh to be made manifest and patent,—and that time is the father of truth and virtue. *Gloss. in 1. 1. cod. de servit. authent. de restit. et ea quae pa. et spec. tit. de requisit. cons.* Therefore is it that, after the manner and fashion of your other worships I defer, protract, delay, prolong, intermit, surcease, pause, linger, suspend, prorogate, drive out, wire-draw, and shift off the time of giving a definitive sentence, to the end that the suit or process, being well fanned and winnowed, tossed, and canvassed to and fro, narrowly, precisely, and nearly garbled, sifted, searched, and examined, and on all hands exactly argued, disputed, and debated, may, by succession of time, come at last to its full ripeness and maturity. By means whereof, when the fatal hazard of the dice ensueth thereupon, the parties cast or condemned by the said aleatory chance will with much greater patience, and more mildly and gently, endure and bear up the disastrous load of their misfortune, than if they had been sentenced at their first arrival unto the court, as *not. gl. ff. de excus. tut. 1. tria. onera. . . .*

.   .   .   .   .

Chapter XLI. How Bridlegoose relateth the history of the reconcilers of parties at variance in matters of law

I remember to the same purpose, quoth Bridlegoose, in continuing his discourse, that in the time when at Poictiers I was a student of law under Brocadium Juris, there was at Semerve one Peter Dandin, a very honest man, careful labourer of the ground, fine singer in a church-desk, of good repute and credit, and older than the most aged of all your worships. . . . This honest man compounded, atoned, and agreed more differences, controversies, and variances at law than had been determined, voided, and finished during his time in the whole palace of Poictiers, in the auditory of Montmorillon, and in the town-house of the old Partenay. This amicable disposition of his rendered him venerable and of great estimation, sway, power, and authority throughout all the neighboring places of Chauvigny, Nouaille, Leguge, Vivonne, Mezeaux, Estables, and other bordering and circumjacent towns, villages, and hamlets. All their debates were pacified by him; he put an end to their brabbling suits at law and wrangling differences. By his advice and counsels were accords and reconcilements no less firmly made than if the verdict of a sovereign judge had been interposed therein, although, in very deed, he was no judge at all, but a right honest man, as you may well conceive,—*arg. in 1. sed si unius. ff. de jure-jur. et de verbis obligatoriis 1. continuus.* There was not a hog killed within three parishes of him whereof he had not some part of the haslet and puddings. He was almost every day invited either to a marriage banquet, christening feast, an uprising or woman-churching treatment, a birthday's anniversary solemnity, a merry frolic gossiping, or otherwise to some delicious entertainment in a tavern, to make some accord and agreement between persons at odds and in debate with one another. . . . He had a son, whose name was Tenot Dandin, a lusty, young, sturdy, frisking roister, so help me God! . . .

And such was his confidence to have no worse success than his father, he assumed unto himself the title of Law-strife-settler. He was likewise in these pacificatory negotiations so active and vigilant—for, *Vigilantibus jura subveniunt. ex 1. pupillus. ff. quae in fraud. cred. et ibid. 1. non enim. et instit. in proaem.*—that when he had smelt, heard, and fully understood—*ut ff. si quando paup. fec. 1. Agaso. gloss. in verb. olfecit, id est, nasum ad culum posuit*—and found that there was anywhere in the country a debatable matter at law, he would incontinently thrust in his advice, and so forwardly intrude his opinion in the business, that he made no bones of making offer, and taking upon him to decide it, how difficult soever it might happen to be, to the full contentment and satisfaction of both parties. . . . But so hugely great was his misfortune in this undertaking, that he never composed any difference, how little soever you may imagine it might have been, but that, instead of reconciling the parties at odds, he did incense, irritate, and exasperate them to a higher point of dissension and enmity than ever they were at before. . . .

It happened a little while thereafter that he made a most heavy regret thereof to his father, attributing the causes of his bad success in pacificatory enterprises to the perversity, stubbornness, froward, cross, and backward inclinations of the people of his time; roundly, boldly, and irreverently upbraiding, that if but a score of years before the world had been so wayward, obstinate, pervacacious, implacable, and out of all square, frame, and order as it was then, his father had never attained to and acquired the honour and title of Strife-appeaser so irrefragably, inviolably, and irrevocably as he had done. . . . To this the honest old father answered thus: My son Dandin, when Don Oportet taketh place, this is the course which we must trace, *gl. c. de appell. 1. eos etiam.* For the road that you went upon was not the way to the fuller's mill, nor in any part thereof was the form to be found wherein the hare did sit. Thou hast not the skill and dexterity of settling and composing differences. Why? Because thou takest them at the beginning, in the very infancy and bud as it were, when they are green, raw, and indigestible. Yet I know handsomely and featly how to compose and settle them all. Why? Because I take them at their decadence, in their weaning, and when they are pretty well digested. So saith Gloss:

Dulcior est fructus post multa pericula ductus.

l. non moriturus. c. de contrahend. et commit. stip. Didst thou ever hear the vulgar proverb, *Happy is the physician whose coming is desired at the declension of a disease?* For the sickness being come to a crisis is then upon the decreasing hand, and drawing towards an end, although the physician should not repair thither for the cure thereof; whereby, though nature wholly do the work, he bears away the palm and praise thereof. My pleaders, after the same manner, before I did interpose my judgment in the reconciling of them, were waxing faint in their contestations. Their altercation heat was much abated, and, in declining from their former strife, they of themselves inclined to a firm accommodation of their differences; because there wanted fuel to that fire of burning rancour and despiteful wrangling whereof the lower sort of lawyers were the kindlers. That is to say, their purses were emptied of coin, they had not a win in their fob, nor penny in their bag, wherewith to solicit and present their actions.

Deficiente pecu, deficit omne, ma.

There wanted then nothing but some brother to supply the place of a paranymph, brawl-broker, proxenete, or mediator, who, acting his part dexterously, should be the first broacher of the motion of an agreement, for saving both the one and the other party from that hurtful and pernicious shame whereof he could not have avoided the imputation when it should have been said that he was the first who yielded and spoke of a reconcilement, and that therefore, his cause not being good, and being sensible where his shoe did pinch him, he was willing to break the ice, and make the greater haste to prepare the way for a condescendment to an amicable and friendly treaty. Then was it that I came in pudding time, Dandin, my son, nor is the fat of bacon more relishing to boiled peas than was my verdict then agreeable to them. This was my luck, my profit, and good fortune. I tell thee, my jolly son Dandin, that by this rule and method I could settle a firm peace, or at least clap up a cessation of arms and truce for many years to come, betwixt the Great King and the Venetian State, the Emperor and the Cantons of Switzerland, the English and the Scots, and betwixt the Pope and the Ferrarians. Shall I go yet further? Yea, as I would have God to help me, betwixt the Turk and the Sophy, the Tartars and the Muskoviters. Remark well what I am to say unto thee. I would take them at that very instant nick of time when both those of the one and the other side should be weary and tired of making war, when they had voided and emptied their own cashes and coffers of all treasure and coin, drained and exhausted the purses and bags of their subjects, sold and mortgaged their domains and proper inheritances, and totally wasted, spent, and consumed the munition, furniture, provision, and victuals that were necessary for the continuance of a military expedition. There, I am sure, by God, or by his Mother, that, would they, would they not, in spite of all their teeth, they should be forced to have a little respite and breathing time to moderate their fury and cruel rage of their ambitious aims. This is the doctrine in *Gl. 37, d. c. siquando.*

Odero, si potero; si non, invitus amabo.

EHRLICH, JUDICIAL FREEDOM OF DECISION: ITS PRINCIPLES AND OBJECTS *

I. Bureaucratic Law as Contrasted with People's Law

§1. *Relations of Legislator and Judge.* Modern systematic legal science inclines to explain each rule of law principally by seeking to discover the intention of the legislator; but sufficient stress has never been laid on the fact that the significance of law in the daily life of a people depends far more on the persons charged with its administration than on the principles according to which it is administered. The same rule is likely to have an essentially different meaning in different countries or at different periods,

---

* [Translated from *"Freie Rechtsfindung und freie Rechtswissenchaft"* in volume 9 of Modern Legal Philosophy Series, *Science of Legal Method.* Bruncken, trans. New York: The Macmillan Company, 1903.]

for no other reason than that the persons sitting on the bench are differently trained, have a different temperament, hold a different official or social position. This is apt to be more vividly realized by the trained historian
of law than by the analytical student. To the historian, the *"praetor"* and
the *"prudentes"* still speak in the Pandects, the *"Schöffen"* in the old German law, and the judges of the Superior Courts with the Chancellor, in
English common law and equity grown out of the same Germanic root.
Similarly, the law prevailing to-day on the European continent must be
viewed as a system of law peculiar to a judiciary composed of learned
bureaucratic judges. . . .

We are all children of the bureaucratic State which has now dominated
our political and social life for several centuries. Hardly one of us is likely,
without great difficulty, to free himself from the conceptions and lines of
thought generated and fostered thereby. In the eyes of a bureaucracy law
is properly nothing but a body of directions given by the Government to
its officials. . . . [Pp. 48-49.]

§2. *Increased Importance of Statutory Law.*

.   .   .   .   .

The essential nature of the bureaucratic State is expressed by the fact
that for us the statute is the predominant form of law. Similarly, the content of the law of the bureaucratic State depends on the essential character
of that form of government. In essence, such a system of law is simply a
rule of decision. Its exclusive or almost exclusive purpose is to direct officials how to deal with the matters intrusted to them, and particularly how
to decide legal controversies. That is, of course, a very one-sided conception; for law as a rule of decision may indeed be the side of law most
interesting to the lawyer, but it is by no means the only and not even
the most important side. Law exists for other very different purposes in
addition to the settlement of controversies. It is the very foundation of
the social organism, or (to use an expression of Schäffle, already growing
antiquated), law is the skeleton of the social body. . . . [Pp. 48-51.]

.   .   .   .   .

§4. *The Importance of Unwritten Law.* But, even of rules of decision,
the smallest part is the result of State action. Every sort of protection of
rights by the State begins with enforcing the payment of compensatory
damages, which in primitive times the injured party sought to recover on
his own authority and by his own power. At the moment when the judgment of a court is substituted for this primitive self-help, there are no rules
of decision in existence except those flowing from the very nature of the
social organization. In other words, they are derived from such sources as
the nature of property in the form it assumed directly under the condi-

tions of primitive ownership; also from the nature of those associations, which are of so much importance in primitive society, like the clan, the family, the community, the guild; from the customary subject-matters and forms of the most ancient contracts, and the primitive forms of intercourse, which are mostly older than any sort of legal protection. Decisions are first preserved by oral tradition, then written down, collected, commented upon, generalized, and at last codified. Thus arise those peculiar systems of law in the special keeping of lawyers, which are, in many different forms, characteristic of the early times of all the nations of the world. They are legal science and legal rule all in one, like the old *"jus civile"* of the Romans which still lives, unchanged in essentials, in the writings of the classical Roman jurists and the great compilation of Justinian.

The decisions, therefore, are not based on the rules of law, but the rules of law are deduced from the decisions. The law on which the decisions are based is the *"jus quod est."* Paulus, who could still observe the actual working of a living law of this kind, puts what he has learned in actual experience tersely into the famous maxim: *"Non ex regula jus sumatur, sed ex jure quod est regula fit."* The decisions are older than the rules,—the law of the lawyers older and incomparably richer than the law of legislatures. . . . [Pp. 53-54.]

§11. *Inadequacy of Mere Statutory Law.*

.   .   .   .   .

No theory of the application of law can get around the difficulty that every body of formulated rules is in its very nature incomplete; that it is really antiquated the very moment it has been formulated. . . . [P. 61.]

II. Statutory Law and Its Obstructions to Free Judicial Decision

.   .   .   .   .

§13. *Legal Technicalism.* . . . Generally speaking, it is undoubtedly much easier to decide a definite case correctly than to establish an abstract rule universally applicable for all imaginable cases; and surely it can hardly be maintained seriously that such a rule will invariably result in the fairest decision, even in those cases which nobody had thought of when the rule was made. As a matter of fact no such thing is attempted by the technical judicial method of decision; its goal is quite different. A rule is to be framed, not necessarily always just, but at least certain, that can be ascertained in advance and will afford protection against arbitrary and biased judgments. In order to attain this end, the judge is to be subjected, bound hand and foot, to a rule that determines all things in advance. [Pp. 61-63.]

.   .   .   .   .

§14. *Further Objections to the Technical Method.* But how about the possibility of foreseeing what the decision of the court will be? In what cases is such foresight actually attained under the technical method? Apparently in those few cases only in which the law is so clear and definite that there is really no need of searching for it. In cases of this sort, however, the method of free decision would make no change, for it would come into play merely when there is no clear provision in the formulated law. There is good reason to claim that a better guaranty for certainty of the law than by the technical method may be found in a method of free decision—bound only by judicial precedents, but not beyond that. Even to-day, a judge feels greater assurance when he can refer to a series of adjudications than when he has nothing but a construction of the statute which may at any time be upset by some other artist in construction.

On still another ground, however, one may venture to call the method of legal technicalism nothing less than the sin against the Holy Spirit. For this method has obscured our eyes to the only true principle at the foundation not merely of a certain and unbiased administration of justice, but also of a justice dominated by great ideals: ... By making legislation the center of our system of law, and by nothing else, has it been possible to hide for so long a period the recognition of the simple truth that the greatest task that can be given a man to discharge, Justice, requires a standard of mental and moral greatness far above the common average. Thus, and thus only, can people fail to see that for such a task a man is not fit merely because by examination and a little practice he has proved that he can, after a fashion, find his way through the sections of a code. [Pp. 65-66.]

.   .   .   .   .

III. *Characteristics of the Principle of Free Judicial Decision*

§17. *Free Decision Not Arbitrary.* A modern judge who assumes it to be his duty always to base his decisions on an express statute naturally will ask what is to serve as foundation for the administration of justice if that of a statute is to be withdrawn.

One might be tempted to reply simply that in every period of time there has existed a justice not hedged about by code sections. Such justice, however, is by no means arbitrary. As already emphasized at the opening of this essay, it grows out of the principles of juridical tradition. Every kind of freedom of decision starts with juridical tradition and tends toward what Stammler has called "correct law" ("*richtiges Recht*"). The very peculiarity of the judicial office is the assumption that the judge's utterance represents, not his personal opinion, but the law. And this law is found primarily in the legal records of the past, in statutes, in decisions of courts, in legal literature. No Roman jurist ever deviated farther from the traditional rules than he was compelled to do by necessity. Blackstone, in a famous passage of his Commentaries, speaking of the English common law, represents the English judge as only declaring, not as making, the rules of law.[10] Free decision is conservative, as every kind of freedom is; for freedom means responsibility, while restraint shifts responsibility upon other shoulders. [Pp. 71-72.]

. . . . .

§ 20. *The Personality of the Judge.* Thus the administration of justice has always contained a personal element. In all ages, social, political and cultural movements have necessarily exerted an influence upon it; but whether any individual jurist yields more or less to such influences whether he is more inclined in his *"quae traditae sunt perseverare"* or rather *"ingenii qualitate et fiducia doctrinae plurima innovare constituit,"* depends of course less on any theory of legal method than on his own personal temperament. The point is that this fact should not be tolerated as something unavoidable, but should be gladly welcomed. For the one important desideratum is that his personality must be great enough to be properly intrusted with such functions. The principle of free decision is really not concerned with the substance of the law, but with the proper selection of judges; in other words, it is the problem of how to organize the judiciary so as to give plenty of scope to strong personalities. Everything depends upon that....[P. 74.]

. . . . .

It would be unfair if we failed to recognize that there are further and perhaps better-founded reasons for the existing antipathy to free legal decision. One such reason may be found especially in traditional conceptions regarding the proper limits of the functions of Government and the separation of powers. In the tendency to make the bureaucratic judge base his judicial opinion invariably on the letter of the statute we may find a good portion of the old-fashioned Liberal distrust of the Government; and on the other hand it will take a long time before the idea will be thoroughly familiar that the function of legislation does not extend to every form of lawmaking but is confined to the passing of express statutes. Those ways of thinking, however, really belong to a theory of the State which is already antiquated, although like every political theory it was the scientific expression of conditions historically developed.

IV. The Tasks Awaiting Freedom of Judicial Decision

§ 21. *The Work of Legal Science.* We may now cast a glance at the science of law, and consider what tasks will remain for it after technicalism has been supplanted by free decision.

---

[10] *Blackstone's Commentaries* (Cooley, 3d ed.), p. 69.

First of all, it becomes plain that after this change there can be no further place for the traditional essay on rules of construction. The moment it is recognized that a statute provides only for what it provides, and that what is not so provided simply remains unprovided, there can be no further excuse for using a hairsplitting machine,—or as it were, for squeezing decisions out of a statute with a hydraulic press.... [P. 76.]

.   .   .   .   .

§ 22. *The Practical Operation of the Law.* ... It is the business of legal science to teach the law as it actually works. Whoever knows but the "intent of the legislator" is still far from knowing the law that is really in effect.

In this sense the traditional, dogmatic conception of law may be contrasted with a dynamic conception. For the latter, the problem is not simply to know what a rule means, but how it lives and works, how it adapts itself to the different relations of life, how it is being circumvented and how it succeeds in frustrating circumvention. ...

Here we must turn first to the decisions of the courts. From these principally we may learn the "*jus quod est*," from them alone we can gather what rules of decision have actually entered into daily life, and how they have done so. But it is not enough to cite decisions in a text, or in notes, and to approve or condemn them according as they are deemed correct or otherwise. A legal decision is always the result of a number of factors influencing the judge; meaning and text of a rule is one of these factors, but not the only one. Every decision expresses some actually existing social movement; even the most abstruse scholastical reason, the most manifest misinterpretations or conscious perversions of law, at least help to show these facts as coefficients of social tendencies. One of the duties of legal science is to examine the origin, nature, effect, and value of the tendencies that become apparent in legal decisions, and thus to furnish a picture of what is going on in the administration of justice and what the causes thereof may be.[15] [Pp. 77-78.]

M. R. COHEN, THE PROCESS OF JUDICIAL LEGISLATION *

Whether because of the general overturning of ordinary interests brought about by the World War, or for some other reason, the con-

---

[15] In my paper on "*Die stillschweigende Willenserklärung,*" I have tried to make use of the decisions in this manner.

* [From *Law and the Social Order,* by M. R. Cohen, copyright, 1933, by Harcourt, Brace and Company, Inc. The major part of this essay was read at the first meeting of the Conference on Legal and Social Philosophy, April 26, 1913, and published under this title in 48 *Am. L. Rev.,* 161 (1914). Portions of the present essay are taken from a paper presented at the thirty-eighth annual meeting of the New York State Bar Association, January 22-23, 1915, and published under the title "Legal Theories and Social Science" in *Internat. Jour. of Ethics,* Vol. XXV (1915), p. 469.]

troversy over the recall of judges and judicial decisions that raged some years ago seems to have disappeared. The leaders of the American bar claim to have settled the matter by a campaign of education. The keynote of this campaign was sounded by Elihu Root when he urged that the public be educated to an appreciation of the true function of the judge, which he expressed as follows: "It is not his function or within his power to enlarge or improve or change the law." [2] In Sharswood's "Essay on Professional Ethics," republished by the American Bar Association, judicial legislation is the one cardinal sin of which jurists must beware. [3]

In spite, however, of the apparent authority back of this theory, a philosopher need not hesitate to declare it demonstrably false, *i.e.*, contrary to fact. If judges never make law, how could the body of rules known as the common law ever have arisen or have undergone the changes which it has?

Moreover, not only is the common law changed from time to time by judicial decisions, but we may with Professor Gray [4] go on to assert that in the last analysis the courts also make our statute law; for it is the court's interpretation of the meaning of a statute that constitutes the law. If anyone needed to be convinced of this, a mere reference to the history of the Sherman Anti-Trust Act would be sufficient. The situation, however, becomes quite transparent in the realm of constitutional law. Who has made the body of law dealing with the police power of the states if not judges within the last forty years? Indeed the same men who insist that judges never make the law also tell us, as Mr. Hornblower does, how much better judge-made law is than that which we get from our legislators. [5] What respectable lawyer is not ready, at a moment's notice, to extol the work of John Marshall in shaping the national Constitution? If the judges are in no way to change or make the law, what business had Marshall to shape the Constitution? [6] [Pp. 112-113.]

.   .   .   .   .

The theory, then, that law pre-exists judicial decision, and that judges, therefore, can and should do their work without at the same time making

---

[2] "The Importance of an Independent Judiciary," *Independent*, Vol. LXXII (1912), p. 704.

[3] American Bar Association, *Reports*, Vol. III (1907), pp. 45 *et seq.*

[4] Gray, *Nature and Sources of the Law*, 1909, sec. 275-76.

[5] Hornblower, "A Century of 'Judge-Made' Law," *Columbia Law Review*, Vol. VII (1907), pp. 453-57. In historical and biographical estimates of various judges it is quite usual to find them praised for developing or creating certain branches of law, *e.g.*, nearly all accounts of Story praise him for having created our admiralty law, which, in truth, he did.

[6] "He (Marshall) was not the commentator upon American Constitutional Law; he was not the expounder of it; he was the author, the creator of it." Phelps, "Annual Address," *Annual Report* American Bar Association, 1879, pp. 173, 176.

new law, can be defended only on the assumption of the eternal self-sufficiency of the existing law. If, however, life is continually developing new and unforeseeable situations not covered by precedent, and judges are obliged to decide every case before them (these decisions serving as binding precedents), it follows that they must in the course of their work develop new rules.[25]

The process according to which this law-making takes place may be viewed under the three headings of finding, interpreting, and applying the law.

1. Finding or Making the Law.

In the physical world no antithesis seems more justified than that between making and finding. Inventing and finding a continent are surely incompatible. When, however, we come to human affairs, the antithesis becomes less sharp. Making and finding an opportunity, making or finding time, making or finding a theory, are not so clearly antagonistic. Hence we need not be surprised that under the pressure of a prevailing theory, embodied in a current terminology, the process of law-making should be called finding the law. Some simple-hearted people believe that the names we give to things do not matter. But though the rose by any other name might smell as sweet, the history of civilization bears ample testimony to the momentous influence of names. At any rate, whether the process of judicial legislation should be called finding or making the law is undoubtedly of great practical moment.

To speak of finding the law seems to connote that the law exists before the decision, and thus tends to minimize the importance of the judicial contribution to the law or of the *arbitrium judicium* and the factors that determine it.

---

[25] The flimsy fiction that judicial decisions do not make the law, but are only the evidence of it, is really inconsistent with the doctrine of *stare decisis*. If decisions were only evidence of the law, why could not courts of coordinate or even inferior jurisdiction entertain evidence that any previous decision or judgment was wrong? Obviously, to the extent that such evidence is excluded, the past decision has made law.

There is no space here to indicate fully the logical confusion in the classical theory that each particular decision embodies a general rule as its *ratio decidendi*. A particular proposition can never uniquely determine a general one, and as a matter of fact any case, no matter how simple, can be cited in our system as an authority for various propositions of law of different degrees of generality. The true relation between decisions or judgments and rules of law is analogous to that between given points and the curves that can be drawn through them.

Professor Geldart and others seem to think it absurd to suppose that when a new case is decided "the facts of the case were previously governed by no law" (*Elements of English Law*, 1911, p. 23). This objection is based on a confusion between potential and actual existence, but we may here meet it by simply calling attention to the undoubted fact that vast regions of human relations, such as informal agreements, formerly not governed by the common law have by judicial decision been brought within its sway.

How is the law found? Consider, to begin with, cases of first impression that have no clear precedent. They are decided, we are told, on principle.[26] But what principle, and where does it come from? If we examine the decisions of the great creative minds in our legal history, of judges like Mansfield, Gibson, or Shaw, we find the prevailing ideas of justice, public convenience, and what is "reasonable" are always appealed to as decisive. (It has been noted that Marshall seldom cited precedents.) Moral rules or considerations of public convenience do not, of course, of themselves have the force of law. It is only when courts, balancing considerations of justice and policy, decide to enforce a moral or political rule that they transform it into a legal rule.[27] At any rate, there can be no doubt that by direct judicial legislation based on supposed principles of justice have been developed the bodies of law known as quasi contract, the common counts, the law of boycott, etc. Principles of public policy can be seen in the law of trade and other fixtures, in the doctrine of contracts void against public policy, the law of agency, the distinction between libel and slander, the law of privileged communications, the law of corporations, etc.[28] A great deal of judicial legislation also takes place under cover of finding what is "reasonable" under given circumstances. Thus our whole law of negligence consists essentially of various standards of conduct set up by courts to which people must conform at their peril. The same process can be observed in the law as to what are the reasonable necessities of an infant, what is a reasonable time for notice of dishonour of a bill, what is reasonable cause in an action for malicious prosecution or false arrest, and what is the reasonable income to which a public service corporation is entitled.[29]

It may be urged that these cases of first impression which constitute the leading cases of any branch of law are rare and must continue to become rarer as the number of precedents increases. To this we may reply that the cases of first impression are rare only because, in consequence of the prevailing theory, we tend to lose sight of them. Every case differs in some respect from previous ones. But the felt necessity of finding precedents produces the tendency to ignore or minimize these differences. Nor

---

[26] See Sneddeker v. Waring, 12 N.Y. 170, 174 (1854).

[27] For modern instances or illustrations see Lefroy, "The Basis of Case Law," *Law Quarterly Review*, Vol. XXII (1906), p. 293 *et seq.* From the Continental and comparative point of view this has been significantly treated by Kohler, "*Die Menschenhülfe in Privatrecht*," *Jherings Jahrbücher für die Dogmatik*, Vol. XXV (1887), pp. 1-141.

[28] For the classical common-law conception of public policy see Co. Litt. 66a (1st Amer. ed., 1853) and Sheppard's *Touchstone*, Chap. 6. The attempt of Baron Parke to narrow the meaning of the term "public policy" to mean simply the policy already established in the law was, as Lefroy has pointed out, rejected by the House of Lords in Egerton v. Earl of Brownlow, 4 H.L.C. 1 (1853).

[29] See Willcox v. The Consolidated Gas Co., 212 U.S. 19, 29 Sup. Ct. 192 (1919). "Reasonableness in these cases belongeth to the knowledge of the law, and therefore to be decided by the justices." (Co. Litt. 56, b.)

is it true that as the number of decided cases increases, the number of cases of first impression must necessarily diminish. The possibility of these latter cases depends not so much on the mass of adjudicated cases as on the rapidity with which conditions of life are changing. Moreover, as the number of precedents increases, skilful counsel can and do all the more readily find precedents on both sides, so that the process of judicial decision is, as a matter of fact, determined consciously or unconsciously by the judges' views of fair play, public policy, and the general nature and fitness of things. It is true that judges of a certain temperament, the so-called strong-minded judges, frequently stop short at most tempting equities with the plea that authoritative precedent or well-settled law will not permit them to mete out the justice that they would like to enforce.[30] This, however, does not mean that justice is not a ground of decision with such judges; for we find them in other cases reasoning that that which leads to unjust or monstrous consequences cannot be the law.

The same judges who could not, because of the Fourteenth Amendment or its equivalent, approve the constitutionality of an admittedly just workmen's compensation law, had no difficulty in declaring unconstitutional a primary law that for all its iniquity did not seem to run afoul of any specific constitutional provision.[31] The simple fact is that the desire to do justice is a constant motive, but the sense for juristic consistency or symmetry is another that sometimes outweighs it. The relative weight of these two, as a matter of fact, varies with the psychology or temperament of the judge. Whatever may be the constitution of the ideal judge, it is not unreasonable to suppose that the minds of most judges work like those of other mortals, that is, having in various ways been unconsciously determined to decide one way or another, they look for and find reasons or precedents for such decisions. It was not a layman but a president of the American Bar Association who said that "a judge may decide almost any question any way, and still be supported by an array of cases."[32] [Pp. 121-124.]

---

[30] E. R. Thayer, "Judicial Legislation," *Harvard Law Review*, Vol. V (1891), pp. 170, 180.

[31] People ex rel. Hotchkiss v. Smith, 206 N. Y. 231, 99 N.E. 568 (1912). The court condemns certain things because "unnecessary" and others pass as "not sufficiently onerous." But "requirements which shock the sense of justice" (p. 242) are not always unconstitutional.

[32] Wigmore, *Evidence*, 2d ed., 1923, Vol. 1, p. xv. Judge Baldwin cites with approval the statement of an English judge that "nine-tenths of the cases which had ever gone to judgment in the highest court of England might have been decided the other way without any violence to the principles of the common law." Baldwin, *The American Judiciary*, 1905, p. 54.

SOUTHERN PACIFIC CO. v. JENSEN
U.S. Supreme Court, 1917
244 U.S. 205

Mr. Justice Holmes [dissenting]. I recognize without hesitation that judges do and must legislate, but they can do so only interstitially; they are confined from molar to molecular motions. A common-law judge could not say I think the doctrine of consideration a bit of historical nonsense and shall not enforce it in my court. No more could a judge exercising the limited jurisdiction of admiralty say I think well of the common-law rules of master and servant and propose to introduce them here *en bloc*. Certainly he could not in that way enlarge the exclusive jurisdiction of the District Courts and cut down the power of the States. If admiralty adopts common-law rules without an act of Congress it cannot extend the maritime law as understood by the Constitution. It must take the rights of the parties from a different authority, just as it does when it enforces a lien created by a State. The only authority available is the common law or statutes of a State. For from the often repeated statement that there is no common law of the United States, *Wheaton v. Peters*, 8 Pet. 591, 658; *Western Union Telegraph Co. v. Call Publishing Co.*, 181 U.S. 92, 101, and from the principles recognized in *Atlantic Transport Co. v. Imbrovek* having been unknown to the maritime law, the natural inference is that in the silence of Congress this court has believed the very limited law of the sea to be supplemented here as in England by the common law, and that here that means, by the common law of the State. *Sherlock v. Alling*, 93 U.S. 99, 104. *Taylor v. Carryl*, 20 How. 583, 598. So far as I know, the state courts have made this assumption without criticism or attempt at revision from the beginning to this day; e. g. *Wilson v. MacKenzie*, 7 Hill (N.Y.), 95. *Gabrielson v. Waydell*, 135 N.Y. 1, 11. *Kalleck v. Deering*, 161 Massachusetts, 469. See *Ogle v. Barnes*, 8 T. R. 188. *Nicholson v. Mounsey*, 15 East, 384. Even where the admiralty has unquestioned jurisdiction the common law may have concurrent authority and the state courts concurrent power. *Schoonmaker v. Gilmore*, 102 U.S. 118. The invalidity of state attempts to create a remedy for maritime contracts or torts, parallel to that in the admiralty, that was established in such cases as *The Moses Taylor*, 4 Wall. 411, and *The Hine v. Trevor*, 4 Wall. 555, is immaterial to the present point.

The common law is not a brooding omnipresence in the sky but the articulate voice of some sovereign or quasi-sovereign that can be identified; although some decisions with which I have disagreed seem to me to have forgotten the fact. It always is the law of some State, and if the District Courts adopt the common law of torts, as they have shown a tendency to do, they thereby assume that a law not of maritime origin and deriving its authority in that territory only from some particular

State of this Union also governs maritime torts in that territory—and if the common law, the statute law has at least equal force, as the discussion in *The Osceola* assumes. On the other hand the refusal of the District Courts to give remedies coextensive with the common law would prove no more than that they regarded their jurisdiction as limited by the ancient lines—not that they doubted that the common law might and would be enforced in the courts of the States as it always has been. . . . [Pp. 221-222.]

. . . . .

As to the spectre of a lack of uniformity I content myself with referring to *The Hamilton*, 207 U.S. 398, 406. The difficulty really is not so great as in the case of interstate carriers by land, which "in the absence of Federal statute providing a different rule are answerable according to the law of the State for nonfeasance of misfeasance within its limits." *The Minnesota Rate Cases*, 230 U.S. 352, 408, and cases cited. The conclusion that I reach accords with the considered cases of *Lindstrom v. Mutual Steamship Co.*, 132 Minnesota, 328; *Kennerson v. Thames Towboat Co.*, 89 Connecticut, 367; and *North Pacific S. S. Co. v. Industrial Accident Commission of California*, 163 Pac. Rep. 199, as well as with the New York decision in this case. 215 N.Y. 514. [P. 223.]

BENJAMIN N. CARDOZO, THE NATURE OF THE JUDICIAL PROCESS *

Lecture I. Introduction. The Method of Philosophy

The work of deciding cases goes on every day in hundreds of courts throughout the land. Any judge, one might suppose, would find it easy to describe the process which he had followed a thousand times and more. Nothing could be farther from the truth. Let some intelligent layman ask him to explain: he will not go very far before taking refuge in the excuse that the language of craftsmen is unintelligible to those untutored in the craft. Such an excuse may cover with a semblance of respectability an otherwise ignominious retreat. It will hardly serve to still the pricks of curiosity and conscience. In moments of introspection, when there is

---

* [New Haven: Yale University Press, 1921.

Benjamin Nathan Cardozo (1870–1938), after practising in New York from 1891 until 1914, was elected a Justice of the New York Supreme Court, and was almost immediately elevated to the Court of Appeals of that State, to which he was twice re-elected. In 1932 President Hoover appointed Cardozo an Associate Justice of the United States Supreme Court, a position which he occupied until his death. His best-known works are: *The Nature of the Judicial Process* (1921); *The Growth of the Law* (1924); *The Paradoxes of Legal Science* (1928); and *Law and Literature and Other Essays* (1931). The best account of Cardozo's significance in American law and jurisprudence will be found in the first chapter of B. L. Shientag, *Moulders of Legal Thought* (1943).]

no longer a necessity of putting off with a show of wisdom the un-
initiated interlocutor, the troublesome problem will recur, and press for
a solution. What is it that I do when I decide a case? To what sources
of information do I appeal for guidance? In what proportions do I permit them to contribute to the result? In what proportions ought they
to contribute? If a precedent is applicable, when do I refuse to follow it?
If no precedent is applicable, how do I reach the rule that will make
a precedent for the future? If I am seeking logical consistency, the
symmetry of the legal structure, how far shall I seek it? At what point
shall the quest be halted by some discrepant custom, by some consideration of the social welfare, by my own or the common standards of justice
and morals? Into that strange compound which is brewed daily in the
caldron of the courts, all these ingredients enter in varying proportions.
I am not concerned to inquire whether judges ought to be allowed to
brew such a compound at all. I take judge-made law as one of the
existing realities of life. There, before us, is the brew. Not a judge
on the bench but has had a hand in the making. The elements have not
come together by chance. *Some* principle, however unavowed and inarticulate and subconscious, has regulated the infusion. It may not have
been the same principle for all judges at any time, nor the same principle for any judge at all times. But a choice there has been, not a
submission to the decree of Fate; and the considerations and motives
determining the choice, even if often obscure, do not utterly resist
analysis. . . . [Pp. 9-11.]

·   ·   ·   ·   ·

Before we can determine the proportions of a blend, we must know
the ingredients to be blended. Our first inquiry should therefore be:
Where does the judge find the law which he embodies in his judgment?
There are times when the source is obvious. The rule that fits the
case may be supplied by the constitution or by statute. If that is so, the
judge looks no farther. The correspondence ascertained, his duty is to
obey. The constitution overrides a statute, but a statute, if consistent with
the constitution, overrides the law of judges. In this sense, judge-made law
is secondary and subordinate to the law that is made by legislators. It is
true that codes and statutes do not render the judge superfluous, nor his
work perfunctory and mechanical. There are gaps to be filled. There are
doubts and ambiguities to be cleared. There are hardships and wrongs
to be mitigated if not avoided. Interpretation is often spoken of as if it
were nothing but the search and the discovery of a meaning which,
however obscure and latent, had none the less a real and ascertainable
pre-existence in the legislator's mind. The process is, indeed, that at
times, but it is often something more. The ascertainment of intention
may be the least of a judge's troubles in ascribing meaning to a statute.

"The fact is," says Gray in his lectures on the "Nature and Sources of the Law," [3] "that the difficulties of so-called interpretation arise when the legislature has had no meaning at all; when the question which is raised on the statute never occurred to it; when what the judges have to do is, not to determine what the legislature did mean on a point which was present to its mind, but to guess what it would have intended on a point not present to its mind, if the point had been present." [4] So Brutt: [5] "One weighty task of the system of the application of law consists then in this, to make more profound the discovery of the latent meaning of positive law. Much more important, however, is the second task which the system serves, namely the filling of the gaps which are found in every positive law in greater or less measure." You may call this process legislation, if you will. In any event, no system of *jus scriptum* has been able to escape the need of it. Today a great school of continental jurists is pleading for a still wider freedom of adaptation and construction. The statute, they say, is often fragmentary and ill-considered and unjust. The judge as the interpreter for the community of its sense of law and order must supply omissions, correct uncertainties, and harmonize results with justice through a method of free decision—"*libre recherche scientifique.*" That is the view of Gény and Ehrlich and Gmelin and others. [6] Courts are to "search for light among the social elements of every kind that are the living force behind the facts they deal with." [7] The power thus put in their hands is great, and subject, like all power, to abuse; but we are not to flinch from granting it. In the long run "there is no guaranty of justice," says Ehrlich, [8] "except the personality of the judge." [9] . . .

. . . Sometimes the rule of constitution or of statute is clear, and then the difficulties vanish. Even when they are present, they lack at times some of that element of mystery which accompanies creative energy. We reach the land of mystery when constitution and statute are silent, and the judge must look to the common law for the rule that fits the case. He is the "living oracle of the law" in Blackstone's vivid phrase. Looking at Sir Oracle in action, viewing his work in the dry light of realism, how does he set about his task?

The first thing he does is to compare the case before him with the prece-

---

[3] Sec. 370, p. 165.

[4] Cf. Pound, "Courts and Legislation," 9 Modern Legal Philosophy Series, p. 226.

[5] "*Die Kunst der Rechtsanwendung,*" p. 72.

[6] "Science of Legal Method," 9 Modern Legal Philosophy Series, pp. 4, 45, 65, 72, 124, 130, 159.

[7] Gény, "*Méthode d'Interprétation et Sources en droit privé positif,*" vol. II, p. 180, sec. 176, ed. 1919; transl. 9 Modern Legal Philosophy Series, p. 45.

[8] P. 65, *supra*; "*Freie Rechtsfindung und freie Rechtswissenschaft,*" 9 Modern Legal Philosophy Series.

[9] Cf. Gnaeus Flavius (Kantorowicz), "*Der Kampf um Rechtswissenschaft,*" p. 48: "*Von der Kultur des Richters hängt im letzten Grunde aller Fortschritt der Rechtsentwicklung ab.*"

dents, whether stored in his mind or hidden in the books. I do not mean that precedents are ultimate sources of the law, supplying the sole equipment that is needed for the legal armory, the sole tools, to borrow Maitland's phrase,[11] "in the legal smithy." Back of precedents are the basic juridical conceptions which are the postulates of judicial reasoning, and farther back are the habits of life, the institutions of society, in which those conceptions had their origin, and which, by a process of interaction, they have modified in turn.[12] None the less, in a system so highly developed as our own, precedents have so covered the ground that they fix the point of departure from which the labor of the judge begins. Almost invariably, his first step is to examine and compare them. If they are plain and to the point, there may be need of nothing more. *Stare decisis* is at least the everyday working rule of our law. I shall have something to say later about the propriety of relaxing the rule in exceptional conditions. But unless those conditions are present, the work of deciding cases in accordance with precedents that plainly fit them is a process similar in its nature to that of deciding cases in accordance with a statute. It is a process of search, comparison, and little more. Some judges seldom get beyond that process in any case. Their notion of their duty is to match the colors of the case at hand against the colors of many sample cases spread out upon their desk. The sample nearest in shade supplies the applicable rule. But, of course, no system of living law can be evolved by such a process, and no judge of a high court, worthy of his office, views the function of his place so narrowly. If that were all there was to our calling, there would be little of intellectual interest about it. The man who had the best card index of the cases would also be the wisest judge. It is when the colors do not match, when the references in the index fail, when there is no decisive precedent, that the serious business of the judge begins. . . .

In the life of the mind as in life elsewhere, there is a tendency toward the reproduction of kind. Every judgment has a generative power. It begets in its own image. Every precedent, in the words of Redlich, has a "directive force for future cases of the same or similar nature."[14] . . . The common law does not work from pre-established truths of universal and inflexible validity to conclusions derived from them deductively. Its method is inductive, and it draws its generalizations from particulars. The process has been admirably stated by Munroe Smith: . . .* [Pp. 14-23.]

·   ·   ·   ·   ·

---

[11] Introduction to Gierke's "Political Theories of the Middle Age," p. viii.

[12] Saleilles, *"De la Personnalité Juridique,"* p. 45; Ehrlich, *"Grundlegung der Soziologie des Rechts,"* pp. 34, 35; Pound, "Proceedings of American Bar Assn. 1919," p. 455.

[14] Redlich, "The Case Method in American Law Schools," Bulletin No. 8, Carnegie Foundation, p. 37.

* Cardozo here refers to Munroe Smith's comment: "In their effort to give to the social sense of justice articulate expression in rules and in principles, the method of

In this perpetual flux, the problem which confronts the judge is in reality a twofold one: he must first extract from the precedents the underlying principle, the *ratio decidendi;* he must then determine the path or direction along which the principle is to move and develop, if it is not to wither and die.

The first branch of the problem is the one to which we are accustomed to address ourselves more consciously than to the other. Cases do not unfold their principles for the asking. They yield up their kernel slowly and painfully. The instance cannot lead to a generalization till we know it as it is. That in itself is no easy task. For the thing adjudged comes to us oftentimes swathed in obscuring dicta, which must be stripped off and cast aside. Judges differ greatly in their reverence for the illustrations and comments and side-remarks of their predecessors, to make no mention of their own. All agree that there may be dissent when the opinion is filed. Some would seem to hold that there must be none a moment thereafter. Plenary inspiration has then descended upon the work of the majority. No one, of course, avows such a belief, and yet sometimes there is an approach to it in conduct. I own that it is a good deal of a mystery to me how judges, of all persons in the world, should put their faith in dicta. A brief experience on the bench was enough to reveal to me all sorts of cracks and crevices and loopholes in my own opinions when picked up a few months after delivery, and re-read with due contrition. The persuasion that one's own infallibility is a myth leads by easy stages and with somewhat greater satisfaction to a refusal to ascribe infallibility to others. But dicta are not always ticketed as such, and one does not recognize them always at a glance. There is the constant need, as every law student knows, to separate the accidental and the nonessential from the essential and inherent. Let us assume, however, that this task has been achieved, and that the precedent is known as it really is. Let us assume too that the principle, latent within it, has been skillfully extracted and accurately stated. Only half or less than half of the work has yet been done. The problem remains to fix the bounds and the tendencies of development and growth, to set the directive force in motion along the right path at the parting of the ways.

The directive force of a principle may be exerted along the line of logical progression; this I will call the rule of analogy or the method of philosophy; along the line of historical development; this I will call the

the lawfinding experts has always been experimental. The rules and principles of case law have never been treated as final truths, but as working hypotheses, continually retested in those great laboratories of the law, the courts of justice. Every new case is an experiment; and if the accepted rule which seems applicable yields a result which is felt to be unjust, the rule is reconsidered. It may not be modified at once, for the attempt to do absolute justice in every single case would make the development and maintenance of general rules impossible; but if a rule continues to work injustice, it will eventually be reformulated. The principles themselves are continually retested; for if the rules derived from a principle do not work well, the principle itself must ultimately be re-examined."

method of evolution; along the line of the customs of the community; this I will call the method of tradition; along the lines of justice, morals and social welfare, the *mores* of the day; and this I will call the method of sociology.

I have put first among the principles of selection to guide our choice of paths, the rule of analogy or the method of philosophy. In putting it first, I do not mean to rate it as most important. On the contrary, it is often sacrificed to others. I have put it first because it has, I think, a certain presumption in its favor. Given a mass of particulars, a congeries of judgments on related topics, the principle that unifies and rationalizes them has a tendency, and a legitimate one, to project and extend itself to new cases within the limits of its capacity to unify and rationalize. It has the primacy that comes from natural and orderly and logical succession. . . . [Pp. 28-31.]

HAINES, GENERAL OBSERVATIONS ON THE EFFECTS OF PERSONAL, POLITICAL, AND ECONOMIC INFLUENCES IN THE DECISIONS OF JUDGES *

The mechanical theory which postulates absolute legal principles, existing prior to and independent of all judicial decisions, and merely discovered and applied by courts,[4] has been characterized as a theory of a "judicial slot machine." [5] According to this theory, it is assumed that provisions have been made in advance for legal principles, so that it is merely necessary to put the facts into the machine and draw therefrom an appropriate decision.[6] This view of the function of a judge has been subjected to constant criticisms,[7] and yet it continues to hold sway in Anglo-American law as one of the strong determining forces guiding lawyers and judges. In fact, despite all influences to the contrary, American courts have clung to the belief that justice must be administered in accordance with fixed rules, which can be applied by a rather mechanical process of

---

* [Reprinted by special permission of the *Illinois Law Review* (Northwestern University School of Law). 17 *Ill. L. Rev.* 96 (1922).

Charles Grove Haines (b. 1879) was professor of history, political science, and law at Ursinus College, Whitman College, University of Chicago, U.C.L.A., and Harvard, and author of many books and articles on the judiciary, among them *The Supreme Court in United States History* (1935) and *Revival of Natural Law Concepts* (1930).]

[4] Pound, in "The Science of Legal Method" 205-206.

[5] Kantorowicz "*Rechtswissenschaft und Soziologie*" 5.

[6] *Cf.* Pound in "The Science of Legal Method" 206; see also Cohen "Legal Theories and Social Science" N.Y. Bar Assn. Reports (1915) at p. 184, in which this theory is styled the "phonograph theory of the judicial function."

[7] For example Austin referred with contempt to "The childish fiction employed by our judges that judiciary or common law is not made by them, but is a miraculous something made by nobody, existing, I suppose, from eternity and merely declared from time to time by the judges": *Jurisprudence* (4 ed.) 655. See also Pound "Mechanical Jurisprudence" *Col. L. Rev.* (1908) VIII 605.

logical reasoning to a given state of facts and can be made to produce an inevitable result.[7a] And it is assumed that the very nature of law requires such a mechanical application of its rules and principles. Due to the general acceptance of this view by the legal fraternity, it has become a habit of those trained in law to bestow little attention upon their individual views or prejudices and to turn attention instead to precedents which are regarded as forming the authoritative basis of the law. [Pp. 97-98.]

.   .   .   .   .

Among the foremost of those who have challenged prevailing traditions as to the judge's function are Holmes and Ehrlich. Justice Holmes expressed his views many years ago in his well known work, "The Common Law":

The very considerations which judges most rarely mention and always with an apology are the secret root from which the law draws all the juices of life. I mean, of course, considerations of what is expedient to the community concerned. Every important principle which is developed by litigation is in fact and at bottom the result of more or less definitely understood views of public policy; most generally, to be sure, under our practice and traditions, the unconscious result of instinctive preferences and inarticulate convictions, but none the less traceable to views of public policy in the last analysis.[26]

In law review articles and numerous opinions he has reiterated this view. A few noteworthy comments deserve repetition here:

I think that the judges themselves have failed adequately to recognize their duty of weighing considerations of social advantage. The duty is inevitable, and the result of the often proclaimed judicial aversion to deal with such considerations is simply to leave the very ground and foundation of judgments inarticulate and often unconscious.[27]

Perhaps one of the reasons why judges do not like to discuss questions of policy, or to put a decision in terms upon their views as lawmakers, is that the moment you leave the path of merely logical deduction you lose the illusion of certainty which makes legal reasoning seem like mathematics. But the certainty is only an illusion, nevertheless. Views of public policy are taught by experience of the interests of life. Those interests are fields of battle. Whatever decisions are made must be against the wishes and opinions of one party, and the distinctions on which they go will be distinctions of degree.[28]

[7a] Note on "Rule and Discretion in the Administration of Justice" *Har. L. Rev.* (1919–20) XXXIII 972.

[26] "The Common Law" 35, 6 and 106.

[27] "The Path of the Law" *Har. L. Rev.* (1896–1897) X 456, 467; "Collected Legal Papers" 184.

[28] "Privilege, Malice, and Intent" *Har. L. Rev.* (1894) VIII 7; "Collected Legal Papers" 126. With regard to the doctrine of *stare decisis* and its main object to secure certainty, Dean Wigmore observes "but the sufficient answer is that it has not in fact secured it. Our judicial law is as uncertain as any law could well be. We possess all the detriment of uncertainty which *stare decisis* was supposed to avoid, and also all the detriment of law-lumber which *stare decisis* concededly involves—the government of the living by the dead as Herbert Spencer has called it": "Problems of Law" 79, 80.

The true grounds of decisions are consideration of policy and of social advantage, and it is vain to suppose that solutions can be attained merely by logic and the general propositions of law which nobody disputes.[29]

Approval is here given to the type of judge who looks at the equities of a cause and then searches for precedents to sustain the desired results.[30] Where no rule has been definitely formulated, it is conceded that judicial decisions must be based on judicial conceptions of public policy.[31] The whole body of the common law is, in fact, made up of "compromises of conflicting individual interests in which we turn to some social interest frequently under the name of public policy, to determine the limits of a reasonable adjustment." [32]

To Ehrlich, likewise, the significance of law in the daily life of a people depends far more on the persons charged with its administration than on the principles according to which it is administered.[33] To continue in his suggestive words—

The administration of justice has always contained a personal element. In all ages, social, political, and cultural movements have necessarily exerted an influence upon it; but whether any individual jurist yields more or less to such influences, whether he is more inclined to follow tradition or is rather disposed to introduce changes and innovations, depends, of course, less on any theory of legal method than on his own personal temperament.[34]

Psychological motives and influences have been subjected to analysis in their effects upon political conduct to some extent, and it is conceded that these motives and influences are not altered when one assumes the role of judge. Just as is the case with other opinions of individuals, judicial opinions necessarily represent in a measure the personal impulses of the judge, in relation to the situation before him, and these impulses are determined by the judge's lifelong series of previous experiences.[35] The psychologists recently have emphasized the fact that all of us have

---

[29] Dissenting opinion in Vegelahn v. Guntner (1896) 167 Mass. 92, 105, 106.

[30] "No man has seen more plainly that the court was measuring the legislature's reasons by its own intellectual yardstick than has Justice Holmes; none more keenly perceived that the notation thereupon marked those results of environment and education which many men seem to regard": C. M. Hough "Due Process of Law—Today" *Har. L. Rev.* (1918–1919) XXXII 232; for comments of Justice Holmes see Lochner v. New York (1905) 198 U.S. 45, 75, and Grant Timber Co. v. Gray (1915) 236 U.S. 133.

[31] See Waite "Public Policy and Personal Opinion" *Mich. L. Rev.* (1920–21) XIX 265, where it is observed "There can be no question but that where no rule at all has been definitely precipitated, judicial decisions are time and again founded on nothing but the judicial apprehension, or conception, of public policy."

[32] Pound "A Theory of Social Interests" *Pub. Am. Soc. Society* XV 17.

[33] Ehrlich in "The Science of Legal Method" p. 48.

[34] *Ibid.* p. 74.

[35] T. Schroeder "The Psychologic Study of Judicial Opinions" *Cal. L. Rev.* (1917–18) VI 93.

predispositions which unconsciously attach themselves to the conscious consideration of any question. Every conclusion is expressive of a dominant personal motive and is a resultant of the evolutionary status of the individual's mind.[36] Apparent as these facts are, they have received scant consideration in the discussion of problems in the administration of justice.[37] A noteworthy exception to the usual attitude of indifference toward psychic or personal influences in judicial administration is found in the reports of the statistician of the City Magistrates' Courts of New York City.

In a survey of the records of the 41 magistrates of the city courts, the percentage of cases discharged or dismissed for the year 1915 varied from 6.7 per cent to 73.7 per cent. The opportunity for a discharge or dismissal therefore depended to a considerable degree upon the magistrate before which the prisoner was arraigned. In 1916, 17,075 persons were charged before the magistrates with intoxication. Of these, 92 per cent were convicted. But the examination of the record of individual judges showed that one judge discharged 79 per cent of this class of cases. In cases for disorderly conduct one judge heard 566 cases and discharged one person, whereas another judge discharged 18 per cent; another 54 per cent. Numerous instances of similar variations in the results of the consideration of cases by different magistrates were presented in the reports of the City Magistrates' Courts for 1914 and 1915. The tabulations of the statistician were prepared in part to discover the personal equation in the administration of justice and they showed that the magistrates differed to an amazing degree in their treatment of similar classes of cases. The conclusion was inescapable that justice is a personal thing, reflecting the temperament, the personality, the education, environment, and personal traits of the magistrates.[38] The results showing to what extent justice is affected by the personality of the judge were so startling and so disconcerting that it seemed advisable to discontinue the comparative tables of the records of the justices. Some time, no doubt, more facts regarding the personal element in the administration of justice will be rendered available, and, perhaps, a better educated public will be prepared to know the truth—namely, that the process of judicial decision is determined to a considerable extent by the judges' views of fair play, public policy, and their general consensus as to what is right and just.[39] Law and politics are indeed inseparable and politics is the very stuff of life. Its motives are interlaced with the whole fibre of experience, private

36 Schroeder *op. cit.* 94.

37 For a discriminating analysis of the relation of psychology to political science and to jurisprudence see J. M. Williams, "The Foundations of Social Science," especially Books I and II (N. Y. 1920).

38 G. Everson "Human Element in Justice" *Jour. Crim. L.* [Vol.] X 98.

39 *Cf.* Cohen *op. cit.* 171.

and public. Its relations are intensely human, and generally intimately personal.[40]

"In approaching the problem, then, of the administration of justice," says Dean Pound, "it is becoming clear that men count for more than machinery and that there are many subtle forces at work of which we are but partially conscious. Tradition, education, physical surroundings, race, class and professional solidarity, and economic, political and social influences of all sorts and degrees make up a complex environment in which men endeavor to reach certain results by means of legal machinery. No discussion simply in terms of men or of legal and political machinery, or both, ignoring this complex environment, will serve. At whatever cost in the loss of dramatic interest or satisfying simplicity of plan, we must insist on plurality of causes and plurality and relativity of remedies." [41]

The role of discretion in the administration of justice, in which the effects of personality are always evident, is a phase of judicial activity as yet largely unexplored.[42] . . . [Pp. 103-106.]

.   .   .   .   .

If considerations of public policy form a vital part in the development of the common law, does it not follow that even greater weight should be given to these considerations in the growth of constitutional law? Justice Holmes frequently warns his associates against "the subtle danger of the unconscious identification of personal views with constitutional sanction" and brings to the fore the fact that our public law is truly one of the living forces in which we have, as in other avenues, the operation of instincts and interests. [P. 107.]

.   .   .   .   .

Judicial legislation, whether it operates in public or in private law, is imbued with certain characteristics which have been suggestively analyzed by Professor Dicey:

The courts or the judges, when acting as legislators, are, of course, influenced by the beliefs and feelings of their time, and are guided to a considerable extent by the dominant current of public opinion; Eldon and Kenyon belonged to the era of old Toryism as distinctly as Denman, Campbell, Erle and Bramwell belonged to the age of Benthamite liberalism. But whilst our tribunals, or the judges of whom they are composed, are swayed by the prevailing beliefs of a particular time, they are also guided by professional opinions and ways of thinking which are to a certain extent independent of and possibly opposed to the general tone of public opinion. The judges are the heads of the legal

[40] Woodrow Wilson "Law and the Facts" *Am. Pol. Sc. Rev.* V 3.
[41] "Criminal Justice in the American City" *The Survey* Oct. 29, 1921.
[42] "Investigation of the essential nature of legal rules develops the conclusion that discretion instead of being a casual defect of legal systems, a vice to be wholly eradicated by the aid of legal science and legislative skill, is a standing and permanent characteristic of law, and one of the great levers of legal evolution": Kocourek "Formal Relation Between Law and Discretion" *Ill. L. Rev.* (1914–1915) IX 225.

professions. They are advanced in life. They are for the most part persons of a conservative disposition. They are in no way dependent for their emoluments, dignity, or reputation upon the favor of the electors, or even of ministers who represent in the long run the wishes of the electorate. They are most likely to be biased by professional habits and feeling than by the popular sentiment of the hour. Hence, judicial legislation will often be marked by certain characteristics rarely found in acts of Parliament.[51]

Judicial legislation thus aims at the maintenance of the logic or the symmetry of the law and great care is exercised to secure consistency. It aims at securing certainty rather than the development of the law and tends toward the maintenance of a fixed legal system. It frequently results also that ideas of expediency or policy accepted by the courts may differ considerably from the ideas which at a given time have acquired predominant influence among the general public.[52] The morality of courts may be higher than the morality of traders or of politicians, but it has, of course, often happened that the ideas entertained by the judges have fallen below the highest and most enlightened public opinion of a particular time.[53] As a general rule, judge-made law represents the conviction of an earlier age and is characterized by conservatism.[54] [P. 110.]

.   .   .   .   .

While in theory, then, we have often been led to believe that constitutional law has been developed solely through the application of the rules of formal logic in accordance with well established principles, in reality we have found it has been to a considerable extent the result of human forces in which the personality of the judges, their education, associations, and individual views are of prime importance. The former of these two elements, legal logic, tradition and precedent, has received extended and adequate treatment at the hands of lawyers and political scientists; the latter, the element of free conception, in which individual views and personal notions have influenced and have frequently predetermined judicial decisions, has received scant attention.[68] To be sure, the subject is a difficult one. It carries the diligent seeker for truth into wide and varied fields wherein the personal and political doctrines of public men are formed. But difficult as is the search, the important bear-

---

[51] Dicey *op. cit.* [*Law and Opinion in England*] 361, 362.

[52] Dicey *op. cit.* 365.

[53] Dicey *op. cit.* 365.

[54] *Ibid.* 367.

[68] In a discussion of the "Spirit of Our Judges," Mr. E. V. Abbott claims "we are overawed by the authority of their position; we let them do many things which they have no business to do; we do not sufficiently examine their decisions to note what they are doing; we are too lenient when we do criticise and we are content to leave them at all times in a position of practically irresponsible power": *Am. L. Rev.* (1920) LIV 240. "If the judges continue," says Dean Lewis, "to act as elder statesmen and to veto acts which shock their sense of justice and fairness, it becomes imperative that public criticism and control be more actively exercised": See *Pro. of Acad. of Pol. Sc.* (Jan. 1913) III 45.

ings of the decisions of our highest courts renders it desirable that more
attention be given than heretofore to the personal and political doctrines
of those favored few who are elevated to the bench and whose decisions
affect profoundly public and private interests. [Pp. 113-114.]

.   .   .   .   .   .

... As an individual's views in political and legal matters are likely
to be in part, at least, determined by his interests, training, environment
and long-continued associations, it is suggestive to analyze these personal
factors with a view of determining some of the influences which affect
federal constitutional law. The factors likely to influence judicial decisions are:

A. Remote and Indirect—
    1. Education—
        (a) General.
        (b) Legal.
    2. Family and personal associations; wealth and social position.

B. Direct—
    1. Legal and political experience.
    2. Political affiliations and opinions.
    3. Intellectual and temperamental traits.

A consideration of all of these factors has been made for only a few of
the justices, and in numerous instances the records and biographical accounts are far from adequate for anything like a complete analysis. But
the evidence available reveals instances of personal and political influences
in decisions on federal constitutional law which deserve careful consideration. [Pp. 115-116.]

HUTCHESON, THE JUDGMENT INTUITIVE: THE FUNCTION
OF THE "HUNCH"[1] IN JUDICIAL DECISION *

Many years ago, at the conclusion of a particularly difficult case both
in point of law and fact, tried to a court without a jury, the judge, a
man of great learning and ability, announced from the Bench that since
the narrow and prejudiced modern view of the obligations of a judge
in the decision of causes prevented his resort to the judgment aleatory

---

[1] "A strong, intuitive impression that something is about to happen." *Webster,
International Dictionary.*

* [14 *Cornell L.Q.* 274 (1929).

Joseph C. Hutcheson, Jr. (b. 1879), long a practising attorney in Houston, Texas,
was appointed to the United States District Court bench in 1918 and to the Circuit
Court of Appeals in 1931. He has written several articles on the judicial process, as
seen from within. See also "Lawyer's Law and the Little, Small Dice" (1932) 7 *Tulane
L. Rev.* 1.]

by the use of his "little, small dice" he would take the case under advisement, and, brooding over it, wait for his hunch.

To me, a young, indeed a very young lawyer, picked, while yet the dew was on me and I had just begun to sprout, from the classic gardens of a University, where I had been trained to regard the law as a system of rules and precedents, of categories and concepts, and the judge had been spoken of as an administrator, austere, remote, "his intellect a cold logic engine," who, in that rarified atmosphere in which he lived coldly and logically determined the relation of the facts of a particular case to some of these established precedents, it appeared that the judge was making a jest, and a very poor one, at that. [P. 274.]

. . . . .

I knew that judges "are the depositories of the laws like the oracles, who must decide in all cases of doubt and are bound by an oath to decide according to the law of the land," [2] but I believed that creation and evolution were at an end, that in modern law only deduction had place, and that the judges must decide "through being long personally accustomed to and acquainted with the judicial decisions of their predecessors." [3] [P. 275.]

. . . . .

As I grew older, however, and knew and understood better the judge to whom I have in this opening referred; as I associated more with real lawyers, whose intuitive faculties were developed and made acute by the use of a trained and cultivated imagination; as I read more after and came more under the spell of those great lawyers and judges whose thesis is that "modification is the life of the law," [4] I came to see that "as long as the matter to be considered is debated in artificial terms, there is danger of being led by a technical definition to apply a certain name and then to deduce consequences which have no relation to the grounds on which the name was applied;" [5] that "the process of inclusion and exclusion so often applied in developing a rule, cannot end with its first enunciation. The rule announced must be deemed tentative. For the many and varying facts to which it will be applied cannot be foreseen." [6]

I came to see that "every opinion tends to become a law." [7] That "regulations, the wisdom, necessity and validity of which as applied to,

---

[2] *Bl. Comm.* 169.

[3] *Ibid.*

[4] Carter, *Law, Its Origin, Growth and Function* (1907). "Modification implies growth. It is the life of the Law." Washington v. Dawson, 264 U.S. 219, 236, 44 Sup. Ct. 302 (1924), Brandeis, J., dissenting.

[5] Guy v. Donald, 203 U.S., 399, 406, 27 Sup. Ct. 63 (1926).

[6] Washington v. Dawson, *supra* note 4.

[7] Lochner v. New York, 198 U.S. 45, 76, 25 Sup. Ct. 539 (1905).

existing conditions, are so apparent that they are now uniformly sustained, a century ago, or even half a century ago, would probably have been rejected as arbitrary and oppressive, . . . and that in a changing world it is impossible that it should be otherwise." [8]

I came to see that "resort to first principles is, in the last analysis, the only safe way to a solution of litigated matters." [9] [P. 276.]

.   .   .   .   .

And so, after eleven years on the Bench following eighteen at the Bar, I, being well advised by observation and experience of what I am about to set down, have thought it both wise and decorous to now boldly affirm that "having well and exactly seen, surveyed, overlooked, reviewed, recognized, read and read over again, turned and tossed about, seriously perused and examined the preparatories, productions, evidences, proofs, allegations, depositions, cross speeches, contradictions . . . and other such like confects and spiceries, both at the one and the other side, as a good judge ought to do, I posit on the end of the table in my closet all the pokes and bags of the defendants—that being done I thereafter lay down upon the other end of the same table the bags and satchels of the plaintiff." [12]

Thereafter I proceed "to understand and resolve the obscurities of these various and seeming contrary passages in the law, which are laid claim to by the suitors and pleading parties," even just as Judge Bridlegoose did, with one difference only. "That when the matter is more plain, clear and liquid, that is to say, when there are fewer bags," and he would have used his "other large, great dice, fair and goodly ones," I decide the case more or less offhand and by rule of thumb. While when the case is difficult or involved, and turns upon a hairsbreadth of law or of fact, that is to say, "when there are many bags on the one side and on the other" and Judge Bridlegoose would have used his "little small dice," I, after canvassing all the available material at my command, and duly cogitating upon it, give my imagination play, and brooding over the cause, wait for the feeling, the hunch—that intuitive flash of understanding which makes the jump-spark connection between question and decision, and at the point where the path is darkest for the judicial feet, sheds its light along the way. [Pp. 277-278.]

.   .   .   .   .

Now, what is this faculty? What are its springs, what its uses? Many men have spoken of it most beautifully. Some call it "intuition"—some "imagination" this sensitiveness to new ideas, this power to range when

---

[8] Euclid Valley v. Ambler, 272 U.S. 365, 47 Sup. Ct. 114 (1926).
[9] Old Colony Trust Co. v. Sugarland Industries, 296 Fed. 129, 138 (S.D. Tex. 1924).
[12] Rabelais, Book III, c. 39.

the track is cold, this power to cast in ever widening circles to find a fresh scent, instead of standing baying where the track was lost.

Imagination, that wondrous faculty, which properly controlled by experience and reflection, becomes the noblest attribute of man, the source of poetic genius, the instrument of discovery in science.[17]

With accurate experiment and observation to work upon, imagination becomes the architect of physical theory. Newton's passage from a falling apple to a falling moon was an act of the prepared imagination without which the laws of Keppler could never have been traced to their foundations.

Out of the facts of chemistry the constructive imagination of Dalton formed the atomic theory. Scientific men fight shy of the word because of its ultra-scientific connotations, but the fact is that without the exercise of this power our knowledge of nature would be a mere tabulation of co-existences and sequences.[16] [Pp. 280-281.]

.   .   .   .   .

"When I once asked the best administrator whom I knew," writes Mr. Wallas, "how he formed his decisions, he laughed, and with the air of letting out for the first time a guilty secret, said: 'Oh, I always decide by feeling. So and so always decides by calculation, and that is no good.' When again I asked an American judge, who is widely admired both for his skill and for his impartiality, how he and his fellows formed their conclusions, he also laughed, and said that he would be stoned in the street if it were known that, after listening with full consciousness to all the evidence, and following as carefully as he could all the arguments, he waited until he 'felt' one way or the other. He had elided the preparation and the brooding, or at least had come to think of them as processes of faint kinship with the state of mind that followed." "When the conclusion is there," says William James, "we have already forgotten most of the steps preceding its attainment." [21] [P. 282.]

.   .   .   .   .

Time was when judges, lawyers, law writers and teachers of the law refused to recognize in the judge this right and power of intuitive decision. It is true that the trial judge was always supposed to have superior facilities for decision, but these were objectivized in formulas, such as— the trial judge has the best opportunity of observing the witnesses, their demeanor,—the trial judge can see the play and interplay of forces as they operate in the actual class of the trial.

Under the influence of this kind of logomachy, this sticking in the "skin" of thought, the trial judge's superior opportunity was granted, but the real reason for that superior position, that the trial creates an atmosphere springing from but more than the facts themselves, in which and

---

[17] Address to the Royal Society of England, November 3, 1859, Sir Benjamin Brodie, quoted from *Fragments of Science*, 109.

[18] "Scientific Use of the Imagination" Address delivered before the British Association at Liverpool, Sept. 16, 1860 by Tyndall, quoted from *Fragments of Science*, III.

[21] Cardozo, *Paradoxes of Legal Science* (1928) 59, 60.

out of which the judge may get the feeling which takes him to the desired end, was deliberately suppressed.

Later writers, however, not only recognize but emphasize this faculty, nowhere more attractively than in Judge Cardozo's lectures before the law schools of Yale University, in 1921 [27] and Columbia University in 1927,[28] while Max Radin, in 1925, in a most sympathetic and charming way, takes the judge's works apart, and shows us how his wheels go round.[29]

He tells us, first, that the judge is a human being; that therefore he does not decide causes by the abstract application of rules of justice or of right, but having heard the cause and determined that the decision ought to go this way or that way, he then takes up his search for some category of the law into which the case will fit.

He tells us that the judge really feels or thinks that a certain result seems desirable, and he then tries to make his decision accomplish that result. "What makes certain results seem desirable to a judge?" he asks, and answers his question that that seems desirable to the judge which, according to his training, his experience, and his general point of view, strikes him as the jural consequence that ought to flow from the facts, and he advises us that what gives the judge the struggle in the case is the effort so to state the reasons for his judgment that they will pass muster.

Now what is he saying except that the judge really decides by feeling, and not by judgment; by "hunching" and not by ratiocination, and that the ratiocination appears only in the opinion?

Now what is he saying but that the vital, motivating impulse for the decision is an intuitive sense of what is right or wrong for that cause, and that the astute judge, having so decided, enlists his every faculty and belabors his laggard mind, not only to justify that intuition to himself, but to make it pass muster with his critics?

There is nothing unreal or untrue about this picture of the judge, nor is there anything in it from which a just judge should turn away. It is true, and right that it is true, that judges really do try to select categories or concepts into which to place a particular case so as to produce what the judge regards as a righteous result, or, to avoid any confusion in the matter of morals, I will say a "proper result."

This is true. I think we should go further, and say it ought to be true. No reasoning applied to practical matters is ever really effective unless motivated by some impulse. [Pp. 284-285.]

· · · · · ·

There is not one among us but knows that while too often cases must be decided without that "feeling" which is the triumphant precursor

[27] Cardozo, The Nature of the Judicial Process (1921).
[28] Supra note 21.
[29] Radin, Theory of Judicial Decision (1925) 2 Am. B. A. J. 359.

of the just judgment, that just as "sometimes a light surprises the Christian while he sings," so sometimes, after long travail and struggle of the mind, there does come to the dullest of us, flooding the brain with the vigorous blood of decision, the hunch that there is, or is not invention; that there is, or is not, anticipation; that the plaintiff should be protected by a decree, or should be denied protection. This hunch, sweeping aside hesitancy and doubt, takes the judge vigorously on to his decision; and yet, the cause decided, the way thither, which was for the blinding moment a blazing trail, becomes wholly lost to view.

Sometimes again that same intuition or hunch, which warming his brain and lighting his feet produced the decision, abides with the decider "while working his judgment backward" as he blazes his trail "from a desirable conclusion back to one or another of a stock of logical premises." [33]

It is such judicial intuitions, and the opinions lighted and warmed by the feeling which produced them, that not only give justice in the cause, but like a great white way, make plain in the wilderness the way of the Lord for judicial feet to follow. [Pp. 287-288.]

LLEWELLYN, A REALISTIC JURISPRUDENCE—THE NEXT STEP *

The Place and Treatment of Paper Rules

Are "rules of law" in the accepted sense eliminated in such a course of thought? Somewhat obviously not. Whether they be pure paper rules, or are the accepted patter of the law officials, they remain present, and their presence remains an actuality—an actuality of importance—but an actuality whose *precise* importance, whose bearing and influence become clear. First of all they appear as what they are: rules of authoritative ought, addressed *to* officials, telling *officials* what the *officials* ought to do.[14] To which telling the officials either pay no heed at all (the pure paper rule; the dead-letter statute; the obsolete case) or listen partly (the rule "construed" out of recognition; the rule to which lip-service only is paid, while practice runs another course) or listen with all care (the rule with which the official practice pretty accurately coincides). I think that every such official precept-on-the-books (statute, doctrine laid down

---

[33] *Supra* note 29.

* [30 *Col. L. Rev.* 431 (1930).]

[14] This I think holds true of *all* official ought-rules, irrespective of their form. I speak of their effects, not of their purposes. And the rights of laymen result through the screen of the official's practice, by a kind of social reflex. Ehrlich described the phenomenon cogently, so far as concerned the rules governing the set-up of the state governmental machine. A legal philosopher or a normatizer, with his mind fixed on the purpose of rules to ultimately affect the conduct of the "governed," will quarrel with this. A sociologist is content to see and describe what happens—and *compare* that with what is purposed.

in the decision of a court, administrative regulation) tacitly contains an element of pseudo-description along with its statement of what officials ought to do; a tacit statement that officials do act according to the tenor of the rule; a tacit prediction that officials will act according to its tenor. Neither statement nor prediction is often true *in toto*. And the first point of the approach here made is skepticism as to the truth of either in the case in hand. Yet it is an accepted convention to act and talk as if this statement and prediction were most solemn truth: a tradition marked peculiarly among the legal profession when engaged officially. It is indeed of first importance to remember that such a tradition contains a tendency to verify itself.[15] But no more so than to remember that such a tendency is no more powerful than its opposite: that other tendency to move quietly into falsifying the prediction in fact, while laying on an ointment of conventional words to soothe such as wish to believe the prediction has worked out.

Thus the problem of official formulations of rules and rights becomes complex. First, as to formulation already present, already existent; the accepted doctrine. There, I repeat, one lifts an eye canny and skeptical as to whether judicial behavior is in fact what the paper rule purports (implicitly) to state. One seeks the real practice on the subject, by study of how the cases do in fact eventuate. One seeks to determine how far the paper rule is real, how far *merely* paper.[16] One seeks an understanding of *actual* judicial behavior, in that comparison of rule with practice; one follows also the use made of the paper rule in argument by judges and by counsel, and the apparent influence of its official presence on decisions. One seeks to determine when it is stated, but ignored; when it is stated and followed; when and why it is *expressly* narrowed or extended or modified, so that a new paper rule is created. One observes the level of *silent* application or modification or escape, in the "interpretation" of the facts of a case, in contrast to that other and quite distinct level of express wrestling with the language of the paper rule. One observes how strongly ingrained is the tradition of requiring a good paper justification, in terms of officially accepted paper rules, before any decision, however appealing on the facts, can be regarded as likely of acceptance. And by the same token, one observes the importance of the official formulae as tools of argument and persuasion; one observes both the stimuli to be derived from, and the limitations set by, their language. Very rapidly, too, one

---

[15] Ehrlich, again, brings this out beautifully.

[16] And on moving into the further fields of contact between judicial or official behavior and lay behavior, one gets into much deeper water: how does the paper rule work out (*i.e.*, have a reflection or a counterpart in behavior) in lower court cases, unappealed? How often does it have any influence? What influence on administrative officials? On transactions between laymen which never reach any officials? All signs point to this being vastly more important than the set-up of doctrine, or even than the actual practices of higher courts. What is documented takes on a specious appearance of value, as against the unexplored.

perceives that neither are all official formulae alike in these regards, nor are all courts, nor are all times and circumstances for the same formula in the same court. The *handling* of the official formulae to influence court behavior then comes to appear as an art, capable only to a limited extent of routinization or (to date) of accurate and satisfying description. And the discrepancy, great or small, between the official formula and what actually results, obtains the limelight attention it deserves. [Pp. 449-451.]

FRANK, WHAT COURTS DO IN FACT *

It is plain where all this leaves lawyers and clients. Jones and Smith enter into a transaction. Later a lawsuit arises concerning that transaction. If it is "contested," the court's decision (judgment) will turn on what the court will guess what that transaction was. That guess, made by the court, as to what happened, is by no means sure to be identical with what actually happened. Ergo, *the decision (judgment) was not knowable when Jones and Smith acted. It was not knowable when Jones consulted his lawyer, or Smith his lawyer.* (To lapse for the moment into verbiage I have promised to forego, the "law" and/or the legal "rights" and "duties" of Jones and Smith were unknown and unknowable when Jones and Smith acted or when they consulted their respective lawyers, because at that time no one could know whether there would be a lawsuit; or whether, if there was a lawsuit, it would be "contested"; or if it was "contested," what the court's guess would be as a result of hearing the conflicting testimony, or what would be the court's reaction to that guess.) [P. 651.]

. . . . . .

But talks with candid judges have begun to disclose that, whatever is said in opinions, the judge often arrives at his decision before he tries to explain it. With little or no preliminary attention to legal rules or a definite statement of facts, he often makes up his mind that Jones should win the lawsuit, not Smith; that Mrs. White should have the custody of the children; that McCarthy should be reinstated as keeper of the dog pound. After the judge has so decided, then the judge writes his "opinion."...

The judge's opinion makes it *appear* as if the decision were a result

---

* [Reprinted by special permission of the *Illinois Law Review* (Northwestern University School of Law). 26 *Ill. L. Rev.* 645 (1932).

Jerome N. Frank (b. 1889), a practising attorney since 1912, served in many government posts after 1933, becoming a United States Circuit Court Judge in 1941. Frank has taught at a number of universities and is presently a visiting professor at Yale Law School. His published works, besides many articles, include: *Law and the Modern Mind* (1930); *If Men Were Angels* (1942) and *Courts on Trial* (1949). Frank is generally considered to be a leader of the "realist" movement in jurisprudence.]

solely of playing the game of law-in-discourse. But this explanation is often truncated, incomplete. Worse, it is frequently unreal, artificial, distorted. It is in large measure an after-thought. It omits all mention of many of the factors which induced the judge to decide the case.[17] Those factors (even to the extent that the judge is aware of them) are excluded from the opinion. So far as opinions are concerned, those factors are tabu, unmentionables.

Opinions, then, disclose but little of how judges come to their conclusions. The opinions are often *ex post facto;* they are *censored expositions.* To study those eviscerated expositions as the principal bases of forecasts of future judicial action is to delude oneself.[18] It is far more unwise than it would be for a botanist to assume that plants are merely what appears above the ground, or for an anatomist to content himself with scrutinizing the outside of the body.

It is helpful for the lawyer to borrow the point of view of the political scientist and look at the judge as one kind of governmental official. When William Howard Taft, as President, gave his reasons for recommending or vetoing a bill, urging the adoption of a treaty, espousing a higher tariff, or finding that charges against his Secretary of the Interior were groundless, many wise students of government recognized that his explanations were sometimes artificial or incomplete and that sometimes he formulated them long after he had reached the decisions which he formally explained.[19] If William Howard Taft, when on the bench, followed a not unlike course, he was adopting the admitted practice of some of the ablest of those governmental officials we call judges. One recalls the story about Marshall (recently quoted by Llewellyn): "Judgment for the plaintiff; Mr. Justice Story will furnish the authorities." [20] Chancellor

---

[17] The artificial character of opinions is usually not due to hypocrisy or intellectual or moral dishonesty. As I have devoted a considerable portion of a book to pointing out the unconscious self-deception involved in many judicial opinions, I shall not redevelop that thesis here. See Frank, *loc. cit.* [*Law and the Modern Mind*] 37, 120, 144-147, 152-153, 362, and the next instalment of this paper.

[18] See Appendix to the next instalment of this article.

[19] *Cf.* Senate Document No. 719, 61st Congress, 3d Session, Vol. I, 60-62.

[20] Put that story in formal-law speech and it reads: "The general rule of law to be applied to a particular case must be conceived as existing before the particular concrete case to which it is applied occurred." *Cf.* Zane "German Legal Philosophy" (1918) 16 *Mich. Law Rev.* 287 at 311. Zane also says (338): "The rule of law and its application may be reached in a thousand different ways, but a judgment of a court is always this pure deduction. Now it must be apparent to any one who is willing to admit the rules governing rational mental action that unless the rule of the major premise exists as antecedent to the ascertainment of the fact or facts put into the minor premise, there is no judicial act in stating the judgment."

Of course, the mere fact that the reason given for an act or a judgment is *ex post facto* does not invalidate that reason. Jones may hit Smith, or vote for Hoover, or make love to a girl, or explore the arctic without reflecting on his conduct. When asked to explain or justify his acts he may give excellent reasons which are entirely satisfactory. But sometimes it is impossible to ascertain the soundness of those reasons

Kent, when off the bench, explained that in arriving at a judicial decision he first made himself "master of the facts." That done, he wrote,

> I saw where justice lay, and the moral sense decided the court half the time. I then sat down to search the authorities ... I might once in a while be embarrassed by a technical rule, but I almost always found principles suited to my view of the case.

A member of an upper court once told me that the chief justice said to him after the oral argument of a case, "We'll have to lick that plaintiff somehow and it's up to you to find some theory and authorities that will help us to it." The chief justice of another important upper court recently wrote to a friend of mine that in his court it was the usual practice for the judges first to determine the "abstract justice" of a case and then to examine the "law."

How then does a judge arrive at his decision? In terse terms, he does so by a "hunch" as to what is fair and just or wise or expedient. So we have recently been advised by one of our ablest federal judges, Hutcheson.[21] The lawyer's task, then, becomes this: The determination of what produces the judge's hunches. What, then, does produce the judicial hunch? The answer must be vague: The effect of innumerable stimuli on what is loosely termed "the personality of the judge." If you have a liking for mathematical formulas you can let S be the stimuli, P be the judge's personality; D be the decision; you can then say "$S \times P = D$."

"The personality of the judge" is a phrase which too glibly describes an exquisitely complicated mass of phenomena.[22] The phrase "judicial hunch" is likewise beautifully vague. But those phrases will do for present purposes. Be it noted then that "the personality of the judge" and the "judicial hunch" are not and cannot be described in terms of legal rules and principles.[23] They are therefore not recognized or referred to by formal law—except in jocular asides or allegedly humorous footnotes. [Pp. 653-655.]

·   ·   ·   ·   ·

For the practicing lawyer and his client the specific decisions of actual specific cases are ultimates. Decisions, not opinions. What the lawyer

---

because it is impossible to ascertain the truth of the facts asserted in his fact premise. This is peculiarly true of judicial opinions because the facts stated in the judge's fact premise are often "subjective." This point is discussed further in the next instalment of this paper.

[21] Hutcheson "The Judgment Intuitive: The Function of the 'Hunch' in Judicial Decisions" (1929) 14 *Cornell Law Quar.* 274. *Cf.* Douglas and Shanks in (1929) *Yale Law Jour.* 193. It should be said that Judge Hutcheson values the jury highly and, generally speaking, considers somewhat excessive such views on the judicial process as those expressed in this paper.

[22] See Frank, *loc. cit.* 104-106, 114, 147, 338, note 7.

[23] The same is true of the innumerable external stimuli which activate the judge's personality and yield the hunch. In the equation $S \times P = D$, both S and P are the loosest of loose symbols. See further in the next instalment of this paper.

and his client want are judgments and decrees—regardless of the presence or absence of concomitant opinions, irrespective of the contents of the opinions, if there are any.[27]. . . [P. 657.]

. . . . . .

8. Let us here take stock. (1) Specific enforceable decisions (*i.e.,* judgments, orders, and decrees) in concrete cases are of the essence of the lawyer's work. All else is subsidiary. (2) Specific decisions are the result of the judge's hunches.[34] (3) To predict or bring about decisions, one should know something about what produces judicial hunches. (4) The so-called legal rules and principles are some of the many hunch producers. (5) Whatever may be the stimuli to the making of those hunches, those stimuli must operate through their effects on what may loosely be described as the judge's personality. (6) Neither the background stimuli nor the congeries labelled "judge's personality" are stated or statable in terms of the conventional legal rules and principles. (7) The failure to recognize the composite nature of this hunch and the artificial breaking up of the decisional process into "rules" and "facts" accounts in part for the delusion of the formalist as to the exclusive value of the "rules." (8) The formalist errs also in overlooking the circumstance that it is impossible to predict what cases will be "contested" and the subjective nature of the "facts" of a "contested" case and the resulting unchallengeability of the judge's statement of those "facts."[35] (9) The formalist conveniently neglects the jury. [Pp. 662-663.]

F. S. COHEN, TRANSCENDENTAL NONSENSE AND THE FUNCTIONAL APPROACH *

3. *The Theory of Legal Decisions*

The uses of the functional approach are not exhausted by "realistic jurisprudence." "Realistic jurisprudence," as that term is currently used,[80] is a theory of the nature of law, and therefore a theory of the

---

[27] Of course, to the extent that the opinion in one case will be one of the stimuli producing decisions in future cases, the lawyer is interested in the opinion. See Frank, *loc. cit.* 104, 126-127, 130-131. This point will be further discussed in the next instalment of this paper. Nothing said in the text of this instalment is to be taken as indicating a belief that there are no such things as "legal rules, principles and precepts" or that they are without any effect on decisions.

[34] As to the jury's, see Frank, *loc. cit.* 170-185.

[35] See further discussion of this point in the Appendix to the next instalment of this paper.

* [35 *Col. L. Rev.* 809, 842-847 (1935).]

[80] See K. N. Llewellyn, A Realistic Jurisprudence—The Next Step (1930) 30 *Columbia Law Rev.* 431; Pound, The Call for a Realist Jurisprudence (1931) 44 *Harv. L. Rev.* 697; Llewellyn, Some Realism about Realism: Responding to Dean Pound (1931) 44 *Harv. L. Rev.* 1222.

nature of legal rules, legal concepts, and legal questions. Its essence is the definition of law as a function of judicial decisions. This definition is of tremendous value in the development of legal science, since it enables us to dispel the supernatural mists that envelop the legal order and to deal with the elements of the legal order in objective, scientific terms. But this process of definition and clarification is only a preliminary stage in the life of legal science. When we have analyzed legal rules and concepts as patterns of decisions, it becomes relevant to ask, "What are judicial decisions made of?"

If we conceive of legal rules and concepts as functions of judicial decisions, it is convenient, for purposes of this analysis, to think of these decisions as hard and simple facts. Just as every physical object may be analyzed as a complex of positive and negative electrons, so every legal institution, every legal rule or concept may be analyzed as a complex of plaintiff decisions and defendant decisions. But simplicity is relative to the level of analysis. For the chemist, the atom is the lowest term of analysis. But the physicist cannot stop the process of analysis with the atom or even the electron. It would be heresy to the faith of science to endow either with final simplicity and perpetual immunity from further analysis. Unfortunately, certain advocates of realistic jurisprudence, after using the functional method to break down rules and concepts into atomic decisions, refuse to go any further with the analytic process. They are willing to look upon decisions as simple unanalyzable products of judicial hunches or indigestion.

The "hunch" theory of law,[81] by magnifying the personal and accidental factors in judicial behavior, implicitly denies the relevance of significant, predictable, social determinants that govern the course of judicial decision. Those who have advanced this viewpoint have performed a real service in indicating the large realm of uncertainty in the actual law. But actual experience does reveal a significant body of predictable uniformity in the behavior of courts. Law is not a mass of unrelated decisions nor a product of judicial bellyaches. Judges are human, but they are a peculiar breed of humans, selected to a type and held to service under a potent system of governmental controls. Their acts are "judicial" only within a system which provides for appeals, re-hearings, impeachments, and legislation. The decision that is "peculiar" suffers erosion—unless it represents the first salient manifestation of a new social force, in which case it soon ceases to be peculiar. It is more useful to analyze a judicial "hunch" in terms of the continued impact of

---

[81] See Hutcheson, The Judgment Intuitive: The Function of the "Hunch" in Judicial Decisions (1929) 14 *Corn. L.Q.* 274; Hutcheson, Lawyer's Law and the Little, Small Dice (1932) 7 *Tulane L. Rev.* 1; Frank, *Law and the Modern Mind* (1930) c. 12-13; T. Schroeder, The Psychologic Study of Judicial Opinions (1918) 6 *Calif. L. Rev.* 89.

a judge's study of precedents, his conversations with associates, his reading of newspapers, and his recollections of college courses, than in
strictly physiological terms.

A truly realistic theory of judicial decisions must conceive every decision as something more than an expression of individual personality, as
concomitantly and even more importantly a function of social forces,
that is to say, as a product of social determinants and an index of social
consequences. A judicial decision is a social event. Like the enactment
of a Federal statute, or the equipping of police cars with radios, a judicial
decision is an intersection of social forces: Behind the decision are social
forces that play upon it to give it a resultant momentum and direction;
beyond the decision are human activities affected by it. The decision
is without significant social dimensions when it is viewed simply at the
moment in which it is rendered. Only by probing behind the decision to
the forces which it reflects, or projecting beyond the decision the lines
of its force upon the future, do we come to an understanding of the
meaning of the decision itself. The distinction between "holding" and
"dictum" in any decision is not to be discovered by logical inspection of
the opinion or by historical inquiry into the actual facts of the case.[82]
That distinction involves us in a prediction, a prophecy of the weight that
courts will give to future citations of the decision rendered. This is a
question not of pure logic but of human psychology, economics and
politics.

What is the meaning of a judicial decision, summed up in the words,
"Judgment for the plaintiff"? Obviously, the significance of the decision,
even for the parties directly involved in the case, depends upon certain
predictable uniformities of official behavior, e.g., that a sheriff or marshall
will enforce the decision, in one way or another, over a period of time,
that the given decision will be respected or followed in the same court
or other courts if the question at issue is relitigated, and that certain procedures will be followed in the event of an appeal, etc. When we go
beyond the merely private significance of an actual decision, we are
involved in a new set of predictions concerning the extent to which other
cases, similar in certain respects, are likely to receive the same treatment
in the same courts or in other courts within a given jurisdiction. Except
in the context of such predictions the announcement of a judicial decision
is only a noise. If reasonably certain predictions of this sort could never

---

[82] Compare the orthodox wild goose chase of Goodhart after a formula which
will determine the "real" *ratio decidendi* of a case (Goodhart, Determining the
Ratio Decidendi of a Case (1930) 40 *Yale L.J.* 161) with the sane description by
Llewellyn of the way in which cases come to stand for propositions of narrow or
wide scope. *The Bramble Bush* (1930) 47, 61-66. *Cf.* also Oliphant, A Return to Stare
Decisis (1928) 6 *Am. L. School Rev.* 215, 217-218; F. S. Cohen, *Ethical Systems and
Legal Ideals* (1933) 33-37.

be made, as Jerome Frank at times seems to say,[83] then all legal decisions would be simply noises, and no better grist for science than the magical phrases of transcendental jurisprudence.

If the understanding of any decision involves us necessarily in prophecy (and thus in history), then the notion of law as something that exists completely and systematically at any given moment in time is false.[84] Law is a social process, a complex of human activities, and an adequate legal science must deal with human activity, with cause and effect, with the past and the future. Legal science, as traditionally conceived, attempts to give an instantaneous snapshot of an existing and completed system of rights and duties. Within that system there are no temporal processes, no cause and no effect, no past and no future. A legal decision is thus conceived as a logical deduction from fixed principles. Its meaning is expressed only in terms of its logical consequences. A legal system, thus viewed, is as far removed from temporal activity as a system of pure geometry. In fact, jurisprudence is as much a part of pure mathematics as is algebra, unless it be conceived as a study of human behavior,—human behavior as it molds and is molded by judicial decisions. Legal systems, principles, rules, institutions, concepts, and decisions can be understood only as functions of human behavior.[85]

Such a view of legal science reveals gaps in our legal knowledge to which, I think, legal research will give increasing attention.

We are still in the stage of guesswork and accidentally collected information, when it comes to formulating the social forces which mold the course of judicial decision. We know, in a general way, that dominant economic forces play a part in judicial decision, that judges usually reflect the attitudes of their own income class on social questions, that their views on law are molded to a certain extent by their past legal experience as counsel for special interests, and that the impact of counsel's skill and eloquence is a cumulative force which slowly hammers the law into forms desired by those who can best afford to hire legal skill and eloquence; but nobody has ever charted, in scientific fashion, the extent of such economic influences.[86] We know, too, that judges are craftsmen, with

---

[83] See Frank, *Law and the Modern Mind* (1930), 7, 53, 104-111, 132-134.

[84] In this, law is no different from other social institutions or physical objects. *Cf.* C. I. Lewis, *op. cit. supra* note 48 [*Mind and the World-Order* (1929)], c. 5.

[85] "To say that a legal institution,—private property, the federal government of the United States, Columbia University,—exists is to say that a group of persons is doing something, is acting in some way. It is to point to a particular aspect of human behavior.... But a legal institution is something more than the way men act on a single occasion.... A legal institution is the happening over and over again of the same kind of behavior." U. Moore, *loc. cit. supra* note 32. ["Rational Basis of Legal Institutions" 23 *Col. L. Rev.* 609 (1923).]

[86] Promising first steps towards such a study have been taken in: Brooks Adams, *op. cit. supra* note 32 [Law under Inequality; Monopoly, in *Centralization and the Law* (1906) Lecture 2]; Gustavus Myers, *History of the Supreme Court* (1912); Boudin, *op. cit. supra* note 27 [*Government by Judiciary*] (1932); Walter Nelles,

aesthetic ideals,[87] concerned with the aesthetic judgments that the bar and the law schools will pass upon their awkward or skillful, harmonious or unharmonious, anomalous or satisfying, actions and theories; but again we have no specific information on the extent of this aesthetic bias in the various branches of the law. We know that courts are, at least in this country, a generally conservative social force, and more like a brake than a motor in the social mechanism, but we have no scientific factual comparison of judicial, legislative, and executive organs of government, from the standpoint of social engineering. Concretely and specifically, we know that Judge So-and-so, a former attorney for a non-union shop, has very definite ideas about labor injunctions, that another judge, who has had an unfortunate sex life, is parsimonious in the fixing of alimony; that another judge can be "fixed" by a certain political "boss"; that a series of notorious kidnappings will bring about a wave of maximum sentences in kidnapping cases. All this knowledge is useful to the practicing lawyer, to the public official, to the social reformer, and to the disinterested student of society. But it is most meager, and what little of it we have, individually, is not collectively available. There is at present no publication showing the political, economic, and professional background and activities of our various judges. Such a reference work would be exceedingly valuable, not only to the practical lawyer who wants to bring a motion or try a case before a sympathetic court, but also to the disinterested student of the law. Such a Judicial Index is not published, however, because it would be disrespectable.[88] According to the classical theory, these things have nothing to do with the way courts decide cases. A witty critic of the functional approach regards it as a *reductio ad absurdum* of this approach that law schools of the future may investigate judicial psychology, teach the art of bribery, and produce graduate detectives.[89] This is far from a *reductio ad absurdum*. Our understanding of the law will be greatly enriched when we learn more about how judges think, about the exact extent of judicial corruption, and about the techniques for investigating legally relevant facts. Of course, this knowledge may be used for improper purposes, but

---

Commonwealth v. Hunt (1932) 32 *Columbia Law Rev.* 1128; Nelles, The First American Labor Case (1931) 41 *Yale L.J.* 165; Max Lerner, The Supreme Court and American Capitalism (1933) 42 *Yale L.J.* 668; W. Hamilton, Judicial Tolerance of Farmers' Cooperatives (1929) 38 *Yale L.J.* 936; articles of Haines [General Observations on the Effects of Personal, Political and Economic Influences in the Decisions of Judges (1922) 17 *Ill. L. Rev.* 96], Brown [Police Power—Legislation for Health and Personal Safety (1929) 42 *Harv. L. Rev.* 545], and Cushman [The Social and Economic Interpretation of the Fourteenth Amendment (1922) 20 *Mich. L. Rev.* 737] cited *supra* note 38.

[87] *Cf.* F. S. Cohen, *Ethical Systems and Legal Ideals* (1933) 56-61; Modern Ethics and the Law (1934) 4 *Brooklyn L. Rev.* 33, 48-50.

[88] Frank reports (*Law and the Modern Mind*, 112-115) the discontinuance of a statistical study of the decisions of various New York magistrates which revealed startling differences in the treatment of certain offenses. [See p. 464 *supra*.]

[89] Kantorowicz, Some Rationalism about Realism (1934) 43 *Yale L.J.* 1240.

cannot the same be said of the knowledge which traditional legal education distributes?

If we know little today of the motivating forces which mold legal decisions, we know even less of the human consequences of these decisions. We do not even know how far the appellate cases, with which legal treatises are almost exclusively concerned, are actually followed in the trial courts.[90] Here, again, the experienced practitioner is likely to have accumulated a good deal of empirical information, but the young law clerk, just out of a first-rate law school, is not even aware that such a problem exists. Likewise, the problem of the actual enforcement of judgments has received almost no critical study. Discussion of the extent to which various statutes are actually enforced regularly moves in the thin air of polemic theory. It is usually practically impossible to find out whether a given statute has ever been enforced unless its enforcement has raised a legal tangle for appellate courts.

When we advance beyond the realm of official conduct and seek to discover the social consequences of particular statutes or decisions, we find a few promising programs of research [91] but almost no factual studies.[92] Today the inclusion of factual annotations in a code, showing the extent and effects of law enforcement, would strike most lawyers as almost obscene. But notions of obscenity change, and every significant intellectual revolution raises to prominence facts once obscure and disrespectable. It is reasonable to expect that some day even the impudencies of Holmes and Llewellyn will appear sage and respectable.

---

[90] The Institute of Law of Johns Hopkins broke the ice in the modern study of trial court decisions. See *Study of Civil Justice in New York* (1931). See also Marshall, *Study of Judicial System of Maryland* (1932); C. E. Clark, Fact Research in Law Administration (1928) 2 *Conn. Bar J.* 211; B. L. Shientag and F. S. Cohen, Summary Judgments in the Supreme Court of New York (1932) 32 *Columbia Law Rev.* 825, and works cited therein, notes 6 and 7; Saxe, Summary Judgments in New York— A Statistical Study (1934) 19 *Corn. L.Q.* 237; B. L. Shientag, Summary Judgment (1935) 4 *Fordham L. Rev.* 186.

[91] See, for example, Pound, The Scope and Purpose of Sociological Jurisprudence (1911–1912) 24 *Harv. L. Rev.* 591, 25 *id.* 140, 489; F. K. Beutel, Some Implications of Experimental Jurisprudence (1934) 48 *Harv. L. Rev.* 169, 191-194.

[92] Notable exceptions are: McCracken, *Strike Injunctions in the New South* (1931); Brissenden and Swayzee, The Use of the Labor Injunction in the New York Needle Trades (1929) 44 *Pol. Sci. Q.* 548, (1930) 45 *id.* 87. In addition to these direct studies of the effects of legal rules or decisions, there is a growing literature on the social materials with which law is concerned. Examples of such work are: Pound and Frankfurter, *Criminal Justice in Cleveland* (1922); R. R. Powell and Looker, Decedents' Estates: Illumination from Probate and Tax Records (1930) 30 *Columbia Law Rev.* 919; Smith, Lilly and Dowling, Compensation for Automobile Accidents: A Symposium (1932) 32 *Columbia Law Rev.* 785; S. and E. T. Glueck, Predictability in the Administration of Criminal Justice (1929) 42 *Harv. L. Rev.* 297.

LEGISLATION

Contents

Introductory Note

A democracy striving to mould its own way of life finds itself met at every turn by an adversary more formless than Peer Gynt's Boig, assuming successively a thousand different shapes. Some of these disguises are called "maxims of statutory construction," thus deriving a presumptive propriety from a pun that links the verbs "construe" and "construct" and gives to the former the good name won by the latter. "Maxims of statutory destruction" would be a more accurately descriptive term for the host of rules by which courts sometimes seek to excuse their unwillingness to follow legislative directions. Behind those maxims lie technical problems of the sort that Frankfurter and Landis point out. But behind the technicalities are basic resistances to the legislative process, which the essay of Spencer herein set forth illustrates, and which the essays of T. V. Smith, Frank Horack, and Max Radin expose.

If our own democracy is ever to achieve a more cooperative relationship between its judicial and its legislative servants than we have yet achieved, we must give more thought than we have yet given to the intellectual and non-intellectual sources of this friction. Ehrlich's challenging appeal for judicial freedom from legislative supervision may serve to remind us that liberalism is not a permanent and exclusive possession of legislatures and that under certain circumstances it is possible that judicial law-making may faithfully serve the values of a free society.

---

1. The Nature and Scope of Legislation

SPENCER, OVER-LEGISLATION *

... Take up a daily paper and you will probably find a leader exposing the corruption, negligence, or mismanagement of some State department. Cast your eye down the next column, and it is not unlikely that you will read proposals for an extension of State-supervision.... Here is a vehement condemnation of the police for stupidly allowing sight-seers to crush each other to death; you look for the corollary that official regulation is not to be trusted; when instead, apropos of a shipwreck, you read an urgent demand for government-inspectors to see that ships always have their boats ready for launching. Thus, while every day chronicles a failure, there every day reappears the belief that it needs but an Act of Parliament and a staff of officers, to effect any end desired. Nowhere is the perennial faith of mankind better seen. Ever since society existed Disappointment has been preaching—"Put not your trust in legislation"; and yet the trust in legislation seems scarcely diminished....

... Badly as government discharges its true duties, any other duties committed to it are likely to be still worse discharged. To guard its subjects against aggression, either individual or national, is a straightforward and tolerably simple matter; to regulate, directly or indirectly, the personal actions of those subjects is an infinitely complicated matter. It is one thing to secure to each man the unhindered power to pursue his own good; it is a widely different thing to pursue the good for him. To do the first efficiently, the State has merely to look on while its citizens act; to forbid unfairness; to adjudicate when called on; and to enforce restitution for injuries. To do the last efficiently, it must become an ubiquitous worker—must know each man's needs better than he knows them himself—must, in short, possess super-human power and intelligence. Even, therefore, had the State done well in its proper sphere, no sufficient warrant would have existed for extending that sphere; but seeing how ill it has discharged those simple offices which we cannot help consigning to it, small indeed is the probability of its discharging well offices of a more complicated nature....

... This transference of power from constituencies to members of par-

---

* [*Herbert Spencer* (1820-1903), a friend of Darwin and Huxley, was popularly regarded as a great philosopher during the half century from 1860 to 1910. He did much to popularize the idea of evolution and gave the theory of anarchism a respectable formulation under the guise of *"laissez faire."* Among his more influential works are: *Social Statics* (1850); *Principles of Psychology* (1855); and *Principles of Sociology* (1896).]

liament, from these to the executive, from the executive to a board, from the board to its inspectors, and from inspectors through their subs down to the actual workers—this operating through a series of levers, each of which absorbs in friction and inertia part of the moving force; is as bad, in virtue of its complexity, as the direct employment by society of individuals, private companies, and spontaneously-formed institutions, is good, in virtue of its simplicity. Fully to realize the contrast, we must compare in detail the working of the two systems.

To the immense positive evils entailed by over-legislation have to be added the equally great negative evils—evils which, notwithstanding their greatness, are scarcely at all recognized, even by the farseeing. It is not simply that the State does those things which it ought not to do, but that, as an *inevitable consequence*, it leaves undone those things which it ought to do. Time and human activity being limited, it necessarily follows that legislators' sins of *commission* entail corresponding sins of *omission*. The injury is unavoidably doubled. Mischievous meddling involves disastrous neglect; and until statesmen are ubiquitous and omnipotent, must ever do so. It is in the very nature of things that an agency employed for two purposes must fulfil both imperfectly; ...

And if an institution undertakes, not two functions, but a score—if a government, whose office it is to defend citizens against aggressors foreign and domestic, engages also to disseminate Christianity, to administer charity, to teach children their lessons, to adjust prices of food, to inspect coalmines, to regulate railways, to superintend house-building, to arrange cabfares, to look into people's stink-traps, to vaccinate their children, to send out emigrants, to prescribe hours of labour, to examine lodging-houses, to test the knowledge of mercantile captains, to provide public libraries, to read and authorize dramas, to inspect passenger-ships, to see that small dwellings are supplied with water, to regulate endless things from a banker's issues down to the boat-fares on the Serpentine—is it not manifest that its primary duty must be ill-discharged in proportion to the multiplicity of affairs it busies itself with? Is it not manifest that its time and energies must be frittered away in schemes, and inquiries, and amendments, in proposals, and debates, and divisions, to the utter neglect of its essential office? And does not a glance over the debates make it manifest that this is the fact? ...

MAINE, EARLY HISTORY OF INSTITUTIONS *

The capital fact in the mechanism of modern States is the energy of legislatures. Until the fact existed, I do not, as I have said, believe that the [analytical] system of Hobbes, Bentham and Austin could have been con-

---

* [3d ed. (1880), pp. 398-400. The first edition of this work appeared in 1874. *Cf.* excerpts on status and contract from Maine's *Ancient Law* at pp. 124-125 *supra*.]

ceived; wherever it exhibits itself imperfectly, I think that the system is never properly appreciated. The comparative neglect with which German writers have treated it seems to me to be explained by the comparative recency of legislative activity in Germany. It is however impossible to observe on the connection between legislation and the analytical theory of law without having the mind carried to the famous addition which Bentham and Austin engrafted on the speculations of Hobbes. This addition consisted in coupling them with the doctrine or theory of utility—of the greatest happiness of the greatest number considered as the basis of law and morals. What, then, is the connection essential or historical, between the utilitarian theory and the analytical theory of law? I certainly do not affect to be able, especially at the close of a lecture, to exhaust a subject of such extent and difficulty, but I have a few words to say of it. To myself the most interesting thing about the theory of Utility is that it presupposes the theory of Equality. The greatest number is the greatest number of men taken as units; "one shall only count for one," said Bentham emphatically and over and over again. In fact, the most conclusive objection to the doctrine would consist in denying this equality; and I have myself heard an Indian Brahmin dispute it on the ground that, according to the clear teaching of his religion, a Brahmin was entitled to twenty times as much happiness as anybody else. Now how did this fundamental assumption of equality which (I may observe) broadly distinguishes Bentham's theories from some systems with which it is supposed to share the reproach of having pure selfishness for its base—how did it suggest itself to Bentham's mind? He saw plainly—nobody more clearly—that men are not as a fact equal; the proposition that men are by nature equal he expressly denounced as an anarchical sophism. Whence then came the equality which is a postulate of his famous doctrine about the greatest happiness of the greatest number? I venture to think that this doctrine is nothing more than a working rule of legislation, and that in this form it was originally conceived by Bentham. Assume a numerous and tolerably homogeneous community— assume a Sovereign whose commands take a legislative shape—assume great energy, actual or potential, in this legislature—the only possible, the only conceivable, principle which can guide legislation on a great scale is the greatest happiness of the greatest number. It is in fact a condition of legislation which, like certain characteristics of laws, has grown out of the distance from which sovereign power acts upon subjects in modern political societies, and of the necessity under which it is thereby placed of neglecting differences, even real differences, between the units of which they are composed. Bentham was in truth neither a jurist nor a moralist in the proper sense of the word. He theorises not on law but on legislation; when carefully examined, he may be seen to be a legislator even in morals. No doubt his language seems sometimes to imply that he is explaining moral phenomena; in reality he wishes to alter or rearrange them according to a working rule gathered from his reflections on legislation. This transfer of his working rule from legislation to morality seems to me the true ground of the criticisms to which Bentham is justly open as an analyst of moral facts.

T. V. SMITH, THE LEGISLATIVE WAY OF LIFE *

Preface

Democracy is government by politicians for citizens who too often reward them with disdain. This disdain of politicians is a dangerous disease. It is peculiarly dangerous for a democracy. Politicians are the secular priests of our common faith in one another. Either they attend to our joint business or that business gets neglected. If it gets neglected, then democracy fails from inefficiency.

Disdain of politicians should be left to dictators. Democrats cannot afford the luxury of such malevolence. [P. ix.]

. . . . .

I. The Problem of the Legislative Way

. . . . .

IV. The Tolerant Person Meets the Trying Problem

I met sometime ago the wife of a man who once had been a member of a middle western legislature. Being always curious as to the attitude of idealistic people toward their legislative bodies, I engaged her in conversation regarding her husband's experiences in politics. She said that she had been originally worried about her husband's getting into politics at all. She had thought politics rotten, you see, calculated to corrupt whomever it touches.

Her husband must have been a very wise man, or at least a very lucky one, seeing how he handled the situation. She said that when he first went off to the capital city, she told him that she asked only two things: that he would keep personally decent and that he would do his duty by voting his convictions on each bill. Presently he invited her to go with him to the legislature. Being himself very busy, he asked her now and then to read

---

* [Chicago: University of Chicago Press, 1940.

The Legislative Way of Life by *T. V. Smith* (b. 1890) consists of lectures originally delivered at Westminster College. It is an attempt to give expression to the underlying realities and human objectives of the contemporary American political scene. Editor of the international journal *Ethics,* professor of philosophy at the University of Chicago, and former State Senator and Congressman-at-large from Illinois, Smith has brought a wealth of learning and practical testing to bear on the analysis of contemporary ethical problems, in the work cited and in several other books and articles.]

certain bills that he had no time to read, and to advise him how to vote upon the bills.

This she undertook to do. The first bill he gave her she read with great care and told him how to vote. But then, she said, there developed a curious situation. After she had advised her husband how to vote, she would go to the committee meetings or hear the debates on the floor. She said that the people on each side would put up such good arguments that after listening to the debates she did not know whether her advice to her husband had been sound or not. This discovery was to her something of a surprise—the double discovery, you see, that each side was reasonable and that both groups were honest. After having this upsetting experience a few times, she said that she told her husband that he would just have to read the bills for himself thereafter, that she did not know anything more about what was right to do than he.

It is a great discovery for the self-righteous to make. It marks the first crack in the shell of elemental egoism. It is a crack which the Hitlers of life never suffer, nor permit others to enjoy. It is a great day when anyone is brought to suspect that he is no wiser than others, and that others are as honest as he. The beginning of collective wisdom is for each man to discover that he is not God. To discover that is to see why legislatures are necessary and to learn how they can be fruitful. For that is a discovery calculated to emancipate one from his natural narrowness and to start him upon the pilgrimage whose mecca is the full-fledged legislative way of life. [Pp. 29-31.]

. . . . .

III. The Product of the Legislative Way

. . . . .

1. Laws, the Direct Product

. . . . .

These direct products of our legislative way [laws] represent the maximum of private conscience which can at any time become social fact. This maximum seems to many so minimal as always to provoke pessimism about democracy. But the curious thing is that if you get too discouraged over the amount of ideality which can be socially realized and impetuously set about to make all your best private ideals effective, action becomes less ideal by your very effort to make it more so. There is a sort of law of diminishing returns in the life of ideals, as in the flow of goods: the more strident the ideals, the weaker; the gentler the ideals, the stronger.

Few people would deny the elemental sincerity of, say, either Lenin or Hitler. Such men feel private ideals so intensely that they are frustrated unless their convictions can be made to pass over, whole bodied, into collective action. But intolerant effort leaves the national course strewn with dead bodies and lays upon the consciences of millions the heavy hand of a single conscience desperate in its demands. As Thomas Hobbes, the old materialist, once said: "The law is the public conscience." Blessed is the man who, through patience, sagacity, and co-operation with other men, can take the purely private thing called conscience and turn it into socially acceptable action through law. [Pp. 71-72.]

.   .   .   .   .

II. Enlarged Opportunity, the Indirect Product

.   .   .   .   .

By the outer process of political compromise, therefore, and by it alone, is brought to birth an inner life free of compromise. By applying a second-best principle to second-best things, we find that for things of the first moment we can operate under the principle of perfection. Compromise for the compromisable, therefore, freedom for the indispensable. This is the final harmony between the political doctrine of accommodation and the moral doctrine of autonomous integrity. A man is not a good man who will compromise the core of himself—that is, the final principles by which he lives. But a man is not a good citizen who does not meet other good citizens halfway....

... The Constitution itself makes this very clear; for, while the document as a whole establishes the machinery of compromise, the first ten amendments—*i.e.*, the Bill of Rights—takes out from under this reign of democratic relativity all things of the very first moment. It excepts conscience from compromise; it excepts free thought from compromise; it excepts free speech from compromise; it excepts from compromise free conduct up to the point where free behavior conflicts with free behavior.

By accepting compromise in things that count for least we achieve autonomy in things that count for most. The dignity of man is thus safeguarded by a price which no dignified man need hesitate to pay. The legislative way requires exactly this wisdom to distinguish first things and this courage to keep first things first. I have known men very tenacious of property rights when personal rights were secure enough to be forgotten with impunity. "The laws of property," said John Stuart Mill, spokesman for *laissez faire*, "have never yet conformed to the principles on which the justification of private property rests. They have made property of things which never ought to be property and absolute property where only a qualified property ought to exist." But when immunity from search of private home and seizure of person passed away, such men, normally tenacious of property, were happy to give up all their property in order to save their persons from indignity and their convictions from surrender. On the latter, ask any intellectual refugee from Italy. And on the former ask a refugee from Czechoslovakia, from Poland, from any totalitarian land in which all things have been confused with first things and in which first things have been lost in the resulting *mêlée*. [Pp. 77-80.]

. . . . .

Jefferson's formulation of what these inalienable rights are may be taken as our own until we can find a better. All property rights Jefferson reserved to politics and left to be settled as best they could be by the process of give-and-take. [P. 80.]

. . . . .

He did not claim, as Frenchmen and Englishmen of the time, claimed, full freedom of "life, liberty, and property." He claimed as inalienable only what is possible of defense, "life, liberty, and the pursuit of happiness." If with him we keep our claim of inalienability to the minimum, we may be able to extend our defenses to the maximum of the Bill of Rights. These, and not otherwise, are the ramparts that we guard.

Here, then, we find the first two indirect fruits of the legislative way—outer peace and inner freedom. [Pp. 80-82.]

. . . . .

III. The Legislative Way in Final Perspective

The outer fruits of the legislative way are very great to those not engaged in lotus-hunting. Legislation is a process slow and cumbersome. It turns out a product—laws—that rarely are liked by everybody, and frequently little liked by anybody. But the legislature is, for all that, the only institution developed by man through the centuries which preserves individuals against gross invasion of their private rights and guarantees some minimum of benefits to all groups alike in their struggle for survival and supremacy. If the legislative way can but keep the qualities of its defects, we must continue to allow it the defects of its qualities. For there is no humane alternative. True, when seen from the shining cliffs of perfection the legislative process of compromise appears shoddy indeed. But when seen from some concentration camp of the only alternative way of life, the compromises of legislation appear but another name for what we call civilization and even revere as Christian forbearance. Compromise makes actual one great good, and it makes possible another great good. What it makes actual is self-expression through free speech and unhampered association. What it makes always possible is a scientific arrangement through which its gracious processes may be continuously improved.

It should be to us, therefore, a matter of great meaning and high hope that no modern nation long seasoned in our legislative way of handling common problems has yet voluntarily given it up. . . .

America is the one country which was legislative-minded from its birth as a nation. Its general way of life makes legislatures possible, and legislatures in turn keep alive and prosperous its way of life.... [Pp. 91-93.]

.   .   .   .   .

Regardless of political party, we Americans believe, for instance, that all children of all the people are entitled to both health and education. Or do we—with about one-third of our children growing up in the South on but one-sixth of the nation's school revenues? We believe that all life is equally sacred and must be equally secure under the law. Or do we—with gangsterdom now and then a-shooting in the cities of the North and barbarism then and now a-lynching in the counties of the South? We believe that all questions that cannot be settled otherwise must be settled by the ballot. Or do we—with more than half the citizens unencouraged to vote in the South and oftentimes a third of them unwilling to vote in the North?

Don't we or do we believe, I mean, in these ideals of equal opportunity, equal protection, equal participation? We do; we do believe in all these ideals. They represent yet and ever our faith, our way of thought, if you will. But they do not fully represent our way of life. We have still to find out how to take up the slack between our way of thought and our way of life. This disturbing leeway between what we love and the way we live is the penance we pay for being at once more than human and less than human—for being both skyborn and earthbound.

Forgetting its pathos, we may with the unknown poet nail this our common shame to the crucifix of fun:

> There was a dachshund, once so long
> He hadn't any notion
> How long it took to notify
> His tail of his emotion;
> And so it happened, while his eyes
> Were filled with woe and sadness,
> His little tail went wagging on
> Because of previous gladness. [Pp. 95-96.]

HORACK, THE COMMON LAW OF LEGISLATION *

Statute law has an unenviable reputation. The common-law lawyer has emphasized its unwholesome bulk,[1] and has alleged that its capricious and

---

* [23 *Iowa L. Rev.* 41 (1937).

Frank Edward Horack, Jr. (b. 1907), professor of law at West Virginia University and Indiana University, Acting Dean of Indiana University School of Law, holder of various state and federal official posts, has been highly influential in persuading American law teachers to give increasing attention to statutes and the legislative process. In addition to the article here quoted, he has set forth his ideas on the role of legislation in considerable detail in several books and articles. See "The Disintegration of Statutory Construction" 24 *Ind. L.J.* 335-352 (1949), cited *infra* at p. 524, and *Cases and Materials on Legislation* (1940).]

[1] Stevenson, Excessive Regulation (1928) 62 *Am. L. Rev.* 619; Verner, Is There Too Much Legislation? (1928) 3 *Ala. L.J.* 257; Hasty Legislation, 162 *The Law*

sporadic method [2] has infused illegitimate legal principles into an otherwise symmetrical jurisprudence.[3] These attacks have discredited the statute books, and the negative implication of common law perfection has added disdain for the entire legislative method. And so commonplace have these assertions become that the temptation is to accept them without analysis. Analysis and comparison of the legislative and judicial processes, however, discloses surprising similarity. Indeed, if there is a common law of cases, there is equally a common law of legislation. . . .

The function of precedent in judge-made law has been discussed elaborately; its similar functions in legislation has been ignored. Nevertheless, legislation, like judge-made law, follows precedent. Save for formal differences of structure, legislation and adjudication spring from similar patterns of human conduct.

Habit and the essential caution of the human mind seek the easy comfort of past decisions and abjures responsibility for new determinations. Consequently, whether the decision involves changing the color of one's house, the breakfast menu, a judge-made rule of tort liability, or a statutory amendment, experience will find friendly reception. But the law of statutory precedents must be looked for, not in the courts, but in the legislative acts. The search is, of course, more perilous and the discoveries more difficult, for legislative assemblies have lost the art of argument and fail to "explain" their decisions.[8] Their books have only the decisions, but behind each decision there will be found a reason.[9]

Statutory precedent grows as case-precedent grows. First, someone

---

Times, 511 (1926); Multiplicity of Laws, 11 *Va. L. Reg.* (N.S.) 687 (1926); Rain of Law, 4 *Can. Bar R.* 402 (1926); Jones, A Tyranny of Laws (1930) 9 *Tenn. L. Rev.* 38.

[2] "It seems scarcely appropriate to apply the term 'law' to that which was one thing yesterday, another today, and still another tomorrow. It is hard to realize that what was proper yesterday can be very wrong today and all right tomorrow." Alter, Presidential Address, 1925 *Pa. Bar Asso.* 3.

[3] Lord Coke once remarked, "If I am asked a question of *common law*, I should be ashamed if I could not immediately answer it; if I am asked a question of *statute law*, I should be ashamed to answer it without referring to the Statute Book."

[8] Statutes have suffered from the abandonment of the preamble. Only recently has the "policy section" reappeared to serve its function. Long ago Bentham suggested its importance. "My practice, . . . is to give to each enactment, or intimately connected with it, its own set of reasons. . . ." 3 *Bentham Works* (Bowring Ed.) 323.

[9] "Legislators who, having freed themselves from the shackles of authority, have learnt to soar above the mists of prejudice, know as well how to make laws for one country as for another: all they need is to be possessed fully of the facts; to be informed of the local situation, the climate, the bodily constitution, the manners, the legal customs, the religion, of those with whom they have to deal. These are the data they require; possessed of these data, all places are alike. If they are more at home in their own country than elsewhere, it is only because the requisite stock of facts in the former situation is already possessed by them without their being obliged to wait the time which, in a foreign country, it would require to seek them out." 7 *Bentham Works* (Bowring Ed.) 801.

bolder than the rest marks a new course.[10] If the course appears satisfactory, others follow. Legal science calls this the doctrine of *stare decisis*. The legislative process is similar. . . .

. . . Important present day legislation is no longer of "wild and sporadic growth." Scientific legislative services have made great strides,[15] national associations[16] follow proposed state and federal legislation, with careful scrutiny, and the conflicting interests represented in every committee room make it as dangerous for proponent or committeeman to be unfamiliar with existing legislation as it is for judge or counsel to argue without "authorities."

It may be objected, of course, that so long as statutes are not applied by analogy in judicial proceedings,[17] care in legislative preparation is unimportant. This overlooks two rather significant possibilities. First, that the history of social control through law usually follows a pattern which eventually shifts from the unwritten to the written law—and, thus, statutes become the significant legal materials.[18] Second, that the lawyer's function today is not limited to litigation. The understanding of administrative action and the prediction of legislative action are chief responsibilities of many lawyers. The job is difficult, of course, but it is not impossible. To achieve a capacity for legislative prediction the lawyer must organize legislative materials along systems similar to the judicial digests. [Pp. 44-45.]

. . . . .

Stare decisis provides courts and litigants a fair standard for the prediction of future judicial action; *stare de statute* enables legislators, public administrators, and those privately interested in legislative development to predict within similar degrees of error the development of statutory rule. It is as Bentham suggested, an understanding of the mores, prejudices and past experience of a people that will provide the key for the prediction of

---

[10] Sometimes the new course is discovered quite by accident. See the strange case related by Lewis in *The Anatomy of Science*, 34-37. Not always do the proponents of a new idea suffer the fate of Mr. Lewis' young man whose ideas were "so heretical in character that he was tried, condemned, and eaten."

[15] See Leek, The Legislative Reference Bureau in Recent Years (1929) 20 *Am. Pol. Sci. Rev.* 832. Arnold, Judicial Councils (1929) 35 *W. Va. L.Q.* 193. Witte, A Law Making Laboratory (1930) 3 *St. Gov.* 3.

[16] The significance of the participation of national organizations in the legislative process is emphasized by their inclusion in *The Book of the States* (1937) published by the Council of State Governments, and the reference in Beardsley, *Legal Bibliography* (1937). Any one conversant with the legislative service bureaus of these associations and their activities before specific state legislatures will recognize the shift that has been made from the insidious private lobby to the public recognized and responsible national association.

[17] See Landis, [The Study of Legislation in Law Schools (1931) 39 *Harv. Grad. Mag.* 433, 434.]

[18] Williston, Written and Unwritten Law (1931) 17 *A.B.A.J.* 39. But see Williston, Change in the Law (1935) 69 *U.S.L. Rev.* 237.

statute law. Legislation develops in an orderly manner. It finds analogy in prior legislative enactment. Unique is the occasion when completely new legislation is enacted.[39]

Mr. Justice v. Mr. Senator

Putting aside the psychological advantages the judicial feathers provide,[40] judges are alleged to be superior because of the advantage of their professional training. It is said that judges are "safer guardians" of the law because they are trained *in law*, serve apprenticeships as lawyers, and because they develop a cautious appreciation of the necessities of certainty and continuity. Legislators, it is said, receive no special training, are frequently swept into office on the tide of political or of economic disaffection and arrive at their desks without training for or appreciation of their responsibilities. Again the comparison is only partially accurate.

Judges, like legislators, may ride the tide of political fortunes. But legislators, unlike judges, are not assured of great power or influence by their election. The new representative must make his way. During his first term, he must sit with quiet respect for those familiar with legislative practice and procedure. The legislative tyro receives training similar to the attorney who practices before he presides. Minor committee assignments will be his first term rewards. With a second term, he may receive more important assignments; but if the seniority rule applies, he must be an "old wheel horse" before he can expect important chairmanships.[41]

The difficulty is that we still see legislation emanating from the oratorical halls and the smoke-filled chambers of state capital hotels. For the most part, this picture exists, today, only in the cartoons. Thus, although formally legislatures are unpredictable, heterogeneous collections of untrained representatives, the informal organization of the legislature makes it a highly trained skillful machine that can when it wants make an examination of policy and write a statute with a skill to be envied by any court.[42] Again, although the forms and symbols differ—the personnels of each system have the same capacities and incapacities for their functions.[43]

---

[39] The Federal Social Security Act is perhaps generally considered the most unique and unprecedented legislation that we have of recent date. Yet it patterns after much continental experience and is almost a duplicate of the act which Jeremy Bentham wrote in 1797. He outlined a plan for old age security, mothers' aid, children's aid, and unemployment compensation. In many respects his plan was more comprehensive than our own. He concluded, however, that the plan would not work. See 8 *Bentham Works* (Bowring Ed. 1843) 166, 367, 442.

[40] Arnold, *Symbols of Government* (1935).

[41] Note the rise of southern Democrats to the chairmanship of important committees, because of the seniority rule, in spite of their opposition to the so-called New Deal policies.

[42] See Wis., *The Assembly Manual* (1927) p. 279, Joint Rule No. 6; hearings before the committee of Bank and Currency, 73d Cong. 1st Sess., C. Rec. 84, 56, 97, Part. 15.

[43] See Caraway, *Good and Bad Lobbies*, and Bellows, In Defence of Lobbying, *Harper's Mag.* (Dec. 1935) p. 96.

Judicial Trial v. Legislative Hearing

Notice and hearing and the give and take of trial procedure long have been unquestioned virtues of common-law procedure, but they are not common law monopolies. Legislation follows the same esoteric path—the essentials of the "trial of a statute" are the essentials of the judicial system.

Legislation of significance inevitably receives complete committee consideration. A hearing is held, witnesses subpoenaed and sworn, evidence presented, policy discussed, and in recent years, an opportunity for proponent and opponent provided.[44] Inasmuch as the determination of legislative policy involves much more than a specific or limited fact inquiry, it is natural that the form of the hearing will not be identical with a judicial trial; but although the form differs, the essential purpose of each procedure is the same—the collection of reliable evidence and a sharp policy judgment based on the evidence. Indeed, when legislatures consider special legislation, the committee hearing assumes not only the objectives of trial procedure but all its forms.[45]

A distinction has frequently been drawn between legislative and judicial procedure on the basis of the care and thoroughness with which each system disposes of its business. The legislative process is frequently attacked because many bills are "rushed through" on the closing days of legislative sessions, apparently without thought or consideration. This is not the true picture. If it were, judges might be criticized because they hand down many opinions on a single day or enter many orders at a single time. Lawyers understand that the opinions handed down and the orders entered are but the final result of careful consideration, thorough conference, and much debate. The same is true of legislative action. Bills speedily enacted have run the gamut of committee hearing, administrative counsel, and have the additional protection that the process has been duplicated in each house of the legislature. Apparent haste might delude the unwary observer; but the trained legislator knows that the committee's time and thought has been expended to perfect the legislative policy. The legislature holds the committee responsible and accepts its judgment.[46]

In many respects the legislative hearing provides greater protection to the essential interests of society than does the trial. Self-limitation has made the judge a referee. The legislator understands that he must bear full

---

[44] Landis, Constitutional Limitations on the Congressional Power of Investigation (1926) 40 *Harv. L. Rev.* 153. Seabury, Herwitz & Mulligan, The Legislative Investigating Committee (1933) 33 *Col. L. Rev.* 1.

[45] Landers, *Private Bills*, 6; Standing Orders Relative to Private Business of the House of Commons (1928); P. B. R., Eyre and Spottiswood's London (1899); Ind. Local Acts (1945–6) c. 18; Ill. Acts (1929) p. 124; W. Va. Acts (2d Extr. Sess. 1933) c. 170.

[46] Wilson pointed out that our government was a "government by the chairman of the standing committees of Congress." Wilson, *Congressional Government*, 102.

responsibility for his decisions, and thus he is not content with the evidence of interested parties. He must search out every source which adds to the understanding and the determination of the question before him.[47]

Committee responsibility usually results in more complete and competent information than the judicial method of brief and argument. The appellate tribunal must depend upon a lawyer's evaluation of a proposed decision. The committee, in addition to its lawyers, enjoys the counsel of economists, public administrators, and business men. And bi-party committee representation insures additional divergent viewpoints. Practical evaluation of proposed legislation is ever available in the committee room.

Committee procedure follows as orderly a pattern as judicial procedure. It is true that some of the lawyers' safeguards are missing, but likewise, many out-moded judicial procedures are avoided.[48] Thus, the form and indeed the practice of trial and hearing are similar in the essentials. This is naturally so; not only because courts and legislatures trace their origin to the single governmental body—the *Curia Regis*,[49] but also because the nature of their work is parallel. Only because lawyers have eulogized the judicial system and spokesmen for the legislative procedure have been few, has the idea become common that legislation is ill-considered and unpredictable.... [Pp. 49-52.]

· · · · ·

A Comprehensive Jurisprudence

· · · · ·

Perhaps the greatest difficulty in advancing the thesis of consistence and order in legislative policy is the inability to make readily available the course and pattern of legislative precedent. Today it is little more than a realization of those persons who have had close contact with the activity of legislatures. Its complete establishment will depend, as the establishment of case precedent depended, upon its growing use. Law schools provide the most effective agency for the advancement of a jurisprudence which combines in an effective way the inter-related development of case and statute law. Unfortunately, even at this late date, there is little appreciation or sympathy for such a movement. All Gaul is still divided into three parts —executive, legislative, and judicial. [P. 56.]

---

[47] See note 43, *supra.*
[48] See note 44, *supra.*
[49] Plucknett, *A Concise History of the Common Law* (2d Ed. 1936) 122.

2. Statutory Interpretation

ARISTOTLE, RHETORIC *

First, then, let us take laws and see how they are to be used in persuasion and dissuasion, in accusation and defense. If the written law tells against our case, clearly we must appeal to the universal law, and insist on its greater equity and justice. We must argue that the juror's oath "I will give my verdict according to my honest opinion" means that one will not simply follow the letter of the written law. We must urge that the principles of equity are permanent and changeless, and that the universal law does not change either, for it is the law of nature, whereas written laws often do change. This is the bearing of the lines in Sophocles' *Antigone*, where Antigone pleads that in burying her brother she had broken Creon's law, but not the unwritten law:

> Not of to-day or yesterday they are,
> But live eternal: (none can date their birth.)
> Not I would fear the wrath of any man,
> (And brave Gods' vengeance) for defying these.[71]

We shall argue that justice indeed is true and profitable, but that sham justice is not, and that consequently the written law is not, because it does not fulfil the true purpose of law. Or that justice is like silver, and must be assayed by the judges, if the genuine is to be distinguished from the counterfeit. Or that the better a man is, the more he will follow and abide by the unwritten law in preference to the written. Or perhaps that the law in question contradicts some other highly-esteemed law, or even contradicts itself. Thus it may be that one law will enact that all contracts must be held binding, while another forbids us ever to make illegal contracts. Or if a law is ambiguous, we shall turn it about and consider which construction best fits the interests of justice or utility, and then follow that way of looking at it. Or if, though the law still exists, the situation to meet which it was passed exists no longer, we must do our best to prove this and to combat the law thereby. If however the written law supports our case, we must urge that the oath "to give my verdict according to my honest opinion" is not meant to make the judges give a verdict that is contrary to the law, but to save them from the guilt of perjury if they misunderstand what the law really means. Or that no one chooses what is absolutely good, but every one what is good for himself.[72] Or that not to use the laws is as bad as to have no laws at all. Or that, as in the other arts, it does not pay to try to be cleverer than the doctor: for less harm comes from the doc-

---

* [Bk. I, Chap. 15.]

[71] Sophocles, *Antigone*, 456.

[72] *sc.*, and our written laws, which were made for us, may not reach the abstract ideal of perfection, but they probably suit us better than if they did.

tor's mistakes than from the growing habit of disobeying authority. Or that trying to be cleverer than the laws is just what is forbidden by those codes of law that are accounted best. . . .

HEYDON'S CASE

EXCHEQUER, 1584

3 Co. 7a, 76 Eng. Rep. 637

. . . And it was resolved by them, that for the sure and true interpretation of all statutes in general (be they penal or beneficial, restrictive or enlarging of the common law,) four things are to be discerned and considered:—

1st. What was the common law before the making of the Act.

2nd. What was the mischief and defect for which the common law did not provide.

3rd. What remedy the Parliament hath resolved and appointed to cure the disease of the commonwealth.

And, 4th. The true reason of the remedy; and then the office of all the Judges is always to make such construction as shall suppress the mischief, and advance the remedy, and to suppress subtle inventions and evasions for continuance of the mischief, and *pro privato commodo*, and to add force and life to the cure and remedy, according to the true intent of the makers of the Act, *pro bono publico*. . . .

POUND, COMMON LAW AND LEGISLATION *

Not the least notable characteristics of American law today are the excessive output of legislation in all our jurisdictions and the indifference, if not contempt, with which that output is regarded by courts and lawyers. Text-writers who scrupulously gather up from every remote corner the most obsolete decisions and cite all of them, seldom cite any statutes except those landmarks which have become a part of our American common law, or, if they do refer to legislation, do so through the judicial decisions which apply it. The courts, likewise, incline to ignore important legislation; not merely deciding it to be declaratory, but sometimes assuming silently that it is declaratory without adducing any reasons, citing prior judicial decisions and making no mention of the statute.[1] In the same way, lawyers in the legislature often conceive it more expedient to make of a statute the barest outline, leaving details of the most vital importance to be filled in by judicial law-making.[2] It is fashionable to point out the deficiencies of legislation and to declare that there are things that legislators

---

* [21 *Harv. L. Rev.* 383 (1908). Footnotes have been renumbered.]

[1] See address of Amasa M. Eaton, Proceedings of Seventeenth Annual Conference of Commissioners on Uniform State Laws, 45.

[2] *E.g.*, the Sherman Anti-Trust Act, also Senator Knox's plan for an Employers' Liability Act.

cannot do try how they will.[3] It is fashionable to preach the superiority of judge-made law.[4] It may be well, however, for judges and lawyers to remember that there is coming to be a science of legislation and that modern statutes are not to be disposed of lightly as off-hand products of a crude desire to do something, but represent long and patient study by experts, careful consideration by conferences or congresses or associations, press discussions in which public opinion is focussed upon all important details, and hearings before legislative committees. It may be well to remember also that while bench and bar are never weary of pointing out the deficiencies of legislation, to others the deficiencies of judge-made law are no less apparent. To economists and sociologists, judicial attempts to force Benthamite conceptions of freedom of contract and common law conceptions of individualism upon the public of today are no less amusing—or even irritating—than legislative attempts to do away with or get away from these conceptions are to bench and bar. The nullifying of these legislative attempts is not regarded by lay scholars with the complacent satisfaction [5] with which lawyers are wont to speak of it. They do not hesitate to say that "the judicial mind has not kept pace with the strides of industrial development." [6] They express the opinion that "belated and anti-social" decisions have been a fruitful cause of strikes, industrial discord, and consequent lawlessness.[7] They charge that "the attitude of the courts has been responsible for much of our political immorality." [8]

---

[3] For examples from the juristic literature of the past two years, see Carter, *Law, Its Origin, Growth and Function,* 3; Parker, The Congestion of Law, 29 *Rep. Am. Bar Ass'n,* 383; Parker, Address as President of the Am. Bar Ass'n 1907, 19 *Green Bag* 581; Dos Passos, *The American Lawyer,* 169; Hughes, *Datum Posts of Jurisp.,* 106; 2 Andrews, *Am. Law,* 2 ed., 1190.

[4] An excellent example may be seen in the Introduction (by Judge Baldwin) to *Two Centuries' Growth of American Law.*

[5] *E.g.,* a recent writer, assuming that certain common law doctrines as to procedure inhere in nature, points out that despite legislative attempts to get away from them, courts have preserved them. This is assumed to show that the legislature had attempted the impossible. 2 Andrews, *Am. Law,* § § 646, 684. Of course, one might answer that there are jurisdictions where such legislation has been given effect by the courts. Gartner v. Corwine, 57 Oh. St. 246; Rogers v. Duhart, 97 Cal. 200. One might also say that if courts had been as zealous to enforce the spirit of the New York Code of 1848 as they were to graft common law upon it and to show that its leading ideas could not be carried out, the cases might tell another story.

[6] Kelley, *Some Ethical Gains through Legislation,* 142. See also Seager, *Introduction to Economics,* § 236.

[7] *Ibid.* 144, 156.

[8] Smith, *Spirit of Am. Gov.,* c. xii. Professor Smith says: "By protecting the capitalist in the possession and enjoyment of privileges unwisely and even corruptly granted, they have greatly strengthened the motive for employing bribery and other corrupt means in securing the grant of special privileges. If the courts had all along held that any proof of fraud or corruption in obtaining a franchise or other legislative grant was sufficient to justify its revocation, the lobbyist, the bribe-giver and the 'innocent purchaser' of rights and privileges stolen from the people, would have found the traffic in legislative favors a precarious and much less profitable mode of acquiring wealth." 329-330.

There are two ways in which the courts impede or thwart social legislation demanded by the industrial conditions of today. The first is narrow and illiberal construction of constitutional provisions, state and federal. "Petty judicial interpretations," says Professor Thayer, "have always been, are now, and will always be, a very serious danger to the country." [9] The second is a narrow and illiberal attitude toward legislation conceded to be constitutional, regarding it as out of place in the legal system, as an alien element to be held down to the strictest limits and not to be applied beyond the requirements of its express language. The second is by no means so conspicuous as the first, but is not on that account the less unfortunate or the less dangerous. Let us see what this attitude is, how it arose, and why it exists in an industrial community and an age of legislation.

Four ways may be conceived of in which courts in such a legal system as ours might deal with a legislative innovation. (1) They might receive it fully into the body of the law as affording not only a rule to be applied but a principle from which to reason, and hold it, as a later and more direct expression of the general will, of superior authority to judge-made rules on the same general subject; and so reason from it by analogy in preference to them. (2) They might receive it fully into the body of the law to be reasoned from by analogy the same as any other rule of law, regarding it, however, as of equal or co-ordinate authority in this respect with judge-made rules upon the same general subject. (3) They might refuse to receive it fully into the body of the law and give effect to it directly only; refusing to reason from it by analogy but giving it, nevertheless, a liberal interpretation to cover the whole field it was intended to cover. (4) They might not only refuse to reason from it by analogy and apply it directly only, but also give to it a strict and narrow interpretation, holding it down rigidly to those cases which it covers expressly. The fourth hypothesis represents the orthodox common law attitude toward legislative innovations. Probably the third hypothesis, however, represents more nearly the attitude toward which we are tending. The second and first hypotheses doubtless appeal to the common law lawyer as absurd. He can hardly conceive that a rule of statutory origin may be treated as a permanent part of the general body of the law. But it is submitted that the course of legal development upon which we have entered already must lead us to adopt the method of the second and eventually the method of the first hypothesis. [Pp. 383-386.]

· · · · ·

... The proposition that statutes in derogation of the common law are to be construed strictly has no such justification. It assumes that legislation is something to be deprecated. As no statute of any consequence dealing with any relation of private law can be anything but in derogation of the

---

[9] Thayer, *Legal Essays,* 159.

common law, the social reformer and the legal reformer, under this doctrine, must always face the situation that the legislative act which represents the fruit of their labors will find no sympathy in those who apply it, will be construed strictly, and will be made to interfere with the *status quo* as little as possible. The New York Code of Civil Procedure of 1848 affords a conspicuous example of how completely this attitude on the part of courts may nullify legislative action.[10] Some regard this attitude toward legislation as a basic principle of jurisprudence.[11] Others are content to make of it an ancient and fundamental principle of the common law.[12] In either event they agree in praising it as a wise and useful institution.[13] It is not difficult to show, however, that it is not necessary to and inherent in a legal system; that it is not an ancient and fundamental doctrine of the common law; that it had its origin in archaic notions of interpretation generally, now obsolete, and survived in its present form because of judicial jealousy of the reform movement; and that it is wholly inapplicable to and out of place in American law of today.

That the attitude of our courts toward legislation is not necessary to and inherent in a legal system is apparent when we turn to a great legal system in which it is wholly unknown. Not only is this view of legislation unknown to Roman law,[14] but quite an opposite doctrine was established in Roman law countries even before they enacted codes.[15] "Where a gap has been left by any statutory rule, it is filled up, according to this method, by reference to another rule, contained in the same statute, in connection with which a point left open in the first mentioned rule is expressly provided for, and the *ratio juris* of the last mentioned expression is taken to be a general rule of law applicable to all cases."[16]... [Pp. 387-388.]

*   *   *   *   *

... As legislation was in point of fact a relatively unimportant element throughout the growing period of our legal system, it was natural that statutes should come to be regarded as furnishing rules for particular, defi-

---

[10] "You have the State of New York before you as a terrible example. I believe our practice today is infinitely more technical than that in New Jersey. Even the attempt to abolish forms of action and especially the attempt to abolish the distinction between law and equity practice have been dismal failures. The distinction between trover and assumpsit is today even more rigidly observed than under the common law practice. It is impossible to amend upon a trial from trover to assumpsit or *vice versa*." W. B. Hornblower, quoted in 2 Andrews, *Am. Law*, 2 ed., § 635, n. 29. But the impossibility of amendment spoken of and the rigid distinction were introduced into code practice by the judges in the teeth of express code provisions upon common law considerations. De Graw v. Elmore, 50 N.Y. 1. See N.Y. Code Civ. Proc. 1848, § § 69, 173, 176.

[11] Robinson, *Am. Jurisp.*, § 301.

[12] *E.g.*, Carter, *Law, Its Origin, Growth and Function*, 308.

[13] Dr. Robinson says of the proposition that statutes in derogation of the common law are to be construed strictly that it is "a positive but reasonable rule." *Am. Jurisp.*, § 301. Mr. Carter says that judges "displayed their wisdom by adopting it."

nite situations, but not principles for cases not within their tenor, or from which to reason by analogy.[17] And the tendency to conceive of a statute as something exceptional and more or less foreign to the body of legal rules in which legislation had endeavored to insert it, which such a doctrine fostered, was furthered by the growth of an idea of limitations upon legislation which, through our doctrine of judicial power over unconstitutional legislation, has become very strong in America. [P. 390.]

. . . . .

If, however, we should concede that an attitude of antipathy toward legislative innovation is a fundamental common law principle, we should have to inquire whether that principle is applicable to American conditions and is a part of our American common law.... For one thing, the political occasions for judicial interference with legislation have come to an end. In the sixteenth and seventeenth centuries the judiciary stood between the public and the crown. It protected the individual from the state when he required that protection. Today, when it assumes to stand between the legislature and the public and thus again to protect the individual from the state, it really stands between the public and what the public needs and desires, and protects individuals who need no protection against society which does need it. Hence the side of the courts is no longer the popular side. Moreover, courts are less and less competent to formulate rules for new relations which require legislation. They have the experience of the past. But they do not have the facts of the present. They have but one case before them, to be decided upon the principles of the past, the equities of the one situation, and the prejudices which the individualism of common law institutional writers, the dogmas learned in a college course in economics, and habitual association with the business and professional class, must inevitably produce.[18] It is a sound instinct in the community that objects to the settlement of questions of the highest social import in private litigations between John Doe and Richard Roe. It is a sound instinct that objects to an agricultural view of industrial legislation.[19] Judicial law-making for sheer lack of means to get at the real situation, operates unjustly and inequitably in a complex social organization. One might find more than one illustration in the conflict between judicial decision and labor legislation. [Pp. 403-404.]

. . . . .

---

[17] The phrase "common law" was borrowed from the canonists in the thirteenth century, meaning, both in its lay and in its ecclesiastical use, general, as opposed to local, law and custom. The use of "common law" in contrast to "statute law" is later, arising from the circumstance that statutes were rare. Maitland, *Canon Law in the Church of England*, 4.

[18] "It is not to be expected from human nature that the *few* should be always attentive to the interests of the *many*." 4 *Bl. Comm.* 379. One must not forget that counsel on both sides belong to the same class and have had the same training as the judges.

[19] Kelley, *Some Ethical Gains through Legislation*, 142.

Formerly it was argued that common law was superior to legislation because it was customary and rested upon the consent of the governed.[20] Today we recognize that the so-called custom is a custom of judicial decision, not a custom of popular action. We recognize that legislation is the more truly democratic form of law-making. We see in legislation the more direct and accurate expression of the general will.[21] We are told that law-making of the future will consist in putting the sanction of society on what has been worked out in the sociological laboratory.[22] That courts cannot conduct such laboratories is self evident. Courts are fond of saying that they apply old principles to new situations.[23] But at times they must apply new principles to situations both old and new. The new principles are in legislation. The old principles are in common law. The former are as much to be respected and made effective as the latter—probably more so as our legislation improves. The public cannot be relied upon permanently to tolerate judicial obstruction or nullification of the social policies to which more and more it is compelled to be committed. [Pp. 406-407.]

M. R. COHEN, THE PROCESS OF JUDICIAL LEGISLATION *

II. Interpretation as a Mode of Judicial Legislation

There are few branches of the law of which the theory is so confused and disorganized as in the case of the interpretation and construction of written instruments. For this condition the theory of judicial passivity is in no slight degree responsible. This theory finds expression in the assertion that legal interpretation consists solely in finding the intention of the writer. But can any one maintain that the accepted rules of legal interpretation are simply scientific rules for the discovery of actual intention? Doubtless judges, like others, do sometimes seek and find the actual intention of parties as revealed in writings before them; but when they do so, they make use of the ordinary knowledge of language and affairs and they do not use any special rules or organon any more than they do in interpreting the oral communications of witnesses. Perhaps the day is not far distant when a scientific psychology of written language will be in a position to offer definite data to the jurist, but the prevailing technical rules of construction are not of this character. They come down to us largely from the Roman law, and their main function, so far as they partake of the nature of the rules, is first, to introduce certainty by fixing a meaning in cases where conflicting meanings are otherwise possible (all questions of mean-

[20] 1 *Wilson's Works*, Andrews' ed., 183 (written 1790).
[21] Bosanquet, *Philosophical Theory of the State*, 120-123.
[22] Ward, *Applied Sociology*, 338.
[23] *E.g.*, Rensselaer Glass Factory v. Reed, 5 Cow. (N.Y.) 587, which has been quoted repeatedly.
* [From *Law and the Social Order*. New York: Harcourt, Brace and Company, 1933. See p. 450 *supra*, for another excerpt from this essay.]

ing for the court arise, of course, through the fact that two different meanings are claimed by the contending parties),[44] and, secondly, to subordinate
the intention of the parties to considerations of public policy and the convenience of judicial administration. Just as the rules of evidence are, in the
main, fashioned to exclude what is logically probative, so our rules of interpretation and construction of written instruments are, for the most part,
rules for the exclusion of inquiry into the actual psychological intention.
Considerations of public policy and of the convenient administration of
justice require us to attach certain consequences to words, irrespective of
the actual intention of the writer.[45] It is because of such considerations,
and not in the interest of scientific truth, that the rules for the interpretation of wills differ from the rules for the interpretation of contracts or
deeds, and the rule of executory from those of executed trusts.[46] Again, a
blind fear of paternalism makes us say that the proper duty of the court is
to interpret people's contracts, to give effect to their actual intention, and
not to make contracts or impose obligations that the parties did not intend
when they contracted. But as a matter of fact most of the disputes about
contracts arise because of the emerging of unexpected conditions that
were not in the contemplation of the parties when they made their agreement. In all such cases the courts do not enforce the real intentions of the
parties, for there were none, but decide on the rights of the contestants in
accordance with their sense of the equities of the case or the suggestion of
analogous rules of legal obligation.

These considerations are suggestive in enabling us to avoid some con-
fusing fiction in the theory of statutory interpretation.

Austin, Lieber, and most eminent writers after them define interpretation as the discovery of the true meaning of a statute or law. In harmony
with the phonograph theory of the judicial function, this true meaning is
lodged in the mind of the legislature, and the upright judge simply finds it
and in no way modifies it. In actual judicial interpretation, however, this is
certainly not always true. If I have any difficulty in interpreting a passage
in a book, I consider myself fortunate if I can interrogate the author himself. But for the courts to ask those who actually drew up a statute what
they meant would be absurd,[47] nay, even an expressed declaration by a
legislature as to what was meant in a previous statute is effective not from

---

[44] A distinction between interpretation and construction is sometimes drawn, the
latter being necessary only when the meaning is doubtful. But when parties are
interested in finding different meanings, "constructions will be found." (This phrase
was used by such a pillar of the orthodox theory as Elihu Root.)

[45] Thayer, *Preliminary Treatise on Evidence*, 1898, p. 204.

[46] Maitland, *Equity*, 1910, p. 66.

[47] Thus Lord Halsbury distinctly asserts that the worst person to construe a statute
is the person who drafted it, because he tends to confuse what he intended to say
with what he actually said. (Hilder v. Dexter (1902) A.C. 474, 477.) A judge who
drafted a bill must thus divest his mind of all past impressions of it. In re Mew and
Thorne, 31 L.J. Bcy. (1862) 87.

the time of the original, but only from the time of the declaratory act.[48] In defence of this rule we are told that the rights acquired under the original act must not be presumed to be divested by a subsequent declaratory act. But if the actual intention of the legislator makes law, how could any rights be acquired contrary to the intention of the law? [49] We can get rid of this and other difficulties by recognizing that the legislative intent is an eliminable fiction. Experience amply shows that the drafters or framers of a law, the committee that reports it, the majority of the members of the two houses that, for various reasons, pass it, and the executive that signs it are by no means always agreed as to its meaning.[50] Hence the rule that parliamentary debates are of no direct value in the interpretation of statutes.[51]

Back, however, of the motives and ideas of the various individuals who constitute the legislature are the various interests concerned in the passing of a measure into law. We do not, of course, avoid fiction altogether by calling the triumph of one of these interests or the final compromise between conflicting claims "the will of the people." But such language brings us nearer to the actual procedure of courts in interpreting statutes, and helps us to understand the real significance of the statement that courts interpret not the actual intention of the legislator but the meaning of the statute before them.

What is the meaning of a statute? The rule that courts must interpret the meaning of the statute rather than the intention of the legislature is frequently conceived as if it implied that the words of a statute are sufficient to determine every question that arises under it. This would lead to a revival of the stage of strict law in which the strictly literal meaning of words is followed no matter how unjust or absurd the consequences. Doubtless there are many who still believe juristic interpretation to be a kind of magic whereby a whole body of law is made to spring out of a few words or phrases. But most modern jurists are outgrowing the super-

---

[48] Odgen, Administrator v. Blackedge, Executor, 2 Cranch 272 (1804); Dash v. Van Kleeck, 7 Johns. R. 477, Kent, J., at p. 512 (1811); Smith v. Syracuse Ins. Co., 161 N.Y. 484, 55 N.E. 1077 (1900). This rule, however, is not followed in England (Attorney General v. Theobald, 24 Q.B.D. 557 (1890) and cases therein cited). This has been carried to the extent of collecting duties, even though property has meanwhile passed to others.

[49] Wahl, *Les successions*, 1902, Vol. I, p. 513. For criticism of the classical theory of retroactivity and vested or acquired rights, see Vareilles-Sommieres in *Nouvelle revue de l'histoire du droit*, 1893, p. 241 *et seq.* Cf. Aubry et Rau, *Cours de droit*, 3d ed., 1856, Vol. I, p. 30; and Planiol, *op. cit.* (note 40) [*Traité élémentaire du droit civil* (1908)], Vol. I, pp. 250 *et seq.*

[50] A striking instance of this is to be found in Art. 757, French Civil Code. It was voted by the Assembly on the assurance by Treilhard, the reporter of the commission that edited it, that it provided for the wife a high rank among the heirs of the husband. As a matter of fact it puts the wife after all relatives, and even after natural children. See Mallieux, *L'exégèse des codes*, 1908, p. 16.

[51] Regina v. Hartford College, 3 Q.B.D. 693, 707.

stitious awe of the printed word and its magic potency. The meaning of a statute consists in the system of social consequences to which it leads or of the solutions to all the possible social questions that can arise under it.[52] These solutions or systems of consequences cannot be determined solely from the words used, but require a knowledge of the social conditions to which the law is to be applied as well as of the circumstances which led to its enactment. Legal rules relate to human life, and grammar or formal logic alone will not enable us to deduce their juridical consequences. The proof of the fact that the interpretation of legal rules is impossible without an intimate knowledge of the factual world to which they are to be applied, is seen in the many rules of Roman law that are today unintelligible because we do not know sufficiently under what conditions they were intended to work. The meaning of a statute, then, is a juridical creation in the light of social demands. It decides not so much what the legislature actually intended, nor what the words of a statute ordinarily mean, but *what the public, taking all the circumstances of the case into account, should act on.*[53]

Consider the rules of statutory interpretation laid down in any textbook, for example, that penal statutes, or statutes in derogation of the common law, should be strictly construed, that remedial statutes should be liberally construed, and that there is an almost conclusive presumption against an unreasonable or inconvenient intention on the part of the legislator. These are not scientific rules for the discovery of actual intentions or the meanings of words, but *maxims of public policy to guide judges in the process of making law out of statutes.* It is notorious that the assumption of legislative reasonableness and regard for public welfare is one that judges privately do not hold, but public policy requires it in the administration of law. It is certainly only from this latter point of view that we can find any rationale in the rules against retroactivity. Why, for instance, can rules against retroactivity be invoked against new rights but not against new remedies, against penal legislation but not against remedial provisions? It is only by the recognition of the fact that judicial interpre-

---

[52] *Scire leges non hoc est verba earum tenere sed vim ac potestatem* (Celsus, Dig. I, 3, 17). On the Continent the movement for "free" creative or sociological interpretation has now met with general acceptance. It was elaborated with unusual keenness by Kohler in articles in *Grünhuts Zeitschrift*, Vol. XIII (1886), pp. 1-61, and *Jherings Jahrbücher*, Vol. XXV (1887), pp. 262-97, but received little attention until the adoption of the German and Swiss civil codes made the topic a pressing one. Since the publication of Geny's *Méthode d'interprétation*, 1899, a whole literature on the subject has grown up, references to which will be found in Sternberg, *Einführung in die Rechtswissenschaft*, 1912, Vol. I, pp. 141-42; Cosentine, *La réforme de la législation civile*, 1913, pp. 268-78; and On Continental Legal Philosophy, pp. 286-318 of this volume [M. R. Cohen, *Law and the Social Order*]. The logical and historical parallel between the rules and methods of legal interpretation and those of Biblical exegesis offers a theme that has not been developed.

[53] It also decides, incidentally, what the public should have understood or have taken the statute to mean.

tation makes law that we can justify the position that decisions, like statutes, are not to be interpreted retroactively;[54] that the judicial construction of a statute is "as much a part of the statute as the text itself, and a change of decision is to all intents and purposes the same in its effects on contracts as an amendment of the law by means of a legislative act or amendment."[55] The whole Gordian knot of controversy over *Gelpoke v. Dubuque*, together with the seeming force of Justice Miller's dissenting opinion, is certainly removed by the recognition that courts do and must make law.[56]

It is generally stated that the reason why questions of interpretation arise at all is because of the necessary obscurity of language; and doubtless it is impossible to formulate regulations that shall be so unequivocal in all situations as to render unnecessary judicial selection from possible meanings. Reference, however, to the rules of interpretation applied by English courts, dealing with statutes very carefully drawn, shows that most of the questions of interpretation arise not so much because of the obscurities of language, but rather because the *courts have to apply a general law to a situation that could not have been foreseen by the legislature*. Take as an instance the Workmen's Compensation Act of 1906. This act was practically an extension of the act of 1897, as amended in 1900. The original act was most carefully drawn, and its workings carefully studied by the Digby Commission, whose report the framers of the act of 1906 had before them. Yet in spite of a mass of supplementary legislation, in the form of orders by the Home Secretary, volumes of court decisions have been necessary to determine whether certain situations shall be brought within the scope of the bill or not. In our own country, where statutes are not so carefully drawn (because of perennially green legislators), where we do not have anything to compare in thoroughness with the English statutory interpretation act of 1889, and where, because of the mischievous dogma that legislative powers cannot be delegated, we do not allow administrative officers ample power of supplementary legislation, all this mass of supplementary legislation has to be enacted by the courts, in the form of judicial interpretations, and no one really knows a law thoroughly unless he knows what the courts have made of it.[57]

Not only must courts supplement legislative enactments by supplying the detailed rules and regulations, but the interests of any workable justice

---

[54] Rowan v. Runnels, 5 How. 134, 139 (1847).

[55] Douglass v. County of Pike, 101 U.S. 677, 687 (1879).

[56] Thayer, *Legal Essays*, 1908, p. 150.

[57] One of the most usual ways in which courts supplement a statute is by supplying definitions, for instance, defining "person" in the Fourteenth Amendment to include corporations. Again, if the legislature in an income-tax law defines "income" to include the unearned increment of land value, there is no doubt that this is substantial legislation. Would it be less so if, in the absence of legislative expression, the courts would so define it?

demand that courts should also in effect exercise a limited power of amending the law. Legislatures are the commissioners of warring social interests. They can draw up general treaties of peace, but the details have at all times been and must be inserted by the courts, else we should have a constant recurrence to a state of lawlessness. Courts must necessarily attach a somewhat different meaning to statutes than do the legislators, owing to the necessarily different point of view. The conditions of legislation make legislators view even the most general statutes exclusively as measures of relief to certain social demands. Courts, however, must construe them as integral parts of the legal system that controls the whole of life. Legislators can never have in mind all the possible consequences of their enactments, and many of them would be shocked and would refuse to pass the bills they do if they could realize these consequences. Hence, every system of legal administration that is not impossibly rigorous allows the judge, who has had the chance of seeing the actual working of the statute in concrete situations, some power of amendment—hard and fast legal and political theories to the contrary notwithstanding.[58]

The process by which the terms of laws are widened or narrowed has been called spurious interpretation. Such interpretation is spurious only so far as it pretends to discover the actual intention of the legislator, but the process of extending or restricting the meaning of a statute is inevitable. Unless we are wilfully to blind ourselves by some dogma of legislative omniscience, we must recognize that supplementary legislation by judges or other administrative officials is absolutely necessary to make statutes workable.[59] Statutes must be expressed in general and more or less abstract terms. *To make a detailed description of specific human actions forbidden or allowed and their consequences would be an endless and impossible task.* The judge, however, must apply the general rule to specific cases. To prevent an impossible uniformity or rigour, and to give statutes a form and content that will adapt them to the complicated needs of life, judges must classify the cases under the rule and use what is called equitable interpretation as a corrective or supplement to the abstract generality of the law before them. That equitable interpretation is not foreign to the essence of the common law can be seen in such writers as Littleton, Coke, and Sheppard. Some of our courts and textbook writers have said that the doctrine of equitable interpretation has

[58] For example, see Thayer, *op. cit.* (note 45) pp. 195-96

[59] It is interesting to note that, in spite of the wide power of supplementary legislation given to administrative officers on the Continent, modern Continental codes recognize the need of judicial legislation, the German Civil Code implicitly (*e.g.*, sec. 626) and the Swiss Code explicitly (Civil Code, Art. 1, 2). Cf. the Italian Civil Code, Art. 3, and the Austrian Civil Code, Art. 7. Even the framers of the Napoleonic Code recognized this. "A host of things are necessarily left to the rule of usage, to the discipline of learned men, and to the decision of judges." Portalis, *"Discours préliminaire"* (1836), Fenet, *Rescueil complet des travaux préparatoires du Code Civil*, p. 476.

been abandoned in modern times. But does not the well established rule and practice that an inconvenient and inequitable interpretation is to be avoided, that the spirit rather than the letter of the statute is to be given effect, amount to the same thing? The extent to which this latter rule is carried can be shown by the fact that courts will, in the interests of equitable interpretation, change the tense of a statute,[60] interpret the phrase "single man" to include widows,[61] or the term "woman" to exclude married women,[62] and the like. Nothing is more usual in the interpretation of statutes than to find them construed as operating between certain persons only, or for certain purposes only, though the language expresses no such limitation;[63] or cases where the language is extended to include things that were not known and could not have been contemplated by the legislators when the statute was passed—for example, when the word "telegraph" is held to cover the telephone invented subsequent to the law in question.[64]

RADIN, STATUTORY INTERPRETATION *

Anglo-American law is in a fair way of becoming statutory, not by a great act of summation like the *Bürgerliches Gesetzbuch* or the Swiss Code, but piecemeal by the relentless annual or biennial grinding of more than fifty legislative machines. . . . [P. 863.]

.   .   .   .   .

Words are certainly not crystals, as Mr. Justice Holmes has wisely and properly warned us,[6] but they are after all not portmanteaus. We can not quite put anything we like into them. And we may not disregard them in statutes. The real question in statutory interpretation is just what we shall do with them. [P. 866.]

.   .   .   .   .

Mr. W. E. Johnson, whose *Logic* [12] is one of the most considerable of recent contributions to this much-discussed subject, has given us in his differentiation of *determinables* and *determinates* a valuable instrument for presenting the meaning of statutes. The situation described in a statute is generally a determinable; that is to say, it is a statement which

---

[60] Malloy v. Chicago & N.W.R. Co., 109 Wis. 29, 85 N.W. 130 (1901).
[61] Silver v. Ladd, 7 Wall. 219 (1868).
[62] R. v. Harrald, L.R. 7 Q.B. 361 (1872).
[63] See cases quoted by Maxwell, *Statutory Interpretation*, 1884, pp. 115, 118, 163-68; and W. H. Loyd, "The Equity of a Statute," *University of Pennsylvania Law Review*, Vol. LVIII (1909), p. 76.
[64] Attorney General v. Edison Tel. Co., 6 Q.B.D. 244 (1880).
* [43 *Harv. L. Rev.* 863 (1930).]
[6] Towne v. Eisner, 245 U.S. 418, 425 (1918).
[12] Johnson, *Logic* (1921) Pt. I, c. 11, at 173-86.

involves a number of possible events or individualizations, any one of which would be correctly described by that determinable. . . . [P. 868.]

.   .   .   .   .

The act of interpretation, however, is not that of rendering a determinable quite determinate. The determinate involved is the actual issue in litigation. As soon as it is made apparent that the statutory determinable does or does not cover this determinate event, the act of interpretation is finished. It consists therefore in making a determinable somewhat more nearly determinate. Our inquiry must then turn to the methods by which this is done.

It has frequently been declared that the most approved method is to discover the intent of the legislator.[13] Did the legislator in establishing this determinable have a series of pictures in mind, one of which was this particular determinate? On this transparent and absurd fiction it ought not to be necessary to dwell. It is clearly enough an illegitimate transference of law of concepts proper enough in literature and theology. The least reflection makes clear that the law maker, *der Gesetzgeber, le législateur*, does not exist,[14] and only worse confusion follows when in his place there are substituted the members of the legislature as a body. A legislature certainly has no intention whatever in connection with words which some two or three men drafted, which a considerable number rejected, and in regard to which many of the approving majority might have had, and often demonstrably did have, different ideas and beliefs. [Pp. 869-870.]

.   .   .   .   .

The legislative history [21] based on the "materials" does not therefore enable us to discover without more ado what determinate situations or

---

[13] It was repeated by Lord Justice Turner in an often cited judgment, Hawkins v. Gathercole, 6 De G.M. & G. I., 22 (1855); by Blackburn, J., in River Wear Comm'rs v. Adamson, 2 Apps. Cas. 743 (1877), and by Birkenhead, L. C., and Lord Wrenbury in Viscountess Rhondda's Claim, [1922] 2 A.C. 339. Tindal, C. J., called it the "only rule," in the Sussex Peerage Case, 11 Cl. & F. 85, 143 (1844), a phrase quoted by Lord MacNaghten in Vacher v. London Soc. of Compositors, [1913] A.C. 107, 118. Cf. Bacon, *Abridgement* Stat. I, (5). It comes in as the last phrase of the fourth of the things which the barons of the exchequer said must be "considered for the sure and true interpretation of statutes." Heydon's Case, 3 Co. 8a (1584). They must advance the remedy "according to the true intent of the makers of the act." *Ibid.* It is the limitation on the golden rule of "plain" interpretation. Jervis, C. J., in Mattison v. Hart, 23 L.J.C.P. 108, 114 (1854). Kent thought the real intent of the legislature was controlling. 1 Kent, *Comm.* 460.

The American cases that have so declared run into the hundreds. One of the most recent is Takao Ozawa v. United States, 260 U.S. 178 (1922).

[14] He is no less a fiction if he is idealized as a presumed *bonus pater patriae* who wishes only the good of the people. Cf. Reichel, *op. cit. supra* note 2 [*Gesetz und Richterspruch* (1915)], at 78.

[21] The "legislative history" of a statute is taken to mean the successive forms in which the statute is found from the first draft presented until its final passage. That

events are included in the small or large group described by the statute. Technical devices have been resorted to, similar in theory to the processes by which, in mathematics or in the Aristotelian syllogism, propositions are reduced, simplified, transposed, and solved. Without examining the question whether these processes are abstractly applicable, it may be of interest to notice two such technical devices, both phrased in Latin and both widely employed. They are, *expressio unius est exclusio alterius*, and *ejusdem generis*.

The rule that the expression of one thing is the exclusion of another is in direct contradiction to the habits of speech of most persons. To say that all men are mortal does not mean that all women are not, or that all other animals are not. There is no such implication, either in usage or in logic, unless there is a very particular emphasis on the word *men*. It is neither customary nor convenient to indicate such emphasis in statutes, and without this indication, the first comment on the rule is that it is not true.

So far from being logical, as some courts have called it, it illustrates one of the most fatuously simple of logical fallacies, the "illicit major," long the *pons asinorum* of schoolboys.[22] And yet in a widely used cyclopedia, there are at least seven hundred cases cited in which the maxim has been "applied or explained." [23] It has been called an axiom by the House of Lords, and it has been said of it that no maxim is of more general and uniform application.[24] Yet in the same case in which the House of Lords called it axiomatic, it was disregarded;[25] and the first case of its "application" cited in *Corpus Juris* is a case in the United States Supreme Court in which it was rejected.[26]

It must be clear that the only value which such a maxim or axiom or rule could have would lie in the existence of an infallible or approximately infallible test of its applicability. Emphasis will help us in ordinary speech, but except for such inferred emphasis as the general purpose of the act will enable us to apply, no other stress on the words will be apparent in the printed page. The question will accordingly be in every case, not whether or not the expression of one thing excludes everything else, but whether we are to deny or affirm this rule in this particular case. We shall evidently deny it or affirm it for some other reason than its axiomatic

---

is different obviously from the history of the agitation which resulted in the fact that such a statute was proposed at all. It is this latter history which is contained in the famous four considerations established by the barons of the exchequer in Heydon's Case, 3 Co. 8a (1584), and popularized by Blackstone, 1 *Comm.* 88 *et seq.*

[22] Cf. Jevons, *Elementary Lesson in Logic* (1918) 132.

[23] (1921) 25 C.J. 220.

[24] See Saunders v. Evans, 8 H.L. Cas. 721, 729 (1861); Broom, *Legal Maxims s.v.*; Johnson v. Jordan, 2 Metc. 234, 261 (Mass. 1841).

[25] Saunders v. Evans, 8 H.L. Cas. 721 (1861).

[26] United States v. Barnes, 222 U.S. 513 (1912).

force, and it will be necessary to search for that other reason. [Pp. 873-874.]

. . . . .

That almost any determinable situation posited by a statute is capable of expansion or contraction is recognized in the frequent differentiation between restrictive and liberal constructions. On the lips of opponents the terms "strict" and "liberal" become changed to "rigid" and "loose," but they are obviously instances in which a small number of determinates is preferred to a great number, or *vice versa*. A strict construction is resorted to when it is desired to exclude a determinate which might readily enough be included within the statute. Liberal construction, as a rule, merely means that no such effort of exclusion will be made.

These tendencies are perfectly intelligible, and to know when a strict interpretation is to be applied and when it is not, would be of distinct value. Unfortunately the statements made on this question do not help us. When we read that laws enacted "in the interest of the public welfare or convenience, for the construction of works of great public utility for the protection of human life or in regard to the rights of citizenship; for the prevention of fraud; or providing remedies against public or private wrongs, should be liberally construed," [32] we are not aided much by an enumeration which includes almost every type of legislation that we can imagine, particularly when we are almost immediately referred to a case in which liberal construction is to be restricted to an attempt at effectuating only the "specified" purposes and objects of the statute. Similarly, the rule that remedial statutes are to be liberally construed [33] has the qualification that this construction is never to be applied so as to extend the application of statutes to cases not within the contemplation of the legislature. The doctrine that statutes in derogation of the common law or common right, statutes conferring privileges, and all penal statutes are to be strictly construed [34] would be a little clearer and easier to deal with if it were not so often disregarded, and if logically indistinguishable precedents were not present for the application and the rejection of the rule of strict construction in these cases. [Pp. 879-880.]

. . . . .

Clarity would manifestly be secured by singleness of avowed method. If we must select one, it is hard to see how we can avoid selecting that method which is the commonest in practice, if the least announced. The

---

[32] The enumeration is found in (1910) 36 *Cyc.* 1173, and is in part derived from 1 *Bl. Comm.* 87-89.

[33] *Ibid.* at 87; Hudler v. Golden, 36 N.Y. 446 (1867); Camunas v. New York & P. R. S. S. Co., 260 Fed. 40 (C.C.A. 1st, 1919).

[34] 1 *Bl. Comm.* 89; Corrigan v. United States, 298 Fed. 610 (S.D.N.Y. 1923). But *cf.* Ash Sheep Co. v. United States, 252 U.S. 159 (1920).

statute—the *lex lata*—creates limits on both sides of strictness and liberality. Within them, any decision to interpret strictly—that is, any decision to exclude a particular determinate—might with advantage be consciously rendered, as is so often done semi-consciously or covertly, on the basis of its probable consequences. Judges will perhaps have to seek special and expert guidance as to what those consequences will be—especially in those many cases in which a limited and highly specialized group of economic activities is involved.

When they have properly equipped themselves with the material competence necessary to make an intelligent conjecture of results, we shall doubtless find a considerable difficulty in making them desire one result rather than another. A judge may well be free from the *sophismes du coeur* which M. Fabreguettes has so eloquently described,[37] but he cannot be free from some preference. When he discovers that the exclusion of a given determinate will have a certain effect, he must decide whether he wishes that effect.[38] If the matter is one which is intimately connected with other elements of the social or economic order, it is worse than idle

---

[37] Fabreguettes, *La Logique judiciaire* 436 *et seq.*

[38] Perhaps the best examples of this effect on interpretation are two much discussed cases. In Holy Trinity Church v. United States, 143 U.S. 457 (1892), the Court examined the contract labor law which forbade the encouragement of an alien to migrate to the United States in order to perform services of any kind, and asked itself whether the employment of an English clergyman by a wealthy and distinguished Protestant Episcopal church was an encouragement to migrate in order to perform services of any kind. It could easily be included, of course, in the large determinables of the statutory expression. The Court found a legislative intention, for which there was not an atom of evidence, that it was not to be included. The only obvious purpose of the statute was to prevent foreign labor from being imported to the United States in order to compete with local labor. But that was not the only purpose the statute might well have had. The narrowing of the determinable so that this determinate was not included was almost certainly motivated by the feeling of men trained to respect an established Christian denomination which by virtue of its history could hardly fail to look abroad frequently for its ministers.

In Caminetti v. United States, 242 U.S. 470 (1917), the so-called Mann Act came into question. 36 Stat. 825 (1910), 18 U.S.C. §398 (1926). The act made it a felony to aid in the transportation of any woman or girl for the purpose of prostitution or debauchery, or for any other immoral purpose; the Court held it applicable to the case of a couple who had voluntarily crossed a state border and after having crossed it were guilty of an offense which in their own state would have been immoral but not criminal. The legislative intent was urged upon the Court and rejected. 242 U.S. at 484. One of the known purposes of the statute was to prevent traffic in prostitution. A great many persons certainly believed this was the sole purpose. The Court chose to make the determinable large enough to include this special case of illicit relations, and it can hardly be doubted that in doing so, it was influenced by the disinclination to seem to condone a moral dereliction. If the Court had considered probable consequences, it might perhaps have foreseen that such an interpretation made the statute a ready instrument of blackmail and did not appreciably decrease the instances of sexual irregularity. But the contrast between the two interpretations illustrates clearly the effect of social motives in deciding where the determinable is to be limited. The Court desired to support religion in every way. It did not desire to connive at sexual immorality in any way.

to profess that he will disregard the connection and select as a desirable consequence something which he does not wish to happen.

There would then be two questions of importance in the interpretative process. The first would be: Can the statutory determinable in the widest range be taken to include the determinate before the court? The more nearly determinate the statute is, the easier that question will be to answer. It is far easier to make a statute which contains large determinables than limited ones, if we wish to see clearly and with brief consideration what the maximum and minimum of extension is, in any determinable, we must avoid words like "just" and "reasonable" and "property" and similar almost indefinitely extensible terms. These words have so little color of their own that they can be made to take almost any hue we desire.

The second question would be: Will the inclusion of this particular determinate in the statutory determinable lead to a desirable result? What is desirable will be what is just, what is proper, what satisfies the social emotions of the judge, what fits into the ideal scheme of society which he entertains. The dangers, whatever they are, which are involved in a *Gefühlsjurisprudenz* can in no system be completely avoided. An attempt to avoid them by declaring that judges must be guided by broad principles and not by particular situations is inevitably futile, because the broader the principle, the wider the scope of the personal predilections of the judge. If there is a glaring contradiction between what the judge thinks desirable and what the great majority of the community so considers, the community must, in its legislative function, limit as carefully as it can by more easily determinable categories the range within which the judge shall select his desirables. But the legislature can not both have its cake and eat it. It can not indulge itself in using large, round, sonorous words and then complain that courts do not treat them as precise, definite, and unreverberant. [Pp. 882-884.]

LANDIS, A NOTE ON "STATUTORY INTERPRETATION" *

A passing acquaintance with the literature of statutory interpretation evokes sympathy with the eminent judge who remarked that books on spiritualism and statutory interpretation were two types of literary ebullitions that he had learned not to read. Mr. Radin's plea for realism in the science of interpreting statutes must thus fall on not unwilling ears. With such a slogan, volunteers for the fray should readily spring to his standard. But to learn, when the smoke of battle has cleared away, that

---

* [43 *Harv. L. Rev.* 886 (1930).

James M. Landis, (b. 1899), after serving as law clerk to the late Justice Brandeis, taught at Harvard Law School until 1934, when he devoted himself exclusively to public service, occupying a number of important posts in the Federal Government. Landis served as Dean of Harvard Law School from 1937 until 1946, since which time he has occupied governmental positions and engaged in the private practice of law.]

the prize of victory is but *Gefühlsjurisprudenz* savors too much of the saddening process of making the world safe for democracy. Surely what Broom, Coke, Bacon, Austin, and Leiber dignified with the conception of a science deserves a better fate than the surrender implicit in the resort to *Gefühlsjurisprudenz.*

The Anglo-American scheme of government conceives of lawgivers apart from and at times paramount over courts. Such a function, commonly vested in a legislature, presupposes an intelligible method of making known to the organs of administration, courts or otherwise, its desires and hopes. . . . [P. 886.]

⋅   ⋅   ⋅   ⋅   ⋅

. . . One further consideration, especially significant to those who advocate the principles of *Gefühlsjurisprudenz*, and pointing to the necessity of preferring from the sociological standpoint the *Gefühl* of the legislator to the *Gefühl* of the judge, is epigrammatically summed up by Dicey when he says: "If a statute . . . is apt to reproduce the public opinion not so much of today as of yesterday, judge-made law occasionally represents the opinion of the day before yesterday." [6] [P. 886.]

⋅   ⋅   ⋅   ⋅   ⋅

The assumption that the meaning of a representative assembly attached to the words used in a particular statute is rarely discoverable, has little foundation in fact. The records of legislative assemblies once opened and read with a knowledge of legislative procedure often reveal the richest kind of evidence. To insist that each individual legislator besides his aye vote must also have expressed the meaning he attaches to the bill as a condition precedent to predicating an intent on the part of the legislature, is to disregard the realities of legislative procedure.[7] Through the committee report,[8] the explanation of the committee chairman,[9] and otherwise,[10]

---

[6] Dicey, *Law and Opinion in England* (1926) 369.

[7] Mr. Radin is correct in his assumption that even in a large representative assembly the debate on statutes passed by it will not call forward external utterances or significant behavior on the part of "hundreds of men." Pp. 870-71. Rarely does a debate evoke more than a handful, and the yea and nay votes of the non-participants by every reasonable intendment must be taken to adopt their views. Of course, no such assumption can be indulged in where the variance between the views of the participants is impossible of such bifurcation as legislative procedure demands. See, *e.g.,* the varying views of the intent of the First Congress upon the President's power of removal. Taft, C. J., and Brandeis, J., in Myers v. United States, 272 U.S. 52, 123-27, 285 (1926); Corwin, *The President's Removal Power* (1927) 12-13.

[8] *Cf.* Tagg Bros. & Moorhead v. United States, 50 Sup. Ct. 220 (U.S. 1930); Shaik Moosa v. Shaik Essa. 8 Ind. L.R. (Bomb.) 241, 247 (1884).

[9] *Cf.* St. Louis Ry. v. United States, 262 U.S. 70, 76 (1923); United States v. St. Paul M. & M. Ry., 247 U.S. 310 (1918).

[10] *Cf.* Penn. Mut. Life Ins. Co. v. Lederer, 252 U.S. 523, 534 (1920).

a mere expression of assent becomes in reality a concurrence in the expressed views of another. A particular determinate thus becomes the common possession of the majority of the legislature, and as such a real discoverable intent.

Legislative history similarly affords in many instances accurate and compelling guides to legislative meaning. Successive drafts of the same act do not simply succeed each other as isolated phenomena, but the substitution of one for another necessarily involves an element of choice often leaving little doubt as to the reasons governing such a choice.[11] The voting down of an amendment or its acceptance upon the statement of its proponent again may disclose real evidence of intent.[12] Changes made in the light of earlier statutes and their enforcement,[13] acquiescence in a known administrative interpretation,[14] the use of interpreted language borrowed from other sources,[15] all give evidence of a real and not a fictitious intent, and should be deemed to govern questions of construction. The real difficulty is twofold: that strong judges prefer to override the intent of the

---

[11] *Cf.* United States v. Pfitsch, 256 U.S. 547 (1921); Hood Rubber Co. v. Commissioner of Corporations, 167 N.E. 670 (Mass. 1929). See also the light thrown upon the interpretation of §34 of the Judiciary Act of Sept. 24, 1789, by the discovery of the original draft of that section, in Warren, New Light on the History of the Federal Judiciary Act of 1789 (1923) 37 *Harv. L. Rev.* 49, 85.

[12] An illustration of this will be found in the debate on the Trade Disputes Act of 1906. Sir Charles Dilke moved the amendment of §3 of that act so as to make non-actionable an act done in furtherance of a trade dispute "on the ground only that it induces some other person to break a contract of employment." 162 *Parliamentary Debates* (4th ser. 1906) 1678. Mr. Rufus Isaacs rightly objected to the ambiguity inherent in the phrase, inasmuch as it was uncertain whether the immunity extended to malicious inducements of breach of contract—malicious in the wide sense in which courts theretofore had used that term as illustrated by South Wales Miners' Fed. v. Glamorgan Coal Co., [1905] A.C. 239—and thus whether the amendment extended any further than restating the existing law. *Ibid.* at 1679. Sir Frederick Banbury then moved to incorporate the Glamorgan doctrine by amending the amendment so as to insert after "induces" the words "otherwise than maliciously." *Ibid.* at 1685. Sir John Walton, attorney-general and spokesman for the administration, refused to accept the Banbury amendment because in his opinion the purpose of the Dilke amendment was to abrogate the rule of the Glamorgan case. *Ibid.* at 1686, 1691. With the voting down of the Banbury amendment and the acceptance of the Dilke amendment, Mr. Isaacs' original query was answered—"malice in law" was insufficient to make actionable inducing a breach of contract in furtherance of a trade dispute. Whether "malice in fact" would make such inducement actionable was, however, left open to "interpretation." It is significant in the light of these events that the later English cases, though hesitate in their conception of the meaning of "trade dispute" and "contract of employment," have never doubted but that mere malice in law was insufficient to make such conduct actionable. *Cf.* Conway v. Wade, [1909] A.C. 506; Valentine v. Hyde, [1919] 2 Ch. 129; White v. Riley [1921] 1 Ch. 1; Brimelow v. Casson, [1924] 1 Ch. 302; Hodges v. Webb, 89 L.J. Ch. (N.S.) 273 (1920); Dallimore v. Williams, 30 T.L.R. 432 (1914); Long v. Larkin, [1914] 2 Ir. R. 285.

[13] *Cf.* Brandeis, J., dissenting, in Dahnke-Walker Co. v. Bondurant, 257 U.S. 282, 299 (1921).

[14] *Cf.* Patterson v. Louisville & Nashville R. R., 269 U.S. 1 (1925).

[15] See Note (1930) 43 *Harv. L. Rev.* 623, for an analysis of the realities of this situation.

legislature in order to make law according to their own views,[16] and that barbaric rules of interpretation too often exclude the opportunity to get at legislative meaning in a realistic fashion.[17] The latter, originating at a time when records of legislative assemblies were not in existence, deserves no adherence in these days of carefully kept journals, debates, and reports. Unfortunately they persist with that tenaciousness characteristic of outworn legal rules. Strong judges are always with us; no science of interpretation can ever hope to curb their propensities. But the effort should be to restrain their tendencies, not to give them free rein in the name of scientific jurisprudence.

When the intent or meaning of the legislature is discoverable, statutory interpretation posits no serious problem except the political one of insistence upon judicial humility. The real problems arise where the meaning of the legislature is not discoverable. Here the gravest sins are perpetrated in the name of the intent of the legislature. Judges are rarely willing to admit their role as actual lawgivers, and such admissions as are wrung from their unwilling lips lie in the field of common and not statute law. To condone in these instances the practice of talking in terms of the intent of the legislature, as if the legislature had attributed a particular meaning to certain words, when it is apparent that the intent is that of the judge, is to condone atavistic practices too reminiscent of the medicine man. No compromise can be had on this issue. But is the alternative *Gefühlsjurisprudenz* or, better, *Freiegesetzfindung?* [18]

A statute rarely stands alone. Back of Minerva was the brain of Jove, and behind Venus the spume of the ocean. So of the statute, it is the culmination often of long legislative processes, too rarely understood by the mere lawyer, and too rarely studied to have been lifted from the contempt bred of ignorance. Such material frequently affords a guide to the intent of the legislature conceived of in terms of purpose. To deal,

---

[16] See, *e.g.*, the protest of Brandeis, J., against the adoption of such methods. Railroad Comm. v. Los Angeles Ry., 50 Sup. Ct. 71, 76 (U.S. 1929).

[17] For example, in Queen-Empress v. Bal Gangadhar Tilak, 22 Ind. L.R. (Bomb.) 112, 126-28 (1897), counsel sought to read the speech of the Legal Member of the Legislative Council, Sir James Stephen, proposing the enactment whose construction was in issue. The court ruled the speech inadmissible but added: "Mr. Pugh can, of course, read any passages from Sir James Stephen's speech as a part of his address, and as stating his own argument in words which he adopts as his own, but he cannot cite them as Sir James Stephen's opinion and as authority showing the construction to be put upon the section." Or compare Fuller, C. J., in Dunlap v. United States, 173 U.S. 65, 75 (1899): "Without questioning the doctrine that debates in Congress are not appropriate sources of information from which to discover the meaning of a statute passed by that body, United States v. Trans-Missouri Freight Ass'n, 166 U.S. 290, 318, it is nevertheless interesting to note that efforts were made in the Senate to amend the bill...." Liberal interpretation is scarcely to be expected of the text, "...let not thy left hand know what thy right hand doeth."

[18] No better evidence of the dangers inherent in *Freierechtsfindung* need be adduced than that in Radin, The Good Judge of Château-Thierry and His American Counterpart (1922) 10 *Calif. L. Rev.* 300.

for example, with the Trade Disputes Act of 1906 without regard to the fact that it followed upon a Liberal-Labor victory, would be to thwart known legislative hopes and desires.[19] It is done unquestionably. The mutilated Clayton Act bears ample testimony to the "day before yesterday" that judges insist is today.[20] But this is simply the price we pay for judicial independence. To ignore legislative processes and legislative history in the processes of interpretation, is to turn one's back on whatever history may reveal as to the direction of the political and economic forces of our time.

It must be insisted that the legislative purposes and aims are the important guideposts for statutory interpretation, not the desiderata of the judge. And there is a world of difference between an attitude of mind that honestly seeks to grasp these and give them effect, and one that cavalierly throws them overboard and leaves us to the mercy of the judge's "day before yesterday." The so-called rules of interpretation are not rules that automatically reach results, but ways of attuning the mind to a vision comparable to that possessed by the legislature ... [Pp. 886-892.]

FRANKFURTER,[1] SOME REFLECTIONS ON THE READING OF STATUTES *

... Inevitably the work of the Supreme Court reflects the great shift in the center of gravity of law-making. Broadly speaking, the number of cases disposed of by opinions has not changed from term to term. But even as late as 1875 more than 40% of the controversies before the Court were common-law litigation, fifty years later only 5%, while today cases not resting on statutes are reduced almost to zero. It is therefore accurate to say that courts have ceased to be the primary makers of law in the sense in which they "legislated" the common law. It is certainly true of the

---

[19] What hearings, departmental reports, committee reports, and the then state of public opinion can furnish as to the direction of legislative purpose, is well illustrated by Omaechevarria v. Idaho, 246 U.S. 343 (1918). Compare the method of construing §611 of the Revenue Act of 1918, of Mack, J., in Regle Coal Co. v. Bowers, 37 F. (2d) 373 (S.D.N.Y. 1929), with that of Foster, J., in United States v. Burden, Smith & Co., 33 F. (2d) 229 (C.C.A. 5th, 1929). See also Piedmont Coal Co. v. Seaboard Fisheries Co., 254 U.S. I (1920).

[20] See Frankfurter and Greene, *The Labor Injunction* (1930) 176; Powell, The Supreme Court's Control Over the Issue of Injunctions in Labor Disputes (1928) 13 *Acad. of Pol. Sci. Proc.* 37, 56.

[1] It gives me pleasure to make acknowledgment to my learned friends, Philip Elman, Louis Henkin and Philip Kurland, Esqs. They have no responsibility for what I have said; they are merely subjected to my gratitude.

* [Sixth Annual Benjamin N. Cardozo Lecture delivered by Justice Felix Frankfurter before the Association of the Bar of the City of New York, March 18, 1947. Published in 2 *The Record of the Ass'n. of the Bar of the City of New York* No. 6 (1947), and 47 *Col. L. Rev.* 528 (1947).]

Supreme Court that almost every case has a statute at its heart or close to it. [P. 527.]

.   .   .   .   .

The Judge's Task

Everyone has his own way of phrasing the task confronting judges when the meaning of a statute is in controversy. Judge Learned Hand speaks of the art of interpretation as "the proliferation of purpose." Who am I not to be satisfied with Learned Hand's felicities? And yet that phrase might mislead judges intellectually less disciplined than Judge Hand. It might justify interpretations by judicial libertines, not merely judicial libertarians. My own rephrasing of what we are driving at is probably no more helpful, and is much longer than Judge Hand's epigram. I should say that the troublesome phase of construction is the determination of the extent to which extraneous documentation and external circumstances may be allowed to infiltrate the text on the theory that they were part of it, written in ink discernible to the judicial eye.

Chief Justice White was happily endowed with the gift of finding the answer to problems by merely stating them. Often have I envied him this faculty but never more than in recent years. No matter how one states the problem of statutory construction, for me at least it does not carry its own answer. Though my business throughout most of my professional life has been with statutes, I come to you empty-handed. I bring no answers. I suspect the answers to the problems of an art are in its exercise. Not that one does not inherit, if one is capable of receiving it, the wisdom of the wise. But I confess unashamedly that I do not get much nourishment from books on statutory construction, and I say this after freshly reexamining them all, scores of them.

. . . An examination of some 2,000 cases, the bulk of which directly or indirectly involves matters of construction, ought to shed light on the encounter between the judicial and the legislative processes, whether that light be conveyed by hints, by explicit elucidation, or, to mix the metaphor, through the ancient test, by their fruits.

And so I have examined the opinions of Holmes, Brandeis and Cardozo and sought to derive from their treatment of legislation what conclusions I could fairly draw, freed as much as I could be from impressions I had formed in the course of the years. [Pp. 529-530.]

.   .   .   .   .

. . . All these years I have avoided speaking of the "legislative intent" and I shall continue to be on my guard against using it. The objection to "intention" was indicated in a letter by Mr. Justice Holmes which the recipient kindly put at my disposal:

Only a day or two ago—when counsel talked of the intention of a legislature, I was indiscreet enough to say I don't care what their intention was. I
only want to know what the words mean. Of course the phrase often is used
to express a conviction not exactly thought out—that you construe a particular clause or expression by considering the whole instrument and any
dominant purposes that it may express. In fact intention is a residuary clause
intended to gather up whatever other aids there may be to interpretation
beside the particular words and the dictionary.

If that is what the term means, it is better to use a less beclouding char-
acterization. Legislation has an aim; it seeks to obviate some mischief, to
supply an inadequacy, to effect a change of policy, to formulate a plan
of government. That aim, that policy is not drawn, like nitrogen, out of
the air; it is evinced in the language of the statute, as read in the light
of other external manifestations of purpose. That is what the judge must
seek and effectuate, and he ought not to be led off the trail by tests that
have overtones of subjective design. We are not concerned with anything
subjective. We do not delve into the mind of legislators or their draftsmen,
or committee members. Against what he believed to be such an attempt
Cardozo once protested:

> The judgment of the court, if I interpret the reasoning aright, does not rest
> upon a ruling that Congress would have gone beyond its power if the purpose
> that it professed was the purpose truly cherished. The judgment of the court
> rests upon the ruling that another purpose, not professed, may be read beneath
> the surface, and by the purpose so imputed the statute is destroyed. Thus the
> process of psychoanalysis has spread to unaccustomed fields. There is a wise
> and ancient doctrine that a court will not inquire into the motives of a legis-
> lative body.... [28]

The difficulty in many instances where a problem of meaning arises is
that the enactment was not directed towards the troubling question. The
problem might then be stated, as once it was by Mr. Justice Cardozo,
"which choice is it the more likely that Congress would have made?" [29]
While in its context the significance and limitations of this question are
clear, thus to frame the question too often tempts inquiry into the subjective and might seem to warrant the court in giving answers based on
an unmanifested legislative state of mind. But the purpose which a court
must effectuate is not that which Congress should have enacted, or would
have. It is that which it did enact, however inaptly, because it may fairly
be said to be imbedded in the statute, even if a specific manifestation was
not thought of, as is often the very reason for casting a statute in very
general terms.

Often the purpose or policy that controls is not directly displayed in
the particular enactment. Statutes cannot be read intelligently if the eye
is closed to considerations evidenced in affiliated statutes, or in the known

---

[28] United States v. Constantine, 296 U.S. 287, 298, 299 (1936) (dissenting).
[29] Burnet v. Guggenheim, 288 U.S. 280, 285 (1933).

temper of legislative opinion. Thus, for example, it is not lightly to be presumed that Congress sought to infringe on "very sacred rights." [30] This improbability will be a factor in determining whether language, though it should be so read if standing alone, was used to effect such a drastic change. [Pp. 538-539.]

·   ·   ·   ·   ·

Search for Purpose

How then does the purpose which a statute expresses reveal itself, particularly when the path of purpose is not straight and narrow? The English courts say: look at the statute and look at nothing else.... [P. 540.]

·   ·   ·   ·   ·

...When not so long ago the Parliamentary mechanism was under scrutiny of the Lord Chancellor's Committee, dissatisfaction was expressed with the prevailing practise of English courts not to go outside the statutes. It was urged that the old practise of preambles be restored or that a memorandum of explanation go with proposed legislation. [36]

At the beginning, the Supreme Court reflected the early English attitude. With characteristic hardheadedness Chief Justice Marshall struck at the core of the matter with the observation "Where the mind labours to discover the design of the legislature, it seizes everything from which aid can be derived." [37] This commonsensical way of dealing with statutes fell into disuse, and more or less catchpenny canons of construction did service instead. To no small degree a more wooden treatment of legislation was due, I suspect, to the fact that the need for keeping vividly in mind the occasions for drawing on all aids in the process of distilling meaning from legislation was comparatively limited. As the area of regulation steadily widened, the impact of the legislative process upon the judicial brought into being, and compelled consideration of, all that convincingly illumines an enactment, instead of merely that which is called, with delusive simplicity, "the end result." Legislatures themselves provided illumination by general definitions, special definitions, explicit recitals of policy, and even directions of attitudes appropriate for judicial construction. Legislative reports were increasingly drawn upon, statements by those in charge of legislation, reports of investigating committees, recommendations of agencies entrusted with the enforcement of laws, etc. When Mr. Justice Holmes came to the Court, the U.S. Reports were practically barren of references to legislative materials. These swarm in current vol-

---

[30] Milwaukee Social Democrat Publishing Co. v. Burleson, 255 U.S. 407, 438 (1921) (dissenting).

[36] Laski, *Note to the Report of the Committee on Minister's Powers, Cmd* 4060, Annex V, 135 (1932).

[37] United States v. Fisher, 2 Cranch 358, 386 (U.S. 1805).

umes. And let me say in passing that the importance that such materials play in Supreme Court litigation carry far-reaching implications for bench and bar.

The change I have summarized was gradual. Undue limitations were applied even after courts broke out of the mere language of a law. We find Mr. Justice Holmes saying, "It is a delicate business to base speculations about the purposes or construction of a statute upon the vicissitudes of its passage." [38] And as late as 1925 he referred to earlier bills relating to a statute under review, with the reservation "If it be legitimate to look at them." [39]

Such hesitations and restraints are in limbo. Courts examine the forms rejected in favor of the words chosen. They look at later statutes "considered to throw a cross light" upon an earlier enactment. [40] The consistent construction by an administrative agency charged with effectuating the policy of an enactment carries very considerable weight. While assertion of authority does not demonstrate its existence, long-continued, uncontested assertion is at least evidence that the legislature conveyed the authority. Similarly, while authority conferred does not atrophy by disuse, failure over an extended period to exercise it is some proof that it was not given. And since "a page of history is worth a volume of logic," [41] courts have looked into the background of statutes, the mischief to be checked and the good that was designed, looking sometimes far afield and taking notice also as judges of what is generally known by men.

Unhappily, there is no table of logarithms for statutory construction. No item of evidence has a fixed or even average weight. One or another may be decisive in one set of circumstances, while of little value elsewhere. A painstaking, detailed report by a Senate Committee bearing directly on the immediate question may settle the matter. A loose statement even by a chairman of a committee, made impromptu in the heat of debate, less informing in cold type than when heard on the floor, will hardly be accorded the weight of an encyclical.

Spurious use of legislative history must not swallow the legislation so as to give point to the quip that only when legislative history is doubtful do you go to the statute. While courts are no longer confined to the language, they are still confined by it. Violence must not be done to the words chosen by the legislature. Unless indeed no doubt can be left that the legislature has in fact used a private code, so that what appears to be violence to language is merely respect to special usage. In the end, language and external aids, each accorded the authority deserved in the circumstances, must be weighed in the balance of judicial judgment. Only

---

[38] Pine Hill Coal Co. v. United States, 259 U.S. 191, 196 (1922).
[39] Davis v. Pringle, 268 U.S. 315, 318 (1925).
[40] United States v. Aluminum Co. of Amer., 148 F.2nd 416, 429 (C.C.A.2d 1945).
[41] New York Trust Co. v. Eisner, 256 U.S. 345, 349 (1921).

if its premises are emptied of their human variables, can the process of statutory construction have the precision of a syllogism. We cannot avoid what Mr. Justice Cardozo deemed inherent in the problem of construction, making "a choice between uncertainties. We must be content to choose the lesser." [42] But to the careful and disinterested eye, the scales will hardly escape appearing to tip slightly on the side of a more probable meaning.

Canons of Construction

Nor can canons of construction save us from the anguish of judgment. Such canons give an air of abstract intellectual compulsion to what is in fact a delicate judgment, concluding a complicated process of balancing subtle and elusive elements. All our three Justices have at one time or another leaned on the crutch of a canon. But they have done so only rarely, and with a recognition that these rules of construction are not in any true sense rules of law. So far as valid, they are what Mr. Justice Holmes called them, axioms of experience. [43] In many instances, these canons originated as observations in specific cases from which they were abstracted, taken out of the context of actuality, and, as it were, codified in treatises. We owe the first known systematic discussion of statutory interpretation in England to the scholarship of Professor Samuel E. Thorne, Yale's Law Librarian. According to Professor Thorne, it was written probably prior to 1567. The latest American treatise on the subject was published in 1943. It is not unfair to say that in the four intervening centuries not much new wisdom has been garnered. But there has been an enormous quantitative difference in expounding the wisdom. "A Discourse upon the Exposicion & Understandinge of Statutes" is a charming essay of not more than thirty pages. Not even the freest use of words would describe as charming the latest edition of Sutherland's *Statutory Construction*, with its three volumes of more than 1500 pages. [Pp. 542-544.]

·   ·   ·   ·   ·

Fair Construction and Fit Legislation

The quality of legislative organization and procedure is inevitably reflected in the quality of legislative draftsmanship. Representative Monroney told the House last July that "ninety-five percent of all the legislation that becomes law passes the Congress in the shape that it came from our committees. Therefore if our committee work is sloppy, if it is bad, if it is inadequate, our legislation in ninety-five percent of the cases will be bad and inadequate as well." [44] And Representative Lane added that

---

[42] Burnet v. Guggenheim, 288 U.S. 280, 288 (1933).
[43] Boston Sand & Gravel Co. v. United States, 278 U.S. 41, 48 (1928).
[44] 92 *Cong. Rec.* 10040 (1946).

"... in the second session of the 78th Congress 953 bills and resolutions were passed, of which only 86 were subject to any real discussion." [45] But what courts do with legislation may in turn deeply affect what Congress will do in the future. Emerson says somewhere that mankind is as lazy as it dares to be. Loose judicial reading makes for loose legislative writing. It encourages the practise illustrated in a recent cartoon in which a senator tells his colleagues "I admit this new bill is too complicated to understand. We'll just have to pass it to find out what it means." A modern Pascal might be tempted at times to say of legislation what Pascal said of students of theology when he charged them with "a looseness of thought and language that would pass nowhere else in making what are professedly very fine distinctions." And it is conceivable that he might go on and speak, as did Pascal, of the "insincerity with which terms are carefully chosen to cover opposite meanings." [46]

But there are more fundamental objections to loose judicial reading. In a democracy the legislative impulse and its expression should come from those popularly chosen to legislate, and equipped to devise policy, as courts are not. The pressure on legislatures to discharge their responsibility with care, understanding and imagination should be stiffened, not relaxed. Above all, they must not be encouraged in irresponsible or undisciplined use of language. In the keeping of legislatures perhaps more than any other group is the well-being of their fellow-men. Their responsibility is discharged ultimately by words. They are under a special duty therefore to observe that "Exactness in the use of words is the basis of all serious thinking. You will get nowhere without it. Words are clumsy tools, and it is very easy to cut one's fingers with them, and they need the closest attention in handling; but they are the only tools we have, and imagination itself cannot work without them. You must master the use of them, or you will wander forever guessing at the mercy of mere impulse and unrecognized assumptions and arbitrary associations, carried away with every wind of doctrine." [47] [Pp. 545-546.]

HORACK, THE DISINTEGRATION OF STATUTORY CONSTRUCTION *

The problem of giving meaning to and finding meaning in symbols is universal. Communication and interpretation are the first requisites of a society. The rules of statutory interpretation purport to express the judicial custom in this general social phenomenon. When a judicial decision

---

[45] 92 *Cong. Rec.* 10054 (1946).

[46] Pater, *Essay on Pascal* in *Miscellaneous Studies* 48, 51 (1895).

[47] Allen, Essay on Jeremy Bentham in *The Social and Political Ideas of the Revolutionary Era* 181, 199 (Hearnshaw ed. 1931).

* [24 *Ind. L.J.* 335 (1949). See p. 491 *supra* for Horack's article on "The Common Law of Legislation."]

is pegged on one rule of interpretation and in a succeeding case the contrary result is dictated by a conflicting but equally authoritarian rule, it is time to recognize that we are dealing neither with "rules" nor with "interpretation," but with "explanations" of decisions independently determined. [P. 335.]

. . . . . .

...In a sense every statute, with the exception of declaratory statutes, alters the common law—either directly or by entering fields previously free of common law regulation. Thus, all statutes potentially may be strictly construed because they are in derogation of the common law. But to presume that the legislature did not intend to change the common law usually is directly contrary to the fact and often is in contradiction to specific legislative rejection of the rule.[31] Realistic acceptance of the situation induced the Minnesota Supreme Court very properly to declare: "We do not consider ourselves at liberty to apply any rule of 'strict construction' to this or any other statute simply because it happens to be in derogation of common law.... Too much judicial indulgence in 'strict construction' of statutes has heretofore disguised 'extraconstitutional obstacles to, or hindrances of, legislative purpose....' "[32]

"Extraconstitutional obstacles" is an excellent euphemism for judicial usurpation of legislative policy making—a usurpation unjustified under our constitutional system even though judges may think that they know better than legislators what the people desire or what is good for them.

Numerous other rules of presumption serve the function of shifting policy determination from the legislature to the court. For example, after what appeared to have been a decent burial,[33] the rule of derogation of sovereignty has appeared again in all its unfortunate vigor in the *Lewis* case.[34] The weak strands of the majority's legislative history are not strengthened by the assertion that "There is an old and well-known rule that statutes which in general terms divest pre-existing rights or privileges will not be applied to the sovereign without express words to that effect."[35] For as Mr. Justice Rutledge pointed out "The issue is not avoided, nor is the effect of final legislative rejection nullified, by the easy device of resting the power ... upon common law rules of statutory con-

---

[31] Approximately one-third of the states have adopted general statutes concerning construction in which this rule is expressly rejected. 3 Sutherland, *Statutory Construction* § 6205 (Horack's ed. 1943).

[32] Teders v. Rothermel, 205 Minn. 470, 472, 286 N.W. 353, 354 (1939).

[33] United States v. California, 297 U.S. 175 (1936); Nardone v. United States, 302 U.S. 379 (1937); and in the case of government agencies, Keifer & Keifer v. Reconstruction Finance Corp., 306 U.S. 381 (1939); Federal Housing Adm'r. v. Burr, 309 U.S. 242 (1940).

[34] United States v. United Mine Workers, 330 U.S. 258 (1947).

[35] *Id.* at 272.

struction" [36]—rules "vague, conveniently selective and often, as here, contradictory...." [37]

Legislatures seldom give helpful information concerning the applicability to the sovereign of a specific statute or of the whole body of statutes and common law.[38] To say that because the legislature has not considered the question, it has decided it, is both fictitious and illogical. To say when the legislature has determined the question, as it did in the *Lewis* case, that because the language of the statute was not explicit the legislature had not decided the question discloses the rule for what it is—a limitation on legislative power—an "extraconstitutional obstacle." [Pp. 345-346.]

· · · · ·

Critical as we may be of the courts, it must also be recognized that legislative draftsmen have obligations to provide statutes capable of judicial administration. It is obvious that draftsmen have not always discharged this responsibility. Legislatures like courts have tended to accept the validity of word symbols and to provide courts with nothing but the "literal words" of the statute. Only Congress and three or four state legislatures publish permanent records of their committee hearings, reports, and legislative memoranda. Not until all state legislatures make data of this character regularly available and published in usable form can bench and bar be expected to give adequate treatment to the interpretative process. [Pp. 347-348.]

· · · · ·

In the twenty-odd years since Cardozo wrote *The Nature of the Judicial Process* much false mysticism has been abandoned. It is recognized today that precedent has its place and that likewise society is entitled to progress. Where the two claims collide the court or the legislature each in its own way must accept the responsibility for decision.[43] [P. 349.]

· · · · ·

When once it is accepted that the process of interpretation is normal and inescapable and that the court must decide from such sources as are relevant, it can be hoped that legislatures will provide adequate sources of interpretation and that the courts will use them without explanation or apology. The test of the decisions will not change: the profession will judge the judicial skills; the public will judge the social results. [P. 352.]

---

[36] *Id.* at 344 n.4.

[37] *Id.* at 349 n.11.

[38] The question which majority and minority assumed in Federal Crop Insurance Corp. v. Merrill, 332 U.S. 380 (1947). Note, Legal Responsibility of Federal Agencies, 24 *Ind. L.J.* 427 (1949).

[43] But neither their ways nor their methods are as diverse as might be expected. Cohen, On the Teaching of 'Legislation', 47 *Col. L. Rev.* 1301 (1947).